Discover the Online Experience!
4ltrpress.cengage.com/econ

FOR STUDENTS:

- Flashcards
- Interactive quizzing
- Games: Crossword Puzzles, Beat the Clock & Quiz Bowl
- PowerPoint® Slides
- Videos
- Stock Market Project
- And More!

FOR INSTRUCTORS:

- First Day of Class Instructions
- Custom Options through 4LTR+ Program
- Instructor's Manual
- Test Bank
- ExamView® on IRCD Instructions
- PowerPoint® Slides
- Instructor Prep Cards
- Student Review Cards
- And More!

"The part I liked most about the text are the **real-world applications that put the concepts into perspective.** I also think the graphs are clear and easy to understand. The review cards are helpful too."

Josh Wittman,
Student
University of Great Falls

"Students bring the text with them to class more often than before, regardless of whether I tell them to bring it. I would say **they are engaging with the text more.**"

Ayman Reda,
Instructor
Grand Valley State University

SOUTH-WESTERN
CENGAGE Learning™

ECON Macro 2010–2011 Edition
William A. McEachern

EVP/Publisher: Jonathan Hulbert

VP/Editorial Director: Jack W. Calhoun

VP/Director of Marketing: Bill Hendee

Publisher: Joe Sabatino

Director, 4LTR Press: Neil Marquardt

Sr. Acquisitions Editor: Steve Scoble

Sr. Developmental Editor:
    Susanna C. Smart

Developmental Editor: David Ferrell,
    B-books, Ltd.

Project Manager, 4LTR Press:
    Clara Goosman

Editorial Assistant: Lena Mortis

Executive Brand Marketing Manager:
    Robin Lucas

Sr. Marketing Manager: John Carey

Marketing Communications Manager:
    Sarah Greber

Production Director: Amy McGuire,
    B-books, Ltd.

Managing Media Editor: Pam Wallace

Media Editor: Deepak Kumar

Sr. Manufacturing Coordinator:
    Sandee Milewski

Production Service: B-books, Ltd.

Sr. Art Director: Michelle Kunkler

Internal Designer: Beckmeyer Design

Cover Designer: Ke Design

Cover Image: © Image Source/
    Jupiter Images

Photography Manager: Deanna Ettinger

Photo Researcher: Charlotte Goldman

For product information and technology assistance, contact us at **Cengage Learning Customer & Sales Support, 1-800-423-0563**

For permission to use material from this text or product, submit all requests online at **www.cengage.com/permissions** Further permissions questions can be emailed to **permissionrequest@cengage.com**

© 2010 Cengage Learning. All Rights Reserved.

Library of Congress Control Number: 2009932862

SE ISBN-13: 978-1-4390-4067-6
SE ISBN-10: 1-4390-4067-2
IE ISBN-13: 978-0-538-75566-5
IE ISBN-10: 0-538-75566-0

South-Western Cengage Learning
5191 Natorp Boulevard
Mason, OH 45040
USA

Cengage Learning is a leading provider of customized learning solutions with office locations around the globe, including Singapore, the United Kingdom, Australia, Mexico, Brazil, and Japan. Locate your local office at **www.cengage.com/global**.

Cengage Learning products are represented in Canada by Nelson Education, Ltd.

For your course and learning solutions, visit academic.cengage.com Purchase any of our products at your local college store or at our preferred online store **www.ichapters.com**

Printed in the United States of America
3 4 5 6 7 12 11 10

MACRO
ECON
Brief Contents

MACRO ECON

Contents

PART 2   Fundamentals of Macroeconomics

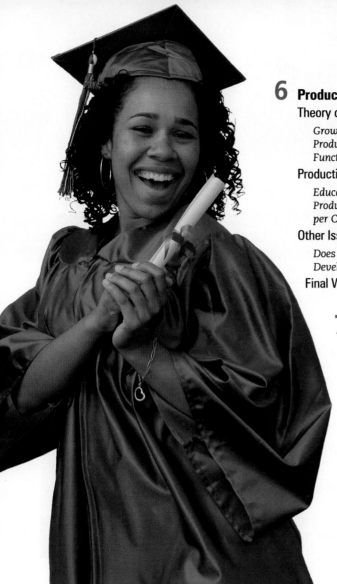

PART 3   Fiscal and Monetary Policy

More Bang for Your Buck

1

The Art and Science of Economic Analysis

Learning Outcomes

LO[1] Explain the economic problem of scarce resources and unlimited wants

LO[2] Describe the forces that shape economic choices

LO[3] Explain the relationship between economic theory and economic reality

LO[4] Identify some pitfalls of economic analysis

LO[5] Describe several reasons to study economics

"How can it be said that in economics 'what goes around comes around'?"

Why are comic-strip characters like Hagar the Horrible, Hi and Lois, Cathy, Monty, and FoxTrot missing a finger on each hand? And where is Dilbert's mouth? Why is there no such thing as a free napkin? In what way are people who pound on vending machines relying on theory? Why is a good theory like a California Closet? What's the big idea with economics? Finally, how can it be said that in economics "what goes around comes around"? These and other questions are answered in this chapter, which introduces the art and science of economic analysis.

You have been reading and hearing about economic issues for years—unemployment, inflation, poverty, federal deficits, college tuition, airfares, stock prices, computer prices, gas prices. When explanations of these issues go into any depth, your eyes may glaze over and you may tune out, the same way you do when a weather forecaster tries to provide an in-depth analysis of high-pressure fronts colliding with moisture carried in from the coast.

What many people fail to realize is that economics is livelier than the dry accounts offered by the news media. Economics is about making choices, and you make economic choices every day—choices about whether to get a part-time job or focus on your studies, live in a dorm or off campus, take a course in accounting or one in history, get married or stay single, pack a lunch or buy a sandwich. You already know much more about economics than you realize. You bring to the subject a rich personal experience, an experience that will be tapped throughout the book to reinforce your understanding of the basic ideas.

What do you think?

Economics is a science, not an art.

Strongly Disagree						Strongly Agree
1	2	3	4	5	6	7

Topics discussed in Chapter 1 include:

- The economic problem
- Rational self-interest
- Marginal analysis
- Scientific method
- Normative versus positive analysis
- Pitfalls of economic thinking

LO¹ The Economic Problem: Scarce Resources, Unlimited Wants

Would you like a new car, a nicer home, better meals, more free time, a more interesting social life, more spending money, more leisure, more sleep? Who wouldn't? But even if you can satisfy some of these desires, others keep popping up. *The problem is that, although your wants, or desires, are virtually unlimited, the resources available to satisfy these wants are scarce.* A resource is *scarce* when it is not freely available—that is, when its price exceeds zero. Because resources are scarce, you must choose from among many wants, and whenever you choose, you must forgo satisfying some other wants. The problem of scarce resources but unlimited wants exists to a greater or lesser extent for each of the 6.6 billion people on earth. Everybody—cab driver, farmer, brain surgeon, dictator, shepherd, student, politician—faces the problem. For example, a cab driver uses time and other scarce resources, such as the taxi, knowledge of the city, driving skills, and gasoline, to earn income. That income, in turn, buys housing, groceries, clothing, trips to Disney World, and thousands of other goods and services that help satisfy some of the driver's unlimited wants. Economics examines how people use their scarce resources to satisfy their unlimited wants. Let's pick apart the definition, beginning with resources, then goods and services, and finally focus on the heart of the matter—economic choice, which arises from scarcity.

economics
the study of how people use their scarce resources to satisfy their unlimited wants

resources
the inputs, or factors of production, used to produce the goods and services that people want; resources consist of labor, capital, natural resources, and entrepreneurial ability

labor
the physical and mental effort used to produce goods and services

capital
the buildings, equipment, and human skills used to produce goods and services

natural resources
all "gifts of nature" used to produce goods and services; includes renewable and exhaustible resources

Resources

Resources are the inputs, or factors of production, used to produce the goods and services that people want. *Goods and services are scarce because resources are scarce.* Resources sort into four broad categories: labor, capital, natural resources, and entrepreneurial ability. Labor is human effort, both physical and mental. Labor includes the effort of the cab driver and the brain surgeon. Labor itself comes from a more fundamental resource: *time.* Without time we can accomplish nothing. We allocate our time to alternative uses: we can *sell* our time as labor, or we can *spend* our time doing other things, like sleeping, eating, studying, playing sports, going online, watching TV, or just relaxing with friends.

Capital includes all human creations used to produce goods and services. Economists often distinguish between physical capital and human capital. *Physical capital* consists of factories, tools, machines, computers, buildings, airports, highways, and other human creations used to produce goods and services. Physical capital includes the cab driver's taxi, the surgeon's scalpel, and the building where your economics class meets. *Human capital* consists of the knowledge and skill people acquire to increase their productivity, such as the cab driver's knowledge of city streets, the surgeon's knowledge of human anatomy, and your knowledge of economics.

Natural resources are all *gifts of nature,* including bodies of water, trees, oil reserves, minerals, and even animals. Natural resources can be divided into renewable resources and exhaustible resources. A *renewable resource* can be drawn on indefinitely if used conservatively. Thus, timber is a renewable resource if felled trees are replaced to provide a steady supply. The air and rivers are renewable resources if they are allowed sufficient time to clean themselves of any pollutants. More generally, biological resources like fish, game, livestock, forests, rivers, groundwater, grasslands, and soil are renewable if managed properly. An *exhaustible resource*—such as oil, coal, or copper ore—does not renew itself and so is available in a limited amount. Once burned, each barrel of oil or ton of coal is gone forever. The world's oil and coal deposits are exhaustible.

A special kind of human skill called entrepreneurial ability is the talent required to dream up a new product or find a better way to produce an existing one. This special skill comes from an entrepreneur. An entrepreneur is a profit-seeking decision maker who starts with an idea, then organizes an enterprise to bring that idea to life, and assumes the risk of operation. An entrepreneur pays resource owners for the opportunity to employ their resources in the firm. Every firm in the world today, such as Ford, Microsoft, Google, and Dell, began as an idea in the mind of an entrepreneur.

Resource owners are paid wages for their labor, interest for the use of their capital, and rent for the use of their natural resources. Entrepreneurial ability is rewarded by profit, which equals the *revenue* from items sold minus the cost of the resources employed to make those items. The word *profit* comes from the Latin *proficere*, which means "to benefit." The entrepreneur benefits from what's left over after paying other resource suppliers. Sometimes the entrepreneur suffers a loss. Resource earnings are usually based on the *time* these resources are employed. Resource payments therefore have a time dimension, as in a wage of $10 *per hour*, interest of 6 percent *per year*, rent of $600 *per month*, or profit of $10,000 *per year*.

Goods and Services

Resources are combined in a variety of ways to produce goods and services. A farmer, a tractor, 50 acres of land, seeds, and fertilizer combine to grow the good: corn. One hundred musicians, musical instruments, chairs, a conductor, a musical score, and a music hall combine to produce the service: Beethoven's Fifth Symphony. Corn is a good because it is something you can see, feel, and touch; it requires scarce resources to produce; and it satisfies human wants. The book you are now holding, the chair you are sitting in, the clothes you are wearing, and your next meal are all goods. The performance of the Fifth Symphony is a service because it is intangible, yet it uses scarce resources to satisfy human wants. Lectures, movies, concerts, phone service, broadband connections, yoga lessons, dry cleaning, and haircuts are all services.

Because goods and services are produced using scarce resources, they are themselves scarce. *A good or service is scarce if the amount people desire exceeds the amount available at a zero price.* Because we cannot have all the goods and services we would like, we must continually choose among them. We must choose among more pleasant living quarters, better meals, nicer clothes, more reliable transporta-

There's no such thing as a free napkin.

© RANDY FARIS/CORBIS

tion, faster computers, and so on. Making choices in a world of scarcity means we must pass up some goods and services. But not everything is scarce. In fact some things we would prefer to have less of. For example, we would prefer to have less garbage, less spam email, and less pollution. Things we want none of even at a zero price are called *bads*. Think of a bad as the opposite of a good.

A few goods and services seem *free* because the amount available at a zero price exceeds the amount people want. For example, air and seawater often seem free because we can breathe all the air we want and have all the seawater we can haul away. Yet, despite the old saying "The best things in life are free," most goods and services are scarce, not free, and even those that appear to be free come with strings attached. For example, *clean air* and *clean* seawater have become scarce. *Goods and services that are truly free are not the subject matter of economics. Without scarcity, there would be no economic problem and no need for prices.*

Sometimes we mistakenly think of certain goods as free because they involve no apparent cost to us. Napkins seem to be free at Starbucks. Nobody stops you from taking a fistful. Supplying napkins, however, costs the company millions each year and prices reflect that cost. Some restaurants make special efforts to keep napkin use down—such as packing them tightly into the dispenser or making you ask for them.

You may have heard the expression "There is no such thing as a free lunch." There is no free lunch because all goods and services involve a cost to someone. The lunch may seem free to us, but it draws scarce resources away from the production of other goods and services, and whoever provides a free lunch often expects something in return. A Russian proverb makes a similar point but with a bit more bite: "The only place you find free cheese is in a mousetrap." Albert Einstein once observed, "Sometimes one pays the most for things one gets for nothing."

Economic Decision Makers

There are four types of decision makers in the economy: households, firms, governments, and the rest of the world. Their interaction determines how an economy's resources are allocated. *Households* play the starring role. As consumers, households demand the goods and services produced. As resource owners, households supply labor, capital, natural resources, and entrepreneurial ability to firms, governments, and the rest of the world. *Firms, governments,* and *the rest of the world* demand the resources that households supply and then use these resources to supply the goods and services that households demand. The rest of the world includes foreign households, firms, and governments that supply resources and products to U.S. markets and demand resources and products from U.S. markets.

Markets are the means by which buyers and sellers carry out exchange. By bringing together the two sides of exchange, markets determine price and quantity. Markets are often physical places, such as supermarkets, department stores, shopping malls, or yard sales. But markets also include other mechanisms by which buyers and sellers communicate, such as classified ads, radio and television ads, telephones, bulletin boards, online sites, and face-to-face bargaining. These market mechanisms provide information about the quantity, quality, and price of products offered for sale. Goods and services are bought and sold in product markets. Resources are bought and sold in resource markets. The most important resource market is the labor, or job, market. Think about your own experience looking for a job, and you get some idea of that market.

market
a set of arrangements by which buyers and sellers carry out exchange at mutually agreeable terms

product market
a market in which a good or service is bought and sold

resource market
a market in which a resource is bought and sold

circular-flow model
a diagram that traces the flow of resources, products, income, and revenue among economic decision makers

A Simple Circular-Flow Model

Now that you have learned a bit about economic decision makers, consider how they interact. Such a picture is conveyed by the circular-flow model, which describes the flow of resources, products, income, and revenue among economic decision makers. The simple circular-flow model focuses on the primary interaction in a market economy—that between households and firms. Exhibit 1 shows households on the left and firms on the right; please take a look.

Households supply labor, capital, natural resources, and entrepreneurial ability to firms through resource markets, shown in the lower portion of the exhibit. In return, households demand goods and services from firms through product markets, shown on the upper portion of the exhibit. Viewed from the business end, firms demand labor, capital, natural resources, and entrepreneurial ability from households through resource markets, and firms supply goods and services to households through product markets.

Exhibit 1

The Simple Circular-Flow Model for Households and Firms

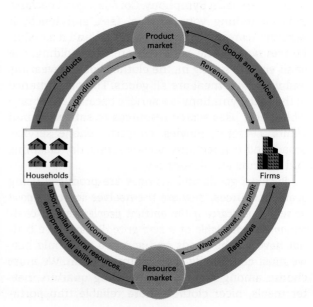

The flows of resources and products are supported by the flows of income and expenditure—that is, by the flow of money. So let's add money. The demand and supply of resources come together in resource markets to determine what firms pay for resources. These resource prices—wages, interest, rent, and profit—flow as *income* to households. The demand and supply of products come together in product markets to determine what households pay for goods and services. These product prices of goods and services flow as *revenue* to firms. Resources and products flow in one direction—in this case, counterclockwise—and the corresponding payments flow in the other direction—clockwise. What goes around comes around. Take a little time now to trace the logic of the circular flows.

> An economy results from the choices that millions of individuals make in attempting to satisfy their unlimited wants.

LO² The Art of Economic Analysis

An economy results from the choices that millions of individuals make in attempting to satisfy their unlimited wants. Because these choices lie at the heart of the economic problem—coping with scarce resources but unlimited wants—they deserve a closer look. Learning about the forces that shape economic choice is the first step toward mastering the art of economic analysis.

Rational Self-Interest

A key economic assumption is that individuals, in making choices, rationally select alternatives they perceive to be in their best interests. By *rational*, economists mean simply that people try to make the best choices they can, given the available information. People may not know with certainty which alternative will turn out to be the best. They simply select the alternatives they *expect* will yield the most satisfaction and happiness. In general, rational self-interest means that individuals try to maximize the expected benefit achieved with a given cost or to minimize the expected cost of achieving a given benefit.

Rational self-interest should not be viewed as blind materialism, pure selfishness, or greed. We all know people who are tuned to radio station WIIFM (What's In It For Me?). For most of us, however, self-interest often includes the welfare of our family, our friends, and perhaps the poor of the world. Even so, our concern for others is influenced by the cost of

that concern. We may readily volunteer to drive a friend to the airport on Saturday afternoon but are less likely to offer a ride if the plane leaves at 6:00 A.M. When we donate clothes to an organization such as Goodwill Industries, they are more likely to be old and worn than brand new. People tend to give more to charities when their contributions are tax deductible. TV stations are more likely to donate airtime for public-service announcements during the dead of night than during prime time (in fact, 80 percent of such announcements air between 11:00 P.M. and 7:00 A.M.[1]). In Asia some people burn money to soothe the passage of a departed loved one. But they burn fake money, not real money. The notion of self-interest does not rule out concern for others; it simply means that concern for others is influenced by the same economic forces that affect other economic choices. *The lower the personal cost of helping others, the more help we offer.*

Choice Requires Time and Information

Rational choice takes time and requires information, but time and information are scarce and therefore valuable. If you have any doubts about the time and information required to make choices, talk to someone who recently purchased a home, a car, or a personal computer. Talk to a corporate official trying to decide whether to introduce a new product, sell online, build a new factory, or buy another firm. Or think back to your own experience of choosing a college. You probably talked to friends, relatives, teachers, and guidance counselors. You likely used school catalogs, college guides, and Web sites. You may have visited some campuses to see the admissions staff and anyone else willing to talk. The decision took time and money, and it probably involved aggravation and anxiety.

Because information is costly to acquire, we are often willing to pay others to gather and digest it for us. College guidebooks, stock analysts, travel agents, real estate brokers, career counselors, restaurant critics, movie reviewers, specialized Web sites, and *Consumer*

rational self-interest individuals try to maximize the expected benefit achieved with a given cost or to minimize the expected cost of achieving a given benefit

1. Sally Goll Beatty, "Media and Agencies Brawl Over Do-Good Advertising," *Wall Street Journal,* 29 September 1997.

> > After armed guards escorted the shipment of *Harry Potter and the Deathly Hallows* to Amazon, the online retailer, it deposited the top-secret books in a guarded security zone. The zone had one entrance, and employees required a special badge to enter. Only longtime employees were allowed to pack the books, and counts were taken multiple times a day to ensure that no copies "went missing." The marginal cost for distributing such a hot title were certainly not insignificant.

the status quo if the expected marginal benefit from the change exceeds the expected marginal cost. For example, Amazon.com compares the marginal benefit expected from adding a new line of products (the additional sales revenue) with the marginal cost (the additional cost of the resources required). Likewise, you compare the marginal benefit you expect from eating dessert (the additional pleasure or satisfaction) with its marginal cost (the additional money, time, and calories).

Typically, the change under consideration is small, but a marginal choice can involve a major economic adjustment, as in the decision to quit school and find a job. For a firm, a marginal choice might mean building a plant in Mexico or even filing for bankruptcy. By focusing on the effect of a marginal adjustment to the status quo, the economist is able to cut the analysis of economic choice down to a manageable size. Rather than confront a bewildering economic reality head-on, the economist begins with a marginal choice to see how this choice affects a particular market and shapes the economic system as a whole. Incidentally, to the noneconomist, *marginal* usually means relatively inferior, as in "a movie of marginal quality." Forget that meaning for this course and instead think of *marginal* as meaning incremental, additional, or extra.

Reports magazine attest to our willingness to pay for information that improves our choices. As we'll see next, *rational decision makers continue to acquire information as long as the additional benefit expected from that information exceeds the additional cost of gathering it.*

Economic Analysis Is Marginal Analysis

Economic choice usually involves some adjustment to the existing situation, or status quo. Amazon.com must decide whether to add an additional line of products. The school superintendent must decide whether to hire another teacher. Your favorite jeans are on sale, and you must decide whether to buy another pair. You are wondering whether to carry an extra course next term. You just finished lunch and are deciding whether to have dessert.

Economic choice is based on a comparison of the *expected marginal benefit* and the *expected marginal* cost of the action under consideration. Marginal means incremental, additional, or extra. Marginal refers to a change in an economic variable, a change in the status quo. A *rational decision maker changes*

marginal
incremental, additional, or extra; used to describe a change in an economic variable

microeconomics
the study of the economic behavior in particular markets, such as that for computers or unskilled labor

Microeconomics and Macroeconomics

Although you have made thousands of economic choices, you probably seldom think about your own economic behavior. For example, why are you reading this book right now rather than doing something else? Microeconomics is the study of your economic behavior and the economic behavior of others who make choices about such matters as how much to study and how much to party, how much to borrow and how much to save, what to buy and what to sell. Microeconomics examines individual economic choices and how markets coordinate the choices of various decision makers. Microeconomics explains how price and quantity are determined in individual markets—the market for breakfast cereal, sports equipment, or used cars, for instance.

You have probably given little thought to what influences your own economic choices. You have likely given even less thought to how your choices link up with those made by millions of others in the U.S. economy to determine economy-wide measures such as total production, employment, and economic growth. Macroeconomics studies the performance of the economy as a whole. Whereas microeconomics studies the individual pieces of the economic puzzle, as reflected in particular markets, macroeconomics puts all the pieces together to focus on the big picture.

To review: The art of economic analysis focuses on how people use their scarce resources in an attempt to satisfy their unlimited wants. Rational self-interest guides individual choice. Choice requires time and information and involves a comparison of the marginal benefit and marginal cost of alternative actions. Microeconomics looks at the individual pieces of the economic puzzle; macroeconomics fits the pieces together to shape the big picture.

LO^3 The Science of Economic Analysis

Economists use scientific analysis to develop theories, or models, that help explain economic behavior. An economic theory, or economic model, is a simplification of economic reality that *is used to make predictions about the real world*. A theory, or model, such as the circular-flow model, captures the important elements of the problem under study but need not spell out every detail and interrelation. In fact, adding more details may make a theory more unwieldy and, therefore, less useful. For example, a wrist watch is a model that tells time, but a watch

A good theory can act like a closet organizer for your mind, helping you understand a messy and confusing world.

festooned with extra features is harder to read at a glance and is therefore less useful as a time-telling model. The world is so complex that we must simplify to make sense of things. Store mannequins simplify the human form (some even lack arms and heads). Comic strips simplify characters—leaving out fingers or a mouth, for instance. You might think of economic theory as a stripped-down, or streamlined, version of economic reality.

A good theory helps us understand a messy and confusing world. Lacking a theory of how things work, our thinking can become cluttered with facts, one piled on another as in a messy closet. You could think of a good theory as a closet organizer for the mind. A good theory offers a helpful guide to sorting, saving, and understanding information.

The Role of Theory

Most people don't understand the role of theory. Perhaps you have heard, "Oh, that's fine in theory, but in practice it's another matter." The implication is that the theory in question provides little aid in practical matters. People who say this fail to realize that they are merely substituting their own theory for a theory they either do not believe or do not understand. They are really saying, "I have my own theory that works better."

All of us employ theories, however poorly defined or understood. Someone who pounds on the Pepsi machine that just ate a quarter has a crude theory about how that machine works. One version of that theory might be "The quarter drops through a series of whatchamacallits, but sometimes it gets stuck. *If* I pound on the machine, *then* I can free up the quarter and send it on its way." Evidently, this theory is widespread enough that people continue to pound on machines that fail to perform (a real problem for the vending machine industry and one reason newer machines are fronted with glass). Yet, if you were to ask these mad pounders to explain their "theory" about how the machine operates, they would look at you as if you were crazy.

The Scientific Method

To study economic problems, economists employ a process of theoretical investigation called *the scientific method*, which consists of four steps, as outlined in Exhibit 2.

macroeconomics
the study of the economic behavior of entire economies

economic theory (economic model)
a simplification of reality used to make predictions about cause and effect in the real world

Exhibit 2

The Scientific Method: Step by Step

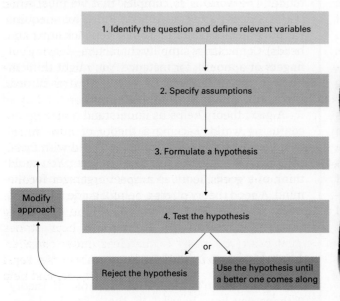

```
┌──────────────────────────────────────────────────┐
│ 1. Identify the question and define relevant variables │
└──────────────────────────────────────────────────┘
                          ↓
            ┌──────────────────────────┐
            │ 2. Specify assumptions    │
            └──────────────────────────┘
                          ↓
            ┌──────────────────────────┐
            │ 3. Formulate a hypothesis │
            └──────────────────────────┘
                          ↓
  ┌──────────┐  ┌──────────────────────────┐
  │ Modify   │  │ 4. Test the hypothesis    │
  │ approach │  └──────────────────────────┘
  └──────────┘            ↓
              or
  ┌──────────────────┐  ┌──────────────────────────┐
  │ Reject the       │  │ Use the hypothesis until  │
  │ hypothesis       │  │ a better one comes along  │
  └──────────────────┘  └──────────────────────────┘
```

Step One: Identify the Question and Define Relevant Variables

The scientific method begins with curiosity: Someone wants to answer a question. Thus, the first step is to identify the economic question and define the variables relevant to a solution. For example, the question might be "What is the relationship between the price of Pepsi and the quantity of Pepsi purchased?" In this case, the relevant variables are price and quantity. A variable is a measure that can take on different values at different times. The variables of concern become the elements of the theory, so they must be selected with care.

Step Two: Specify Assumptions

The second step is to specify the assumptions under which the theory is to apply. One major category of assumptions is the other-things-constant assumption—in Latin, the *ceteris paribus* assumption. The idea is to identify the variables of interest and then focus exclusively on the relationships among them, assuming that nothing else important changes—that other things remain constant. Again, suppose we are interested in how the price of Pepsi influences the amount purchased. To isolate the relation between these two variables, we assume that there are no changes in other relevant variables such as consumer income, the average temperature, or the price of Coke.

We also make assumptions about how people behave; these are called behavioral assumptions. The primary behavioral assumption is rational self-interest. Earlier we assumed that individual decision makers pursue self-interest rationally and make choices accordingly. Rationality implies that each consumer buys the products expected to maximize his or her level of satisfaction. Rationality also implies that each firm supplies the products expected to maximize the firm's profit. These kinds of assumptions are called behavioral assumptions because they specify how we expect economic decision makers to behave—what makes them tick, so to speak.

Step Three: Formulate a Hypothesis

The third step in the scientific method is to formulate a hypothesis, which is a theory about how key variables relate to each other. For example, one hypothesis holds that if the price of Pepsi goes up, other things constant, then the quantity purchased declines. The hypothesis becomes a prediction of what happens to the quantity purchased if the price increases. *The purpose of this hypothesis, like that of any theory, is to help make predictions about cause and effect in the real world.*

Step Four: Test the Hypothesis

In the fourth step, by comparing its predictions with evidence, we test the validity of a hypothesis. To test a hypothesis, we must focus on the variables in question, while carefully controlling for other effects assumed not to change. The test leads us either to (1) reject the hypothesis, or theory, if it predicts worse than the best alternative theory or (2) use the hypothesis, or theory, until a better one comes along. If we reject the hypothesis, we can go back and modify our approach in light of the results. Please spend a moment now reviewing the steps of the scientific method in Exhibit 2.

Normative Versus Positive

Economists usually try to explain how the economy works. Sometimes they concern themselves not with how the economy *does* work but how it *should*

variable
a measure, such as price or quantity, that can take on different values at different times

other-things-constant assumption
the assumption, when focusing on the relation among key economic variables, that other variables remain unchanged; in Latin, *ceteris paribus*

behavioral assumption
an assumption that describes the expected behavior of economic decision makers—what motivates them

hypothesis
a theory about how key variables relate

work. Compare these two statements: "The U.S. unemployment rate is 9.5 percent" and "The U.S. unemployment rate should be lower." The first, called a positive economic statement, is an assertion about economic reality that can be supported or rejected by reference to the facts. Positive economics, like physics or biology, attempts to understand the world around us. The second, called a normative economic statement, reflects an opinion. And an opinion is merely that—it cannot be shown to be true or false by reference to the facts. Positive statements concern what is; normative statements concern what, in someone's opinion, *should be*. Positive statements need not necessarily be true, but they must be subject to verification or refutation by reference to the facts. Theories are expressed as positive statements such as "If the price of Pepsi increases, then the quantity demanded decreases."

Most of the disagreement among economists involves normative debates—such as the appropriate role of government—rather than statements of positive analysis. To be sure, many theoretical issues remain unresolved, but economists generally agree on most fundamental theoretical principles—that is, about positive economic analysis. For example, in a survey of 464 U.S. economists, only 6.5 percent disagreed with the statement "A ceiling on rents reduces the quantity and quality of housing available." This is a positive statement because it can be shown to be consistent or inconsistent with the evidence. In contrast, there was much less agreement on normative statements such as "The distribution of income in the United States should be more equal." Half the economists surveyed "generally agreed," a quarter "generally disagreed," and a quarter "agreed with provisos."[2]

Normative statements, or value judgments, have a place in a policy debate such as the proper role of government, provided that statements of opinion are distinguished from statements of fact. In such policy debates, you are entitled to your own opinion, but you are not entitled to your own facts.

> **"** Economists explain their theories by telling stories about how they think the economy works. **"**

2. Richard M. Alston et al., "Is There a Consensus Among Economists in the 1990s?" *American Economic Review* 82 (May 1992): pp. 203–209, Table 1.

Economists Tell Stories

Despite economists' reliance on the scientific method for developing and evaluating theories, economic analysis is as much art as science. Formulating a question, isolating the key variables, specifying the assumptions, proposing a theory to answer the question, and devising a way to test the predictions all involve more than simply an understanding of economics and the scientific method. Carrying out these steps requires good intuition and the imagination of a storyteller. Economists explain their theories by telling stories about how they think the economy works. To tell a compelling story, an economist relies on case studies, anecdotes, parables, the personal experience of the listener, and supporting data. Throughout this book, you'll hear stories that bring you closer to the ideas under consideration. The stories, such as the one about the Pepsi machine, breathe life into economic theory and help you personalize abstract ideas.

Predicting Average Behavior

The goal of an economic theory is to predict the impact of an economic event on economic choices and, in turn, the effect of these choices on particular markets or on the economy as a whole. Does this mean that economists try to predict the behavior of particular consumers or producers? Not necessarily, because a specific individual may behave in an unpredictable way. But the unpredictable actions of numerous individuals tend to cancel one another out, so the *average behavior* of groups can be predicted more accurately. For example, if the federal government cuts personal income taxes, certain households may decide to save the entire tax cut. On average, however, household spending increases. Likewise, if Burger King cuts the price of Whoppers, the manager can better predict how much sales will increase than how a specific customer coming through the door will respond. *The random actions of individuals tend to offset one another, so the average behavior of a large group can be predicted more accurately than the behavior of a particular individual.* Consequently, economists tend to focus on the average, or typical, behavior of people in groups—for example, as average taxpayers or average Whopper consumers—rather than on the behavior of a specific individual.

positive economic statement
a statement that can be proved or disproved by reference to facts

normative economic statement
a statement that reflects an opinion, which cannot be proved or disproved by reference to the facts

LO⁴ Some Pitfalls of Faulty Economic Analysis

Economic analysis, like other forms of scientific inquiry, is subject to common mistakes in reasoning that can lead to faulty conclusions. Here are three sources of confusion.

The Fallacy That Association Is Causation

In the last two decades, the number of physicians specializing in cancer treatment increased sharply. At the same time, the incidence of some cancers increased. Can we conclude that physicians cause cancer? No. To assume that event A caused event B simply because the two are associated in time is to commit the association-is-causation fallacy, a common error. The fact that one event precedes another or that the two events occur simultaneously does not necessarily mean that one causes the other. Remember: Association is not necessarily causation.

The Fallacy of Composition

Perhaps you have been to a rock concert where everyone stands to get a better view. At some concerts, most people even stand on their chairs. But even standing on chairs does not improve the view if others do the same. Likewise, arriving early to buy game tickets does not work if many others have the same idea. These are examples of the fallacy of composition, which is an erroneous belief that what is true for the individual, or the part, is also true for the group, or the whole.

association-is-causation fallacy the incorrect idea that if two variables are associated in time, one must necessarily cause the other

fallacy of composition the incorrect belief that what is true for the individual, or part, must necessarily be true for the group, or the whole

secondary effects unintended consequences of economic actions that may develop slowly over time as people react to events

The Mistake of Ignoring the Secondary Effects

In many cities, public officials have imposed rent controls on apartments. The primary effect of this policy, the effect policy makers focus on, is to keep rents from rising. Over time, however, fewer new apartments get built because renting them becomes less profitable. Moreover, existing rental units deteriorate because owners have plenty of customers anyway. Thus, the quantity and quality of housing may decline as a result of what appears to be a reasonable measure to keep rents from rising. The mistake was to ignore the secondary effects, or the unintended consequences, of the policy. Economic actions have secondary effects that often turn out to be more important than the primary effects. Secondary effects may develop more slowly and may not be immediately obvious, but good economic analysis tries to anticipate them and take them into account.

LO⁵ Why Study Economics (Or, If Economists Are So Smart, Why Aren't They Rich?)

Why aren't economists rich? Well, some are, earning over $25,000 per appearance on the lecture circuit. Others top $2 million a year as consultants and expert witnesses.[3] Economists have been appointed to federal cabinet posts, such as Secretaries of Commerce, Defense, Labor, State, and Treasury, and to head the U.S. Federal Reserve System. Economics is the only social science and the only business discipline for which the prestigious Nobel Prize is awarded, and pronouncements by economists are reported in the media daily. *The Economist*, a widely respected news weekly from London, has argued that economic ideas have influenced policy "to a degree that would make other social scientists drool."[4]

The economics profession thrives because its models usually do a better job of making economic sense out of a confusing world than do alternative approaches. But not all economists are wealthy, nor is personal

3. As reported by George Anders, "An Economist's Courtroom Bonanza," *Wall Street Journal,* 19 March 2007.
4. "The Puzzling Failure of Economics," *The Economist,* 23 August 1997, p. 11.

wealth the goal of the discipline. In a similar vein, not all doctors are healthy (some even smoke), not all carpenters live in perfectly built homes, not all marriage counselors are happily married, and not all child psychologists have well-adjusted children. Still, those who study economics do reap financial rewards.

Among college graduates, all kinds of factors affect earnings, such as general ability, occupation, college attended, college major, and highest degree earned. To isolate the effects of the college major on earnings, a National Science Foundation study surveyed people in specific age groups who worked full time and had earned a bachelor's as their highest degree. Exhibit 3 shows the median earnings by major for men and women ages 35 to 44. As a point of reference, the *median* annual earnings for men was $43,199 (half earned more and half earned less). The median earnings for women was $32,155, only 74 percent that of men. Among men, the top pay was the $53,286 median earned by engineering majors; that pay was 23 percent above the median for all men surveyed. Among women, the top pay was the $49,170 median earned by economics majors; that pay was 53 percent above the median for all women surveyed.

Incidentally, men who majored in economics earned a median of $49,377, ranking them seventh among 27 majors and 14 percent above the median for all men surveyed. Thus, even though the median pay for all women was only 74 percent of the median pay for all men, women who majored in economics earned about the same as men who majored in economics. We can say that *economics majors earned more than most, and they experienced no pay difference based on gender.*

Note that among both men and women, the majors ranked toward the top of the list tend to be more quantitative and analytical. According to the study's author, "Employers may view certain majors as more difficult and may assume that graduates in these fields are more able and hard working, whereupon they offer them higher salaries."[5] The selection of a relatively more challenging major such as economics sends a favorable signal to future employers.

The study also examined the kinds of jobs different majors actually found. Those who majored in economics became mid- and top-level managers,

Are you the next successful economics major?

{ Famous Economics Majors }

A number of world leaders majored in economics, including three of the last seven U.S. presidents, Philippines President Gloria Macapagal-Arroyo, who earned a Ph.D. in the subject, U.S. Supreme Court Justices Steven Breyer and Anthony Kennedy, and former Justice Sandra Day O'Connor. Other economics majors include billionaire Donald Trump, former eBay President (and billionaire) Meg Whitman, Microsoft chief executive officer (and billionaire) Steve Ballmer, CNN founder (and billionaire) Ted Turner, Intel President Paul Otellini, NFL Patriot's coach Bill Belichick, Governor Arnold Schwarzenegger, high-tech guru Esther Dyson, and Scott Adams, creator of Dilbert, the mouthless wonder.

SOURCE: "The World's Billionaires," *Forbes,* 11 March 2009.

executives, and administrators. They also worked in sales, computer fields, financial analysis, and economic analysis. Remember, the survey was limited to those whose highest degree was the baccalaureate, so it excluded the many economics majors who went on to pursue graduate studies in law, business administration, economics, public administration, journalism, and other fields.[6]

Final Word

This textbook describes how economic factors affect individual choices and how all these choices come together to shape the economic system. Economics is not the whole story, and economic factors are not always the most important. But economic considerations have important and predictable effects on individual choices, and these choices affect the way we live.

Sure, economics is a challenging discipline, but it is also an exciting and rewarding one. The good news is that you already know a lot about economics. To use this knowledge, however, you must cultivate the art and science of economic analysis. You must be able to simplify the world to formulate questions, isolate the relevant variables, and then tell a persuasive story about how these variables relate.

An economic relation can be expressed in words, represented as a table of quantities, described by a mathematical equation, or illustrated as a graph. The

5. Daniel E. Hecker, "Earnings of College Graduates, 1993," *Monthly Labor Review* (December 1995): p. 15.

6. For a survey of employment opportunities, go to the U.S. Labor Department's Occupational Outlook Handbook at http://www.bls.gov/oco/.

Exhibit 3

Median Annual Earnings of 35- to 44-Year-Olds with Bachelor's as Highest Degree, by Major

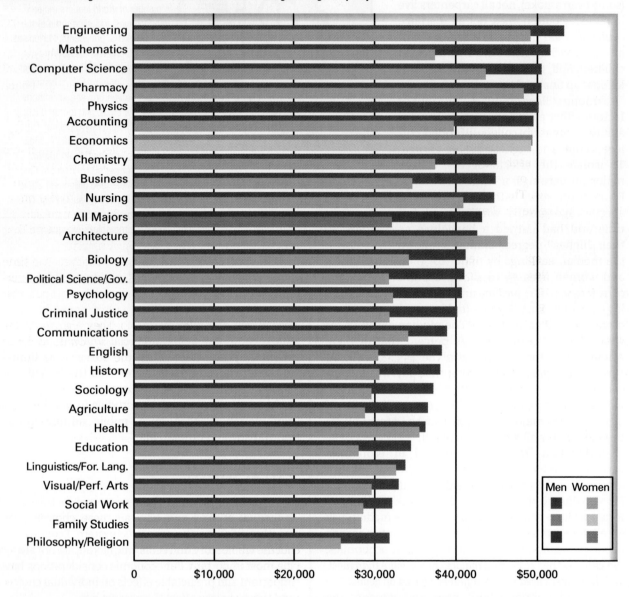

SOURCE: Earnings are for 1993 based on figures reported by Daniel Hecker in "Earnings of College Graduates, 1993." *Monthly Labor Review* (December 1995): pp. 3–17.

appendix to this chapter introduces graphs. You may find this unnecessary. If you are already familiar with relations among variables, slopes, tangents, and the like, you can probably just browse. But if you have little recent experience with graphs, you might benefit from a more careful reading with pencil and paper in hand.

The next chapter introduces key tools of economic analysis. Subsequent chapters use these tools to explore economic problems and to explain economic behavior that may otherwise seem puzzling. You must walk before you can run, however, and in the next chapter, you take your first wobbly steps.

Appendix
Understanding Graphs

Take out a pencil and a blank piece of paper. Go ahead. Put a point in the middle of the paper. This is your point of departure, called the origin. With your pencil at the origin, draw a straight line off to the right. This line is called the horizontal axis. The value of the variable x measured along the horizontal axis increases as you move to the right of the origin. Now mark off this line from 0 to 20, in increments of 5 units each. Returning to the origin, draw another line, this one straight up. This line is called the vertical axis. The value of the variable y measured along the vertical axis increases as you move upward. Mark off this line from 0 to 20, in increments of 5 units each.

Within the space framed by the two axes, you can plot possible combinations of the variables measured along each axis. Each point identifies a value measured along the horizontal, or x, axis *and* a value measured along the vertical, or y, axis. For example, place point *a* in your graph to reflect the combination where x equals 5 units and y equals 15 units. Likewise, place point *b* in your graph to reflect 10 units of x and 5 units of y. Now compare your results with the points shown in Exhibit 4.

A graph is a picture showing how variables relate, and a picture can be worth a thousand words. Take a look at Exhibit 5, which shows the annual U.S. unemployment rate since 1900. The years are measured along the horizontal axis and the unemployment rate is measured as a percentage along the vertical axis. Exhibit 5 is a *time-series graph*, which shows the value of a variable, in this case the percentage of the labor

force unemployed, over time. If you had to describe the information presented in Exhibit 5 in words, the explanation could take many words. The picture shows not only how one year compares to the next but also how one decade compares to another and how the rate trends over time. The sharply higher unemployment rate during the Great Depression of the 1930s is unmistakable. *Graphs convey information in a compact and efficient way.*

This appendix shows how graphs express a variety of possible relations among variables. Most graphs of interest in this book reflect the relationship between two economic variables, such as the unemployment rate and the year, the price of a product and the quantity demanded, or the price of production and the quantity supplied. Because we focus on just two variables at a time, we usually assume that other relevant variables remain constant.

One variable often depends on another. The time it takes you to drive home depends on your average speed. Your weight depends on how much you eat. The amount of Pepsi people buy depends on its price. A *functional relation* exists between two variables when the value of one variable *depends* on the value of another variable. The value of the dependent variable depends on the value of the independent variable. The task of the economist is to isolate economic relations and determine the direction of causality, if any. Recall that one of the pitfalls of economic thinking is the erroneous belief that association is causation. We cannot conclude that, simply because two events relate in time, one causes the other. There may be no relation between the two events.

Drawing Graphs

Let's begin with a simple relation. Suppose you are planning to drive across country and want to determine how far you will travel each day. You plan to average 50 miles per hour. Possible combinations of driving time and distance traveled per day appear in Exhibit 6. One column lists the hours driven per day, and the next column lists the number of

origin
on a graph depicting two-dimensional space, the zero point

horizontal axis
line on a graph that begins at the origin and goes to the right and left; sometimes called the x axis

vertical axis
line on a graph that begins at the origin and goes up and down; sometimes called the y axis

graph
a picture showing how variables relate in two-dimensional space; one variable is measured along the horizontal axis and the other along the vertical axis

dependent variable
a variable whose value depends on that of the independent variable

independent variable
a variable whose value determines that of the dependent variable

Exhibit 4

Basics of a Graph

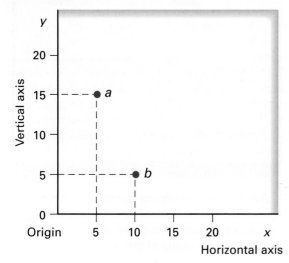

Exhibit 5

U.S. Unemployment Rate Since 1900

A time-series graph depicts the behavior of some economic variable over time.

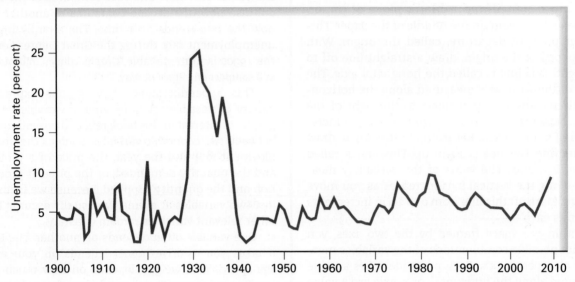

SOURCE: *Bicentennial Edition: Historical Statistics of the United States, Colonial Times to 1970,* U. S. Census Bureau, and *The Economic Report of the President, 2009.*

miles traveled per day, assuming an average speed of 50 miles per hour. The distance traveled, the *dependent* variable, depends on the number of hours driven, the *independent* variable. Combinations of hours driven and distance traveled are shown as *a, b, c, d,* and *e.* Each combination of hours driven and distance traveled is represented by a point in Exhibit 7. For example, point *a* shows that if you drive for 1 hour, you travel 50 miles. Point *b* indicates that if you drive for 2 hours, you travel 100 miles. By connecting the points, or possible combinations, we create a line running upward and to the right. This makes sense, because the longer you drive, the farther you travel. Assumed constant along this line is your average speed of 50 miles per hour.

Types of relations between variables include the following:

1. As one variable increases, the other increases—as in Exhibit 7; this is called a positive, or direct, relation between the variables.

2. As one variable increases, the other decreases; this is called a negative, or inverse, relation.

3. As one variable increases, the other remains unchanged; the two variables are said to be *independent,* or *unrelated.* One of the advantages of graphs is

positive relation (direct relation) occurs when two variables increase or decrease together; the two variables move in the same direction

negative relation (inverse relation) occurs when two variables move in opposite directions; when one increases, the other decreases

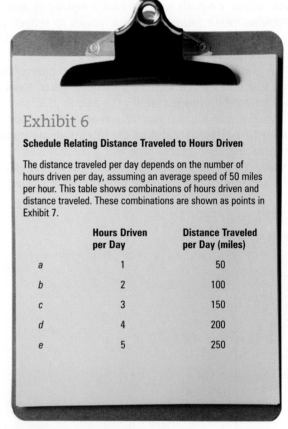

Exhibit 6

Schedule Relating Distance Traveled to Hours Driven

The distance traveled per day depends on the number of hours driven per day, assuming an average speed of 50 miles per hour. This table shows combinations of hours driven and distance traveled. These combinations are shown as points in Exhibit 7.

	Hours Driven per Day	Distance Traveled per Day (miles)
a	1	50
b	2	100
c	3	150
d	4	200
e	5	250

that they easily convey the relation between variables. We do not need to examine the particular combinations of numbers; we need only focus on the shape of the curve.

Exhibit 7

Graph Relating Distance Traveled to Hours Driven

Points *a* through *e* depict different combinations of hours driven per day and the corresponding distances traveled. Connecting these points graphs a line.

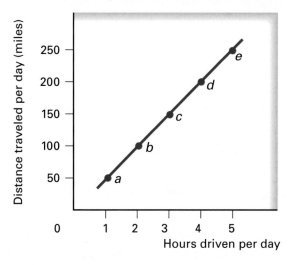

The Slopes of Straight Lines

A more precise way to describe the shape of a curve is to measure its slope. The **slope of a line** indicates how much the vertical variable changes for a given increase in the horizontal variable. Specifically, the slope between any two points along any straight line is the vertical change between these two points divided by the horizontal increase, or

$$\text{Slope} = \frac{\text{Change in the vertical distance}}{\text{Increase in the horizontal distance}}$$

Each of the four panels in Exhibit 8 indicates a vertical change, given a 10-unit increase in the horizontal variable. In panel (a), the vertical distance increases by 5 units when the horizontal distance increases by 10 units. The slope of the

> **slope of a line**
> a measure of how much the vertical variable changes for a given increase in the horizontal variable; the vertical change between two points divided by the horizontal increase

Exhibit 8

Alternative Slopes for Straight Lines

(a) Positive relation

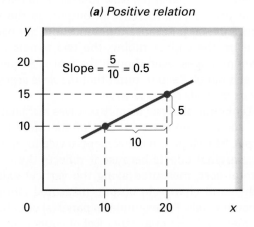

(b) Negative relation

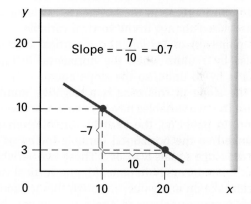

(c) No relation: zero slope

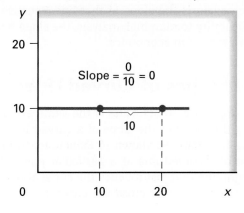

(d) No relation: infinite slope

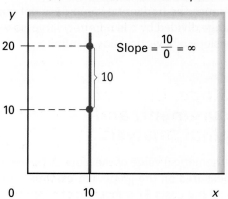

Exhibit 9

Slope Depends on the Unit of Measure

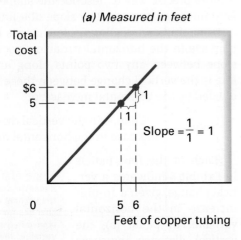

(a) Measured in feet

Slope = $\frac{1}{1}$ = 1

Feet of copper tubing

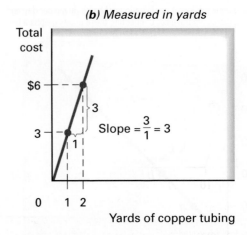

(b) Measured in yards

Slope = $\frac{3}{1}$ = 3

Yards of copper tubing

line is therefore 5/10, or 0.5. Notice that the slope in this case is a positive number because the relation between the two variables is positive, or direct. This slope indicates that for every 1-unit increase in the horizontal variable, the vertical variable increases by 0.5 units. The slope, incidentally, does not imply causality; the increase in the horizontal variable does not necessarily *cause* the increase in the vertical variable. The slope simply measures the relation between an increase in the horizontal variable and the associated change in the vertical variable.

In panel (b) of Exhibit 8, the vertical distance declines by 7 units when the horizontal distance increases by 10 units, so the slope equals –7/10, or –0.7. The slope in this case is a negative number because the two variables have a negative, or inverse, relation. In panel (c), the vertical variable remains unchanged as the horizontal variable increases by 10, so the slope equals 0/10, or 0. These two variables are not related. Finally, in panel (d), the vertical variable can take on any value, although the horizontal variable remains unchanged. Again, the two variables are not related. In this case, any change in the vertical measure, for example a 10-unit change, is divided by 0, because the horizontal value does not change. Any change divided by 0 is infinitely large, so we say that the slope of a vertical line is infinite.

The Slope, Units of Measurement, and Marginal Analysis

The mathematical value of the slope depends on the units measured on the graph. For example, suppose copper tubing costs $1 a foot. Graphs depicting the

relation between total cost and quantity purchased are shown in Exhibit 9. In panel (a), the total cost increases by $1 for each 1-foot increase in the amount of tubing purchased. Thus, the slope equals 1/1, or 1. If the cost per foot remains the same but units are measured not in *feet* but in *yards*, the relation between total cost and quantity purchased is as depicted in panel (b). Now total cost increases by $3 for each 1-*yard* increase in output, so the slope equals 3/1, or 3. Because different units are used to measure the copper tubing, the two panels reflect different slopes, even though the cost is $1 per foot in each panel. Keep in mind that *the slope depends in part on the units of measurement.*

Economic analysis usually involves *marginal analysis,* such as the marginal cost of one more unit of output. The slope is a convenient device for measuring marginal effects because it reflects the change in total cost, measured along the vertical axis, for each 1-unit change in output, measured along the horizontal axis. For example, in panel (a) of Exhibit 9, the marginal cost of another *foot* of copper tubing is $1, which also equals the slope of the line. In panel (b), the marginal cost of another *yard* of tubing is $3, which again is the slope of that line. Because of its applicability to marginal analysis, the slope has special relevance in economics.

The Slopes of Curved Lines

The slope of a straight line is the same everywhere along the line, but the slope of a curved line differs along the curve, as shown in Exhibit 10. To find the slope of a curved line at a particular point, draw a straight line that just touches the curve at that point but does not cut or cross the curve. Such a line is

Exhibit 10

Slope at Different Points on a Curved Line

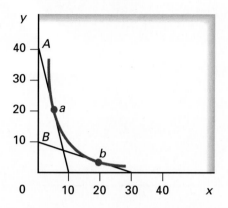

called a **tangent** to the curve at that point. The slope of the tangent gives the slope of the curve at that point. Look at line A, which is tangent to the curve at point a. As the horizontal value increases from 0 to 10, the vertical value drops along A from 40 to 0. Thus, the vertical change divided by the horizontal change equals –40/10, or –4, which is the slope of the curve at point a. This slope is negative because the vertical value decreases as the horizontal value increases. Line B, a line tangent to the curve at point b, has the slope –10/30, or –0.33. As you can see, the curve depicted in Exhibit 10 gets flatter as the horizontal variable increases, so the value of its slope approaches zero.

Other curves, of course, will reflect different slopes as well as different changes in the slope along the curve. Downward-sloping curves have negative slopes, and upward-sloping curves, positive slopes. Sometimes curves, such as those in Exhibit 11, are more complex, having both positive and negative ranges, depending on the horizontal value. In the hill-shaped curve, for small values of x, there is a positive relation between x and y, so the slope is positive. As the value of x increases, however, the slope declines and eventually becomes negative. We can divide the curve into two segments: (1) the segment between the origin and point a, where the

Exhibit 11

Curves with Both Positive and Negative Slopes

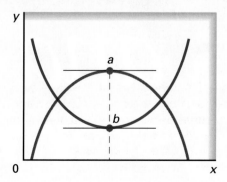

Exhibit 12

Shift of Line Relating Distance Traveled to Hours Driven

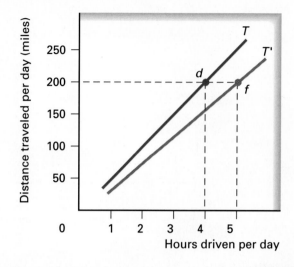

slope is positive, and (2) the segment of the curve to the right of point a, where the slope is negative. The slope of the curve at point a is 0. The U-shaped curve in Exhibit 11 represents the opposite relation: x and y are negatively related until point b is reached; thereafter, they are positively related. The slope equals 0 at point b.

Line Shifts

Let's go back to the example of your cross-country trip, where we were trying to determine how many miles you would travel per day. Recall that we measured hours driven per day on the horizontal axis and miles traveled per day on the vertical axis, assuming an average speed of 50 miles per hour. That same relation is shown as line T in Exhibit 12. What happens if the average speed is 40 miles per hour? The entire relation between hours driven and distance traveled would change, as shown by the shift to the right of line T to T'. With a slower average speed, any distance traveled per day now requires more driving time. For example, 200 miles traveled requires 4 hours of driving when the average speed is 50 miles per hour (as shown by point d on curve T), but 200 miles takes 5 hours when your speed averages 40 miles per hour (as shown by point f on curve T'). Thus, *a change in the assumption about average speed changes the relationship between the two variables observed.* This changed relationship is expressed by a shift of the line that shows how the two variables relate.

That ends our once-over of graphs. Return to this appendix when you need a review.

tangent
a straight line that touches a curve at a point but does not cut or cross the curve; used to measure the slope of a curve at a point

2

Learning Outcomes

LO 1 Describe the impact of choice on opportunity

LO 2 Explain how comparative advantage, specialization, and exchange affect economic outcomes (output)

LO 3 Outline how economies function as production systems

LO 4 Describe different economic systems and the decision-making rules that define them

Economic Tools *and* Economic Systems

> **"What goods and services should different economies produce, how should they produce them, and for whom should they produce them?"**

Why are you reading this book right now rather than doing something else? What is college costing you? Why will you eventually major in one subject rather than continue to take courses in different ones? Why is fast food so fast? Why is there no sense crying over spilt milk? These and other questions are addressed in this chapter, which introduces some tools of economic analysis—some tools of the trade.

Chapter 1 introduced the idea that scarcity forces us to make choices, but the chapter said little about how to make economic choices. This chapter develops a framework for evaluating economic alternatives. First, we consider the cost involved in selecting one alternative over others. Next, we develop tools to explore the choices available to individuals and to the economy as a whole. Finally, we examine the questions that different economies must answer—questions about what goods and services to produce, how to produce them, and for whom to produce them.

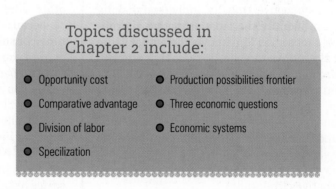

What do you think?

I have more stuff than I have opportunity to make use of.

Strongly Disagree						Strongly Agree
1	2	3	4	5	6	7

Topics discussed in Chapter 2 include:

- Opportunity cost
- Comparative advantage
- Division of labor
- Specilization
- Production possibilities frontier
- Three economic questions
- Economic systems

LO¹ Choice and Opportunity Cost

Think about a decision you just made: the decision to begin reading this chapter right now rather than use the time to study for another course, play sports, watch TV, go online, get some sleep, hang with friends, or do **something else.** Suppose your best alternative to reading right now is getting some sleep. The cost of reading is passing up the opportunity of sleep. Because of scarcity, whenever you make a choice, you must pass up another opportunity; you must incur an *opportunity cost.*

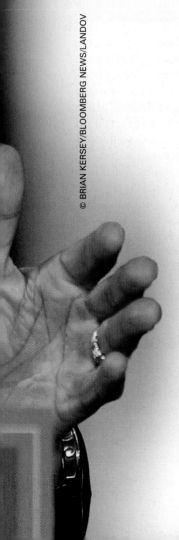

Opportunity Cost

What do we mean when we talk about the cost of something? Isn't it what we must give up—must forgo—to get that thing? The opportunity cost of the chosen item or activity is *the value of the best alternative that is forgone*. You can think of opportunity cost as the *opportunity lost*. Sometimes opportunity cost can be measured in terms of money, although, as we shall see, money is usually only part of opportunity cost.

How many times have you heard people say they did something because they "had nothing better to do"? They actually mean they had nothing else going on. Yet, according to the idea of opportunity cost, people *always* do what they do because they have nothing better to do. The choice selected seems, at the time, preferable to any other possible alternative. You are reading this chapter right now because you have nothing better to do. In fact, you are attending college for the same reason: College appears more attractive than your best alternative.

{ **The Opportunity Cost of Change** }

Consider the following major issues of the beginning of President Barack Obama's term and what they might cost to address:

1. **Fiscal Stimulus vs. The Federal Deficit**—Aggressive spending programs proposed by the new administration (infrastructure building, for instance) could certainly help jumpstart the economy. After years of government deficit spending, however, funds might be better used to address already looming debts and expenses, like Medicare.

2. **Health Care Coverage vs. Competition**—Many Americans have inadequate health insurance coverage, and increased price regulation could help make coverage more affordable. Alternately, reducing restrictions on corporations could result in increased competition and new opportunities for innovation and greater value.

3. **Energy Cost vs. Energy Cleanliness**—The new administration faces many programs competing for its limited resources, including initiatives designed to reduce pollution and U.S. dependence on foreign oil. Consumers, taxpayers, and the government will have to decide which benefits are most worthy of the necessary investment.

SOURCE: Geoff Colvin, "Obama's Opportunity Costs," *Fortune,* 8 December 2008. p. 20.

Opportunity Cost Is Subjective

Like beauty, opportunity cost is in the eye of the beholder. It is subjective. Only the individual making the choice can identify the most attractive alternative. But the chooser seldom knows the actual value of the best alternative forgone, because that alternative is "the road not taken." If you give up an evening of pizza and conversation with friends to work on a term paper, you will never know exactly what you gave up. You know only what you *expected*. Evidently, you expected the value of working on that paper to exceed the value of the best alternative. (Incidentally, focusing on the best alternative forgone makes all lesser alternatives irrelevant.)

Calculating Opportunity Cost Requires Time and Information

opportunity cost
the value of the best alternative forgone when an item or activity is chosen

Economists assume that people rationally choose the most valued alternative. This does not mean you exhaus-

tively assess the value of all possibilities. You assess alternatives as long as the expected marginal benefit of gathering more information about your options exceeds the expected marginal cost (even if you are not aware of making such conscious calculations). In other words, you do the best you can for yourself.

Because learning about alternatives is costly and time consuming, some choices are based on limited or even wrong information. Indeed, some choices may turn out badly (you went for a picnic but it rained; the movie you rented stank; your new shoes pinch; your new exercise equipment gets no exercise; the stock you bought tanked). Regret about lost opportunities is captured in the common expression "coulda, woulda, shoulda." At the time you made the choice, however, you thought you were making the best use of all your scarce resources, including the time required to gather and evaluate information about your alternatives.

Time: The Ultimate Constraint

The Sultan of Brunei is among the richest people on earth, with wealth topping $20 billion based on huge oil revenues that flow into his tiny country. He and his royal family (which has ruled for six centuries) live in a palace with 1,788 rooms, 250 toilets, and a throne room the size of a football field. The family owns hundreds of cars, including dozens of Rolls-Royces. Supported by such wealth, the Sultan would appear to have overcome the economic problem of scarcity. Though he can buy just about whatever he wants, he lacks the time to enjoy his stuff. If he pursues one activity, he cannot at the same time do something else. Each activity involves an opportunity cost. Consequently, the Sultan must choose from among the competing uses of his scarcest resource, time. Although your alternatives are less exotic, you too face time constraints, especially toward the end of the college term.

© AP IMAGES

Opportunity Cost Varies with Circumstance

Opportunity cost depends on your alternatives. This is why you are more likely to study on a Tuesday night than on a Saturday night. On a Tuesday night, the opportunity cost of studying is lower because your alternatives are less attractive than on a Saturday night, when more is happening. Suppose you go to a movie on Saturday night. Your opportunity cost is the value of your best alternative forgone, which might be attending a college game. For some of you, studying on Saturday night may be well down the list of alternatives—perhaps ahead of reorganizing your closet but behind doing your laundry.

Opportunity cost is subjective, but in some cases, money paid for goods and services is a reasonable approximation. For example, the opportunity cost of the new DVD player you bought is the value of spending that $100 on the best forgone alternative. The money measure may leave out some important elements, however, particularly the value of the time involved. For example, renting a movie costs you not just the $4 rental fee but the time and travel required to get it, watch it, and return it.

Even religious practices are subject to opportunity cost. For example, about half the population attends religious services at least once a month. In some states, so called "blue laws" prohibit retail activity on Sunday. Many states have repealed these laws in recent years, thus raising the opportunity cost of church attendance. Researchers have found that when a state repeals its blue laws, religious attendance declines as do church donations. These results do not seem to be linked to any decline in religiosity before the repeal.[1]

❖❖❖
1. See Jonathan Gruber and Daniel Hungerman, "The Church vs. the Mall: What Happens When Religion Faces Increased Secular Competition?" *Quarterly Journal of Economics* (May 2008).

> You should ignore sunk cost in making economic choices.

Sunk Cost and Choice

Suppose you have just finished grocery shopping and are wheeling your cart toward the checkout counters. How do you decide which line to join? Easy. You pick the shortest one. Suppose that it barely moves for 10 minutes, when you notice that a cashier has opened a new line and invites you to check out. Do you switch to the open cashier, or do you think, "Since I've already spent 10 minutes in this line, I'm staying put"? The 10 minutes you waited represents a sunk cost, which is a cost that has already been incurred and cannot be recovered, regardless of what you do next. You should ignore sunk cost in making economic choices. Hence, you should switch. *Economic decision makers should consider only those costs that are affected by the choice. Sunk costs have already been incurred and are not affected by the choice, so they are irrelevant.* Likewise, you should walk out on a bad movie, even if you spent $10 to get in. Your $10 is gone, and sitting through that stinker only makes you worse off. The irrelevance of sunk costs is underscored by proverbs such as "Don't throw good money after bad," "Let bygones be bygones," "That's water over the dam," and "There's no sense crying over spilt milk." The milk has already spilled, so whatever you do now cannot change that. Or, as Tony Soprano would say, "Fuhgeddaboutit!"

Now that you have some idea about opportunity cost, let's see how it helps solve the economic problem.

sunk cost
a cost that has already been incurred, cannot be recovered, and thus is irrelevant for present and future economic decisions

LO² Comparative Advantage, Specialization, and Exchange

Suppose you live in a dormitory. You and your roommate have such tight schedules that you each can spare only about an hour a week for mundane tasks like ironing shirts and typing papers (granted, in reality you may not iron shirts or type papers, but this example will help you understand some important principles). Each of you must turn in a typed three-page paper every week, and you each prefer ironed shirts when you have the time. Let's say it takes you a half hour to type a handwritten paper. Your roommate is from the hunt-and-peck school and takes about an hour. But your roommate is a talented ironer and can iron a shirt in 5 minutes flat (or should that be, iron it flat in 5 minutes?). You take twice as long, or 10 minutes, to iron a shirt.

During the hour set aside each week for typing and ironing, typing takes priority. If you each do your own typing and ironing, you type your paper in a half hour and iron three shirts in the remaining half hour. Your roommate takes the entire hour typing the paper, leaving no time for ironing. Thus, if you each do your own tasks, the combined output is two typed papers and three ironed shirts.

The Law of Comparative Advantage

Before long, you each realize that total output would increase if you did all the typing and your roommate did all the ironing. In the hour available for these tasks, you type both papers and your roommate irons 12 shirts. As a result of specialization, total output increases by 9 shirts! You strike a deal to exchange your typing for your roommate's ironing, so you each end up with a typed paper and 6 ironed shirts. Thus, *each of you is better off as a result of specialization and exchange.* By specializing in the task that you each do better, you are using the law of comparative advantage, which states that the individual with the lower opportunity cost of producing a particular output should specialize in producing that output. You face a lower opportunity cost of typing than does your roommate, because in the time it takes to type a paper, you could iron 3 shirts whereas your roommate could iron 12 shirts in the time it takes your roommate to type the paper. And if you face a lower opportunity cost of typing, your roommate must face a lower opportunity cost of ironing (try working that out).

Absolute Advantage Versus Comparative Advantage

The gains from specialization and exchange so far are obvious. A more interesting case is if you are faster at both tasks. Suppose the example changes only in one respect: your roommate takes 12 minutes to iron a shirt compared with your 10 minutes. You now have an *absolute advantage* in both tasks, meaning each task takes you less time than it does your roommate. More generally, having an absolute advantage means making something using fewer resources than other producers require.

Does your absolute advantage in both activities mean specialization is no longer a good idea? Recall that the law of comparative advantage states that the individual with the *lower opportunity cost* of producing a particular good should specialize in that good. You still take 30 minutes to type a paper and 10 minutes to iron a shirt, so your opportunity cost

> 66 Does your absolute advantage in both activities mean specialization is no longer a good idea? 99

SPECIALIZATION

law of comparative advantage
the individual, firm, region, or country with the lowest opportunity cost of producing a particular good should specialize in that good

absolute advantage
the ability to make something using fewer resources than other producers use

 = 5 ×  + 2 ×

of typing the paper remains at three ironed shirts. Your roommate takes an hour to type a paper and 12 minutes to iron a shirt, so your roommate could iron five shirts in the time it takes to type a paper. Your opportunity cost of typing a paper is ironing three shirts; for your roommate it's ironing five shirts. *Because your opportunity cost of typing is lower than your roommate's, you still have a comparative advantage in typing.* Consequently, your roommate must have a comparative advantage in ironing (again, try working this out to your satisfaction). Therefore, you should do all the typing and your roommate, all the ironing. Although you have an absolute advantage in both tasks, your comparative advantage calls for specializing in the task for which you have the lower opportunity cost—in this case, typing.

If neither of you specialized, you could type one paper and iron three shirts. Your roommate could still type just the one paper. Your combined output would be two papers and three shirts. If you each specialized according to comparative advantage, in an hour you could type both papers and your roommate could iron five shirts. Thus, specialization increases total output by two ironed shirts. Even though you are better at both tasks than your roommate, you are comparatively better at typing. Put another way, your roommate, although worse at both tasks, is not quite as bad at ironing as at typing.

Don't think that this is just common sense. Common sense would lead you to do your own ironing and typing, because you are better at both. *Absolute advantage focuses on who uses the fewest resources, but comparative advantage focuses on what else those resources could produce—that is, on the opportunity cost of those resources.* Comparative advantage is the better guide to who should do what.

The law of comparative advantage applies not only to individuals but also to firms, regions of a country, and entire nations. Individuals, firms, regions, or countries with the lowest opportunity cost of producing a particular good should specialize in producing that good. Because of such factors as climate, workforce skills, natural resources, and capital stock, certain parts of the country and certain parts of the world have a comparative advantage in producing particular goods. From Washington State apples to Florida oranges, from software in India to hardware in Taiwan—*resources are allocated most efficiently across the country and around the world when production and trade conform to the law of comparative advantage.*

Specialization and Exchange

In the previous example, you and your roommate specialized and then exchanged output. No money was involved. In other words, you engaged in barter, where products are traded directly for other products. Barter works best in simple economies with little specialization and few traded goods. But for economies with greater specialization, *money* facilitates exchange. Money—coins, bills, checks, and debit cards—is a *medium of exchange* because it is the one thing that everyone accepts in return for goods and services.

Because of specialization and comparative advantage, most people consume little of what they produce and produce little of what they consume. Each individual specializes, then exchanges that product for money, which in turn is exchanged for goods and services. Did you make anything you are wearing? Probably not. Think about the degree of specialization that went into your cotton shirt. A farmer in a warm climate grew the cotton and sold it to someone who spun it into thread, who sold it to someone who wove it into fabric, who sold it to someone who sewed the shirt, who sold it to a wholesaler, who sold it to a retailer, who sold it to you. Many specialists created that shirt.

> The degree of specialization is limited by the extent of the market.

Evidence of specialization is all around us. Shops at the mall specialize in products ranging from luggage to lingerie. Restaurants range from subs to sushi. Or let your fingers do the walking through the help-wanted ads or *Yellow Pages*, where you will find thousands of specializations. Without moving a muscle, you can observe the division of labor within a single industry by watching the credits roll at the end of a movie. The credits show scores of specialists—from gaffer (lighting electrician) to assistant location scout. TV is no different. A typical TV drama, such as *Grey's Anatomy*, requires hundreds of specialists.

Some specialties may seem odd. For example, professional mourners in Taiwan are sometimes hired by grieving families to scream, wail, and otherwise demonstrate the deep anguish befitting a proper funeral. The degree of specialization is perhaps most obvious online, where the pool of potential customers is so vast that individual sites become sharply focused. For example, you can find sites specializing in musical bowls, tongue studs, toe rings,

comparative advantage the ability to make something at a lower opportunity cost than other producers face

barter the direct exchange of one good for another without using money

> **66** Adam Smith said the degree of specialization is limited by the extent of the market. **99**

brass knuckles, mouth harps, ferret toys, and cat bandannas—just to name a few of the hundreds of thousands of specialty sites. You won't find such precise specialization at the mall. Adam Smith said the degree of specialization is limited by the extent of the market. Online sellers draw on the broadest customer base in the world to find a market niche.

Division of Labor and Gains from Specialization

Picture a visit to McDonald's: "Let's see, I'll have a Big Mac, an order of fries, and a chocolate shake." Less than a minute later your order is ready. It would take you much longer to make a homemade version of this meal. Why is the McDonald's meal faster, cheaper, and—for some people—tastier than one you could make yourself? Why is fast food so fast? McDonald's takes advantage of the gains resulting from the division of labor. Each worker, rather than preparing an entire meal, specializes in separate tasks. This division of labor allows the group to produce much more.

How is this increase in productivity possible? First, the manager can assign tasks according to *individual preferences and abilities*—that is, according to the law of comparative advantage. The worker with the toothy smile and pleasant personality can handle the customers up front; the one with the strong back but few social graces can handle the heavy lifting out back. Second, a worker who performs the same task again and again gets better at it (experience is a good teacher). The worker filling orders at the drive-through, for example, learns to deal with special problems that arise. As another example, consider the experience gained by someone screening bags at the airport. Experience helps the screener distinguish the harmful from the harmless. Third, specialization means no time is lost moving from one task to another. Finally, and perhaps most importantly, the specialization of labor allows for the introduction of more sophisticated production techniques—techniques that would not make sense on a smaller scale. For example, McDonald's large shake machine would be impractical in the home. *Specialized machines make workers more productive.*

To review: The specialization of labor (1) takes advantage of individual preferences and natural abilities, (2) allows

> ONLINE SELLERS DRAW ON THE BROADEST CUSTOMER BASE IN THE WORLD TO FIND A MARKET NICHE.

division of labor
breaking down the production of a good into separate tasks

specialization of labor
focusing work effort on a particular product or a single task

workers to develop more experience at a particular task, (3) reduces the need to shift between different tasks, and (4) permits the introduction of laborsaving machinery. Specialization and the division of labor occur not only among individuals but also among firms, regions, and indeed entire countries. The cotton shirt mentioned earlier might involve growing cotton in one country, turning it into cloth in another, making the shirt in a third, and selling it in a fourth.

We should also acknowledge the downside of specialization. Doing the same thing all day can become tedious. Consider, for example, the assembly-line worker whose sole task is to tighten a particular bolt. Such a job could drive that worker bonkers or lead to repetitive motion injury. Thus, the gains from dividing production into individual tasks must be weighed against any problems caused by assigning workers to repetitive, tedious, and potentially harmful jobs. Fortunately, many routine tasks, particularly on assembly lines, can be turned over to robots.

LO³ The Economy's Production Possibilities

The focus to this point has been on how individuals choose to use their scarce resources to satisfy their unlimited wants or, more specifically, how they specialize based on comparative advantage. This emphasis on the individual has been appropriate because the economy is shaped by the choices of individual decision makers, whether they are consumers, producers, or public officials. Just as resources are scarce for the individual, they are also scarce for the economy as a whole (no fallacy of composition here). An economy has millions of different resources that can be combined in all kinds of ways to produce millions of different goods and services. This section steps back from the immense complexity of the real economy to develop another model, which explores the economy's production options.

Efficiency and the Production Possibilities Frontier

Let's develop a model to get some idea of how much an economy can produce with the resources available. What are the economy's production capabilities? Here are the model's assumptions:

1. To simplify matters, output is limited to just two broad classes of products: consumer goods and capital goods.

2. The focus is on production during a given period—in this case, a year.

3. The economy's resources are fixed in both quantity and quality during that period.

4. Society's knowledge about how these resources combine to produce output—that is, the available *technology*—does not change during the year.

5. Also assumed fixed during the period are the "rules of the game" that facilitate production and exchange. These include such things as the legal system, property rights, tax laws, patent laws, and the manners, customs, and conventions of the market.

The point of these simplifying assumptions is to freeze in time the economy's resources, technology, and rules of the game so we can focus on the economy's production options.

Given the resources, technology, and rules of the game available in the economy, the production possibilities frontier, or PPF, identifies possible combinations of the two types of goods that can be produced when all available resources are employed efficiently. *Resources are employed efficiently when there is no change that could increase the production of one good without decreasing the production of the other good.* Efficiency involves getting the most from available resources.

The economy's PPF for consumer goods and capital goods is shown by the curve *AF* in Exhibit 1. Point A identifies the amount of consumer goods produced per year if all the economy's resources are used efficiently to produce consumer goods. Point F identifies the amount of capital goods produced per year if all the economy's resources are used efficiently to produce capital goods. Points along the curve between A and F identify possible combinations of the two goods that can be produced when *all* the economy's resources *are used efficiently.*

Inefficient and Unattainable Production

Points inside the PPF, such as *I* in Exhibit 1, identify combinations that do not employ resources efficiently. Note that point *C* yields more consumer goods and no fewer capital goods than *I*. And point *E* yields more capital goods and no fewer consumer goods than *I*. Indeed, any point along the PPF between *C* and *E*, such as point *D*, yields both more consumer goods and more capital goods than *I*. Hence, point *I* is *inefficient.* By using resources more efficiently, the economy can produce more of at least one good without reducing the production of the other good. Points outside the PPF, such as *U* in Exhibit 1, identify *unattainable* combinations, given the availability of resources, technology,

Exhibit 1

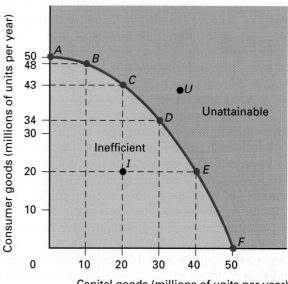

The Economy's Production Possibilities Frontier

and rules of the game. Thus, *the PPF not only shows efficient combinations of production but also serves as the boundary between inefficient combinations inside the frontier and unattainable combinations outside the frontier.*

The Shape of the Production Possibilities Frontier

Focus again on point A in Exhibit 1. Any movement along the PPF involves giving up some of one good to get more of the other. Movements down along the curve indicate that the opportunity cost of more capital goods is fewer consumer goods. For example, moving from point A to point B *increases* capital production from none to 10 million units but *reduces* consumer units from 50 million to 48 million. Increasing capital to 10 million units reduces consumer goods only a little. Capital production initially employs resources (such as heavy machinery used to build factories) that add few consumer units but are quite productive in making capital.

As shown by the dashed lines in Exhibit 1, each additional 10 million capital units reduces consumer units by a successively larger amount. The resources used to produce more capital were increasingly better suited to producing consumer goods.

production possibilities frontier (PPF) a curve showing alternative combinations of goods that can be produced when available resources are used efficiently; a boundary line between inefficient and unattainable combinations

efficiency the condition that exists when there is no way resources can be reallocated to increase the production of one good without decreasing the production of another; getting the most from available resources

The opportunity cost of making more capital goods inceases, because resources in the economy are not all perfectly adaptable to the production of both types of goods. The shape of the production possibilities frontier reflects the law of increasing opportunity cost. If the economy uses all resources efficiently, the law of increasing opportunity cost states that each additional increment of one good requires the economy to sacrifice successively larger and larger increments of the other good.

The PPF derives its bowed-out shape from the law of increasing opportunity cost. For example, whereas the first 10 million units of capital have an opportunity cost of only 2 million consumer units, the final 10 million units of capital—that is, the increase from point E to point F—have an opportunity cost of 20 million consumer units. Notice that the slope of the PPF shows the opportunity cost of an increment of capital. As the economy moves down the curve, the curve becomes steeper, reflecting the higher opportunity cost of capital goods in terms of forgone consumer goods. The law of increasing opportunity cost also applies when moving from the production of capital goods to the production of consumer goods. If resources were perfectly adaptable to alternative uses, the PPF would be a straight line, reflecting a constant opportunity cost along the PPF.

What Can Shift the Production Possibilities Frontier?

Any production possibilities frontier assumes the economy's resources

law of increasing opportunity cost to produce more of one good, a successively larger amount of the other good must be sacrificed

economic growth an increase in the economy's ability to produce goods and services; reflected by an outward shift of the economy's production possibilities frontier

and technology are fixed during the period under consideration. Over time, however, the PPF may shift if resources, technology, or the rules of the game change. Economic growth is an expansion in the economy's production possibilities as reflected by an outward shift of the PPF.

Changes in Resource Availability

If people decide to work longer hours, the PPF shifts outward, as shown in panel (a) of Exhibit 2. An increase in the size or health of the labor force, an increase in the skills of the labor force, or an increase in the availability of other resources, such as new oil discoveries, also shifts the PPF outward. In contrast, a decrease of resources shifts the PPF inward, as depicted in panel (b). For example, in 1990 Iraq invaded Kuwait, setting oil fields ablaze and destroying much of Kuwait's physical capital. In West Africa, the encroaching sands of the Sahara destroy thousands of square miles of farmland each year.

Exhibit 2

Shifts of the Economy's Production Possibilities Frontier

(a) Increase in available resources

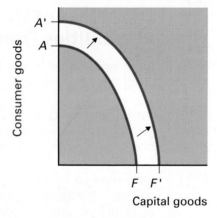

(b) Decrease in available resources

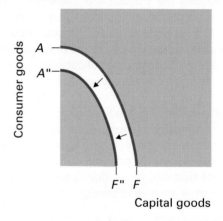

(c) Change in resources, technology, or rules that benefits consumer goods

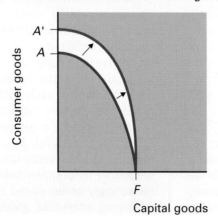

(d) Change in resources, technology, or rules that benefits capital goods

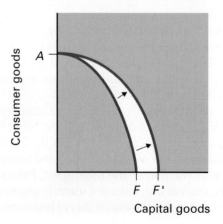

Disasters cause an inward shift or retraction of the PPF.

© REUTERS/LANDOV

of both consumer goods and capital goods, as shown in panel (a) of Exhibit 2. For example, the Internet has increased each firm's ability to identify available resources. A technological discovery that benefits consumer goods only, such as more disease resistant crops, is reflected by a rotation outward of the PPF along the consumer goods axis, as shown in panel (c). Note that point F remains unchanged because the breakthrough does not affect the production of capital goods. Panel (d) shows a technological advance in the production of capital goods, such as better software for designing heavy machinery.

And in northwest China, a rising tide of wind-blown sand has claimed grasslands, lakes, and forests and swallowed entire villages, forcing tens of thousands of people to flee.

The new PPFs in panels (a) and (b) appear to be parallel to the original ones, indicating that the resources that changed could produce both capital goods and consumer goods. For example, an increase in electrical power can enhance the production of both, as shown in panel (a). If a resource such as farmland benefits just consumer goods, then increased availability or productivity of that resource shifts the PPF more along the consumer goods axis, as shown in panel (c). Panel (d) shows the effect of an increase in a resource such as construction equipment that is suited only to capital goods.

Increases in the Capital Stock

An economy's PPF depends in part on the stock of human and physical capital. The more capital an economy produces during one period, the more output can be produced in the next period. Thus, producing more capital goods this period (for example, more machines in the case of physical capital or more education in the case of human capital) shifts the economy's PPF outward the next period. The choice between consumer goods and capital goods is really the choice between present consumption and future production. Again, the more capital goods produced this period, the greater the economy's production possibilities next period.

Technological Change

A technological discovery that employs resources more efficiently could shift the economy's PPF outward. Some discoveries enhance the production

Improvements in the Rules of the Game

The rules of the game are the formal and informal institutions that support the economy—the laws, customs, manners, conventions, and other institutional underpinnings that encourage people to pursue productive activity. A more stable political environment and more reliable property rights increase the incentive to work and to invest, and thus help the economy grow. For example, people have more incentive to work if taxes claim less of their paychecks. People have more incentive to invest if they are more confident that their investment will not be appropriated by government, stolen by thieves, destroyed by civil unrest, or blown up by terrorists. Improvements in the rules of the game shift the economy's PPF outward. On the other hand, greater instability reduces the economy's productive capacity, as reflected by in inward shift of the PPF. Rankings like the ones in Exhibit 3 on the next page illustrate how rules of the game of a particular country affect how easy it is to conduct business there.

What We Learn from the PPF

The PPF demonstrates several ideas introduced so far. The first is *efficiency*: The PPF describes efficient combinations of outputs, given the economy's resources, technology, and rules of the game. The second idea is *scarcity*: Given the resources,

> **rules of the game** the formal and informal institutions that support the economy—the laws, customs, manners, conventions, and other institutional underpinnings that encourage people to pursue productive activity

Exhibit 3

Best 10 and Worst 10 Among 181 Countries Based on Ease of Doing Business, According to the World Bank

Best 10	Worst 10
1. Singapore	172. Niger
2. New Zealand	173. Eritrea
3. United States	174. Venezuela
4. Hong Kong	175. Chad
5. Denmark	176. São Tomé and Principe
6. United Kingdom	177. Burundi
7. Ireland	178. Republic of Congo
8. Canada	179. Guinea-Bissau
9. Australia	180. Central African Republic
10. Norway	181. Democratic Republic of Congo

SOURCE: *Doing Business in 2009: Economy Rankings,* World Bank Publications, http://www.doingbusiness.org/economyrankings/

technology, and rules of the game, the economy can produce only so much. The PPF slopes downward, so more of one good means less of the other good, thus demonstrating *opportunity cost.* The PPF's bowed-out shape reflects the *law of increasing opportunity cost,* which arises because some resources are not perfectly adaptable to the production of each good. And a shift outward in the PPF reflects *economic growth.*

Finally, because society must somehow select a specific combination of output—a single point—along the PPF, the PPF also underscores the need for *choice.* Selecting a particular combination determines not only consumer goods available this period but also the capital stock available next period. One thing the PPF does not tell us is which combination to choose. The PPF tells us only about the costs, not the benefits, of the two goods. To make a selection, we need to know about both costs *and* benefits. How society goes about choosing a particular combination depends on the nature of the economic system, as you will see next.

economic system
the set of mechanisms and institutions that resolve the what, how, and for whom questions

LO⁴ Economic Systems

Each point along the economy's production possibilities frontier is an efficient combination of outputs. Whether the economy produces efficiently and how the economy selects the most preferred combination depends on the decision-making rules employed. But regardless of how decisions are made, each economy must answer three fundamental questions.

Three Questions Every Economic System Must Answer

What goods and services are to be produced? How are they to be produced? And for whom are they to be produced? An *economic system* is the set of mechanisms and institutions that resolve the *what, how,* and *for whom* questions. Some criteria used to distinguish among economic systems are (1) who owns the resources, (2) what decision-making process is used to allocate resources and products, and (3) what types of incentives guide economic decision makers.

What Goods and Services Are to Be Produced?

Most of us take for granted the incredible number of choices that go into deciding what gets produced—everything from which new kitchen appliances are introduced, which roads get built, to which of the 10,000 movie scripts purchased by U.S. studios each year get to be among the 500 movies made.[2] Although different economies resolve these and millions of other questions using different decision-making rules and mechanisms, all economies must somehow make such choices.

How Are Goods and Services to Be Produced?

The economic system must determine how output gets produced. Which resources should be used, and how should they be combined to produce each product? How much labor should be used and at what skill

"Of the 10,000 movie scripts Hollywood studios buy each year, only 500 get made into movies."

2. As reported in Ian Parker, "The Real McKee," *New Yorker,* 20 October 2003.

levels? What kinds of machines should be used? What new technology should be incorporated into the latest video games? Should the office complex be built in the city or closer to the interstate highway? Millions of individual decisions determine which resources are employed and how these resources are combined.

For Whom Are Goods and Services to Be Produced?

Who will actually consume the goods and services produced? The economic system must determine how to allocate the fruits of production among the population. Should everyone receive equal shares? Should the weak and the sick get more? Should those willing to wait in line get more? Should goods be allocated according to height? Weight? Religion? Age? Gender? Race? Looks? Strength? Political connections? The value of resources supplied? The question "For whom are goods and services to be produced?" is often referred to as the *distribution question*.

Although the three economic questions were discussed separately, they are closely related. The answer to one depends on the answers to the others. For example, an economy that distributes goods and services uniformly to all will, no doubt, answer the what-will-be-produced question differently than an economy that somehow allows more personal choice. As we have seen, laws about resource ownership and the role of government determine the "rules of the game"—the set of conditions that shape individual incentives and constraints. Along a spectrum ranging from the freest to the most regimented types of economic systems, *pure capitalism* would be at one end and the *pure command system* at the other.

Pure Capitalism

Under **pure capitalism**, the rules of the game include the private ownership of resources and the market distribution of products. Owners have *property rights* to the use of their resources and are therefore free to supply those resources to the highest bidder. **Private property rights** allow individuals to use resources or to charge others for their use. Any income derived from supplying labor, capital, natural resources, or entrepreneurial ability goes to the individual resources owners. Producers are free to make and sell whatever they think will be profitable. Consumers are free to buy whatever goods they can afford. All this voluntary buying and selling is coordinated by unrestricted markets, where buyers and sellers make their intentions known. Market prices guide resources to their most productive use and channel goods and services to the consumers who value them the most.

Under pure capitalism, markets answer the what, how, and for whom questions. That's why capitalism is also referred to as a *market system*. Markets transmit information about relative scarcity, provide individual incentives, and distribute income among resource suppliers. No individual or small group coordinates these activities. Rather, it is the voluntary choices of many buyers and sellers responding only to their individual incentives and constraints that direct resources and products to those who value them the most.

According to Adam Smith (1723–1790), market forces allocate resources as if by an "invisible hand"—an unseen force that harnesses the pursuit of self-interest to direct resources where they earn the greatest payoff. According to Smith, *although each individual pursues his or her self-interest, the "invisible hand" of markets promotes the general welfare.* Capitalism is sometimes called *laissez-faire*; translated from the French, this phrase means "to let do," or to let people do as they choose without government intervention. Thus, under capitalism, voluntary choices based on rational self-interest are made in unrestricted markets to answer the questions what, how, and for whom.

As we will see in later chapters, pure capitalism has its flaws. The most notable market failures are:

1. No central authority protects property rights, enforces contracts, and otherwise ensures that the rules of the game are followed.

2. People with no resources to sell could starve.

3. Some producers may try to monopolize markets by eliminating the competition.

4. The production or consumption of some goods involves side effects that can harm or benefit people not involved in the market transaction.

5. Private firms have no incentive to produce so-called *public goods,* such as national defense, because private firms cannot prevent nonpayers from enjoying the benefits of public goods.

Because of these limitations, countries have modified pure capitalism to allow some role for government. Even Adam Smith believed government should play a role. The United States is among the most market-oriented economies in the world today.

pure capitalism
an economic system characterized by the private ownership of resources and the use of prices to coordinate economic activity in unregulated markets

private property rights
an owner's right to use, rent, or sell resources or property

Common ownership often leads to common neglect.

Pure Command System

In a pure command system, resources are directed and production is coordinated not by market forces but by the "command," or central plan, of government. In theory at least, instead of private property, there is public, or *communal*, ownership of property. That's why central planning is sometimes called *communism*. Government planners, as representatives of all the people, answer such questions through *central plans* spelling out how much steel, how many cars, and how much housing to produce. They also decide how to produce these goods and who gets them.

In theory, the pure command system incorporates individual choices into collective choices, which, in turn, are reflected in the central plans. In fact, command economies often have names that focus on collective choice, such as the People's Republic of China and the Democratic People's Republic of Korea (North Korea). In practice, the pure command system also has flaws, most notably:

pure command system
an economic system characterized by the public ownership of resources and centralized planning

mixed system
an economic system characterized by the private ownership of some resources and the public ownership of other resources; some markets are regulated by government

1. Running an economy is so complicated that some resources are used inefficiently.

2. Because nobody in particular owns resources, each person has less incentive to employ them in their highest-valued use, so some resources are wasted.

3. Central plans may reflect more the preferences of central planners than those of society.

4. Because government is responsible for all production, the variety of products tends to be more limited than in a capitalist economy.

5. Each individual has less personal freedom in making economic choices.

Because of these limitations, countries have modified the pure command system to allow a role for markets. North Korea is perhaps the most centrally planned economy in the world today.

Mixed and Transitional Economies

No country on earth exemplifies either type of economic system in its pure form. Economic systems have grown more alike over time, with the role of government increasing in capitalist economies and the role of markets increasing in command economies. The United States represents a mixed system, with government directly accounting for about one-third of all economic activity. What's more, government regulates the private sector in a variety of ways. For example, local zoning boards determine lot sizes, home sizes, and the types of industries allowed. Federal bodies regulate workplace safety, environmental quality, competitive fairness, food and drug quality, and many other activities.

Although both ends of the spectrum have moved toward the center, capitalism has gained the most converts in recent decades. Perhaps the benefits of markets are no better illustrated than where a country, as a result of war or political upheaval, became divided by ideology into a capitalist economy and a command economy, such as with Taiwan and China or South Korea and North Korea. In each case, the economies began with similar human and physical resources, but once they went their separate ways, economic growth diverged sharply, with the capitalist economies outperforming the command economies. For example, Taiwan's production per capita in 2006 was four times that of China, and South Korea's production per capita was 12 times that of North Korea.

Consider the experience of the pilgrims in 1620 while establishing Plymouth Colony. They first tried communal ownership of the land. That turned out badly. Crops were neglected and food shortages developed. After three years of near starvation, the system was changed so that each family was assigned a private plot of land and granted the fruits of that plot. Yields increased sharply. The pilgrims learned that people take better care of what they own individually; common ownership often leads to common neglect.

Recognizing the incentive power of property rights and markets, some of the most die-hard central planners are now allowing a role for markets. For example, about one-fifth of the world's population lives in China, which grows more market oriented each day, even going so far as to give private property constitutional protection on a par with state property. In a poll of Chinese citizens, 74 percent agreed that "the free enterprise system is the best system

on which to base the future of the world." Among Americans polled, 71 percent agreed with that statement.[3] More than a decade ago, the former Soviet Union dissolved into 15 independent republics; most converted state-owned enterprises into private firms. From Moscow to Beijing, from Hungary to Mongolia, the transition to mixed economies now under way in former command economies will shape the world for decades to come.

Economies Based on Custom or Religion

Finally, some economic systems are molded largely by custom or religion. For example, caste systems in India and elsewhere restrict occupational choices. Charging interest is banned under Islamic law. Family relations also play significant roles in organizing and coordinating economic activity. Even in the United States, some occupations are still dominated by women, others by men, largely because of tradition. Your own pattern of consumption and choice of occupation may be influenced by some of these considerations.

Final Word

Although economies can answer the three economic questions in a variety of ways, this book focuses primarily on the mixed market system, such as exists in the United States. This type of economy blends *private choice,* guided by the price system in competitive markets, with *public choice,* guided by democracy in political markets. The study of mixed market systems grows more relevant as former command economies try to develop markets. The next chapter focuses on the economic actors in a mixed economy and explains why government gets into the act.

❂❂❂

3. As reported in "Capitalism, Comrade," *Wall Street Journal,* 18 January 2006.

Scripts bought by Hollywood studios each year > 10,000

Notable limitations of pure command and pure capitalism > 5

Multiple by which per capita production in South Korea exceeded that of North Korea > 12

Main questions every economic system must answer > 3

Learning Outcomes

LO [1] Explain the role of the household in an economic system

LO [2] Identify the different types of firms and describe their roles in the economy

LO [3] Outline the ways governments affect their economies

LO [4] Outline the international influences on an economy

3

Economic
Decision Makers

"What happens to personal income once it comes into the household?"

If we live in the age of specialization, then why haven't specialists taken over all production? For example, why do most of us still do our own laundry and perform dozens of other tasks for ourselves? In what sense has production moved from the household to the firm and then back to the household? If the "invisible hand" of competitive markets is so efficient, why does government get into the act? Answers to these and other questions are addressed in this chapter, which discusses the four economic decision makers: households, firms, governments, and the rest of the world.

To develop a better feel for how the economy works, you must get more acquainted with the key players. You already know more about them than you may realize. You grew up in a household. You have dealt with firms all your life, from Sony to Subway. You know much about governments, from taxes to public schools. And you have a growing awareness of the rest of the world, from online sites, to imports, to foreign travel. This chapter draws on your abundant personal experience with economic decision makers to consider their makeup and objectives.

What do you think?

If I could afford it, I would hire a housekeeper.

Strongly Disagree						Strongly Agree
1	2	3	4	5	6	7

Topics discussed in Chapter 3 include:

- Evolution of the household
- Evolution of the firm
- Types of firms
- Market failures and government remedies
- Taxing and public spending
- International trade and finance

LO¹ The Household

Households **play the starring role in a market economy.** Their demand for goods and services determines what gets produced. And their supplies of labor, capital, natural resources, and entrepreneurial ability produce that output. As demanders of goods and services and suppliers of resources, households make all kinds of choices, such as what to buy, how much to save, where to live, and where to work. Although a household usually consists of several individuals, we will view each household as acting like a single decision maker.

The Evolution of the Household

In earlier times, when the economy was primarily agricultural, a farm household was largely self-sufficient. Each family member specialized in a specific farm task—cooking meals, making clothes, tending livestock, planting crops, and so on. These early households produced what they consumed and consumed what they produced. With the introduction of new seed varieties, better fertilizers, and laborsaving machinery, farm productivity increased sharply. Fewer farmers were needed to grow enough food to feed a nation. At the same time, the growth of urban factories increased the demand for factory labor. As a result, workers moved from farms to cities, where they became more specialized but less self-sufficient.

Households evolved in other ways. For example, in 1950, only about 15 percent of married women with young children were in the labor force. Since then, higher levels of education among women and a growing demand for their labor increased women's earnings, thus raising their opportunity cost of working in the home. This higher opportunity cost contributed to their growing labor force participation. Today 70 percent of women with children under 18 are in the labor force.

The rise of two-earner households has affected the family as an economic unit.

utility
the satisfaction received from consumption; sense of well-being

Households produce less for themselves and demand more from the market. For example, child-care services and fast-food restaurants have displaced some household production (Americans consume about one-third of their calories away from home). The rise in two-earner families has reduced specialization within the household—a central feature of the farm family. Nonetheless, some production still occurs in the home, as we'll explore later.

Households Maximize Utility

There are more than 115 million U.S. households. All those who live together under one roof are considered part of the same household. What exactly do households attempt to accomplish in making decisions? Economists assume that people try to maximize their level of satisfaction, sense of well-being, happiness, and overall welfare. In short, households attempt to maximize utility. Households, like other economic decision makers, are viewed as rational, meaning that they try to act in their best interests and do not deliberately make themselves less happy. Utility maximization depends on each household's subjective goals, not on some objective standard. For example, some households maintain neat homes with well-groomed lawns; others pay little attention to their homes and use their lawns as junkyards.

70% of women with children under 18 are in the labor force.

© REGINE MAHAUX/STONE/GETTY IMAGES

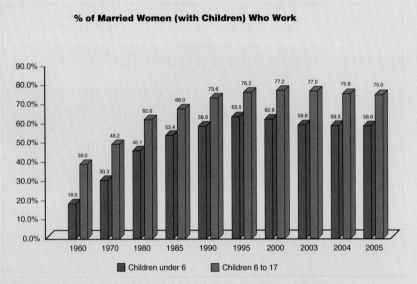

% of Married Women (with Children) Who Work

	1960	1970	1980	1985	1990	1995	2000	2003	2004	2005
Children under 6	18.6	30.3	45.1	53.4	58.9	63.5	62.8	59.8	59.3	58.8
Children 6 to 17	39.0	49.2	62.0	68.0	73.6	76.2	77.2	77.0	75.6	75.0

SOURCES: U.S. Census Bureau, *Statistical Abstract of the United States, 1999, 2001, and 2004–2005* (Washington, D.C.: U.S. Government Printing Office, 1999, 2001, and 2004), "Employment Status of Women by Marital Status and Presence and Age of Children: 1960 to 1998," Table No. 631; "Employment Status of Women by Marital Status and Presence and Age of Children: 1970 to 2005," Table No. 580.

Households as Resource Suppliers

Households use their limited resources—labor, capital, natural resources, and entrepreneurial ability—in an attempt to satisfy their unlimited wants. They can use these resources to produce goods and services in their homes. For example, they can prepare meals, mow the lawn, and fix a leaky faucet. They can also sell these resources in the resource market and use the income to buy goods and services in the product market. The most valuable resource sold by most households is labor.

Panel (a) of Exhibit 1 shows the sources of personal income received by U.S. households in 2007, when personal income totaled $11.7 trillion. As you can see, 62 percent of personal income came from wages and salaries. A distant second was transfer payments (to be discussed next), at 13 percent of personal income, followed by personal interest at 10 percent, and proprietors' income at 8 percent. *Proprietors* are people who work for themselves rather than for employers; farmers, plumbers, and doctors are often self-employed. Proprietors' income should also be considered a form of labor income. *Over two-thirds of personal income in the United States comes from labor earnings rather than from the ownership of other resources such as capital or natural resources.*

Because of a poor education, disability, discrimination, time demands of caring for small children, or bad luck, some households have few resources that are valued in the market. Society has made the political decision that individuals in such circumstances should receive short-term public assistance. Consequently, the government gives some households transfer payments, which are outright grants. *Cash transfers* are monetary payments, such as welfare benefits, Social Security, unemployment compensation, and disability benefits. *In-kind transfers* provide for specific goods and services, such as food stamps, health care, and housing.

Households as Demanders of Goods and Services

What happens to personal income once it comes into the household? Most goes to personal consumption, which sorts into three broad spending categories: (1) *durable goods*—that is, goods expected to last three or more years—such as an automobile or a refrigerator; (2) *nondurable goods,* such as food, clothing, and gasoline; and (3) *services,* such as haircuts, air travel, and medical care. As you can see from panel (b) of Exhibit 1, spending on durable goods in 2007 claimed 9 percent of U.S. personal income; nondurables, 24 percent; and services, 50 percent. Taxes claimed 13

> **transfer payments**
> cash or in-kind benefits given to individuals as outright grants from the government

Exhibit 1

Where U.S. Personal Income Comes From and Where It Goes

(a) Over two-thirds of personal income in 2007 was from wages, salaries, and proprietors' income

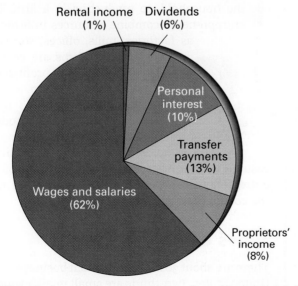

(b) Half of U.S. personal income in 2007 was spent on services

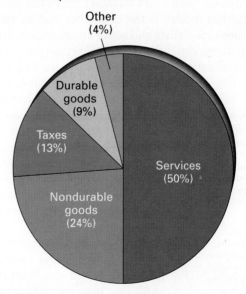

SOURCE: Based on figures from *Survey of Current Business,* Bureau of Economic Analysis, October 2008, Tables 2.1 and 2.3.5. For the latest figures, go to http://www.bea.gov/scb/index.htm.

percent, and all other categories, including savings, claimed just 4 percent. So half of all personal income went for services—the fastest growing sector, because many services, such as child care, are shifting from do-it-yourself home production to market production.

LO² The Firm

Households members once built their own homes, made their own clothes and furniture, grew their own food, and amused themselves with books, games, and hobbies. Over time, however, the efficiency arising from comparative advantage resulted in a greater specialization among resource suppliers. This section takes a look at firms, beginning with their evolution.

The Evolution of the Firm

Specialization and comparative advantage explain why households are no longer self-sufficient. But why is a firm the natural result? For example, rather than make a woolen sweater from scratch, couldn't a consumer take advantage of specialization by negotiating with someone who produced the wool, another who spun the wool into yarn, and a third who knitted the yarn into a sweater? Here's the problem with that model: If the consumer had to visit each of these specialists and strike an agreement, the resulting *transaction costs* could easily erase the gains from specialization. Instead of visiting and bargaining with each specialist, the consumer can pay someone to do the bargaining—an entrepreneur, who hires all the resources necessary to make the sweater. *An entrepreneur, by contracting for many sweaters rather than just one, is able to reduce the transaction costs per sweater.*

For about two hundred years, profit-seeking entrepreneurs relied on "putting out" raw material, like wool and cotton, to rural house-

> SPECIALIZATION AND COMPARATIVE ADVANTAGE EXPLAIN WHY HOUSEHOLDS ARE NO LONGER SELF-SUFFICIENT.

holds that turned it into finished products, like woolen goods made from yarn. The system developed in the British Isles, where workers' cottages served as tiny factories, especially during winter months, when farming chores were light (so the opportunity cost was low). This approach, which came to be known as the *cottage industry system*, still exists in some parts of the world. You might think of this system as part way between household self-sufficiency and the modern firm.

As the British economy expanded in the 18th century, entrepreneurs began organizing the stages of production under one roof. Technological developments, such as waterpower and later steam power, increased the productivity of each worker and contributed to the shift of employment from rural areas to urban factories. *Work, therefore, became organized in large, centrally powered factories that (1) promoted a more efficient division of labor, (2) allowed for the direct supervision of production, (3) reduced transportation costs, and (4) facilitated the use of machines far bigger than anything used in the home.* The development of large-scale factory production, known as the Industrial Revolution, began in Great Britain around 1750 and spread to the rest of Europe, North America, and Australia.

Production, then, evolved from self-sufficient rural households to the cottage industry system, where specialized production occurred in the household, to production in a firm. Today, entrepreneurs combine resources in firms such as factories, mills, offices, stores, and restaurants. Firms are economic units formed by profit-seeking entrepreneurs who combine labor, capital, and natural resources to produce goods and services. Just as we assume that households try to maximize utility, we assume that firms try to *maximize profit*. Profit, the entrepreneur's reward, equals sales revenue minus the cost of production.

Types of Firms

There are about 30 million for-profit businesses in the United States. Two-thirds are small retail businesses, small service operations, part-time home-based businesses, and small farms. Each year more than a million new businesses start up and many fail. Firms are organized in one of three ways: as a sole proprietorship, as a partnership, or as a corporation.

Sole Proprietorships

The simplest form of business organization is the **sole proprietorship**, a single-owner firm. Examples are self-employed plumbers, farmers, and dentists. Most sole proprietorships consist of just the self-employed proprietor—there are no hired employees. To organize a sole proprietorship, the owner simply opens for business by, for example, taking out a classified ad announcing availability for plumbing or whatever. The owner is in complete control. But he or she faces unlimited liability and could lose everything, including a home and other personal assets, to settle business debts or other claims against the business. Also, since the sole proprietor has no partners or other financial backers, raising enough money to get the business going can be a challenge. One final disadvantage is that a sole proprietorship usually goes out of business when the proprietor dies or leaves the business. Still, a sole proprietorship is the most common type of business, accounting most recently for 72 percent of all U.S. businesses. Nonetheless, because this type of firm is typically small, proprietorships generate just a tiny portion of all U.S. business sales—only 4 percent.

Partnerships

A more complicated form of business is the **partnership**, which involves two or more individuals who agree to combine their funds and efforts in return for a share of the profit or loss. Law, accounting, and medical partnerships typify this business form. Partners have strength in numbers and often find it easier than sole proprietors to raise enough funds to get the business going. But partners may not always agree. Also, each partner usually faces unlimited liability for any debts or claims against the partnership, so one partner could lose everything because of another's mistake. Finally, the death or departure of one partner can disrupt the firm's continuity and require a complete reorganization. The partnership is the least common form of U.S. business, making up only 10 percent of all firms and 12 percent of all business sales.

Corporations

By far the most influential form of business is the corporation. A **corporation** is a legal entity established through articles of incorporation. Shares of stock confer corporate ownership, thereby entitling stockholders to a claim on any profit. A major advantage of the corporate form is that many investors—hundreds, thousands, even millions—can pool their funds, so incorporating represents the easiest way to amass large sums to finance the business. Also, stockholder liability for any loss is limited to the value of their stock, meaning stockholders enjoy *limited liability*. A final advantage of this form of organization is that the corporation has a life apart from its owners. The corporation survives even if ownership changes hands, and it can be taxed, sued, and even charged with a crime as if it were a person.

The corporate form has some disadvantages as well. A stockholder's ability to influence corporate policy is limited to voting for a board of directors, which oversees the operation of the firm. Each share of stock usually carries with it one vote. The typical stockholder of a large corporation owns only a tiny fraction of the shares and thus has little say. Whereas the income from sole proprietorships and partnerships is taxed only once, corporate income gets whacked twice—first as corporate profits and second as stockholder income, either as corporate dividends or as realized capital gains. A *realized capital gain* is any increase in the market price of a share that occurs between the time the share is purchased and the time it is sold.

A hybrid type of corporation has evolved to take advantage of the limited liability feature of the corporate structure while reducing the impact of double taxation. The *S corporation* provides owners with limited liability, but profits are taxed only once—as income on each shareholder's personal income tax return. To qualify as an S corporation, a firm must have no more than 100 stockholders and no foreign stockholders.

Corporations make up only 18 percent of all U.S. businesses, but because they tend to be much larger than the other two business forms, corporations account for 84 percent of all business sales. Exhibit 2 on the next page shows, by business type, the percentages of U.S. firms and the percentages of U.S. sales. *The sole proprietorship is the most important in sheer numbers, but the corporation is the most important in terms of total sales.*

> Corporations account for 84 percent of all business sales.

sole proprietorship a firm with a single owner who has the right to all profits but who also bears unlimited liability for the firm's losses and debts

partnership a firm with multiple owners who share the profits and bear unlimited liability for the firm's losses and debts

corporation a legal entity owned by stockholders whose liability is limited to the value of their stock ownership

Exhibit 2

Number and Sales of Each Type of Firm

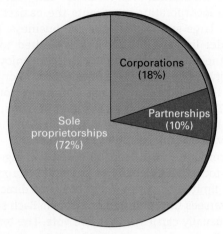

(a) *Most firms are sole proprietorships*

Corporations (18%)

Partnerships (10%)

Sole proprietorships (72%)

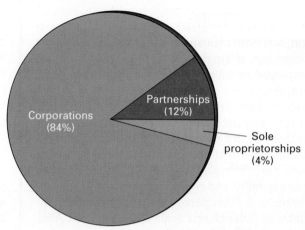

(b) *Corporations account for most sales*

Partnerships (12%)

Corporations (84%)

Sole proprietorships (4%)

SOURCE: U.S. Census Bureau, *Statistical Abstract of the United States: 2007.* U.S. Bureau of the Census, Table No. 724 and Table No. 806. For the latest figures go to http://www.census.gov/compendia/statab/.

Cooperatives

A cooperative, or "co-op" for short, is a group of people who cooperate by pooling their resources to buy and sell more efficiently than they could independently. Cooperatives try to minimize costs and operate with limited liability of members. The government grants most cooperatives tax-exempt status. There are two types: consumer cooperatives and producer cooperatives.

cooperative
an organization consisting of people who pool their resources to buy and sell more efficiently than they could individually

Consumer Cooperatives

A *consumer cooperative* is a retail business owned and operated by some or all of its customers in order to reduce costs. Some cooperatives require members to pay an annual fee and others require them to work a certain number of hours each year. Members sometimes pay lower prices than other customers or may share in any revenues that exceed costs. In the United States, consumer cooperatives operate credit unions, electric-power facilities, health plans, apartment buildings, and grocery stores, among other businesses. Many college bookstores are cooperatives. For example, the UConn Co-op is owned by about 30,000 students, faculty, and staff. These members receive discounts on their purchases.

Producer Cooperatives

In a *producer cooperative*, producers join forces to buy supplies and equipment and to market their output. Each producer's objective is to reduce costs and

>> Ocean Spray is one of the best known producer cooperatives in the United States. Through product development (think Craisins), Ocean Spray has been able to increase the price it pays its farmers 100 percent over a three-year period.

© MATHIEU BELANGER/REUTERS/LANDOV

increase profits. Federal legislation allows farmers to cooperate without violating antitrust laws. Firms in other industries could not do this legally. Farmers pool their funds to purchase machinery and supplies, provide storage and processing facilities, and transport goods to market. Sunkist, for example, is a farm cooperative owned and operated by 6,500 citrus growers in California and Arizona.

Not-for-Profit Organizations

So far, you have learned about organizations that try to maximize profits or, in the case of cooperatives, to minimize costs. Some organizations have neither as a goal. Not-for-profit organizations engage in charitable, educational, humanitarian, cultural, professional, and other activities, often with a social purpose. Government agencies do not have profit as a goal either, but governments are not included in this definition of not-for-profit organizations.

Like businesses, not-for-profit organizations evolved to help people accomplish their goals. Examples include nonprofit hospitals, private schools and colleges, religious organizations, the Red Cross, Greenpeace, charitable foundations, soup kitchens, orchestras, museums, labor unions, and professional organizations. There are about two million not-for-profit organizations in the United States. They employ about 10 million workers, with not-for-profit hospitals being the biggest employer. But even not-for-profit organizations must somehow pay the bills. Revenues typically include some combination of voluntary contributions and service charges, such as college tuition and hospital charges. In the United States, not-for-profit organizations are usually exempt from taxes.

> 66 Although you wouldn't hire someone to brush your teeth, dental work is not for amateurs 99

Why Does Household Production Still Exist?

If firms are so efficient at reducing transaction and production costs, why don't they make everything? Why do households still perform some tasks, such as cooking and cleaning? *If a household's opportunity cost of performing a task is below the market price, then the household usually performs that task.* People with a lower opportunity cost of time do more for themselves. For example, janitors are more likely to mow their lawns than are physicians. Let's look at some reasons for household production.

Do it yourself, or pay someone to do it for you?

© COMSTOCK IMAGES/JUPITERIMAGES

No Skills or Special Resources Are Required

Some activities require so few skills or special resources that householders find it cheaper to do the jobs themselves. Sweeping the kitchen floor requires only a broom and some time, so it's usually performed by household members. Sanding a wooden floor, however, involves special machinery and expertise, so this service is usually left to professionals. Similarly, although you wouldn't hire someone to brush your teeth, dental work is not for amateurs. *Households usually perform domestic chores that demand neither expertise nor special machinery.*

Household Production Avoids Taxes

Suppose you are deciding whether to pay someone $3,000 to paint your house or to do it yourself. If the income tax rate is one-third, you must earn $4,500 before taxes to have the $3,000 after taxes to

not-for-profit organizations groups that do not pursue profit as a goal; they engage in charitable, educational, humanitarian, cultural, professional, or other activities, often with a social purpose

pay for the job. And the painter who charges you $3,000 nets only $2,000 after paying $1,000 in taxes. Thus, you must earn $4,500 so that the painter can take home $2,000. If you paint the house yourself, no taxes are involved. The tax-free nature of do-it-yourself activity favors household production over market transactions.

Household Production Reduces Transaction Costs

Getting estimates, hiring a contractor, negotiating terms, and monitoring job performance all take time and require information. Doing the job yourself reduces these transaction costs. Household production also allows for more personal control over the final product than is usually available through the market. For example, some people prefer home-cooked meals, because they can season home-cooked meals to individual tastes.

Technological Advances Increase Household Productivity

Technological breakthroughs are not confined to market production. Vacuum cleaners, washers and dryers, dishwashers, microwave ovens, and other modern appliances reduce the time and often the skill required to perform household tasks. Also, new technologies such as DVD players, HDTV, broadband downloads, and computer games enhance home entertainment. Indeed, microchip-based technologies have shifted some production from the firm back to the household.

LO³ The Government

You might think that production by households and firms could satisfy all consumer wants. Why must yet another economic decision maker get into the act? After all, governments play some role in every nation on earth.

The Role of Government

Sometimes the unrestrained operation of markets yields undesirable results. Too many of some goods and too few of other goods get produced. This section discusses the sources of **market failure** and how society's overall welfare may be improved through government intervention.

market failure a condition that arises when the unregulated operation of markets yields socially undesirable results

Establishing and Enforcing the Rules of the Game

Market efficiency depends on people like you using your resources to maximize your

Financial Weapons of Mass Destruction

This is the title that billionaire investor Warren Buffet gave to Credit Default Swaps, or CDSs. CDSs, which the Federal Reserve under Alan Greenspan had long opposed regulating, proved one of the biggest question marks during the credit crisis and financial meltdown in 2008. CDSs on the surface are basically types of insurance contracts. The buyer pays a premium and the seller agrees to make a specific payment if a certain event occurs, such as a bond defaulting. In many instances, CDSs were used as a kind of "insurance" policy on extremely risky mortgages during the recent housing bubble. Furthermore, CDSs could be taken out on practically anything, even bonds or assets not owned by the buyer. In October 2008, outstanding CDSs amounted to roughly $54.6 trillion, up from $919 billion in 2001.

SOURCE: Nicholas Varchaver and Katie Benner, "The $55 Trillion Question," *Fortune,* 13 October 2008. pp.134–140.

utility. But what if you were repeatedly robbed of your paycheck on your way home from work? Or what if, after you worked two weeks in a new job, your boss called you a sucker and said you wouldn't get paid? Why bother working? The market system would break down if you could not safeguard your private property or if you could not enforce contracts. Governments safeguard private property through police protection and enforce contracts through a judicial system. More generally, governments try to make sure that market participants abide by the rules of the game. These rules are established through government laws and regulations and also through the customs and conventions of the marketplace.

Promoting Competition

Although the "invisible hand" of competition usually promotes an efficient allocation of resources, some firms try to avoid competition through *collusion,* which is an agreement among firms to divide the market and fix the price. Or an individual firm may try to eliminate the competition by using unfair business practices. For example, to drive out local competitors, a large firm may temporarily sell at a price below cost. Government antitrust laws try to promote competition by prohibiting collusion and other anti-competitive practices.

Regulating Natural Monopolies

Competition usually keeps the product price below what it would be without competition—that is, below the price charged by a monopoly, a sole supplier to the market. In rare instances, however, a monopoly can produce and sell the product for less than could competing firms. For example, electricity is delivered more efficiently by a single firm that wires the community than by competing firms each stringing its own wires. When it is cheaper for one firm to serve the market than for two or more firms to do so, that one firm is called a natural monopoly. Since a natural monopoly faces no competition, it maximizes profit by charging a higher price than would be optimal from society's point of view. A lower price and greater output would improve social welfare. Therefore, the government usually regulates the natural monopoly, forcing it to lower its price and increase output.

> THE SUPPLIER OF A PRIVATE GOOD CAN EASILY EXCLUDE THOSE WHO FAIL TO PAY.

Providing Public Goods

So far this book has been talking about private goods, which have two important features. First, private goods are *rival* in consumption, meaning that the amount consumed by one person is unavailable for others to consume. For example, when you and some friends share a pizza, each slice they eat is one less available for you. Second, the supplier of a private good can easily exclude those who fail to pay. Only paying customers get pizza. Thus, private goods are said to be *exclusive*. So private goods, such as pizza, are both rival in consumption and exclusive. In contrast, public goods are *nonrival* in consumption. For example, your family's benefit from a safer neighborhood does not reduce your neighbor's benefit. What's more, once produced, public goods are available to all. Suppliers cannot easily prevent consumption by those who fail to pay. For example, reducing terrorism is *nonexclusive*. It benefits all in the community, regardless of who pays for it and who doesn't. Because public goods are *nonrival* and *nonexclusive*,

private firms cannot sell them profitably. The government, however, has the authority to enforce tax collections for public goods. Thus, the government provides public goods and funds them with taxes.

Dealing with Externalities

Market prices reflect the private costs and private benefits of producers and consumers. But sometimes production or consumption imposes costs or benefits on third parties—on those who are neither suppliers nor demanders in a market transaction. For example, a paper mill fouls the air breathed by nearby residents, but the price of paper fails to reflect such costs. Because these pollution costs are outside, or external to, the market, they are called *externalities*.

An externality is a cost or a benefit that falls on a third party. A negative externality imposes an external cost, such as factory pollution or auto emissions. A positive externality confers an external benefit, such as getting a good education or driving carefully. Because market prices do not reflect externalities, governments often use taxes, subsidies, and regulations to discourage negative externalities and encourage positive externalities. For example, a polluting factory often faces taxes and regulations aimed at curbing that pollution. And because more educated people can read road signs and have options that pay better than crime, governments try to encourage education with free public schools and subsidized higher education and by keeping people in school until their 16th birthdays.

A More Equal Distribution of Income

As mentioned earlier, some people, because of poor education, mental or physical disabilities, or perhaps the need to care for small children, are unable to support themselves and their families. Because resource markets do not guarantee even a minimum level of income, transfer payments reflect

---

monopoly
a sole supplier of a product with no close substitutes

natural monopoly
one firm that can supply the entire market at a lower per-unit cost than could two or more firms

private good
a good that is both rival in consumption and exclusive, such as pizza

public good
a good that, once produced, is available for all to consume, regardless of who pays and who doesn't; such a good is nonrival and nonexclusive, such as a safer community

externality
a cost or a benefit that affects neither the buyer or seller, but instead affects people not involved in the market transaction

society's attempt to provide a basic standard of living to all households. Most citizens agree that government should redistribute income to the poor (note the normative nature of this statement). Opinions differ about who should receive benefits, how much they should get, what form benefits should take, and how long benefits should last.

Full Employment, Price Stability, and Economic Growth

Perhaps the most important responsibility of government is fostering a healthy economy, which benefits just about everyone. The government—through its ability to tax, to spend, and to control the money supply—attempts to promote full employment, price stability, and economic growth. Pursuing these objectives by taxing and spending is called fiscal policy. Pursuing them by regulating the money supply is called monetary policy. Macroeconomics examines both policies.

Government's Structure and Objectives

fiscal policy
the use of government purchases, transfer payments, taxes, and borrowing to influence economy-wide variables such as inflation, employment, and economic growth

monetary policy
regulation of the money supply to influence economy-wide variables such as inflation, employment, and economic growth

The United States has a *federal system* of government, meaning that responsibilities are shared across levels of government. State governments grant some powers to local governments and surrender some powers to the national, or federal, government. As the system has evolved, the federal government has primary responsibility for national security, economic stability, and market competition. State governments fund public higher education, prisons, and—with aid from the federal government—highways and welfare. Local governments provide primary and secondary education with aid from the state, plus police and fire protection. Here are some distinguishing features of government.

Difficulty in Defining Government Objectives

We assume that households try to maximize utility and firms try to maximize profit, but what about governments—or, more specifically, what about government decision makers? What do they try to maximize? One problem is that our federal system consists of not one but many governments—more than 87,600 separate jurisdictions in all including 1 nation, 50 states, 3,034 counties, 35,933 cities and towns, 13,506 school districts, and 35,052 special districts. What's more, because the federal government relies on offsetting, or countervailing, powers across the executive, legislative, and judicial branches, government does not act as a single, consistent decision maker. Even within the federal executive branch, there are so many agencies and bureaus that at times they seem to work at cross-purposes. For example, at the same time as the U.S. Surgeon General required health warnings on cigarette packages, the U.S. Department of Agriculture pursued policies to benefit tobacco growers. Given this thicket of jurisdictions, branches, and bureaus, one useful theory of government behavior is that elected officials try to maximize the number of votes they will get in the next election. So let's assume that elected officials are vote maximizers. In this theory, vote maximization guides the decisions of elected officials who, in turn, oversee government employees.

Voluntary Exchange Versus Coercion

Market exchange relies on the voluntary behavior of buyers and sellers. Don't like tofu? No problem—don't buy it. But in political markets, the situation is different. Any voting rule except unanimous consent must involve some government coercion. Public choices are enforced by the police power of the state. Those who fail to pay their taxes could go to jail, even though they may object to some programs those taxes support, such as the war in Iraq or capital punishment.

No Market Prices

Another distinguishing feature of governments is that public output is usually offered at either a zero price or at a price below the cost of providing it. If

you now pay in-state tuition at a public college or university, your tuition probably covers only about half the state's cost of providing your education. Because the revenue side of the government budget is usually separate from the expenditure side, there is no necessary link between the cost of a program and the benefit. In the private sector, the expected marginal benefit is at least as great as marginal cost; otherwise, market exchange would not occur.

The Size and Growth of Government

One way to track the impact of government over time is by measuring government outlays relative to the U.S. *gross domestic product,* or *GDP,* which is the total value of all final goods and services produced in the United States. In 1929, the year the Great Depression began, all government outlays, mostly by state and local governments, totaled about 10 percent of GDP.

At the time, the federal government played a minor role. In fact, during the nation's first 150 years, federal outlays, except during war years, never exceeded 3 percent relative to GDP.

The Great Depression, World War II, and a change in macroeconomic thinking boosted the share of government outlays to 38 percent of GDP in 2008, with about two-thirds of that by the federal government. In comparison, government outlays relative to GDP were 36 percent in Japan; 39 percent in Canada; 43 percent in Germany; 45 percent in the United Kingdom; 49 percent in Italy; and 52 percent in France. Government outlays by the 28 largest industrial economies averaged 41 percent of GDP in 2009.[1] Thus, government outlays in the United States relative to GDP are below those of most other advanced economies.

Let's look briefly at the composition of federal outlays. Since 1960, defense spending has declined from over half of federal outlays to about one-fifth by 2009, as shown in Exhibit 3. Redistribution—Social Security, Medicare, and welfare programs—has been the mirror image of defense spending, jumping from only about one-fifth of federal outlays in 1960 to nearly half by 2009.

Sources of Government Revenue

Taxes provide the bulk of revenue at all levels of government. The federal government relies primarily on the individual income tax, state governments rely on income and sales taxes, and local governments rely on the property tax. Other revenue sources include user charges, such as highway tolls, and borrowing. For additional revenue, some states also monopolize certain markets, such as for lottery tickets and liquor.

Exhibit 4 on the next page focuses on the composition of federal revenue since 1960. The share made up by the individual income tax has remained relatively constant, ranging from a low of 42 percent in the mid-1960s to 47 percent in 2009. The share from payroll taxes more than doubled from 15 percent in 1960 to

Exhibit 3

Redistribution Has Grown and Defense Has Declined as Share of Federal Outlays Since 1960

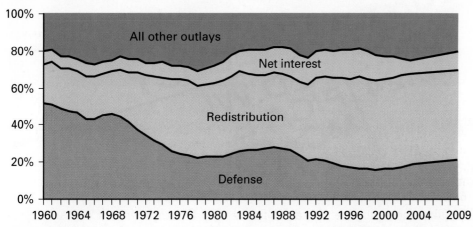

SOURCE: Computed based on figures from the *Economic Report of the President,* February 2008. Table B-80. For the latest figures, go to http://www.gpoaccess.gov/eop/.

1. The Organization of Economic Cooperation and Development, OECD *Economic Outlook* (June 2008): Annex Table 25.

Exhibit 4

Payroll Taxes Have Grown as a Share of Federal Revenue Since 1960

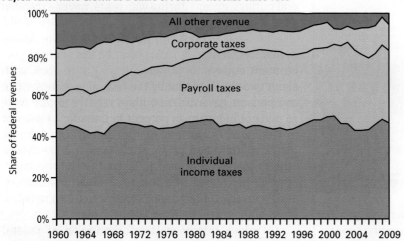

SOURCE: Computed based on figures from the *Economic Report of the President,* February 2008. Table B-80. For the latest figures, go to http://www.gpoaccess.gov/eop/.

35 percent in 2009. *Payroll taxes* are deducted from paychecks to support Social Security and Medicare, which funds medical care for the elderly. Corporate taxes and revenue from other sources, such as excise (sales) taxes and user charges, have declined as a share of the total since 1960.

Tax Principles and Tax Incidence

The structure of a tax is often justified on the basis of one of two general principles. First, a tax could relate to the individual's ability to pay, so those with a greater ability pay more taxes. Income taxes or property taxes often rely on this ability-to-pay tax principle. Alternatively, the benefits-received tax principle relates taxes to the benefits taxpayers receive from the government activity funded by the tax. For example, the tax on gasoline funds highway construction and maintenance, thereby linking tax payment to road use, since those who drive more pay more gas taxes.

Tax incidence indicates who actually bears the burden of the tax. One way to evaluate tax incidence is by measuring the tax as a percentage of income. Under proportional taxation, taxpayers at all income levels pay the same percentage of their income in taxes. A proportional income tax is also called a flat tax, since the tax as a percentage of income remains constant, or flat, as income increases. Note that under proportional taxation, although taxes remain constant as a percentage of income, the dollar amount of taxes increases as income increases.

Under progressive taxation, the percentage of income paid in taxes increases as income increases. The marginal tax rate indicates the percentage of each additional dollar of income that goes to taxes. Because high marginal rates reduce the after-tax return from working or investing, high marginal

ability-to-pay tax principle
those with a greater ability to pay, such as those earning higher incomes or those owning more property, should pay more taxes

benefits-received tax principle
those who get more benefits from the government program should pay more taxes

tax incidence
the distribution of tax burden among taxpayers; who ultimately pays the tax

proportional taxation
the tax as a percentage of income remains constant as income increases; also called a flat tax

progressive taxation
the tax as a percentage of income increases as income increases

marginal tax rate
the percentage of each additional dollar of income that goes to the tax

{ Decoding the taxes on your pay stub }

FICA (aka Social Security) stands for Federal Insurance Contributions Act: 6.2% paid by you, 6.2% paid by your employer

FUTA (aka unemployment) stands for Federal Unemployment Tax Act: 6.2% of taxable wages, paid by your employer

Exhibit 5

Top Marginal Rate on Federal Personal Income Tax Since 1913

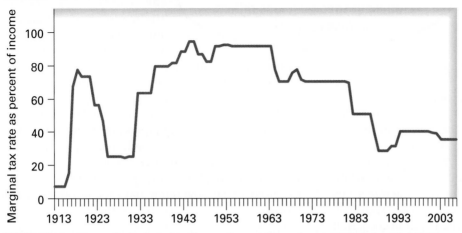

SOURCE: U.S. Internal Revenue Service. For the latest figures on the personal income tax go to http://www.irs.gov/individuals/index.html.

rates can reduce people's incentives to work and invest. The six marginal rates applied to the U.S. personal income tax ranged from 10 to 35 percent in 2008, down from a range of 15 to 39.6 percent in 2000. President Barack Obama, during the campaign, proposed increasing the top marginal rate while reducing taxes on other workers.

The top marginal tax bracket each year during the history of the personal income tax is shown by Exhibit 5. Although the top marginal rate is now lower than it was during most other years, high income households still pay most of the federal income tax collected. For example, according to the U.S. Internal Revenue Service, the top 1 percent of tax filers, based on income, paid 39.4 percent of all income taxes collected in 2006. Their average tax rate was 23.8 percent. And the top 10 percent of tax filers paid 70.5 percent of all income taxes collected. Their average tax rate

> > In France, a house's property taxes used to be assessed on the basis of the number stories of livable space in the building. Attic space was not counted as livable space, so houses designed with Mansard roofs became increasingly popular. (More usable space, less taxes.)

Mansard roof

was 19.3 percent. In contrast, the bottom 50 percent of tax filers paid only 3.1 percent of all income taxes collected. Their tax rate averaged only 3.0 percent. Whether we look at marginal tax rates or average tax rates, the U.S. income tax is progressive. High-income filers pay the overwhelming share of income taxes.

> International trade occurs because the opportunity cost of producing specific goods differs across countries.

Finally, under regressive taxation, the percentage of income paid in taxes decreases as income increases, so the marginal tax rate declines as income increases. Most U.S. payroll taxes are regressive, because they impose a flat rate up to a certain level of income, above which the marginal rate drops to zero. For example, Social Security taxes were levied on the first $106,800 of workers' pay in 2009. Half of the 12.4 percent tax is paid by employers and half by employees (the self-employed pay the entire 12.4 percent).

Taxes often do more than fund public programs. Some taxes discourage certain activity. For example, a pollution tax can help clean the air. A tax on gasoline can encourage people to work at home, carpool, or use public transportaion. Some taxes have unintended consequences. For example, in Egypt a property tax is not imposed until a building is complete. To avoid such taxes, builders never finish the job; multistory dwellings are usually missing the top floor. As another example of how taxes can distort the allocation of resources, property taxes in Amsterdam and Vietnam were originally based on the width of the building. As a result, buildings in those places are extremely narrow.

This discussion of revenue sources brings to a close, for now, our examination of the role of government in the U.S. economy. Government has a pervasive influence on the economy, and its role is discussed throughout the book.

regressive taxation the tax as a percentage of income decreases as income increases

merchandise trade balance the value during a given period of a country's exported goods minus the value of its imported goods

balance of payments a record of all economic transactions during a given period between residents of one country and residents of the rest of the world

LO⁴ The Rest of the World

So far, the focus has been on institutions within the United States—that is, on *domestic* households, firms, and governments. This focus is appropriate because our primary objective is to understand the workings of the U.S. economy, by far the largest in the world. But the rest of the world affects what U.S. households consume and what U.S. firms produce. For example, Japan and China supply us with all kinds of manufactured goods, thereby affecting U.S. prices, wages, and profits. Likewise, political events in the Persian Gulf can affect what Americans pay for oil. Foreign decision makers, therefore, influence the U.S. economy—what we produce and what we consume. The *rest of the world* consists of the households, firms, and governments in the two hundred or so sovereign nations throughout the world.

International Trade

In the previous chapter, you learned about comparative advantage and the gains from specialization. These gains explain why householders stopped doing everything for themselves and began to specialize. *International trade arises for the same reasons. International trade occurs because the opportunity cost of producing specific goods differs across countries.* Americans import raw materials like crude oil, diamonds, and coffee beans and finished goods like cameras, DVD players, and automobiles. U.S. producers export sophisticated products like computer software, aircraft, and movies, as well as agricultural products like wheat and corn.

Trade between the United States and the rest of the world has increased in recent decades. In 1970, U.S. exports of goods and services amounted to only 6 percent of the gross domestic product. That has increased to 12 percent. The top 10 destinations for U.S. exports in order of importance are Canada, Mexico, Japan, China, United Kingdom, Germany, South Korea, Netherlands, France, and Taiwan.

The merchandise trade balance equals the value of exported goods minus the value of imported goods. Goods in this case are distinguished from services, which show up in another trade account. For the last quarter century, the United States has imported more goods than it has exported, resulting in a merchandise trade deficit. Just as a household must pay for its spending, so too must a nation. The merchandise trade deficit must be offset by a surplus in one or more of the other *balance-of-payments* accounts. A nation's balance of payments is the record of all economic transactions between its residents and residents of the rest of the world.

Exchange Rates

The lack of a common currency complicates trade between countries. How many U.S. dollars buy a Porsche? An American buyer cares only about the dollar cost; the German carmaker cares only about the *euros* (€) received (the common currency of 16 European countries). To facilitate trade funded by different currencies, a market for foreign exchange has developed. Foreign exchange is foreign currency needed to carry out international transactions. The supply and demand for foreign exchange comes together in *foreign exchange markets* to determine the exchange rate. The *exchange rate* measures the price of one currency in terms of another. For example, the exchange rate between the euro and the dollar might indicate that one euro exchanges for $1.20. At that exchange rate, a Porsche selling for €100,000 costs $120,000. The exchange rate affects the prices of imports and exports and thus helps shape the flow of foreign trade.

Trade Restrictions

Despite clear gains from international specialization and exchange, nearly all nations restrict trade to some extent. These restrictions can take the form of (1) tariffs, which are taxes on imports; (2) quotas, which are limits on the quantity of a particular good that can be imported from a country; and (3) other trade restrictions. If specialization according to comparative advantage is so beneficial, why do most countries restrict trade? Restrictions benefit certain domestic producers that lobby their governments for these benefits. For example, U.S. growers of sugar cane have benefited from legislation restricting imports, thereby raising U.S. sugar prices. These higher prices hurt domestic consumers, but consumers are usually unaware of this harm. Trade restrictions interfere with the free flow of products across borders and tend to hurt the overall economy.

Final Word

This chapter examined the four economic decision makers: households, firms, governments, and the rest of the world. Domestic households are by far the most important, for they supply resources and demand goods and services.

If you were to stop reading right now, you would already know more economics than most people. But to understand market economies, you must learn how markets work. The next chapter introduces demand and supply.

> **foreign exchange**
> foreign money needed to carry out international transactions
>
> **tariff**
> a tax on imports
>
> **quota**
> a legal limit on the quantity of a particular product that can be imported

---

$II.7 < Trillion of personal income in the United States

72% < Of all U.S. businesses are sole proprietorships

Number of separate government jurisdictions in the United States > 87,600

Number of for-profit businesses in the United States > 30 million

Start of Industrial Revolution in Britain > 1750

Student, faculty, and staff owners of UConn bookstore co-op > 30,000

4

Demand, Supply, and Markets

Learning Outcomes

LO **1** Explain how the law of demand affects market activity

LO **2** Explain how the law of supply affects market activity

LO **3** Describe how the interaction between supply and demand creates markets

LO **4** Describe how markets reach equilibrium

LO **5** Explain how markets react during periods of disequilibrium

" *Why do roses cost more on Valentine's Day than during the rest of the year?* "

Why do roses cost more on Valentine's Day than during the rest of the year? Why do TV ads cost more during the Super Bowl ($3.0 million for 30 seconds in 2009) than during *Nick at Nite* reruns? Why do Miami hotels charge more in February than in August? Why do surgeons earn more than butchers? Why do basketball pros earn more than hockey pros? Why do economics majors earn more than most other majors? Answers to these and most economic questions boil down to the workings of demand and supply—the subject of this chapter.

This chapter introduces demand and supply and shows how they interact in competitive markets. *Demand and supply are the most fundamental and the most powerful of all economic tools*—important enough to warrant a chapter. Indeed, some believe that if you program a computer to answer "demand and supply" to every economic question, you could put many economists out of work. An understanding of the two ideas will take you far in mastering the art and science of economic analysis. This chapter uses graphs, so you may need to review the Chapter 1 appendix as a refresher.

What do you think?

Professional athletes should earn comparable salaries regardless of the sport they play.

Strongly Disagree						*Strongly Agree*
1	2	3	4	5	6	7

Topics discussed in Chapter 4 include:

- Demand and quantity demanded
- Movement along a demand curve
- Shift of a demand curve
- Supply and quantity supplied
- Movement along a supply curve
- Shift of a supply curve
- Markets and equilibrium
- Disequilibrium

LO¹ Demand

How many six-packs of Pepsi will people buy each month at a price of $3? What if the price is $2? What if it's $4? The answers reveal the relationship between the price of Pepsi and the quantity demanded. Such a relationship is called the *demand* for Pepsi. Demand indicates the quantity consumers are both *willing and able* to buy at each possible price during a given time period,

> **demand**
> a relation between the price of a good and the quantity that consumers are willing and able to buy per period, other things constant

other things constant. Because demand pertains to a specific period—a day, a week, a month—think of demand as the *amounts purchased per period* at each possible price. Also, notice the emphasis on *willing and able*. You may be *able* to buy a new Harley-Davidson XL 883 Sportster for $6,999 because you can afford one, but you may not be *willing* to buy one if motorcycles don't interest you.

> Sell for less, and the world will beat a path to your door.

The Law of Demand

In 1962, Sam Walton opened his first store in Rogers, Arkansas, with a sign that read "Wal-Mart Discount City. We sell for less." Wal-Mart now sells more than any other retailer in the world because prices are among the lowest around. As a consumer, you understand why people buy more at a lower price. Sell for less, and the world will beat a path to your door. Wal-Mart, for example, sells on average over 20,000 pairs of shoes *an hour*. This relation between the price and the quantity demanded is an economic law. The law of demand says that quantity demanded varies inversely with price, other things constant. Thus, the higher the price, the smaller the quantity demanded; the lower the price, the greater the quantity demanded.

Demand, Wants, and Needs

Consumer demand and wants are not the same. As we have seen, wants are unlimited. You may want a new Mercedes SL600 Roadster convertible, but the $139,975 price tag is likely beyond your budget (that is, the quantity you demand at that price is zero). Nor is demand the same as need. You may need a new muffler for your car, but a price of $300 is just too high for you. If, however, the price drops enough—say, to $200—then you become both willing and able to buy one.

The Substitution Effect of a Price Change

What explains the law of demand? Why, for example, is more demanded at a lower price? The explanation begins with unlimited wants confronting scarce resources. Many goods and services could satisfy particular wants. For example, you can satisfy your hunger with pizza, tacos, burgers, chicken, or hundreds of other foods. Similarly, you can satisfy your desire for warmth in the winter with warm clothing, a home-heating system, a trip to Hawaii, or in many other ways. Clearly, some alternatives have more appeal than others (a trip to Hawaii is more fun than warm clothing). In a world without scarcity, everything would be free, so you would always choose the most attractive alternative. Scarcity, however, is a reality, and the degree of scarcity of one good relative to another helps determine each good's relative price.

Notice that the definition of *demand* includes the other-things-constant assumption. Among the "other things" assumed to remain constant are the prices of other goods. For example, if the price of pizza declines while other prices remain constant, pizza becomes relatively cheaper. Consumers are more *willing* to purchase pizza when its relative price falls; they substitute pizza for other goods. This principle is called the substitution effect of a price change. On the other hand, an increase in the price of pizza, other things constant, increases the opportunity cost of pizza. This higher opportunity cost causes consumers to substitute other goods for the now higher-priced pizza, thus reducing their quantity of pizza demanded. Remember that it is *the change in the relative price—the price of one good relative to the prices of other goods—that causes the substitution effect*. If all prices changed by the same percentage, there would be no change in relative prices and no substitution effect.

The Income Effect of a Price Change

A fall in the price increases the quantity demanded for a second reason. Suppose you earn $30 a week from a part-time job, so $30 is your money income. Money income is simply the number of dollars received per period, in this case, $30 per week. Suppose you spend all that income on pizza, buying three a week at $10 each. What if the price drops to $6? At the lower price you can now afford five pizzas a week. Your money income remains at $30 per week, but the decrease in the price has increased your real income—that is, your income measured in terms of what it can buy. The price reduction, other things constant, increases the purchasing power of your income, thereby increasing your ability to buy pizza. The quantity of pizza you demand will likely increase because of this

---

law of demand
the quantity of a good that consumers are willing and able to buy per period relates inversely, or negatively, to the price, other things constant

substitution effect of a price change
when the price of a good falls, that good becomes cheaper compared to other goods so consumers tend to substitute that good for other goods

money income
the number of dollars a person receives per period, such as $400 per week

real income
income measured in terms of the goods and services it can buy; real income changes when the price changes

income effect of a price change. You may not increase your quantity demanded to five pizzas, but you could. If you decide to purchase four pizzas a week when the price drops to $6, you would still have $6 remaining to buy other goods. Thus, the income effect of a lower price increases your real income and thereby increases your ability to purchase all goods. Because of the income effect, consumers typically increase their quantity demanded when the price declines.

Conversely, an increase in the price of a good, other things constant, reduces real income, thereby reducing the *ability* to purchase all goods. Because of the income effect, consumers typically reduce their quantity demanded when the price increases. Again, note that money income, not real income, is assumed to remain constant along a demand curve. A change in price changes your real income, so real income varies along a demand curve. The lower the price, the greater your real income.

The Demand Schedule and Demand Curve

Demand can be expressed as a *demand schedule* or as a *demand curve*. Exhibit 1a shows a hypothetical demand schedule for pizza. In describing demand, we must specify the units measured and the period

Exhibit 1a

The Demand Schedule for Pizza

	Price per Pizza	Quantity Demanded per Week (millions)
a	$15	8
b	12	14
c	9	20
d	6	26
e	3	32

© THINKSTOCK IMAGES/JUPITERIMAGES

considered. In our example, the unit is a 12-inch regular pizza and the period is a week. The schedule lists possible prices, along with the quantity demanded at each price. At a price of $15, for example, consumers demand 8 million pizzas per week. As you can see, the lower the price, other things constant, the greater the quantity demanded. Consumers substitute pizza for other foods. And as the price falls, real income increases, causing consumers to increase the quantity of pizza they demand.

If the price drops as low as $3, consumers demand 32 million per week.

The demand schedule in Exhibit 1a appears as a **demand curve** in Exhibit 1b, with price measured on the vertical axis and the quantity demanded per week on the horizontal axis. Each price-quantity combination listed in the demand schedule in Exhibit 1a becomes a point in Exhibit 1b. Point *a*, for example, indicates that if the price is $15, consumers demand 8 million pizzas per week. These points connect to form the demand curve for pizza, labeled D. (By the way, some demand curves are straight lines, some are curved lines, and some are even jagged lines, but all are called demand *curves*.)

Exhibit 1b

The Demand Curve for Pizza

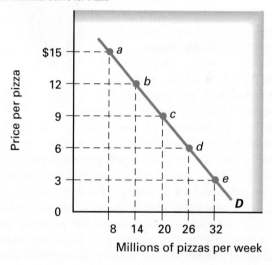

A demand curve slopes downward, reflecting the *law of demand*: Price and quantity demanded are inversely related, other things constant. Besides money income, also assumed constant along the demand curve are the prices of other goods. Thus, along the demand curve for pizza, the price of pizza changes *relative to the prices of other goods*. The demand curve shows the effect of a change in the *relative price* of pizza—that is, relative to other prices, which do not change.

Take care to distinguish between *demand* and *quantity demanded*. The *demand* for pizza is not a specific amount, but rather

income effect of a price change
a fall in the price of a good increases consumers' real income, making consumers more able to purchase goods; for a normal good, the quantity demanded increases

demand curve
a curve showing the relation between the price of a good and the quantity consumers are willing and able to buy per period, other things constant

the *entire relationship* between price and quantity demanded—represented by the demand schedule or the demand curve. An individual point on the demand curve indicates the quantity demanded at a particular price. For example, at a price of $12, the quantity demanded is 14 million pizzas per week. If the price drops from $12 to, say, $9, this is shown in Exhibit 1b by *a movement along the demand curve—* in this case from point *b* to point *c*. Any movement along a demand curve reflects a *change in quantity demanded*, not a change in demand.

The law of demand applies to the millions of products sold in grocery stores, department stores, clothing stores, shoe stores, drugstores, music stores, bookstores, hardware stores, travel agencies, and restaurants, as well as through mail-order catalogs, the Yellow Pages, classified ads, online sites, stock markets, real estate markets, job markets, flea markets, and all other markets. The law of demand applies even to choices that seem more personal than economic, such as whether or not to own a pet. For example, after New York City passed an anti-dog-litter law, law-abiding owners had to follow their dogs around the city with scoopers, plastic bags—whatever would do the job. Because the law raised the personal cost of owning a dog, the quantity of dogs demanded decreased. Some owners simply abandoned their dogs, raising the number of strays in the city. The number of dogs left at animal shelters doubled. The law of demand predicts this inverse relation between cost, or price, and quantity demanded.

It is useful to distinguish between individual demand, which is the demand of an individual consumer, and market demand, which is the sum of the individual demands of all consumers in the market. In most markets, there are many consumers, sometimes millions. Unless otherwise noted, when we talk about demand, we are referring to market demand, as shown in Exhibit 1.

quantity demanded
the amount of a good consumers are willing and able to buy per period at a particular price, as reflected by a point on a demand curve

individual demand
a relation between the price of a good and the quantity purchased by an individual consumer per period, other things constant

market demand
the relation between the price of a good and the quantity purchased by all consumers in the market during a given period, other things constant; sum of the individual demands in the market

Shifts of the Demand Curve

A demand curve isolates the relation between the price of a good and quantity demanded when other factors that could affect demand remain unchanged. What are those other factors, and how do changes in them affect demand? Variables that can affect market demand are (1) the money income of consumers, (2) prices of other goods, (3) consumer expectations, (4) the number or composition of consumers in the market, and (5) consumer tastes. How do changes in each affect demand?

Changes in Consumer Income

Exhibit 2 shows the market demand curve *D* for pizza. This demand curve assumes a given level of money income. Suppose consumer income increases. Some consumers will then be willing and able to buy more pizza at each price, so market demand increases. The demand curve shifts to the right from *D* to *D'*. For example, at a price of $12, the amount of pizza demanded increases from 14 million to 20 million per week, as indicated by the movement from point *b* on demand curve *D* to point *f* on demand curve *D'*. In short, *an increase in demand—that is, a rightward shift of the demand curve—means that consumers are willing and able to buy more pizza at each price.*

Exhibit 2

An Increase in the Market Demand for Pizza

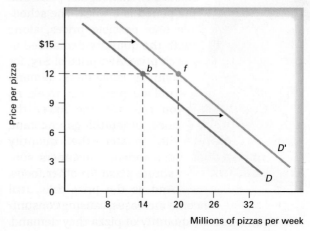

© THINKSTOCK IMAGES/JUPITERIMAGES

Goods are classified into two broad categories, depending on how demand responds to changes in money income. The demand for a normal good increases as money income increases. Because pizza is a normal good, its demand curve shifts rightward when money income increases. Most goods are normal. In contrast, demand for an inferior good actually decreases as money income increases, so the demand curve shifts leftward. Examples of inferior goods include bologna sandwiches, used furniture, and used clothing. As money income increases, consumers tend to switch from these inferior goods to normal goods (such as roast beef sandwiches, new furniture, and new clothing).

Changes in the Prices of Other Goods

Again, the prices of other goods are assumed to remain constant along a given demand curve. Now let's bring these other prices into play. Consumers have various ways of trying to satisfy any particular want. Consumers choose among substitutes based on relative prices. For example, pizza and tacos are substitutes, though not perfect ones. An increase in the price of tacos, other things constant, reduces the quantity of tacos demanded along a given taco demand curve. An increase in the price of tacos also increases the demand for pizza, shifting the demand curve for pizza to the right. Two goods are considered substitutes if an increase in the price of one shifts the demand for the other rightward and, conversely, if a decrease in the price of one shifts demand for the other leftward.

Goods used in combination are called *complements*. Examples include Coke and pizza, milk and cookies, computer software and hardware, and airline tickets and rental cars. Two goods are considered complements if an increase in the price of one decreases the demand for the other, shifting that demand curve leftward. For example, an increase in the price of pizza shifts the demand curve for Coke leftward. But most pairs of goods selected at random are *unrelated*—for example, pizza and housing, or milk and gasoline. Still, an increase in the price of an unrelated good reduces the consumer's real income and can reduce the demand for pizza and other goods. For example, a sharp increase in housing prices reduces the amount of income people have to spend on other goods, such as pizza.

Changes in Consumer Expectations

Another factor assumed constant along a given demand curve is consumer expectations about factors that influence demand, such as incomes or prices. A change in consumers' *income expectations* can shift the demand curve. For example, a consumer who learns about a pay raise might increase demand well before the raise takes effect. A college senior who lands that first real job may buy a new car even before graduation. Likewise, a change in consumers' *price expectations* can shift the demand curve. For example, if you expect the price of pizza to jump next week, you may buy an extra one today for the freezer, shifting this week's demand for pizza rightward. Or if consumers come to believe that home prices will climb next month, some will increase their demand for housing now, shifting this month's demand for housing rightward. On the other hand, if housing prices are expected to fall next month, some consumers will postpone purchases, thereby shifting this month's housing demand leftward.

Changes in the Number or Composition of Consumers

As mentioned earlier, the market demand curve is the sum of the individual demand curves of all consumers in the market. If the number of consumers changes, the demand curve will shift. For example, if the population grows, the demand curve for pizza will shift rightward. Even if total population remains unchanged, demand could shift with a change in the composition of the population. For example, a bulge in the teenage population could shift pizza demand rightward. A baby boom would shift rightward the demand for car seats and baby food. A growing Latino population would affect the demand for Latino foods.

Changes in Consumer Tastes

Do you like anchovies on your pizza? How about sauerkraut on your hot dogs?

normal good
a good, such as new clothes, for which demand increases, or shifts rightward, as consumer income rises

inferior good
a good, such as used clothes, for which demand decreases, or shifts leftward, as consumer income rises

substitutes
goods, such as Coke and Pepsi, that relate in such a way that an increase in the price of one shifts the demand for the other rightward

complements
goods, such as milk and cookies, that relate in such a way that an increase in the price of one shifts the demand for the other leftward

Are you into tattoos and body piercings? Is music to your ears more likely to be rock, country, hip-hop, reggae, R&B, jazz, funk, Latin, gospel, new age, or classical? Choices in food, body art, music, clothing, books, movies, TV—indeed, all consumer choices—are influenced by consumer tastes. Tastes are nothing more than your likes and dislikes as a consumer. What determines tastes? Your desires for food when hungry and drink when thirsty are largely biological. So too is your desire for comfort, rest, shelter, friendship, love, status, personal safety, and a pleasant environment. Your family background affects some of your tastes—your taste in food, for example, has been shaped by years of home cooking. Other influences include the surrounding culture, peer pressure, and religious convictions. So economists can say a little about the origin of tastes, but they claim no special expertise in understanding how tastes develop and change over time. Economists recognize, however, that tastes have an important impact on demand. For example, although pizza is popular, some people just don't like it, and those who are lactose intolerant can't stomach the cheese topping. Thus, most people like pizza but some don't.

In our analysis of consumer demand, *we will assume that tastes are given and are relatively stable.* Tastes are assumed to remain constant along a given demand curve. A change in the tastes for a particular good would shift that good's demand curve. For example, a discovery that the tomato sauce and cheese combination on pizza promotes overall health could change consumer tastes, shifting the demand curve for pizza to the right. But because a change in tastes is so difficult to isolate from other economic changes, we should be reluctant to attribute a shift of the demand curve to a change in tastes. We try to rule out other possible reasons for a shift of the demand curve before accepting a change in tastes as the explanation.

tastes
consumer preferences; likes and dislikes in consumption; assumed to remain constant along a given demand curve

movement along a demand curve
change in quantity demanded resulting from a change in the price of the good, other things constant

shift of a demand curve
movement of a demand curve right or left resulting from a change in one of the determinants of demand other than the price of the good

supply
a relation between the price of a good and the quantity that producers are willing and able to sell per period, other things constant

law of supply
the amount of a good that producers are willing and able to sell per period is usually directly related to its price, other things constant

supply curve
a curve showing the relation between the price of a good and the quantity producers are willing and able to sell per period other things constant

That wraps up our look at changes in demand. Before we turn to supply, you should remember the distinction between a movement along a given demand curve and a shift of a demand curve. A change in *price,* other things constant, causes a *movement along a demand curve,* changing the quantity demanded. A change in one of the determinants of demand other than price causes a *shift of a demand curve,* changing demand.

LO² Supply

Just as demand is a relation between price and quantity demanded, supply is a relation between price and quantity supplied. Supply indicates how much producers are *willing* and *able* to offer for sale per period at each possible price, other things constant. The law of supply states that the quantity supplied is usually directly related to its price, other things constant. Thus, the lower the price, the smaller the quantity supplied; the higher the price, the greater the quantity supplied.

© THINKSTOCK IMAGES/JUPITERIMAGES

The Supply Schedule and Supply Curve

Exhibit 3 presents the market *supply schedule* and market supply curve S for pizza. Both show the quantities supplied per week at various possible prices by the thousands of pizza makers in the economy. As you can see, price and quantity supplied are directly, or positively, related. Producers offer more at a higher price than at a lower price, so the supply curve slopes upward.

Exhibit 3a

The Supply Schedule for Pizza

Price per Pizza	Quantity Supplied per Week (millions)
$15	28
12	24
9	20
6	16
3	12

There are two reasons why producers offer more for sale when the price rises. First, as the price increases, other things constant, a producer becomes more *willing* to supply the good. Prices act as signals to existing and potential suppliers about the rewards for producing various goods. A higher pizza price attracts resources from lower-valued uses. *A higher price makes producers more willing to increase quantity supplied.*

Higher prices also increase the producer's *ability* to supply the good. The law of increasing opportunity cost, as noted in Chapter 2, states that the opportunity cost of producing more of a particular good rises as output increases—that is, the *marginal cost* of production increases as output increases. Because producers face a higher marginal cost for additional output, they need to get a higher price for that output to be *able* to increase the quantity supplied. *A higher price makes producers more able to increase quantity supplied.* As a case in point, a higher price for gasoline increases oil companies' ability to extract oil from tar sands, to drill deeper, and to explore in less accessible areas, such as the remote jungles of the Amazon, the stormy waters of the North Sea, and the frozen tundra above the Arctic Circle. For example, at a market price of $20 per barrel, extracting oil from tar sands is unprofitable, but at price of $25 per barrel, producers are able to supply millions of barrels per month from tar sands.

>> **Higher gasoline prices increase a company's ability to explore and drill in less accessible areas.**

Exhibit 3b

The Supply Curve for Pizza

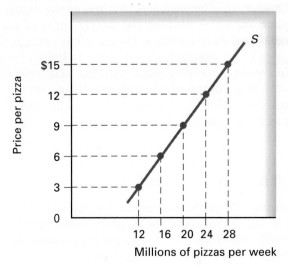

Thus, a higher price makes producers more *willing* and more *able* to increase quantity supplied. Producers are more *willing* because production becomes more profitable than other uses of the resources involved. Producers are more *able* because they can afford to cover the higher marginal cost that typically results from increasing output.

As with demand, we distinguish between *supply* and quantity supplied. *Supply* is the entire relationship between prices and quantities supplied, as reflected by the supply schedule or supply curve. *Quantity supplied* refers to a particular amount offered for sale at a particular price, as reflected by a point on a given supply curve. We also distinguish between individual supply, the supply of an individual producer, and market supply, the sum of individual supplies of all producers in the market. Unless otherwise noted, the term *supply* refers to market supply.

quantity supplied
the amount offered for sale per period at a particular price, as reflected by a point on a given supply curve

individual supply
the relation between the price of a good and the quantity an individual producer is willing and able to sell per period, other things constant

market supply
the relation between the price of a good and the quantity all producers are willing and able to sell per period, other things constant

Shifts of the Supply Curve

The supply curve isolates the relation between the price of a good and the quantity supplied, other things constant. Assumed constant along a supply curve are the determinants of supply other than the price of the good, including (1) the state of technology, (2) the prices of relevant resources, (3) the prices of alternative goods, (4) producer expectations, and (5) the number of producers in the market. Let's see how a change in each affects the supply curve.

Changes in Technology

Recall from Chapter 2 that the state of technology represents the economy's knowledge about how to combine resources efficiently. Along a given supply curve, technology is assumed to remain unchanged. If a better technology is discovered, production costs will fall, so suppliers will be more willing and able to supply the good at each price. Consequently, supply will increase, as reflected by a rightward shift of the supply curve. For example, suppose a new high-tech oven that costs the same as existing ovens bakes pizza in half the time. Such a breakthrough would shift the market supply curve rightward, as from S to S' in Exhibit 4, where more is supplied at each possible price. For example, at a price of $12, the amount supplied increases from 24 million to 28 million pizzas, as shown in Exhibit 4 by the movement from point g to point h. In short, *an increase in supply—that is, a rightward shift of the supply curve—means that producers are willing and able to sell more pizza at each price.*

Changes in the Prices of Relevant Resources

Relevant resources are those employed in the production of the good in question. For example, suppose the price of mozzarella cheese falls. This price decrease reduces the cost of making pizza, so producers are more willing and better able to supply it. The supply curve for pizza shifts rightward, as shown in Exhibit 4. On the other hand, an increase in the price of a relevant resource

relevant resources resources used to produce the good in question

alternative goods other goods that use some or all of the same resources as the good in question

Exhibit 4

An Increase in the Supply of Pizza

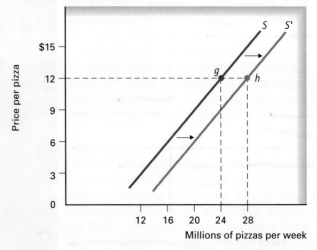

reduces supply, meaning a shift of the supply curve leftward. For example, a higher price of mozzarella increases the cost of making pizza. Higher production costs decrease supply, as reflected by a leftward shift of the supply curve.

Changes in the Prices of Alternative Goods

Nearly all resources have alternative uses. The labor, building, machinery, ingredients, and knowledge needed to run a pizza business could produce other baked goods. Alternative goods are those that use some of the same resources employed to produce the good under consideration. For example, a decrease in the price of Italian bread reduces the opportunity cost of making pizza. As a result, some bread makers become pizza makers so the supply of pizza increases, shifting the supply curve of pizza rightward as in Exhibit 4. On the other hand, if the price of an alternative good, such as Italian bread, increases, supplying pizza becomes relatively less attractive compared to supplying Italian bread. As resources shift from pizza to bread, the supply of pizza decreases, or shifts to the left.

Changes in Producer Expectations

Changes in producer expectations can shift the supply curve. For example, a pizza maker expecting higher pizza prices in the future may expand his or her pizzeria now, thereby shifting the supply of pizza rightward. When a good can be easily stored (crude oil, for example, can be left in the ground), expecting higher prices in the future might prompt some producers to *reduce* their current supply while awaiting the higher price. Thus, an expectation of higher prices in the future could either increase or decrease current supply, depending on the good. More generally, any change affecting future profitability, such as a change in business taxes, could shift the supply curve now.

Supply and Demand in the Video Game Industry

Traditionally, the primary customer base in the video game industry has been teenage and young-adult males. With the current generation of consoles—the Nintendo Wii, Sony's PlayStation 3, and Microsoft's Xbox 360—having been out for several years, console makers began looking for ways to expand their markets with more family-oriented games, like Wii Music and Cooking, and Sony's fantastic puzzle-adventure game LittleBig-Planet. Nearly two-thirds of Sony's 20 titles during the 2008 holiday season were slated as casual or family oriented. Furthermore, some consoles like the Xbox have experienced price cuts, and at $50–$60, video games can provide relatively cheap family entertainment. Some analysts, however, think the demand for family-friendly games is still not that high. One potential Wii buyer, for instance, characterized the game Hasbro Family Game Night, a compilation of classic board games, as an expensive board game substitute.

SOURCE: Christopher Lawton and Yukari Iwatani Kane, "Game Makers Push 'Family' Fare," *Wall Street Journal,* 29 October 2008. Available at http://online.wsj.com/article/SB122523218232077657.html (accessed 11 December 2008).

Changes in the Number of Producers

Because market supply sums the amounts supplied at each price by all producers, market supply depends on the number of producers in the market. If that number increases, supply will increase, shifting supply to the right. If the number of producers decreases, supply will decrease, shifting supply to the left. As an example of increased supply, the number of gourmet coffee bars in the United States has more than quadrupled since 1990 (think Starbucks), shifting the supply curve of gourmet coffee to the right.

Finally, note again the distinction between a *movement along a supply curve* and a *shift of a supply curve.* A change in *price,* other things constant, causes *a movement along a supply curve,* changing the quantity supplied. A change in one of the determinants of supply other than price causes a *shift of a supply curve,* changing supply.

You are now ready to bring demand and supply together.

LO³ Demand and Supply Create a Market

Demanders and suppliers have different views of price. Demanders pay the price and suppliers receive it. Thus, a higher price is bad news for consumers but good news for producers. As the price rises, consumers reduce their quantity demanded along the demand curve and producers increase their quantity supplied along the supply curve. How is this conflict between producers and consumers resolved?

Markets

A market sorts out differences between demanders and suppliers. A *market,* as you know from Chapter 1, includes all the arrangements used to buy and sell a particular good or service. Markets reduce transaction costs—the costs of time and information required for exchange. For example, suppose you are looking for a summer job. One approach might be to go from employer to employer looking for openings. But this could have you running around for days or weeks. A more efficient strategy would be to pick up a copy of the local newspaper or go online and look for openings. Classified ads and Web sites, which are elements of the job market, reduce the transaction costs of bringing workers and employers together.

The coordination that occurs through markets takes place not because of some central plan but because of Adam Smith's "invisible hand." For example, the auto dealers in your community tend to locate together, usually on the outskirts of town, where land is cheaper. The dealers congregate not because they all took an economics course or because they like

movement along a supply curve change in quantity supplied resulting from a change in the price of the good, other things constant

shift of a supply curve movement of a supply curve left or right resulting from a change in one of the determinants of supply other than the price of the good

transaction costs the costs of time and information required to carry out market exchange

one another's company but because together they become a more attractive destination for car buyers. A dealer who makes the mistake of locating away from the others misses out on a lot of business. Similarly, stores locate together so that more shoppers will be drawn by the call of the mall. From Orlando theme parks to Broadway theaters to Las Vegas casinos, suppliers congregate to attract demanders. Some groupings can be quite specialized. For example, shops selling dress mannequins cluster along Austin Road in Hong Kong. And diamond merchants congregate within a few city blocks in New York City.

Market Equilibrium

To see how a market works, let's bring together market demand and supply. Exhibit 5 shows the market for pizza, using schedules in panel (a) and curves in panel (b). Suppose the price initially is $12. At that price, producers supply 24 million pizzas per week, but consumers demand only 14 million, resulting in an *excess quantity supplied*, or a surplus, of 10 million pizzas per week. Suppliers don't like getting stuck with unsold pizzas. Their desire to eliminate the surplus puts downward pressure on the price, as shown by the arrow pointing down in the graph. As the price falls, producers reduce their quantity supplied and consumers increase their quantity demanded. The price continues to fall as long as quantity supplied exceeds quantity demanded.

surplus
at a given price, the amount by which quantity supplied exceeds quantity demanded; a surplus usually forces the price down

shortage
at a given price, the amount by which quantity demanded exceeds quantity supplied; a shortage usually forces the price up

Alternatively, suppose the price initially is $6. You can see from Exhibit 5 that at that price, consumers demand 26 million pizzas but producers supply only 16 million, resulting in an *excess quantity demanded,* or a shortage, of 10 million pizzas per week. Producers quickly notice that they have sold out and those customers still demanding pizzas are grumbling. Profit-maximizing producers and frustrated consumers create market pressure for a higher price, as shown by the arrow pointing up in the graph. As the price rises, producers increase their quantity supplied and consumers reduce their quantity demanded. The price continues to rise as long as quantity demanded exceeds quantity supplied.

Thus, *a surplus creates downward pressure on the price, and a shortage creates upward pressure.* As long as quantity demanded differs from quantity supplied, this difference forces a price change. Note that a shortage or a surplus depends on the price. There is no such thing as a general shortage or a general surplus, only a shortage or a surplus at a particular price.

Exhibit 5

Equilibrium in the Pizza Market

(a) Market schedules

Millions of Pizzas per Week

Price per Pizza	Quantity Demanded	Quantity Supplied	Surplus or Shortage	Effect on Price
$15	8	28	Surplus of 20	Falls
12	14	24	Surplus of 10	Falls
9	20	20	Equilibrium	Remains the same
6	26	16	Shortage of 10	Rises
3	32	12	Shortage of 20	Rises

(b) Market curves

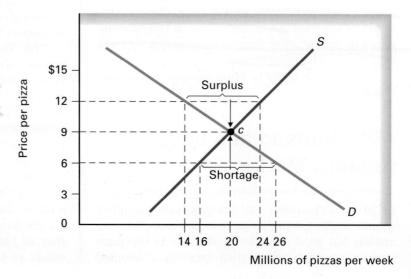

A market reaches equilibrium when the quantity demanded equals quantity supplied. In equilibrium, the independent plans of both buyers and sellers exactly match, so market forces exert no pressure for change. In Exhibit 5, the demand and supply curves intersect at the *equilibrium point,* identified as point c. The *equilibrium price* is $9 per pizza, and the *equilibrium quantity* is 20 million per week. At that price and quantity, the market *clears.* Because there is no shortage or surplus, there is no pressure for the price to change. The demand and supply curves form an "x" at the intersection. The equilibrium point is found where "x" marks the spot.

A market finds equilibrium through the independent actions of thousands, or even millions, of buyers and sellers. In one sense, the market is personal because each consumer and each producer makes a personal decision about how much to buy or sell at a given price. In another sense, the market is impersonal because it requires no conscious communication or coordination among consumers or producers. The price does all the talking. *Impersonal market forces synchronize the personal and independent decisions of many individual buyers and sellers to achieve equilibrium price and quantity.*

LO⁴ Changes in Equilibrium Price and Quantity

Equilibrium occurs when the intentions of demanders and suppliers exactly match. Once a market reaches equilibrium, that price and quantity prevail until something happens to demand or supply. A change in any determinant of demand or supply usually changes equilibrium price and quantity in a predictable way, as you'll see.

Shifts of the Demand Curve

In Exhibit 6, demand curve D and supply curve S intersect at point c to yield the initial equilibrium price of $9 and the initial equilibrium quantity of 20 million 12-inch regular pizzas per week. Now suppose that one of the determinants of demand changes in a way that increases demand, shifting the demand curve to the right from D to D'. Any of the following could shift the

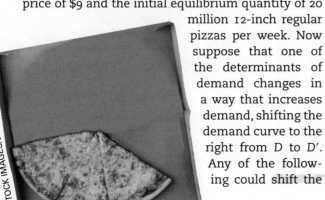

© THINKSTOCK IMAGES/JUPITERIMAGES

Exhibit 6

Effects of an Increase in Demand

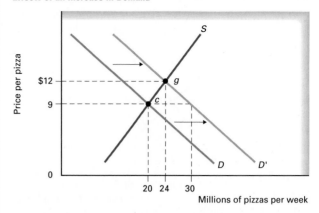

demand for pizza rightward: (1) an increase in the money income of consumers (because pizza is a normal good); (2) an increase in the price of a substitute, such as tacos, or a decrease in the price of a complement, such as Coke; (3) a change in consumer expectations that causes people to demand more pizzas now; (4) a growth in the number of pizza consumers; or (5) a change in consumer tastes—based, for example, on a discovery that the tomato sauce on pizza has antioxidant properties that improve overall health.

After the demand curve shifts rightward to D' in Exhibit 6, the amount demanded at the initial price of $9 is 30 million pizzas, which exceeds the amount supplied of 20 million by 10 million pizzas. This shortage puts upward pressure on the price. As the price increases, the quantity demanded decreases along the new demand curve D', and the quantity supplied increases along the existing supply curve S until the two quantities are equal once again at equilibrium point g. The new equilibrium price is $12, and the new equilibrium quantity is 24 million pizzas per week. Thus, given an upward-sloping supply curve, an increase in demand increases both equilibrium price and quantity. A decrease in demand would lower both equilibrium price and quantity. These results can be summarized as follows: *Given an upward-sloping supply curve, a rightward shift of the demand curve increases both equilibrium price and quantity and a leftward shift decreases both equilibrium price and quantity.*

Shifts of the Supply Curve

Let's consider shifts of the supply curve. In Exhibit 7, as before, we begin with demand curve D and supply curve S intersecting at point c

equilibrium
the condition that exists in a market when the plans of buyers match those of sellers, so quantity demanded equals quantity supplied and the market clears

Exhibit 7

Effects of an Increase in Supply

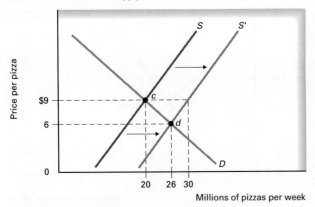

Millions of pizzas per week

to yield an equilibrium price of $9 and an equilibrium quantity of 20 million pizzas per week. Suppose one of the determinants of supply changes, increasing supply from S to S'. Changes that could shift the supply curve rightward include (1) a technological breakthrough in pizza ovens; (2) a reduction in the price of a relevant resource, such as mozzarella cheese; (3) a decline in the price of an alternative good, such as Italian bread; (4) a change in expectations that encourages pizza makers to expand production now; or (5) an increase in the number of pizzerias.

After the supply curve shifts rightward in Exhibit 7, the amount supplied at the initial price of $9 increases from 20 million to 30 million, so producers now supply 10 million more pizzas than consumers demand. This surplus forces the price down. As the price falls, the quantity supplied declines along the new supply curve but the quantity demanded increases along the existing demand curve until a new equilibrium point *d* is established. The new equilibrium price is $6, and the new equilibrium quantity is 26 million pizzas per week. In short, an increase in supply reduces the price and increases the quantity. On the other hand, a decrease in supply increases the price but decreases the quantity. Thus, *given a downward-sloping demand curve, a rightward shift of the supply curve decreases price but increases quantity, and a leftward shift increases price but decreases quantity.*

Simultaneous Shifts of Demand and Supply Curves

As long as only one curve shifts, we can say for sure how equilibrium price and quantity will change. If both curves shift, however, the outcome is less obvious. For example, suppose both demand and supply increase, or shift rightward, as in Exhibit 8. Note that in panel (a), demand shifts more than supply, and in panel (b),

supply shifts more than demand. In both panels, equilibrium quantity increases. The change in equilibrium price, however, depends on which curve shifts more. If demand shifts more, as in panel (a), equilibrium price increases. For example, between 1995 and 2005, the demand for housing increased more than the supply, so both price and quantity increased. But if supply shifts more, as in panel (b), equilibrium price decreases. For example, in the last decade, the supply of personal computers has increased more than the demand, so price has decreased and quantity increased.

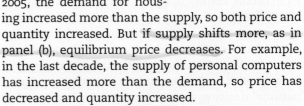

Conversely, if both demand and supply decrease, or shift leftward, equilibrium quantity decreases. But, again, we cannot say what will happen to equi-

Exhibit 8

Indeterminate Effect of an Increase in Both Demand and Supply

(a) *Shift of demand dominates*

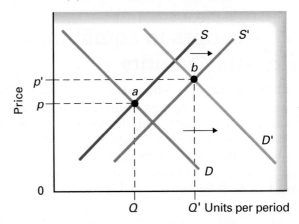

(b) *Shift of supply dominates*

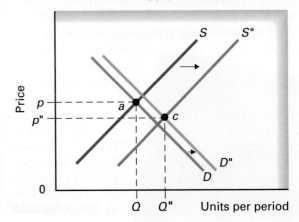

librium price unless we examine relative shifts. (You can use Exhibit 8 to consider decreases in demand and supply by viewing D' and S' as the initial curves.) If demand shifts more, the price will fall. If supply shifts more, the price will rise.

If demand and supply shift in opposite directions, we can say what will happen to equilibrium price. Equilibrium price will increase if demand increases and supply decreases. Equilibrium price will decrease if demand decreases and supply increases. Without reference to particular shifts, however, we cannot say what will happen to equilibrium quantity.

These results are no doubt confusing, but Exhibit 9 summarizes the four possible combinations of changes. Using Exhibit 9 as a reference, please take the time right now to work through some changes in demand and supply to develop a feel for the results.

Exhibit 9

Effects of Shifts of Both Demand and Supply

	Change in demand	
	Demand increases	**Demand decreases**
Supply increases	Equilibrium price change is indeterminate. Equilibrium quantity increases.	Equilibrium price falls. Equilibrium quantity change is indeterminate.
Supply decreases	Equilibrium price rises. Equilibrium quantity change is indeterminate.	Equilibrium price change is indeterminate. Equilibrium quantity decreases.

(left axis label: Change in supply)

The Market for Professional Basketball

Take a look at Exhibit 10 depicting the market for NBA players, with demand and supply in 1980 as D_{1980} and S_{1980}. The intersection of these two curves generated an average pay in 1980 of \$170,000, or \$0.17 million, for the 300 or so players in the league. Since 1980, the talent pool expanded somewhat, shifting the supply curve a bit rightward from S_{1980} to S_{2007} (almost by definition, the supply of the top few hundred players in the world is limited). But demand exploded from D1980 to D2007. With supply relatively fixed, the greater demand boosted average pay for NBA players to \$4.9 million by 2007 for the 450 or so players in the league. Such pay attracts younger and younger players. NBA players are now the highest-paid team

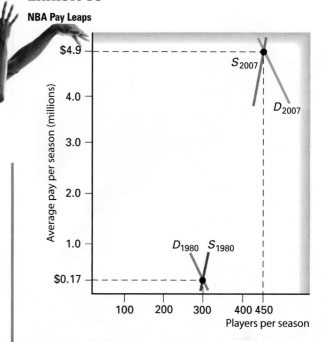

Average annual pay \$4.9 million.

Exhibit 10

NBA Pay Leaps

(Graph: vertical axis "Average pay per season (millions)" with values \$0.17, 1.0, 2.0, 3.0, 4.0, \$4.9; horizontal axis "Players per season" with values 100, 200, 300, 400, 450. Curves D_{1980} and S_{1980} intersect at about 300 players at \$0.17; curves S_{2007} and D_{2007} intersect at about 450 players at \$4.9.)

athletes in the world—earning 60 percent more than pro baseball's average and at least double that for pro football and pro hockey.

But rare talent alone does not command high pay. Top rodeo riders, top bowlers, and top women basketball players also possess rare talent, but the demand for their talent is not sufficient to support pay anywhere near NBA levels. Some sports aren't even popular enough to support professional leagues.

LO⁵ Disequilibrium

A surplus exerts downward pressure on the price, and a shortage exerts upward pressure. Markets, however, don't always reach equilibrium quickly. During the time required to adjust, the market is said to be in disequilibrium. Disequilibrium is usually temporary as the market gropes for equilibrium. But sometimes, often as a result of government intervention, disequilibrium can last a while, perhaps decades, as we will see next.

Price Floors

Sometimes public officials set prices above their equilibrium levels. For example, the federal government regulates some agriculture

disequilibrium
the condition that exists in a market when the plans of buyers do not match those of sellers; a temporary mismatch between quantity supplied and quantity demanded as the market seeks equilibrium

Rare talent alone doesn't command high pay. Only the 300 or so top riders can earn a living. Only the top 50 or so make more than $100,000.

© HANS-PETER MERTEN/MAURITIUS DIE BILDAGENTUR GMBH/PHOTOLIBRARY

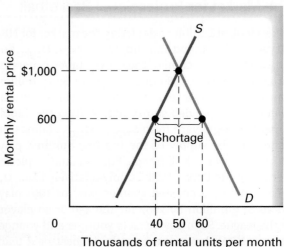

© THINKSTOCK IMAGES/JUPITERIMAGES

prices in an attempt to ensure farmers a higher and more stable income than they would otherwise earn. To achieve higher prices, the federal government sets a price floor, or a *minimum* selling price that is above the equilibrium price. Exhibit 11a shows the effect of a $2.50 per gallon price floor for milk. At that price, farmers supply 24 million gallons per week, but consumers demand only 14 million gallons, yielding a surplus of 10 million gallons. This surplus milk will pile up on store shelves, eventually souring. To take it off the market, the government usually agrees to buy the surplus milk. The federal government, in fact, spends billions buying and storing surplus agricultural products. Note, to have an impact, a price floor must be set above the equilibrium price. A price floor set at or below the equilibrium price would be nonbinding (how come?). Price floors distort markets and reduce economic welfare.

price floor
a minimum legal price below which a product cannot be sold; to have an impact, a price floor must be set above the equilibrium price

price ceiling
a maximum legal price above which a product cannot be sold; to have an impact, a price ceiling must be set below the equilibrium price

Price Ceilings

Sometimes public officials try to keep a price below the equilibrium level by setting a price ceiling, or a *maximum* selling price. Concern about the rising cost of rental housing in some cities has prompted city officials to impose rent ceilings. Exhibit 11b depicts the demand and supply of rental housing. The vertical axis shows monthly rent, and the horizontal axis shows the quantity of rental units. The equilibrium, or market-clearing, rent is $1,000 per month, and the equilibrium quantity is 50,000 housing units. Suppose city officials set a maximum rent of $600 per month. At that ceiling price, 60,000 rental units are demanded, but only 40,000 supplied, resulting in a housing shortage of 20,000 units. Because of the price ceiling, the rental price no longer rations housing to those who value it the most. Other devices

Exhibit 11a

Price Floors for Milk

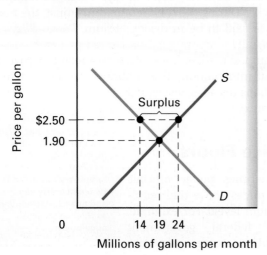

Millions of gallons per month

Exhibit 11b

Price Ceilings for Rent

Thousands of rental units per month

emerge to ration housing, such as long waiting lists, personal connections, and the willingness to make under-the-table payments, such as "key fees," "finder's fees," high security deposits, and the like. To have an impact, a price ceiling must be set below the equilibrium price. A price ceiling set at or above the equilibrium level would be nonbinding. Price floors and ceilings distort markets and reduce economic welfare.

Government intervention is not the only source of market disequilibrium. Sometimes, when new products are introduced or when demand suddenly changes, it takes a while to reach equilibrium. For example, popular toys, best-selling books, and chart-busting CDs sometimes sell out. On the other hand, some new products attract few customers and pile up unsold on store shelves, awaiting a "clearance sale."

Final Word

Demand and supply are the building blocks of a market economy. Although a market usually involves the interaction of many buyers and sellers, few markets are consciously designed. Just as the law of gravity works whether or not we understand Newton's principles, market forces operate whether or not participants understand demand and supply. These forces arise naturally, much the way car dealers cluster on the outskirts of town to attract more customers.

Markets have their critics. Some observers may be troubled, for example, that an NBA star like Kevin Garnett earns a salary that could pay for 500 new schoolteachers, or that movie stars earn enough to pay for 1,000 new schoolteachers, or that U.S. consumers spend over $40 billion on their pets. On your next trip to the supermarket, notice how much shelf space goes to pet products—often an entire aisle. PetSmart, a chain store, sells over 12,000 pet items. Veterinarians offer cancer treatment, cataract removal, root canals, even acupuncture. Kidney dialysis for a pet can cost over $75,000 per year.

In a market economy, consumers are kings and queens. Consumer sovereignty rules, deciding what gets produced. Those who don't like the market outcome usually look to government for a solution through price ceilings and price floors, regulations, income redistribution, and public finance more generally.

Year that October was designated National Pizza Month. > 1987

350 < Slices per second rate at which Americans eat pizza, which amounts to approximately 100 acres of pizza each day.

Annual sales of the pizza industry. > $30 billion

69,000 < Pizzerias in the United States.

Amount of pizza each man, woman, and child in America eats on average in a year. > 23 pounds

3 billion < Number of pizzas sold in the U.S. each year.

© THINKSTOCK IMAGES/JUPITERIMAGES

SOURCES: *Pizza Today* magazine; National Association of Pizza Operators; http://pizzaware.com/facts.htm; Blumenfeld and Associates, Darien, CT; Packaged Facts, New York.

CHAPTER 5

Learning Outcomes

LO[1] Discuss macroeconomics and the national economy

LO[2] Discuss economic fluctuations and growth

LO[3] Explain aggregate demand and aggregate supply

LO[4] Describe the history of the U.S. economy

Introduction *to* Macroeconomics

> ## "Which has more impact on your standard of living, the economy's short-term ups and downs or its long-term growth trend?"

What's the big idea with macroeconomics? Why is its focus the national economy? How do we measure the economy's performance over time? Which has more impact on your standard of living, the economy's short-term ups and downs or its long-term growth trend? Answers to these and related questions are provided in this chapter, which introduces macroeconomics. Macroeconomics looks at the big picture—not the demand for iPhones but the demand for everything produced in the economy; not the price of gasoline but the average price of all goods and services produced in the economy; not consumption by the Martinez household but consumption by all households; not investment by Google but investment by all firms in the economy.

Macroeconomists develop and test theories about how the economy as a whole works—theories that can help predict the impact of economic policies and events. Macroeconomists are concerned not only with what determines such big-picture indicators as production, employment, and the price level but also with understanding how and why they change over time. Macroeconomists are especially interested in what makes an economy grow, because a growing economy creates more jobs and more goods and services— in short, more growth means a rising standard of living. What determines the economy's ability to use resources productively, to adapt, to grow? This chapter begins exploring such questions.

What do you think?

Keynes' economic theory is more applicable to our present economic state than Smith's.

Strongly Disagree						Strongly Agree
1	2	3	4	5	6	7

Topics discussed in Chapter 5 include:

- The national economy
- Economic fluctuations
- Aggregate demand
- Aggregate supply
- Equilibrium price level and aggregate output
- The history of the U.S. economy
- Demand-side economics
- Supply-side economics

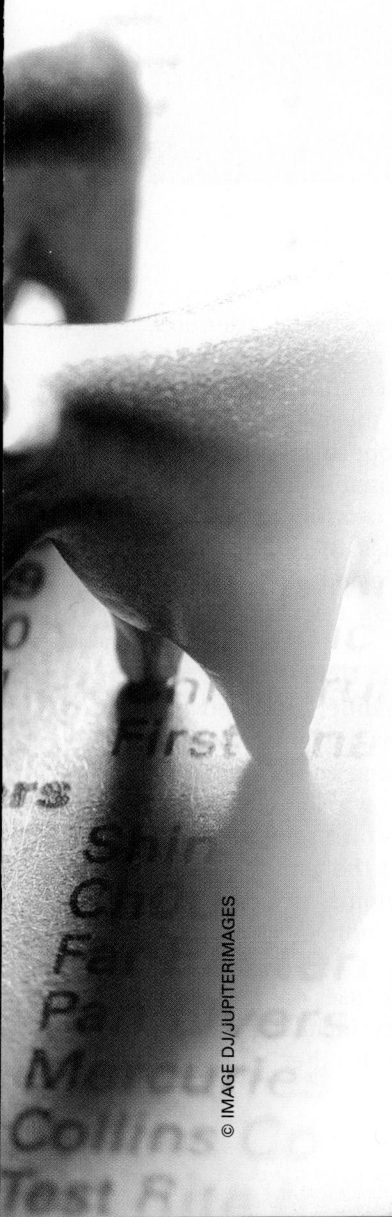

LO¹ The National Economy

Macroeconomics concerns the overall performance of the *economy*. The term economy describes the structure of economic life, or economic activity, in a community, a region, a country, a group of countries, or the world. We could talk about the Chicago economy, the Illinois economy, the Midwest economy, the U.S. economy, the North American economy, or the world economy.

economy
the structure of economic activity in a community, a region, a country, a group of countries, or the world

The United States and Mexico usually allow people and goods to move more freely *within* their borders than *across* their borders.

We measure an economy's size in different ways, such as the amount produced, the number of people working, or their total income. The most common yardstick is *gross product,* which measures the market value of final goods and services produced in a particular geographical region during a given period, usually one year.

If the focus is the Illinois economy, we consider the *gross state product*. If the focus is the U.S. economy, we consider the gross domestic product, or GDP, which measures the market value of all final goods and services produced in the United States during a given period, usually a year. GDP adds up production of the economy's incredible variety of goods and services, from trail bikes to pedicures. We can use the gross domestic product to compare different economies at the same time or to track the same economy over time. We could also consider the gross world product, which measures the value of all final goods and services produced in the world during a given period, usually a year. But the focus of macroeconomics is usually the national economy.

gross domestic product (GDP)
the market value of all final goods and services produced in the nation during a particular period, usually a year

gross world product
the market value of all final goods and services produced in the world during a given period, usually a year

What's Special About the National Economy?

The national economy deserves special attention. Here's why. If you were to drive west on Interstate 10 in Texas, you would hardly notice crossing into New Mexico. But if, instead, you took the Juarez exit south into Mexico, you would be stopped at the border, asked for identification, and possibly searched. You would become quite aware of crossing an international border. Like most countries, the United States and Mexico usually allow people and goods to move more freely *within* their borders than *across* their borders.

The differences between the United States and Mexico are far greater than the differences between Texas and New Mexico. For example, each country has its own standard of living and currency, its own culture and language, its own communication and transportation systems, its own system of government, and its own "rules of the game"—that is, its own laws, regulations, customs, manners, and conventions for conducting economic activity both within and across its borders.

Macroeconomics typically focuses on the performance of the national economy, including how the national economy interacts with other economies around the world. The U.S. economy is the largest and most complex in world history, with about 116 million households, 30 million for-profit businesses, and 89,500 separate government jurisdictions. The world economy includes about 200 sovereign nations, ranging from tiny Liechtenstein, with only 34,500 people, to China, with 1.3 billion people. These numbers offer snapshots, but the economy is a motion picture, a work in progress—too complex to capture in snapshots. This is why we use theoretical models to focus on key relationships. To help you get your mind around the economy, let's begin with a simple analogy.

The Human Body and the U.S. Economy

Consider the similarities and differences between the human body and the economy. The body consists of millions of cells, each performing particular functions yet each linked to the entire body. Similarly, the U.S. economy is composed of millions of decision makers, each acting with some independence yet each connected with the economy as a whole. The economy, like the body, is continually renewing itself, with new households, new businesses, a changing group of public officials, and new foreign competitors and customers. Blood circulates throughout the body, facilitating the exchange of oxygen and vital nutrients among cells. Similarly, money circulates throughout the economy, facilitating the exchange of resources and products among individual economic units. In fact, blood and money are each called a *medium of exchange.* In Chapter 1 we saw that the movement of money, products, and resources throughout the economy follows a *circular flow,* as does the movement of blood, oxygen, and nutrients throughout the body.

Flow and Stock Variables

Just as the same blood recirculates as a medium of exchange in the body, the same dollars recirculate as a medium of exchange in the economy to finance transactions. The dollars you spend on bagels are spent by the baker on butter and then spent by the dairy farmer on work boots. Dollars *flow* through the economy. To measure a flow, we use a flow variable, which is an amount per unit of time, such as your average spending per week or your heartbeats per minute. In contrast, a stock variable is an amount measured at a particular point in time, such as the amount of money you have with you right now or your weight this morning.

Testing New Theories

Physicians and other natural scientists test their theories using controlled experiments. Macroeconomists, however, have no laboratories and little ability to run economy-wide experiments of any kind. Granted, they can study different economies around the world, but each economy is unique, so comparisons are tricky. Controlled experiments also provide the natural sciences with something seldom available to economists—the opportunity for chance, or serendipitous, discovery (such as penicillin). Macroeconomists studying the U.S. economy have only one patient, so they can't introduce particular policies in a variety of alternative settings. You can't squeeze economies into a test tube. Cries of "Eureka!" are seldom heard from macroeconomists.

Knowledge and Performance

Throughout history, little was known about the human body, yet many people still enjoyed good health. For example, the fact that blood circulates in the body was not established until 1638; it took scientists another 150 years to figure out why. Similarly, over the millennia, various complex economies developed and flourished, although at the time there was little understanding about how an economy worked.

The economy is much like the body: As long as it functions smoothly, policy makers need not understand how it works. But if a problem develops—severe unemployment, high inflation, or sluggish growth, for example—we must know how a healthy economy works before we can consider whether anything can be done about it. We need not know every detail

flow variable
a variable that measures something over an interval of time, such as your income per week

stock variable
a variable that measures something at a particular point in time, such as the amount of money you have with you right now

theory about how the economy works. At one time, for example, a nation's economic vitality was thought to spring from the stock of precious metals accumulated in the public treasury. This theory spawned a policy called mercantilism, which held that, as a way of accumulating gold and silver, a nation should try to export more than it imports. To achieve this, nations restricted imports by such barriers as tariffs and quotas. But these restrictions led to retaliations by other countries, reducing international trade and the gains from specialization. Another flawed economic theory prompted President Herbert Hoover to introduce a major tax *increase* during the Great Depression. Economists have since learned that such a policy does more harm than good. In addition, debates about whether policies are helpful or harmful were prevalent as policy makers responded to the 2008–2009 economic downturn.

We turn now to the performance of the U.S. economy.

LO² Economic Fluctuations and Growth

The U.S. economy and other industrial market economies historically have experienced alternating periods of expansion and contraction in economic activity. Economic fluctuations are the rise and fall of economic activity relative to the long-term growth trend of the economy. These fluctuations, or *business cycles,* vary in length and intensity, yet some features appear common to all. The ups and downs usually involve the entire nation and often many other economies around the world, and they affect nearly all dimensions of economic activity, not just production and employment.

U.S. Economic Fluctuations

Perhaps the easiest way to understand the business cycle is to examine its components. During the 1920s

© HULTON ARCHIVE/GETTY IMAGES

of the economy, just as we need not know every detail of the body. But we must understand essential relationships among key variables. For example, does the economy work well on its own, or does it often perform poorly? If it performs poorly, are there remedies? Can we be sure that a proposed remedy would not do more harm than good? When doctors didn't understand how the human body worked, their attempted "cures" were often worse than the diseases. Much of the history of medicine describes misguided efforts to deal with maladies. Even today, medical care is based on less scientific evidence than you might think. According to one study, only one in seven medical interventions is supported by reliable scientific evidence.[1] For example, acetaminophen (e.g., Tylenol) is a popular pain reliever, but nobody really knows how it works.

Likewise, policy makers may adopt the wrong prescription because of a flawed

mercantilism
the incorrect theory that a nation's economic objective should be to accumulate precious metals in the public treasury; this theory prompted trade barriers to cut imports, but other countries retaliated, reducing trade and the gains from specialization

economic fluctuations
the rise and fall of economic activity relative to the long-term growth trend of the economy; also called business cycles

1. As reported by Sherwin Nuland, "Medical Fads: Bran, Midwives and Leeches," *New York Times,* 25 January 1995.

and 1930s, Wesley C. Mitchell, director of the National Bureau of Economic Research (NBER), analyzed business cycles, noting that the economy has two phases: *expansions* and *contractions*. During an expansion, the economy's output increases. During a contraction, the economy's output decreases. Prior to World War II, a contraction might be so severe as to be called a depression, which is a sharp reduction in the nation's total production lasting more than a year and accompanied by high unemployment. A milder contraction is called a recession, traditionally defined as a decline in total output lasting at least two consecutive quarters, or at least six months. The U.S. economy experienced both recessions and depressions before World War II. So far, there have been recessions but no depressions, so things have improved.

Despite these ups and downs, the U.S. economy has grown dramatically over the long term. The economy now produces about 13 times more output than it did in 1929. Output is measured by real GDP, the value of final goods and services after stripping away changes due to inflation, which is an increase in the economy's average price level. Production increased because of (1) increases in the amount and quality of resources, especially labor and capital; (2) better technology; and (3) improvements in the *rules of the game* that facilitate production and exchange, such as property rights, patent laws, the legal system, and market practices.

Exhibit 1 shows such a long-term growth trend in real GDP as an upward-sloping straight line. Economic fluctuations reflect movements around this growth trend. A contraction begins after the previous expansion has reached a *peak,* or high point, and continues until the economy reaches a *trough,* or low point. The period between a peak and trough is a *contraction,* and the period between a trough and subsequent peak is an *expansion.* Note that expansions last longer than contractions, but the length of the full cycle varies.

Analysts at NBER have tracked the U.S. economy back to 1854. Since then, the nation has experienced 32 peak-to-trough-to-peak cycles. No two have been exactly alike. During the 22 business cycles prior to

Exhibit 1

Hypothetical Business Cycles

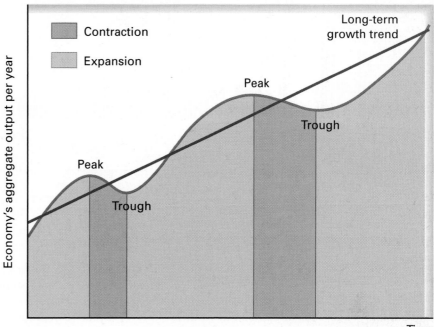

1945, expansions averaged 29 months and contractions 21 months. During the 11 cycles since 1945, expansions stretched twice as long to 57 months, and recessions fell by half to 11 months. Thus since 1945 expansions are longer and recessions are shorter. Both developments have been hugely beneficial for economic growth and the U.S. standard of living. The longest expansion on record lasted 10 years, from March 1991 to March 2001. The longest contraction lasted five and a half years, from 1873 to 1879.

Exhibit 2 shows annual percentage changes in real GDP since 1929. Years of declining real GDP are shown as red bars and years of increasing real GDP as blue bars. The big decline during the Great Depression of the early 1930s and the sharp jump during World War II stand in stark contrast. Growth since 1929 averaged 3.4 percent a year. Although official data are not yet available, eventually the 2008–2009 recession will appear on charts like Exhibit 2.

expansion
a period during which the economy's output increases

contraction
a period during which the economy's output declines

depression
a sharp reduction in an economy's total output accompanied by high unemployment lasting more than a year

recession
a sustained decline in the economy's total output lasting at least two consecutive quarters, or six months; an economic contraction

inflation
an increase in the economy's average price level

Exhibit 2

Annual Percentage Change in U.S. Real GDP Since 1929

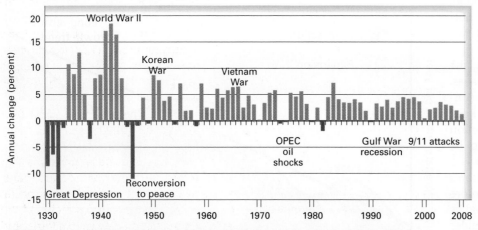

SOURCE: Bureau of Economic Analysis, U.S. Dept. of Commerce. For the latest data, go to http://www.bea.gov/index.htm.

The intensity of U.S. economic fluctuations varies across regions. A recession hits hardest those regions that produce capital goods, such as heavy machinery, and durable goods, such as appliances, furniture, and automobiles. The demand for these goods falls more during hard times than does the demand for other goods and services, such as breakfast cereal, gasoline, and haircuts. In addition, housing, banks and financial institutions particularly suffered in 2008

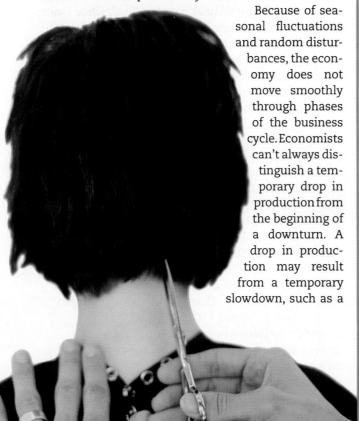

Because of seasonal fluctuations and random disturbances, the economy does not move smoothly through phases of the business cycle. Economists can't always distinguish a temporary drop in production from the beginning of a downturn. A drop in production may result from a temporary slowdown, such as a snowstorm or a poor growing season. Turning points—peaks and troughs—are thus identified by the NBER only after the fact. Because a recession means output declines for at least two consecutive quarters, a recession is not so designated until at least six months after it begins.

As noted, fluctuations usually involve the entire nation. Indeed, major economies around the world often move together. For example, the Great Depression was a worldwide calamity. The unemployment rate in Germany reached 34 percent, which helped bring Hitler to power. The following section compares the year-to-year output changes in the United States with those in another major economy, the United Kingdom, during the last three decades.

The Global Economy

Though business cycles are not perfectly synchronized across countries, a link is often apparent. Consider the experience of two leading economies—the United States and the United Kingdom. Exhibit 3 shows for each economy the year-to-year percentage change in real GDP since 1978. By examining the annual changes in each economy, you can see some similarities. Both economies went into recession in the early 1980s, in 1991, in 2001, and in 2008. Notice also that over time, the countries' growth rates have fluctuated less and become more similar.

When linkage across economies occurs, a slump in one major economy could worsen a recession in the other, and vice versa. For example, the terrorist attacks on the United States in September 2001 affected economies around the world, reducing airline travel and lowering stock market prices. On the other hand, economic strength overseas can give the U.S. economy a lift, with overseas profits helping companies offset a weak home market. The same pattern of worldwide decline occurred with the housing and banking crisis of 2008–2009.

Leading Economic Indicators

Certain events foreshadow a turning point in economic activity. Months before a recession is under

Exhibit 3

U.S. and U.K. Annual Growth Rates in Output Are Similar

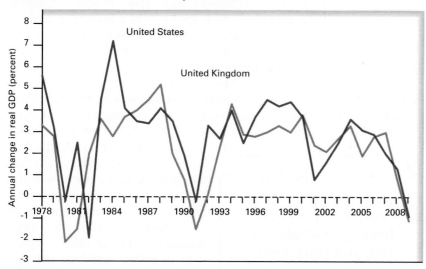

SOURCE: U.S. growth estimates from Bureau of Economic Analysis, U.S. Department of Commerce. For the latest, go to http://www.bea.gov/index.htm, then click on Gross Domestic Product. U.K. growth estimates from *OECD Economic Outlook* 84 (November 2008), Annex Table 1. Growth rates for 2008 in the United Kingdom and 2009 in both countries are OECD projections.

way, changes in leading economic indicators point to the coming storm. In the early stages of a recession, business slows down, orders for machinery and computers slip, and the stock market, anticipating lower profits, turns down. Consumer confidence in the economy also begins to sag, so households spend less, especially on big-ticket items like homes and automobiles. Unsold goods start piling up. All these signs are called **leading economic indicators** because

they usually predict, or *lead to,* a downturn. Likewise, upturns in leading indicators point to an economic recovery. But leading indicators cannot predict precisely *when* a turning point will occur, or even *whether* one will occur. Sometimes leading indicators sound a false alarm.

Some economic indicators measure what's going on in the economy right now. **Coincident economic indicators** are those measures that reflect expansions, contractions, peaks, and troughs as they occur. Coincident indicators include total employment, personal income, and industrial production. And some economic indicators measure what has already happened. **Lagging economic indicators** follow, or trail, changes in overall economic activity. Lagging indicators, which look at the economy through the rearview mirror, include interest rates and how long people remain unemployed.

Our introduction to business cycles has been largely mechanical, focusing on the history and measurement of these fluctuations. We have not discussed why economies fluctuate, in part because such a discussion requires firmer footing in macroeconomic theory and in part because the causes remain in dispute. In the next section, we begin to build a macroeconomic framework by introducing a key model of analysis.

LO³ Aggregate Demand and Aggregate Supply

The economy is so complex that we need to simplify matters, or to abstract from the millions of relationships to isolate the important ones. We must step back from all

{ Pegging a Recession }

On November 28, 2008, the National Bureau of Economic Research determined that the U.S. economy entered its most recent recession after peaking in December 2007. So what did the leading indicators say? The Dow Jones Industrial Average ended 2008 down 38% from its peak in October 2007. Orders for manufactured goods decreased 6% and 4.6% in October and November, amidst some of the worst months of the Wall Street meltdown. Home sales were down 8.6% in November as well.

SOURCES: Jeff Bater, "Factory Orders Fall, as Service Sector Contracts," *Wall Street Journal,* 6 January 2009. Available at http://online.wsj.com/article/SB123125322355257355.html (accessed 9 January 2009); E. S. Browning, "After the Collapse, Guarded Hope for '09," *Wall Street Journal,* 2 January 2009. Available at http://online.wsj.com/article/SB123084159289047143.html (accessed 9 January 2009); Rob Curran, "U.S. Entered a Recession a Year Ago, NBER Says," *Wall Street Journal,* 1 December 2008. Available at http://online.wsj.com/article/SB122815252673269395.html (accessed 9 January 2009); Sudeep Reddy, "Recession, Tight Credit Compound Housing Woes," *Wall Street Journal,* 24 December 2008. Available at http://online.wsj.com/article/SB123003859646029853.html (accessed 24 December 2008).

leading economic indicators
variables that predict, or lead to, a recession or recovery; examples include consumer confidence, stock market prices, business investment, and big-ticket purchases, such as automobiles and homes

coincident economic indicators
variables that reflect peaks and troughs in economic activity as they occur; examples include employment, personal income, and industrial production

lagging economic indicators
variables that follow, or trail, changes in overall economic activity; examples include the interest rate and the average duration of unemployment

the individual economic transactions to survey the resulting mosaic.

Aggregate Output and the Price Level

Let's begin with something you already know. Picture a pizza. Now picture food more generally. Food, of course, includes not just pizza but thousands of other items. Although food is more general than pizza, you probably have no difficulty picturing food. Now make the leap from food to all goods and services produced in the economy—food, housing, clothing, entertainment, transportation, health care, and so on. Economists call this aggregate output. Because *aggregate* means total, aggregate output is the total amount of goods and services produced in the economy during a given period. Because output is measured per period, it's a flow measure. The best measure of aggregate output is *real GDP*, which you'll soon learn more about.

Just as we can talk about the demand for pizza, or the demand for food, we can talk about the demand for aggregate output. Aggregate demand is the relationship between the average price of aggregate output in the economy and the quantity of aggregate output demanded. The average price of aggregate output is called the economy's price level. You are more familiar than you may think with these aggregate measures. Headlines refer to the growth of aggregate output—as in "Growth Slows in Second Quarter." News accounts also report on changes in the "cost of living," reflecting movements in the economy's price level—as in "Prices Jump in June."

In a later chapter, you will learn how the economy's price level is computed. All you need to know now is that the price level in any year is an *index number,* or a reference number, comparing average prices that year with average prices in some base, or reference, year. If we say that the price level is higher, we mean compared with where it was. In Chapter 4, we talked about the price of a particular product, such as pizza, *relative to the prices of other products.* Now we talk about the *average price* of all goods and services produced in the economy *relative to the price level in some base year.*

The price level in the *base year* is standardized to a benchmark value of 100, and price levels in other years are expressed relative to the base-year price level. For example, in 2008, the U.S. price level, or price index, was 122.4, indicating that the price level that year was 22.4 percent higher than its value of 100 in the base year of 2000. The price level, or price index, is used not only to make comparisons in prices over time but also to make accurate comparisons of real aggregate output over time. Economists use the *price index* to eliminate year-to-year changes in GDP due solely to changes in the price level. What's left is the change in real output—the change in the amount of goods and services produced. After adjusting GDP for price level changes, we end up with what is called the real gross domestic product, or real GDP. So the price index (1) shows how the economy's price level changes over time and (2) can be used to figure out real GDP each year. You get a better idea of these two roles as we discuss the U.S. economy.

> The price level in the *base year* is standardized to a benchmark value of 100, and price levels in other years are expressed relative to the base-year price level.

Aggregate Demand Curve

In Chapter 4, you learned about the demand for a particular product. Now let's talk about the demand for our composite measure of output—aggregate output, or real GDP. The aggregate demand curve shows the relationship between the price level in the economy and real GDP demanded, other things constant. Exhibit 4 shows a hypothetical aggregate demand curve, *AD*. The vertical axis measures an index of the economy's price level relative to a 2000 base-year price level of 100. The horizontal axis shows real GDP, which measures output in dollars of constant purchasing power (here we use 2000 prices).

The aggregate demand curve in Exhibit 4 reflects an inverse relationship between the price level in the economy and real GDP demanded. Aggregate demand sums demands of the four economic decision makers: households, firms, governments, and the rest of the world. As the price level increases, other things constant, households demand less housing and fur-

aggregate output
a composite measure of all final goods and services produced in an economy during a given period; real GDP

aggregate demand
the relationship between the economy's price level and aggregate output demanded, with other things constant

price level
a composite measure reflecting the prices of all goods and services in the economy relative to prices in a base year

real gross domestic product (real GDP)
the economy's aggregate output measured in dollars of constant purchasing power

aggregate demand curve
a curve representing the relationship between the economy's price level and real GDP demanded per period, with other things constant

Exhibit 4

Aggregate Demand Curve

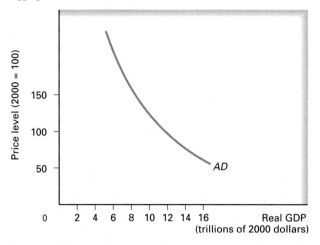

niture, firms demand fewer trucks and tools, governments demand less computer software and military hardware, and the rest of the world demands less U.S. grain and U.S. aircraft.

The reasons behind this inverse relationship get a closer look in later chapters, but here's a quick summary. Real GDP demanded depends in part on household *wealth*. Some wealth is usually held in bank accounts and currency. An increase in the price level, other things constant, decreases the purchasing power of bank accounts and currency. Households are therefore poorer when the price level increases, so the quantity of real GDP they demand decreases. Conversely, a reduction in the price level increases the purchasing power of bank accounts and currency. Because households are richer as the price level decreases, the quantity of real GDP demanded increases.

Factors held constant along a given aggregate demand curve include the price levels in other countries as well as the exchange rates between the U.S. dollar and foreign currencies. When the U.S. price level increases, U.S. products become more expensive relative to foreign products. Consequently, households, firms, and governments both here and abroad decrease the quantity of U.S. products demanded. On the other hand, a lower U.S. price level makes U.S. products cheaper relative to foreign products, so the quantity of U.S. products demanded increases.

Consider the demand for a particular product versus aggregate demand. If the price of a particular product, such as pizza, increases, quantity demanded declines in part because pizza becomes more costly compared to substitutes. If the economy's price level increases, the quantity of U.S. real GDP demanded declines in part because U.S. products become more costly compared to foreign products.

Aggregate Supply Curve

The aggregate supply curve shows how much U.S. producers are willing and able to supply at each price level, other things constant. How does quantity supplied respond to changes in the price level? The upward-sloping aggregate supply curve, AS, in Exhibit 5 on the next page shows a positive relationship between the price level and the quantity of real GDP supplied. Assumed constant along an aggregate supply curve are (1) resource prices, (2) the state of technology, and (3) the rules of the game that provide production incentives, such as patents and business practices. With regard to resource prices, wage rates are typically assumed to be constant along the aggregate supply curve. With wages constant, firms find a higher price level more profitable, so they increase real GDP supplied. *As long as the prices firms receive for their products rise faster than their cost of production, firms find it profitable to expand output, so real GDP supplied varies directly with the economy's price level.*

Equilibrium

The aggregate demand curve intersects the aggregate supply curve to determine the equilibrium levels of price and real GDP in the economy. Exhibit 5 is a rough depiction of aggregate demand and aggregate supply in 2008. Equilibrium real GDP that year was about $11.7 trillion (measured in dollars of 2000 purchasing power). The equilibrium price level was 122.3 (compared with a price level of 100 in the base year of 2000). At any other price level, quantity demanded would not match quantity supplied.

Incidentally, although employment is not measured directly along the horizontal axis, firms usually must hire more workers to produce more output. So higher levels of real GDP can be beneficial because (1) more goods and services

> Household demand
> Firm demand
> Government demand
> + World demand
> ――――――――――――
> Aggregate demand

aggregate supply curve
a curve representing the relationship between the economy's price level and real GDP supplied per period, with other things constant

Exhibit 5

Aggregate Demand and Aggregate Supply in 2008

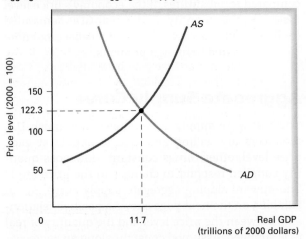

LO⁴ Short History of the U.S. Economy

The history of the U.S. economy can be divided roughly into four economic eras: (1) before and during the Great Depression, (2) after the Great Depression to the early 1970s, (3) from the early 1970s to the early 1980s, and (4) since the early 1980s. The first era suffered from recessions and depressions, culminating in the Great Depression of the 1930s. These depressions were often accompanied by a falling price level. The second era was one of generally strong economic growth, with only moderate increases in the price level. The third era saw both high unemployment and high inflation at the same time. And the fourth era was more like the second, with good economic growth on average and only moderate increases in the price level. It remains to be seen if the 2008–2009 recession marks an end to the fourth era or just a temporary setback.

The Great Depression and Before

Before World War II, the U.S. economy alternated between hard times and prosperity. As noted earlier, the longest contraction on record occurred between 1873 and 1879, when 80 railroads went bankrupt and most of the nation's steel industry shut down. During the 1890s, the economy contracted about half the time, and the unemployment rate topped 18 percent. In October 1929, the stock market crash began what was to become the deepest, though not the longest, economic contraction in our nation's history, the Great Depression of the 1930s.

In terms of aggregate demand and aggregate supply, the Great Depression can be viewed as a shift to the left of the aggregate demand curve, as shown in Exhibit 6. AD_{1929} is the aggregate demand curve in 1929, before the onset of the depression. Real GDP in 1929 was $865 billion (measured in dollars of 2000 purchasing power), and the price level was 12.0 (relative to a 2000 base-year price level of 100). By 1933, aggregate demand shifted leftward, decreasing to AD_{1933}. Why did aggregate demand decline? Though economists still debate the exact causes, most agree that the stock market crash of 1929 was the trigger. From there, grim business expectations cut investment, consumer spending fell, banks failed, the nation's money supply dropped by one-third, and world trade was severely restricted by high tariffs. All this contributed to a big decline in aggregate demand. The aggregate supply curve probably also

become available in the economy, and (2) more people are usually employed. Perhaps the best way to understand aggregate demand and aggregate supply is to apply these tools to the U.S. economy. The following section simplifies U.S. economic history to review changes in the price and output levels over time.

{ The Wealth of Nations }

Before the Great Depression, macro-economic policy was based primarily on the *laissez-faire* philosophy of Adam Smith. Smith, you may recall, argued in his famous book, *The Wealth of Nations,* that if people were allowed to pursue their self-interest in free markets, resources would be guided as if by an "invisible hand" to produce the most efficient and most valued level of aggregate output. Although the U.S. economy suffered many sharp contractions even before the Great Depression, most economists of the day viewed these as a natural phase of the economy—unfortunate but ultimately therapeutic and *self-correcting.*

shifted somewhat during this period, but the drop in aggregate demand was the dominant force.

Because of the decline in aggregate demand, both the price level and real GDP dropped. Real GDP fell 27 percent, from $865 billion in 1929 to $636 billion in 1933, and the price level fell 26 percent, from 12.0 to 8.9. As real GDP declined, unemployment soared from only 3 percent of the labor force in 1929 to 25 percent in 1933, the highest U.S. rate ever recorded.

The Age of Keynes: After the Great Depression to the Early 1970s

The Great Depression was so severe that it stimulated new thinking about how the economy worked (or didn't work). In 1936, John Maynard Keynes (1883–1946) published *The General Theory of Employment, Interest, and Money,* the most famous economics book of the 20th century. In it, Keynes argued that aggregate demand was inherently unstable, in part because investment decisions were often guided by the unpredictable "animal spirits" of business expectations. If businesses grew pessimistic about the economy, they would invest less, which would reduce aggregate demand, output, and employment. For example, investment dropped more than 80 percent between 1929 and 1933. Keynes saw no natural market forces operating to ensure that the economy, even if allowed a reasonable time to adjust, would get output and employment growing again.

Keynes proposed that the government jolt the economy out of its depression by increasing aggregate demand. He recommended an expansionary fiscal policy to offset contractions. The government could achieve this stimulus either directly by increasing its own spending or indirectly by cutting taxes to stimulate consumption and investment. But either action could create a federal budget deficit. A **federal budget deficit** is a flow variable that measures, for a particular period, the amount by which federal outlays exceed federal revenues.

To understand what Keynes had in mind, look at Exhibit 6 and imagine federal budget policies that would increase aggregate demand, shifting the aggregate demand curve to the right, back to its original position. Such a shift would raise real GDP, which would increase employment. According to the Keynesian prescription, the miracle drug of fiscal policy—changes in government spending and taxes—could compensate for what he viewed as the instability of private-sector spending, especially investment. If demand in the private sector declined, Keynes said the government should pick up the slack. We can think of the Keynesian approach as demand-side economics because it focused on how changes in aggregate demand could promote full employment. Keynes argued

Exhibit 6

The Decrease in Aggregate Demand from 1929 to 1933

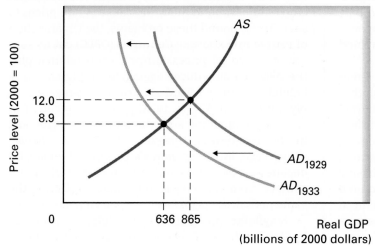

federal budget deficit
a flow variable measuring the amount by which federal government outlays exceed federal government revenues in a particular period, usually a year

demand-side economics
macroeconomic policy that focuses on shifting the aggregate demand curve as a way of promoting full employment and price stability

<< **Keynes proposed that the government jolt the economy out of its depression by increasing aggregate demand.**

that government stimulus could shock the economy out of its depression. Once investment returned to normal levels, and the economy started growing on its own, the government's shock treatment would no longer be necessary.

The U.S. economy bounced back beginning in 1933, growing four years in a row (see Exhibit 2 on page 72 again). The outbreak of World War II boosted employment to make tanks, ships, aircraft, and the like. Federal government spending increased 10-fold between 1940 and 1944. The explosion of output and the sharp drop in unemployment seemed to confirm the powerful role government spending could play in the economy. The increase in government spending, with no significant increase in tax rates, created federal deficits during the war.

Immediately after the war, memories of the Great Depression were still vivid. Trying to avoid another depression, Congress approved the *Employment Act of 1946,* which imposed a clear responsibility on the federal government to promote "maximum employment, production, and purchasing power." The act also required the president to appoint a *Council of Economic Advisers,* a three-member team of econ-

stagflation
a contraction, or *stagnation,* of a nation's output accompanied by in*flation* in the price level

omists to provide economic advice and report on the economy.

The economy seemed to prosper during the 1950s largely without added stimulus from fiscal policy. The 1960s, however, proved to be the *golden age of Keynesian economics,* a period when fiscal policy makers thought they could "fine-tune" the economy for top performance—just as a mechanic fine-tunes a race car. During the early 1960s, nearly all advanced economies around the world enjoyed low unemployment and healthy growth with only modest inflation.

The U.S. economy was on such a roll that toward the end of the 1960s some economists believed the business cycle was history. As a sign of the times, the name of a federal publication, *Business Cycle Developments,* was changed to *Business Conditions Digest.* In the early 1970s, however, fluctuations returned with a fury. Worse yet, the problems of recession were compounded by inflation, which increased during the recessions of 1973–1975 and 1980. Prior to that, high inflation was limited primarily to periods of expansion. Confidence in demand-side policies was shaken, and the expression "fine-tuning" dropped from the economic vocabulary. What ended the golden age of Keynesian economics?

Stagflation: 1973 to 1980

During the late 1960s, federal spending increased on both the war in Vietnam and social programs at home. This combined stimulus increased aggregate demand enough that in 1968 the *inflation rate,* the annual percentage increase in the price level, rose to 4.4 percent, after averaging only 2.0 percent during the previous decade. Inflation climbed to 4.7 percent in 1969 and to 5.3 percent in 1970. These rates were so alarming that in 1971, President Richard Nixon imposed ceilings on prices and wages. Those ceilings were eliminated in 1973, about the time that crop failures around the world caused grain prices to soar. To compound these problems, the Organization of Petroleum Exporting Countries (OPEC) cut its supply of oil, so oil prices jumped. Crop failures plus the OPEC action reduced aggregate supply, shown in Exhibit 7 by the leftward shift of the aggregate supply curve from AS_{1973} to AS_{1975}. This resulted in stagflation, meaning a *stag*nation, or a contraction, in the economy's aggregate output and in*flation,* or increase, in the economy's price level. Real GDP declined between 1973 and 1975, and unemployment climbed from 4.9 percent to 8.5 percent. During the same period, the price level jumped 19 percent.

Stagflation hit again five years later, stoked again by OPEC cutbacks. Between 1979 and 1980, real GDP

Exhibit 7

Stagflation from 1973 to 1975

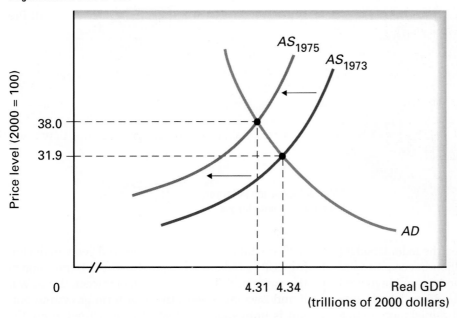

declined, but the price level increased by 9.1 percent. Macroeconomics has not been the same since. Because stagflation was on the supply side, not on the demand side, the demand-management prescriptions of Keynes seemed ineffective. Increasing aggregate demand might reduce unemployment but would worsen inflation.

Since 1980

Increasing aggregate supply seemed an appropriate way to combat stagflation, for such a move would both lower the price level and increase output and employment. Attention thus turned from aggregate demand to aggregate supply. A key idea behind supply-side economics was that the federal government, by lowering tax rates, would increase after-tax wages, which would provide incentives to increase the supply of labor and other resources. According to advocates of the supply-side approach, the resulting increase in aggregate supply would achieve the happy result of expanding real GDP and reducing the price level. But this was more easily said than done.

In 1981, to provide economic incentives to increase aggregate supply, President Ronald Reagan and Congress cut personal income tax rates by an average of 23 percent to be phased in over three years. Their belief was that lower tax rates would increase aggregate supply, thereby expanding output and employment. They hoped that higher tax revenue from a larger economy would more than make up for the cut in tax rates. In other words, the gov-

ernment's smaller share of a bigger pie would exceed what had been its larger share of a smaller pie.

But even before the tax cut took effect, recession hit in 1981, contracting output and pushing the unemployment rate to 10 percent. Once the recession ended, the economy began to grow, and this growth continued for the rest of the decade. But the growth in federal spending exceeded the growth in federal tax revenues during this period, so federal budget deficits swelled.

Deficits worsened with the onset of a recession in 1990. Even though that recession officially bottomed in March 1991, the federal deficit climbed, topping $290 billion in 1992. Annual deficits accumulated as a huge federal debt. The federal debt is a stock variable that measures the net accumulation of prior federal deficits. To reduce federal deficits, President George H. W. Bush increased taxes in 1990, President William Clinton in 1993 increased tax rates for those in the highest tax bracket, and in 1995 a newly elected Republican Congress slowed the growth in federal spending. Higher tax rates and a slower growth in federal spending combined with an improving economy to cut federal deficits. By 1998, the federal budget had turned into a surplus. By early 2001, the U.S. economic expansion became the longest on record, a stretch during which 22 million jobs were added, the unemployment rate dropped from 7.5 percent to 4.2 percent, and inflation remained modest.

But after achieving the longest expansion on record, the economy slipped into recession aggravated by the terrorist attacks of September 2001. The recession lasted only eight months, but the recovery was slow and uneven. The unemployment rate continued to rise, peaking at 6.3 percent in June 2003. President Bush pushed through tax cuts "to get the economy moving again." Output was growing even though employment was not because those working had become more productive. But the tax cuts

supply-side economics
macroeconomic policy that focuses on a rightward shift of the aggregate supply curve through tax cuts or other changes to increase production incentives

federal debt
a stock variable that measures the net accumulation of annual federal deficits

Large Pie

Small Pie

<< 1/8 of a bigger pie is larger
than 1/7 of a smaller pie.

© CORBIS/JUPITERIMAGES

and spending programs increased the federal budget deficit, which exceeded $400 billion in 2004. Despite uncertainty created by the war in Iraq and higher oil prices, the U.S. economy began adding jobs in late 2003 and by the end of 2007 had gained more than 8 million. This job growth helped cut the federal budget deficit to about $160 billion in 2007.

The recession that began officially in December 2007 reversed those recent gains. After spikes in the price of oil and other commodities and the collapse of the housing market, the U.S. economy lost 2.5 million jobs in 2008. The federal budget deficit swelled to $450 billion in 2008. With lower tax revenues and increased stimulus spending, the deficit was sharply higher in 2009.

Focusing on the ups and downs of the economy can miss the point that the U.S. economy over the long run has been an incredible creator of jobs and output—the most productive economy in the world. To underscore that point, we close with a look at U.S. economic growth since 1929.

Eight Decades of Real GDP and Price Levels

Exhibit 8 traces the U.S. real GDP and price level for each year since 1929. Aggregate demand and aggregate supply curves are shown for 2008, but all points in the series reflect such intersections. Years of growing

GDP are indicated as blue points and years of declining GDP as red ones. Despite the Great Depression of the 1930s and the 10 recessions between World War II and December 2007, the long-term growth in output is unmistakable. Real GDP, measured along the horizontal axis in 2000 constant dollars, grew from $0.9 trillion in 1929 to $11.7 trillion in 2008. The price index also rose from 12.0 in 1929 to 122.4 in 2008.

Because the U.S. population is growing, the economy must create more jobs just to employ the addi-

Exhibit 8

Tracking U.S. Real GDP and Price Level Since 1929

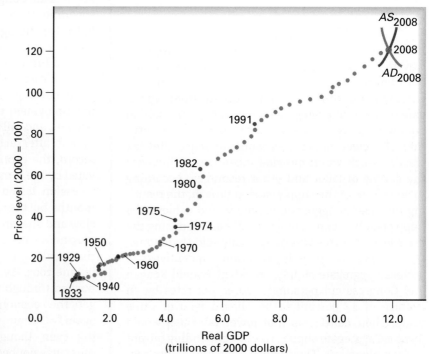

SOURCE: Developed from estimates by the Bureau of Economic Analysis, U.S. Dept. of Commerce. For the latest data, go to http://bea.gov/index.htm.

> " Though the U.S. population increased by 151 percent from 1929 to 2008, fortunately, employment grew even faster, by 210 percent, over the same period . . . real GDP *per capita* jumped five-fold from 1929 to 2008. "

tional people entering the work force. Though the U.S. population increased by 151 percent from 1929 to 2008, fortunately, employment grew even faster, by 210 percent, over the same period.

Real GDP is important, but the best measure of the average standard of living is an economy's real GDP per capita, which tells us how much an economy produces on average per resident. Because real GDP grew much faster than the population, real GDP per capita jumped five-fold from 1929 to 2008.[2]

***

2. For the latest population data, go to http://www.census.gov. For the latest employment data, go to http://www.bls.gov. For the latest real GDP and price level data, go to http://www.bea.doc.gov.

Final Word

Because macroeconomists have no test subjects and cannot rely on luck, they hone their craft by developing models of the economy and then searching for evidence to support or reject these models. In this sense, macroeconomics is retrospective, always looking at recent developments for hints about which model works best. The macroeconomist is like a traveler who can see only the road behind and must find the way using a collection of poorly drawn maps. The traveler must continually check each map (or model) against the landmarks to see whether one map is more consistent with the terrain than the others. Each new batch of information about the economy causes macroeconomists to shuffle through their "maps" to check their models. Macroeconomics often emphasizes what can go wrong with the economy. Sagging output, high unemployment, and rising inflation capture much of the attention. But perhaps the most important performance measure is economic growth, which is examined in the next chapter. In a later chapter, we discuss two potential problems confronting the economy: unemployment and inflation.

real GDP per capita
real GDP divided by the population; the best measure of an economy's standard of living

Learning Outcomes

LO ^{1} Explain the theory of productivity and growth

LO ^{2} Describe productivity and growth in practice

LO ^{3} Discuss other issues of technology and growth

Productivity *and* Growth

"Why is the long-term growth rate more important than short-term fluctuations in economic activity?"

Why is the standard of living so much higher in some countries than in others? How does an economy increase its living standard? Why is the long-term growth rate more important than short-term fluctuations in economic activity? What is labor productivity, why did it slow down for a while, and why did it pick up again? What's been the impact of computers and the Internet on labor productivity? Answers to these and other questions are addressed in this chapter, which focuses on arguably the most important criteria for judging an economy's performance—productivity and growth.

The single most important determinant of a nation's standard of living in the long run is the productivity of its resources. Even seemingly low growth in productivity, if sustained for years, can have a substantial effect on the average living standard—that is, on the average availability of goods and services per capita. Growing productivity is therefore critical to a rising standard of living and has kept the U.S. economy a world leader.

Economic growth is a complicated process, one that even experts do not yet fully understand. Since before Adam Smith inquired into the *Wealth of Nations,* economists have puzzled over what makes some economies prosper while others founder. Because a market economy is not the product of conscious design, it does not reveal its secrets readily, nor can it be easily manipulated in pursuit of growth. We can't simply push here and pull there to achieve the desired result. Changing the economy is not like remodeling a home by knocking out a wall to expand the kitchen. Because we have no clear blueprint of the economy, we cannot make changes to specifications.

Still, there is much economists do know. In this chapter, we first develop a few simple models to examine productivity and growth. Then, we use these models to help explain why some nations are rich and some poor. U.S. performance gets special attention, particularly compared with other major economies around the world. We close with some controversies of technology and growth.

What do you think?

Governments should be closely involved in the technological development of domestic industries.

Strongly Disagree						Strongly Agree
1	2	3	4	5	6	7

Topics discussed in Chapter 6 include:

- Labor productivity
- The production function
- U.S. productivity and growth
- Technological change and unemployment
- Research and development
- Convergence

LO¹ Theory of Productivity and Growth

Two centuries ago, 90 percent of the American workforce was in agriculture, where the hours were long and rewards unpredictable. Other workers had it no better, toiling from sunrise to sunset for a wage that bought just the bare necessities. People had little intellectual stimulation and little contact with the outside world. A skilled worker's home in 1800 was described as follows: "Sand sprinkled on the floor did duty as a carpet. . . . What a stove was he did not know. Coal he had never seen. Matches he had never heard of. . . . He rarely tasted fresh meat. . . . If the food of a [skilled worker] would now be thought coarse, his clothes would be thought abominable."[1]

Over the last two centuries, there has been an incredible increase in the U.S. *standard of living* as measured by the amount of goods and services available on average per person. Perhaps the easiest way to introduce economic growth is by beginning with something you have already read about, the production possibilities frontier.

Growing Standard of Living

An economy's standard of living grows over the long run because of

- increases in the amount and quality of resources, especially labor and capital,

- better technology, and

- improvements in the *rules of the game* that facilitate production and exchange, such as tax laws, property rights, patent laws, the legal system, and the manners, customs, and conventions of the market.

Growth and the Production Possibilities Frontier

The *production possibilities frontier*, or PPF, first introduced in Chapter 2, shows what the economy can produce if available resources are used efficiently. Let's briefly review the assumptions made in developing the frontier shown in Exhibit 1. During the period under consideration, usually a year, the quantity of resources in the economy and the level of technology are assumed to be fixed. Also assumed fixed during

1. E. L. Bogart, *The Economic History of the United States* (New York: Longmans, Green, and Co., 1912), pp. 157–158.

> " Economic growth is shown by an outward shift of the production possibilities frontier. "

the period are the rules of the game that facilitate production and exchange. We classify all production into two broad categories—in this case, consumer goods and capital goods. Capital goods are used to produce other goods. For example, the economy can bake pizzas and make pizza ovens. Pizzas are consumer goods and ovens are capital goods.

When resources are employed efficiently, the production possibilities frontier, *CI* in Exhibit 1, shows the possible combinations of consumer goods and capital goods that can be produced in a given year. Point C depicts the quantity of consumer goods produced if all the economy's resources are employed efficiently to produce them. Point *I* depicts the same for capital goods. Points inside the frontier are inefficient combinations, and points outside the frontier are unattainable combinations, given the resources, technology, and rules of the game. The production possibilities frontier is bowed out because resources are not perfectly adaptable to the production of both goods; some resources are specialized.

Economic growth is shown by an outward shift of the production possibilities frontier, as reflected in Exhibit 1. What can cause growth? An increase in resources, such as a growth in the labor supply or in the capital stock, shifts the frontier outward. Labor supply can increase either because of population growth or because the existing population works more. The capital stock increases if the economy produces more capital this year. The more capital produced this year, the more the economy grows, as reflected by an outward shift of the production frontier.

Breakthroughs in technology also shift out the frontier by making more efficient use of resources. Technological change often improves the quality of capital, but it can enhance the productivity of any resource. And technological change can free up resources for other uses. For example, the development of synthetic dyes in the 19th century freed up millions of acres of agricultural land that had been growing dye crops such as madder (red) and indigo (blue). The development of fiber-optic cable and cellular technology freed up the world's largest stock of copper in the form of existing telephone wires strung on poles across the nation.

Exhibit 1

Economic Growth Shown by a Shift Outward in the Production Possibilities Frontier

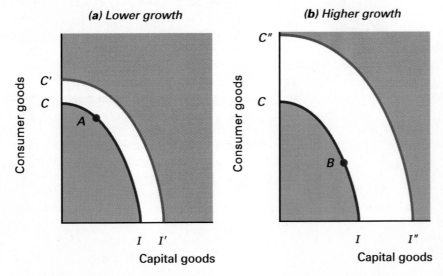

(a) Lower growth

(b) Higher growth

What Is Productivity?

Production is a process that transforms resources into goods and services. Resources coupled with technology produce output. Productivity measures how efficiently resources are employed. In simplest terms, the greater the productivity, the more can be produced from a given amount of resources, and the farther out the production possibilities frontier. Economies that use resources more efficiently create a higher standard of living, meaning that more goods and services are produced per capita.

Productivity is defined as the ratio of total output to a specific measure of input. Productivity usually reflects an average, expressing total output divided by the amount of a particular kind of resource employed to produce that output. For example, labor productivity is the output per unit of labor and measures total output divided by the hours of labor employed to produce that output.

We can talk about the productivity of any resource, such as labor, capital, or natural resources. When agriculture accounted for most output in the economy, land productivity, such as bushels of grain per acre, was a key measure of economic welfare. Where soil was rocky and barren, people were poorer than where soil was fertile and fruitful. Even today, soil productivity determines the standard of living in some economies. Industrialization and trade, however, have liberated many from dependence on soil fertility. Today, some of the world's most productive economies have little land or have land of poor fertility. For example, Japan has a high living standard even though its population, which is nearly half that of the United States, lives on a land area only one twenty-fifth the U.S. land area.

Finally, any improvement in the rules of the game that nurtures production and exchange promotes growth and expands the frontier. For example, the economy can grow as a result of improved patent laws that encourage more inventions[2] or legal reforms that reduce transaction costs. Thus, *the economy grows because of a greater availability of resources, an improvement in the quality of resources, technological change that makes better use of resources, or improvements in the rules of the game that enhance production.*

The amount of capital produced this year shapes the PPF next year. For example, in Exhibit 1a, the economy has chosen point A from possible points along CI. The capital produced this year shifts the PPF from CI this year out to C′I′ next year. But if fewer consumer goods and more capital goods are produced this year, as reflected by point B in Exhibit 1b, the PPF shifts farther out next year, to C″I″.

An economy that produces more capital this year is said to *invest* more in capital. As you can see, to invest more, people must give up some consumer goods this year. Thus, the opportunity cost of more capital goods is fewer consumer goods. More generally, we can say that people must *save* more now—that is, forgo some current consumption—to invest in capital. *Investment cannot occur without saving.* Economies that save more can invest more, as we'll see later. But let's get back to production.

Labor Productivity

Labor is the resource most commonly used to measure productivity. Why labor? First, labor accounts for most production cost—about 70 percent on average. Second, labor is more

productivity
the ratio of a specific measure of output, such as real GDP, to a specific measure of input, such as labor; in this case productivity measures real GDP per hour of labor

labor productivity
output per unit of labor; measured as real GDP divided by the hours of labor employed to produce that output

2. For evidence how the greater protection of intellectual property stimulates technological change, see Sunil Kanwar and Robert Evenson, "Does Intellectual Property Protection Spur Technological Change?" *Oxford Economic Papers* 55 (April 2003): 235–264.

easily measured than other inputs, whether we speak of hours per week or full-time workers per year. Statistics about employment and hours worked are more readily available and more reliable than those about other resources.

But the resource most responsible for increasing labor productivity is capital. As introduced in Chapter 1, the two broad categories are human capital and physical capital. *Human capital* is the accumulated knowledge, skill, and experience of the labor force. As workers acquire more human capital, their productivity and their incomes grow. That's why surgeons earn more than butchers and accountants earn more than file clerks. You are reading this book right now to enhance your human capital. *Physical capital* includes the machines, buildings, roads, airports, communication networks, and other human creations used to produce goods and services. Think about digging a ditch with bare hands versus using a shovel. Now switch the shovel for a backhoe. More physical capital obviously makes diggers more productive. Or consider picking oranges with bare hands versus using a picking machine that combs the trees with steel bristles. In less than 15 minutes the machine can pick 18 tons of oranges from 100 trees, catch the fruit, and drop it into storage carts. Without the machine, that would take four workers all day.[3] The operator of the picking machine is at least 128 times more productive than a regular orange picker.

In poorer countries labor is cheap and capital dear, so producers substitute labor for capital. For example, in India a beverage truck makes its rounds festooned with workers so as to minimize the time the truck, the valuable resource, spends at each stop. In the United States, where labor is more costly (compared with capital), the truck makes its rounds with just the driver. As another example, in Haiti, the poorest country in the

© CHET TOWNSEND/ULTIMATE CITRUS

Western Hemisphere, a ferry service could not afford to build a dock, so it hired workers to carry passengers through the water to and from the ferry on their shoulders.[4]

As an economy accumulates more capital per worker, labor productivity increases and the standard of living grows. The most productive combination of all is human capital combined with physical capital. For example, one certified public accountant with a computer and specialized software can sort out a company's finances more quickly and more accurately than could a thousand high-school-educated file clerks with pencils and paper.

Per-Worker Production Function

We can express the relationship between the amount of capital per worker and the output per worker as an economy's per-worker production function. Exhibit 2 shows the amount of capital per worker, measured along the horizontal axis, and average output per worker, or labor productivity, measured along the vertical axis, other things constant—including the level of technology and rules of the game. Any point on the production function, PF, shows the average output per worker on the vertical axis for each level of capital

per-worker production function
the relationship between the amount of capital per worker in the economy and average output per worker

3. Eduardo Porter, "In Florida Groves, Cheap Labor Means Machines," *New York Times,* 22 March 2004.

4. This example was noted by Tyler Cowen, "The Ricardo Effect in Haiti," 23 February 2004, http://www.marginalrevolution.com.

Exhibit 2

Per-Worker Production Function

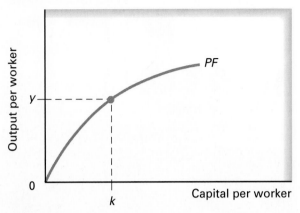

per worker on the horizontal axis. For example, with k units of capital per worker, the average output per worker in the economy is y. The curve slopes upward from left to right because an increase in capital per worker helps each worker produce more output. For example, bigger trucks make truck drivers more productive.

An increase in the amount of capital per worker is called capital deepening and is one source of rising productivity. *Capital deepening contributes to labor productivity and economic growth.* As the quantity of capital per worker increases, output per worker increases but at a diminishing rate, as reflected by the shape of the per-worker production function. The diminishing slope of this curve reflects the *law of diminishing marginal returns from capital,* which says that beyond some level of capital per worker, increases in capital add less and less to output per worker. For example, increasing the size of trucks beyond some point has dimishing returns as trucks become too large to negotiate some public roads. Thus, given the supply of other resources, the level of technology, and the rules of the game, additional gains from more capital per worker eventually diminish and could turn negative.

Technological Change

Held constant along a per-worker production function is the level of technology in the economy. Technological change usually improves the *quality* of capital and represents another source of increased productivity. For example, a tractor is more productive than a horse-drawn plow, a word processor more productive than a typewriter, and an Excel spreadsheet more productive than pencil and paper. Better technology is reflected in Exhibit 3 by an upward rotation in the per-worker produc-

tion function from PF to PF'. As a result of a technological breakthrough, more is produced at each level of capital per worker. For example, if there are k units of capital per worker, a major breakthrough in technology increases the output per worker in the economy from y to y'.

Simon Kuznets, who won a Nobel Prize in part for his analysis of economic growth, claimed that technological change and the ability to apply such breakthroughs to all aspects of production are the driving forces behind economic growth in market economies. Kuznets argued that changes in the *quantities* of labor and capital account for only one-tenth of the increase in economic growth. Nine-tenths came from improvements in the *quality* of these inputs. As technological breakthroughs become *embodied* in new capital, resources are combined more efficiently, increasing total output. *From the wheel to the assembly-line robot, capital embodies the fruits of discovery and drives economic growth.*

Thus, two kinds of changes in capital improve worker productivity: (1) an increase in the *quantity* of capital per worker, as reflected by a movement along the per-worker production function, and (2) an improvement in the *quality* of capital per worker, as reflected by technological change that rotates the curve upward. More capital per worker and better capital per worker result in more output per worker, which, over time, translates into more output per capita, meaning a higher standard of living.

> **capital deepening**
> an increase in the amount of capital per worker; one source of rising labor productivity

Exhibit 3

Impact of a Technological Breakthrough on the Per-Worker Production Function

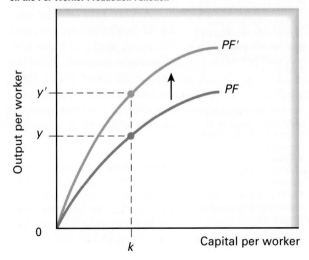

Rules of the Game

Perhaps the most elusive ingredients for productivity and growth are the rules of the game, the formal and informal institutions that promote economic activity: the laws, customs, manners, conventions, and other institutional elements that encourage people to undertake productive activity. A stable political environment and system of well-defined property rights are important. Less investment occurs if potential investors believe their capital could be seized by the government, stolen by thieves, destroyed by civil unrest, or blown up by terrorists. Improvements in the rules of the game could result in more output for each level of capital per worker, thus reflected in a rotation up in the per-worker production function.

We tend to think that laws are the backbone of market exchange, but we should not underestimate the role of manners, customs, and conventions. According to the 18th century British philosopher Edmund Burke, "Manners are of more importance than law. . . . The law touches us but here and there and now and then. Manners are what vex or soothe, corrupt or purify, exalt or debase, barbarize or refine us, by a constant, steady, uniform and insensible operation like that of the air we breathe in."[5] The Russian proverb, "Custom is stronger than law," makes a similar point.

Simply put, a more stable political climate could benefit productivity just like a technological improvement. Conversely, events that foster instability can harm an economy's productivity and rotate the per-worker production function downward. The terrorist attack on the World Trade Center and Pentagon was such a destabilizing event. According to Albert Abadie, a Harvard economist, the attack affected "the spinal cord of any favorable business environment"—the ability of business and workers "to meet and communicate effectively without incurring risks."[6] As other examples, a greater threat to airport security adds to the time and cost of flying. Shops in countries

plagued by suicide bombers must hire security guards to deter such horror, and this increases the cost of doing business. And the mortgage meltdown of 2008–2009 reduced the trust that one bank had in another, thereby freezing up credit markets and increasing the cost of borrowing.

Now that you have some idea about the theory of productivity and growth, let's look at them in practice, beginning with the vast difference in performance among economies around the world. Then we turn to the United States.

LO² Productivity and Growth in Practice

Differences in the standard of living among countries are vast. To give you some idea, per capita output in the United States, the world leader among major economies, is about 150 times that of the world's poorest countries. Poor countries are poor because they experience low labor productivity. We can sort the world's economies into two broad groups. Industrial market countries, or *developed countries*, make up about 16 percent of the world's population. They consist of the economically advanced capitalist countries of Western Europe, North America, Australia, New Zealand, and Japan, plus the newly industrialized Asian countries of Taiwan, South Korea, Hong Kong, and Singapore. Industrial market countries were usually the first to experience long-term economic growth during the 19th century, and today have the world's highest standard of living based on abundant human and

rules of the game the formal and informal institutions that promote economic activity; the laws, customs, manners, conventions, and other institutional elements that determine transaction costs and thereby affect people's incentive to undertake production and exchange

industrial market countries economically advanced capitalist countries of Western Europe, North America, Australia, New Zealand, and Japan, plus the newly industrialized Asian economies of Taiwan, South Korea, Hong Kong, and Singapore

❖❖❖
5. Edmund Burke, *Letters to Parliament*, 2nd ed. (London: Rivington, 1796): 105.
6. As quoted in Greg Ip and John McKinnon, "Economy Likely Won't See Gain from War Against Terrorism," *Wall Street Journal*, 25 September 2001.

physical capital. Industrial market countries produce about 74 percent of the world's output. The rest of the world, the remaining 84 percent of the world's population, consists of **developing countries**, which have a lower standard of living because they have less human and physical capital. Many workers in developing countries are farmers. Because farming methods there are primitive, labor productivity is low and most people barely subsist, much like Americans two centuries ago. Developing countries produce about 26 percent of the world's output.

Exhibit 4

Percent of Adult Population with at Least a College Education: 2003 and 2006

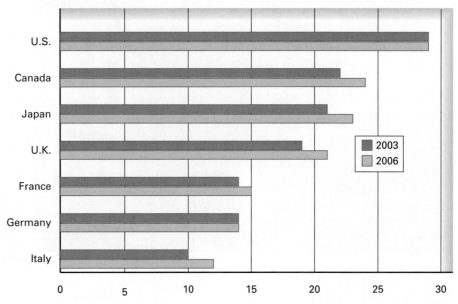

SOURCES: Based on figures in *Education at a Glance: 2006* and *Education at a Glance: 2008,* OECD at http://www.oecd.org.

Education and Economic Development

Another important source of productivity is human capital—the skill, experience, and education of workers. If knowledge is lacking, other resources may not be used efficiently. *Education makes workers aware of the latest production techniques and more receptive to new approaches and methods.* Exhibit 4 shows the percentage of the population ages 25 to 64 who have at least a college education. Figures are presented for the United States and six other industrial market economies, together called the *Group of Seven,* or G-7 (sometimes Russia is added to form the G-8, but Russia is not yet an industrial market economy and has a per capita income about half as much as any G-7 country). In 2003, 29 percent of the U.S. adult population had at least a college degree, the highest percentage in the world. Among other advanced economies, figures ranged from a low of 10 percent in Italy to 22 percent in Canada. The U.S. percentage remained at 29 in 2006, still topping the list. Second-ranked Canada rose to 24 percent.

But a focus on younger adults, those ages 25 to 34, indicates that other countries have closed the gap with the United States. Whereas 30 percent of Americans ages 25 to 34 had at least a college degree in 2006, so did 30 percent of the Japanese and 29 percent of Canadians. And beyond the largest economies, six countries matched or exceeded America. For example, among those ages 25 to 34, 34 percent of Dutch had a college degree and 40 percent of Norwegians did. So some other countries are catching up. The U.S. share of the global college-educated workforce declined from 30 percent in the 1970s to 14 percent more recently.

Not shown in Exhibit 4 are developing countries, which have far lower education levels on average. For example, while the literacy rate exceeds 99 percent in industrial market economies, more than half the adults in the world's poorest countries can't read or write.

developing countries countries with a low living standard because of less human and physical capital per worker

If a roofer in 1870 could shingle one roof in a day, today's roofer could shingle nearly 18 roofs in a day.

since 1870 would have jumped 3,367 percent! The wheels of progress seem to grind slowly but they grind very fine, and the cumulative effect is powerful.

So far, we have averaged productivity growth for all workers. Productivity has grown more in some industries than in others. In ocean shipping, for example, cargo carried per worker hour is more than 85 times greater now than in 1900, for an average annual growth of 4.3 percent. On the other hand, those making wooden office furniture are only three times more productive today than in 1900, for an average annual growth in productivity of only 1.1 percent.

U.S. Labor Productivity

What has been the record of labor productivity in the United States? Exhibit 5 offers a long-run perspective, showing growth in real output per work hour. Annual productivity growth is averaged by decade. The huge dip during the Great Depression and the strong rebound during World War II are unmistakable. Growth slowed during the 1970s and 1980s but recovered since 1990. Labor productivity has grown an average of 2.1 percent per year since 1870. This may not impress you, but because of the power of compounding, output per hour has jumped 1,680 percent during the period. To put this in perspective, if a roofer in 1870 could shingle one roof in a day, today's roofer could shingle nearly 18 roofs in a day.

Over long periods, small differences in productivity can make huge differences in the economy's ability to produce and therefore on the standard of living. For example, if productivity grew only 1.0 percent per year instead of 2.1 percent, output per work hour since 1870 would have increased by only 287 percent, not 1,680 percent. On the other hand, if productivity grew 2.6 percent per year (the average since 1996), output per work hour

Slowdown and Rebound in Productivity Growth

You can see in Exhibit 5 that productivity growth slowed to 1.8 percent per year during the 1970s and 1980s, and has recovered since 1990. By breaking the data down into intervals other than decades, we can get a better feel for years since World War II. Exhibit 6 offers average annual growth for four periods. Labor productivity growth averaged 2.9 percent per year between 1948 and 1973; these could be called

Exhibit 5

Long-Term Trend in U.S. Labor Productivity Growth: Annual Average by Decade

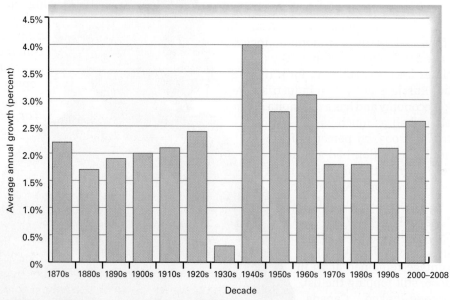

SOURCES: Angus Maddison, *Phases of Capitalist Development* (New York: Oxford University Press, 1982) and U.S. Bureau of Labor Statistics. For the latest data, go to http://www.bls.gov/lpc/.

Exhibit 6

U.S. Labor Productivity Growth Slowed During 1974 to 1982 and Then Rebounded

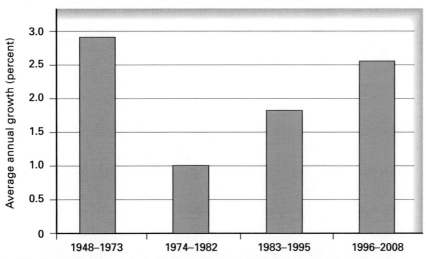

SOURCE: Averages based on annual estimates from the U.S. Bureau of Labor Statistics. For the latest data go to http://www.bls.gov/lpc/home.htm.

the golden days of productivity growth. But, between 1974 and 1982, productivity growth slowed to about a third of that, averaging only 1.0 percent. Why the slowdown? First, oil prices jumped from 1973 to 1974 and again from 1979 to 1980 as a result of OPEC actions, boosting inflation and contributing to stagflation and three recessions. Second, legislation in the early 1970s necessary to protect the environment and improve workplace safety increased production costs.

Fortunately, productivity rebounded off the 1974–1982 low, averaging 1.8 percent from 1983 to 1995 and 2.6 percent from 1996 to 2008. Why the rebound? The information revolution powered by the computer chip started paying off.

Computers boost productivity through two channels: (1) efficiency gains in the production of computers and semiconductors and (2) greater computer use by industry. These two channels account for much of the gain in productivity growth since 1996. Although computer hardware manufacturers make up only a small fraction of the U.S. economy, their pace of innovation quickened enough since 1996 to boost overall U.S. productivity growth.

What really set the productivity gains in motion was the big drop in semiconductor prices during the last half of the 1990s. Computers per worker increased, which boosted labor productivity throughout the entire economy but especially in the service sector.

Northwestern University's Robert Gordon argues that the economy enjoyed a one-time boost from computers and the Internet, but that the effect has already faded and productivity growth is likely to be disappointing during the next several years. Other economists are more upbeat, but they acknowledge that it takes a steady stream of innovations to keep the U.S. productivity on the march.

Higher labor productivity growth can easily make up for output lost from recessions. For example, if over the next 10 years the U.S. labor productivity grew an average of 2.6 percent per year (the average from 1996 to 2008) instead of 1.8 percent (the average from 1983 to 1995), that higher growth would add nearly $1.4 trillion to GDP in the 10th year—more than enough to make up for the output lost during two typical recessions. *This cumulative power of productivity growth is why economists now pay less attention to short-term fluctuations in output and more to long-term growth.*

Output per Capita

As noted earlier, the best measure of an economy's standard of living is output per capita. *Output per capita,* or GDP divided by the population, indicates how much an economy produces on average per resident. Exhibit 7 on the next page presents real GDP per capita for the United States since 1959. Notice the general upward trend, interrupted by eight recessions, indicated by the pink bars. Real GDP per capita nearly tripled (in 2000 dollars) for an average annual growth rate of 2.2 percent. Incidentally, since 1959, labor productivity grew an average of 2.1 percent, which is also the average since 1870. Output per capita since 1959 grew slightly faster than did labor productivity because the number of workers grew slightly faster than did the population (give that a little thought).

International Comparisons

How does U.S. output per capita compare with that of other industrial countries? Exhibit 8 on page 93 compares GDP per capita in 2008 for the United States and the six other leading industrial nations. Local currencies have been converted to U.S. dollars of 2008 purchasing power. With nominal GDP per capita of $48,000 in 2008, the United States stood alone at the top, with a per capita income 19 percent above

Exhibit 7

U.S. Real GDP per Capita Has Nearly Tripled Since 1959

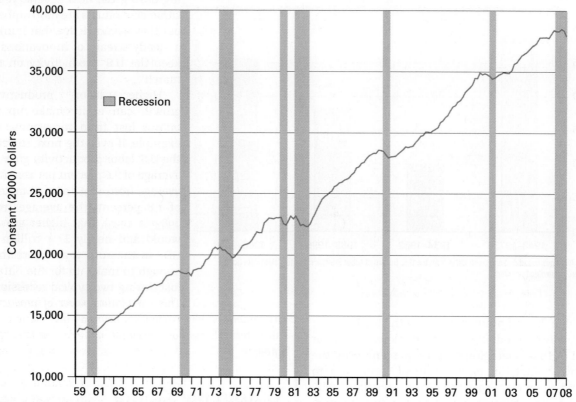

SOURCE: *Survey of Current Business* 89 (January 2009). For the latest data, go to http://www.bea.gov/sbc. Select the most recent month, go to the "National Data" section toward the end of the page, and then select "Charts."

second-ranked Canada and at least 28 percent above the rest. Thus, the United States produced more per capita than any other major economy.

Exhibit 8 looks at the *level* of output per capita. What about the *growth* in output per capita? Exhibit 9 shows growth in real GDP per capita from 1982 to 2007. With an average growth of 2.1 percent per year, the United States ranked second among the seven major economies. The United Kingdom ranked first, thanks in part to Prime Minister Margaret Thatcher, who converted some crusty government enterprises into dynamic for-profit firms. Industries she *privatized* during the 1980s include coal, iron and steel, gas, electricity, railways, trucking, airlines, telecommunications, and the water supply. She also cut income tax rates.

To Review: U.S. labor productivity growth has averaged 2.1 percent per year over the long term. Productivity growth slowed between 1974 and 1982 because of spikes in energy prices and implementation of necessary but costly new environmental and workplace regulations. Since 1982 labor productivity growth has picked up, especially since 1996, due primarily to breakthroughs in information technology. Among the seven major economies, the United States

experienced the second fastest growth in real GDP per capita income from 1982 to 2007, and in 2008 boasted the highest GDP per capita among major economies.

LO³ Other Issues of Technology and Growth

In this section we consider some other issues of technology and growth, beginning with the question of whether technological change creates unemployment.

Does Technological Change Lead to Unemployment?

Because technological change usually reduces the labor needed to produce a given amount of output, some observers fear technological change increases unemployment. True, technological change can create dislocations as displaced workers try to find jobs elsewhere. But technological change can also make products more affordable. For example, the assembly line cut the cost of automobiles, making them more

Exhibit 8

U.S. GDP per Capita Is Highest of Major Economies

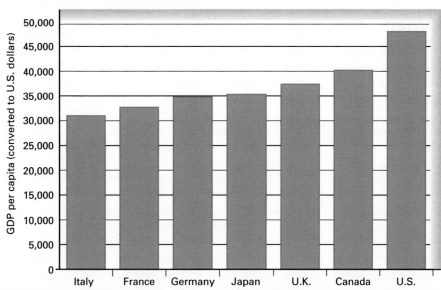

SOURCES: Based on 2008 dollar estimates from the OECD at http://www.oecd.org/home/ and *The World Factbook: 2008* at www.cia.gov/library/publications/the-world-factbook/index.html. Estimates have been adjusted across countries using the purchasing power of the local currency in 2008.

affordable for the average household. This increased the quantity of automobiles demanded, boosting production and employment. Even in industries where machines displace some workers, those who keep their jobs become more productive, so they earn more. And *because human wants are unlimited, displaced workers usually find jobs producing other goods*

Exhibit 9

U.S. Real GDP per Capita Outgrew That of Most Other Major Economies Since 1982

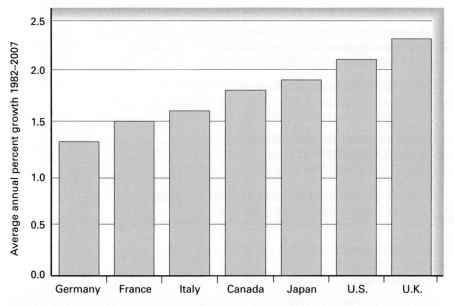

SOURCES: Based on annual figures from 1982 through 2007 from the U.S. Bureau of Labor Statistics at http://www.stats. bls.gov/fls/flsgdp.pdf. Figures were converted into U.S. dollars based on the purchasing power of local currency. The German growth rate dates from 1991, after the reunification between East Germany and West Germany. For the latest data, go to http://www.stats.bls.gov/fls/.

and services demanded in a growing economy.

Although job data from the 19th century are sketchy, there is no evidence that the unemployment rate is any higher today than it was in 1870. Since then, worker productivity has increased nearly 1,700 percent, and the length of the average workweek has been cut nearly in half. Although technological change may displace some workers in the short run, long-run benefits include higher real incomes and more leisure—in short, a higher standard of living.

If technological change caused unemployment, then the recent spurt in productivity growth should have increased unemployment compared to the slow-growth years from 1974 to 1982. But the unemployment rate, the percentage of the workforce looking for jobs, averaged 7.2 percent during 1974 to 1982, compared to only 5.3 percent since 1996. And if technological change causes unemployment, then unemployment rates should be lower in economies where the latest technology has not yet been adopted, such as in developing countries. But unemployment is much worse there, and those fortunate enough to find work earn little because they are not very productive.

Again, there is no question that technological change sometimes creates job dislocations and hardships in the short run, as workers scramble to adjust to a changing world. Some workers with specialized skills made obsolete by technology may be unable to find jobs that pay as well as the ones they lost. These temporary dislocations are one price of progress. Over time, however, most displaced workers find other jobs, often in new industries created by technological change. In a typical year, the U.S. economy eliminates about 10 million jobs but creates nearly 12 million new ones. Out with the old, in with the new.

Research and Development

As noted several times already, a prime contributor to labor productivity growth has been an improvement in the quality of human and physical capital. Human capital has benefited from better education and more job training. Better technology embodied in physical capital has also helped labor productivity. For example, because of extensive investments in cellular transmission, new satellites, and fiber-optic technology, labor productivity in the telecommunications industry has increased by an average of 5.5 percent per year during the past three decades.

Improvements in technology arise from scientific discovery, which is the fruit of research. We can distinguish between basic research and applied research. Basic research, the search for knowledge without regard to how that knowledge will be used, is a first step toward technological advancement. In terms of economic growth, however, scientific discoveries are meaningless until they are implemented, which requires applied research. Applied research seeks to answer particular questions or to apply scientific discoveries to the development of specific products. Because technological breakthroughs may or may not have commercial possibilities, the payoff is less immediate with basic research than with applied research. *Yet basic research yields a higher return to society as a whole than does applied research.*

Because technological change is the fruit of

research and development (R&D), investment in R&D improves productivity through technological discovery. One way to track R&D spending is to measure it relative to GDP. Exhibit 10 shows R&D spending as a share of GDP for the United States and the six other major economies for the 1980s, 1990s, and 2006. Overall R&D spending in the United States during the last quarter century has remained nearly constant, averaging 2.7 percent of GDP in the 1980s and the 1990s, and 2.6 percent in 2006. During the 1990s and in 2006, the United States was second among the major economies, behind Japan.

Bar segments in the chart distinguish between R&D by businesses (shown as green segments) and R&D by governments and nonprofit institutions (shown as orange segments). Business R&D is more likely to target applied research and innovations. R&D spending by governments and nonprofits, such as universities, may generate basic knowledge that has applications in the long run (for example, the Internet sprang from R&D spending on national defense). R&D by U.S. businesses ranged between 1.6 and 1.9 percent of GDP in all three periods. Again,

basic research
the search for knowledge without regard to how that knowledge will be used

applied research
research that seeks answers to particular questions or to apply scientific discoveries to develop specific products

Exhibit 10

R&D Spending as a Percentage of GDP for Major Economies during the 1980s, 1990s, and 2006

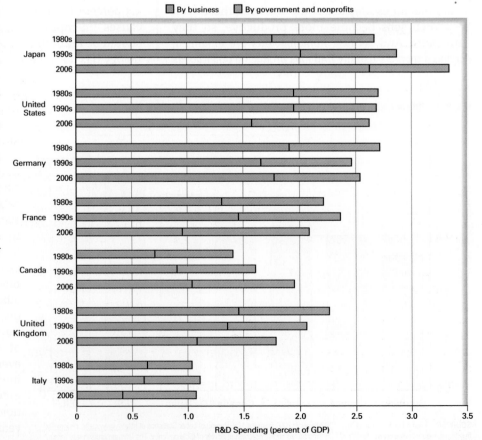

SOURCE: Based on estimates developed by the OECD at www.oecd.org.

only Japan had higher business R&D than the United States in the 1990s and in 2006. In short, the United States devotes more resources to R&D than most other advanced economies, and this helps America maintain a higher standard of living.

Industrial Policy

Policy makers have debated whether government should become more involved in shaping an economy's technological future. One concern is that technologies of the future will require huge sums to develop, sums that an individual firm cannot easily raise and put at risk. Another concern is that some technological breakthroughs spill over to other firms and other industries, but the firm that develops the breakthrough may not be in a position to reap benefits from these spillover effects, so individual firms may underinvest in such research. One possible solution is more government involvement in economic planning.

Industrial policy is the idea that government, using taxes, subsidies, regulations, and coordination of the private sector, could help nurture the industries and technologies of the future to give domestic industries an advantage over foreign competitors. The idea is to secure a leading role for domestic industry in the world economy. One example of European industrial policy is Airbus Industrie, a four-nation aircraft consortium. With an estimated $20 billion in government aid, the aircraft maker has become Boeing's main rival. When Airbus seeks aircraft orders around the world, it can draw on government backing to promise favorable terms, such as landing rights at key European airports and an easing of regulatory constraints. U.S. producers get less government backing.

U.S. industrial policy over the years was aimed at creating the world's most advanced military production capacity. With the demise of the Soviet Union, however, defense technologies became less important, but the war in Iraq shifted some attention back to military applications. Some argue that U.S. industrial policy should shift from a military to a civilian focus. Many state governments are also trying to identify what industries to support. Economists have long recognized that firms in some industries gain a performance advantage by *clustering*—that is, by locating in a region already thick with firms in the same industry

© AP IMAGES

or in related industries. Clusters such as Hollywood studios, Wall Street brokers, Broadway theaters, Las Vegas casinos, Boston colleges, Orlando theme parks, and Silicon Valley software makers facilitate communication and promote healthy competition among cluster members. The flow of information and cooperation between firms, as well as the competition among firms in close proximity, stimulates regional innovation and propels growth. By locating in a region already settled with similar firms, a firm can also tap into established local markets for specialized labor and for other inputs.

But skeptics wonder whether the government should be trusted to identify emerging technologies and to pick the industry clusters that will lead the way. Critics of industrial policy believe that markets allocate scarce resources better than governments do. For example, European governments' costly attempt to develop the supersonic transport Concorde never became cost efficient. Airbus has also run into financial difficulties, and sponsoring governments have tried to distance themselves from the company. As a U.S. example, in the early 1980s, the U.S. government spent $1 billion to help military contractors develop a high-speed computer circuit. But Intel, a company getting no federal aid, was the first to develop the circuit.

industrial policy the view that government—using taxes, subsidies, and regulations—should nurture the industries and technologies of the future, thereby giving these domestic industries an advantage over foreign competition

There is also concern that an industrial policy would evolve into a government giveaway program. Rather than going to the most promising technologies, the money and the competitive advantages would go to the politically connected. Critics also wonder how wise it is to sponsor corporate research when beneficiaries may share their expertise with foreign companies or even build factories abroad. Most economists would prefer to let Microsoft, General Electric, Google, or some start-up bet their own money on the important technologies of the future.

Do Economies Converge?

If given enough time, will poor countries eventually catch up with rich ones? The convergence theory argues that developing countries can grow faster than advanced ones and should eventually close the gap. Here's why: It is easier to copy existing technology than to develop new technology. Countries that are technologically backward can grow faster by adopting existing technology. But economies already using the latest technology must come up with a steady stream of new breakthroughs to grow faster.

Leading countries, such as the United States, find growth limited by the rate of creation of new knowledge and better technology. But follower countries can grow more quickly by, for example, adding computers where they previously had none. Until 1995, the United States, which makes up just 5 percent of the world's population, accounted for most of the world's computer purchases by households. But by 2000, most computers were bought by non-U.S. households.

What's the evidence on convergence? Some poor countries have begun to catch up with richer ones. For example, the newly industrialized Asian economies of Hong Kong, Singapore, South Korea, and Taiwan, by adopting the latest technology and investing in human resources, are closing the gap with the world leaders. Real output per capita in South Korea has grown three times faster than the average for the seven major economies. These *Asian Tigers* have graduated from developing economies to industrial market economies. But these are the exceptions. Among the nations that comprise the poorest third of the world's population, consumption per capita has grown only about 1.0 percent per year over the past two decades compared with a 2.5 percent growth in the rest of the world,[7] so the standard of living in the poorest third of the world has grown somewhat in absolute terms but has fallen farther behind in relative terms. Worse yet, a billion people seem trapped in poor economies that are going nowhere.

One reason per capita consumption has grown so slowly in the poorest economies is that birthrates there are double those in richer countries, so poor economies must produce still more just to keep up with a growing population. Another reason why convergence has not begun, particularly for the poorest third of the world, is the vast difference in the quality of human capital across countries. Whereas technology is indeed portable, the knowledge, skill, and training needed to take advantage of that technology are not. Countries with a high level of human capital can make up for other shortcomings. For example, much of the capital stock in Japan and Germany was destroyed during World War II. But the two countries retained enough of their well-educated and highly skilled labor force to rejoin elite industrial market economies in little more than a generation. But some countries, such as those in Africa, simply lack the human capital needed to identify and absorb new technology. As noted already, such poor economies tend to have low education levels and low literacy rates. What's more, some countries lack the stable macroeconomic environment and the established institutions needed to nurture economic growth. Many developing countries have serious deficiencies in their infrastructures, lacking, for example, the reliable source of electricity to power new technologies. For example, in Northern Nigeria, near the Sahara, 90 percent of the villages have no electricity. Some of the poorest nations have been ravaged by civil war for years. And simply communicating can be challenging in some developing countries. In Nigeria, for example, more than 400 languages are spoken by 250 distinct ethnic groups. (To learn more about the challenges facing the poorest nations, read the

> " Whereas technology is indeed portable, the knowledge, skill, and training needed to take advantage of that technology are not. "

convergence
a theory predicting that the standards of living in economies around the world will grow more similar over time, with poorer countries eventually catching up with richer ones

7. Based on figures developed by the World Bank in *World Development Report 2007* (Washington, D.C.: World Bank Publications 2006), Tables 1 and 2.

final chapter of this book, entitled "Developing and Transitional Economies.")

Final Word

Productivity and growth depend on the supply and quality of resources, the level of technology, and the rules of the game that nurture production and exchange. These elements tend to be correlated with one another. An economy with an unskilled and poorly educated workforce usually is deficient in physical capital, in technology, and in the institutional support that promotes production and exchange. Similarly, an economy with a high-quality workforce likely excels in the other sources of productivity and growth.

We should distinguish between an economy's standard of living, as measured by output per capita, and improvements in that standard of living, as measured by the growth in output per capita. Growth in output per capita can occur when labor productivity increases or when the number of workers in the economy grows faster than the population. *In the long run, productivity growth and the growth in workers relative to the growth in population will determine whether or not the United States continues to enjoy the world's highest standard of living.*

In the next chapter, you learn how to measure output in the economy and how to adjust for changes in the price level. In later chapters, you develop aggregate demand and aggregate supply curves to build a model of the economy. Once you have an idea how a healthy economy works, you can consider the policy options in the face of high unemployment, high inflation, or both.

© AP IMAGES

30   < percent of Americans between 25 and 34 with at least a college degree

percent of the world's population coming from industrial market countries > 16

2 million
< net number of jobs the U.S. economy adds in a typical year

2012   < year by which President Obama wants 1 million electric cars on the road

250   < distinct ethnic groups in Nigeria

percent of the world's output coming from industrial market countries > 74

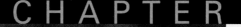

Tracking *the* U.S. Economy

Learning Outcomes

LO^1 Explain the gross domestic product

LO^2 Discuss the circular flow of income and expenditure

LO^3 Assess the limitations of national income accounting

LO^4 Explain how to account for price changes

"How do we keep track of the most complex economy in world history?"

How do we keep track of the most complex economy in world history? What's gross about the gross domestic product? What's domestic about it? If you make yourself a tuna sandwich, how much does your effort add to the gross domestic product? Because prices change over time, how can we compare the economy's production in one year with that in other years? Answers to these and other questions are addressed in this chapter, which introduces an economic scorecard for a $14 trillion U.S. economy. That scorecard is the national income accounting system, which reduces a huge network of economic activity to a few aggregate measures.

As you will see, aggregate output is measured either by the spending on that output or by the income derived from producing it. We examine each approach and learn why they are equivalent. The major components and important equalities built into the national income accounts are offered here as another way of understanding how the economy works—not as a foreign language to be mastered before the next exam. The emphasis is more on economic intuition than on accounting precision. The body of the chapter provides the background you need for later chapters.

What do you think?

I should spend as much as I can, because consumer spending keeps the economy healthy.

Strongly Disagree   Strongly Agree
1   2   3   4   5   6   7

LO¹ The Product of a Nation

How do we measure the economy's performance? During much of the 17th and 18th centuries, when the dominant economic policy was mercantilism, many thought that economic prosperity was best measured by the stock of precious metals a nation accumulated in the public treasury. Mercantilism led to restrictions on international trade, but this had the unintended consequence of reducing the gains from comparative advantage. In the latter half of the 18th century, François Quesnay became the first to measure economic activity as a *flow*. In 1758 he published his *Tableau Économique*, which described the *circular flow* of output and income through different sectors of the economy. His insight was

Topics discussed in Chapter 7 include:

- National income accounts
- Expenditure approach to GDP
- Income approach to GDP
- Circular flow of income and expenditure
- Leakages and injections
- Limitations of national income accounting
- Consumer price index
- GDP price index

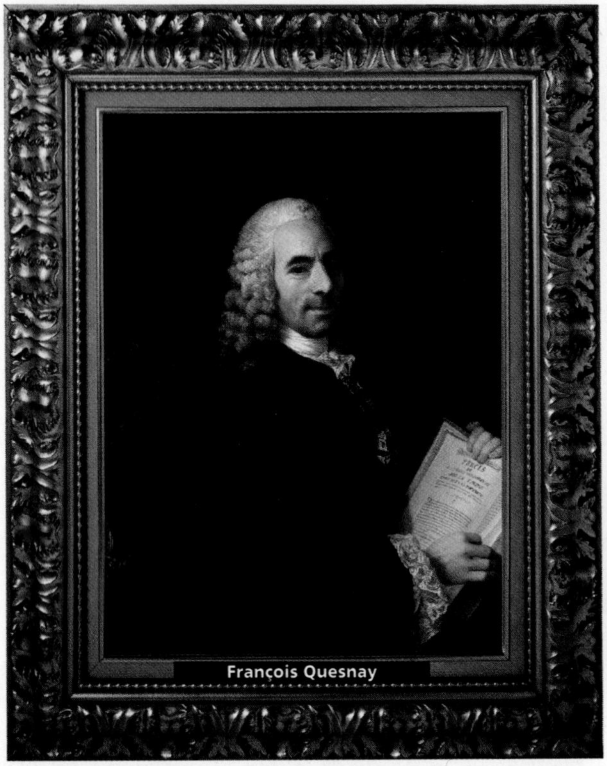

© MATHIAS DE BEER/ALAMY / © BURKE/TRIOLO/BRAND X PICTURES/JUPITERIMAGES

likely inspired by his knowledge of blood's *circular flow* in the body—Quesnay was court physician to King Louis XV of France.

Rough measures of national income were developed in England two centuries ago, but detailed calculations built up from microeconomic data were refined in the United States during the Great Depression. The resulting *national income accounting system* organizes huge quantities of data collected from a variety of sources across America. These data were summarized, assembled into a coherent framework, and reported by the federal government. The conception and implementation of these accounts has been hailed as one of the greatest achievements of the 20th century. The U.S. national income accounts are the most widely copied and most highly regarded in the world and earned their developer, Simon Kuznets, the Nobel Prize in 1971 for "giving quantitative precision to economic entities."

expenditure approach to GDP calculating GDP by adding up spending on all final goods and services produced in the nation during the year

income approach to GDP calculating GDP by adding up all earnings from resources used to produce output in the nation during the year

final goods and services goods and services sold to final, or end, users

intermediate goods and services goods and services purchased by firms for additional processing and resale

double counting the mistake of including both the value of intermediate products and the value of final products in calculating gross domestic product; counting the same production more than once

National Income Accounts

How do the national income accounts keep track of the economy's incredible variety of goods and services, from hiking boots to Pilates classes? The *gross domestic product*, or *GDP*, measures the market value of all final goods and services produced during a year by resources located in the United States, regardless of who owns the resources. For example, GDP includes production in the United States by foreign firms, such as a Toyota plant in Kentucky, but excludes foreign production by U.S. firms, such as a Ford plant in Mexico.

The national income accounts are based on the simple fact that *one person's spending is another person's income*. GDP can be measured either by total spending on U.S. production or by total income received from that production. The expenditure approach adds up spending on all final goods and services produced during the year. The income approach adds up earnings during the year by those who produce all that output. In the *double-entry bookkeeping system* used to track the economy, spending on aggregate output is recorded on one side of the ledger and income from producing that aggregate output is recorded on the other side.

Gross domestic product includes only final goods and services, which are goods and services sold to the final, or end, user. A toothbrush, a pair of contact lenses, and a bus ride are examples of final goods and services. Whether a sale is to the final user depends on who buys the product. When you buy chicken, that's reflected in GDP. When KFC buys chicken, however, that's not counted in GDP because KFC is not the final consumer. Only after the chicken is cooked and sold by KFC is the transaction counted in GDP.

Intermediate goods and services are those purchased for additional processing and resale, like KFC's chicken. This change may be imperceptible, as when a grocer buys canned goods to restock the shelves. Or the intermediate goods can be dramatically altered, as when a painter transforms a $100 canvas and $30 in oils into a work of art that sells for $5,000. Sales of intermediate goods and services are excluded from GDP to avoid the problem of double counting, which is counting an item's value more than once. For example, suppose the grocer buys a can of tuna for $0.60 and sells it for $1.00. If GDP counted both the intermediate transaction of $0.60 and the final transaction of $1.00, the recorded value

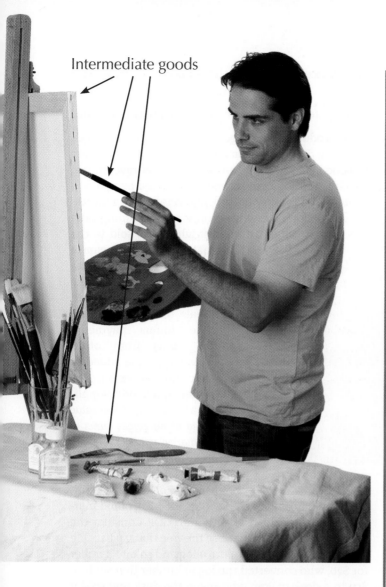

Intermediate goods

© TETRA IMAGES/JUPITERIMAGES

of $1.60 would exceed its final value by $0.60. Hence, GDP counts only the final value. As another example, in 2008 Wal-Mart paid $287 billion for products it sold for $375 billion. If GDP counted intermediate transactions and final transactions, it would be $287 billion too high. GDP also ignores most of the secondhand value of used goods, such as existing homes, used cars, and used textbooks. These goods were counted in GDP when they were produced. But just as the services provided by the grocer and by Wal-Mart are captured in GDP, so are the services provided by real estate agents, used-car dealers, and used-book sellers.

GDP Based on the Expenditure Approach

As noted already, one way to measure GDP is to add spending on all final goods and services produced in the economy during the year. The easiest way to understand the spending approach is to divide aggregate expenditure into its components: consumption, investment, government purchases, and net exports. Consumption, or more specifically, *personal consumption expenditures,* consists of purchases of final goods and services by households during the year. Consumption is the largest spending category, averaging about two-thirds of U.S. GDP during the last decade. Along with *services* like dry cleaning, haircuts, and air travel, consumption includes *nondurable goods,* like soap and soup, and *durable goods,* like furniture and kitchen appliances. Durable goods are expected to last at least three years.

Investment, or more specifically, *gross private domestic investment,* consists of spending on new capital goods and on net additions to inventories. The most important investment is physical capital, such as new buildings and new machinery. Investment also includes new residential construction. Although it fluctuates from year to year, investment averaged about one-sixth of U.S. GDP during the last decade. More generally, investment consists of spending on current production that is not used for current consumption. A net increase to inventories also counts as investment because it represents current production not used for current consumption. Inventories are stocks of goods in process, such as computer parts, and stocks of finished goods, such as new computers awaiting sale. Inventories help manufacturers cope with unexpected changes in the supply of their resources or in the demand for their products.

Although investment includes purchasing a new residence, it excludes purchases of *existing* buildings and machines and purchases of financial assets, such as stocks and bonds. Existing buildings and machines were counted in GDP when they were produced. Stocks and bonds are not investments themselves but simply indications of ownership.

Government purchases, or more specifically, *government consumption and gross investment,* include government spending for goods and services—from clearing snowy roads to clearing court dockets, from buying library books to paying

consumption
household purchases of final goods and services, except for new residences, which count as investment

investment
the purchase of new plants, new equipment, new buildings, and new residences, plus net additions to inventories

physical capital
manufactured items used to produce goods and services; includes new plants and new equipment

residential construction
building new homes or dwelling places

inventories
producers' stocks of finished and in-process goods

government purchases
spending for goods and services by all levels of government; government outlays minus transfer payments

librarians. Government purchases averaged a bit less than one-fifth of U.S. GDP during the last decade. Government purchases, and therefore GDP, exclude transfer payments, such as Social Security, welfare benefits, and unemployment insurance. Such payments are not true purchases by the government or true earnings by the recipients.

The final spending component, net exports, reflects international trade in goods and services. Goods, or *merchandise* traded, include physical items such as bananas and DVD players (stuff you can put in a box). Services, or so-called *invisibles,* include intangible items, such as European tours and online customer service from India. Foreign purchases of U.S. goods and services are counted as part of U.S. GDP. But U.S. purchases of foreign goods and services are subtracted from U.S. GDP. Net exports equal the value of U.S. exports of goods and services minus the value of U.S. imports of goods and services. U.S. imports have exceeded U.S. exports nearly every year since the 1960s, meaning U.S. net exports have been negative. During the last decade, net exports averaged a negative 2 percent of GDP, but this has become a negative 5 or 6 percent of GDP in recent years.

GDP Based on the Income Approach

The expenditure approach sums, or aggregates, spending on production. The income approach sums, or aggregates, income arising from that production. Again, double-entry bookkeeping ensures that the value of aggregate output equals the aggregate income paid for resources used to produce that output: the wages, interest, rent, and profit arising from production. The price of a Hershey bar reflects the income earned by resource suppliers along the way. Aggregate income equals the sum of all the income earned by resource suppliers in the economy. Thus, we can say that

Aggregate expenditure = GDP = Aggregate income

A product usually goes through several stages involving different firms on its way to the consumer. A wooden desk, for example, starts as raw timber, which is typically cut by one firm, milled by another, made into a desk by a third, and retailed by a fourth. We avoid double counting either by including only the market value of the desk when it is sold to the final user or by *summing the value added at each stage of production.* The value added by each firm equals that firm's selling price minus payments for inputs from other firms. The value added at each stage is the income earned by resource suppliers at that stage. *The value added at all stages sums to the market value of the final good, and the value added for all final goods sums to GDP based on the income approach.* For example, suppose you buy a wooden desk for $200. This final market value gets added directly into GDP. Consider the history of that desk. Suppose the tree that gave its life for your studies was cut into a log and sold to a miller for $20, who converted the log to lumber that sold for $50 to a desk maker, who made the desk and sold it for $120 to a retailer, who sold it to you for $200.

Column (1) of Exhibit 1 lists the selling price at each stage of production. If all these transactions were added up, the total of $390 would exceed the $200 market value of the desk. To avoid double counting, we include only the value added at each stage, listed in column (3) as the difference between the purchase price and the selling price at that stage. Again,

GDP: The Nation's Aggregate Expenditure

With the expenditure approach, the nation's **aggregate expenditure** sums consumption, investment, government purchases, and net exports.

$$C + I + G + (X - M) = \text{Aggregate expenditure} = \text{GDP}$$
$$C = \text{Consumption}$$
$$I = \text{Investment}$$
$$G = \text{Government purchases}$$
$$(X - M) = \text{Net exports} = \text{Exports} - \text{Imports}$$

net exports
the value of a country's exports minus the value of its imports

aggregate expenditure
total spending on final goods and services in an economy during a given period, usually a year

aggregate income
all earnings of resource suppliers in an economy during a given period, usually a year

value added
at each stage of production, the selling price of a product minus the cost of intermediate goods purchased from other firms

Exhibit 1

Computation of Value Added for a New Desk

Stage of Production	(1) Sale Value	(2) Cost of Intermediate Goods	(3) Value Added (3) = (1) − (2)
Logger	$ 20	—	$ 20
Miller	50	$ 20	30
Manufacturer	120	50	70
Retailer	200	120	80
		Market value of final good	$200

the value added at each stage equals the income earned by those who supply their resources at that stage. For example, the $80 in value added by the retailer consists of income to resource suppliers at that stage, from the salesperson to the janitor who cleans the showroom to the trucker who provides "free delivery" of your desk. The value added at all stages totals $200, which is both the final market value of the desk and the total income earned by all resource suppliers along the way.

> The value added at each stage equals the income earned by those who supply their resources at that stage.

To reinforce your understanding of the equality of income and spending, let's return to something introduced in the first chapter, the circular-flow model.

LO² Circular Flow of Income and Expenditure

The model in Exhibit 2 outlines the circular flow of income and spending in the economy for not only households and firms, as was the case in Chapter 1, but governments and the rest of the world. The main stream flows clockwise around the circle, first as income from firms to households (in the lower half of the circle), and then as spending from households back to firms (in the upper half of the circle). For each flow of money, there is an equal and opposite flow of products or resources. Here we follow the money.

Income Half of the Circular Flow

In the process of developing a circular flow of income and spending, we must make some simplifying assumptions. Specifically, by assuming that physical capital does not wear out (i.e., no capital depreciation) and that firms pay out all profits to firm owners (i.e., firms

retain no earnings), we can say that *GDP equals aggregate income.* The circular flow is a continuous process, but the logic of the model is clearest if we begin at juncture (1) in Exhibit 2, where U.S. firms make production decisions. After all, production must occur before output can be sold and income earned. As Henry Ford explained, "It is not the employer who pays the wages—the employer only handles the money. It is the product that pays wages."

Households supply their labor, capital, natural resources, and entrepreneurial ability to make products that sell to pay wages, interest, rent, and profit. Production of aggregate output, or GDP, gives rise to an equal amount of aggregate income.

Thus, at juncture (1), aggregate output equals aggregate income. But not all that income is available to spend. At juncture (2), governments collect taxes. Some of these tax dollars return as transfer payments

Exhibit 2

Circular Flow of Income and Expenditure

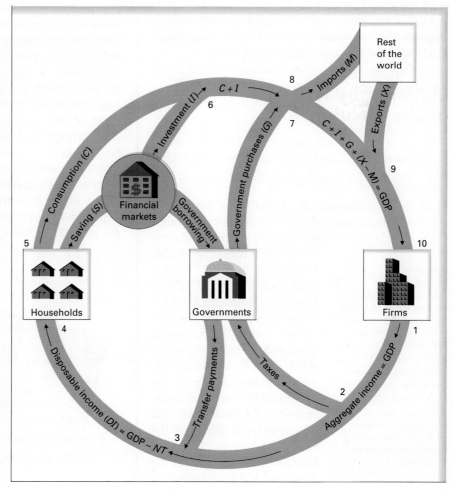

to the income stream at juncture (3). By subtracting taxes and adding transfers, we transform aggregate income into disposable income, (DI), which flows to households at juncture (4). Disposable income is take-home pay, which households can spend or save.

The bottom half of this circular flow is the *income half* because it focuses on the income arising from production. Aggregate income is the total income from producing GDP, and disposable income is the income remaining after taxes are subtracted and transfers added. To simplify the discussion, we define net taxes, (NT), as taxes minus transfer payments. So *disposable income equals GDP minus net taxes*. Put another way, we can say that aggregate income equals disposable income plus net taxes:

$$GDP = \text{Aggregate income} = DI + NT$$

At juncture (4), firms have produced output and have paid resource suppliers; governments have collected taxes and made transfer payments. With the resulting disposable income in hand, households now decide how much to spend and how much to save. Because firms have already produced the output and have paid resource suppliers, firms wait to see how much consumers want to spend. Any unsold production gets added to firm inventories.

Expenditure Half of the Circular Flow

Disposable income splits at juncture (5). Part is spent on consumption, C, and the rest is saved, S. Thus,

$$DI = C + S$$

Spending on consumption remains in the circular flow and is the biggest aggregate expenditure, about two-thirds of the total. Household saving flows to financial markets, which consist of banks and other financial institutions that link savers to borrowers. For simplicity, Exhibit 2 shows households as the only savers, though governments, firms, and the rest of the world could save as well. The primary borrowers are firms and governments, but households borrow too, particularly for new homes, and the rest of the world also borrows. In reality, financial markets should be connected to all four economic

disposable income (DI) the income households have available to spend or to save after paying taxes and receiving transfer payments

net taxes (NT) taxes minus transfer payments

financial markets banks and other financial institutions that facilitate the flow of funds from savers to borrowers

$$GDP = DI + NT$$
$$DI = C + S$$

decision makers, but we have simplified the flows to keep the model from looking like a plate of spaghetti.

In our simplified model, firms pay resource suppliers an amount equal to the entire value of output. With nothing left for investment, firms must borrow to finance purchases of physical capital plus any increases in their inventories. Households also borrow to purchase new homes. Therefore, investment, I, consists of spending on new capital by firms, including inventory changes, plus spending on residential construction. Investment enters the circular flow at juncture (6), so aggregate spending at that point totals C + I.

Governments must also borrow whenever they incur deficits, that is, whenever their total *outlays*—transfer payments plus purchases of goods and services—exceed their revenues. Government purchases of goods and services, represented by G, enter the spending stream in the upper half of the circular flow at juncture (7). Remember that G *excludes* transfer payments, which already entered the stream as income at juncture (3).

Some spending by households, firms, and governments goes for imports. Because spending on imports flows to foreign producers, spending on imports, M, leaks from the circular flow at juncture (8). But the rest of the world buys U.S. products, so foreign spending on U.S. exports, X, enters the spending flow at juncture (9). Net exports, the impact of the *rest of the world* on aggregate expenditure, equal exports minus imports, X−M, which can be positive, negative, or zero.

The upper half of the circular flow, the *expenditure half*, tracks the four components of aggregate expenditure: consumption, C, investment, I, government purchases, G, and net exports, X−M. Aggregate expenditure flows into firms at juncture (10). Aggregate expenditure equals the market value of aggregate output, or GDP. For short,

$$C + I + G + (X−M) = \text{Aggregate expenditure} = GDP$$

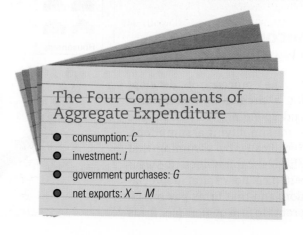

The Four Components of Aggregate Expenditure

- consumption: C
- investment: I
- government purchases: G
- net exports: $X − M$

© SAMUEL KESSLER/ISTOCKPHOTO.COM

>> The labor of working mothers is reflected in the GDP; the labor of those who stay home is not.

© ELYSE LEWIN/BRAND X PICTURES/JUPITERIMAGES

Leakages Equal Injections

Let's step back now to view the big picture. In the upper half of the circular flow, aggregate expenditure is total spending on U.S. output. In the lower half, aggregate income is the income arising from that spending. This is the first accounting identity. Aggregate expenditure (spending by each sector) equals aggregate income (disposable income plus net taxes), or

$$C + I + G + (X-M) = DI + NT$$

Because disposable income equals consumption plus saving, we can substitute $C + S$ for DI in the above equation to yield

$$C + I + G + (X-M) = C + S + NT$$

After subtracting C from both sides and adding M to both sides, the equation reduces to

$$I + G + X = S + NT + M$$

Note that, injections into the main stream occur at various points around the circular flow. Investment, I, government purchases, G, and exports, X, are *injections* of spending into the circular flow. At the same time, some of the circular flow leaks from the main stream. Saving, S, net taxes, NT, and imports, M, are leakages from the circular flow. As you can see from the equation, *injections into the circular flow equal leakages from the flow.* This injections-leakages equality demonstrates a second accounting identity based on double-entry bookkeeping.

LO³ Limitations of National Income Accounting

Imagine the difficulty of developing an accounting system that must capture such a complex and dynamic economy. In the interest of clarity and simplicity, certain features get neglected. In this section, we examine some limitations of the national income accounting system, beginning with production not captured by GDP.

Some Production Is Not Included in GDP

With some minor exceptions, GDP includes only those products that are sold in markets. This ignores all do-it-yourself production—child care, meal preparation, house cleaning, laundry, home maintenance and repair. Thus, an economy in which householders are largely self-sufficient has a lower GDP than an otherwise similar economy in which households specialize and sell products to one another—taking in each other's laundry, so to speak. During the 1950s, more than 80 percent of American mothers with small children remained at home caring for the family, but all this care added not one cent to GDP. Today most mothers with small children are in the workforce, where their labor gets counted in GDP. Meals, child care, and the like are now often purchased in markets and thus get reflected in GDP. In less developed economies, more economic activity is do-it-yourself.

GDP also ignores off-the-books production. The term underground economy describes market activity that goes unreported either because it's illegal or because people want to evade taxes on otherwise legal activity. Although there is no official measure of the underground economy, most economists agree that it is substantial. A federal study suggests the equivalent of 10 percent of U.S. GDP is underground production; this would have amounted to about $1.4 trillion in 2009.

For some economic activity, income must be *imputed*, or assigned, because market exchange does not occur. For example, included in

injection
any spending other than by households or any income other than from resource earnings; includes investment, government purchases, exports, and transfer payments

leakage
any diversion of income from the domestic spending stream; includes saving, taxes, and imports

underground economy
market transactions that go unreported either because they are illegal or because people involved want to evade taxes

GDP is an *imputed rental income* that homeowners receive from home ownership, even though no rent is actually paid or received. Also included in GDP is an imputed dollar amount for (1) wages paid *in kind,* such as employers' payments for employees' medical insurance, and (2) food produced by farm families for their own consumption. *GDP therefore includes some economic production that does not involve market exchange.*

Leisure, Quality, and Variety

The average U.S. workweek is much shorter now than it was a century ago, so people work less to produce today's output. People also retire earlier and live longer after retirement. As a result of a shorter workweek and earlier retirement, more leisure is available. But leisure is not reflected in GDP because it is not directly bought and sold in a market. The quality and variety of products available have also improved on average over the years because of technological advances and greater competition. For example, the magazine *Consumer Reports* finds a consistent improvement in the quality of the automobile over time. Yet most of these improvements are not reflected in GDP. Recording systems, computers, tires, running shoes, cell phones, and hundreds of other products have gotten better over the years. Also, new products are being introduced all the time, such as MP3 players, HDTV, and energy drinks. *The gross domestic product fails to capture changes in the availability of leisure time and often fails to reflect changes in the quality of products or in the availability of new products.*

What's Gross about Gross Domestic Product?

In the course of producing GDP, some capital wears out, such as the delivery truck that finally dies, and some capital becomes obsolete, such as an aging computer that can't run the latest software. A new truck that logs 100,000 miles its first year has been subject to wear and tear, and therefore has a diminished value as a resource. A truer picture of the net production that actually occurs during a year is found by subtracting this capital *depreciation* from GDP.

depreciation
the value of capital stock used up to produce GDP or that becomes obsolete during the year

net domestic product
gross domestic product minus depreciation

> 66 Gross domestic product is called "gross" because it fails to take into account this depreciation. 99

Depreciation measures the value of the capital stock that is used up or becomes obsolete in the production process. Gross domestic product is called "gross" because it fails to take into account this depreciation. Net domestic product equals gross domestic product minus depreciation, the capital stock used up in the production process.

We now have two measures of investment. *Gross investment* is the value of all investment during a year and is used in computing GDP. *Net investment* equals gross investment minus depreciation. The economy's production possibilities depend on what happens to net investment. If net investment is positive—that is, if gross investment exceeds depreciation—the economy's capital stock increases, so its contribution to output increases as well. If net investment is zero, the capital stock remains constant, as does its contribution to output. And in the unlikely event that net investment is negative, the capital stock declines, as does its contribution to output.

As the names imply, *gross* domestic product reflects gross investment and *net* domestic product reflects net investment. But estimating depreciation involves some guesswork. For example, what is the appropriate measure of depreciation for the roller coasters at Busch Gardens, the metal display shelves at Wal-Mart, or the parking lots at Mall of America in Minnesota?

GDP Does Not Reflect All Costs

Some production and consumption degrades the quality of our environment. Trucks and automobiles pump pollution into the atmosphere, which may contribute to global warming. Housing developments displace scenic open space and forests. Paper mills foul the lungs and burn the eyes. These negative externalities—costs that fall on those not directly involved in the transactions—are mostly ignored in GDP calculations, even though they diminish the quality of life now and in the future. To the extent that growth in GDP generates negative externalities, a rising GDP may not be as attractive as it would first appear.

Although the national income accounts reflect the depreciation of buildings, machinery, vehicles, and other manufactured capital, this accounting ignores the depletion of natural resources, such as standing timber, oil reserves, fish stocks, and soil fertility. So national income accounts reflect depreciation of the physical capital stock but not the natural

capital stock. For example, intensive farming may raise productivity and boost GDP temporarily, but this depletes soil fertility. Worse still, some production may speed the extinction of certain plants and animals. The U.S. Commerce Department is now in the process of developing so-called *green accounting*, or *green GDP*, trying to register the impact of production on air pollution, water pollution, soil depletion, and the loss of other natural resources.

GDP and Economic Welfare

In computing GDP, the market price of output is the measure of its value. Therefore, each dollar spent on handguns or cigarettes is counted in GDP the same as each dollar spent on baby formula or fitness programs. Positive economic analysis tries to avoid making value judgments about *how* people spend their money. Because GDP, as a total, provides no information about its composition, some economists question whether GDP is the best measure of the nation's economic welfare.

Despite the limitations of official GDP estimates, GDP offers a useful snapshot of the U.S. economy at a point in time. Inflation, however, clouds comparability over time. In the next section, we discuss how to adjust GDP for changes in the economy's price level.

LO⁴ Accounting for Price Changes

As noted earlier, the national income accounts are based on the market values of final goods and services produced in a particular year.

Initially, gross domestic product measures the value of output in *nominal dollars*—that is, in the dollar values at the time production occurs. When GDP is based on nominal dollars, the national income accounts measure the *nominal value* of national output. Thus, nominal GDP is based on the prices prevailing when production takes place. National income accounts based on nominal dollars allow for comparisons among income or expenditure components in a particular year. Because the economy's average price level changes over time, however, nominal-dollar comparisons across years can be misleading. For example, between 1979 and 1980, nominal GDP increased by about 9 percent. That sounds impressive, but the economy's average price level rose more than 9 percent. So the growth in nominal GDP came entirely from inflation. Real GDP, or GDP measured in terms of the goods and services produced, in fact declined. If nominal GDP increases in a given year, part of this increase may simply reflect inflation—pure hot air. To make meaningful comparisons of GDP across years, we must take out the hot air, or *deflate* nominal GDP. We focus on *real* changes in production by eliminating changes due solely to inflation.

Price Indexes

To compare the price level over time, let's first establish a point of reference, a base year to which prices in other years can be compared. An *index number* compares the value of some variable in a particular year to its value in a base year, or reference year. Think about the simplest of index numbers. Suppose bread is the only good produced in an economy. As a reference point, let's look at its price in some specific year. The year selected is called the base year; prices in other years are expressed relative to the base-year price.

Suppose the base year is 2008, when a loaf of bread in our simple economy sold for $1.25. Let's say the price of bread increased to $1.30 in 2009 and to $1.40 in 2010. We construct a price index by dividing each year's price by the price in the base year and then multiplying by 100, as shown in Exhibit 3. For 2008, the base year, we divide the base price of bread by itself, $1.25/$1.25, which equals 1, so the price index in 2008 equals 1 × 100 = 100. *The price index in the base year is always*

nominal GDP
GDP based on prices prevailing at the time of production

base year
the year with which other years are compared when constructing an index; the index equals 100 in the base year

price index
a number that shows the average price of products; changes in a price index over time show changes in the economy's average price level

Exhibit 3

Hypothetical Example of a Price Index (base year = 2008)

The price index equals the price in the current year divided by the price in the base year, all multiplied by 100.

Year	(1) Price of Bread in Current Year	(2) Price of Bread in Base Year	(3) Price Index (3) = (1)/(2) × 100
2008	$1.25	$1.25	100
2009	1.30	1.25	104
2010	1.40	1.25	112

100. The price index in 2009 is $1.30/$1.25, which equals 1.04, which when multiplied by 100 equals 104. In 2010, the index is $1.40/$1.25, or 1.12, which when multiplied by 100 equals 112. Thus, the index is 4 percent higher in 2009 than in the base year and 12 percent higher in 2010. The price index permits comparisons across years. For example, what if you were provided the indexes for 2009 and 2010 and asked what happened to the price level between the two years? By dividing the 2010 price index by the 2009 price index, 112/104, you find that the price level rose 7.7 percent.

This section has shown how to develop a price index assuming we already know the price level each year. Determining the price level is a bit more involved, as we'll now see.

Consumer Price Index

The price index most familiar to you is the consumer price index, or CPI, which measures changes over time in the cost of buying a "market basket" of goods and services purchased by a typical family. For simplicity, suppose a typical family's market basket for the year includes 365 packages of Twinkies, 500 gallons of heating oil, and 12

consumer price index (CPI)
a measure of inflation based on the cost of a fixed market basket of goods and services

months of cable TV. Prices in the base year are listed in column (2) of Exhibit 4. The total cost of each product in the base year is found by multiplying price by quantity, as shown in column (3). The cost of the market basket in the base year is shown at the bottom of column (3) to be $1,184.85.

Prices in the current year are listed in column (4). Notice that not all prices changed by the same percentage since the base year. The price of fuel oil increased by 50 percent, but the price of Twinkies declined. The cost of that same basket in the current year increased to $1,398.35, shown as the sum of column (5). To compute the consumer price index for the current year, we simply divide the cost in the current year by the cost of that same basket in the base year, $1,398.35/$1,184.85, and then multiply by 100. This yields a price index of 118. We could say that between the base period and the current year, the "cost of living" increased by 18 percent, although not all prices increased by the same percentage.

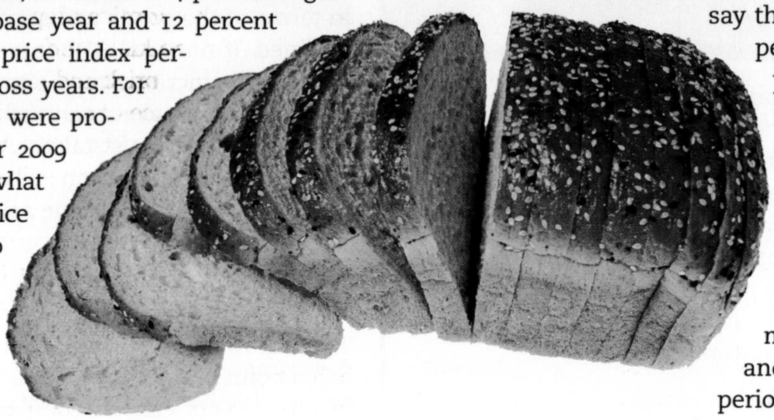

The federal government uses the 36 months of 1982, 1983, and 1984 as the base period for calculating the CPI for a market basket consisting of hundreds of goods and services. The CPI is reported monthly based on prices collected from about 23,000 sellers across the country in 87 metropolitan areas. In reality, each household consumes a unique market basket, so we could theoretically develop about 117 million CPIs—one for each household.

Exhibit 4

Hypothetical Market Basket Used to Develop the Consumer Price Index

The cost of a market basket in the current year, shown at the bottom of column (5), sums the quantities of each item in the basket, shown in column (1), times the price of each item in the current year, shown in column (4).

Product	(1) Quantity in Market Basket	(2) Prices in Base Year	(3) Cost of Basket in Base Year (3) = (1) × (2)	(4) Prices in Current Year	(5) Cost of Basket in Current Year (5) = (1) × (4)
Twinkies	365 packages	$ 0.89/package	$ 324.85	$ 0.79	$ 288.35
Fuel oil	500 gallons	1.00/gallon	500.00	1.50	750.00
Cable TV	12 months	30.00/month	360.00	30.00	360.00
			$1,184.85		$1,398.35

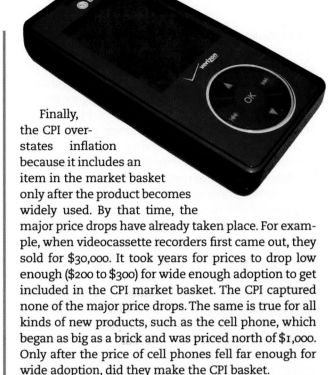

Problems with the CPI

COURTESY OF CHAPEL HOUSE PHOTOGRAPHY

There is no perfect way to measure changes in the price level. As we have already seen, the quality and variety of some products are improving all the time, so some price increases may be as much a reflection of improved quality as of inflation. Thus, there is a *quality bias* in the CPI, because it assumes that the quality of the market basket remains relatively constant over time. *To the extent that the CPI ignores quality improvements, it overstates the true extent of inflation.* Those who come up with the CPI each month try to make some quality adjustments.

But the CPI tends to overstate inflation for another reason. Recall that the CPI holds constant over time the kind and amount of goods and services in the typical market basket. Because not all items in the market basket experience the same rate of price change, relative prices change over time. A rational household would respond to changes in relative prices by buying less of the more expensive products and more of the cheaper products. But, because the CPI holds the market basket constant for long periods, the CPI is slow to incorporate consumer responses to changes in relative prices. *The CPI calculations, by not allowing households to shift away from goods that have become more costly, overestimate the true extent of inflation experienced by the typical household.*

The CPI has also failed to keep up with the consumer shift toward discount stores such as Wal-Mart, Target, and Home Depot. Government statisticians consider goods sold by discounters as different from goods sold by regular retailers. Hence, the discounter's lower price does not translate into a reduction in the cost of living, simply as a different consumer purchase decision.

Finally, the CPI overstates inflation because it includes an item in the market basket only after the product becomes widely used. By that time, the major price drops have already taken place. For example, when videocassette recorders first came out, they sold for $30,000. It took years for prices to drop low enough ($200 to $300) for wide enough adoption to get included in the CPI market basket. The CPI captured none of the major price drops. The same is true for all kinds of new products, such as the cell phone, which began as big as a brick and was priced north of $1,000. Only after the price of cell phones fell far enough for wide adoption, did they make the CPI basket.

Experts conclude the CPI has overestimated inflation by about 1 percent per year. This problem is of more than academic concern because changes in the CPI determine changes in tax brackets and in an array of payments, including wage agreements that include a cost-of-living adjustment, Social Security benefits totaling more than $500 billion annually, welfare benefits, even alimony. In fact, about 30 percent of federal outlays are tied to changes in the CPI. A 1 percent correction in the upward bias of the CPI would save the federal budget nearly $200 billion annually by 2014.

Overstating the CPI also distorts other measures, such as wages, that use the CPI to adjust for inflation.

Price Check on Aisle 2

© CREATAS IMAGES/JUPITERIMAGES

The Bureau of Labor Statistics (BLS) is the government agency that calculates the CPI each month, employing dozens of economists to analyze the impact of any quality changes to products in the CPI market basket. Most price adjustments are straightforward. For example, if a candy bar shrinks 10 percent but still sells for the same price, the CPI shows this as a 10 percent price increase. But sometimes a product changes in a more complicated way. For example, the price of a 57-inch TV dropped from $2,239 to $1,910, for an apparent decline of 15 percent. But upon closer inspection, the analyst found that the new model lacked an HDTV tuner that had been included in the model it replaced. This tuner would be valued by consumers at $514. So, instead of declining 15 percent, the price of the 57-inch TV actually rose 11 percent [= 1,910/(2,239 − 514)]. For more on how the BLS calculates the CPI, read the case at 4ltrpress.cengage.com/econ.

SOURCES: Justin Lahart, "Is Inflation View from Fed Worth Taking to Bank?" *Wall Street Journal,* 21 February 2001; Timothy Aeppel, "An Inflation Debate Brews Over Intangibles at the Mall," *Wall Street Journal,* 9 May 2005; and Mary Kokoski, Keith Waehrer, and Patricia Rosaklis, "Using Hedonic Methods for Quality Adjustment in the CPI," U.S. Bureau of Labor Statistics Working Paper (2000) found at http://www.bls.gov/cpi/cpiaudio.htm.

For example, based on the official CPI, the average real wage in the U.S. economy fell by a total of about 2 percent in the last two decades. But if the CPI overstated inflation by 1 percent per year, as researchers now believe, then the average real wage, instead of dropping by 2 percent, actually increased by about 20 percent. The Bureau of Labor Statistics, the group that estimates the CPI, is now working on these problems and has introduced an experimental version of the CPI that would reduce measured inflation. One experiment uses scanner data at supermarkets to find out how consumers respond, for example, to a rise in the price of romaine lettuce relative to iceberg lettuce, two products assumed to be reasonable substitutes.

GDP price index
a comprehensive inflation measure of all goods and services included in the gross domestic product

chain-weighted system
an inflation measure that adjusts the weights from year to year in calculating a price index, thereby reducing the bias caused by a fixed-price weighting system

The GDP Price Index

A price index is a weighted sum of various prices. Whereas the CPI focuses on just a sample of consumer purchases, a more complex and more comprehensive price index, the GDP price index, measures the average price of all goods and services produced in the economy. To calculate the GDP price index, we use the formula

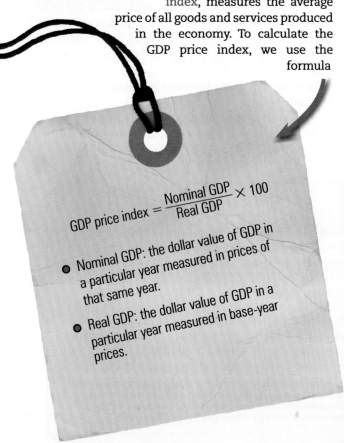

$$\text{GDP price index} = \frac{\text{Nominal GDP}}{\text{Real GDP}} \times 100$$

- Nominal GDP: the dollar value of GDP in a particular year measured in prices of that same year.
- Real GDP: the dollar value of GDP in a particular year measured in base-year prices.

The challenge is finding real GDP in a particular year. Any measure of real GDP is constructed as the weighted sum of thousands of different goods and services produced in the economy. The question is what weights, or prices, to use. Prior to 1995, the Bureau of Economic Analysis (BEA) used prices for a particular base year (most recently 1987) to estimate real GDP. In this case, the quantity of each output in a particular year was valued by using the 1987 price of each output. So real GDP in, say, 1994 was the sum of 1994 output valued at 1987 prices.

Moving from Fixed Weights to Chain Weights

Estimating real GDP by using prices from a base year yields an accurate measure of real GDP as long as the year in question is close to the base year. But BEA used prices that prevailed in 1987 to value production from 1929 to 1995. In early 1996, BEA switched from a fixed-price weighting system to a chain-weighted system, using a complicated process that changes price weights from year to year. All you need to know is that the chain-weighted real GDP adjusts the weights more or less continuously from year to year, reducing the bias caused by a fixed-price weighting system.

Even though the chain-type index adjusts the weights from year to year, any index, by definition, must still use some year as an anchor, or reference point—that is, any index must answer the question, "Compared to what?" To provide such a reference point, BEA measures U.S. real GDP and its components in *chained (2000) dollars*. Exhibit 5 presents nominal-dollar estimates of GDP as well as chained (2000) dollar estimates of real GDP. The blue line indicates nominal-dollar GDP since 1959. The red line indicates real GDP since 1959, or GDP measured in chained (2000) dollars. The two lines intersect in 2000, because that's when real GDP equaled nominal GDP. Nominal GDP is below real GDP in years prior to 2000 because real GDP is based on chained (2000) prices, which on average are higher than prices prior to 2000. Nominal GDP reflects growth in real GDP and in the price level. Chained-dollar GDP reflects growth only in real GDP. So nominal-dollar GDP grows faster than chained-dollar GDP.

Final Word

This chapter discussed how GDP is measured and how it's adjusted for changes in the price level over time. The national income accounts have limitations, but they offer a reasonably accurate picture of the economy at a point in time as well as year-to-year movements in the economy. Subsequent chapters will refer to the distinction between real and nominal values.

Exhibit 5

U.S. Gross Domestic Product in Nominal Dollars and Chained (2000) Dollars

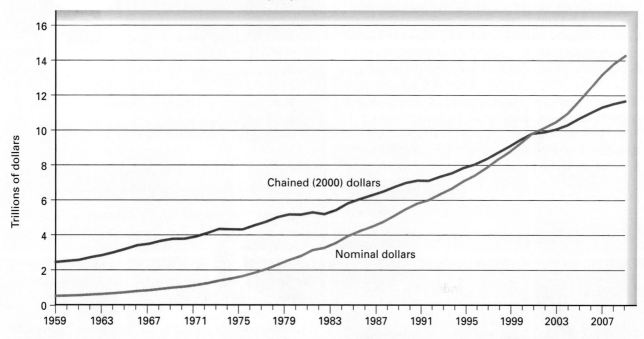

SOURCE: Based on annual estimates from the Bureau of Economic Analysis, U.S. Department of Commerce. For the latest data, go to http://bea.gov/national/index.htm#gdp.

3 < Minimum years of expected lifespan for a durable good

Investment as a fraction of U.S. GDP on average during last decade > **1/6**

$1.4 Trillion < Estimated size of the underground economy in 2009

Apparent price decline in 57-inch TV > **15%**

30% < Federal outlays tied to CPI

11% < Actual price increase in 57-inch TV when absence of HDTV tuner taken into account

Approximate price of a first-generation VCR > **$30,000**

Unemployment
and Inflation

Learning Outcomes

LO[1] Discuss the effects of unemployment on the economy

LO[2] Discuss the effects of inflation on the economy

"What's so bad about inflation?"

Who among the following would be counted as unemployed: a college student who is not working, a bank teller displaced by an automatic teller machine, Jennifer Aniston between movies, or baseball slugger Manny Ramirez in the off-season? What type of unemployment might be healthy for the economy? What's so bad about inflation? Why is anticipated inflation less of a problem than unanticipated inflation? These and other questions are answered in this chapter, where we explore two macroeconomic problems: unemployment and inflation.

To be sure, unemployment and inflation are not the only problems an economy could face. Sluggish growth and widespread poverty are others. But low unemployment and low inflation go a long way toward reducing other economic problems. Although unemployment and inflation are often related, each is introduced separately. The causes of each and the relationship between the two will become clearer as you learn more about how the economy works.

This chapter shows that not all unemployment or all inflation harms the economy. Even in a healthy economy, a certain amount of unemployment reflects the voluntary choices of workers and employers seeking their best options. And low inflation that is fully anticipated creates fewer distortions than does unanticipated inflation.

What do you think?

Inflation is harmful to the health of the economy.

Strongly Disagree						Strongly Agree
1	2	3	4	5	6	7

Topics discussed in Chapter 8 include:

- Measuring unemployment
- Frictional, seasonal, structural, and cyclical unemployment
- Full employment
- Sources and consequences of inflation
- Relative price changes
- Nominal and real interest rates

LO¹ Unemployment

"They scampered about looking for work. . . . They swarmed on the highways. The movement changed them; the highways, the camps along the road, the fear of hunger and the hunger itself, changed them. The children without dinner changed them, the endless moving changed them."[1] There is no question, as John Steinbeck writes in *The Grapes of Wrath*, that a long stretch of unemployment profoundly affects the jobless and

1. John Steinbeck, *The Grapes of Wrath* (New York: Viking Press, 1939), p. 392.

their families. The most obvious loss is a steady paycheck, but the unemployed often lose self-esteem and part of their identity as well. According to psychologists, in terms of stressful events, the loss of a good job ranks only slightly below a divorce or the death of a loved one. Moreover, unemployment appears to be linked to a greater incidence of crime and to a variety of afflictions, including heart disease, suicide, and clinical depression.[2] No matter how often people complain about their jobs, they rely on those same jobs not only for their livelihood but for part of their personal identity. When strangers meet, one of the first questions asked is "what do you do for a living?" Alfred Marshall wrote that your job is often the main object of your thoughts and intellectual development.

In addition to the personal costs, unemployment imposes a cost on the economy as a whole because fewer goods and services are produced. When those who are willing and able to work can't find jobs, their labor is lost forever. *This lost output coupled with the economic and psychological cost of unemployment on the individual and the family are the true costs of unemployment.* As we begin our analysis, keep in mind that the national unemployment rate reflects millions of individuals with their own stories. As President Harry Truman once remarked, "It's a recession when your neighbor loses his job; it's a depression when you lose your own." For some lucky people, unemployment is a brief vacation between jobs. For some others, a long stretch can have a lasting effect on family stability, economic welfare, self-esteem, and personal identity.

Measuring Unemployment

The unemployment rate is the most widely reported measure of the nation's economic health. What does

> **"** The college student, the displaced bank teller, Jennifer Aniston, and Manny Ramirez would all be counted as unemployed if they want a job and looked for work in the previous month. **"**

the unemployment rate measure? What are the sources of unemployment? How has unemployment changed over time? These are some of the questions explored in this section. Let's first see how to measure unemployment.

We begin with the U.S. *civilian noninstitutional adult population,* which consists of all civilians 16 years of age and older, except those in prison or in mental hospitals. The adjective *civilian* means the definition excludes those in the military. From here on, references to the *adult population* mean the civilian noninstitutional adult population. The labor force consists of the people in the adult population who are either working or looking for work. *Those who want a job but can't find one are unemployed.* The Bureau of Labor Statistics interviews 60,000 households monthly and counts people as unemployed if they have no job but want one and have looked for work at least once during the preceding four weeks. Thus, the college student, the displaced bank teller, Jennifer Aniston, and Manny Ramirez would all be counted as unemployed if they want a job and looked for work in the previous month. The unemployment rate measures the percentage of those in the labor force who are unemployed. Hence, the unemployment rate, which is reported monthly, equals the number unemployed—that is, people without jobs who are looking for work—divided by the number in the labor force.

Only a fraction of adults who are not working are considered unemployed. The others may have retired, are students, are caring for children at home, or simply don't want to work. Others may be unable to work because of long-term illness or disability. Some may have become so discouraged by a long, unfruitful job search that they have given up in frustration. These discouraged workers have, in effect, dropped out of the labor force, so they are not counted as unemployed. Finally, about one-third of those working part time would prefer to work full time, yet all part-timers are counted as employed. Because the official unemployment rate does not include dis-

labor force
those 16 years of age and older who are either working or looking for work

unemployment rate
the number unemployed as a percentage of the labor force

discouraged workers
those who drop out of the labor force in frustration because they can't find work

❋❋❋
2. For a study linking a higher incidence of suicides to recessions, see Christopher Ruhm, "Are Recessions Good for Your Health?" *Quarterly Journal of Economics,* 115 (May 2000): 617–650. Clinical depression is also higher among the unemployed, as demonstrated in Frederick Zimmerman and Wayne Katon, "Socioeconomic Status, Depression Disparities, and Financial Strain: What Lies Behind the Income-Depression Relationship?" *Health Economics,* 14 (December 2004): 1197–1215.

February 2009:

12.5 million people unemployed
÷ labor force of 154.2 million
= unemployment rate of 8.1%

Exhibit 1

The Adult Population Sums the Employed, the Unemployed, and Those Not in the Labor Force: February 2009 (in millions)

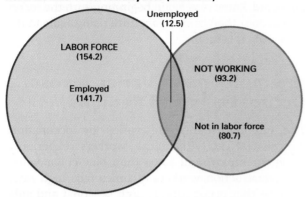

SOURCE: Figures are for February 2009, from the U.S. Bureau of Labor Statistics. For the latest data, go to http://www.bls.gov/news.release/empsit.toc.htm.

couraged workers and counts all part-time workers as employed, it may underestimate the true extent of unemployment in the economy. Later we consider some reasons why the unemployment rate may exaggerate the true extent of unemployment.

These definitions are illustrated in Exhibit 1, where circles represent the various groups, and the number (in millions) of individuals in each category and subcategory is shown in parentheses. The circle on the left depicts the entire U.S. labor force, including both employed and unemployed people. The circle on the right represents those in the adult population who, for whatever reason, are not working. These two circles combined show the adult population. The overlapping area identifies the number

of *unemployed* workers—that is, people in the labor force who are not working. The unemployment rate is found by dividing the number unemployed by the number in the labor force.

Labor Force Participation Rate

The productive capability of any economy depends in part on the proportion of adults in the labor force, measured as the *labor force participation rate*. In Exhibit 1, the U.S. adult population equals those in the labor force (154.2 million) plus those not in the labor force (80.7 million)—a total of 234.9 million. The labor force participation rate therefore equals the number in the labor force divided by the adult population, or 65.6 percent (=154.2 million/234.9 million). So, on average, two out of three U.S. adults are in the labor force. The labor force participation rate increased from about 60 percent in 1970 to about 67 percent in 1990 and has remained relatively steady since then.

One striking development since World War II has been the convergence in the labor force participation rates of men and women. In 1950, only 34 percent of adult women were in the labor force. Today 60 percent are, with the greatest increase among younger women. The labor force participation rate among men has declined from 86 percent in 1950 to about 75 percent today, primarily because of earlier retirement. The participation rate is slightly higher among white males than black males but higher among black females than white females. Finally, the participation rate climbs with education—from 45.9 percent for those without a high school diploma to 77.8 percent among those with a college degree.

Unemployment over Time

Exhibit 2 shows the U.S. unemployment rate since 1900, with shaded bars to indicate periods of recession and depression. As you can see, rates rise during contractions and fall during expansions. Most

Exhibit 2

The U.S. Unemployment Rate Since 1900

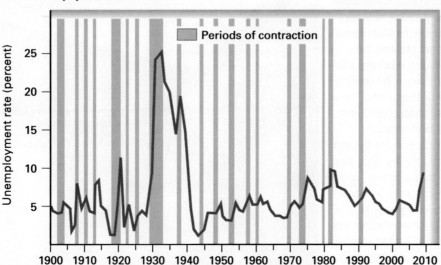

SOURCES: U.S. Census Bureau, *Historical Statistics of the United States: Colonial Times to 1970* (Washington, D.C. U.S. Government Printing Office, 1975): *Economic Report of the President*, January 2009; and U.S. Bureau of Labor Statistics. Figure for 2009 is as of June, seasonally adjusted. For the latest unemployment rate, go to http://www.bls.gov/news.release/empsit.toc.htm.

labor force participation rate
the labor force as a percentage of the adult population

striking is the jump during the Great Depression of the 1930s, when the rate topped 25 percent. Note that the rate trended upward from the end of World War II in the mid-1940s until the early 1980s; then it backed down, from a high of 9.7 percent in 1982 to a low of 3.9 percent in late 2000. With the recession of 2001, the rate increased until it peaked at 6.0 percent in 2003. The rate then declined over the next four years. The unemployment rate increased again during the financial crisis and recession of 2008–2009.

Why did the unemployment rate trend down from the early 1980s to 2000? First, the overall economy was on a roll during that period, interrupted by a brief recession from July 1990 to March 1991, which was triggered by the first war in Iraq. By adding 35 million jobs between 1982 and late 2000, the U.S. economy became an incredible job machine and the envy of the world. The unemployment rate also trended down because there were fewer teenagers in the workforce. Teenagers have an unemployment rate about three times that of adults, so the declining share of teenage workers helped cut the overall unemployment rate.

Unemployment in Various Groups

The unemployment rate says nothing about who is unemployed or for how long. Even a low rate can mask wide differences in unemployment rates based on age, race, gender, geography, and occupation. For example, when the U.S. unemployment rate in February 2009 was 8.1 percent, the rate was 21.6 percent among teenagers, 13.4 percent among black workers, and 10.9 percent among people of Hispanic ethnicity. Why are unemployment rates among teenagers so much higher than among older workers? Young workers enter the job market with little training, so they take unskilled jobs and are the first to be fired if the economy softens. Young workers also move in and out of the job market more frequently as they juggle school demands. Even those who have left school often shop around more than older workers, quitting one job in search of a better one.

Unemployment rates for different groups appear in Exhibit 3. Each panel shows the rate by race and by gender since 1972 (historical data are not available for those of Hispanic ethnicity). Panel (a) shows the rates for people 20 and older, and panel (b) the rates for 16- to 19-year olds. Years of recession are shaded pink. As you can see, rates are higher among black workers than among whites, and rates are higher among teenagers than among those 20 and older. During recessions, rates climbed for all groups. Rates peaked during the recession of 1982 and then trended down. After the recession of the early 1990s, unemployment rates continued downward, with the rate among black people falling in 2000 to the lowest on record. Rates rose again beginning with the recession of 2001 then came down until rising again in the 2008–2009 recession.

Unemployment Varies Across Occupations and Regions

The unemployment rate varies by occupation. Professional and technical workers experience lower unemployment rates than blue-collar workers. Construction workers at times face high rates because that occupation is both seasonal and subject to wide swings over the business cycle.

Partly because certain occupations dominate labor markets in certain regions, unemployment rates also vary by region. For example, because of pressure on blue-collar jobs in smokestack industries such as autos, in January 2009 unemployment rates in Michigan and Indiana were double those in emerging western states of Wyoming and Utah. Even within a state, unemployment can vary widely. For example, the California city of El Centro had three times the unemployment rate of the city of Napa.

Exhibit 4 on page 118 shows unemployment rates for 27 major metropolitan areas. As you can see, Detroit had the highest unemployment rate, at 10.6 percent. This was more than double the rate for the city with the lowest rate, Honolulu, at 4.2 percent. The point is that *the national unemployment rate masks differences across the country and even across an individual state.* Still, most cities in Exhibit 4 had rates between 4.0 percent and 6.5 percent.

© CORBIS/JUPITERIMAGES

Exhibit 3

Unemployment Rates for Various Groups

(a) 20 years of age or older

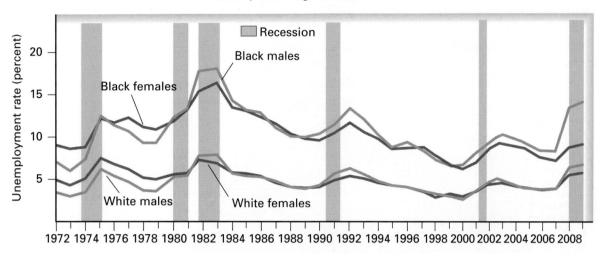

(b) 16 to 19 years of age

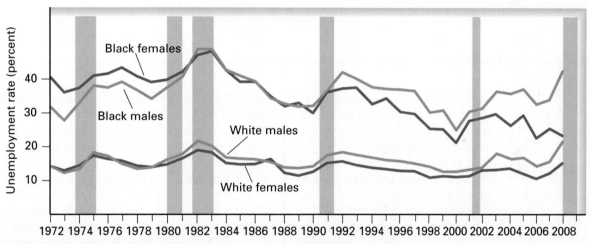

SOURCES: *Economic Report of the President,* January 2009, Table B–43; and U.S. Bureau of Labor Statistics. Figure for 2009 is of January. For the latest data, go to http://www.bls.gov/news.release/empsit.toc.htm.

Sources of Unemployment

Pick up any metropolitan newspaper and thumb through the classifieds. The help-wanted section may include thousands of jobs, from accountants to X-ray technicians. Online job sites such as Monster.com list hundreds of thousands of openings. Why, when millions are unemployed, are so many jobs available? To understand this, we must think about all the reasons why people are unemployed. They may be looking for a first job, or they may be reentering the labor force after an absence. They may have quit or been fired from their last job. Sixty-two percent of those unemployed in February 2009 lost their previous job, 7 percent quit, 8 percent

entered the labor market for the first time, and 23 percent reentered the labor market. *Thus, 38 percent were unemployed either because they quit jobs or because they were just joining or rejoining the labor force.*

There are four sources of unemployment: frictional, seasonal, structural, and cyclical.

Frictional Unemployment

Just as employers do not always hire the first applicant who comes through the door, job seekers do not always accept the first offer. Both employers and job seekers need time to explore the job market. Employers need time to learn about the talent available, and job seekers need time to learn about

Exhibit 4

Unemployment Rates Differ Across U.S. Metropolitan Areas

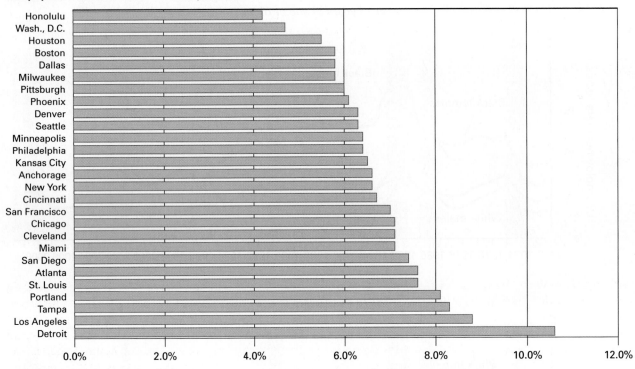

SOURCE: Based on figures for December 2008 from the U.S. Bureau of Labor Statistics. For the latest figures, go to http://www.bls.gov/lau/home.htm.

employment opportunities. The time required to bring together employers and job seekers results in frictional unemployment. Although unemployment often creates economic and psychological hardships, not all unemployment is necessarily bad. Frictional unemployment does not usually last long and it results in a better match between workers and jobs, so the entire economy works more efficiently. Policy makers and economists are not that concerned about frictional unemployment.

Seasonal Unemployment

Unemployment caused by seasonal changes in labor demand during the year is called seasonal unemployment. During cold winter months, demand for farm hands, lifeguards, landscapers, and construction workers shrinks, as it does for dozens of other seasonal occupations. Likewise, tourism in winter destinations such as Miami and Phoenix melts in the heat of summer. The Christmas season increases the demand for sales clerks, postal workers, and Santa Clauses. Those in seasonal jobs know their jobs disappear in the off-season. Some even choose seasonal occupations to complement their lifestyles or academic schedules. To eliminate seasonal unemployment, we would have to outlaw winter and abolish Christmas. Monthly employment data are *seasonally adjusted* to smooth out the unemployment bulges that result from seasonal factors. Policy makers and economists are not that concerned about seasonal unemployment.

Structural Unemployment

A third reason why job vacancies and unemployment coexist is that unemployed workers often do not have the skills in demand or do not live where their skills are demanded. For example, the Lincoln Electric Company in Euclid, Ohio, could not fill 200 openings because few among the thousands who applied could operate computer-controlled machines. Unemployment arising from a mismatch of skills or geographic location is called structural unemployment. *Structural unemployment occurs because changes in tastes, technology, taxes, and competition reduce the demand for certain skills and increase the demand for other skills.* In our dynamic economy, some workers, such as

frictional unemployment unemployment that occurs because job seekers and employers need time to find each other

seasonal unemployment unemployment caused by seasonal changes in the demand for certain kinds of labor

structural unemployment unemployment because (1) the skills demanded by employers do not match those of the unemployed, or (2) the unemployed do not live where the jobs are

coal miners in West Virginia, are stuck with skills no longer demanded. Likewise, golf carts replaced caddies, ATMs replaced bank tellers, and office technology is replacing clerical staff. For example, because of e-mail, voice mail, PCs, PDAs, BlackBerries, cell phones, and other wireless devices, the number of secretaries, typists, and administrative assistants in the United States has fallen by more than half over the past two decades. Structural unemployment may also arise from a change in tastes and preferences. For example, because Americans smoke less, some tobacco farmers have lost their jobs. And because Americans buy fewer newspapers, employment in that industry has declined.

Whereas most frictional unemployment is short-term and voluntary, structural unemployment poses more of a problem because workers must either develop the skills demanded in the local job market or look elsewhere. Moving is not easy. Most people prefer to remain near friends and relatives. Those laid off from good jobs hang around in hopes of getting rehired. Married couples with one spouse still employed may not want to give up one good job, especially one with health benefits, to look for two jobs elsewhere. Finally, available jobs may be in regions where the living cost is much higher. So those structurally unemployed often stay put. Some federal retraining programs aim to reduce structural unemployment.

Cyclical Unemployment

As output declines during recessions, firms reduce their demand for nearly all resources, including labor. Cyclical unemployment increases during recessions and decreases during expansions. Between 1932 and 1934, when unemployment averaged about 24 percent, there was clearly much cyclical unemployment. Between 1942 and 1945, when unemployment averaged less than 2 percent, there was no cyclical unemployment. Cyclical unemployment means the economy is operating inside its production possibilities frontier. Government policies that stimulate aggregate demand aim to reduce cyclical unemployment.

The Meaning of Full Employment

In a dynamic economy such as ours, changes in product demand and in technology continually alter the supply and demand for particular types of labor. Thus, even in a healthy economy, there is some frictional, structural, and seasonal unemployment. The economy is viewed as operating at *full employment* if there is no cyclical unemployment. When economists talk about "full employment," they do not mean zero unemployment but low unemployment, with estimates ranging from 4 to 6 percent. Even when the economy is at **full employment**, there is some frictional, structural, and seasonal unemployment. Even during the recession of 2008–2009, nearly 40 percent of those unemployed in February 2009 quit their previous job or were new entrants or reentrants into the labor force. We can't expect people to find jobs overnight. Many in this group would be considered frictionally unemployed.

cyclical unemployment unemployment that fluctuates with the business cycle, increasing during contractions and decreasing during expansions

full employment employment level when there is no cyclical unemployment

Unemployment Compensation

As noted at the outset, unemployment often imposes an economic and psychological hardship. For a
variety of reasons, however, the burden of unemployment on the individual and the family may not be as
severe today as it was during the Great Depression.
Today, many households have two or more workers
in the labor force, so if one loses a job, another may
still have one—a job that could provide health insurance and other benefits for the family. *Having more
than one family member in the labor force cushions the
shock of unemployment.*

Moreover, unlike the experience during the Great
Depression, most who lose their jobs now collect
unemployment benefits. In response to the Great
Depression, Congress passed the Social Security Act
of 1935, which provided unemployment insurance
financed by a tax on employers. Unemployed workers
who meet certain qualifications can receive unemployment benefits for up to six months, provided
they actively look for work. During recessions, benefits
often extend beyond six months in states with especially high unemployment or nationwide during the
recession of 2008–2009. Benefits go mainly to people
who have lost jobs. Those just entering or reentering
the labor force are not covered, nor are those who quit
their last job or those fired for just cause, such as exces-
sive absenteeism or theft. Because of these restrictions,
about half of those unemployed receive benefits.

unemployment benefits
cash transfers to
those who lose their
jobs and actively seek
employment

Unemployment benefits
replace on average about 40
percent of a person's take-
home pay, with a higher
share for those whose jobs
paid less. Benefits averaged
about $280 per week in 2008.

Because these benefits reduce the opportunity cost
of remaining unemployed, they may reduce the
incentives to find work. For example, if faced with
a choice of washing dishes for $300 per week or col-
lecting $250 per week in unemployment benefits,
which would you choose? Evidence suggests that
those collecting unemployment benefits remain out
of work weeks longer than those without benefits.
Many leave the labor force once their benefits are
exhausted.[3] So although unemployment insurance
provides a safety net, it may reduce the urgency of
finding work, thereby increasing unemployment. On
the plus side, because beneficiaries need not take
the first job that comes along, unemployment insurance allows for a higher quality search. As a result of
a higher quality job search, there is a better match
between job skills and job requirements, and this
promotes economic efficiency.

International Comparisons of Unemployment

How do U.S. unemployment rates compare with
those around the world? Exhibit 5 shows rates since
1980 for the United States, Japan, and the average of
four major Western European economies (France,
Germany, Italy, and the United Kingdom). Over the
last quarter century, unemployment trended down
in the United States, trended up in Japan, and
remained high in Western Europe. At the beginning
of the period, the United States had the highest
rates among the three economies. After declines in
the U.S. rate, it spiked above that of Western Europe
because of the 2008–2009 recession. The rate in Japan
remained relatively low.

Why are rates traditionally so high in Western
Europe? The ratio of unemployment benefits to
average pay is higher in Western Europe than in
the United States, and unemployment benefits last
longer there, sometimes years. So those collecting
unemployment benefits have less incentive to find
work. What's more, government regulations make
European employers more reluctant to hire new
workers because firing them is difficult. For example,
Germany imposes penalties on firms for "socially
unjustified" layoffs. As a result of extended unemployment benefits and employer reluctance to hire
workers because they are so difficult to fire, nearly
60 percent of those unemployed in Germany in 2006
had been out of work more than a year. In contrast,

---

3. See David Card, Raj Chetty, and Andrea Weber, "The Spike at Benefits
Exhaustion: Leaving the Unemployment System or Starting a New Job?"
NBER Working Paper No. 12893 (February 2007).

Exhibit 5

During the Last Quarter Century, the U.S. Unemployment Rate Fell, Europe's Remained High, and Japan's Rose

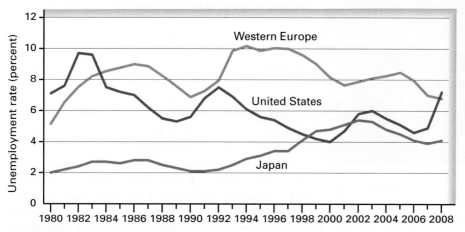

SOURCES: Based on standardized rates in *OECD Economic Outlook* 84 (November 2008) and *Economic Report of the President,* January 2009. Figures for Western Europe are the averages for France, Germany, Italy, and the United Kingdom. For the latest international data, go to http://www.bls.gov/fls/home.htm.

fewer than 10 percent of those unemployed in the United States had been out that long. The recession of 2008–2009 will likely reduce that difference.

Historically, unemployment has been low in Japan because many firms there offered job security for life. Thus, some employees who do little or no work are still carried on company payrolls. Both labor laws and social norms limit layoffs in Japan. Unemployment increased there since the early 1990s because more firms went bankrupt.

Problems with Official Unemployment Figures

Official unemployment statistics are not problem free. As we saw earlier, not counting discouraged workers as unemployed understates unemployment. Official employment data also ignore the problem of underemployment, which arises because people are counted as employed even if they can find only part-time work or are vastly overqualified for their jobs, as when someone with a Ph.D. in literature can find only a clerk's position. Counting overqualified and part-time workers as employed tends to understate the actual amount of unemployment.

On the other hand, because unemployment benefits and most welfare programs require recipients to seek employment, some people may go through the motions of looking for work just to qualify for these programs. If they do not in fact want a job, counting them as unemployed overstates actual unemployment. Likewise, some people who would prefer to work part time can find only full-time jobs, and some

forced to work overtime and weekends would prefer to work less. To the extent that people must work more than they would prefer, the official unemployment rate overstates the actual rate. Finally, people in the underground economy may not admit they have jobs because they are breaking the law. For example, someone working off the books or someone selling illegal drugs would not admit to being employed.

On net, however, because discouraged workers aren't counted as unemployed and because underemployed workers are counted as employed, most experts believe that official U.S. unemployment figures tend to underestimate unemployment. Still, the size of this underestimation may not be large. For example, counting discouraged workers as unemployed would have raised the unemployment rate in February 2009 from 8.1 percent to 8.5 percent.

Despite these qualifications and limitations, the U.S. unemployment rate is a useful measure of trends over time.

We turn next to inflation.

LO² Inflation

As noted already, inflation is a sustained increase in the economy's average price level.

We have already discussed inflation in different contexts. If the price level bounces around—moving up one month, falling back the next month—any particular increase in the price level would not necessarily be called inflation in a meaningful sense. We typically measure inflation on an annual basis. The annual *inflation rate* is the percentage increase in the average price level from one year to the next. For example, between December 2007 and December 2008, the U.S. *consumer price index* increased 3.8 percent. Extremely high inflation, as in Zimbabwe, is called hyperinflation. A sustained decrease in the average price level is called deflation, as occurred in

underemployment
workers are overqualified for their jobs or work fewer hours than they would prefer

hyperinflation
a very high rate of inflation

deflation
a sustained decrease in the price level

<< As the economic situation in Zimbabwe continued to deteriorate, even the most basic transactions required huge stacks of money. In February 2009, the government legalized the use of foreign currency.

the United States during the Great Depression and recently in Japan, Hong Kong, and Taiwan. And a reduction in the rate of inflation is called disinflation, as occurred in the United States from 1981 to 1986, 1991 to 1994, and 2001 to 2003.

In this section, we first consider two sources of inflation. Then, we examine the extent and consequences of inflation in the United States and around the world.

Two Sources of Inflation

Inflation is a sustained increase in the economy's price level; it results from an increase in aggregate demand, a decrease in aggregate supply, or both. Panel (a) of Exhibit 6 shows that an increase in aggregate demand raises the economy's price level from P to P'. In such cases, a shift to the right of the aggregate demand curve *pulls up* the price level. Inflation resulting from increases in aggregate demand is called demand-pull inflation. To generate continuous demand-pull inflation, the aggregate demand curve would have to keep shifting out along a given aggregate supply curve. Rising U.S. inflation dur-

ing the late 1960s resulted from demand-pull inflation, when federal spending for the Vietnam War and expanded social programs boosted aggregate demand.

Alternatively, inflation can arise from reductions in aggregate supply, as shown in panel (b) of Exhibit 6, where a leftward shift of the aggregate supply curve raises the price level. For example, crop failures and OPEC price hikes reduced aggregate supply during 1974 and 1975, thereby raising the price level. Inflation stemming from decreases in aggregate supply is called cost-push inflation, suggesting that increases in the cost of production *push up* the price level. Prices increase and real GDP decreases, a combination identified earlier as *stagflation*. Again, to generate sustained and continuous cost-push inflation, the aggregate supply curve would have to keep shifting left along a given aggregate demand curve.

A Historical Look at Inflation and the Price Level

The consumer price index is the inflation measure you most often encounter, so it gets the most attention here. As you learned in the previous chapter, the *consumer price index,* or *CPI,* measures the cost of a market basket of consumer goods and services over time. Exhibit 7 shows prices in the United States since 1913, using the consumer price index. Panel (a) shows the price *level,* measured by an index relative to the base period of 1982 to 1984. As you can see,

disinflation
a reduction in the rate of inflation

demand-pull inflation
a sustained rise in the price level caused by a rightward shift of the aggregate demand curve

cost-push inflation
a sustained rise in the price level caused by a leftward shift of the aggregate supply curve

Exhibit 6

Inflation Caused by Shifts of Aggregate Demand and Aggregate Supply Curves

Panel (a) illustrates demand-pull inflation. An outward shift of the aggregate demand to AD' "pulls" the price level up from P to P'. Panel (b) shows cost-push inflation. A decrease of aggregate supply to AS' "pushes" the price level up from P to P'.

(a) *Demand-pull inflation: inflation caused by an increase of aggregate demand*

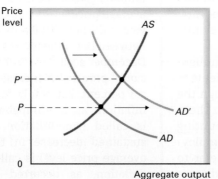

(b) *Cost-push inflation: inflation caused by a decrease of aggregate supply*

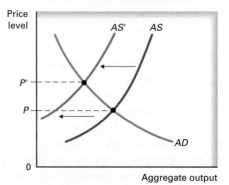

the price level was lower in 1940 than in 1920. Since 1940, however, it has risen steadily, especially during the 1970s.

People are concerned less about the price level and more about year-to-year changes in that level. The lower panel shows the *annual rate of change* in the CPI, or the annual rate of *inflation* or *deflation*. The 1970s was not the only period of high inflation. Inflation exceeded 10 percent from 1916 to 1919 and in 1947—periods associated with world wars. Prior to the 1950s, high inflation was war related and was usually followed by deflation. Such an inflation-deflation cycle stretches back over the last two centuries. In fact, between the Revolutionary War and World War II, the price level fell in about as many years as it rose. At the end of World War II, the price level was about where it stood at the end of the Civil War.

So fluctuations in the price level are nothing new. But prior to World War II, years of inflation and deflation balanced out over the long run. Therefore, people had good reason to believe the dollar would retain its purchasing power over the long term. Since the end of World War II, however, the CPI has increased by an average of 3.8 percent per year. That may not sound like much, but it translates into a tenfold increase in the consumer price index since 1947. *Inflation erodes confidence in the value of the dollar over the long term.*

Anticipated Versus Unanticipated Inflation

What is the effect of inflation on the economy? *Unanticipated inflation* creates more problems than *anticipated inflation.* To the extent that inflation is higher or lower than anticipated, it arbitrarily creates winners and losers. For example, suppose inflation is expected to be 3 percent next year, and you agree to sell your labor to your employer for a 4 percent increase in your nominal, or money, wage. You expect your *real* wage—that is, your wage measured in dollars of constant purchasing power—to increase by 1 percent. If inflation turns out to be 3 percent, as expected, you and the buyer of your labor are both satisfied with your nominal wage increase of 4 percent. If inflation turns out to be 5 percent, your real wage will fall by 1 percent, so you are a loser and the buyer of your labor a winner. If inflation turns out to be only 1 percent, your real wage increased by 3 percent, so you are a winner and your employer a loser.

If inflation is higher than expected, the losers are those who agreed to sell at a price that anticipated lower inflation and the winners are those who agreed to pay that price. If inflation is lower than expected, the situation is reversed: The losers are those who agreed to pay a price that anticipated higher inflation, and the winners are those who agreed to sell at that price. *The arbitrary gains and losses arising from unanticipated inflation is one reason inflation is so unpopular. Inflation just doesn't seem fair.*

Exhibit 7

Consumer Price Index Since 1913

(a) Consumer price index

(b) Annual percentage change

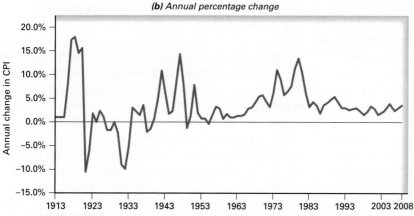

SOURCE: The CPI home page of the U.S. Bureau of Labor Statistics is at http://www.bls.gov/cpi/home.htm. Go there for the latest figures.

The Costs of Variable Inflation

During long periods of price stability, people correctly believe that they can predict future prices and can therefore plan accordingly. If inflation changes unexpectedly, however, the future is cloudier, so planning gets harder. Uncertainty about inflation undermines money's ability to link the present with the future. U.S. firms dealing with the rest of the world face an added burden. Not only must they plan for U.S. inflation, they must also anticipate how the value of the dollar will change relative to foreign currencies. Inflation uncertainty and the resulting exchange-rate uncertainty complicate international transactions. In this more uncertain environment, managers must shift their attention from production decisions to anticipating the effects of inflation and exchange-rate changes on the firm's finances. Market transactions, particularly long-term contracts, become more complicated as inflation becomes more unpredictable. Some economists believe that the high and variable U.S. inflation during the 1970s and early 1980s cut economic growth during those periods.

Inflation Obscures Relative Price Changes

Even with no inflation, some prices would increase and some would decrease, reflecting normal activity in particular markets. For example, since the early 1980s the U.S. price level has doubled, yet the prices of flat-screen TVs, computers, long-distance phone service, and many other products have declined sharply. Because the prices of various goods change by different amounts, *relative prices* change. Consider price changes over a longer period. In the last hundred years, consumer prices overall increased about 2,000 percent, but the price of a hotel room in New York City jumped 7,500 percent, while the price of a three-minute phone call from New York to Chicago dropped 99 percent. Whereas the economy's price level describes the exchange rate between a market basket and *money*, relative prices describe the exchange rate between goods—that is, how much one good costs compared to another.

Inflation does not necessarily cause a change in relative prices, but it can obscure that change. During periods of volatile inflation, there is greater uncertainty about the price of one good relative to another—that is, about relative prices. But relative price changes are important signals for allocating the economy's resources efficiently. If all prices

> Unanticipated inflation creates more problems than anticipated inflation.

moved together, suppliers could link the selling prices of their goods to the overall inflation rate. Because prices usually do not move in unison, however, tying a particular product's price to the overall inflation rate may result in a price that is too high or too low based on market conditions. The same is true of agreements to link wages with inflation. If the price of an employer's product grows more slowly than the rate of inflation in the economy, the employer may be hard-pressed to increase wages by the rate of inflation. Consider the problem confronting oil refiners who signed labor contracts agreeing to pay their workers cost-of-living wage increases. In some years, those employers had to provide pay increases at a time when the price of oil was falling like a rock.

Inflation Across Metropolitan Areas

Inflation rates differ across regions mostly because of differences in housing prices, which rise or fall faster in some places than in others. But most prices, such as for automobiles, refrigerators, or jeans, do not differ that much across regions. The federal government tracks separate CPIs for each of 27 U.S. metropolitan areas. Based on these CPIs from 2004 to 2008, the average annual inflation rate is presented in Exhibit 8. Annual inflation between 2004 and 2008 averaged from a low of 2.3 percent in Houston to a high of 5.0 percent in Honolulu. Most cities averaged between 3.1 percent and 4.0 percent. Again, the metropolitan inflation rate is heavily influenced by what's happening in the local housing market. We can conclude that the housing market in Honolulu was hotter than in Houston.

International Comparisons of Inflation

Exhibit 9 on page 126 shows annual inflation based on the CPI for the past quarter century in the United States, Japan, and the Western European economies, represented here as the average of four major nations (France, Germany, Italy, and the United Kingdom). All three economies show a similar trend, with declining inflation, or disinflation, during the first half of the 1980s, rising inflation during the second half of the 1980s to a peak in the early 1990s, and then another trend lower. The overall trend since 1980 has been toward lower inflation. Inflation rates in Western Europe were similar to those in the United

Exhibit 8

Average Annual Inflation from 2004 to 2008 Differed across U.S. Metropolitan Areas

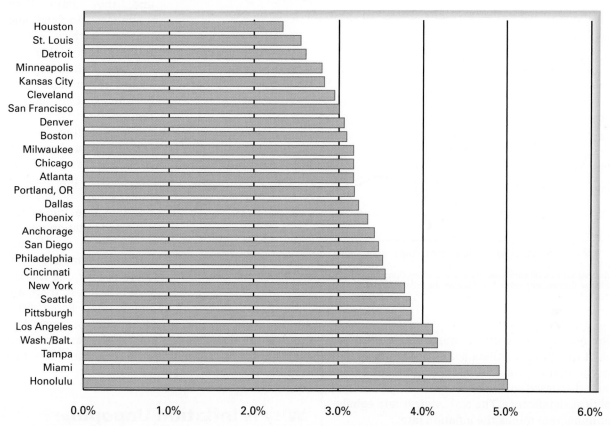

SOURCE: Annual averages for 2004 to 2008 based on CPI estimates from the U.S. Bureau of Labor Statistics. For the latest figures, go to http://www.bls.gov/cpi/home.htm and find "Regional Resources."

States. Rates in Japan were consistently lower, even dipping into deflation in recent years. Inflation since 1980 averaged 3.8 percent in Western Europe, 3.4 percent in the United States, and 1.0 percent in Japan.

The quantity and quality of data going into the price index varies across countries. Governments in less-developed countries sample fewer products and measure prices only in the capital city. Whereas hundreds of items are sampled to determine the U.S. consumer price index, as few as 30 might be sampled in some developing countries.

Inflation and Interest Rates

No discussion of inflation would be complete without some mention of the interest rate. Interest is the dollar amount paid by borrowers to lenders. Lenders must be rewarded for forgoing present consumption, and borrowers are willing to pay a premium to spend now. The interest rate is the amount paid per year as a percentage of the amount borrowed. For example, an interest rate of 5 percent means $5 per year on a $100 loan. The greater the interest rate, other things

constant, the greater the reward for lending money. The amount of money people are willing to lend, called *loanable funds,* increases as the interest rate rises, other things constant. The supply curve for loanable funds therefore slopes upward, as indicated by curve S in Exhibit 10 on the next page.

These funds are demanded by households, firms, and governments to finance homes, buildings, machinery, college, and other major purchases. The lower the interest rate, other things constant, the cheaper the cost of borrowing. So the quantity of loanable funds demanded increases as the interest rate decreases, other things constant. That is, the interest rate and the quantity of loanable funds demanded are inversely related. The demand curve therefore slopes downward, as indicated by curve D in Exhibit 10. The downward-sloping demand curve and the upward-sloping supply curve intersect to yield the equilibrium nominal rate of interest, i.

interest
the dollar amount paid by borrowers to lenders

interest rate
interest per year as a percentage of the amount loaned

Exhibit 9

Inflation Rates in Major Economies Have Trended Lower over the Past Quarter Century

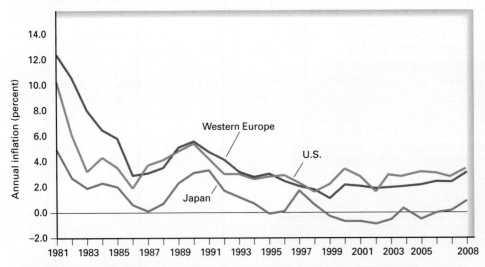

SOURCE: Developed from CPI inflation reported in *OECD Economic Outlook* 81 (*May 2007). Figures for Western Europe are the averages for France, Germany, Italy, and the United Kingdom. For the latest data, go to http://www.bls.gov/fls/home.htm.

The nominal interest rate measures interest in terms of the current dollars paid. The nominal rate is the one that appears on the loan agreement; it is the rate discussed in the news media and is often of political significance. The real interest rate equals the nominal rate minus the inflation rate:

$$\text{Real interest rate} = \text{Nominal interest rate} - \text{Inflation rate}$$

For example, if the nominal interest rate is 5 percent and the inflation rate is 3 percent, the real interest rate is 2 percent. With no inflation, the nominal rate and the real rate would be identical. But with inflation, the nominal rate exceeds the real rate. If inflation is unexpectedly high—higher, for example, than the nominal rate—then the real interest rate would be negative. In this case, the nominal interest earned for lending money would not even cover the loss in spending power caused by inflation. Lenders would lose purchasing power. This is why lenders and borrowers are concerned more about the real rate than the nominal rate. The real interest rate, however, is known only after the fact— that is, only after inflation actually occurs.

Because the future is uncertain, lenders and bor-

nominal interest rate
the interest rate expressed in dollars of current value (that is, not adjusted for inflation) as a percentage of the amount loaned; the interest rate specified on the loan agreement

real interest rate
the interest rate expressed in dollars of constant purchasing power as a percentage of the amount loaned; the nominal interest rate minus the inflation rate

rowers must form expectations about inflation, and they base their willingness to lend and borrow on these expectations. The higher the *expected* inflation, the higher the nominal rate of interest that lenders require and that borrowers are willing to pay. Lenders and borrowers base their decisions on the *expected* real interest rate, which equals the nominal rate minus the expected inflation rate.

Although the discussion has implied that there is only one market rate of interest, there are many rates. Rates differ depending on such factors as the duration of the loan, the tax treatment of the interest, and the risk that the loan will not be repaid.

Why Is Inflation Unpopular?

Whenever the price level increases, spending must increase just to buy the same amount of goods and services. If you think of inflation only in terms of spending, you consider only the problem of paying those higher prices. But if you think of inflation in terms of the higher money income that results, you see that higher prices mean higher receipts for resource suppliers, including higher wages for work-

Exhibit 10

The Market for Loanable Funds

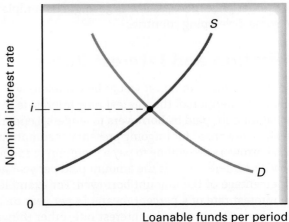

$$\text{Real interest rate} = \text{Nominal interest rate} - \text{Inflation rate}$$

ers. When viewed from the income side, inflation is not so bad.

If every higher price is received by some resource supplier, why are people so troubled by inflation? People view their higher incomes as well-deserved rewards for their labor, but they see inflation as a penalty that unjustly robs them of purchasing power. Most people do not stop to realize that unless their labor productivity increases, higher wages *must* result in higher prices. Prices and wages are simply two sides of the same coin. To the extent that nominal wages on average keep up with inflation, workers retain their purchasing power.

Presidents Ford and Carter could not control inflation and were turned out of office. Inflation slowed significantly during President Reagan's first term, and he won reelection easily, even though the unemployment rate was higher during his first term than during President Carter's tenure. During the 1988 election, George H. W. Bush won in part by reminding voters what inflation was in 1980, the last time a Democrat was president. But he lost his bid at reelection in part because inflation spiked to 6.0 percent in 1990, the highest in nearly a decade. Inflation remained under 3.0 percent during President Clinton's first term, and he was reelected easily. In the elections of 2000, 2004, and 2008, inflation was low enough not to be an issue in those presidential elections.

Although inflation affects everyone to some extent, it hits hardest those whose incomes are fixed in nominal terms. For example, pensions are often fixed amounts and are eroded by inflation. And retirees who rely on fixed nominal interest income also see their incomes shrunk by inflation. But the benefits paid by the largest pension program, Social Security, are adjusted annually for changes in the CPI. Thus, Social Security recipients get a cost-of-living adjustment, or a COLA. For example, Social Security benefits for 2009 increased 5.8 percent to keep up with changes in the cost of living as measured by the CPI.

In summary: Anticipated inflation is less of a problem than unanticipated inflation. *Unanticipated inflation arbitrarily redistributes income and wealth from one group to another, reduces the ability to make long-term plans, and forces people to focus more on money and prices.* The more unpredictable inflation becomes, the harder it is to negotiate long-term contracts. Productivity suffers because people must spend more time coping with inflation, leaving less time for production.

Final Word

This chapter has focused on unemployment and inflation. Although we have discussed them separately, they are related in ways that will unfold in later chapters. Politicians sometimes add the unemployment rate to the inflation rate to come up with what they refer to as the "misery index." In 1980, for example, an unemployment rate of 7.1 percent combined with a CPI increase of 13.6 percent to yield a misery index of 20.7—a number that helps explain why President Carter was not reelected. By 1984 the misery index had dropped to 11.8, and by 1988 to 9.6; Republicans retained the White House in both elections. In 1992, the index climbed slightly to 10.4 percent, spelling trouble for President George H. W. Bush. And in 1996, the index fell back to 8.4 percent, helping

COLA
cost-of-living adjustment; an increase in a transfer payment or wage that is tied to the increase in the price level

President Clinton's reelection. During the election of 2000, the misery index was down to 7.7, which should have helped Al Gore, the candidate of the incumbent party. But during the campaign, Gore distanced himself from President Clinton and thus was not able to capitalize on the strong economy. In the 2004 election the misery index remained about the same as in 2000, which helps explains why challenger John Kerry had difficulty making much of an issue of the economy. And a misery index of 10.4 the month before the 2008 election helped defeat the incumbent party and put Barack Obama in office.

© CHRISTOPHER ZACHAROW/STOCK ILLUSTRATION SOURCE/GETTY IMAGES

Households interviewed by the Bureau of Labor Statistics each month > **60,000**

Average U.S. inflation rate since World War II > **3.8%**

U.S. unemployment rate during worst years of the Great Depression > **25%**

6 < Months of unemployment benefits usually paid by the federal government

$280 < Average weekly unemployment check in 2008

Misery index in 1980 > **20.7**

Misery index the month before the 2008 election > **10.4**

Speak Up!

ECON was built on a simple principle: to create a new teaching and learning solution that reflects the way today's faculty teach and the way you learn.

Through conversations, focus groups, surveys, and interviews, we collected data that drove the creation of the current version of *ECON* that you are using today. But it doesn't stop there -- in order to make *ECON* an even better learning experience, we'd like you to SPEAK UP and tell us how *ECON* worked for you. What did you like about it? What would you change? Are there additional ideas you have that would help us build a better product for next semester's principles of economics students?

At **4ltrpress.cengage.com/econ** you'll find all of the resources you need to succeed in principles of economics -- **printable flash cards, interactive quizzes, videos** and more!

Speak Up! Go to **4ltrpress.cengage.com/econ**.

[Faculty, check out **4ltrpress.cengage.com/econ** to see what students think about this new learning solution!]

Learning Outcomes

LO **1** Explain the role of consumption   LO **2** Discuss gross private domestic investment   LO **3** Analyze the effects of government purchases of goods and services   LO **4** Explain how net exports affect aggregate expenditure   LO **5** Examine aggregate spending as a whole

9

Aggregate Expenditure

"How would your spending change if your summer job paid more?"

When driving through a neighborhood new to you, how can you figure out the income of the residents? How would your spending change if your summer job paid more? What's the most predictable and useful relationship in macroeconomics? Why are consumer confidence and business confidence in the economy so important? Answers to these and other questions are addressed in this chapter, which focuses on the makeup of aggregate expenditure. Consumption is the most important, accounting for about two-thirds of all spending. But in this short chapter, we also examine investment, government purchases, and net exports. We discuss how each relates to income in the economy. Let's see where this leads.

LO¹ Consumption

What if a college friend invites you home for the weekend? On your first visit, you would get some idea of the family's standard of living. Is their house a mansion, a dump, or in between? Do they drive a new BMW or take the bus? The simple fact is that consumption tends to reflect income. Although some people can temporarily live beyond their means and others still have the first nickel they ever earned, in general, consumption depends on income. *The positive and stable relationship between consumption and income, both for the household and for the economy as a whole, is the main point of this chapter.*

A key decision in the circular-flow model developed two chapters back was how much households spent and how much they saved. Consumption depends primarily on income. Although this relationship seems obvious, the link between consumption and income is fundamental to understanding how the economy works. Let's look at this link in the U.S. economy over time.

Topics discussed in Chapter 9 include:

- Consumption and income
- Marginal propensities to consume and to save
- Changes in consumption and in saving
- Investment
- Government purchases
- Net exports
- Composition of spending

Exhibit 1

Disposable Income, Consumption, and Saving in the United States

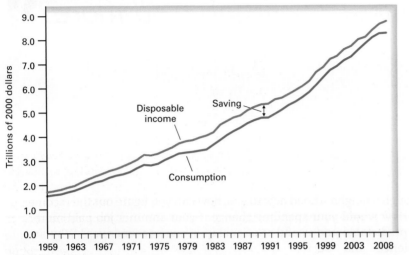

SOURCE: Based on estimates from the Bureau of Economic Analysis, U.S. Department of Commerce. For the latest data, go to http://bea.gov/.

disposable income and consumption. For example, the combination for 1985, identified by the red point, shows that when disposable income (measured along the horizontal axis) was $4.6 trillion, consumption (measured along the vertical axis) was $4.1 trillion.

As you can see, there is a clear and direct relationship between consumption and disposable income, a relationship that should come as no surprise after Exhibit 1. You need little imagination to see that by connecting the dots in Exhibit 2, you could trace a line relating consumption to income. This relationship has special significance in macroeconomics.

A First Look at Consumption and Income

Exhibit 1 shows consumer spending, or consumption, in the United States since 1959 as the red line and *disposable income* as the blue line. Disposable income, remember, is the income actually available for consumption and saving. Data have been adjusted for inflation so that dollars are of constant purchasing power—in this case, 2000 dollars. Notice that consumer spending and disposable income move together over time. Both increased nearly every year, and the relationship between the two appears relatively stable. Specifically, consumer spending has averaged about 90 percent of disposable income. Disposable income minus consumption equals saving. In Exhibit 1, saving is measured by the vertical distance between the two lines. Saving has averaged about 10 percent of disposable income, but in recent years saving has been squeezed as consumption claimed a larger percentage of disposable income—about 94 percent in 2008. Exhibit 1 reflects the flow each year of disposable income, consumption, and saving.

Another way to graph the relationship between consumption and income over time is shown in Exhibit 2, where consumption is measured along the

consumption function
the relationship in the economy between consumption and income, other things constant

vertical axis and disposable income along the horizontal axis. Notice that each axis measures the same units: trillions of 2000 dollars. Each year is depicted by a point that reflects two flow values:

The Consumption Function

After examining the link between consumption and income, we found it to be quite stable. Based on their disposable income, households decide how much to consume and how much to save. So consumption depends on disposable income. *Consumption is the dependent variable and disposable income, the independent variable.* Because consumption depends on income, we say that consumption is a *function* of income. Exhibit 3 presents for the economy a hypothetical consumption function, which shows that consump-

Exhibit 2

U.S. Consumption Depends on Disposable Income

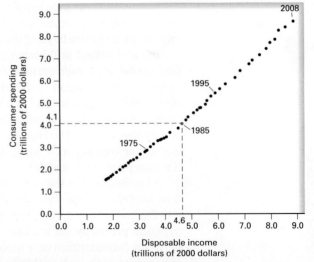

SOURCE: Based on estimates from the Bureau of Economic Analysis, U.S. Department of Commerce. For the latest data, go to http://bea.gov.

Exhibit 3

The Consumption Function

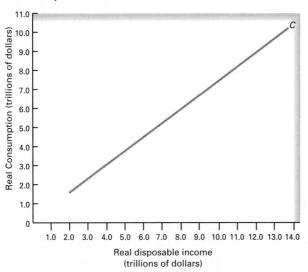

tion increases with disposable income, assuming that other determinants of consumption remain constant. Again, both consumption and disposable income are in real terms, or in inflation-adjusted dollars. Notice that this hypothetical consumption function reflects the historical relationship between consumption and income shown in Exhibit 2.

Marginal Propensities to Consume and to Save

$$MPC + MPS = 1$$

In Chapter 1, you learned that economic analysis focuses on activity at the margin. For example, what happens to consumption if income changes by a certain amount? Suppose U.S. households receive another billion dollars in disposable income. Some is spent on consumption, and the rest is saved. The fraction of the additional income that is spent is called the marginal propensity to consume. More precisely, the **marginal propensity to consume**, or MPC, equals the change in consumption divided by the change in income. Likewise, the fraction of that additional income that is saved is called the marginal propensity to save. More precisely, the **marginal propensity to save**, or MPS, equals the change in saving divided by the change in income.

For example, if U.S. income increases from $14.0 trillion to $14.5 trillion, consumption increases by $0.4 trillion and saving by $0.1 trillion. The marginal propensity to consume equals the change in consumption divided by the change in income. In this case, the change in consumption is $0.4 trillion and the change in income is $0.5 trillion, so the marginal propensity to consume is 0.4/0.5, or 4/5. Income not spent is saved. Saving increases by $0.1 trillion as a result of the $0.5 trillion increase in income, so the marginal propensity to save equals 0.1/0.5, or 1/5. Because disposable income is either spent or saved, the marginal propensity to consume plus the marginal propensity to save must sum to 1. In our example, 4/5 + 1/5 = 1. We can say more generally that MPC + MPS = 1.

MPC, MPS, and the Slope of the Consumption and Saving Functions

The slope of a straight line is the vertical distance between any two points divided by the horizontal distance between those same two points. Consider, for example, the slope

marginal propensity to consume (MPC) the fraction of a change in income that is spent on consumption; the change in consumption divided by the change in income that caused it

marginal propensity to save (MPS) the fraction of a change in income that is saved; the change in saving divided by the change in income that caused it

Exhibit 4

Marginal Propensities to Consume and to Save

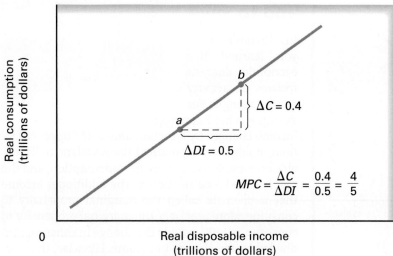

(a) Consumption function

$$MPC = \frac{\Delta C}{\Delta DI} = \frac{0.4}{0.5} = \frac{4}{5}$$

$\Delta C = 0.4$
$\Delta DI = 0.5$

Real consumption (trillions of dollars)

Real disposable income (trillions of dollars)

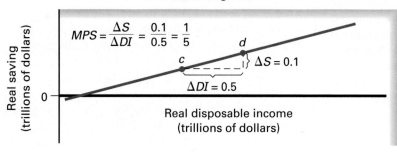

(b) Saving function

$$MPS = \frac{\Delta S}{\Delta DI} = \frac{0.1}{0.5} = \frac{1}{5}$$

$\Delta S = 0.1$
$\Delta DI = 0.5$

Real saving (trillions of dollars)

Real disposable income (trillions of dollars)

function is a straight line, though it need not be.

Panel (b) of Exhibit 4 presents the saving function, S, which relates savings to income. The slope between any two points on the saving function measures the change in saving divided by the change in income. For example, between points c and d in panel (b) of Exhibit 4, the change in income is $0.5 trillion and the resulting change in saving is $0.1 trillion. The slope between these two points therefore equals 0.1/0.5, or 1/5, which by definition equals the marginal propensity to save. Because the marginal propensity to consume and the marginal propensity to save are simply different sides of the same coin, from here on we focus more on the marginal propensity to consume.

Nonincome Determinants of Consumption

Along a given consumption function, consumer spending depends on disposable income in the economy, other things constant. Now let's see what factors are held constant and how changes in them could shift the entire consumption function up or down.

Net Wealth and Consumption

Given the economy's income, an important influence on consumption is each household's net wealth—that is, the value of all assets that each household

between points a and b on the consumption function in panel (a) of Exhibit 4, where Δ means "change in." The horizontal distance between these points shows the change in disposable income, denoted as ΔDI—in this case, $0.5 trillion. The vertical distance shows the change in consumption, denoted as ΔC—in this case, $0.4 trillion. The slope equals the vertical distance divided by the horizontal distance, or 0.4/0.5, which equals the marginal propensity to consume of 4/5.

Thus, the marginal propensity to consume is measured graphically by the slope of the consumption function. After all, the slope is nothing more than the increase in consumption divided by the increase in income. *Because the slope of any straight line is constant everywhere along the line, the MPC for any linear, or straight-line, consumption function is constant at all incomes.* We assume here for convenience that the consumption

saving function
the relationship between saving and income, other things constant

net wealth
the value of all assets minus liabilities

owns minus any liabilities, or debts. Net wealth is a *stock* variable. Consumption and income are *flow* variables. Your family's assets may include a home, furnishings, automobiles, bank accounts, corporate stocks and bonds, cash, and the value of any pensions. Your family's liabilities, or debts, may include a mortgage, car loans, student loans, credit card balances, and the like. According to the Federal Reserve, the net wealth of U.S. households totaled $51.5 trillion at the end of 2008, down 18% from a year earlier.[1]

Net wealth is assumed to be constant along a given consumption function. A decrease in net wealth would make consumers less inclined to spend and more inclined to save at each income level. To see why, suppose prices fall sharply on the stock market. Stockholders are poorer than they were, so they spend less. For example, stock market declines in 2008 cut into consumption, especially of luxury goods. Our original consumption function is depicted as line C in Exhibit 5. If net wealth declines, the consumption function shifts from C down to C', because households now spend less and save more at every income level.

Conversely, suppose stock prices increase sharply. This increase in net wealth increases the desire to spend. For example, stock prices surged in 1999, increasing stockholders' net wealth. Consumers spent 94 percent of disposable income that year compared with an average of about 90 percent during the first half of the 1990s. Purchases of homes and cars soared. Because of an increase in net wealth, the consumption function shifts from C up to C", reflecting households' desire to spend more at each income level. Research by the Federal Reserve indicates that consumer spending eventually rises or falls between

❖❖❖❖
1. S. Mitra Kalita, "Americans See 18% of Wealth Vanish," *Wall Street Journal,* 13 March 2009.

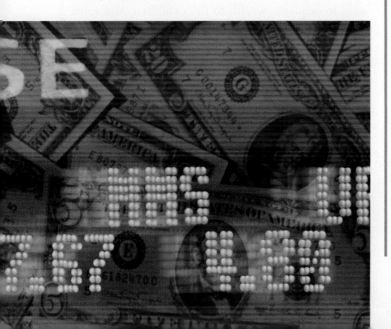

Exhibit 5

Shifts of the Consumption Function

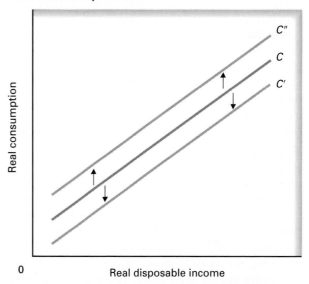

three to five cents for every dollar rise or fall in the value of stock market holdings.

Again, *it is a change in net wealth, not a change in disposable income, that shifts the consumption function. A change in disposable income, other things constant, means a movement along a given consumption function, not a shift of that function.* Be mindful of the difference between a movement along the consumption function, which results from a change in income, and a shift of the consumption function, which results from a change in one of the nonincome determinants of consumption, such as net wealth.

The Price Level

Another variable that affects the consumption function is the price level prevailing in the economy. As we have seen, net wealth is an important determinant of consumption. The greater the net wealth, other things constant, the greater the consumption at each income level. Some household wealth is held as money, such as cash and bank accounts. When the price level changes, so does the real value of cash and bank accounts.

For example, suppose your wealth consists of a $20,000 bank account. If the economy's price level increases by 5 percent, your bank account buys about 5 percent less in real terms. You feel poorer because you are poorer. To rebuild the real value of your money holdings to some desired comfort level, you decide to spend less and save more. *An increase in the price level reduces the purchasing power of money holdings, causing households to consume less and save more at each income level.* So the consumption function would shift downward from C to C', as shown in Exhibit 5.

Conversely, should the price level ever fall, as it did frequently before World War II and recently in Japan, Hong Kong, and Taiwan, the real value of money holdings increases. Households would be wealthier, so they would decide to consume more and save less at each income level. For example, if the price level declined by 5 percent, your $20,000 bank account would then buy about 5 percent more in real terms. A drop in the price level would shift the consumption function from C up to C". *At each income, a change in the price level influences consumption by affecting the real value of money holdings.*

The Interest Rate

Interest is the reward savers earn for deferring consumption and the cost borrowers pay for current spending power. When graphing the consumption function, we assume a given interest rate in the economy. If the interest rate increases, other things constant, savers or lenders are rewarded more, and borrowers are charged more. The higher the interest rate, the less is spent on those items typically purchased on credit, such as cars. Thus, at a higher interest rate, households save more, borrow less, and spend less. Greater saving at each income level means less consumption. Simply put, *a higher interest rate, other things constant, shifts the consumption function downward. Conversely, a lower interest rate, other things constant, shifts the consumption function upward.*

Expectations

Expectations influence economic behavior in a variety of ways. For example, suppose as a college senior you land a good job that starts after graduation. Your consumption probably jumps long before the job actually begins because you expect an increase in your income. You might buy a car, for example. On the other hand, a worker who gets a layoff notice to take effect at the end of the year likely reduces consumption immediately, well before the actual layoff. More generally, if people grow more concerned about their job security, they reduce consumption at each income level.

life-cycle model of consumption and saving young people borrow, middle-agers pay off debts and save, and older people draw down their savings; on average, net savings over a lifetime is usually little or nothing

A change in expectations about price levels or interest rates also affects consumption. For example, a change that leads householders to expect higher car prices or higher interest rates in the future prompts some to buy a new car now. On the other hand, a change leading householders to expect lower car prices or lower interest rates in the future causes some to defer a car purchase. Thus, expectations affect spending, and a change in expectations can shift the consumption function. This is why economic forecasters monitor consumer confidence so closely.

Keep in mind the distinction between *a movement along a given consumption function,* which results from a change in income, and a *shift of the consumption function,* which results from a change in one of the factors assumed to remain constant along the consumption function.

The Life-Cycle Hypothesis

Do people with high incomes save a larger fraction of their incomes than those with low incomes? Both theory and evidence suggest they do. The easier it is to make ends meet, the more income is left over for saving. Does it follow from this that richer economies save more than poorer ones—that economies save a larger fraction of total disposable income as they grow? You might think so, but evidence suggests that *the fraction of disposable income saved in an economy seems to stay constant as the economy grows.*

So how can it be that richer people save more than poorer people, yet richer countries do not necessarily save more than poorer ones? According to the **life-cycle model of consumption and saving,** young people tend to borrow to finance education and home purchases. In middle age, people pay off debts and save more. In old age, they draw down their savings, or dissave. Some still have substantial wealth at death, because they are not sure when death will occur and because some parents want to bequeath wealth to their children. And some people die in debt. But on average net savings over a per-

How would your spending change if you were expecting an increase in income?

Under normal circumstances, saving can be very beneficial to the economy. During a recession, however, increased saving can actually make things worse, starving an economy of growth when it needs it most.

During the third quarter of 2008, consumer spending fell in the United States for the first time in 17 years, and U.S. household debt declined for the first time since the Federal Reserve started tracking it in 1952. The debt trend has been led primarily by people below 35, who have been estimated to spend as much as $117 for every $100 of income. The 35- to 55-year-old age range is thought to have a negative saving rate almost as large. Only the over 55 age group, which traditionally has a high double-digit savings rate, has been able to keep the savings rate above zero until recently. In 2009, however, the savings rate is expected to rise to 3% to 5%, with some analysts even predicting as high as 10%.

SOURCE: Kelly Evans, "Hard-Hit Families Finally Start Saving, Aggravating Nation's Economic Woes," *Wall Street Journal,* 6 January 2009. Available at http://online.wsj.com/article/SB123120525879656021.html (accessed 16 January 2009).

son's lifetime tend to be small. The life-cycle hypothesis suggests that the saving rate for an economy as a whole depends on, among other things, the relative number of savers and dissavers in the population.[2]

Other factors that influence the saving rate across countries include the tax treatment of interest, the convenience and reliability of saving institutions, national customs, and the relative cost of a household's major purchase—housing.

We turn next to the second component of aggregate expenditure—investment. Keep in mind that our initial goal is to understand the relationship between total spending and income.

LO² Investment

The second component of aggregate expenditure is investment, or, more precisely, *gross private domestic investment.*

Investment consists of spending on:

1. new factories, office buildings, malls, and new equipment, such as computers;
2. new housing; and
3. net increases to inventories.

Investment here does **NOT** include financial assets such as stocks or bonds.

2. Martin Browning and Thomas Crossley, "The Life-Cycle Model of Consumption and Saving," *Journal of Economic Perspective* 15 (Summer 2001): 3–22.

Firms invest now in the expectation of a future return. Because the return is in the future, a would-be investor must estimate how much a particular investment will yield this year, next year, the year after, and in all years during the productive life of the investment. *Firms buy new capital goods only if they expect this investment to yield a higher return than other possible uses of their funds.*

The Demand for Investment

To understand the investment decision, let's consider a simple example. The operators of the Hacker Haven Golf Course are thinking about buying some solar-powered golf carts. The model under consideration, called the Weekend Warrior, sells for $2,000, requires no maintenance or operating expenses, and is expected to last indefinitely. *The expected rate of return of each cart equals the expected annual earnings divided by the cart's purchase price.* The first cart is expected to generate rental income of $400 per year. This income, divided by the cost of the cart, yields an expected rate of return on the investment of $400/$2,000, or 20 percent per year. Additional carts will be used less. A second is expected to generate $300 per year in rental income, yielding a rate of return of $300/$2,000, or 15 percent; a third cart, $200 per year, or 10 percent; and a fourth cart, $100 per year, or 5 percent. They don't expect a fifth cart to get rented at all, so it has a zero expected rate of return.

Should the operators of Hacker Haven invest in golf carts, and if so, how many? Suppose they plan to borrow the money to buy the carts. The number of carts they purchase depends on the interest rate they must pay for borrowing. If the market interest rate exceeds 20 percent, the cost of borrowing would exceed the expected rate of return for even the first cart, so the club would buy no carts. What if the operators have enough cash on hand to buy the carts? Suppose the market interest rate also reflects what club owners could earn on savings. If the interest rate earned on savings exceeded 20 percent, course owners would earn more saving their money than buying golf carts. *The market interest rate is the opportunity cost of investing in capital.*

What if the market rate is 8 percent per year? At that rate, the first three carts, all with expected returns exceeding 8 percent, would each yield more than the market rate. A fourth cart would lose money, because its expected rate of return is only 5 percent. Exhibit 6 on the next page measures the nominal interest rate along the vertical axis and the amount invested in golf carts along the horizontal axis. The step-like relationship shows the expected rate of return earned on

Exhibit 6

Rates of Return on Golf Carts and the Opportunity Cost of Funds

The chart shows nominal interest rate (percent) on the vertical axis ranging from 5 to 25, and investment on the horizontal axis from $2,000 to $10,000. The step-like "Expected rate of return" curve declines from 20 percent, and a horizontal "Market rate of interest" line is at 8 percent.

additional dollars invested in golf carts. This relationship also indicates the amount invested in golf carts at each interest rate, so you can view this step-like relationship as Hacker Haven's demand curve for this type of investment. For example, the first cart costs $2,000 and earns a rate of return of 20 percent. A firm should reject any investment with an expected rate of return that falls below the market rate of interest.

The horizontal line at 8 percent indicates the market interest rate, which is Hacker Haven's opportunity cost of investing. The course operators' objective is to choose an investment strategy that maximizes profit. Profit is maximized when $6,000 is invested in the carts—that is, when three carts are purchased. The expected return from a fourth cart is 5 percent, which is below the opportunity cost of funds. Therefore, investing in four or more carts would reduce total profit.

From Micro to Macro

So far, we have looked at the investment decision for a single golf course, but there are over 13,000 golf courses in the United States. The industry demand for golf carts shows the relationship between the amount all courses invest and the expected rate of return. Like the step-like relationship in Exhibit 6, the investment demand curve for the golf industry slopes downward.

Let's move beyond golf carts and consider the investment decisions of all industries: publishing, software, farming, fast food, sporting goods, and thousands more. Individual industries have downward-sloping demand curves for investment. More is invested when the opportunity cost of borrowing is lower, other things constant. A downward-sloping investment demand curve for the entire economy can be derived, with some qualifications, from a horizontal summation of all industries' downward-sloping investment demand curves. The economy's *investment demand curve* is depicted as D in Exhibit 7, which shows the inverse relationship between the quantity of investment demanded and the market interest rate, other things—including business expectations—held constant. For example, in Exhibit 7, when the market rate is 8 percent, the quantity of investment demanded is $1.0 trillion. If the interest rate rises to 10 percent, investment declines to $0.9 trillion, and if the rate falls to 6 percent, investment increases to $1.1 trillion. Assumed constant along the investment demand curve are business expectations about the economy. If firms grow more optimistic about profit prospects, the demand for investment increases, so the investment demand curve shifts to the right.

Exhibit 7

Investment Demand Curve for the Economy

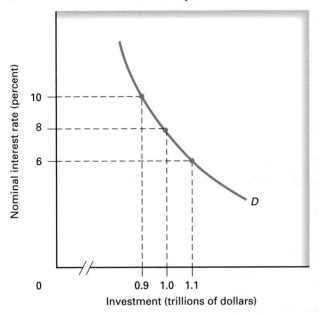

Investment in a particular year shows little relation to income that year. *Investment depends more on interest rates and on business expectations than on the prevailing income level.* One reason investment is less related to income is that some investments, such as a new power plant, take years to build. And investment, once in place, is expected to last for years, sometimes decades. The investment decision is thus said to be *forward looking,* based more on expected profit than on current income.

So how does the amount firms plan to invest relate to income? The simplest investment function assumes that *investment is unrelated to disposable income. Investment is assumed to be autonomous* with respect to disposable income. For example, suppose that, given current business expectations and an interest rate of 8 percent, firms plan to invest $1.0 trillion per year, regardless of the economy's income level. Exhibit 8 measures disposable income on the horizontal axis and investment on the vertical axis. Investment of $1.0 trillion is shown by the flat investment function, *I.* As you can see, along *I,* investment does not vary even though disposable income does.

Investment and Disposable Income

To integrate the discussion of investment with our earlier analysis of consumption, we need to know if and how investment varies with income in the economy. Whereas we were able to present evidence relating consumption to income over time, the link between investment and income is weaker.

Nonincome Determinants of Investment

The investment function isolates the relationship between income in the economy and *investment—* the amount firms plan to invest, other things constant. We have already introduced two determinants that are assumed to be constant: the interest rate and business expectations. Now let's look at how changes in each factor would affect investment.

Exhibit 8

Investment Function

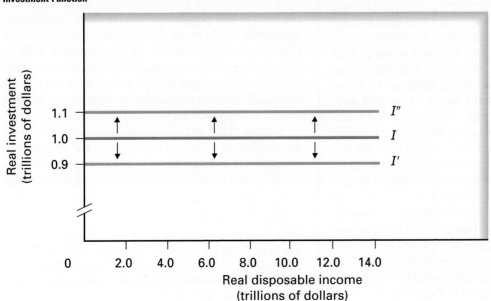

investment function
the relationship between the amount businesses plan to invest and the economy's income, other things constant

autonomous
a term that means "independent"; for example, autonomous investment is independent of income

Market Interest Rate

Exhibit 7 shows that if the interest rate is 8 percent, investment is $1.0 trillion. This investment is also shown as I in Exhibit 8. If the interest rate increases because of, say, a change in the nation's monetary policy (as happened in 2004), the cost of borrowing increases, which increases the opportunity cost of investment. For example, if the interest rate increases from 8 percent to 10 percent, investment drops from $1.0 trillion to $0.9 trillion. This decrease is reflected in Exhibit 8 by a shift of the investment function from I down to I'. Conversely, if the interest rate decreases because of, say, a change in the nation's monetary policy (as happened in 2001, 2002, 2007, and 2008), the cost of borrowing decreases, which reduces the opportunity cost of investment. For example, a drop in the rate of interest from 8 percent to 6 percent, other things remaining constant, reduces the cost of borrowing and increases investment from $1.0 trillion to $1.1 trillion, as reflected by the upward shift of the investment function from I to I''. Notice that the shifts in Exhibit 8 match interest rate movements along the investment demand curve in Exhibit 7.

Business Expectations

Investment depends primarily on business expectations, or on what Keynes called the "animal spirits" of business. Suppose investment initially is $1.0 trillion, as depicted by I in Exhibit 8. If firms now become more pessimistic about their profit prospects, perhaps expecting the worst, as in 2008 during the global financial crisis, investment decreases at every income, as reflected in Exhibit 8 by a shift of the investment function from I down to I'. On the other hand, if profit expectations become rosier, as they did in 2004, firms become more willing to invest, thereby increasing the investment function from I up to I''. *Examples of factors that could affect business expectations, and thus investment plans, include wars, technological change, tax changes, and destabilizing events such as terrorist attacks or the meltdown of financial institutions.* Changes in business expectations would shift the investment demand curve in Exhibit 7.

Exhibit 9

Annual Percentage Change in U.S. Real GDP, Consumption, and Investment

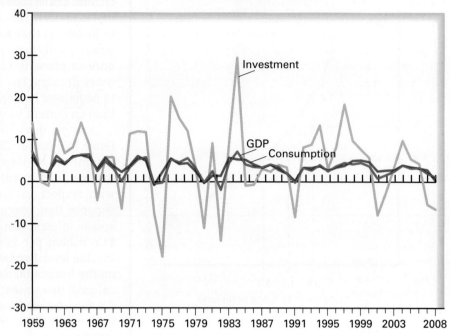

SOURCE: Bureau of Economic Analysis, U.S. Department of Commerce. For the latest data, go to http://bea.gov/.

Variability of Investment and Consumption

We already know that consumption makes up about two-thirds of GDP and that investment varies from year to year, but averaged about one-sixth of GDP over the last decade.[3] Now let's compare the year-to-year variability of consumption and investment. Exhibit 9 shows the annual percentage changes in GDP, consumption, and investment, all measured in real terms. Two points are obvious. First, investment fluctuates much more than either consumption or GDP. Second, fluctuations in consumption and in GDP appear to be entwined, although consumption varies a bit less than GDP. Consumption varies less than GDP because consumption depends on disposable income, which varies less than GDP.

During years of falling GDP since 1959, the average decline in GDP was 0.6 percent, but investment dropped an average of 11.7 percent. Consumption actually increased 0.6 percent. So *while consump-*

<hr>

3. Sources for the section on variability are: *Economic Report of the President,* February 2009; U.S. Department of Commerce, *Survey of Current Business* 89, various months for 2009; and *OECD Economic Outlook* 84 (November 2008). For data and articles about economic aggregates, go to the Bureau of Economic Analysis site at http://bea.gov/.

tion is *the largest spending component, investment varies much more than consumption and accounts for nearly all the year-to-year variability in real GDP.* Note that GDP does not always fall during years in which a recession occurs. That's because the economy is not necessarily in recession for the entire year. To account for these fluctuations, economic forecasters pay special attention to business expectations and investment plans.

LO³ Government

The third component of aggregate expenditure is government purchases of goods and services.

Government Purchase Function

The government purchase function relates government purchases to income in the economy, other things constant. Decisions about government purchases are largely under the control of public officials, such as the decision to build an interstate highway, boost military spending, or hire more teachers. These spending decisions do not depend directly on income in the economy. We therefore assume that *government purchases* are autonomous, or independent of income. Such a function would relate to income as a flat line similar to the investment function shown in Exhibit 8. An increase in government purchases would result in an upward shift of the government purchase function. And a decrease in government purchases would result in a downward shift of the government purchase function.

Transfer Payments

As noted earlier, government purchases represent only one of the two components of government outlays; the other is *transfer payments,* such as for Social Security, welfare benefits, and unemployment insurance. Transfer payments, which make up about a third of government outlays, are outright grants from governments to households and are thus not considered part of aggregate expenditure. Transfer payments vary inversely with income—as income increases, transfer payments decline.

Net Taxes

To fund government outlays, governments impose taxes. Taxes vary directly with income; as income increases, so do taxes. *Net taxes* equal taxes minus transfers. Because taxes tend to increase with income but transfers tend to decrease with income, for simplicity, let's assume that net taxes do not vary with income. Thus, we assume for now that *net taxes* are *autonomous,* or independent of income.

Net taxes affect aggregate spending indirectly by changing disposable income, which in turn changes consumption. We saw from the discussion of circular flow that by subtracting net taxes, we transform real GDP into *disposable income.* Disposable income is take-home pay—the income households can spend or save. We examine the impact of net taxes in the next few chapters.

LO⁴ Net Exports

The rest of the world affects aggregate expenditure through imports and exports and has a growing influence on the U.S. economy. The United States, with only one-twentieth of the world's population, accounts for about one-sixth of the world's imports and one-ninth of the world's exports.

<< Federal, state, and local governments buy thousands of goods and services, ranging from weapon systems, to traffic lights, to education. During the last decade, government purchases in the United States accounted for slightly less than one-fifth of GDP, most of that by state and local governments.

government purchase function
the relationship between government purchases and the economy's income, other things constant

© IMAGE SOURCE/JUPITERIMAGES / © HISHAM IBRAHIM/PHOTODISC/GETTY IMAGES

Net Exports and Income

How do imports and exports relate to the economy's income? When incomes rise, Americans spend more on all normal goods, including imports. Higher incomes lead to more spending on Persian rugs, French wine, Korean DVD players, German cars, Chinese toys, European vacations, African safaris, and thousands of other foreign goods and services.

How do U.S. exports relate to the economy's income? U.S. exports depend on the income of foreigners, not on U.S. income. U.S. disposable income does not affect Europe's purchases of U.S. DVDs or Africa's purchases of U.S. grain. The net export function shows the relationship between net exports and U.S. income, other things constant. Because our exports are insensitive to U.S. income but our imports tend to increase with income, *net exports*, which equal the value of exports minus the value of imports, tend to decline as U.S. incomes increase. For simplicity, we assume now that net exports are *autonomous*, or independent of income.

If exports exceed imports, net exports are positive; if imports exceed exports, net exports are negative; and if exports equal imports, net exports are zero. U.S. net exports have been negative nearly every year during the past three decades, so let's suppose net exports are autonomous and equal to −$0.4 trillion, or −$400 billion, as shown by the net export function X − M in Exhibit 10.

Nonincome Determinants of Net Exports

Factors assumed constant along the net export function include the U.S. price level, price levels in other countries, interest rates here and abroad, foreign income levels, and the exchange rate between the dollar and foreign currencies. Consider the effects of a change in one of these factors. Suppose the value of the

net export function the relationship between net exports and the economy's income, other things constant

Exhibit 10

Net Export Function

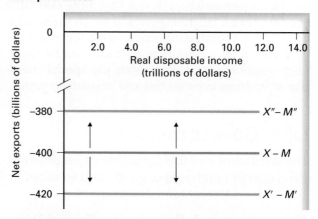

dollar increases relative to foreign currencies such as those of Asia, as happened in 1998. With the dollar worth more on world markets, foreign products become cheaper for Americans, and U.S. products become more costly for foreigners. A rise in the dollar's exchange value increases imports and decreases exports, thus reducing net exports, shown in Exhibit 10 by a parallel drop in the net export line from X − M down to X′ − M′, a decline from −$400 billion to −$420 billion.

A decline in the value of the dollar, as occurred in 2002 and 2003, has the opposite effect, increasing exports and decreasing imports. An increase in autonomous net exports is shown in our example by a parallel increase in the net export function, from X − M up to X″ − M″, reflecting an increase in autonomous net exports from −$400 billion to −$380 billion. A country sometimes tries to devalue its currency in an attempt to increase its net exports and thereby increase employment. The effect of changes in net exports on aggregate spending are taken up in the next chapter.

LO⁵ Composition of Aggregate Expenditure

Now that we have examined each component of aggregate spending, let's get a better idea of spending over time. Exhibit 11 shows the composition of spending in the United States since 1959. As you can see, consumption's share of GDP appears stable from year to year, but the long-term trend shows an increase from an average of 62 percent during the 1960s to 69 percent during the most recent decade.

© THOMAS MCCONVILLE/PHOTOGRAPHER'S CHOICE/GETTY IMAGES

Government purchases as a percent of GDP declined from 22 percent during the 1960s to an average of 18 percent in the last decade due primarily to decreases in defense spending.

© ROGER L. WOLLENBERG/UPI/LANDOV

Investment fluctuates more year to year but with no long-term trend up or down.

Government purchases declined from an average of 22 percent of GDP during the 1960s to an average of 18 percent during the last decade, due primarily to decreases in defense spending since the 1960s. Remember, government purchases do not include transfer payments, which have grown more. Net exports averaged 0.3 percent of GDP in the 1960s but were negative nearly every year since then, averaging a minus 4 percent of GDP during the last decade. Negative net exports means that the sum of consumption, investment, and government purchases exceeds GDP, the amount produced in the U.S. economy. Americans are spending more than they make, and they are covering the difference by borrowing from abroad. U.S. spending exceeds U.S. GDP by the amount shown as negative net exports. Because the spending components must sum to GDP, *negative* net exports are expressed in Exhibit 11 by the red portion of spending that exceeds 100 percent of GDP.

In summary: During the last four decades, consumption's share of total spending increased and government purchases decreased. Investment's share bounced around and net exports' share turned negative, meaning that imports exceeded exports.

Exhibit 11

U.S. Spending Components as Percentages of GDP Since 1959

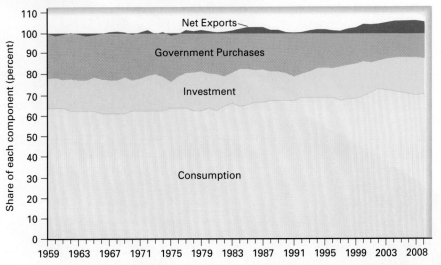

SOURCE: Computed from annual estimates from the U.S. Dept. of Commerce. For the latest data, go to http://bea.gov/.

Final Word

This chapter has focused on the relationship between spending and income. We considered the four components of aggregate expenditure: consumption, investment, government purchases, and net exports. Consumption increases with income. Investment relates more to interest rates and business expectations than it does to income. Government purchases also tend to be autonomous, or independent of income. And net exports are assumed, for now, to be affected more by such factors as the exchange rate than by U.S. income.

CHAPTER 10

Learning Outcomes

LO¹ Explain how total spending in the economy changes with income

LO² Discuss how the simple spending multiplier accounts for changes in spending plans

LO³ Describe the aggregate demand curve

Aggregate Expenditure *and* Aggregate Demand

"How does a change in spending affect the economy?"

Now that we have considered consumption, investment, government purchases, and net exports, how do they combine to yield total spending in the economy? How is spending linked to income? How does a change in spending affect the economy? For example, did the grounding of all commercial airlines following the 9/11 attacks affect other sectors of the economy? Answers to these and other questions are covered in this chapter, which develops the aggregate demand curve.

Your economic success depends in part on the overall performance of the economy. When the economy grows, job opportunities expand, so your chances of finding a good job increase. When the economy contracts, job opportunities shrink, and so do your job prospects. Thus, you have a personal stake in the economy's success.

The previous chapter discussed how each spending component relates to income in the economy. In this chapter, these components add up to show how total spending, or aggregate expenditure, relates to income. We then see how a change in the economy's price level affects aggregate expenditure. All this is aimed at getting to the economy's aggregate demand curve. Aggregate supply will be developed in the next chapter. The effects of government spending and taxing will be explored in the chapter after that.

LO¹ Aggregate Expenditure and Income

In the previous chapter, the big idea was that consumption depends on income, a link that is the most stable in all of macroeconomics. In this section, we build on that connection to learn how total spending in the economy changes with income. If we try to confront the economy head-on, it soon becomes a bewildering maze, which is why we make progress by starting with simple models. We continue to assume, as we did in developing the circular-flow model, that there is no capital depreciation and no business saving. Thus, we can say that *each dollar of spending translates directly into a dollar of income*. Therefore, gross domestic product, or GDP, equals aggregate income.

> **Topics discussed in Chapter 10 include:**
>
> - Aggregate expenditure line
> - Real GDP demanded
> - Changes in aggregate expenditure
> - Simple spending multiplier
> - Changes in the price level
> - Aggregate demand curve

<< Confront the economy head-on
and it becomes a bewildering maze.

The Components of Aggregate Expenditure

When income increases, consumption increases. As noted in the previous chapter, the marginal propensity to consume indicates the fraction of each additional dollar of income that is spent on consumption. For example, if the marginal propensity to consume is 4/5, spending increases by $4 for every $5 increase in income. The consumption function shows how much consumption increases with income.

For simplicity we continue to assume that the other spending components do not vary with income; thus, investment, government purchases, and net exports are autonomous, or independent of the economy's income level. Specifically, we'll assume that investment and government purchases each equals $1.0 trillion for the year in question and net exports are a negative $0.4 trillion. We'll also assume that government purchases equal net taxes, so the government budget is balanced. We first want to see how a balanced budget works before we consider the effects of budget deficits or surpluses.

If we stack up the consumption function, the investment function, the government purchase function, and the net export function, we get the aggregate expenditure line presented in Exhibit 1 as $C + I + G + (X - M)$. Real GDP is measured on the horizontal axis, and aggregate expenditure is measured on the vertical axis. The aggregate expenditure line shows how much households, firms, governments, and the rest of the world plan to spend on U.S. output at each level of real GDP, or real income. Again, the only spending component that varies with real GDP is consumption. Since only consumption varies with income, the slope of the aggregate expenditure line equals the marginal propensity to consume.

aggregate expenditure line a relationship tracing, for a given price level, spending at each level of income, or real GDP; the total of $C + I + G + (X - M)$ at each level of income, or real GDP

income-expenditure model a relationship that shows how much people plan to spend at each income level; this model identifies, for a given price level, where the amount people plan to spend equals the amount produced in the economy

Real GDP Demanded

Let's begin developing the aggregate demand curve by asking how much aggregate output would be demanded at a given price level. By finding the quantity demanded at a given price level, we'll end up identifying a single point on the aggregate demand curve. We begin by considering the relationship between aggregate spending in the economy and aggregate income. To get us started, suppose the price level in the economy is 130, or 30 percent higher than in the base year price level. We want to find out how much is spent at various levels of real income, or real GDP. By real GDP, we mean GDP measured in terms of real goods and services produced. Exhibit 1 combines the relationships introduced in the previous chapter—consumption, saving, investment, government purchases, net taxes, and net exports. Although the entries are hypothetical, they bear some relation to levels observed in the U.S. economy. For example, GDP in the U.S. economy is about $14 trillion a year.

Real GDP, measured along the horizontal axis in Exhibit 1, can be viewed in two ways—as the value of *aggregate output* and as the *aggregate income* generated by that output. Because real GDP, or aggregate income, is measured on the horizontal axis and aggregate expenditure is measured on the vertical axis, this graph is often called the income-expenditure model. To gain perspective on the relationship between income and expenditure, we use a handy analytical tool: the 45-degree ray from the origin. The special feature of this line is that any point along it is the same distance from each axis. Thus, the 45-degree line identifies all points where spending equals real GDP. *Aggregate output demanded at a given price level occurs where aggregate expenditure, measured along the vertical axis, equals real GDP, measured along the horizontal axis.* In Exhibit 1, this occurs at point *e*, where the aggregate expenditure line intersects the 45-degree line. At point *e*, the amount people spend equals the amount produced. We conclude that, at the given price level of 130, the quantity of real GDP demanded equals $14.0 trillion.

Exhibit 1

Deriving the Real GDP Demanded for a Given Price Level

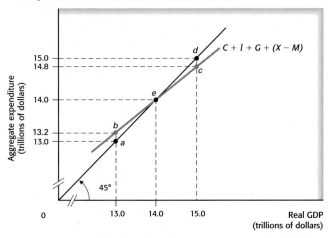

What If Spending Exceeds Real GDP?

To find the real GDP demanded at the given price level, consider what happens if real GDP is initially less than $14.0 trillion. As you can see from Exhibit 1, when real GDP is less than $14.0 trillion, the aggregate expenditure line is above the 45-degree line, indicating that spending exceeds the amount produced (give this a little thought). For example, if real GDP is $13.0 trillion, spending is $13.2 trillion, as indicated by point *b* on the aggregate expenditure line, so spending exceeds output by $0.2 trillion. When the amount people want to spend exceeds the amount produced, something has to give. Ordinarily what gives is the price, but remember that we are seeking the real GDP demanded for a given price level, so the price level is assumed to remain constant, at least for now. What gives in this model are *inventories*. Unplanned reductions in inventories cover the $0.2 trillion shortfall in output. Because firms can't draw down inventories indefinitely, *inventory reductions* prompt firms to produce more output. That increases employment and consumer income, leading to more spending. As long as spending exceeds output, firms increase production to make up the difference. This process of more output, more income, and more spending continues until spending equals real GDP, an equality achieved at point *e* in Exhibit 1.

When output reaches $14.0 trillion, spending exactly matches output, so no unintended inventory adjustments occur. More importantly, when output reaches $14.0 trillion, the amount people want to spend equals the amount produced and equals the total income generated by that production. Earlier we assumed a price level of 130. Therefore, $14.0 trillion is the real GDP demanded at that price level.

What If Real GDP Exceeds Spending?

To reinforce the logic of the model, consider what happens when the amount produced exceeds the amount people want to spend. Notice in Exhibit 1 that, to the right of point *e*, spending falls short of production. For example, suppose real GDP is $15.0 trillion. Spending, as indicated by point *c* on the aggregate expenditure line, is $0.2 trillion less than real GDP, indicated by point *d* on the 45-degree line. Because real GDP exceeds spending, unsold goods accumulate. This swells inventories by $0.2 trillion more than firms planned. Rather than allow inventories to pile up indefinitely, firms cut production, which reduces employment and income. As an example of such behavior, a recent news account read, "General Motors will idle two assembly plants in a move to trim inventories in the wake of slowing sales." *Unplanned inventory buildups* cause firms to cut production until the amount they produce equals

{ **Retail Sales, Retail Inventories, and Unemployment** }

In June 2008, U.S. retail sales posted a gain just under 0.1%, which was then followed by six consecutive months of declines. The table below compares the percentage change in retail sales, in retail inventories, and the unemployment rate by month. When inventories increase while sales decrease, as in July and September, this means production (real GDP) is exceeding spending. Despite the leveling out of retail sales seen in January and February of 2009, the unemployment rate still increased. Unemployment usually trails sales increases, as firms wait until revenues increase before they start hiring again.

	% Change in Retail Sales	% Change in Retail Inventories	Unemployment Rate
July 08	−0.6	1.3	5.7
August 08	−0.7	−0.7	6.1
September 08	−1.6	0.2	6.1
October 08	−3.4	−0.2	6.6
November 08	−2.4	−1.8	6.8
December 08	−3.1	−1.5	7.2
January 09	1.8	−1.7	7.6
February 09	−0.1	−1.2	8.1

SOURCES: Kelly Evans, "Consumers' Spending Appears to Be Stabilizing," *Wall Street Journal*, 13 March, 2009. Available at http://online.wsj.com/article/SB123686041609006861.html (accessed 13 March, 2009); Unemployment rates based on estimates by the U.S. Bureau of Labor Statistics, available at http://www.bls.gov/bls/unemployment.htm; Retail sales data based on estimates by the U.S. Census Bureau, *Time Series Data: Monthly Retail Sales & Seasonal Factors 1992–2009,* available at http://www.census.gov/marts/www/timeseries.html; Adjusted inventories data based on estimates by the U.S. Census Bureau, available at http://www.census.gov/mrts/www/mrts.html.

aggregate spending, which occurs, again, where real GDP is $14.0 trillion. Given the price level, real GDP demanded is found where the amount people spend equals the amount produced. *For a given price level, there is only one point along the aggregate expenditure line at which spending equals real GDP.*

We have now discussed the forces that determine real GDP demanded for a given price level. In the next section, we examine changes that can affect spending plans.

LO² The Simple Spending Multiplier

In the previous section, we used the aggregate expenditure line to find real GDP demanded for a particular price level. In this section, we continue to assume that the price level remains unchanged as we trace the effects of other changes that could affect spending plans. Like a stone thrown into a still pond, the effect of any change in spending ripples through the economy, generating changes in aggregate output that exceed the initial change in spending.

An Increase in Spending

We begin at point *e* in Exhibit 2, where spending equals real GDP at $14.0 trillion. Now let's consider the effect of an increase in one of the components of spending. Suppose that firms become more optimistic about profit prospects and decide to increase their investment from $1.0 trillion to $1.1 trillion per year at each level of real GDP. Exhibit 2 reflects this change by an upward shift of the aggregate expenditure line by $0.1 trillion, from $C + I + G + (X - M)$ to $C + I' + G + (X - M)$.

What happens to real GDP demanded? An instinctive response is to say that real GDP demanded increases by $0.1 trillion as well. In this case, however, instinct is a poor guide. As you can see, the new spending line intersects the 45-degree line at point *e'*, where real GDP demanded is $14.5 trillion. How can a $0.1 trillion increase in spending increase real GDP demanded by $0.5 trillion? What's going on?

The idea of the circular flow is central to an understanding of the adjustment process. As noted earlier, real GDP can be thought of as both the value of production and the income arising from that production. Recall that production yields income, which generates spending. We can think of each trip around the circular flow as a "round" of income and spending.

Round One

An upward shift of the aggregate expenditure line means that, at the initial real GDP of $14.0 trillion, spending now exceeds output by $0.1 trillion, or $100 billion. This is shown in Exhibit 2 as the distance between point e and point f. Initially, firms match this increased investment spending by an unplanned reduction in inventories. John Deere, for example, satisfies the increased demand for tractors by drawing down tractor inventories. But reduced inventories prompt firms to expand production by $100 billion, as shown by the movement from point *f* to point *g*. This generates $100 billion more income. The movement from *e* to *g* shows the first round in the multiplier process. The income-generating process does not stop there, however, because those who earn this additional income spend some of it and save the rest, leading to round two of spending and income.

Round Two

Given a marginal propensity to consume of 0.8, those who earn the additional $100 billion will spend $80 billion on toasters, backpacks, gasoline, restaurant meals, and thousands of other goods and services. They save the other $20 billion. The move from point *g* to point *h* in Exhibit 2 shows this $80 billion spending increase. Firms respond by increasing their output by $80 billion, shown by the movement from point *h* to point *i*. Thus, the $100 billion in new income increases real GDP by $80 billion during round two.

Round Three and Beyond

We know that four-fifths of the $80 billion earned during round two will get spent during round three

Exhibit 2

Effect of an Increase in Investment on Real GDP Demanded

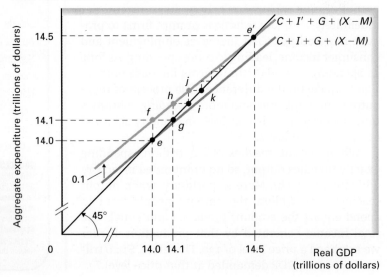

PART 2 Fundamentals of Macroeconomics

Exhibit 3

Tracking the Rounds of Spending Following a $100 Billion Increase in Investment (billions of dollars)

Round	New Spending This Round	Cumulative New Spending	New Saving This Round	Cumulative New Saving
1	100	100	—	—
2	80	180	20	20
3	64	244	16	36
⋮	⋮	⋮	⋮	⋮
10	13.4	446.3	3.35	86.6
⋮	⋮	⋮	⋮	⋮
∞	0	500	0	100

and one-fifth will get saved. Thus, $64 billion is spent during round three on still more goods and services, as reflected by the movement from point i to point j. The remaining $16 billion gets saved. The added spending causes firms to increase output by $64 billion, as shown by the movement from point j to point k. Round three's additional production generated $64 billion more income, which sets up subsequent rounds of spending, output, and income. *As long as spending exceeds output, production increases, thereby creating more income, which generates still more spending.*

Exhibit 3 summarizes the multiplier process, showing the first three rounds, round 10, and the cumulative effect of all rounds. The new spending each round is shown in the second column and the accumulation of new spending appears in the third column. For example, the new spending as of the third round totals $244 billion—the sum of the first three rounds of spending ($100 billion + $80 billion + $64 billion). The new saving from each round appears in the fourth column, and the accumulation of new saving appears in the final column.

Using the Simple Spending Multiplier

In our model, consumers spend four-fifths of the change in income each round, with each fresh round equal to the change in spending from the previous round times the marginal propensity to consume, or the MPC. This goes on round after round, leaving less and less to fuel more spending and income. At some point, the new rounds of income and spending become so small that they disappear and the process stops. The question is, by how much does total spending increase? We can get some idea of the total by working through a limited number of rounds. For example, as shown in Exhibit 3, total new spending after 10 rounds sums to $446.3 billion. But calculating the exact total for all rounds would require us to work through an infinite number of rounds—an impossible task.

Fortunately, we can borrow a shortcut from mathematicians, who have shown that the sum of an infinite number of rounds, each of which is MPC times the previous round, equals $1/(1 - MPC)$ times the initial change. Translated, the cumulative spending change equals $1/(1 - MPC)$, which, in our example, was 1/0.2, or 5, times the initial increase in spending, which was $100 billion. In short, the increase in investment eventually boosts real GDP demanded by 5 times $100 billion, or $500 billion.

The **simple spending multiplier** is the factor by which real GDP demanded changes for a given initial change in spending.

$$\text{Simple spending multiplier} = \frac{1}{1 - MPC}$$

The simple spending multiplier provides a shortcut to the total change in real GDP demanded. This multiplier depends on the MPC. The larger the MPC, the larger the simple spending multiplier. That makes sense—the more people spend from each dollar of fresh income, the more total

simple spending multiplier the ratio of a change in real GDP demanded to the initial change in spending that brought it about; the numerical value of the simple spending multiplier is $1/(1 - MPC)$; called "simple" because only consumption varies with income

© BRIAN HAGIWARA/BRAND X PICTURES/JUPITERIMAGES

spending increases. For example, if the MPC was 0.9 instead of 0.8, the denominator of the multiplier formula would equal 1.0 minus 0.9, or 0.1, so the multiplier would be 1/0.1, or 10. With an MPC of 0.9, a $0.1 trillion investment increase would boost real GDP demanded by $1.0 trillion. On the other hand, an MPC of 0.75 would yield a denominator of 0.25 and a multiplier of 4. So a $0.1 trillion investment increase would raise real GDP demanded by $0.4 trillion.

Let's return to Exhibit 2. The $0.1 trillion rise in autonomous investment raised real GDP demanded from $14.0 trillion to $14.5 trillion. Note that real GDP demanded would have increased by the same amount if consumers had decided to spend $0.1 trillion more at each income level—that is, if the consumption function, rather than the investment function, had shifted up by $0.1 trillion. Real GDP demanded likewise would have increased if government purchases or net exports increased $0.1 trillion. *The change in aggregate output demanded depends on how much the aggregate expenditure line shifts, not on which spending component causes the shift.*

In our example, investment increased by $0.1 trillion in the year in question. *If this greater investment is not sustained the following year, real GDP demanded would fall back.* For example, if investment returns to its initial level, other things constant, real GDP demanded would return to $14.0 trillion. Finally, recall from the previous chapter that the MPC and the MPS sum to 1, so 1 minus the MPC equals the MPS. With this information, we can define the simple spending multiplier in terms of the MPS as follows:

$$\text{Simple spending multiplier} = \frac{1}{1 - \text{MPC}} = \frac{1}{\text{MPS}}$$

We can see that the smaller the MPS, the less leaks from the spending stream as saving. Because less is saved, more gets spent each round, so the spending multiplier is greater. Incidentally, this spending multiplier is called "simple" because consumption is the only spending component that varies with income.

LO³ The Aggregate Demand Curve

In this chapter, we have used the aggregate expenditure line to find real GDP demanded *for a given price level.* But what happens to spending plans if the price level changes? As you will see, for

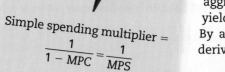

Simple spending multiplier = $\dfrac{1}{1 - \text{MPC}} = \dfrac{1}{\text{MPS}}$

each price level, there is a unique aggregate expenditure line, which yields a unique real GDP demanded. By altering the price level, we can derive the aggregate demand curve.

A Higher Price Level

What is the effect of a higher price level on spending and, in turn, on real GDP demanded? Recall that consumers hold many assets that are fixed in dollar terms, such as currency and bank accounts. A higher price level decreases the real value of these money holdings. This cuts consumer wealth, making people less willing to spend at each income level. For reasons that will be explained in a later chapter, a higher price level also tends to increase the market interest rate, and a higher interest rate reduces investment. Finally, a higher U.S. price level, other things constant, means that foreign goods become cheaper for U.S. consumers, and U.S. goods become more expensive abroad. So imports rise and exports fall, decreasing net exports. Therefore, *a higher price level reduces consumption, investment, and net exports, which all reduce aggregate spending.* This decrease in spending reduces real GDP demanded.

Exhibit 4 represents two different ways of expressing the effects of a change in the price level on real GDP demanded. Panel (a) offers the income-expenditure model, and panel (b) offers the aggregate demand curve, showing the inverse relationship between the price level and real GDP demanded. The idea is to find the real GDP demanded for a given price level in panel (a) and then show that price-quantity combination as a point on the aggregate demand curve in panel (b). The two panels measure real GDP on the horizontal axes. At the initial price level of 130 in panel (a), the aggregate expenditure line, now denoted simply as AE, intersects the 45-degree line at point *e* to yield real GDP demanded of $14.0 trillion. Panel (b) shows more directly the link between real GDP demanded and the price level. As you can see, when the price level is 130, real GDP demanded is $14.0 trillion. This combination is identified by point *e* on the aggregate demand curve.

What if the price level increases from 130 to, say, 140? As you've just learned, an increase in the price level reduces consumption, investment, and net exports. This reduction in spending is reflected in panel (a) by a downward shift of the aggregate expenditure line from AE to AE'. As a result, real GDP demanded declines from $14.0 trillion to $13.5 trillion. Panel (b) shows that an increase in the price

Exhibit 4

The Income-Expenditure Approach and the Aggregate Demand Curve

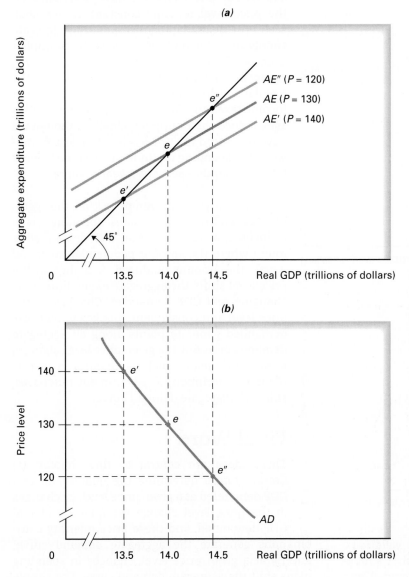

(a)

(b)

and imports decrease. *Because of a decline in the price level, consumption, investment, and net exports increase at each real GDP.*

Refer again to Exhibit 4 and suppose the price level declines from 130 to, say, 120. This increases spending at each income level, as reflected by an upward shift of the spending line from AE to AE″ in panel (a). An increase in spending increases real GDP demanded from $14.0 trillion to $14.5 trillion, as indicated by the intersection of the top aggregate expenditure line with the 45-degree line at point e″. This same price decrease can be viewed more directly in panel (b). As you can see, when the price level decreases to 120, real GDP demanded increases to $14.5 trillion.

The aggregate expenditure line and the aggregate demand curve present real output from different perspectives. The aggregate expenditure line shows, for a given price level, how spending relates to income, or the amount produced in the economy. Real GDP demanded is found where spending equals income, or the amount produced. The aggregate demand curve shows, for various price levels, the quantities of real GDP demanded.

The Multiplier and Shifts in Aggregate Demand

Now that you have some idea how changes in the price level shift the aggregate expenditure line to generate the aggregate demand curve, let's reverse course and return to the situation where the price level is assumed to remain constant. What we want to do now is trace through the effects of a shift of a spending component on aggregate demand, assuming the price level does not change. For example, suppose that a jump in business confidence spurs a $0.1 trillion increase in investment at each real GDP level. Each panel of Exhibit 5 shows a different way of expressing the effects of an increase in spending on real GDP demanded, assuming the price level remains unchanged. Panel (a) presents the income-expenditure model and panel (b), the aggregate demand model. Again, the two panels measure real GDP on the horizontal axes. At a price level of 130 in panel (a), the aggregate expenditure line, $C + I + G + (X - M)$,

level from 130 to 140 decreases real GDP demanded from $14.0 trillion to $13.5 trillion, as reflected by the movement from point *e* to point *e′*.

A Lower Price Level

The opposite occurs if the price level falls. At a lower price level, the value of bank accounts, currency, and other money holdings increases. Consumers on average are wealthier and thus spend more at each real GDP. A lower price level also tends to decrease the market interest rate, which increases investment. Finally, a lower U.S. price level, other things constant, makes U.S. products cheaper abroad and foreign products more expensive here, so exports increase

Exhibit 5

**A Shift of the Aggregate Expenditure Line
That Shifts the Aggregate Demand Curve**

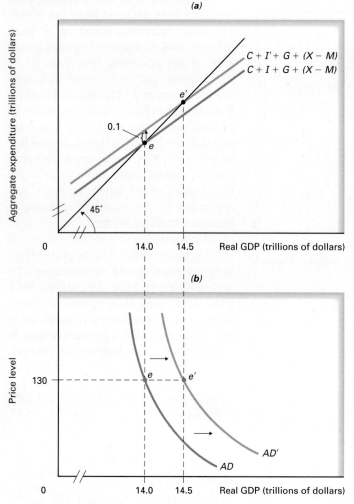

(a)

(b)

Our discussion of the simple spending multiplier exaggerates the actual effect we might expect. For one thing, we have assumed that the price level remains constant. As we shall see in the next chapter, incorporating aggregate supply into the analysis reduces the multiplier because of the resulting price change. Moreover, as income increases, there are leakages from the circular flow in addition to saving, such as higher income taxes and additional imports; these leakages reduce the multiplier. Finally, although we have presented the process in a timeless framework, the spending multiplier takes time to work through rounds—perhaps a year or more.

In summary: For a given price level, the aggregate expenditure line relates spending plans to income, or real GDP. Real GDP demanded is found where the amount people plan to spend equals the amount produced. A change in the price level shifts the aggregate expenditure line, changing real GDP demanded. Changes in the price level and consequent changes in real GDP demanded generate points along an aggregate demand curve. But at a given price level, changes in spending plans, such as changes in investment, consumption, or government purchases, shift the aggregate demand curve.

Final Word

Three ideas are central to this chapter: (1) Certain forces determine the quantity of real GDP demanded at a given price level; (2) changes in the price level change the quantity of real GDP demanded, and these price-quantity combinations generate the aggregate demand curve; and (3) at a given price level, changes in spending plans shift the aggregate demand curve. The simple multiplier provides a crude but exaggerated idea of how a change in spending plans affects real GDP demanded.

This chapter focused on aggregate spending. A simplifying assumption used throughout was that imports do not vary with income, but a more realistic model would also consider what happens when imports increase with income. Because spending on imports leak from the circular flow, this more realistic approach reduces the spending multiplier.

So far, we have derived real GDP demanded using intuition, examples, and graphs. With the various approaches, we find that for each price level there is a specific quantity of real GDP demanded, other things constant.

intersects the 45-degree line at point *e* to yield $14.0 trillion in real GDP demanded. Panel (b) shows more directly the link between real GDP demanded and the price level. As you can see, when the price level is 130, real GDP demanded is $14.0 trillion, identified as point *e* on the aggregate demand curve.

Exhibit 5 shows how a shift of the aggregate expenditure line relates to a shift of the aggregate demand curve, given a constant price level. In panel (a), a $0.1 trillion increase in investment shifts the aggregate expenditure line up by $0.1 trillion. Because of the multiplier effect, real GDP demanded climbs from $14.0 trillion to $14.5 trillion. Panel (b) shows the effect of the increase in spending on the aggregate demand curve, which shifts to the right, from *AD* to *AD'*. At the prevailing price level of 130, real GDP demanded increases from $14.0 trillion to $14.5 trillion as a result of the $0.1 trillion increase in investment.

Test coming up? Now what?

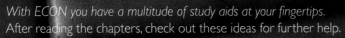

With ECON you have a multitude of study aids at your fingertips. After reading the chapters, check out these ideas for further help.

Chapter in Review cards include all learning outcomes, definitions, and summaries for each chapter.

Online printable flash cards give you three additional ways to check your comprehension of key concepts.

Other great ways to help you study include **interactive quizzes** and **videos**.

You can find it all at **4ltrpress.cengage.com/econ**.

11

Aggregate
Supply

Learning Outcomes

LO   Explain how aggregate supply
operates in the short run

LO   Discuss short-run aggregate supply
in relation to the long run

LO   Analyze shifts of the aggregate
supply curve

> ## "How might a long stretch of high unemployment reduce the economy's ability to produce in the future?"

What is your normal capacity for academic work, and when do you exceed that effort? If the economy is already operating at full employment, how can it produce more? What valuable piece of information do employers and workers lack when they negotiate wages? Why do employers and workers fail to agree on pay cuts that could save jobs? How might a long stretch of high unemployment reduce the economy's ability to produce in the future? These and other questions are answered in this chapter, which develops the aggregate supply curve in the short run and in the long run.

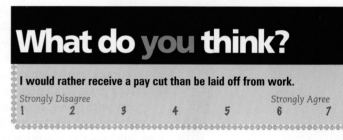

What do you think?

I would rather receive a pay cut than be laid off from work.

Strongly Disagree   Strongly Agree

1   2   3   4   5   6   7

Up to this point, we have focused on aggregate demand. We have not yet examined aggregate supply in any detail, a much debated topic. The debate involves the shape of the aggregate supply curve and the reasons for that shape. This chapter develops a single, coherent approach to aggregate supply. Although the focus continues to be on economic aggregates, you should keep in mind that aggregate supply reflects billions of production decisions made by millions of individual resource suppliers and firms in the economy. Each firm operates in its own little world, dealing with its own suppliers and customers and keeping a watchful eye on existing and potential competitors. Yet each firm recognizes that success also depends on the performance of the economy as a whole. The theory of aggregate supply described here must be consistent with both the microeconomic behavior of individual suppliers and the macroeconomic behavior of the economy.

Topics discussed in Chapter 11 include:

- Short-run aggregate supply
- Potential output
- Expected price level and long-term contracts
- Long-run aggregate supply
- Expansionary gap
- Contractionary gap
- Changes in aggregate supply

LO¹ Aggregate Supply in the Short Run

Aggregate supply is the relationship between the economy's price level and the amount of output firms are willing and able to supply, with other things constant. Assumed constant along a given aggregate supply curve are resource prices, the state of technology, and the set of formal and informal institutions that structure production incentives, such as the system of property rights, patent laws, tax systems, respect for the laws, and the customs and conventions of the marketplace. The greater the supply of resources, the better the technology, and the more effective the production incentives provided by the economic institutions, the greater the aggregate supply. Let's begin with the key resource—labor.

Labor and Aggregate Supply

Labor is the most important resource, accounting for about 70 percent of production cost. The supply of labor in an economy depends on the size and abilities of the adult population and preferences for work versus leisure. Along a given labor supply curve—that is, for a given adult population with given abilities and preferences for work and leisure—the quantity of labor supplied depends on the wage. The higher the wage, other things constant, the more labor supplied.

So far, so good. But things start getting complicated once we recognize that the purchasing power of any given nominal wage depends on the economy's price level. *The higher the price*

^^
Preferences for work and leisure influence the labor supply curve.

nominal wage
the wage measured in dollars of the year in question; the dollar amount on a paycheck

real wage
the wage measured in dollars of constant purchasing power; the wage measured in terms of the quantity of goods and services it buys

level, the less any given money wage purchases, so the less attractive that wage is to workers. Consider wages and the price level over time. Suppose a worker in 1970 was offered a job paying $20,000 per year. That salary may not impress you today, but its real purchasing power back then would exceed $80,000 in today's dollars. Because the price level matters, we must distinguish between the nominal wage, or money wage, which measures the wage in dollars of the year in question (such as 1970), and the real wage, which measures the wage in constant dollars—that is, dollars measured by the goods and services they buy. A higher real wage means workers can buy more goods and services.

Both workers and employers care more about the real wage than about the nominal wage. The problem is that nobody knows for sure how the price level will change during the life of the wage agreement, so labor contracts must be negotiated in terms of nominal wages, not real wages. Some resource prices, such as wages set by long-term contracts, remain in force for extended periods, often for two or three years. Workers as well as other resource suppliers must therefore negotiate based on the *expected* price level.

Even where there are no explicit labor contracts, there is often an implicit agreement that the wage, once negotiated, will not change for a while. For example, in many firms the standard practice is to revise wages annually. So wage agreements may be either *explicit* (based on a labor contract) or *implicit* (based on labor market practices). These explicit and implicit agreements are difficult to renegotiate while still in effect, even if the price level in the economy turns out to be higher or lower than expected.

Potential Output and the Natural Rate of Unemployment

Here's how resource owners and firms negotiate resource price agreements for a particular period, say, a year. Firms and resource suppliers expect a certain price level to prevail in the economy during the year. You could think of this as the *consensus* view for the upcoming year. Based on consensus expectations, firms and resource suppliers reach agreements on resource prices, such as wages. For example, firms and workers may expect the price level to increase 3 percent next year, so they agree on a nominal wage increase of 4 percent, which would increase the real wage by 1 percent. If these price-level expectations are realized, the agreed-on nominal wage translates into the expected real wage, so everyone is satisfied with the way things work out—after all, that's what they willingly negotiated. When the actual price

© BRAND X PICTURES/JUPITERIMAGES

level turns out as expected, we call the result the economy's potential output. Potential output is the amount produced when there are no surprises about the price level. So, at the agreed-on real wage, workers are supplying the quantity of labor they want and firms are hiring the quantity of labor they want. Both sides are content with the outcome.

We can think of potential output as the economy's maximum sustainable output, given the supply of resources, the state of technology, and the formal and informal production incentives offered by the rules of the game. Potential output is also referred to by other terms, including the *natural rate of output* and the *full-employment rate of output*.

The unemployment rate that occurs when the economy produces its potential GDP is called the natural rate of unemployment. That rate prevails when cyclical unemployment is zero. When the economy produces its potential output, the number of job openings equals the number of people unemployed for frictional, structural, and seasonal reasons. Widely accepted estimates of the natural rate of unemployment range from about 4 percent to about 6 percent of the labor force.

Potential output provides a reference point, an anchor, for the analysis in this chapter. *When the price level expectations of both workers and firms are fulfilled, the economy produces its potential output.* Complications arise, however, when the actual price level differs from expectations, as we'll see next.

Actual Price Level Is Higher Than Expected

As you know, each firm's goal is to maximize profit. Profit equals total revenue minus total cost. Suppose workers and firms reach a wage agreement. What if the economy's price level turns out to be higher than expected? What happens *in the short run* to real GDP supplied? The short run in macroeconomics is a period during which some resource prices remain fixed by contract. Does output in the short run exceed the economy's potential, fall short of that potential, or equal that potential?

Because the prices of many resources are fixed for the duration of contracts, firms welcome a higher than expected price level. After all, the selling prices of their products, on average, are higher than expected, while the costs of at least some of the resources they employ remain constant. *A price level that is higher than expected results in a higher profit per unit, so firms have a profit incentive in the short run to increase production beyond the economy's potential level.*

At first it might appear odd to talk about producing beyond the economy's potential, but remember

© HULTON ARCHIVE/GETTY IMAGES

that potential output means not zero unemployment but the natural rate of unemployment. Even in an economy producing its potential output, there is some unemployed labor and some unused production capacity. If you think of potential GDP as the economy's *normal capacity*, you get a better idea of how production can temporarily exceed that capacity. For example, during World War II, the United States pulled out all the stops to win the war. Factories operated around the clock. Overtime was common. The unemployment rate dropped below 2 percent—well under the natural rate. People worked longer and harder for the war effort than they normally would have.

Think about your own study habits. During most of the term, you display your normal capacity for

potential output
the economy's maximum sustainable output, given the supply of resources, technology, and rules of the game; the output level when there are no surprises about the price level

natural rate of unemployment
the unemployment rate when the economy produces its potential output

short run
in macroeconomics, a period during which some resource prices, especially those for labor, are fixed by explicit or implicit agreements

academic work. As the end of the term draws near, however, you may shift into high gear, finishing term papers, studying late into the night for final exams, and generally running yourself ragged trying to pull things together. During those final frenzied days of the term, you study beyond your normal capacity, beyond the schedule you follow on a regular or sustained basis. We often observe workers exceeding their normal capacity for short bursts: fireworks technicians around the Fourth of July, accountants during tax time, farmers during harvest time, and elected officials toward the end of a campaign or legislative session. Similarly, firms and their workers are able, *in the short run,* to push output beyond the economy's potential. But that higher rate of output is not normal and not sustainable.

Why Costs Rise When Output Exceeds Potential

The economy is flexible enough to expand output beyond potential GDP, but as output expands, the cost of additional output increases. Although many workers are bound by contracts, wage agreements may require overtime pay for extra hours or weekends. As the economy expands and the unemployment rate declines, additional workers are harder to find. Retirees, homemakers, and students may require extra pay to draw them into the labor force. If few additional workers are available or if workers require additional pay for overtime, the nominal cost of labor increases as output expands in the short run, even though most wages remain fixed by implicit or explicit agreements.

As production increases, the demand for nonlabor resources increases as well, so the prices of those resources in markets where prices are flexible—such as the market for oil—will increase, reflecting their greater scarcity. Also, as production increases, firms use their machines and trucks more intensively, so equipment wears out faster and is more likely to break down. Thus, the nominal cost per unit of output rises when production is pushed beyond the economy's potential output. But *because the prices of some resources are fixed by contracts, the price level rises faster than the per-unit production cost, so firms find it profitable to increase the quantity supplied.*

When the economy's actual price level exceeds the expected price level, the real value of an agreed-on nominal wage declines. We might ask why workers would be willing to increase the quantity of labor they supply when the price level is higher than expected. One answer is that labor agreements require workers to do so, at least until workers have a chance to renegotiate.

In summary: If the price level is higher than expected, firms have a profit incentive to increase the quantity of goods and services supplied. At higher rates of output, however, the per-unit cost of additional output increases. Firms expand output as long as the revenue from additional production exceeds the cost of that production.

An Actual Price Level Lower Than Expected

We have learned that if the price level is greater than expected, firms expand output in the short run, but as they do, the marginal cost of production increases. Now let's look at the effects of a price level that turns out to be lower than expected. Again, suppose that firms and resource suppliers have reached an agreement based on an expected price level. If the price level turns out to be lower than expected, firms find production less profitable. The prices firms receive for their output are on average lower than they expected, yet many of their production costs, such as nominal wages, do not fall.

Because production is less profitable when prices are lower than expected, firms reduce their quantity supplied, so the economy's output is below its potential. As a result, some workers are laid off, some work fewer hours, and unemployment exceeds the natural rate. Not only is less labor employed, but machines go unused, delivery trucks sit idle, and entire plants may shut down—for example, automakers sometimes halt production for weeks.

Just as some costs increase in the short run when output is pushed beyond the economy's potential, some costs decline when output falls below that potential. As resources become unemployed,

resource prices decline in markets where prices are flexible.

To *review*: If the economy's price level turns out to be higher than expected, firms maximize profit by increasing the quantity supplied beyond the economy's potential output. As output expands, the per-unit cost of additional production increases, but firms expand production as long as prices rise more than costs. If the price level turns out to be lower than expected, firms produce less than the economy's potential output because prices fall more than costs. All of this is a long way of saying that *there is a direct relationship in the short run between the actual price level and real GDP supplied.*

The Short-Run Aggregate Supply Curve

What we have been describing so far traces out the short-run aggregate supply (SRAS) curve, which shows the relationship between the actual price level and real GDP supplied, other things constant. Again, the short run in this context is the period during which some resource prices, especially those for labor, are fixed by implicit or explicit agreements. For simplicity, we can think of the short run as the duration of labor contracts, which are based on the expected price level.

Suppose the expected price level is 130. The short-run aggregate supply curve in Exhibit 1, $SRAS_{130}$, is based on that expected price level (hence the subscript 130). If the price level turns out as expected, producers supply the economy's *potential output*,

Exhibit 1

Short-Run Aggregate Supply Curve

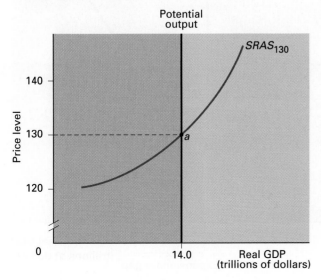

which in Exhibit 1 is $14.0 trillion. Although not shown in the exhibit, the aggregate demand curve would intersect the aggregate supply curve at point *a*. If the economy produces its potential output, unemployment is at the *natural rate*. Nobody is surprised, and all are content with the outcome. There is no tendency to move away from point *a* even if workers and firms could renegotiate wages.

In Exhibit 1, output levels that fall short of the economy's potential are shaded red, and output levels that exceed the economy's potential are shaded blue. The slope of the short-run aggregate supply curve depends on how sharply the marginal cost of production rises as real GDP expands. If costs increase modestly as output expands, the supply curve is relatively flat. If these costs increase sharply as output expands, the supply curve is relatively steep. Much of the controversy about the short-run aggregate supply curve involves its shape. Shapes range from flat to steep. Notice that the short-run aggregate supply curve becomes steeper as output increases, because some resources become scarcer and thus more costly as output increases.

LO² From the Short Run to the Long Run

This section begins with the price level exceeding expectations in the short run to see what happens in the long run. The long run is long enough that firms and resource suppliers can renegotiate all agreements based on knowledge of the actual price level. So *in the long run, there are no surprises about the price level.*

Closing an Expansionary Gap

Let's begin our look at the long-run adjustment in Exhibit 2 on the next page with an expected price level of 130. The short-run aggregate supply curve for that expected price level is $SRAS_{130}$. Given this short-run aggregate supply curve, the equilibrium price level and real GDP depend on the aggregate demand curve. The actual price level would equal the expected price level only if the aggregate demand curve intersects the aggregate supply curve at point *a*—that is, where the short-run quantity equals potential output. Point *a* reflects potential output of $14.0 trillion and a price level of 130, which is the expected price level.

> **short-run aggregate supply (SRAS) curve** a curve that shows a direct relationship between the actual price level and real GDP supplied in the short run, other things constant, including the expected price level

But what if aggregate demand turns out to be greater than expected, such as AD, which intersects the short-run aggregate supply curve SRAS$_{130}$ at point b. Point b is the short-run equilibrium, reflecting a price level of 135 and a real GDP of $14.2 trillion. The actual price level in the short run is higher than expected, and output exceeds the economy's potential of $14.0 trillion.

The amount by which short-run output exceeds the economy's potential is called an expansionary gap. In Exhibit 2, that gap is the short-run output of $14.2 trillion minus potential output of $14.0 trillion, or $0.2 trillion. When real GDP exceeds its potential, the unemployment rate is less than its natural rate. Employees are working overtime, machines are being pushed to their limits, and farmers are sandwiching extra crops between usual plantings. Remember that the nominal wage was negotiated based on an expected price level of 130; because the actual price level is higher, that nominal wage translates into a lower-than-expected real wage. As we will see, output exceeding the economy's potential creates inflationary pressure. *The more that short-run output exceeds the economy's potential, the larger the expansionary gap and the greater the upward pressure on the price level.*

What happens in the long run? The long run is a period during which firms and resource suppliers know about market conditions, particularly aggregate demand and the actual price level, and have the time to renegotiate resource payments based on that knowledge. Because the higher-than-expected price level cuts the real value of the nominal wage originally agreed to, workers will try to negotiate a higher nominal wage at their earliest opportunity. Workers and other resource suppliers negotiate higher nominal payments, raising production costs for firms, so the short-run aggregate supply curve shifts leftward, resulting in cost-push inflation. In the long run, the expansionary gap causes the short-run aggregate supply curve to shift leftward to SRAS$_{140}$, which results in an expected price level of 140. Notice that the short-run aggregate supply curve shifts until the equilibrium output equals the economy's potential output. *Actual output can exceed the economy's potential in the short run but not in the long run.*

As shown in Exhibit 2, the expansionary gap is closed by long-run market forces that shift the short-run aggregate supply curve from SRAS$_{130}$ left to SRAS$_{140}$. Whereas SRAS130 was based on resource contracts reflecting an expected price level of 130, SRAS$_{140}$ is based on resource contracts reflecting an expected price level of 140. At point c the expected price level and the actual price level are identical, so the economy is not only in short-run equilibrium but also is in long-run equilibrium. Consider all the equalities that hold at point c: (1) the expected price

short-run equilibrium
the price level and real GDP that result when the aggregate demand curve intersects the short-run aggregate supply curve

expansionary gap
the amount by which actual output in the short run exceeds the economy's potential output

long run
in macroeconomics, a period during which wage contracts and resource price agreements can be renegotiated; there are no surprises about the economy's actual price level

long-run equilibrium
the price level and real GDP that occurs when (1) the actual price level equals the expected price level, (2) real GDP supplied equals potential output, and (3) real GDP supplied equals real GDP demanded

Exhibit 2

Long-Run Adjustment When the Price Level Exceeds Expectations

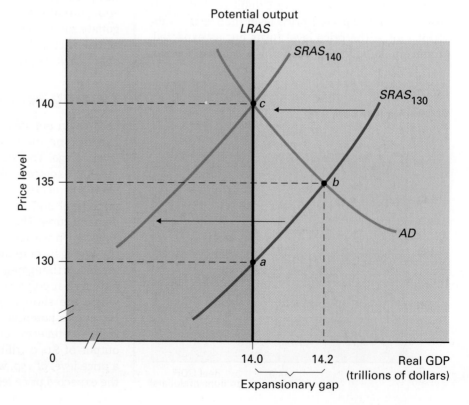

Production exceeding the economy's potential creates inflationary pressure, which causes the short-run aggregate supply curve to shift to the left, reducing output, increasing the price level, and closing the expansionary gap.

© CHRIS BATSON/ALAMY

level equals the actual price level; (2) the quantity supplied in the short run equals potential output, which also equals the quantity supplied in the long run; and (3) the quantity supplied equals the quantity demanded. Looked at another way, *long-run equilibrium occurs where the aggregate demand curve intersects the vertical line drawn at potential output.* Point c continues to be the equilibrium point unless there is some change in aggregate demand or in aggregate supply.

Note that the situation at point c is no different *in real terms* from what had been expected at point a. At both points, firms supply the economy's potential output of $14.0 trillion. The same amounts of labor and other resources are employed, and although the price level, the nominal wage, and other nominal resource payments are higher at point c, the real wage and the real return to other resources are the same as they would have been at point a. For example, suppose the nominal wage averaged $13 per hour when the expected price was 130. If the expected price level increased from 130 to 140, an increase of 7.7 percent, the nominal wage would also increase by that same percentage to an average of $14 per hour, leaving the real wage unchanged. With no change in real wages between points a and c, firms demand enough labor and workers supply enough labor to produce $14.0 trillion in real GDP.

Thus, if the price level turns out to be higher than expected, the short-run response is to increase quantity supplied. But production exceeding the economy's potential creates inflationary pressure. In the long run this causes the short-run aggregate supply curve to shift to the left, reducing output, increasing the price level, and closing the expansionary gap.

If an increase in the price level is predicted accurately year after year, firms and resource suppliers would build these expectations into their long-term agreements. The price level would move up each year by the expected amount, but the economy's output would remain at potential GDP, thereby skipping the round-trip beyond the economy's potential and back.

Closing a Contractionary Gap

Let's begin again with an expected price level of 130 as presented in Exhibit 3, where blue shading indicates output exceeding potential and red shading indicates output below potential. If the price level turned out as

Exhibit 3

Long-Run Adjustment When the Price Level Is Below Expectations

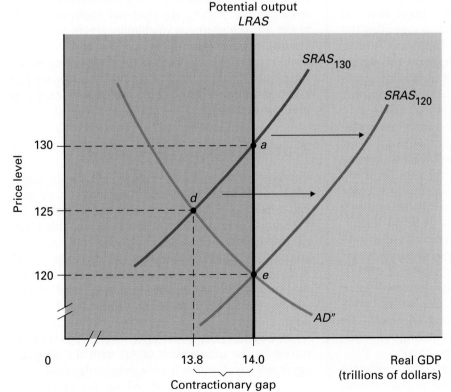

expected, the resulting equilibrium combination would occur at *a*, which would be both a short-run and a long-run equilibrium. Suppose this time that the aggregate demand curve intersects the short-run aggregate supply curve to the left of potential output, yielding a price level below that expected. The intersection of the aggregate demand curve, AD'', with $SRAS_{130}$ yields the short-run equilibrium at point *d*, where the price level is below expectations and production is less than the economy's potential. The amount by which actual output falls short of potential GDP is called a contractionary gap. In this case, the contractionary gap is $0.2 trillion, and unemployment exceeds its natural rate.

Because the price level is less than expected, the nominal wage, which was based on the expected price level, translates into a higher real wage in the short run. What happens in the long run? With the price level lower than expected, employers are no longer willing to pay as high a nominal wage. And with the unemployment rate higher than the natural rate, more workers are competing for jobs, putting downward pressure on the nominal wage. If the price level and the nominal wage are flexible enough, the combination of a lower price level and a pool of unemployed workers competing for jobs should make workers more willing to accept lower nominal wages next time wage agreements are negotiated.

If firms and workers negotiate lower nominal wages, the cost of production decreases, shifting the short-run aggregate supply curve rightward, leading to deflation and greater output. The short-run supply curve continues to shift rightward until it intersects the aggregate demand curve where the economy produces its potential output. This is reflected in Exhibit 3 by a rightward shift of the short-run aggregate supply curve from $SRAS_{130}$ to $SRAS_{120}$. *If the price level and nominal wage are flexible enough, the short-run aggregate supply curve shifts rightward until the economy produces its potential output.* The new short-run aggregate supply curve is based on an expected price level of 120. Because the expected price level and the actual price level are now identical, the economy is in long-run equilibrium at point *e*.

Although the nominal wage is lower at point *e* than

> If wages and prices are not flexible, they will not adjust quickly to a contractionary gap.

contractionary gap
the amount by which actual output in the short run falls short of the economy's potential output

long-run aggregate supply (LRAS) curve
a vertical line at the economy's potential output; aggregate supply when there are no surprises about the price level and all resource contracts can be renegotiated

that originally agreed to when the expected price level was 130, the real wage is the same at point *e* as it was at point *a*. Because the real wage is the same, the amount of labor that workers supply is the same and real output is the same. All that has changed between points *a* and *e* are nominal measures—the price level, the nominal wage, and other nominal resource prices.

We conclude that when incorrect expectations cause firms and resource suppliers to overestimate the actual price level, output in the short run falls short of the economy's potential. As long as wages and prices are flexible enough, however, firms and workers should be able to renegotiate wage agreements based on a lower expected price level. The negotiated drop in the nominal wage shifts the short-run aggregate supply curve to the right until the economy once again produces its potential output. If wages and prices are not flexible, they will not adjust quickly to a contractionary gap, so shifts of the short-run aggregate supply curve may be slow to move the economy to its potential output. The economy can therefore get stuck at an output and employment level below its potential.

We are now in a position to provide an additional interpretation of the red- and blue-shaded areas of our exhibits. *If a short-run equilibrium occurs in the blue-shaded area, that is, to the right of potential output, then market forces in the long run increase nominal resource costs, shifting the short-run aggregate supply to the left. If a short-run equilibrium occurs in the red-shaded area, then market forces in the long run reduce nominal resource costs, shifting the short-run aggregate supply curve to the right.* Closing an expansionary gap involves inflation and closing a contractionary gap involves deflation.

Tracing Potential Output

If wages and prices are flexible enough, the economy produces its potential output in the long run, as indicated in Exhibit 4 by the vertical line drawn at the economy's potential GDP of $14.0 trillion. This vertical line is called the economy's long-run aggregate supply (LRAS) curve. *The long-run aggregate supply curve depends on the supply of resources in the economy, the level of technology, and the production incentives provided by the formal and informal institutions of the economic system.*

In Exhibit 4, the initial price level of 130 is determined by the intersection of AD with the long-run aggregate supply curve. If the aggregate demand curve shifts out to AD', then in the long run, the equilibrium

Exhibit 4

Long-Run Aggregate Supply Curve

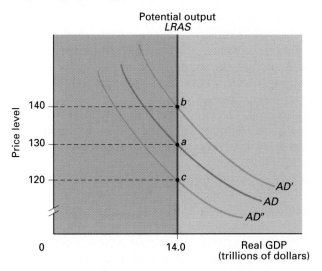

price level increases to 140 but equilibrium output remains at $14.0 trillion, the economy's potential GDP. Conversely, a decline in aggregate demand from *AD* to *AD″*, in the long run, leads only to a fall in the price level from 130 to 120, with no change in output. Note that these long-run movements are more like tendencies than smooth and timely adjustments. It may take a long time for resource prices to adjust, particularly when the economy faces a contractionary gap. But as long as wages and prices are flexible, the economy's potential GDP is consistent with any price level. *In the long run, equilibrium output equals long-run aggregate supply, which is also potential output. The equilibrium price level depends on the aggregate demand curve.*

Wage Flexibility and Employment

What evidence is there that a vertical line drawn at the economy's potential GDP depicts the long-run aggregate supply curve? Except during the Great Depression, unemployment over the last century has varied from year to year but typically has returned to what would be viewed as a natural rate of unemployment—again, estimates range from 4 percent to 6 percent.

An *expansionary* gap creates a labor shortage that eventually results in a higher nominal wage and a higher price level. But a *contractionary* gap does not necessarily generate enough downward pressure to lower the nominal wage. Studies indicate that nominal wages are slow to adjust to high unemployment. Nominal wages have declined in particular industries; during the 1980s, for example, nominal wages fell in airlines, steel, and trucking. But seldom have we observed actual declines in nominal wages across the

economy, especially since World War II. Nominal wages do not adjust downward as quickly or as substantially as they adjust upward, and the downward response that does occur tends to be slow and modest. Consequently, we say that nominal wages tend to be "sticky" in the downward direction. *Because nominal wages fall slowly, if at all, the supply-side adjustments needed to close a contractionary gap may take so long as to seem ineffective.* What, in fact, usually closes a contractionary gap is an increase in aggregate demand as the economy pulls out of its funk.

Although the nominal wage seldom falls, an actual decline in the nominal wage is not necessary to close a contractionary gap. All that's needed is a fall in the real wage. And the *real wage falls if the prices increase more than nominal wages.* For example, if the price level increases by 4 percent and the nominal wage increases by 3 percent, the real wage falls by 1 percent. If the real wage falls enough, firms demand enough additional labor to produce the economy's potential output.

Coordination Failure

When actual output falls short of potential output, the output gap is negative and the economy suffers a contractionary gap. As long as unemployment exceeds its natural rate, the economy suffers a contractionary gap.

Contractionary gaps can thus be viewed as resulting from a coordination failure, in which workers, who produce goods and services, and employers, who provide jobs, fail to reach an agreement that seems possible and that all would prefer. For more on coordination failure, wage flexibility, and output gaps, read the online case at 4ltrpress.cengage.com/econ.

To review: When the actual price level differs from the expected price level, output in the short run departs from the economy's potential. In the long run,

coordination failure
a situation in which workers and employers fail to achieve an outcome that all would prefer

however, market forces shift the short-run aggregate supply curve until the economy once again produces its potential output. Thus, surprises about the price level change real GDP in the short run but not in the long run. Shifts of the aggregate demand curve change the price level but do not affect potential output, or long-run aggregate supply.

LO³ Shifts of the Aggregate Supply Curve

In this section, we consider factors other than changes in the expected price level that may affect aggregate supply. We begin by distinguishing between long-term trends in aggregate supply and supply shocks, which are unexpected events that affect aggregate supply, sometimes only temporarily.

Aggregate Supply Increases

The economy's potential output is based on the willingness and ability of households to supply resources to firms, the level of technology, and the institutional underpinnings of the economic system. Any change in these factors could affect the economy's potential output. Changes in the economy's potential output over time were introduced in the earlier chapter that focused on U.S. productivity and growth. The supply of labor may change over time because of a change in the size, composition, or quality of the labor force or a change in preferences for labor versus leisure. For example, the U.S. labor force has more than doubled since 1948 as a result of population growth and a growing labor force participation rate, especially among women with children. At the same time, job training, education, and on-the-job experience increased the quality of labor. Increases in the quantity and the quality of the labor force have increased the economy's potential GDP, or long-run aggregate supply.

The quantity and quality of other resources also change over time. The capital stock—machines, buildings, and trucks—increases when gross investment exceeds capital depreciation. And the capital stock improves with technological breakthroughs. Even the quantity and quality of land can be increased—for example, by claiming land from the sea, as is done in the

supply shocks unexpected events that affect aggregate supply, sometimes only temporarily

beneficial supply shocks unexpected events that increase aggregate supply, sometimes only temporarily

Netherlands and Hong Kong, or by revitalizing soil that has lost its fertility. These increases in the quantity and quality of resources increase the economy's potential output.

Finally, institutional changes that define property rights more clearly or make contracts more enforceable, such as the introduction of clearer patent and copyright laws, will increase the incentives to undertake productive activity, thereby increasing potential output. *Changes in the labor force, in the quantity and quality of other resources, and in the institutional arrangements of the economic system tend to occur gradually.* Exhibit 5 depicts a gradual shift of the economy's potential output from $14.0 trillion to $14.5 trillion. The long-run aggregate supply curve shifts from *LRAS* out to *LRAS'*.

In contrast to the gradual, or long-run, changes that often occur in the supply of resources, *supply shocks* are unexpected events that change aggregate supply, sometimes only temporarily. Beneficial supply shocks increase aggregate supply; examples include (1) abundant harvests that increase the food supply, (2) discoveries of natural resources, such as oil in Alaska or the North Sea, (3) technological breakthroughs that allow firms to combine resources more efficiently, such as faster computers or the Internet, and (4) sudden changes in the economic system that promote more production, such as tax cuts that stimulate production incentives or new limits on frivolous product liability suits.

Exhibit 6 shows the effect of a beneficial supply shock from a technological breakthrough. The beneficial supply shock shown here shifts the short-run and long-run aggregate supply curves rightward. Along the aggregate demand curve, *AD*, the equilibrium combination of price and output moves from point *a*

Exhibit 5

Effect of a Gradual Increase in Resources on Aggregate Supply

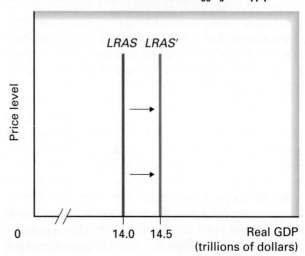

Reclaiming land from the sea increases that economy's potential output, or long-run aggregate supply.

© FRANS LEMMENS/PHOTOGRAPHER'S CHOICE/GETTY IMAGES

to point *b*. *For a given aggregate demand curve, the happy outcome of a beneficial supply shock is an increase in output and a decrease in the price level.* The new equilibrium at point *b* is a short-run and a long-run equilibrium in the sense that there is no tendency to move from that point as long as whatever caused the beneficial effect continues, and a technological discovery usually has a lasting effect. Likewise, substantial new oil discoveries usually benefit the economy for a long time. On the other hand, an unusually favorable growing

Exhibit 6

Effects of a Beneficial Supply Shock on Aggregate Supply

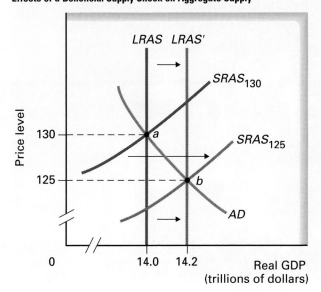

season won't last. When a normal growing season returns, the short-run and long-run aggregate supply curves return to their original equilibrium position—back to point *a* in Exhibit 6.

Decreases in Aggregate Supply

Adverse supply shocks are sudden, unexpected events that reduce aggregate supply, sometimes only temporarily. For example, a drought could reduce the supply of a variety of resources, such as food, building materials, and water-powered electricity. An overthrow of a government could destabilize the economy. Or terrorist attacks could shake the institutional underpinnings of the economy, as occurred in America, England, and Spain. Such attacks add to the cost of doing business—everything from airline screening to building security.

An adverse supply shock is depicted as a leftward shift of both the short-run and long-run aggregate supply curves, as shown in Exhibit 7 on the next page, moving the equilibrium combination from point *a* to point *c* and reducing potential output from $14.0 trillion to $13.8 trillion. As mentioned earlier, the combination of reduced output and a higher price level is often referred to as stagflation. The United States encountered stagflation during the 1970s, when the economy was rocked by a series of adverse supply shocks, such as crop failures around the globe and the oil price hikes by OPEC in 1974 and 1979. If the effect of the adverse supply shock is temporary, such as a poor growing season, the aggregate supply curve returns to its original position once things return to normal. But some economists question an economy's ability to bounce back. For example, for most of the 20th century, unemployment in Western Europe was low, often never even reaching 4 percent. That changed when the worldwide recession of the mid-1970s caused unemployment rates to rise, but well after the recession ended, unemployment continued to climb in Continental Europe, topping 10 percent during the 1990s, and was still 8 percent to 9 percent in 2009. Some observers claim that the natural rate of unemployment has increased in these countries.

adverse supply shocks unexpected events that reduce aggregate supply, sometimes only temporarily

Exhibit 7

Effects of an Adverse Supply Shock on Aggregate Supply

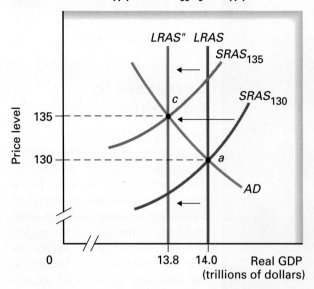

Economists have borrowed a term from physics, **hysteresis** (pronounced *his-ter-eé-sis*), to argue that the natural rate of unemployment depends in part on the recent history of unemployment.[1] *The longer the actual unemployment rate remains above what had been the natural rate, the more the natural rate itself increases.*

No consensus exists regarding the validity of hysteresis. The theory seems to be less relevant in the United States and Great Britain, where unemployment fell from 10 percent in 1982 to 4.5 and 5.5, respectively, in 2007. It remains to be seen how increases in unemployment during the 2008–2009 recession did or did not affect the theory. An alternative explanation for high unemployment in Continental Europe is that legislation introduced there in the 1970s made it more difficult to lay off workers so firms grew more reluctant to hire workers.

Final Word

This chapter explains why the aggregate supply curve slopes upward in the short run and is vertical at the economy's potential output in the long run. Firms and resource suppliers negotiate contracts based on the economy's expected price level, which depends on expectations about aggregate demand. Unexpected changes in the price level can move output in the short run away from its potential level. But as firms and resource suppliers fully adjust to price surprises, the economy in the long run moves toward its potential output. Potential output is the anchor for analyzing aggregate supply in the short run and long run.

1. Sources for the section on hysteresis are Magnus Gustavsson and Par Osterholm, "Hysteresis and Non-Linearities in Unemployment Rates," *Applied Economic Letters,* 13 (July 2006): 545–548; Russell Smyth, "Unemployment Hysteresis in Australian States and Territories," *Australian Economic Review,* 36 (June 2003): 181–192; Horst Siebert, "Labor Market Rigidities: At the Root of Unemployment in Europe," *Journal of Economic Perspectives,* 11 (Summer 1997): 37–54; "Economic and Financial Indicators," *Economist,* 14 March 2009; and OECD *Economic Outlook,* 84 (November 2008).

hysteresis
the theory that the natural rate of unemployment depends in part on the recent history of unemployment; high unemployment rates increase the natural rate of unemployment

>> **Workers in many European countries have guaranteed vacation time; Americans have no minimum vacation guarantee.**

© DYNAMIC GRAPHICS/CREATAS IMAGES/JUPITERIMAGES

Speak Up!

ECON was built on a simple principle: to create a new teaching and learning solution that reflects the way today's faculty teach and the way you learn.

Through conversations, focus groups, surveys, and interviews, we collected data that drove the creation of the current version of *ECON* that you are using today. But it doesn't stop there -- in order to make *ECON* an even better learning experience, we'd like you to SPEAK UP and tell us how *ECON* worked for you. What did you like about it? What would you change? Are there additional ideas you have that would help us build a better product for next semester's principles of economics students?

At **4ltrpress.cengage.com/econ** you'll find all of the resources you need to succeed in principles of economics -- **printable flash cards, interactive quizzes, videos** and more!

Speak Up! Go to **4ltrpress.cengage.com/econ**.

[Faculty, check out **4ltrpress.cengage.com/econ** to see what students think about this new learning solution!]

Fiscal Policy

Learning Outcomes

LO^1 Explain the theory of fiscal policy

LO^2 Describe how aggregate supply affects fiscal policy

LO^3 Discuss the evolution of fiscal policy

"What is the proper role of fiscal policy in the economy?"

President Barack Obama pushed through tax cuts and new government spending plans to "get the country moving again." The Japanese government cut taxes and increased spending to stimulate its troubled economy. These are examples of *fiscal policy*, which focuses on the effects of taxing and public spending on aggregate economic activity. What is the proper role of fiscal policy in the economy? Can fiscal policy reduce swings in the business cycle? Why did fiscal policy fall on hard times for nearly two decades, and what brought it to life? Does fiscal policy affect aggregate supply? Answers to these and other questions are addressed in this chapter, which examines the theory and practice of fiscal policy.

What do you think?

A federal budget deficit is of less concern than a downturn in the nation's economy.

Strongly Disagree						*Strongly Agree*
1	2	3	4	5	6	7

In this chapter, we first explore the effects of fiscal policy on aggregate demand. Next, we bring aggregate supply into the picture. Then, we examine the role of fiscal policy in moving the economy to its potential output. Finally, we review U.S. fiscal policy as it has been practiced since World War II. Throughout the chapter, we use simple tax and spending programs to explain fiscal policy.

LO¹ Theory of Fiscal Policy

Our macroeconomic model so far has viewed government as passive. But government purchases and transfer payments at all levels in the United States total more than $4 trillion a year, making government an important player in the economy. From highway construction, to unemployment compensation, to income taxes,

Topics discussed in Chapter 12 include:

- Theory of fiscal policy
- Discretionary fiscal policy
- Automatic stabilizers
- Lags in fiscal policy
- Limits of fiscal policy
- Deficits, surpluses, and more deficits

to federal deficits, fiscal policy affects the economy in myriad ways. We now move fiscal policy to center stage. As introduced in Chapter 3, *fiscal policy* refers to government purchases, transfer payments, taxes, and borrowing as they affect macroeconomic variables such as real GDP, employment, the price level, and economic growth. When economists study fiscal policy, they usually focus on the federal government, although governments at all levels affect the economy.

Fiscal Policy Tools

The tools of fiscal policy sort into two broad categories: automatic stabilizers and discretionary fiscal policy. Automatic stabilizers are revenue and spending programs in the federal budget that automatically adjust with the ups and downs of the economy to stabilize disposable income and, consequently, consumption and real GDP. For example, the federal income tax is an automatic stabilizer because (1) once adopted, it requires no congressional action to operate year after year, so it's *automatic*, and (2) it reduces the drop in disposable income during recessions and reduces the jump in disposable income during expansions, so it's a *stabilizer*, a smoother. Discretionary fiscal policy, on the other hand, requires the deliberate manipulation of government purchases, transfer payments, and taxes to promote macroeconomic goals like full employment, price stability, and economic growth. President Obama's stimulus plan is an example of discretionary fiscal policy. Some discretionary policies are temporary, such as a one-time boost in government spending to fight a recession. President Bush's tax cuts were originally scheduled to expire, and thus would remain discretionary fiscal policy measures unless they are made permanent.

Using the income-expenditure framework developed earlier, we initially focus on the demand side to consider the effect of changes in government purchases, transfer payments, and taxes on real GDP demanded. The short story is this: *At any given price level, an increase in government purchases or in transfer payments increases real GDP demanded, and an increase in net taxes decreases real GDP demanded, other things constant.* Next, we see how and why.

automatic stabilizers structural features of government spending and taxation that reduce fluctuations in disposable income, and thus consumption, over the business cycle

discretionary fiscal policy the deliberate manipulation of government purchases, taxation, and transfer payments to promote macroeconomic goals, such as full employment, price stability, and economic growth

Changes in Government Purchases

Let's begin by looking at Exhibit 1, with real GDP demanded of $14.0 trillion, as reflected at point *a*, where the aggregate expenditure line crosses the 45-degree line. You may recall that this equilibrium was determined two chapters back, where government purchases and net taxes equaled $1.0 trillion each and did not vary with income—that is, they were

Exhibit 1

Effect of a $0.1 Trillion Increase in Government Purchases on Aggregate Expenditure and Real GDP Demanded

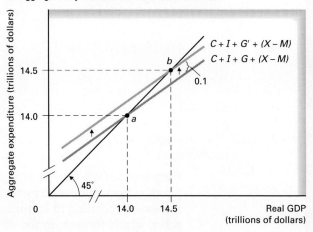

autonomous, or independent of income. Because government purchases equal net taxes, the government budget is balanced.

Now suppose federal policy makers, believing that unemployment is too high, decide to stimulate aggregate demand by increasing government purchases $0.1 trillion, or by $100 billion. To consider the effect on aggregate demand, let's initially assume that nothing else changes, including the price level and net taxes. This additional spending shifts the aggregate expenditure line up by $0.1 trillion, to $C + I + G' + (X - M)$. At real GDP of $14.0 trillion, spending now exceeds output, so production increases. This increase in production increases income, which in turn increases spending, and so it goes through the series of spending rounds.

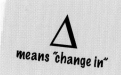

means "change in"

The initial increase of $0.1 trillion in government purchases eventually increases real GDP demanded at the given price level from $14.0 trillion to $14.5 trillion, shown as point *b* in Exhibit 1. Because output demanded increases by $0.5 trillion as a result of an increase of $0.1 trillion in government purchases, the multiplier in our example is equal to 5. *As long as consumption is the only spending component that varies with income, the multiplier for a change in government purchases, other things constant, equals* 1/(1 − MPC), or 1/(1 − 0.8) in our example. Thus, we can say that for a given price level, and assuming that only consumption varies with income,

$$\Delta \text{ Real GDP demanded} = \Delta G \times \frac{1}{1 - MPC}$$

where, again, Δ means "change in." This same multiplier appeared two chapters back, when we discussed shifts of the consumption function, the investment function, and the net exports function.

Changes in Net Taxes

A change in net taxes also affects real GDP demanded, but the effect is less direct. A *decrease* in net taxes, other things constant, *increases* disposable income at each level of real GDP, so consumption increases. In Exhibit 2, we begin again at equilibrium point *a*, with real GDP demanded equal to $14.0 trillion. To stimulate aggregate demand, suppose federal policy makers cut net taxes by $0.1 trillion, or by $100 billion, other things constant. We continue to assume that net taxes are autonomous—that is, that they do not vary with income. A $100 billion reduction in net taxes could result from a tax cut, an increase in transfer payments, or some combination of the two. The $100 billion decrease in net taxes increases disposable income by $100 billion at each level of real GDP. Because households now have more disposable income, they spend more and save more at each level of real GDP.

Because households save some of the tax cut, consumption increases in the first round of spending by less than the full tax cut. Specifically, *consumption spending at each level of real GDP rises by the decrease in net taxes multiplied by the marginal propensity to consume*. In our example, consumption at each level of real GDP increases by $100 billion times 0.8, or $80 billion. Cutting net taxes by $100 billion causes the aggregate expenditure line to shift up by $80 billion, or $0.08 trillion, at all levels of real GDP, as shown in Exhibit 2. This initial increase in spending triggers

subsequent rounds of spending, following a now-familiar pattern in the income-expenditure cycle based on the marginal propensities to consume and to save. For example, the $80 billion increase in consumption increases output and income by $80 billion, which in the second round leads to $64 billion in consumption and $16 billion in saving, and so on through successive rounds. As a result, real GDP demanded eventually increases from $14.0 trillion to $14.4 trillion per year, or by $400 billion.

The effect of a change in net taxes on real GDP demanded equals the resulting shift of the aggregate expenditure line times the simple spending multiplier. Thus, we can say that the effect of a change in net taxes is

$$\Delta \text{ Real GDP demanded} = (-MPC \times \Delta \, NT) \times \frac{1}{1 - MPC}$$

The simple spending multiplier is applied to the shift of the aggregate expenditure line that results from the change in net taxes. This equation can be rearranged as

$$\Delta \text{ Real GDP demanded} = \Delta \, NT \times \frac{-MPC}{1 - MPC}$$

where $-MPC/(1 - MPC)$ is the simple tax multiplier, which can be applied directly to the change in net taxes to yield the change in real GDP demanded at a given price level. This tax multiplier is called *simple* because, by assumption, only consumption varies with income (taxes do not vary with income). For example, with an MPC of 0.8, the simple tax multiplier equals −4. In our example, a *decrease* of $0.1 trillion in net taxes results in an *increase* in real GDP demanded of $0.4 trillion, assuming a given price level. As another example, an *increase* in net taxes of $0.2 trillion would, other things constant, *decrease* real GDP demanded by $0.8 trillion.

Exhibit 2

Effect of a $0.1 Trillion Decrease in Net Taxes on Aggregate Expenditure and Real GDP Demanded

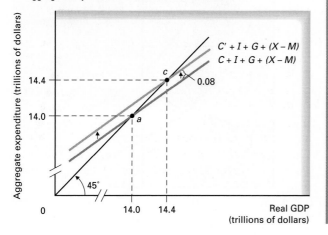

> **simple tax multiplier**
> the ratio of a change in real GDP demanded to the initial change in autonomous net taxes that brought it about; the numerical value of the simple tax multiplier is $-MPC/(1 - MPC)$

> **To summarize:**
>
> An increase in government purchases or a decrease in net taxes, other things constant, increases real GDP demanded. Although not shown, the combined effect of changes in government purchases and in net taxes is found by summing their individual effects.

LO² Including Aggregate Supply

To this point in the chapter, we have focused on the amount of real GDP demanded at a given price level. We are now in a position to bring aggregate supply into the picture. The previous chapter introduced the idea that natural market forces may take a long time to close a contractionary gap. Let's consider the possible effects of using discretionary fiscal policy in such a situation.

Discretionary Fiscal Policy to Close a Contractionary Gap

What if the economy produces less than its potential? Suppose the aggregate demand curve *AD* in Exhibit 3 intersects the aggregate supply curve at point *e*, yielding the short-run output of $13.5 trillion and price level of 125. Output falls short of the economy's potential, opening up a contractionary gap of $0.5 trillion. Unemployment exceeds the natural rate. If markets adjusted naturally to high unemployment, the short-run aggregate supply curve would shift rightward in

Exhibit 3

Discretionary Fiscal Policy to Close a Contractionary Gap

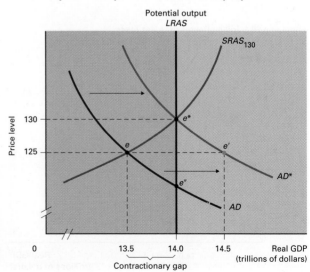

Note two differences between the government purchase multiplier and the simple tax multiplier. First, the government purchase multiplier is positive, so an increase in government purchases leads to an increase in real GDP demanded. The simple tax multiplier is negative, so an increase in net taxes leads to a decrease in real GDP demanded. Second, the multiplier for a given change in government purchases is larger by 1 than the absolute value of the multiplier for an identical change in net taxes. In our example, the government purchase multiplier is 5, while the absolute value of the tax multiplier is 4. This holds because changes in government purchases affect aggregate spending directly—a $100 billion increase in government purchases increases spending in the first round by $100 billion. In contrast, a $100 billion decrease in net taxes increases consumption indirectly by way of a change in disposable income. Thus, each $100 billion decrease in net taxes increases disposable income by $100 billion, which, given an MPC of 0.8, increases consumption in the first round by $80 billion; people save the other $20 billion. In short, an increase in government purchases has a greater impact on real GDP demanded than does an identical tax cut because some of the tax cut gets saved, so it leaks from the spending flow.

the long run to achieve equilibrium at the economy's potential output, point *e″*. History suggests, however, that wages and other resource prices could be slow to respond to a contractionary gap. Suppose policy makers believe that natural market forces will take too long to return the economy to potential output. They also believe that the appropriate increase in government purchases, decrease in net taxes, or some combination of the two could increase aggregate demand just enough to return the economy to its potential output. A $0.2 trillion increase in government purchases reflects an **expansionary fiscal policy** that increases aggregate demand, as shown in Exhibit 3 by the rightward shift from *AD* to *AD**. If the price level remained at 125, the additional spending would increase the quantity demanded from $13.5 to $14.5 trillion. This increase of $1.0 trillion reflects the simple spending multiplier effect, given a constant price level.

At the original price level of 125, however, excess quantity demanded causes the price level to rise. As the price level rises, real GDP supplied increases, but real GDP demanded decreases along the new aggregate demand curve. The price level rises until quantity demanded equals quantity supplied. In Exhibit 3, the new aggregate demand curve intersects the aggregate supply curve at *e**, where the price level is 130, the one originally expected, and output equals potential GDP of $14.0 trillion. Note that *an expansionary fiscal policy aims to close a contractionary gap.*

The intersection at point *e** is not only a short-run equilibrium but a long-run equilibrium. If fiscal policy makers are accurate enough (or lucky enough), the appropriate fiscal stimulus can close the contractionary gap and foster a long-run equilibrium at potential GDP. But the increase in output results in a higher price level. What's more, if the federal budget was in balance before the fiscal stimulus, the increase in government spending creates a budget deficit. In fact, the federal government has run deficits in 90 percent of the years since the early 1970s.

What if policy makers overshoot the mark and stimulate aggregate demand more than necessary to achieve potential GDP? In the short run, real GDP exceeds potential output. In the long run, the short-run aggregate supply curve shifts back until it intersects the aggregate demand curve at potential output, increasing the price level further but reducing real GDP to $14.0 trillion, the potential output.

Discretionary Fiscal Policy to Close an Expansionary Gap

Suppose output exceeds potential GDP. In Exhibit 4, the aggregate demand curve, *AD′*, intersects the aggregate supply curve to yield short-run output of

Exhibit 4

Discretionary Fiscal Policy to Close an Expansionary Gap

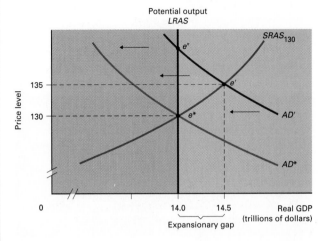

$14.5 trillion, an amount exceeding the potential of $14.0 trillion. The economy faces an expansionary gap of $0.5 trillion. Ordinarily, this gap would be closed by a leftward shift of the short-run aggregate supply curve, which would return the economy to potential output but at a higher price level, as shown by point *e″*.

But the use of discretionary fiscal policy introduces another possibility. By reducing government purchases, increasing net taxes, or employing some combination of the two, the government can implement a **contractionary fiscal policy** to reduce aggregate demand. This could move the economy to potential output without the resulting inflation. If the policy succeeds, aggregate demand in Exhibit 4 shifts leftward from *AD′* to *AD**, establishing a new equilibrium at point *e**. Again, with just the right reduction in aggregate demand, output falls to $14.0 trillion, the potential GDP. Closing an expansionary gap through fiscal policy rather than through natural market forces results in a lower price level, not a higher one. Increasing net taxes or reducing government purchases also reduces a government deficit or increases a surplus. So a contractionary fiscal policy could reduce inflation and reduce

expansionary fiscal policy an increase in government purchases, decrease in net taxes, or some combination of the two aimed at increasing aggregate demand enough to reduce unemployment and return the economy to its potential output; fiscal policy used to close a contractionary gap

contractionary fiscal policy a decrease in government purchases, increase in net taxes, or some combination of the two aimed at reducing aggregate demand enough to return the economy to potential output without worsening inflation; fiscal policy used to close an expansionary gap

a federal deficit. Note that *a contractionary fiscal policy aims to close an expansionary gap.*

© BEN MOLYNEUX/ALAMY

> The proper execution of expansionary and contractionary fiscal policies assumes that:
>
> - potential output is accurately gauged
> - the relevant spending multiplier can be predicted accurately
> - aggregate demand can be shifted by just the right amount
> - various government entities can somehow coordinate their fiscal efforts
> - the shape of the short-run aggregate supply curve is known and remains unaffected by the fiscal policy itself.

The Multiplier and the Time Horizon

In the short run, the aggregate supply curve slopes upward, so a shift of aggregate demand changes both the price level and the level of output. When aggregate supply gets in the act, we find that the simple multiplier overstates the amount by which output changes. The exact change of equilibrium output in the short run depends on the steepness of the aggregate supply curve, which in turn depends on how sharply production costs increase as output expands. *The steeper the short-run aggregate supply curve, the less impact a given shift of the aggregate demand curve has on real GDP and the more impact it has on the price level, so the smaller the spending multiplier.*

If the economy is already producing its potential, then in the long run, any change in fiscal policy aimed at stimulating demand increases the price level but does not affect output. Thus, *if the economy is already producing its potential, the spending multiplier in the long run is zero.*

classical economists
a group of 18th- and 19th-century economists who believed that economic downturns corrected themselves through natural market forces; thus, they believed the economy was self-correcting and needed no government intervention

> The exact change of equilibrium output in the short run depends on the steepness of the aggregate supply curve.

LO³ The Evolution of Fiscal Policy

Now that you have some idea of how fiscal policy can work in theory, let's take a look at fiscal policy in practice, beginning with the approach used before the Great Depression.

Prior to the Great Depression

Before the 1930s, discretionary fiscal policy was seldom used to influence the macroeconomy. Public policy was shaped by the views of classical economists, who advocated *laissez-faire,* the belief that free markets were the best way to achieve economic prosperity. Classical economists did not deny that depressions and high unemployment occurred from time to time, but they argued that the sources of such crises lay outside the market system, in the effects of wars, tax increases, poor growing seasons, changing tastes, and the like. Such external shocks could reduce output and employment, but classical economists believed that natural market forces, such as changes in prices, wages, and interest rates, could correct these problems.

Simply put, classical economists argued that if the economy's price level was too high to sell all that was produced, prices would fall until the quantity supplied equaled the quantity demanded. If wages were too high to employ all who wanted to work, wages would fall until the quantity of labor supplied equaled the quantity demanded. And if the interest rate was too high to invest all that had been saved, interest rates would fall until the amount invested equaled the amount saved.

So the classical approach implied that natural market forces, through flexible prices, wages, and interest rates, would move the economy toward potential

GDP. There appeared to be no need for government intervention. What's more, the government, like households, was expected to live within its means. The idea of government running a deficit was considered immoral. Thus, before the onset of the Great Depression, most economists believed that discretionary fiscal policy could do more harm than good. Besides, the federal government itself was a bit player in the economy. At the onset of the Great Depression, for example, federal outlays were less than 3 percent of GDP (compared to about 24 percent today).

The Great Depression and World War II

Although classical economists acknowledged that capitalistic, market-oriented economies could experience high unemployment from time to time, the depth and duration of the depression strained belief in the economy's ability to mend itself. The Great Depression was marked by four consecutive years of contraction during which unemployment reached 25 percent. Investment plunged 80 percent. Many factories sat idle. With vast unemployed resources, output and income fell well short of the economy's potential.

The stark contrast between the natural market adjustments predicted by classical economists and the years of high unemployment during the Great Depression represented a collision of theory and fact. In 1936, John Maynard Keynes of Cambridge University, England, published *The General Theory of Employment, Interest, and Money,* a book that challenged the classical view and touched off what would later be called the Keynesian revolution. *Keynesian theory and policy were developed in response to the problem of high unemployment during the Great Depression.* Keynes's main quarrel with the classical economists was that prices and wages did not seem to be flexible enough to ensure the full employment of resources.

According to Keynes, prices and wages were relatively inflexible in the downward direction—they were "sticky"—so natural market forces would not return the economy to full employment in a timely fashion. Keynes also believed business expectations might at times become so grim that even very low interest rates would not spur firms to invest all that consumers might save.

It is said that geologists learn more about the nature of the Earth's crust from one major upheaval, such as a huge earthquake or major volcanic eruption, than from a dozen lesser events. Likewise, economists learned more about the economy from the Great Depression than from many more-modest business cycles. Even though this depression began about eight decades ago, economists continue to sift through the rubble, looking for clues about how the economy really works.

Three developments in the years following the Great Depression bolstered the use of discretionary fiscal policy in the United States. The first was the influence of Keynes's *General Theory,* in which he argued that natural forces would not necessarily close a contractionary gap. Keynes thought the economy could get stuck well below its potential, requiring the government to increase aggregate demand to boost output and employment. The second development was the impact of World War II on output and employment. The demands of war greatly increased production and erased cyclical unemployment during the war years, pulling the U.S. economy out of its depression. The third development, largely a consequence of the first two, was the passage of the Employment Act of 1946, which gave the federal government responsibility for promoting full employment and price stability.

Prior to the Great Depression, the dominant fiscal policy was a balanced budget. Indeed, to head off a modest deficit in 1932, federal tax rates were raised, which only deepened the depression. In the wake of Keynes's *General Theory* and World War II, however, policy makers grew more receptive to the idea that fiscal policy could improve economic stability. The objective of fiscal policy was no longer to balance the budget but to promote full employment with price stability even if budget deficits resulted.

Automatic Stabilizers

This chapter has focused mostly on discretionary fiscal policy—conscious decisions to change taxes and

Employment Act of 1946 law that assigned to the federal government the responsibility for promoting full employment and price stability

government spending to achieve the economy's potential output. Now let's get a clearer picture of automatic stabilizers. *Automatic stabilizers smooth out fluctuations in disposable income over the business cycle by stimulating aggregate demand during recessions and dampening aggregate demand during expansions.* Consider the federal income tax. For simplicity, we have assumed that net taxes are independent of income. In reality, the federal income tax system is progressive, meaning that the fraction of income paid in taxes increases as a taxpayer's income increases. During an economic expansion, employment and incomes rise, moving some taxpayers into higher tax brackets. As a result, taxes claim a growing fraction of income. This slows the growth in disposable income and, hence, slows the growth in consumption. Therefore, the progressive income tax relieves some of the inflationary pressure that might otherwise arise as output increases during an economic expansion. Conversely, when the economy is in recession, output declines, employment and incomes fall, mov-

ing some people into lower tax brackets. As a result, taxes take a smaller bite out of income, so disposable income does not fall as much as GDP. Thus, the progressive income tax cushions declines in disposable income, in consumption, and in aggregate demand.

Another automatic stabilizer is unemployment insurance. During economic expansions, the system automatically increases the flow of unemployment insurance taxes from the income stream into the unemployment insurance fund, thereby moderating consumption and aggregate demand. During contractions, unemployment increases and the system reverses itself. Unemployment payments automatically flow from the insurance fund to the unemployed, increasing disposable income and propping up consumption and aggregate demand. Likewise, welfare payments automatically increase during hard times as more people become eligible. *Because of these automatic stabilizers, GDP fluctuates less than it otherwise would, and disposable income varies proportionately less than does GDP.* Because disposable income varies less than GDP does, consumption also fluctuates less than GDP does.

The progressive income tax, unemployment insurance, and welfare benefits were initially designed not so much as automatic stabilizers but as income redistribution programs. Their roles as automatic stabilizers were secondary effects of the legislation. Automatic stabilizers do not eliminate economic fluctuations, but they do reduce their magnitude. The stronger and more effective the automatic stabilizers are, the less need for discretionary fiscal policy. Because of the greater influence of automatic stabilizers, *the economy is more stable today than it was during the Great Depression and before.* As a measure of just how successful these automatic stabilizers have become in cushioning the impact of recessions, consider this: Between 1948 and 2008, real GDP declined during seven years, but real consumption fell during only two years—by 0.8 percent in 1974 and by 0.3 percent in 1980. Real consumption declined in only two of the last 60 years. *Without much fanfare, automatic stabilizers have been quietly doing their work, keeping the economy on a more even keel.*

From the Golden Age to Stagflation

The 1960s was the Golden Age of fiscal policy. John F. Kennedy was the first president to propose a federal budget deficit to stimulate an economy experiencing a contractionary gap. Fiscal policy was also used on occasion to provide an extra kick to an expansion already under way, as in 1964, when Kennedy's successor, Lyndon B. Johnson, cut income tax rates to keep an expansion alive. *This tax cut, introduced to*

The Economy

Progressive Income Tax

Welfare Benefits

Unemployment Insurance

stimulate business investment, consumption, and employment, was perhaps the shining example of fiscal policy during the 1960s. The tax cut seemed to work wonders, increasing disposable income and consumption. The unemployment rate dropped under 5 percent for the first time in seven years, the inflation rate dipped under 2 percent, and the federal budget deficit in 1964 equaled only 0.9 percent of GDP (compared with an average of 2.6 percent since 1980).

Discretionary fiscal policy is a demand-management policy; the objective is to increase or decrease aggregate demand to smooth economic fluctuations. Demand-management policies were applied during much of the 1960s. But the 1970s brought a different problem—stagflation, the double trouble of higher inflation and higher unemployment resulting from a decrease in aggregate supply. The aggregate supply curve shifted left because of crop failures around the world, sharply higher OPEC-driven oil prices, and other adverse supply shocks. Demand-management policies are ill suited to cure stagflation because an increase of aggregate demand would increase inflation, whereas a decrease of aggregate demand would increase unemployment.

Other concerns also caused policy makers and economists to question the effectiveness of discretionary fiscal policy. These concerns included the difficulty of estimating the natural rate of unemployment, the time lags involved in implementing fiscal policy, the distinction between current income and permanent income, and the possible feedback effects of fiscal policy on aggregate supply. We consider each in turn.

> ## "Discretionary fiscal policy is a demand-management policy; the objective is to increase or decrease aggregate demand to smooth economic fluctuations."

Fiscal Policy and the Natural Rate of Unemployment

As we have seen, the unemployment that occurs when the economy is producing its potential GDP is called the *natural rate of unemployment*. Before adopting discretionary policies, public officials must correctly estimate this natural rate. Suppose the economy is producing its potential output of $14.0 trillion, as in Exhibit 5, where the natural rate of unemployment is 5.0 percent. Also suppose that public officials mistakenly believe the natural rate to be 4.0 percent, and they attempt to reduce unemployment and increase real GDP through discretionary fiscal policy. As a result of their policy, the aggregate demand curve shifts to the right, from *AD*

Exhibit 5

When Discretionary Fiscal Policy Overshoots Potential Output

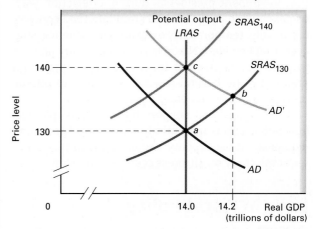

to *AD'*. In the short run, this stimulation of aggregate demand expands output to $14.2 trillion and reduces unemployment to 4.0 percent, so the policy appears successful. But stimulating aggregate demand opens up an expansionary gap, which in the long run results in a leftward shift of the short-run aggregate supply curve. This reduction in aggregate supply pushes up prices and reduces real GDP to $14.0 trillion, the economy's potential. Thus, policy makers initially believe their plan worked, but pushing production beyond the economy's potential leads only to inflation in the long run.

Fiscal Policy and Politics

Given the effects of fiscal policy, particularly in the short run, we should not be surprised that elected officials might try to use it to get reelected. The link between economic performance and reelection success has a long history. Ray Fair of Yale University examined presidential elections dating back to 1916 and found, not surprisingly, that the state of the economy during the election year affected the outcome.[1] Specifically, Fair found that a declining unemployment rate and strong growth rate in GDP per capita increased election prospects for the incumbent party. Clearly, a weak economy in 2008 helped Barack Obama defeat the incumbent party candidate, John McCain.

❖❖❖

1. Ray Fair, *Predicting Presidential Elections and Other Things* (Stanford, Calif.: Stanford University Press, 2002).

Another Yale economist, William Nordhaus, developed a theory of political business cycles, arguing that incumbent presidents, during an election year, use expansionary policies to stimulate the economy, often only temporarily. For example, evidence suggests that President Nixon used expansionary policies to increase his chances for reelection in 1972, even pressuring the Federal Reserve chairman to pursue an expansionary monetary policy.

The evidence to support the theory of political business cycles is not entirely convincing. Read more details about fiscal policy and elections in this chapter's case study on 4ltrpress.cengage.com/econ.

Lags in Fiscal Policy

The time required to approve and implement fiscal legislation may hamper its effectiveness and weaken discretionary fiscal policy as a tool of macroeconomic stabilization. Even if a fiscal prescription is appropriate for the economy at the time it is proposed, the months and sometimes years required to approve and implement legislation means the medicine could do more harm than good. The policy might kick in only after the economy has already turned itself around. Because a recession is not usually identified until at least six months after it begins, and because the 10 recessions between 1945 and 2001 lasted only 10 months on average, discretionary fiscal policy allows little room for error (more later about timing problems).

Discretionary Fiscal Policy and Permanent Income

It was once believed that discretionary fiscal policy could be turned on and off like a water faucet, stimulating or dampening the economy at the right time by just the right amount. Given the marginal propensity to consume, tax changes could increase or decrease disposable income to bring about

desired change in consumption. A more recent view suggests that people base their consumption decisions not merely on changes in their current income but on changes in their permanent income.

Permanent income is the income a person expects to receive on average over the long term. Changing tax rates does not affect consumption much if people view the changes as only temporary. In 1967, for example, the escalating war in Vietnam increased military spending, pushing real GDP beyond its potential. The combination of a booming domestic economy and higher defense spending opened up an expansionary gap by 1968. That year, Congress approved a *temporary* tax hike. The higher tax rates were scheduled to last only 18 months. Higher taxes were supposed to soak up some disposable income to relieve inflationary pressure in the economy. But the reduction in aggregate demand turned out to be disappointingly small, and inflation was hardly affected. The *temporary* nature of the tax increase meant that consumers faced only a small cut in their permanent income. Because permanent income changed little, consumption changed little. Consumers simply saved less. As another example, in late 1997, Japanese officials introduced an income tax cut intended to stimulate Japan's flat economy. People expected the cut would be repealed after a year, so economists were skeptical that the plan would work, and it didn't. Likewise, the stimulative effects of the $600 per family tax rebates in 2008 were disappointing. In short, *to the extent that consumers base spending decisions on their permanent income, attempts to fine-tune the economy with temporary tax changes are less effective.*

The Feedback Effects of Fiscal Policy on Aggregate Supply

So far we have limited the discussion of fiscal policy to its effect on aggregate demand. Fiscal policy may also affect aggregate supply, although this is usually unintentional. For example, suppose the government increases unemployment benefits, paid with higher taxes on earnings. If the marginal propensity to consume is the same for both groups, the increased spending by beneficiaries just offsets the reduced spending by workers. There would be no change in aggregate demand and thus no change in equilibrium real GDP, simply a redistribution of disposable income from the employed to the unemployed.

But could the program affect labor supply? Higher unemployment benefits reduce the opportunity cost of not working, so some job seekers may decide to search at a more leisurely pace. Meanwhile, higher tax rates reduce the opportunity cost of leisure, so

political business cycles
economic fluctuations that occur when discretionary policy is manipulated for political gain

permanent income
income that individuals expect to receive on average over the long term

some with jobs may decide to work fewer hours. In short, the supply of labor could decrease as a result of higher unemployment benefits funded by higher taxes on earnings. A decrease in the supply of labor would decrease aggregate supply, reducing the economy's potential GDP.

Both automatic stabilizers, such as unemployment insurance and the progressive income tax, and discretionary fiscal policies, such as changes in tax rates, may affect individual incentives to work, spend, save, and invest, although these effects are usually unintended consequences. We should keep these secondary effects in mind when we evaluate fiscal policies. It was concern about the effects of taxes on the supply of labor that motivated the tax cuts approved in 1981.

To find out more about these tax cuts and if they worked, read the case study at http://4ltrpress.cengage.com/econ.

Since 1990: From Deficits to Surpluses Back to Deficits

The large federal budget deficits of the 1980s and first half of the 1990s reduced the use of discretionary fiscal policy as a tool for economic stabilization. Because deficits were already high during economic expansions, it was hard to justify increasing deficits to stimulate the economy. For example, President Clinton proposed a modest stimulus package in early 1993 to help the recovery that was already under way. His opponents blocked the measure, arguing that it would increase the budget deficit. President Bush's tax cuts during his first term were widely criticized by the opposition as budget-busting sources of a widening deficit.

Clinton did not get his way with his stimulus package, but in 1993, he did manage to substantially increase taxes on high-income households, a group that pays the lion's share of federal income taxes (the top 10 percent of earners pay about two-thirds of federal income taxes collected). The Republican Congress elected in 1994 imposed more discipline on federal spending as part of its plan to balance the budget. Meanwhile, the economy experienced a strong recovery fueled by growing consumer spending and rising business optimism based on technological innovation, market globalization, and the strongest stock market in history. The confluence of these events—higher taxes on the rich, more spending discipline, and a strengthening economy—changed the dynamic of the federal budget. Tax revenues gushed into Washington, growing an average of 8.3 percent per year between 1993 and 1998; meanwhile, federal outlays remained in check, growing only 3.2 percent per year. By 1998, that one-two punch knocked out the federal deficit, a deficit that only six years earlier reached a record at the time of $290 billion. The federal surplus grew from $70 billion in 1998 to $236 billion in 2000.

But in early 2001, the economy suffered a recession, so newly elected President George W. Bush pushed through an across-the-board $1.35 trillion, 10-year tax cut to "get the economy moving again." Then on September 11, 2001, nineteen men in four hijacked airplanes ended thousands of lives and reduced the chances of a strong economic recovery. Although the recession lasted only eight months, the recovery was weak, and jobs did not start growing again until the second half of 2003. But, between 2003 and 2007, the economy added more than 8 million jobs. The strengthening economy helped cut the federal deficit from about $400 billion in 2004 to $163 billion in 2007. The recession that began officially in December 2007 reversed those recent gains. The federal budget deficit increased to $450 billion in 2008. With lower tax revenues, bailouts, and increased stimulus spending, deficits have been forecast between $1 trillion and $2 trillion. Further implications of federal deficits and the resulting federal debt are discussed in the next chapter.

Final Word

This chapter discussed fiscal policy in theory and in practice. It also examined several factors that reduce the size of the spending and taxing multipliers. In the

{ Government Spending }

On February 13, 2009, Congress passed the American Recovery and Reinvestment Act of 2009, a $787 billion piece of legislation designed to create jobs and help stimulate the struggling economy. So where does all that money go? Here are a few of the areas to which federal funds were allocated as part of this Act.

$27.5 billion—Federal Highway Administration: Highway Infrastructure Investment

$16.8 billion—Department of Energy: Energy Efficiency and Renewable Energy

$13 billion—Department of Education: Education for the Disadvantaged

$1 billion—NASA

$650 million—the Digital-to-Analog Converter Box Program

$300 million—Department of Defense: Research, Development, Test and Evaluation

$100 million—Border Security Fencing, Infrastructure, and Technology

For a full transcript of the American Recovery and Reinvestment Act of 2009, go to: http://www.whitehouse.gov/the_press_office/arra_public_review/.

Part of the 1990s economic boom time was fueled by market globalization.

short run, the aggregate supply curve slopes upward, so the impact on equilibrium output of any change in aggregate demand is blunted by a change in the price level. In the long run, aggregate supply is a vertical line, so if the economy is already producing at its potential, the spending multiplier is zero. To the extent that consumers respond primarily to changes in their permanent incomes, temporary changes in taxes affect consumption less, so the tax multiplier is smaller.

Throughout this chapter, we assumed net taxes and net exports would remain unchanged with changes in income. In reality, income taxes increase with income and net exports decrease with income.

$4 trillion < Annual government purchases and transfer payments at all levels

Recessions since 1945 > **11**

Year when John Keynes published *The General Theory of Employment, Interest, and Money* > **1936**

6 < Months before a recession is usually identified

Federal deficit in 2008 > **$450 billion**

Federal surplus in 2000 > **$236 billion**

23% < Reduction in average income tax rates in 1981

aplia™

Federal Budgets *and* Public Policy

Learning Outcomes

LO ^{1} Examine the federal budget process

LO ^{2} Discuss the fiscal impact of the federal budget

LO ^{3} Explain the national debt

"How big is the federal budget, and where does the money go?"

How big is the federal budget, and where does the money go? Why is the federal budget process such a tangled web? In what sense is the federal budgeting process at odds with discretionary fiscal policy? How is a sluggish economy like an empty res-

taurant? Why has the federal budget been in deficit most years, and why did a surplus briefly materialize at the end of the 1990s? What is the federal debt, and who owes it to whom? Answers to these and other questions are examined in this chapter, which considers federal budgeting in theory and practice.

The word *budget* derives from the Old French word *bougette,* which means "little bag." The federal budget is now about $4,000,000,000,000.00—$4 trillion a year. That's big money! If this "little bag" held $100 bills, it would weigh more than 40,000 *tons!* These $100 bills could paper over a 24-lane highway stretching from northern Maine to southern California. This total could pay every U.S. family's mortgage and car payments for the year. Here's another way to grasp the size of the federal budget: If all 4.6 thousand tons of gold stored in Fort Knox were sold at market rates of $900 per ounce, the proceeds would fund the federal government only about 12 days.

Government budgets have a tremendous impact on the economy. Government outlays at all levels amount to about 39 percent relative to GDP. Our focus in this chapter will be the federal budget, beginning with the budget process. We then look at the source of federal deficits and how they briefly became surpluses. We also examine the national debt and its impact on the economy.

Topics discussed in Chapter 13 include:

- The federal budget process
- Rationale for deficit spending
- Impact of federal deficits
- Crowding out and crowding in
- The short-lived budget surplus
- The burden of the federal debt

LO¹ The Federal Budget Process

The federal budget is a plan of outlays and revenues for a specified period, usually a year. Federal *outlays* include both government purchases and transfer payments. Exhibit 1 shows U.S. federal outlays by major category since 1960. As you can see, the share of outlays going to national defense dropped from over half in 1960 to only 22 percent in 2009. Social Security's share has grown every decade. Medicare, medical care for the elderly, was introduced in 1965 and has also grown since then. In fact, Social Security and Medicare, programs aimed primarily at the elderly, combined for 34 percent of federal outlays in 2009.

federal budget
a plan for federal government outlays and revenues for a specified period, usually a year

Exhibit 1

Defense's Share of Federal Outlays Declined Since 1960 and Redistribution Increased

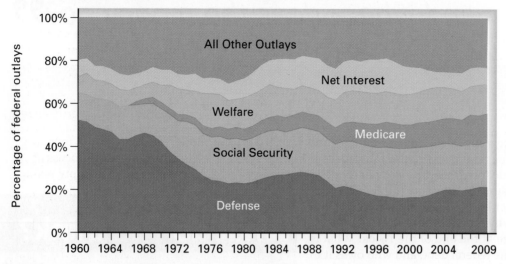

SOURCES: Computed based an budget totals from *Economic Report of the President,* February 2009, Table B-80; and the Office of Management and Budget. For the latest data, go to http://www.gpoaccess.gov/eop/. Percentage shares for 2009 are estimates.

For the last two decades, welfare spending, which consists of cash and in-kind transfer payments, has remained relatively stable and in 2009 accounted for 14 percent of federal outlays. And, thanks to low interest rates, interest payments on the national debt were 7 percent of federal outlays in 2009, down from 15 percent as recently as 1996. So 48 percent, or nearly half the federal budget in 2009, redistributed income (Social Security, Medicare, and welfare); 22 percent went toward defense; 7 percent serviced the national debt; and the remaining 23 percent paid for everything else in the federal budget—from environmental protection to federal prisons to federal aid to education. The federal government has shifted the focus from national defense to redistribution.

The Presidential and Congressional Roles

The president's budget proposal begins to take shape a year before it is submitted to Congress, with each agency preparing a budget request. In late January or early February, the president submits to Congress *The Budget of the United States Government,* a big pile of books detailing spending and revenue proposals for the upcoming fiscal year, which begins October 1. At this stage, the president's budget is little more than detailed suggestions for congressional consideration. About the same time,

budget resolution
a congressional agreement about total outlays, spending by major category, and expected revenues; it guides spending and revenue decisions by the many congressional committees and subcommittees

the president's Council of Economic Advisors sends Congress the *Economic Report of the President,* which offers the president's take on the economy.

Budget committees in both the House and the Senate rework the president's budget until they agree on total outlays, spending by major category, and expected revenues. This agreement, called a **budget resolution,** guides spending and revenue decisions made by the many congressional committees and subcommittees. The budget cycle is supposed to end before October 1, the start of the new fiscal year. Before that date, Congress should have approved detailed plans for outlays along with revenue projections. Thus, the federal budget has a congressional gestation period of about nine months—though, as noted, the president's budget usually begins taking shape a year before it's submitted to Congress.

The size and composition of the budget and the difference between outlays and revenues measure the budget's fiscal impact on the economy. *When outlays exceed revenues, the budget is in deficit. A deficit stimulates aggregate demand in the short run but reduces national saving, which in the long run could impede economic growth. Alternatively, when revenues exceed outlays, the federal budget is in surplus. A surplus dampens aggregate demand in the short run but boosts domestic saving, which in the long run could promote economic growth.*

Problems with the Federal Budget Process

The federal budget process sounds good on paper, but it does not work that well in practice. There are several problems.

Continuing Resolutions Instead of Budget Decisions

Congress often ignores the timetable for developing and approving a budget. Because deadlines are frequently missed, budgets typically run from year to year based on continuing resolutions, which are agreements to allow agencies, in the absence of an approved budget, to spend at the rate of the previous year's budget. Poorly conceived programs continue through sheer inertia; successful programs cannot expand. On occasion, the president must temporarily shut down some agencies because not even the continuing resolution can be approved on time. For example, in late 1995 and early 1996, most federal offices closed for 27 days.

Lengthy Budget Process

You can imagine the difficulty of using the budget as a tool of discretionary fiscal policy when the budget process takes so long. Given that the average recession lasts only 10 months and that budget preparations begin more than a year and a half before the budget takes effect, planning discretionary fiscal measures to reduce economic fluctuations is difficult. That's one reason why attempts to stimulate an ailing economy often seem so halfhearted; by the time Congress and the president agree on a fiscal remedy, the economy has often recovered on its own.

Uncontrollable Budget Items

Congress has only limited control over much of the budget. *About three-fourths of federal budget outlays are determined by existing laws.* For example, once Congress establishes eligibility criteria, entitlement programs, such as Social Security, Medicare, and Medicaid, take on lives of their own, with each annual appropriation simply reflecting the amount required to support the expected number of entitled beneficiaries. Congress has no say in such appropriations unless it chooses to change benefits or eligibility criteria. Most entitlement programs have such politically powerful constituencies that Congress is reluctant to mess with the structure.

No Separate Capital Budget

Congress approves a single budget that mixes *capital* expenditures, like new federal buildings or aircraft carriers, with *operating* expenditures, like employee payrolls or military meals. Budgets for businesses and for state and local governments usually distinguish between a *capital budget* and an *operating budget*. The federal government, by mixing the two, offers a fuzzier picture of what's going on.

Overly Detailed Budget

The federal budget is divided into thousands of accounts and subaccounts, which is why it fills volumes. To the extent that the budget is a way of making political payoffs, such micromanagement allows elected officials to reward friends and punish enemies with great precision. For example, a recent budget included $176,000 for the Reindeer Herders Association in Alaska, $400,000 for the Southside Sportsman Club in New York, and $5 million for an insect-rearing facility in Mississippi. By budgeting in such detail, Congress may lose sight of the big picture. When economic conditions change or when the demand for certain public goods shifts, the federal government cannot easily reallocate funds. Detailed budgeting is not only time consuming, it reduces the flexibility of discretionary fiscal policy and is subject to political abuse.

Possible Budget Reforms

Some reforms might improve the budget process. First, the annual budget could become a two-year budget, or *biennial budget*. As it is, Congress spends nearly all of the year working on the budget. The executive branch is always dealing with three budgets: administering an approved budget, defending a proposed budget before congressional committees, and preparing the next budget for submission to Congress. With a two-year budget, Congress would not be continually involved with budget deliberations, and cabinet members could focus more on running their agencies (many states have adopted two-year budgets). A two-year budget, however, would require longer-term economic forecasts and would be less useful than a one-year budget as a tool of discretionary fiscal policy.

Another possible reform would be to simplify the budget document by concentrating only on major groupings and eliminating line items. Each agency head would receive a total budget, along with the discretion to allocate that budget in a

continuing resolutions budget agreements that allow agencies, in the absence of an approved budget, to spend at the rate of the previous year's budget

entitlement programs guaranteed benefits for those who qualify for government transfer programs such as Social Security and Medicare

manner consistent with the perceived demands for agency services. The drawback is that agency heads may have different priorities than those of elected representatives. On the plus side, elected officials would be less able to insert in the budget favorite pork-barrel projects.

A final reform is to sort federal spending into a capital budget and an operating budget. A *capital budget* would include spending on physical capital such as buildings, highways, computers, military equipment, and other public infrastructure. An *operating budget* would include spending on the payroll, building maintenance, computer paper, transfer programs, and other ongoing outlays.

LO² The Fiscal Impact of the Federal Budget

When government outlays—government purchases plus cash and in-kind transfer programs—exceed government revenue, the result is a *budget deficit*, a flow measure already introduced. Although the federal budget was in surplus from 1998 to 2001, before that it had been in deficit every year but one since 1960 and in all but eight years since 1930. After 2001 the budget slipped back into the red, where it remains. To place deficits in perspective, let's first examine the economic rationale for deficit financing.

The Rationale for Deficits

Deficit financing has been justified for outlays that increase the economy's productivity—capital outlays for investments such as highways, waterways, and dams. The cost of these capital projects should be borne in part by future taxpayers, who will also benefit from these investments. Thus, there is some justification for government borrowing to finance capital projects and for future taxpayers helping to pay for them. State and local governments issue debt to fund capital projects, such as schools and infrastructure. But, as noted already, the federal government does not budget capital projects separately, so there is no explicit link between capital budgets and federal deficits.

Before the Great Depression, federal deficits

<<An annually balanced budget magnifies fluctuations in the business cycle, overheating the economy during expansions and increasing unemployment during recessions.

occurred only during wartime. Because wars often involve great personal hardship, public officials are understandably reluctant to tax citizens much more to finance war-related spending. Deficits during wars were largely self-correcting, however, because military spending dropped after a war, but tax revenue did not.

The Great Depression led John Maynard Keynes to argue that public spending should offset any drop in private spending. As you know by now, Keynes argued that a federal budget deficit would stimulate aggregate demand. As a result of the Great Depression, automatic stabilizers were also introduced, which increased public outlays during recessions and decreased them during expansions. Deficits increase during recessions because tax revenues decline while spending programs such as unemployment benefits and welfare increase. For example, during the 1990–1991 recession, corporate tax revenue fell 10 percent but welfare spending jumped 25 percent. An economic expansion reverses these flows. As the economy picks up, so do personal income and corporate profits, boosting tax revenue. Unemployment compensation and welfare spending decline. Thus, federal deficits usually fall during the recovery stage of the business cycle.

Budget Philosophies and Deficits

Several budget philosophies have emerged over the years. Prior to the Great Depression, fiscal policy focused on maintaining an **annually balanced budget**, except during wartime. Because tax revenues rise during expansions and fall during recessions, an annually balanced budget means that spending increases during expansions and declines during recessions. But such a pattern magnifies fluctuations in the business cycle, overheating the economy during expansions and increasing unemployment during recessions.

A second budget philosophy calls for a **cyclically balanced budget**, meaning that budget deficits during recessions are covered by budget surpluses dur-

annually balanced budget
budget philosophy prior to the Great Depression; aimed at matching annual revenues with outlays, except during times of war

cyclically balanced budget
a budget philosophy calling for budget deficits during recessions to be financed by budget surpluses during expansions

ing expansions. Fiscal policy dampens swings in the business cycle without increasing the national debt. Nearly all states have established "rainy day" funds to build up budget surpluses during the good times for use during hard times.

A third budget philosophy is functional finance, which says that policy makers should be concerned less with balancing the budget annually, or even over the business cycle, and more with ensuring that the economy produces its potential output. If the budgets needed to keep the economy producing its potential involve chronic deficits, so be it. Since the Great Depression, budgets in this country have seldom balanced. *Although budget deficits have been larger during recessions than during expansions, the federal budget has been in deficit in all but a dozen years since 1930.*

Federal Deficits Since the Birth of the Nation

Between 1789, when the U.S. Constitution was adopted, and 1930, the first full year of the Great Depression, the federal budget was in deficit 33 percent of the years, primarily during war years. After a war, government spending dropped more than government revenue. Thus, deficits arising during wars were largely self-correcting once the wars ended.

Since the Great Depression, however, federal budgets have been in deficit 85 percent of the years. Exhibit 2 shows federal deficits and surpluses as a percentage of GDP since 1934. Unmistakable are the huge deficits during World War II, which dwarf deficits in other years. Turning now to the last thirty years, we see the relatively large deficits of the 1980s. These resulted from large tax cuts along with higher defense spending. Supply-side economists argued that tax cuts would stimulate enough economic activity to keep tax revenues from falling. Unspecified spending cuts were supposed to erase a projected deficit, but Congress never made the promised spending cuts. In short, the president and Congress cut tax rates but not expenditures.

As the economy improved during the 1990s, the deficit decreased and then disappeared, turning into a surplus by 1998. But a recession in 2001, tax cuts, and higher federal spending turned surpluses into deficits. A weak recovery and the cost of fighting the war against terrorism worsened the deficits to 3.5 percent relative to GDP by 2003. But over the next four years, a stronger economy along with a rising stock market increased federal revenue enough to drop the deficit to about 1.2 percent relative to GDP in 2007. After that year, the deficit is projected to grow again because of the deep recession of 2008–2009 and increased government spending on stimulus and bailout programs. The Congressional Budget Office projects a 2009 deficit of $1.8 trillion, or 13.1 percent relative to GDP, by far the largest since World War II.

That's a short history of federal deficits. Now let's consider why the federal budget has been in deficit so long.

Why Have Deficits Persisted?

As we have seen, large deficits in the 1980s and more recently came from a combination of tax cuts and spending increases. But why has the budget been in deficit for all but 12 years since 1930? The most obvious answer is that, unlike budgeters in 49 states, federal officials are not required to balance the budget. But why deficits rather than surpluses? One widely accepted

functional finance
a budget philosophy using fiscal policy to achieve the economy's potential GDP, rather than balancing budgets either annually or over the business cycle

Exhibit 2

After Decades of Federal Budget Deficits, Surpluses Appeared from 1998 to 2001, But Deficits Are Back

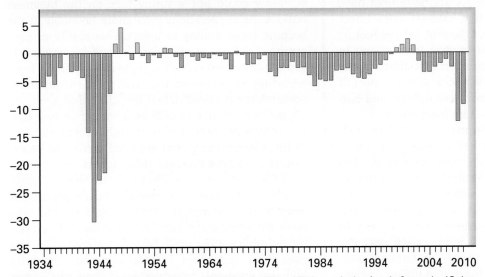

SOURCES: *Economic Report of the President,* February 2009. Deficits for 2009 and 2010 are projections from the Congressional Budget Office. For the latest data, go to http://www.gpoaccess.gov/eop/.

model of the public sector assumes that elected officials try to maximize their political support, including votes and campaign contributions. Voters like spending programs but hate paying taxes, so public spending wins support and taxes lose it. Candidates try to maximize their chances of getting elected and reelected by offering budgets long on benefits but short on taxes. Moreover, members of Congress push their favorite programs with little concern about the overall budget. For example, a senator from Mississippi was able to include $1.5 billion in a recent budget for an amphibious assault ship to be built in his hometown of Pascagoula. The Navy never even asked for the ship.

Deficits, Surpluses, Crowding Out, and Crowding In

What effect do federal deficits and surpluses have on interest rates? Recall that interest rates affect investment, a critical component of economic growth. What's more, year-to-year fluctuations in investment are the primary source of shifts in the aggregate demand curve. Let's look at the impact of government deficits and surpluses on investment.

Suppose the federal government increases spending without raising taxes, thereby increasing the budget deficit. How will this affect national saving, interest rates, and investment? An increase in the federal deficit reduces the supply of national saving, leading to higher interest rates. Higher interest rates

crowding out
the displacement of interest-sensitive private investment that occurs when higher government deficits drive up market interest rates

crowding in
the potential for government spending to stimulate private investment in an otherwise dead economy

discourage, or *crowd out,* some private investment, reducing the stimulating effect of the government's deficit. The extent of crowding out is a matter of debate. Some economists argue that although government deficits may displace some private-sector borrowing, expansionary fiscal policy results in a net increase in aggregate demand, leading to greater output and employment in the short run. Others believe that the crowding out is more extensive, so borrowing from the public in this way results in little or no net increase in aggregate demand and output. Public spending merely substitutes for private spending.

Although crowding out is likely to occur to some degree, there is another possibility. If the economy is operating well below its potential, the additional fiscal stimulus provided by a higher government deficit could encourage firms to invest more. Recall that an important determinant of investment is business expectations. Government stimulus of a weak economy could put a sunny face on the business outlook. As expectations grow more favorable, firms become more willing to invest. This ability of government deficits to stimulate private investment is sometimes called crowding in, to distinguish it from crowding out. Between 1993 and 2009, the Japanese government pursued deficit spending that averaged 5.3 percent relative to GDP as a way of getting that flat economy going, but with only recent success. Unfortunately, the global financial crisis and recession of 2008–2009 reversed that success.

Were you ever unwilling to patronize a restaurant because it was too crowded? You simply did not want to put up with the hassle and long wait and were thus "crowded out." As that baseball-player-turned-philosopher Yogi Berra once said, "No one goes there nowadays. It's too crowded." Similarly, high government deficits may "crowd out" some investors by driving up interest rates. On the other hand, did you ever pass up an unfamiliar restaurant because the place seemed dead—it had no customers? Perhaps you wondered why? If you had seen just a few customers, you might have stopped in—you might have been willing to "crowd in." Similarly, businesses may be reluctant to invest in a seemingly lifeless economy. The economic stimulus resulting from deficit spending could encourage some investors to "crowd in."

The Twin Deficits

To finance the huge deficits, the U.S. Treasury must sell a lot of government IOUs. To get people to buy these Treasury securities, the government must offer higher interest rates. So funding a higher deficit pushes up the market interest rates. With U.S. interest rates higher, foreigners find Treasury securities more attractive. But to buy them, foreigners must first exchange their currencies for dollars. This greater demand for dollars causes the dollar to appreciate relative to foreign currencies, as happened during the first half of the 1980s. The rising value of the dollar makes foreign goods cheaper in the United States and U.S. goods more expensive abroad. Thus, U.S. imports increase and U.S. exports decrease, so the trade deficit increases.

Higher trade deficits mean that foreigners have dollars left over after they buy all the U.S. goods and services they want. With these accumulated dollars, foreigners buy U.S. assets, including U.S. government securities, and thereby help fund federal deficits. The increase in funds from abroad is both good news and bad news for the U.S. economy. The supply of foreign saving increases investment spending in the United States over what would have occurred in the absence of these funds. Ask people what they think of foreign investment in their town; they will likely say it's great. But foreign funds to some extent simply offset a decline in U.S. saving. Such a pattern could pose problems in the long run. The United States has surrendered a certain amount

of control over its economy to foreign investors. And the return on foreign investments in the United States flows abroad. For example, a growing share of the federal government's debt is now owed to foreigners, as discussed later in the chapter.

America was once the world's leading creditor. Now it's the lead debtor nation, borrowing huge sums from abroad, helping in the process to fund the federal deficit. Some critics blame U.S. fiscal policy as reflected in the large federal deficits for the switch from creditor to debtor nation. Japan and China are big buyers of U.S. Treasury securities. A debtor country becomes more beholden to those countries that supply credit.

The Short-Lived Budget Surplus

Exhibit 3 on the next page summarizes the federal budget since 1970, showing outlays relative to GDP as the red line and revenues relative to GDP as the blue line. These percentages offer an overall look at the federal government's role in the economy. Between 1970 and 2009, federal outlays averaged 20.7 percent and revenues averaged 18.2 percent relative to GDP. When outlays exceed revenues, the federal budget is in deficit, measured each year by the vertical distance between the blue and red lines. Thus, on average, the federal budget had a deficit of 2.5 percent relative to GDP. The pink shading shows the annual deficit as a percent of GDP. In the early 1990s, outlays started to decline relative to GDP, while revenues increased. This shrank the deficit and, by 1998, created a surplus, as indicated by the blue shading. Specifically, the deficit in 1990, which amounted to 3.8 percent relative to GDP, became a surplus by 1998, which lasted through 2001. What turned a hefty deficit into a surplus, and why has the surplus turned back into a deficit? The previous chapter explained in broad outline what happened. Here are more details.

Exhibit 3

During the 1990s, Federal Outlays Declined Relative to GDP and Revenues Increased, Turning Deficits into Surpluses, But Not for Long

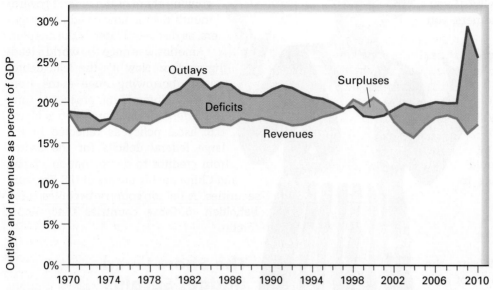

SOURCES: *Economic Report of the President,* February 2009, Table B-79; and the Office of Management and Budget, and the Congressional Budget Office for projections of 2009 and 2010. For the latest data, go to http://www.gpoaccess.gov/eop/.

Tax Increases

With concern about the deficit growing, Congress and President George H. W. Bush agreed in 1990 to a package of spending cuts and tax increases aimed at trimming budget deficits. Ironically, those tax increases not only may have cost President Bush reelection in 1992 (because it violated his 1988 election promise of "no new taxes"), but they also began the groundwork for erasing the budget deficit, for which President Clinton was able to take credit. For his part, President Clinton increased taxes on high-income households in 1993, boosting the top marginal tax rate from 31 percent to 40 percent. The economy also enjoyed a vigorous recovery during the 1990s, fueled by rising worker productivity, growing consumer spending, globalization of markets, and a strong stock market. The combined effects of higher taxes on the rich and a strengthening economy raised federal revenue from 17.8 percent of GDP in 1990 to 20.6 percent in 2000. That may not seem like much of a difference, but it translated into an additional $275 billion in federal revenue in 2000.

Slower Growth in Federal Outlays

Because of spending discipline imposed by the 1990 legislation, growth in federal outlays slowed compared to the 1980s. What's more, the collapse of the Soviet Union reduced U.S. military commitments abroad. Between 1990 and 2000, military personnel dropped one-third and defense spending dropped 30 percent in real terms. An additional impetus for slower spending growth came from Republicans, who attained

congressional majority in 1994. Between 1994 and 2000, domestic spending grew little in real terms. Another beneficial development was the drop in interest rates, which fell to their lowest level in 30 years, saving billions in interest charges on the national debt. In short, federal outlays dropped from 21.6 percent relative to GDP in 1990 to 18.2 percent in 2000. Again, if federal outlays remained the same percentage of GDP in 2000 as in 1990, spending in 2000 would have been $330 billion higher than it was.

A Reversal of Fortune in 2001

Thanks to the tax-rate increases and the strong economy, revenues gushed into Washington, growing an average of 8.4 percent per year between 1993 and 2000. Meanwhile, federal outlays remained in check, growing only 3.5 percent per year. By 2000, that combination created a federal budget surplus of $236 billion, quite a turnaround from a deficit that had topped $290 billion in 1992. But in 2001 unemployment increased, the stock market sank, and terrorists crashed jets and spread anthrax. All this slowed federal revenues and accelerated federal spending. To counter the recession and cope with terrorism, Congress and the president cut taxes and increased federal spending. As a result, the federal budget surplus returned to a deficit by 2002 and has been in the red ever since. The era of federal budget surpluses was short-lived. Stimulus spending, bailouts, and lower tax revenues during the recession of 2008–2009 sharply increased projections for deficits in 2009 and 2010. Worse yet, two major programs— Social Security and Medicare—spell more trouble for the federal budget in the long run.

The Relative Size of the Public Sector

So far, we have focused on the federal budget, but a fuller picture includes state and local governments as well. For added context, we can look at government budgets over time compared to other major econo-mies. Exhibit 4 shows government outlays at all lev-els relative to GDP in 10 industrial economies in 1994 and in 2008. Government outlays in the United States in 2008 were 39 percent relative to GDP, among the smallest in the group. Outlays declined in seven of these other major economies. The 10-country aver-age dropped from 46 percent to 42 percent. Why the drop? The demise of the Soviet Union in the early 1990s reduced defense spending in major economies, and the failure of the Soviet socialist experiment shifted sentiment more toward free markets, thus diminishing the role of government.

Let's now turn our attention to a consequence of federal deficits—a sizable federal debt.

LO^3 The National Debt

Federal deficits add up. It took 39 presidents, six wars, the Great Depression, and more than 200 years for the federal debt to reach $1 trillion, as it did in 1981. It took only 3 presidents and another 15 years for that debt to triple in real terms, as it did by 1996. Ironically, the biggest growth in debt occurred under President Reagan, who ran on a promise to balance the budget. The federal deficit is a flow variable mea-suring the amount by which outlays exceed revenues in a particular year. The federal debt, or the **national debt**, is a stock variable measuring the net accumu-lation of past deficits, the amount owed by the fed-eral government.

This section puts the national debt in perspective by looking at:

(1) changes over time

(2) U.S. debt levels compared with those in other countries

(3) interest payments on the debt

(4) who bears the burden of the debt

(5) what impact the debt has on the nation's capital formation.

Measuring the National Debt

In talking about the national debt, we should distin-guish between the gross debt and debt held by the public. The *gross debt* includes U.S. Treasury securities purchased by various federal agencies. Because the federal government owes this debt to itself, analysts often focus instead on *debt held by the public,* which includes U.S. Treasury securities held by households, firms, banks (including Federal Reserve Banks), and foreign entities. As of 2008, the gross federal debt stood at $10.0 trillion, and the debt held by the public stood at $5.8 trillion.

One way to measure debt over time is relative to the economy's production and income, or GDP (just as a bank might compare the size of a mortgage to a borrower's income). Exhibit 5 on the next page shows federal debt held by the public relative to GDP. The cost of World War II ballooned the debt from 44 percent

Exhibit 4

Government Outlays as a Percentage of GDP Declined Between 1994 and 2008 in Most Major Economies

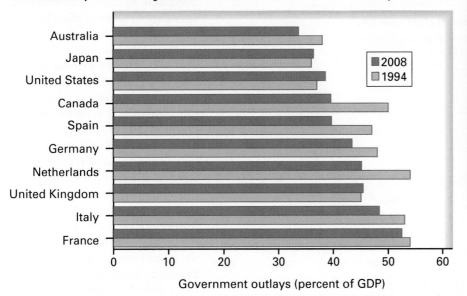

Government outlays (percent of GDP)

Legend: 2008, 1994

Countries (top to bottom): Australia, Japan, United States, Canada, Spain, Germany, Netherlands, United Kingdom, Italy, France

SOURCES: *OECD Economic Outlook,* Vol. 84 (November 2008), Annex Table 25. For the latest data, go to http://www.oecd.org/home/, click on "Statistics," then find the most recent issue of *OECD Economic Outlook.*

Note that the national debt ignores the projected liabilities of Social Secu-rity, Medicare, or other fed-eral retirement programs. If these liabilities were included, the national debt would easily triple.

Read more about Social Security, Medicare, and their impact on the budget in the long run in this chapter's case study on 4ltrpress. cengage.com/econ.

national debt
the net accumulation of federal budget deficits

relative to GDP in 1940 to 109 percent in 1946. After the war, the economy grew much faster than the debt, so that by 1980, debt fell to only 26 percent relative to GDP. But high deficits in the 1980s and early 1990s nearly doubled debt to 49 percent relative to GDP by 1993. Budget surpluses from 1998 to 2001 cut debt to 33 percent relative to GDP by 2001. A recession, a stock market slump, tax cuts, and higher federal spending increased debt to 37 percent relative to GDP in 2004, where it remained through 2007. Deficits from the 2008–2009 recession increased federal debt relative to GDP. According to projections from the Congressional Budget Office based on President Obama's budget, debt relative to GDP by 2010 will exceed all years except those during World War II. But, again, this measure of the debt ignores the fact that the federal government is on the hook to pay Social Security and Medicare benefits that will create a big hole in the budget.

International Perspective on Public Debt

Exhibit 5 shows federal debt relative to GDP over time, but how does the United States compare with other major economies around the world? Because different economies have different fiscal structures—for example some rely more on a central government—we should consider the debt at all government levels. Exhibit 6 compares the net government debt in the United States relative to GDP with those of nine other industrial countries. *Net debt* includes outstanding liabilities of federal, state, and local governments minus government financial assets, such as loans to stu-

Social Security and Medicare create a big hole in the budget.

dents and farmers, securities, cash on hand, and foreign exchange on reserve. Net debt for the ten nations averaged 40 percent in 2008 relative to GDP. The United States is somewhat above this average, at 46 percent. Australia was the lowest with no net debt, and Japan was the highest at 88 percent relative to GDP. Much of Japan's debt accumulated during the "lost decade" of the 1990s as the government borrowed to fund infrastructure spending in order to stimulate the economy.

Italy has the second highest public debt, at 87 percent of GDP. Because political power in Italy is fragmented across a dozen parties, a national government can be formed only through a fragile coalition of parties that could not withstand the voter displeasure from hiking taxes or cutting public spending. Thus, huge government deficits in Italy persisted until quite recently, adding to an already high national debt. Lately, as a condition for joining the European Monetary Union, member countries have been forced to reduce their deficits. Italy, for

Exhibit 5

Federal Debt Held by the Public as a Percentage of GDP Since 1940

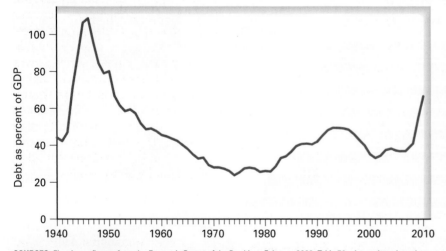

SOURCES: Fiscal year figures from the *Economic Report of the President,* February 2009, Table 79, plus updates based on more recent estimates. Percentage shares for 2008 and 2009 are estimates. Figures for 2009 and 2010 are projections from the Congressional Budget Office. For the latest data go to http://www.gpoaccess.gov/eop/.

Exhibit 6

Relative to GDP, U.S. Net Public Debt in 2008 Was Above Average for Major Economies

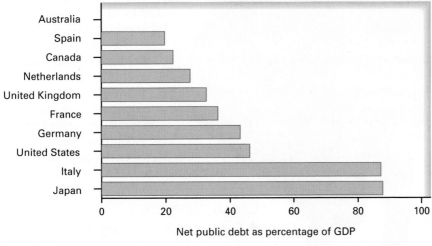

Net public debt as percentage of GDP

SOURCE: *OECD Economic Outlook,* 84 (November 2008), Annex Table 33. For the latest data, go to http://www.oecd.org/home/, click on "Statistics," then find the latest *OECD Economic Outlook.*

example, went from a deficit of 11.4 percent relative to GDP in 1990 to only 2.5 percent by 2008.

Interest on the National Debt

Purchasers of federal securities range from individuals who buy $25 U.S. savings bonds to institutions that buy $1 million Treasury securities. Because most Treasury securities are short term, nearly half the debt is refinanced every year. Based on a $5.8 trillion debt held by the public, a 1 percentage point increase in the nominal interest rate ultimately increases interest costs by $58 billion a year.

Exhibit 7

Interest Payments on Federal Debt Held by the Public as a Percentage of Federal Outlays Peaked in 1996

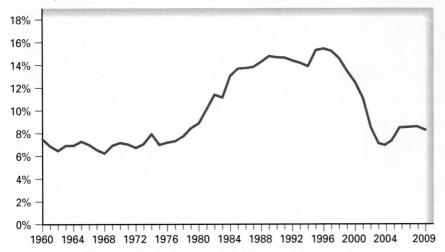

SOURCE: *Economic Report of the President,* February 2009. Figure for 2009 is a projection. For the latest figures, go to http://www.gpoaccess.gov/eop/.

Exhibit 7 shows interest on the federal debt held by the public as a percentage of federal outlays since 1960. After remaining relatively constant for two decades, interest payments climbed in the 1980s because growing deficits added to the debt and because of higher interest rates. Interest payments peaked at 15.4 percent of outlays in 1996, then began falling first because of budget surpluses and later because of lower interest rates. In 2009, interest payments were 7.3 percent of outlays, nearly the same as in 1977. Interest's share of federal outlays will likely climb as interest rates rise from historic lows of recent years.

Who Bears the Burden of the Debt?

Deficit spending is a way of billing future taxpayers for current spending. The national debt raises moral questions about the right of one generation of taxpayers to bequeath to the next generation the burden of its borrowing. To what extent do deficits and debt shift the burden to future generations? Let's examine two arguments about the burden of the federal debt.

We Owe It to Ourselves

It is often argued that the debt is not a burden to future generations because, although future generations must service the debt, those same generations receive the payments. It's true that if U.S. citizens forgo present consumption to buy bonds, they or their heirs will be repaid, so debt service payments stay in the country. Thus, future generations both service the debt and receive the payments. In that sense, the debt is not a burden on future generations. It's all in the family, so to speak.

Foreign Ownership of Debt

But the "we-owe-it-to-ourselves" argument does not apply to that portion of the national debt owed to foreigners. Foreigners who buy U.S. Treasury securities forgo present consumption and are paid back in the future. Foreign buyers reduce the amount of current consumption that Americans must sacrifice to finance a deficit. *A reliance on foreigners, however, increases the burden of the debt on future generations of Americans because future debt service payments no longer remain in the country.* Foreigners held more than half of all federal debt held by the public in January 2009, more than double the share of a decade earlier. So the burden of the debt on future generations of Americans has increased both absolutely and relatively.

Exhibit 8 shows the major foreign holders of U.S. Treasury securities in January 2009, when foreigners held a total of $3.1 trillion of the $5.8 trillion debt held by the public. China is the leader with $740 billion, or 24 percent of foreign-held U.S. debt. Japan ranks second, and a group of oil exporting countries third. Together, Asian countries (including some not shown) own about 60 percent of foreign-held federal debt. Despite

the growth in federal debt, U.S. Treasury securities are considered the safest in the world because they are backed by the U.S. government. Whenever there is trouble around the world, investors flock to U.S. Treasury securities in a "flight to quality." Some other countries have proven to be less trustworthy borrowers. Argentina, Mexico, and Russia, for example, defaulted on some national debt.

© TOLEDANO/STONE/GETTY IMAGES

Crowding Out and Capital Formation

As we have seen, government borrowing can drive up interest rates, crowding out some private investment. The long-run effect of deficit spending depends on how the government spends the borrowed funds. If the funds are invested in better highways and a more educated workforce, this could enhance productivity in the long run.

If, however, borrowed dollars go toward current expenditures such as more farm subsidies or higher retirement benefits, less capital formation results. With less investment today, there will be less capital in the future, thus hurting labor productivity and our future standard of living.

Ironically, despite the large federal deficits during the last few decades, public investments in roads, bridges, and airports—so-called *public capital*—declined, perhaps because a growing share of the federal budget goes toward income redistribution, especially for the elderly. The United States spent 3 percent of GDP building and maintaining the public infrastructure between 1950 and 1970. Since 1980 that share has averaged only 2 percent. A study by the American Society of Civil Engineers found the overall quality of the U.S. public infrastructure declined from 2001 to 2009. For example, governments were spending only half the amount needed to support the nation's transportation systems. The study concludes that $2.2 trillion should be spent to upgrade the infrastucture.[1] Some argue that declining investment in the public infrastructure slows productivity growth. For example, the failure to invest sufficiently in airports and in the air traffic control system has

Exhibit 8

Foreign Holders of U.S. Treasury Securities (Figures in Billions)

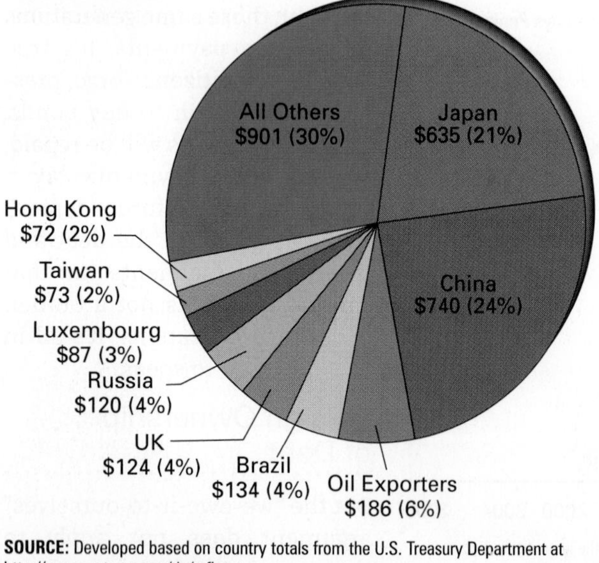

All Others $901 (30%)
Japan $635 (21%)
Hong Kong $72 (2%)
Taiwan $73 (2%)
Luxembourg $87 (3%)
Russia $120 (4%)
UK $124 (4%)
Brazil $134 (4%)
Oil Exporters $186 (6%)
China $740 (24%)

SOURCE: Developed based on country totals from the U.S. Treasury Department at http://www.ustreas.gov/tic/mfh.txt.

● ● ●

1. American Society of Civil Engineers, "Report Card For America's Infrastructure: 2009," at http://www.asce.org/reportcard/2009.

<<The Minneapolis bridge collapse in 2007 focused public attention on the real risks of insufficient investment in the U.S. public infrastructure.

© AP IMAGES

led to congested air travel and flight delays, a problem compounded by the threat of terrorism.

Government deficits of one generation can affect the standard of living of the next. Note again that our current measure of the national debt does not capture all burdens passed on to future generations. As mentioned earlier, if the unfunded liabilities of government retirement programs, especially Medicare, were included, this would triple the national debt.

Final Word

John Maynard Keynes introduced the idea that federal deficit spending is an appropriate fiscal policy when private aggregate demand is insufficient to achieve potential output. The federal budget has not been the same since. Beginning in 1960, the federal budget was in deficit every year but one until 1998. And beginning in the early 1980s, large federal deficits dominated the fiscal policy debate, tripling the national debt in real terms and putting discretionary fiscal policy on hold. But after peaking at $290 billion in 1992, the deficit disappeared briefly later in the decade because of higher tax rates on high-income households, lower growth in federal outlays, and a rip-roaring economy fueled by faster labor productivity growth and a dazzling stock market. The softening economy of 2001 and the terrorist attacks

brought discretionary fiscal policy back in the picture. A recession and weak recovery, tax cuts, and spending increases swelled the federal deficit by 2004 to more than $400 billion, rivaling deficits of the 1980s and early 1990s. But the addition of 8 million more jobs helped cut the deficit more than half by 2007. The deficit is projected to climb again to $1.8 trillion in 2009 because of the recession. Much of this results from one-time stimulus and bailout spending. The deficit is projected to fall to $660 billion by 2012 but then will start rising again, reaching $1 trillion by 2018. Rising health care costs and retirement of baby-boomers continue putting upward pressure on the deficit.

During the years when high deficits diminished the role of discretionary fiscal policy, monetary policy took center stage as the tool of economic stabilization. Monetary policy is the regulation of the money supply by the Federal Reserve. The next three chapters introduce money and financial institutions, review monetary policy, and discuss the impact of monetary and fiscal policy on economic stability and growth. Once we bring money into the picture, we consider yet another reason why the simple spending multiplier is overstated.

© BARBARA PENOYAR/PHOTODISC/GETTY IMAGES

{ For more details on the intergenerational view of deficits and debt, read the case study for Chapter 13 on 4ltrpress.cengage.com/econ

Learning Outcomes

LO^1 Discuss the evolution of money

LO^2 Identify types of financial institutions in the United States

LO^3 Discuss the origin and powers of the Federal Reserve

LO^4 Describe the history of the U.S. banking system from the Great Depression to today

Money *and* the Financial System

Why are you willing to exchange a piece of paper bearing Alexander Hamilton's portrait and the number 10 in each corner for a pepperoni pizza with extra cheese? Has the penny outlived its usefulness? If Russia can't pay its bills, why don't they simply print more rubles? What's the difference between the *Fed* and the *Feds*. Why was someone able to cash a check written on a clean but frayed pair of underpants? And why is there so much fascination with money? These and other questions are answered in this chapter, which introduces money and banking.

The word *money* comes from the name of the goddess (*Juno Moneta*) in whose temple Rome's money was coined. Money has come to symbolize all personal and business finance. You can read *Money* magazine and the "Money" section of *USA Today,* and visit Web sites such as money.cnn.com, moneycentral .msn.com/home.asp, and smartmoney.com (a Google search for "money" returned over a billion hits—four times as many as "economics").

With money, you can articulate your preferences—after all, money talks. And when it talks, it says a lot, as in, "Put your money where your mouth is" and "Show me the money." Money is the grease that lubricates the wheels of market exchange (in fact, an old expression "grease the palm" means to pay someone). Just as grease makes for an easier fit among gears, money reduces the friction—the transaction costs—of exchange. Too little leaves some parts creaking; too much gums up the works.

This chapter is obviously about money. We begin with the evolution of money, tracing its use in broad strokes from primitive economies to our own. Then we turn to developments in the United States.

What do you think?

The government has an obligation to protect failing banks during depressions.

Strongly Disagree						Strongly Agree
1	2	3	4	5	6	7

Topics discussed in Chapter 14 include:

- Barter
- Functions of money
- Commodity and fiat money
- The Federal Reserve System
- Depository institutions
- U.S. Banking history and structure

LO¹ The Evolution of Money

In the beginning, there was no money. The earliest families were largely self-sufficient. Each produced all it consumed and consumed all it produced, so there was little need for exchange. Without exchange, there was no need for money. When specialization first emerged, as some people went hunting and others took up farming, hunters and farmers had to trade. Thus, the specialization of labor resulted in exchange, but the assortment of goods traded was limited enough that people could easily exchange their products directly for other products—a system called *barter*.

Barter and the Double Coincidence of Wants

Barter depends on a double coincidence of wants, which occurs when one trader is willing to exchange his or her product for something another trader has to offer. If a hunter was willing to exchange hides for a farmer's corn, that was a coincidence. But if the farmer was also willing to exchange corn for the hunter's hides, that was a double coincidence—a *double coincidence of wants*. As long as specialization was limited, to, say, two or three goods, mutually beneficial trades were relatively easy to come by—that is, trade wasn't much of a coincidence. As specialization increased, however, finding the particular goods that each trader wanted became more difficult.

In a barter system, traders must not only discover a double coincidence of wants, they must also agree on an exchange rate. How many bushels of corn should the hunter get for a hide? If only two goods are produced, only one exchange rate needs to

double coincidence of wants
two traders are willing to exchange their products directly

money
anything that is generally accepted in exchange for goods and services

be worked out. As the variety of goods traded increased, however, exchange rates increased too. Specialization increased the transaction costs of barter. A huge difference in the values of the units to be exchanged also made barter difficult. For example, a hunter wanting to buy a home that exchanged for 1,000 hides would be hard-pressed finding a home seller needing that many. High transaction costs of barter gave birth to money.

The Earliest Money and Its Functions

Nobody actually recorded the emergence of money. We can only speculate about how it first came into use. Through experience with barter, traders may have found they could always find buyers for certain goods. If a trader could not find a good that he or she desired personally, some other good with a ready market could be accepted instead. So traders began to accept a certain good not for immediate consumption but because that good could be easily traded later. For example, corn might become acceptable because traders knew that it was always in demand. As one good became generally accepted in return for all other goods, that good began to function as money. *Any commodity that acquires a high degree of acceptability throughout an economy becomes money.*

Money fulfills three important functions:

1. a *medium of exchange*
2. a *unit of account*
3. a *store of value.*

3

<< Any commodity that acquires a high degree of acceptability throughout an economy becomes money.

<< **Roman soldiers received part of their pay in salt.**

people can price everything using a single measure, such as corn. For example, if a pair of shoes sells for 2 bushels of corn and a 5-gallon pot sells for 1 bushel of corn, then a pair of shoes has the same value in exchange as two 5-gallon pots.

Store of Value

Because people do not want to buy something every time they sell something, the purchasing power acquired through a sale must somehow be preserved. Money serves as a store of value when it retains purchasing power over time. The better it preserves purchasing power, the better money serves as a store of value, and the more willing people are to hold it. Consider again the distinction between a stock and a flow. Recall that a stock is an amount measured at a particular point in time, such as the amount of food in your refrigerator, or the amount of money you have with you right now. In contrast, a *flow* is an amount per unit of time, such as the calories you consume per day, or the income you earn per week. *Money* is a stock and *income* is a flow. Don't confuse money with income. The role of money as a stock is best reflected by money's role as a store of value.

Medium of Exchange

Separating the sale of one good from the purchase of another requires an item acceptable to all involved in the transactions. If a society, by luck or by design, can find a commodity that everyone accepts in exchange for whatever is sold, traders can save time, disappointment, and sheer aggravation. Suppose corn takes on this role, a role that clearly goes beyond its role as food. We then call corn a medium of exchange because it is accepted in exchange by all buyers and sellers, whether or not they want corn for food. A medium of exchange is anything that is generally accepted in payment for goods and services. The person who accepts corn in exchange for some product believes corn can be traded later for whatever is desired.

In this example, corn is both a *commodity* and *money,* so we call it commodity money. The earliest money was commodity money. Gold and silver have been used as money for at least 4,000 years. Cattle served as money, first for the Greeks, then for the Romans. In fact, the word *pecuniary* (meaning "of or relating to money") comes from the Latin word for cattle, *pecus.* Roman soldiers received part of their pay in salt; the salt portion was called the *salarium,* the origin of the word *salary.* Also used as money were wampum (polished strings of shells) and tobacco in colonial America, tea pressed into small cakes in Russia, rice in Japan, and palm dates in North Africa. Note that commodity money is a good, not a service; a service is intangible and cannot be held for later exchange.

Unit of Account

A commodity such as corn that grows to be widely accepted becomes a unit of account, a standard on which prices are based. The price of hides or shoes or pots is measured in bushels of corn. Thus, corn serves not only as a medium of exchange; it also becomes a common denominator, a yardstick, for *measuring the value* of each product exchanged in the economy. Rather than having to determine exchange rates among all products, as with a barter economy,

Properties of the Ideal Money

The introduction of commodity money reduced the transaction costs of exchange compared with barter, but commodity money also involves some transaction costs. First, if the commodity money is perishable, as is corn, it must be properly stored or its quality deteriorates; even then, it won't maintain its quality for long. U.S. coins have a projected life of 30 years (a dollar note, only 18 months). So the ideal money should be *durable.* Second, if the commodity money is bulky, major purchases can become unwieldy. For example, truckloads of corn would be needed to purchase a home selling for 5,000 bushels of corn. So the ideal money should be *portable,* or easily carried. Dollar notes are easier to carry than dollar coins, which may explain why dollar coins never become popular in the United States. Third, some commodity money was not easily divisible into smaller units. For example, when cattle served as money, any price involving a fraction of a cow posed

medium of exchange
anything that facilitates trade by being generally accepted by all parties in payment for goods or services

commodity money
anything that serves both as money and as a commodity; money that has intrinsic value

unit of account
a common unit for measuring the value of each good or service

store of value
anything that retains its purchasing power over time

Exhibit 1

Six Properties of Ideal Money

Quality	Rationale	Good Examples	Bad Examples
1. Durable	Money should not wear out quickly	Coins; sea shells	Strawberries; seafood
2. Portable	Money should be easy to carry, even relatively large sums	Diamonds; paper money	Lead bars; potatoes
3. Divisible	Market exchange is easier if denominations support a range of possible prices	Honey; paper money and coins	Cattle; diamonds
4. Uniform Quality	If money is not of uniform quality, people will hoard the best and spend the rest, reducing its quality	Salt bricks; paper money; coins	Diamonds
5. Low Opportunity Cost	The fewer resources tied up in creating money, the more available for other uses	Iron coins; paper money	Gold; diamonds
6. Stable Value	People are more willing to accept and hold money if they believe it will keep its value over time	Anything whose supply can be controlled by issuing authority, such as paper money	Farm crops

an exchange problem. So the ideal money should be *divisible*.

Fourth, if commodity money like corn is valued equally in exchange, regardless of its quality, people keep the best corn and trade away the rest. As a result, the quality remaining in circulation declines, reducing its acceptability. Sir Thomas Gresham wrote back in the 16th century that "bad money drives out good money;" this has come to be known as Gresham's law. People tend to trade away inferior money and hoard the best. Over time, the quality of money in circulation becomes less acceptable and, therefore, less useful as a medium of exchange. To avoid this problem, the ideal money should be of *uniform quality*.

Fifth, commodity money usually ties up otherwise valuable resources, so it has a higher opportunity cost than, say, paper money. For example, corn that is used for money cannot at the same time be used for corn on the cob, corn flour, popcorn, or other food. So the ideal money should have a low *opportunity cost*.

If the supply or demand for money fluctuates unpredictably, so will the economy's price level, and this is the final problem with commodity money. For example, if a bumper crop increases the supply of corn, more corn is required to purchase other goods. This we call *inflation*. Likewise, any change in the demand for corn *as food* from, say, the growing popularity of corn chips, would affect the exchange value of corn. Erratic fluctuations in the market for corn limit its use-

> **Ideal money:**
>
> **is durable**
> **is portable**
> **is divisible**
> **is of uniform quality**
> **has a low opportunity cost**
> **is relatively stable in value**

fulness as money, particularly as a unit of account and a store of value. So the ideal money *should maintain a relatively stable value over time*. Money supplied by a responsible issuing authority is likely to retain its value better over time than money whose supply depends on uncontrollable forces of nature such as good or bad growing seasons.

What all this boils down to is that the *ideal money is durable, portable, divisible, of uniform quality, has a low opportunity cost, and is relatively stable in value*. These qualities are reinforced in Exhibit 1, which also lists the rationale, good examples, and bad examples. Please spend a minute now reviewing the table.

Coins

The division of commodity money into units was often natural, as in bushels of corn or heads of cattle. When rock salt was used as money, it was cut into uniform bricks. Because salt was usually of consistent quality, a trader had only to count the bricks to determine the total amount of money. When silver and gold were used as money, both their quantity and quality were open to question. Because precious metals could be *debased* with cheaper metals, the quantity and the quality of the metal had to be determined with each exchange.

This quality control problem was addressed by coining precious metals. *Coinage determined both the amount and quality of the metal.* Coins allowed payment by count rather than by weight. A flat surface on which this money was counted came to be called the *counter*, a term still used today. Initially, an image was stamped on only one side of a coin, leaving the

Gresham's Law
people tend to trade away inferior money and hoard the best

other side blank. But people began shaving precious metal from the blank side. To prevent this, images were stamped on both sides. But another problem arose because bits of metal could still be clipped from the coin's edge. To prevent clipping, coins were bordered with a well-defined rim. If you have a dime or a quarter, notice the tiny serrations on the edge. These serrations, throwbacks from the time when these coins were silver, reduced the chances of "getting clipped."

The power to issue coins was vested in the *seignior*, or feudal lord. Counterfeiting was considered an act of treason. If the face value of the coin exceeded the cost of coinage, minting coins was profitable. **Seigniorage** (pronounced "seen´-your-edge") refers to the profit earned by the seignior from coinage. **Token money** is money whose face value exceeds its production cost. Coins and paper money now in circulation in the United States are token money. For example, the 25-cent coin costs the U.S. Mint only about 9 cents to make. Minting 25-cent coins nets the U.S. Treasury hundreds of millions of dollars a year in seigniorage. But the penny and even the nickel now cost more to mint than they are worth in exchange.

Money and Banking

The word *bank* comes from the Italian word *banca*, meaning "bench," which was a money changer's table. Banking spread from Italy to England, where

London goldsmiths offered safekeeping for money and other valuables. The goldsmith gave depositors their money back on request, but because deposits by some tended to offset withdrawals by others, the amount of idle cash, or gold, in the vault changed little over time. Goldsmiths found that they could earn interest by lending from this pool of idle cash.

Goldsmiths offered depositors safekeeping, but visiting the goldsmith to get money to pay for each purchase became a nuisance. For example, a farmer might visit the goldsmith to withdraw enough money to buy a horse. The farmer would then pay the horse trader, who would promptly deposit the receipts with the goldsmith. Thus, money took a round trip from goldsmith to farmer to horse trader and back to goldsmith. Because depositors soon grew tired of visiting the goldsmith every time they needed money, they began instructing the goldsmith to pay someone from their account. The payment amounted to moving gold from one stack (the farmer's) to another stack (the horse trader's). *These written instructions to the goldsmith were the first checks.* **Checks** have since become official-looking, but they need not be, as evidenced by the actions of a Montana man who paid a speeding fine with instructions written on clean but frayed underpants. The Western Federal Savings and Loan of Missoula honored the check.

By combining the ideas of cash loans and checks, the goldsmith soon discovered how to make loans by check. Rather than lend idle cash, the goldsmith could simply create a checking balance for the borrower. *The goldsmith could extend a loan by creating an account against which the borrower could write checks. In this way goldsmiths, or banks, were able to create a medium of exchange, or to "create money."* This money, based only on an entry in the goldsmith's ledger, was accepted because of the public's confidence that these claims would be honored.

The total claims against the goldsmith consisted of claims by people who had deposited their money plus claims by borrowers for whom the goldsmith had created deposits. Because these claims exceeded the value of gold on reserve, this was the beginning of a **fractional reserve banking system**, a system in which bank reserves amounted to just a fraction of total deposits. The *reserve ratio* measured reserves as a

seigniorage
the difference between the face value of money and the cost of supplying it; the "profit" from issuing money

token money
money whose face value exceeds its cost of production

check
a written order instructing the bank to pay someone from an amount deposited

fractional reserve banking system
bank reserves amount to only a fraction of funds on deposit with the bank

Value   **Cost to Mint**

>> Find out more about values and costs of small change in the chapter case study at **4ltrpress.cengage.com/econ**.

© PETER SPIRO/ISTOCKPHOTO.COM / © STEPHEN HILGER/BLOOMBERG NEWS/LANDOV percentage of total claims against the goldsmith, or total deposits. For example, if the goldsmith had reserves of $4,000 but deposits of $10,000, the reserve ratio would be 40 percent. The goldsmith was relying on the fact that not everyone would ask for their deposits at the same time.

Representative Money and Fiat Money

Another way a bank could create money was by issuing bank notes. Bank notes were pieces of paper promising the bearer specific amounts of gold or silver when the notes were presented to the issuing bank for redemption. In London, goldsmith bankers introduced bank notes about the same time they introduced checks. *Whereas checks could be redeemed only if endorsed by the payee, notes could be redeemed by anyone who presented them.* Paper money was often "as good as gold," because the bearer could redeem it for gold. In fact, paper money was more convenient than gold because it was less bulky and more portable. Bank notes that exchange for a specific commodity, such as gold, were called representative money. The paper money *represented* gold in the bank's vault.

The amount of paper money issued by a bank depended on that bank's estimate of the share of notes that would be redeemed. The higher the redemption rate, the fewer notes could be issued based on a given amount of reserves. Initially, these promises to pay were issued by private individuals or banks, but over time, governments took a larger role in printing and circulating notes. Once paper money became widely accepted, it was perhaps inevitable that governments would begin issuing fiat money, which derives its status as money from the power of the state, or by *fiat*. Fiat (pronounced "fee´at") money is money because the government says so. The word *fiat* is from the Latin and means "so be it." Fiat money is not redeemable for anything other than more fiat money; it is not backed by something of intrinsic value. You can think of fiat money as mere paper money. It is acceptable not because it is intrinsically useful or valuable—as is corn or gold—but because the government says it's money. Fiat money is declared legal tender by the government, meaning that you have made a valid and legal offer of payment of your debt when you pay with such money. *Gradually, people came to accept fiat money because they believed that others would accept it as well.* The currency issued in the United States and throughout most of the world is fiat money.

A well-regulated system of fiat money is more efficient for an economy than commodity money. Fiat money uses only paper (a dollar note costs about 7 cents to make), but commodity money ties up something intrinsically valuable. Paper money makes up only part of the money supply. Modern money also includes checking accounts, which are electronic entries in bank computers.

bank notes
originally, pieces of paper promising a specific amount of gold or silver to anyone who presented them to issuing banks for redemption; today, Federal Reserve notes are mere paper money

representative money
bank notes that exchange for a specific commodity, such as gold

fiat money
money not redeemable for any commodity; its status as money is conferred initially by government decree but eventually by common experience

legal tender
currency that constitutes a valid and legal offer of payment of debt

Is It Counterfeit?

Here Boggs is holding a drawing of a $20 bill which he exchanged for a shipment of lobsters.

J. S. G. Boggs, one of the most famous money artists, has used his art to raise questions about the value of money and art. Boggs draws copies of currency bills, adding small changes to distinguish them from real currency. He considers the work of art incomplete, however, until he makes a transaction in which he offers his notes at face value for real goods or services. He always explains that he is exchanging art for goods—a form of barter or trade rather than an attempt to pass them off as real money—and he keeps the change, the receipt, and sometimes the goods, and sells them as a piece of art representing the transaction. Art collectors can then use the receipt to track down Boggs' notes and purchase them to complete the collection. Boggs has been arrested in Australia and England for counterfeiting (he was acquitted), and in 1991 the Secret Service raided his apartment, seizing many of his notes. Is Boggs counterfeiting? How much are his notes really worth? For more about Boggs, watch Philip Haas' documentary *Money Man.*

SOURCE: Olav Velthius, "In *Boggs* We Trust," *tout-fait: The Marcel Duchamp Studies Online Journal* (January 2002), (2)4. Available at http://www.toutfait .com/issues/volume2/issue_4/articles/velthuis/velthuis1.html (accessed 26 March 2009).

Exhibit 2

Purchasing Power of $1 Measured in 1982–1984 Constant Dollars

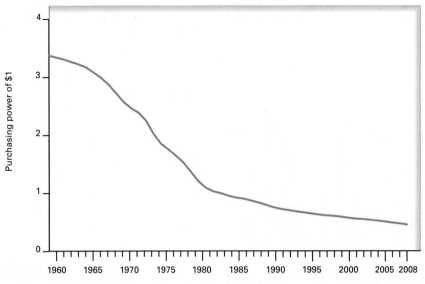

SOURCE: Developed using CPI figures from the U.S. Bureau of Labor Statistics. For the latest CPI, go to http://www.bls.gov/cpi/home.htm.

To measure the purchasing power of the dollar in a particular year, you first compute the price index for that year and then divide 100 by that price index. For example, relative to the base period of 1982 through 1984, the consumer price index for February 2009 was 212. The purchasing power of a dollar was therefore 100/212, or $0.47, measured in 1982–1984 dollars. Exhibit 2 shows the steady decline in the value of the dollar since 1960, when it was worth $3.38 in 1982–1984 dollars.

When Money Performs Poorly

One way to understand the functions of money is to look at instances where money did not perform well. In an earlier chapter, we mentioned hyperinflation in Zimbabwe. With prices growing by the hour, money no longer served as a reliable store of value, so people couldn't wait to exchange their money for goods or for some "hard" currency—that is, a more stable currency. If inflation gets high enough, people no longer accept the nation's money and instead resort to some other means of exchange. On the other hand, if the supply of money dries up or if the price system is not allowed to function properly, barter may be the only alternative.

LO² Financial Institutions in the United States

You have already learned about the origin of modern banks: Goldsmiths lent money from deposits held for safekeeping. So you already have some idea of how banks work. Recall from the circular-flow model that household saving flows into financial markets, where it is lent to investors. Financial institutions, such as banks, mortgage companies, and finance companies, accumulate funds from savers and lend them to borrowers. Financial institutions, or financial intermediaries, earn a profit by "buying low and selling high"—that is, by paying a lower interest rate to savers than they charge borrowers.

financial intermediaries institutions such as banks, mortgage companies, and finance companies that serve as go-betweens, borrowing from people who have saved to make loans to others

The Value of Money

Money has grown increasingly more abstract—from a physical commodity, to a piece of paper representing a claim on a physical commodity, to a piece of paper of no intrinsic value, to an electronic entry representing a claim on a piece of paper of no intrinsic value. So why does money have value? The commodity feature of early money bolstered confidence in its acceptability. Commodities such as corn, tobacco, and gold had value in use even if for some reason they became less acceptable in exchange. When paper money came into use, its acceptability was initially fostered by the promise to redeem it for gold or silver. But because most paper money throughout the world is now fiat money, there is no promise of redemption. So why can a piece of paper bearing the portrait of Alexander Hamilton and the number 10 in each corner be exchanged for a pizza or anything else selling for $10? *People accept these pieces of paper because, through experience, they believe that others will do so as well.* The acceptability of money, which we now take for granted, is based on years of experience with the stability of its value and with the willingness of others to accept it as payment. As we will soon see, when money's value becomes questionable, so does its acceptability.

The *purchasing power* of money is the rate at which it exchanges for goods and services. The higher the price level in the economy, the less can be purchased with each dollar, so the less each dollar is worth. The purchasing power of each dollar over time varies inversely with the economy's price level. As the price level increases, the purchasing power of money falls.

Commercial Banks and Thrifts

A wide variety of financial intermediaries respond to the economy's demand for financial services. Depository institutions—such as commercial banks, savings banks, and credit unions—obtain funds primarily by accepting customer *deposits*. Depository institutions play a key role in providing the nation's money supply. Depository institutions can be classified broadly into commercial banks and thrift institutions.

Commercial banks are the oldest, largest, and most diversified of depository institutions. They are called commercial banks because historically they made loans primarily to *commercial* ventures, or businesses, rather than to households. Commercial banks hold about 75 percent of all deposits. Thrift institutions, or thrifts, include savings banks and credit unions. Historically, savings banks specialized in making home mortgage loans. Credit unions, which are more numerous but smaller than savings banks, extend loans only to their "members" to finance homes or other major consumer purchases, such as new cars.

LO³ Birth of the Fed

Before 1863, banks were chartered by the states in which they operated, so they were called *state banks*. These banks, like the English goldsmiths, issued bank notes. Notes from thousands of different banks circulated and most were redeemable for gold. The National Banking Act of 1863 and later amendments created a new system of federally chartered banks called *national banks*. National banks were authorized to issue notes and were regulated by the Office of the Comptroller of the Currency, part of the U.S. Treasury. State bank notes were taxed out of existence, but state banks survived by creating checking accounts for borrowers. To this day, the United States has a *dual banking system* consisting of state banks and national banks.

During the 19th century, the economy experienced a number of panic "runs" on banks by depositors seeking to withdraw their money. A panic was usually set off by the failure of some prominent financial institution. Fearful customers besieged their banks. Borrowers wanted additional loans and extensions of credit, and depositors wanted their money back. As *many depositors tried to withdraw their money, they couldn't because each bank held only a fraction of its deposits as cash reserves.* To reduce such panics, Congress created the Federal Reserve System in 1913 as the central bank and monetary authority of the United States.

Nearly all industrialized countries had formed central banks by 1900—such as the Bundesbank in Germany, the Bank of Japan, and the Bank of England. But the American public's suspicion of monopoly power led to the establishment of not one central bank but separate banks in each of the 12 Federal Reserve districts around the country. The new banks were named after the cities in which they were located—the Federal Reserve Banks of Boston, New York, Chicago, San Francisco, and so on, as shown in Exhibit 3 (which district are you in?). *Throughout most of its history, the United States had what is called*

depository institutions
commercial banks and thrift institutions; financial institutions that accept deposits from the public

commercial banks
depository institutions that historically made short-term loans primarily to businesses

thrift institutions (thrifts)
savings banks and credit unions; depository institutions that historically lent money to households

Federal Reserve System (the Fed)
the central bank and monetary authority of the United States

Exhibit 3

The Twelve Federal Reserve Districts

Alaska and Hawaii are part of the San Francisco District

SOURCE: Federal Reserve Board Web page at http://www.federalreserve.gov/otherfrb.htm.

Ben Bernanke
Federal Reserve Chairman

© AP IMAGES / © BURKE/TRIOLO/BRAND X PICTURES/JUPITERIMAGES

as depository institutions hold deposits of the public, and they extend loans to member banks, just as depository institutions extend loans to the public. The name *reserve bank* comes from the responsibility to hold member bank *reserves* on deposit.

Reserves are funds that banks have on hand or on deposit with the Fed to promote banking safety, to facilitate interbank transfers of funds, to satisfy the cash demands of their customers, and to comply with Federal Reserve regulations. By holding bank reserves, a reserve bank can clear a check written by a depositor at one bank and deposited at another bank, much like the goldsmith's moving of gold reserves from the farmer's account to the horse trader's account. Reserve banks are also authorized to lend to banks in need of reserves; the interest rate charged is called the *discount rate*.

A member bank is required to own stock in its district Federal Reserve Bank, and this entitles the bank to a 6 percent annual dividend. Any additional profit earned by the reserve banks is turned over to the U.S. Treasury. So, technically, the reserve banks are owned by the member banks in the district.

LO⁴ History of U.S. Banking System

From the Great Depression to today, the U.S. banking system has followed a trajectory of tight regulation followed by deregulation, followed then by a gradual loosening of various regulatory strictures. Let's take a look at the historic stops along the evolution of the U.S. banking system during the 20th and early 21st centuries.

Banking Troubles During the Great Depression

From 1913 to 1929, both the Federal Reserve System and the national economy performed relatively well. But the stock market crash of 1929 was followed by the Great Depression, creating a new set of problems for the Fed, such as bank runs caused by panicked depositors. The Fed, however, dropped the ball by failing to act as a lender of last resort—that is, the Fed did not lend banks the money they needed to satisfy deposit withdrawals in cases of runs on otherwise sound banks. Many banks did not survive. Between 1930 and 1933, about 10,000

a decentralized banking system. The Federal Reserve Act moved the country toward a system that was partly centralized and partly decentralized. All national banks had to joined the Federal Reserve System and thus were subject to new regulations issued by the Fed, as it came to be called (don't confuse *the Fed* with *the Feds,* shorthand for the FBI and other federal crime fighters). For state banks, membership was voluntary, and, to avoid the new regulations, most did not join.

Powers of the Federal Reserve System

The Federal Reserve was authorized to ensure sufficient money and credit in the banking system to support a growing economy. The power to issue bank notes was taken away from national banks and turned over to Federal Reserve Banks. (Take out a $1 note and notice what it says across the top: "Federal Reserve Note." On the $1 note, the seal to the left of George Washington's portrait identifies which Federal Reserve Bank issued the note.) The Federal Reserve was also granted other powers: *to buy and sell government securities, to extend loans to member banks, to clear checks in the banking system,* and *to require that member banks hold reserves equal to at least some specified fraction of their deposits.*

Federal Reserve Banks do not deal with the public directly. Each may be thought of as a bankers' bank. Reserve banks hold deposits of member banks, just

> **reserves**
> funds that banks use to satisfy the cash demands of their customers and the reserve requirements of the Fed; reserves consist of cash held by banks plus deposits at the Fed

banks failed—about one-third of all banks. Most depositors at the failed banks lost everything.

In his first inaugural address in 1933, newly elected President Franklin D. Roosevelt said, "The only thing we have to fear is fear itself," a statement especially apt for a fractional reserve banking system. Most banks were sound as long as people had confidence in the safety of their deposits. But if many depositors, fearing the safety of their deposits, tried to withdraw their money, they could not do so because each bank held only a fraction of deposits as reserves. Bank legislation passed during the Great Depression shored up the banking system and centralized power with the Fed in Washington. Here are some features of this legislation.

Board of Governors

The *Board of Governors*, which consists of seven members appointed by the president and confirmed by the Senate, became responsible for setting and implementing the nation's monetary policy. *Monetary policy*, a term introduced in Chapter 3, is the regulation of the economy's money supply and interest rates to promote macroeconomic objectives. The Board of Governors now oversees the 12 reserve banks, making the system more centralized. Each governor serves a 14-year nonrenewable term, with one governor appointed every two years. *The long tenure is designed to insulate board members from political pressure.* A new U.S. president can be sure of appointing only two members during a presidential term, so a new president could not change much. One governor is also appointed to chair the board for a four-year renewable term.

Federal Open Market Committee

Federal Open Market Committee (FOMC)
the 12-member group that makes decisions about open-market operations—purchases and sales of U.S. government securities by the Fed that affect the money supply and interest rates; consists of the seven board governors plus five of the 12 presidents of the Reserve Banks

open-market operations
purchases and sales of government securities by the Fed in an effort to influence the money supply

The Federal Open Market Committee (FOMC) makes decisions about the key tool of monetary policy, open-market operations—the Fed's buying and selling of government securities (tools of monetary policy are examined in the next chapter). The FOMC consists of the seven board governors plus five of the 12 presidents of the reserve banks; the chair of the Board of Governors heads the group. Because the New York Federal Reserve Bank carries out open-market operations, that bank's president always sits on the FOMC. The structure of the Federal Reserve System is presented in Exhibit 4. The FOMC and, less significantly, the Federal Advisory Committee (which consists of a banker from each of the 12 reserve bank districts) advise the board.

Regulating the Money Supply

Because reserves amount to just a fraction of deposits, the United States has a *fractional reserve* banking system, as already noted. The Federal Reserve System has a variety of tools to regulate the money supply, including *(1) conducting open-market operations—buying and selling U.S. government securities; (2) setting the discount rate—the interest rate charged by reserve banks for loans to member banks; and (3) setting legal reserve requirements for member banks.* We explore these tools in greater detail in the next chapter.

Deposit Insurance

Panic runs on banks stemmed from fears about the safety of bank deposits. The *Federal Deposit Insurance Corporation (FDIC)* was established in 1933 to insure the first $2,500 of each deposit account. Today the insurance ceiling is $250,000 per depositor per bank. Over 90 percent of all banks now purchase FDIC insurance. Other insurance programs take care of the rest. *Deposit insurance, by calming fears about the safety of bank deposits, worked wonders to reduce bank runs.*

Banks Lost Deposits When Inflation Increased

Prior to the 1930s, banks could own corporate stock and bonds, financial assets that fluctuate widely in value and contributed to instability of the banking system. Reforms enacted during the Great Depression limited bank assets primarily to loans and government securities—bonds issued by federal, state, and local governments. A *bond* is an IOU, so a government bond is an IOU from the government. Also, bank failures during the 1930s were thought to have resulted in part from fierce interest-rate competition among banks for customer deposits. To curb such competition, the Fed was empowered to set a ceiling on interest rates that banks could pay depositors.

These restrictions made banking a heavily regulated industry. Banks lost much of their freedom to wheel and deal, and the federal government insured most deposits. The assets banks could acquire were carefully limited, as were the interest rates they could offer depositors (checking deposits earned no interest). Banking thus became a highly regulated, even stuffy, industry. The term "banker's hours" was applied derisively to someone who had a short workday.

Exhibit 4

Organization Chart of the Federal Reserve System

Members of the Board of Governors are appointed by the president and confirmed by the Senate. The seven board members also belong to the 12-member Federal Open Market Committee, which advises the board. The Board of Governors controls the Reserve Banks in each of the 12 districts, which in turn control the U.S. banking system.

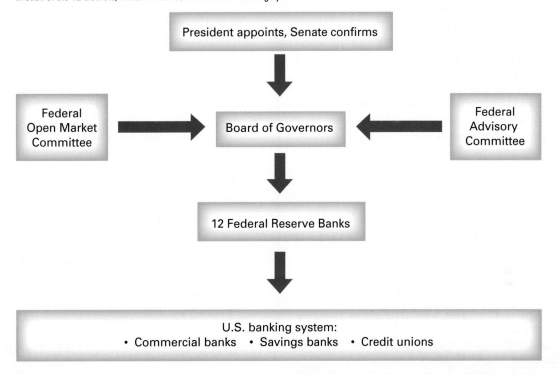

President appoints, Senate confirms

Federal Open Market Committee → Board of Governors ← Federal Advisory Committee

12 Federal Reserve Banks

U.S. banking system:
- Commercial banks
- Savings banks
- Credit unions

Ceilings on interest rates reduced interest-rate competition for deposits *among* banks. But a surge of inflation during the 1970s increased interest rates in the economy. Banking has not been the same since. When market interest rates rose above what banks could legally offer depositors, many withdrew their deposits and put them into higher-yielding alternatives. In 1972, Merrill Lynch, a major brokerage house, introduced an account combining a **money market mutual fund** with limited check-writing privileges. Money market mutual fund shares are claims on a portfolio, or collection, of short-term interest-earning assets. These mutual funds became stiff competition for bank deposits, especially checkable deposits, which at the time paid no interest at banks.

Banking Deregulation

In response to the loss of deposits and other problems, Congress tried to ease regulations, giving banks greater discretion in their operations. For example, interest-rate ceilings for deposits were eliminated, and all depository institutions were allowed to offer money market deposit accounts. Such deposits jumped from only $8 billion in 1978 to $200 billion in 1982. Some states, like California and Texas, also deregulated state-chartered savings banks. The combination of deposit insurance, unregulated interest rates, and wider latitude in the kinds of assets that savings banks could purchase gave them a green light to compete for large deposits in national markets. Once-staid financial institutions moved into the fast lane.

Banks could wheel and deal but with the benefit of

money market mutual fund a collection of short-term interest-earning assets purchased with funds collected from many shareholders

6 Goals of Today's Fed

Over the years, the Fed has accumulated additional responsibilities. Here are 6 frequently mentioned goals of the Fed:

- a high level of employment in the economy
- economic growth
- price stability
- interest rate stability
- financial market stability
- exchange rate stability.

These goals boil down to high employment; economic growth; and stability in prices, interest rates, financial markets, and exchange rates. As we will see, not all of these objectives can be achieved simultaneously.

deposit insurance. The combination of deregulation and deposit insurance encouraged some on the verge of failing to take bigger risks—to "bet the bank"—because their depositors would be protected by deposit insurance. This created a *moral hazard*, which in this case was the tendency of bankers to take unwarranted risks in making loans because deposits were insured. Banks that were virtually bankrupt—so-called "zombie" banks—were able to attract additional deposits because of deposit insurance. Zombie banks, by offering higher interest rates, also drew deposits away from healthier banks. Meanwhile, because deposits were insured, most depositors paid less attention to their banks' health. Thus, *deposit insurance, originally introduced during the Great Depression to prevent bank panics, caused depositors to become complacent about the safety of their deposits. Worse still, it caused those who ran troubled banks to take wild gambles to survive.*

Savings Banks on the Ropes

Many of these gambles didn't pay off, particularly loans to real estate developers, and banks lost a ton of money. The insolvency and collapse of a growing number of banks prompted Congress in 1989 to approve what was then the largest financial bailout of any U.S. industry in history—a measure that would eventually cost about $150 billion. Taxpayers paid 80 percent of the total, and banks paid the remaining 20 percent through higher deposit insurance premiums. The money was spent to close down failing banks, pay off insured depositors, and find healthier banks to take over the deposit accounts.

Exhibit 5 shows the number of savings bank failures in the United States by year since 1980. From their 1989 peak of 328, annual failures dropped to 2 or fewer between 1995 and 2008. Because of failures and mergers, the number of FDIC-insured savings banks fell from 3,418 in 1984 to 1,220 in 2008, a drop of 64 percent. But the financial crisis contributed to a spike in bank failures in 2009.

Credit unions, which make up the bulk of thrift institutions, got into less trouble than savings banks because credit unions typically lent for shorter periods. Still, because of failures and mergers, the number of federally insured credit unions declined by 34 percent from 12,596 in 1992 to 7,904 in 2008.

bank branches
a bank's additional offices that carry out banking operations

Commercial Banks Were Failing Too

The U.S. banking system experienced more change and upheaval during the 1980s and early 1990s than at any other time since the Great Depression. As was the case of savings banks, risky decisions based on deposit insurance hastened the demise of many commercial banks. Banks in Texas and Oklahoma failed when loans to oil drillers and farmers proved unsound. Banks in the Northeast failed because of falling real estate values, which caused borrowers to default. Hundreds of troubled banks, like Continental Illinois Bank, First Republic Bank of Dallas, and the Bank of New England, were taken over by the FDIC or forced to merge with healthier competitors. Exhibit 6 shows commercial bank failures since 1980. The rising tide during the 1980s is clear, with failures peaking at 280 in 1988. But by the mid 1990s, failures declined sharply and were in single digits from 1995 to 2007. The subprime mortgage and global financial crises caused an increase in the number of commercial bank failures in 2008 and early 2009. Because of failures, mergers, and acquisitions, the number of FDIC-insured commercial banks fell from 14,496 in 1984 to 7,085 by 2008, a drop of 51 percent.

U.S. Banking Structure Today

As failed banks disappeared or merged with stronger banks, the industry got healthier. Bank profits grew fourfold during the 1990s. Although the number of commercial banks fell by half since the mid 1980s, the United States still has more than any other country. Other major economies have fewer than 1,000 commercial banks. The large number of U.S. banks reflects past restrictions on bank branches, which are additional offices that carry out banking operations. Again, Americans,

Exhibit 5

Failures of U.S. Savings Banks Peaked in 1989

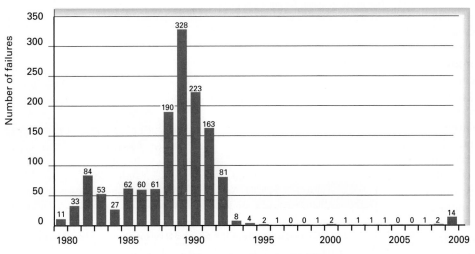

SOURCE: Based on annual reports from the Federal Deposit Insurance Corporation. For the latest figures, go to http://www.fdic.gov/bank/individual/failed/banklist.html. Figure for 2009 is as of July 2, 2009.

fearing monopoly power, did not want any one bank to become too large and too powerful. The combination of intrastate and interstate restrictions on branching spawned the many commercial banks that exist today, most of which are relatively small. For example, the bottom 92 percent of U.S. banks hold just 13 percent of all deposits. Branching restrictions create inefficiencies, because banks cannot achieve optimal size and cannot easily diversify their portfolios of loans across different regions. Branching restrictions were one reason for bank failures during the Depression. Such restrictions meant a bank made loans primarily in one community—it had all its eggs in that basket.

In recent years, federal legislation has lifted some restrictions on interstate branching and on the kinds of assets that banks can own. Two developments allowed banks to get around branching restrictions: bank holding companies and mergers. A *bank holding company* is a corporation that may own several different banks. The *Gramm-Leach-Bliley Act* of 1999 repealed some Depression-era restrictions on the kinds of assets a bank could own. A holding company can provide other services that banks are not authorized to offer, such as financial advising, leasing, insurance, credit cards, and securities trading. Thus, holding companies have blossomed in recent years. More than three-quarters of the nation's checking deposits are in banks owned by holding companies. In the aftermath of the subprime mortgage and global financial crises, policymakers are debating the pros and cons of re-regulating the kinds of assets a bank could own.

Another important development that allowed banks to expand their geographical reach is *bank mergers*, which have spread the presence of some banks across the country. Banks are merging because they want more customers and expect the higher volume of transactions to reduce operating costs per customer. Nationwide banking is also seen as a way of avoiding the concentration of bad loans that sometimes occur in one geographical area. The merger movement was fueled by a rising stock market and by federal legislation that facilitates consolidation of merged banks. In addition, several banks weakened by the

Exhibit 6

Failures of U.S. Commercial Banks Peaked in 1988

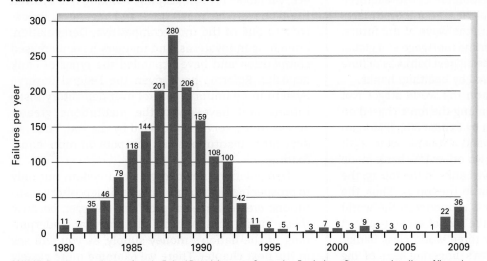

SOURCE: Based on annual reports from the Federal Deposit Insurance Corporation. For the latest figures, go to http://www.fdic.gov/bank/individual/failed/banklist.html. Figure for 2009 is as of July 2, 2009.

bank holding company
a corporation that owns banks

2008 global financial crisis merged with stronger banks.

Bank holding companies and bank mergers have reduced the number of banks but increased the number of branches. Exhibit 7 shows the number of commercial banks and bank branches in the United States since 1934. The number of banks, as indicated by "main offices," remained relatively constant between 1934 and the mid-1980s but then fell nearly in half after 1984 as a result of failures, mergers, and holding companies. The number of bank branches increased steadily, however, nearly doubling since 1984. So the number of branches per bank increased. In 1984, the average U.S. bank had about three branches; by 2008, the average bank had about 12 branches.

Exhibit 7

The Number of Commercial Banks Declined over the Last Two Decades, but the Number of Branches Continues to Grow

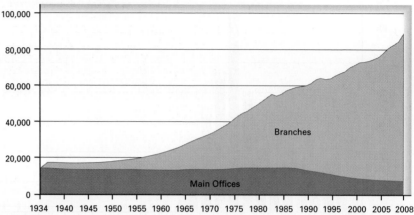

SOURCE: Figures are for FDIC-insured commercial banks in the United States based on Federal Deposit Insurance Corporation data.

Top Banks in America and the World

Exhibit 8(a) shows the top 10 U.S. banks based on their domestic deposits as of June 2008. Notice the wide range in size, with the top bank holding more than seven times the deposits as the bank ranked tenth. The top banks grew mostly through mergers and acquisitions. For example, BankAmerica and NationsBank merged to form Bank of America (BoA), which then acquired FleetBoston, a major bank in the Northeast, which itself was a product of several mergers. BoA now stretches from coast to coast with more than 5,700 branches. As another example of growth through merger, JPMorgan Chase acquired Bank One, which had been the nation's sixth largest bank. National banks are the wave of the future. Finally, because of the subprime mortgage and global financial crisis, several of the biggest banks as of June 2008 ended up being acquired by healthier banks.

How big are U.S. banks on the world stage? Not very. No U.S. bank ranked among the top 10 based on worldwide assets, as shown by Exhibit 8(b); JPMorgan Chase, Bank of America, and Citibank were 13th through 15th, respectively. No other U.S. bank made the top 25. France placed five banks in the top 25; the United Kingdom placed four in the top 25. Thus, the United States has the largest economy in the world by far, almost three times the size of second-ranked Japan, but is home to only three world-class banks. This partly reflects America's lingering fear of big banks. A federal regulation prohibits any merger if

the resulting bank holds more than 10 percent of U.S. deposits (BoA now holds 7 percent).

Final Word

Money has grown increasingly more abstract over time, moving from commodity money to paper money that represented a claim on some commodity such as gold, to paper money with no intrinsic value. As you will see, paper money constitutes only a fraction of the money supply. Modern money also consists of electronic entries in the banking system's computers. So money has changed from a physical commodity to an electronic entry. Money today does not so much change hands as change computer accounts.

Money and banking have been intertwined ever since the early goldsmiths offered to hold customers' valuables for safekeeping. Banking has evolved from one of the most staid and regulated industries to one of the most competitive. Deregulation, branching innovations, and mergers have increased competition and have expanded the types of bank deposits. Reforms have given the Federal Reserve System more uniform control over depository institutions and have given the institutions greater access to the services provided by the Fed. Thus, all depository institutions can compete on more equal footing.

Deregulation provided greater freedom not only to prosper but also to fail. Failures of depository institutions create a special problem, however, because these institutions provide the financial underpinning of the nation's money supply, as you will see in the next chapter. There we examine more closely how banks operate and supply the nation's money.

Exhibit 8

Top 10 Banks in America and the World

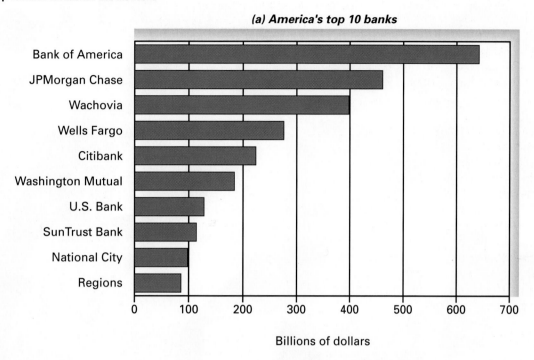

(a) America's top 10 banks

Billions of dollars

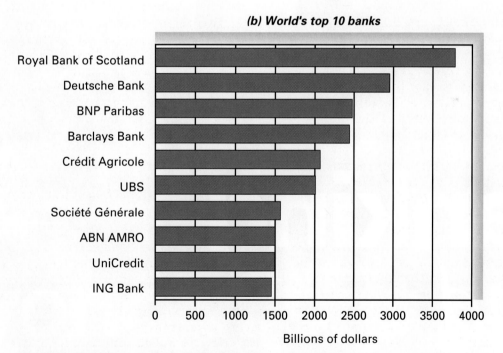

(b) World's top 10 banks

Billions of dollars

(A) SOURCE: Federal Deposit Insurance Corporation as of June 30, 2008.
NOTE: Figures in this panel account for only the banks' U.S. deposits.

(B) SOURCE: "Top 50 Banks in the World," *Bankers' Almanac.* Available at http://www.bankersalmanac.com/addcon/infobank/wldrank.aspx. Figures are total assets in U.S. dollars as of December 31, 2007.

Banking
and the Money Supply

"How is the Fed both literally and figuratively a money machine?"

How do banks create money? Why are banks called First Trust or Security National rather than Benny's Bank or Loadsamoney? How is the Fed both literally and figuratively a money machine? Why are we so interested in banks, anyway? After all, isn't banking a business like any other, such as dry cleaning, auto washing, or home remodeling? Why not devote a chapter to the home-remodeling business? Answers to these and related questions are provided in this chapter, which examines banking and the money supply.

In this chapter, we take a closer look at the unique role banks play in the economy. Banks are special in macroeconomics because, like the London goldsmiths, they can convert a borrower's IOU into money, one key to a healthy economy. Because regulatory reforms have eliminated many of the distinctions between commercial banks and thrift institutions, all depository institutions are usually referred to more simply as *banks*.

We begin by going over the definitions of money, from the narrow to the broader view. Then, we look at how banks work and how they create money. We also consider the Fed in more detail. As you will see, the Fed attempts to control the money supply directly by issuing currency and indirectly by regulating bank reserves.

What do you think?

Most banks don't take part in risky lending.

Strongly Disagree						Strongly Agree
1	2	3	4	5	6	7

Topics discussed in Chapter 15 include:

- Money aggregates
- Checkable deposits
- Balance sheets
- Money creation
- Money multiplier
- Tools of the Fed

LO¹ Money Aggregates

When you think of money, what comes to mind is probably currency—dollar notes and coins. But as you learned in the last chapter, dollar notes and coins account for only part of the money supply. In this section, we consider two definitions of money.

Narrow Definition of Money: M1

Suppose you have some cash with you right now—dollar notes and coins. Dollar notes and coins are part of the money supply as narrowly defined. If you were to deposit this cash in your checking account, you could then write checks directing your bank to

© ISTOCKPHOTO.COM

pay someone from your account. **Checkable deposits** are bank deposits that allow the account owner to write checks to third parties. Checkable deposits are included in the narrow definition of money and can also be tapped with an ATM card or a debit card. Banks hold a variety of checkable deposits. In recent years, financial institutions have developed other kinds of accounts that carry check-writing privileges but also earn interest.

Money aggregates are measures of the money supply defined by the Federal Reserve. The narrow definition, called M1, consists of currency (including coins) held by the nonbanking public, checkable deposits, and traveler's checks. Note that currency in bank vaults is not counted as part of the money supply because it is not being used as a medium of exchange—it's just sitting there. But checkable deposits are money because their owners can write checks or use debit cards to tap them. Checkable deposits are the liabilities of the issuing banks, which stand ready to convert them into cash. But unlike cash, checks are *not* legal tender, as signs that say "No Checks!" attest.

The currency circulating in the United States consists mostly of Federal Reserve notes, which are produced by the U.S. Bureau of Engraving and Printing and are issued by and are liabilities of the 12 Federal Reserve Banks. Over 40 percent of the Fed's liabilities consist of Federal Reserve notes, although prior to the financial crisis of 2008–2009, this amount was over 90 percent. The Fed spends about $600 million a year printing, storing, and distributing notes. Because Federal Reserve notes are redeemable for nothing other than more Federal Reserve notes, U.S. currency is *fiat money*. The other component of currency is coins, manufactured and distributed by the U.S. Mint. Like paper money, U.S. coins are token money because their metal value is usually less than their face value.

As much as 60 percent of Federal Reserve notes now circulate abroad. Some countries such as Panama, Ecuador, and El Salvador use U.S. dollars as their currency. In other countries, especially those that have experienced high inflation, U.S. dollars circulate alongside the local currency. In Vietnam, for example, some restaurants list prices in U.S. dollars, not in dong, the national currency. Dollars circulating abroad is actually a good deal for Americans because a $100 note that costs only about 7 cents to print can be "sold" to foreigners for $100 worth of goods and services. It's as if these countries were granting us an interest-free loan during the period the $100 note circulates abroad, usually several years.

Broader Definition of Money: M2

Economists regard currency and checkable deposits as money because each serves as a medium of exchange, a unit of account, and a store of value. Some other financial assets perform the store-of-value function and can be converted into currency or to checkable deposits. Because these are so close to money, they are called near-monies and are included under a broader definition.

checkable deposits
bank deposits that allow the account owner to write checks to third parties; ATM or debit cards can also access these deposits and transmit them electronically

money aggregates
measures of the economy's money supply

M1
the narrow measure of the money supply, consisting of currency and coins held by the nonbanking public, checkable deposits, and traveler's checks

This is the menu of a restaurant in Ecuador, where prices are in U.S. dollars.

Savings deposits earn interest but have no specific maturity date. Banks often allow depositors to shift funds from savings accounts to checking accounts by phone, ATM card, or online, so distinctions between narrow and broad definitions of money have become blurred. Time deposits (also called *certificates of deposit,* or CDs) earn a fixed rate of interest if held for a specified period, ranging from several months to several years. Premature withdrawals are penalized by forfeiture of several months' interest. Neither savings deposits nor time deposits serve directly as media of exchange, so they are not included in M1, the narrow definition of money.

Money market mutual fund accounts, mentioned in the previous chapter, are another component of money when defined more broadly. But, because of restrictions on the minimum balance, on the number of checks that can be written per month, and on the minimum amount of each check, these popular accounts are not viewed as money when narrowly defined.

Recall that M1 consists of currency (including coins) held by the nonbanking public, checkable deposits, and traveler's checks. M2 includes M1 as well as savings deposits, small-denomination time deposits, money market mutual fund accounts, and other miscellaneous near-monies. Exhibit 1 shows the size and relative importance of each money aggregate. As you can see, compared to M1, M2 is nearly five times larger. Thus, the narrow definition of money is only a fraction of the broader aggregate.

Exhibit 1

Measures of the Money Supply (February 2009)

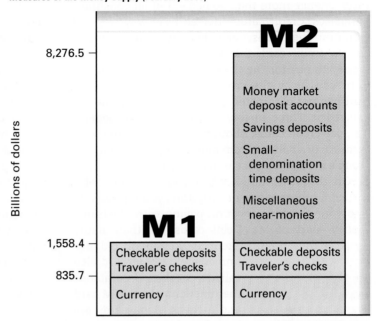

SOURCE: Based on seasonally adjusted monthly figures from the Federal Reserve Board. For the latest data, go to http://www.federalreserve.gov/releases/h6/Current/.

But distinctions between M1 and M2 become less meaningful as banks allow depositors to transfer funds from one account to another.

Credit Cards and Debit Cards: What's the Difference?

You may be curious why the narrow definition includes debit cards but not credit cards. After all, most sellers accept credit cards as readily as they

{ Real or Fake?
(Counterfeiting Facts) }

- The supernote is a counterfeit $100 note of extremely high quality, including sequential serial numbers and a polymer security thread.

- Crane & Company has supplied the paper for U.S. currency since 1879.

- On U.S. soil, the Secret Service seizes most counterfeit money before it circulates.

For more counterfeiting facts, read the online case study at 4ltrpress.cengage.com/econ.

SOURCES: Benny Avni, "U.N. Officials Knew Earlier of North Korean Fake Currency," *New York Sun,* 3 April 2007; Bill Fairies, "Made in South America: New Breed of Fake U.S. Dollars," *Christian Science Monitor,* 14 April 2005; and "The Use and Counterfeiting of U.S. Currency Abroad, Part 3," *A Final Report to the Congress by the Secretary of the Treasury,* September 2006. The U.S. Treasury also has a Web site providing information about new notes at http://www.moneyfactory.com/section.cfm/4.

savings deposits
deposits that earn interest but have no specific maturity date

time deposits
deposits that earn a fixed interest rate if held for the specified period, which can range from several months to several years; also called certificates of deposit

M2
a money aggregate consisting of M1 plus savings deposits, small-denomination time deposits, and money market mutual funds

accept cash, checks, or debit cards (some, such as Internet sites, even prefer credit cards), and credit cards finance more than 20 percent of all consumer purchases. Credit cards offer an easy way to get a loan from the card issuer. If you buy an airline ticket with a credit card, the card issuer lends you the money to pay for the ticket. You don't need money until you repay the credit card issuer. The credit card has not eliminated your use of money, merely delayed it. Three in four households have general purpose credit cards. About half of those with credit cards carry a balance from month to month, and that group's median balance is about $3,000.

On the other hand, when you use your debit card at a grocery store or drugstore, you tap directly into your checking account, paying with electronic money—part of M1. Debit cards get their name because they *debit*, or reduce, your bank balance immediately. A debit card, also called a check card, combines the functions of an ATM card and a check. Debit cards are issued by banks, sometimes jointly with Visa, MasterCard, or other major card issuers. Even though debit cards look like credit cards, and even may bear a name such as Visa, they are not credit cards.

debit card
card that taps directly into the depositor's bank account to fund purchases; also called a check card, and often doubles as an ATM card

Many people prefer debit cards to checks because no checkbook is required and payments are made directly and immediately. Transactions using debit cards and other electronic transfers now exceed payments by check. Like ATM cards, debit cards usually require a personal identification number, or PIN, to use. In that regard, debit cards are safer than credit cards, which could be used more easily by a thief. But debit cards have some disadvantages. Whereas debit cards draw down your checking account immediately, credit cards provide a grace period between a purchase and required payment. And some people prefer to borrow beyond the grace period—that is, they carry a balance from month to month. Also, because debit cards immediately reduce your bank account, you can't dispute a bill or withhold payment as you can with a credit card and you can't stop payment as you can with a check. Still, debit cards came from nowhere a few years ago to be used by more than 60 percent of households today.

LO² How Banks Work

Banks attract deposits from savers to lend to borrowers, earning a profit on the difference between the interest paid depositors and the interest charged borrowers. Savers need a safe place for their money, and borrowers need credit; banks try to earn a profit by serving both groups. To inspire depositor confidence, banks usually present an image of trust and assurance with impressive offices, a big safe often visible from the lobby, and names that impress. Banks are more apt to be called Fidelity Trust, First National, or U.S. Bankcorp than Benny's Bank, Loans 'R' Us, or Loadsamoney. In contrast, *finance companies* are financial intermediaries that do not get their funds from depositors, so they can choose names aimed more at borrowers—names such as Household Finance or The Money Store. Likewise, mortgage companies do not rely on depositors, so they pick names aimed at home buyers, names such as Lender's Depot or Get Home Loans Fast.com.

Banks Are Financial Intermediaries

By bringing together both sides of the money market, banks serve as financial intermediaries, or as go-betweens. They gather various amounts from savers and repackage these funds into the amounts demanded by borrowers. Some savers need their money next week, some next year, some only after retirement. Likewise, borrowers need credit for different lengths of time. Banks,

© JOHN HARDING/TIME-LIFE PICTURES/GETTY IMAGES

as intermediaries, offer desirable durations to both groups. *In short, banks reduce the transaction costs of channeling savings to creditworthy borrowers. Here's how.*

Coping with Asymmetric Information

Banks, as lenders, try to identify borrowers who are willing to pay interest and are able to repay the loan. But borrowers have more reliable information about their own credit history and financial plans than do lenders. Thus, in the market for loans, there is asymmetric information—an inequality in what's known by each party to the transaction. Asymmetric information is unequal information. This wouldn't be a problem if borrowers could be trusted to report relevant details to lenders. Some borrowers, however, have an incentive to suppress important information, such as other debts outstanding, a troubled financial history, or plans to use the borrowed money to fund a risky venture. Borrowers willing to pay a higher interest rate can apply for loans with no income verification. These are commonly called "liars loans" because some applicants overstate their incomes. Liars loans got some financial intermediaries in trouble in 2007–2009, when falling housing prices and rising interest rates caused some borrowers to default on their loans. Because of their experience and expertise in evaluating loan applicants, banks can better cope with asymmetric information than could an individual saver.

Banks also know more about lending agreements than do individual savers. Thus, savers, rather than lending their money directly, are better off depositing their money in banks and letting banks do the lending. *The economy is more efficient because banks develop expertise in evaluating creditworthiness, structuring loans, and enforcing loan contracts.*

Reducing Risk Through Diversification

By developing a diversified portfolio of assets rather than lending funds to a single borrower, banks reduce the risk to each individual saver. A bank, in effect, lends a tiny fraction of each saver's deposits to each of its many borrowers. If one borrower fails to repay a loan, it hardly affects a large, diversified bank. Certainly such a default does not represent the personal disaster it would if one saver's entire nest egg was loaned directly to that defaulting borrower.

Starting a Bank

We could consider the operation of any type of depository institution (commercial bank, savings bank, or credit union), but let's focus on starting a commercial bank because they are the most important in terms of total assets. What's more, the operating principles apply to other depository institutions as well. Suppose some business leaders in your hometown want to establish a commercial bank called Home Bank. To obtain a *charter,* or the right to operate, they must apply to the state banking authority in the case of a state bank or to the U.S. Comptroller of the Currency in the case of a national bank. The chartering agency reviewing the application judges the quality of management, the need for another bank in the region, the proposed bank's funding, and the likely success of the bank.

Suppose the founders plan to invest $500,000 in the bank, and they so indicate on their application for a national charter. If their application is approved, they incorporate, issuing themselves shares of stock—certificates of ownership. Thus, they exchange $500,000 for shares of stock in the bank. These shares are called the *owners' equity,* or the net worth, of the bank. Part of the $500,000, say $50,000, is used to buy shares in their district Federal Reserve Bank. So Home Bank is now a member of the Federal Reserve System. With the remaining $450,000, the owners acquire and furnish the bank building.

© MARY GASCHO/ISTOCKPHOTO.COM

Is this a credible borrower? Banks are generally better than individuals at making these kinds of judgements.

asymmetric information
a situation in which one side of the market has more reliable information than the other side

net worth
assets minus liabilities; also called owners' equity

Exhibit 2

Home Bank's Balance Sheet

Assets		Liabilities and Net Worth	
Building and furniture	$450,000	Net worth	$500,000
Stock in district Fed	50,000		
Total	$500,000	Total	$500,000

To focus our discussion, we examine the bank's balance sheet, presented in Exhibit 2. As the name implies, a balance sheet shows a balance between the two sides of the bank's accounts. The left side lists the bank's assets. An asset is any physical property or financial claim owned by the bank. At this early stage, assets include the building and equipment owned by Home Bank plus its stock in the district Federal Reserve Bank. The right side lists the bank's liabilities and net worth. A liability is an amount the bank owes. So far the bank owes nothing, so the right side includes only the net worth of $500,000. The two sides of the ledger must always be equal, or in *balance*, which is why it's called a *balance sheet*. So assets must equal liabilities plus net worth:

$$\text{Assets} = \text{Liabilities} + \text{Net worth}$$

The bank is now ready for business. Opening day is the bank's lucky day, because the first customer carries in a briefcase full of $100 notes and deposits $1,000,000 into a new checking account. In accepting this, the bank promises to repay the depositor that amount. The deposit therefore is an amount the bank owes—it's a liability of the bank. As a result of this deposit, the bank's assets increase by $1,000,000 in cash and its liabilities increase by $1,000,000 in checkable deposits. Exhibit 3 shows the effects of this transaction on Home Bank's balance sheet. The right side now shows two claims on the bank's assets: claims by the owners, called net worth, and claims by nonowners, called liabilities, which at this point consist of checkable deposits.

balance sheet
a financial statement at a given point in time that shows assets on one side and liabilities and net worth on the other side; because assets must equal liabilities plus net worth, the two sides of the statement must be in balance

asset
anything of value that is owned

liability
anything that is owed to other people or institutions

required reserves
the dollar amount of reserves a bank is obligated by regulation to hold as cash in the bank's vault or on account at the Fed

required reserve ratio
the ratio of reserves to deposits that banks are obligated by regulation to hold

excess reserves
bank reserves exceeding required reserves

Reserve Accounts

Where do we go from here? As mentioned in the previous chapter, banks are required by the Fed to set aside, or to hold in reserve, a percentage of their checkable deposits. The dollar amount that must be held in reserve is called required reserves—checkable deposits multiplied by the required reserve ratio. The required reserve ratio dictates the minimum proportion of deposits the bank must hold in reserve. The current reserve requirement is 10 percent on checkable deposits (other types of deposits have no reserve requirement). All depository institutions are subject to the Fed's reserve requirements. Reserves are held either as cash in the bank's vault, which earns the bank no interest, or as deposits at the Fed, which earn some interest. Home Bank must therefore hold $100,000 as reserves, or 10 percent times $1,000,000.

Suppose Home Bank deposits $100,000 in a reserve account with its district Federal Reserve Bank. Home Bank's reserves now consist of $100,000 in required reserves on deposit with the Fed and $900,000 in excess reserves held as cash in the vault. Home Bank earns no interest on cash in the vault. Excess reserves, however, can be used to make loans or to purchase interest-bearing assets, such as government bonds. By law, the bank's interest-bearing assets are limited primarily to loans and to government securities (if a bank is owned by a holding company, the holding company has broader latitude in the kinds of assets it can hold).

Exhibit 3

Home Bank's Balance Sheet After $1,000,000 Deposit into Checking Account

Assets		Liabilities and Net Worth	
Cash	$1,000,000	Checkable deposits	$1,000,000
Building and furniture	450,000	Net worth	500,000
Stock in district Fed	50,000		
Total	$1,500,000	Total	$1,500,000

© DON FARRALL/PHOTODISC/GETTY IMAGES

Liquidity Versus Profitability

Like the early goldsmiths, modern banks must be prepared to satisfy depositors' requests for funds. A bank loses reserves whenever a depositor withdraws cash or writes a check that gets deposited in another bank. The bank must be in a position to satisfy all depositor demands, even if many depositors ask for their money at the same time. Required reserves are not meant to be used to meet depositor requests for funds; therefore, banks often hold excess reserves or other assets, such as government bonds, that can be easily converted to cash to satisfy any unexpected demand for funds. Banks may also want to hold excess reserves in case a valued customer needs immediate credit.

The bank manager must therefore structure the portfolio of assets with an eye toward liquidity but must not forget that survival also depends on profitability. Liquidity is the ease with which an asset can be converted into cash without a significant loss of value. *The objectives of liquidity and profitability are at odds.* For example, more liquid assets yield lower interest rates than less liquid assets do. The most liquid asset is bank reserves, either in the bank's vault as cash, which earns no interest, or on account with the Fed which earns some interest.

At one extreme, suppose a bank is completely liquid, holding all its assets as cash in its vault. Such a bank would have no difficulty meeting depositors' demands for funds. This bank is playing it safe—too safe. The bank earns no interest and will fail. At the other extreme, suppose a bank uses all its excess reserves to acquire high-yielding but illiquid assets, such as long-term home loans. Such a bank runs into problems whenever withdrawals exceed new deposits. There is a trade-off between liquidity and profitability. The portfolio manager's task is to strike the right balance between liquidity, or safety, and profitability.

Because vault cash earns no interest, banks prefer to hold reserves at the Fed. Banks that are short and require reserves at the end of the day can borrow from other banks that have excess reserves at the Fed. The federal funds market provides for day-to-day lending and borrowing among banks of excess reserves on account at the Fed. These funds usually do not leave the Fed—instead, they shift among accounts. For example, suppose that at the end of the business day, Home Bank has excess reserves of $100,000 on account with the Fed and wants to lend that amount to another bank that finished the day short $100,000 in required reserves. These two

banks are brought together by a broker who specializes in the market for federal funds—that is, the market for reserves at the Fed. The interest rate paid on this loan is called the federal funds rate; this is the rate the Fed targets as a tool of monetary policy, but more on that later.

LO³ How Banks Create Money

Let's now discuss how the Fed, Home Bank, and the banking system as a whole can create fiat money. Excess reserves are the raw material the banking system uses to create money. Again, our discussion focuses on commercial banks because they are the largest and most important depository institutions, although thrifts operate the same way.

Creating Money Through Excess Reserves

Suppose Home Bank has already used its $900,000 in excess reserves to make loans and buy government bonds and has no excess reserves left. In fact, let's assume there are no excess reserves in the banking system. With that as a point of departure, let's walk through the money creation process.

Round One

To start, suppose the Fed buys a $1,000 U.S. government bond from a securities dealer, with the transaction handled by the dealer's bank—Home Bank. The Fed pays the dealer by crediting Home Bank's reserve account with $1,000, so Home Bank can increase the dealer's checking account by $1,000. Where does the Fed get these reserves? It makes them up—creates them out of thin air, out of electronic ether! The securities dealer has exchanged one asset, a U.S. bond, for another asset, checkable deposits. A U.S.

liquidity
a measure of the ease with which an asset can be converted into money without a significant loss of value

federal funds market
a market for overnight lending and borrowing of reserves among banks; the interbank market for reserves on account at the Fed

federal funds rate
the interest rate charged in the federal funds market; the interest rate banks charge one another for overnight borrowing; the Fed's target interest rate

> ❝ More liquid asssets yield lower interest rates than less liquid assets do. ❞

Exhibit 4

**Changes in Home Bank's Balance Sheet
After Fed Buys a $1,000 Bond from Securities Dealer**

Assets		Liabilities and Net Worth	
Reserves at Fed	+ $1,000	Checkable deposits	+ $1,000

bond is not money, but checkable deposits are, so the money supply increases by $1,000 in this first round. Exhibit 4 shows changes in Home Bank's balance sheet as a result of the Fed's bond purchase. On the assets side, Home Bank's reserves at the Fed increase by $1,000. On the liabilities side, checkable deposits increase by $1,000. Of the dealer's $1,000 checkable deposit, Home Bank must set aside $100 in required reserves (based on a 10 percent required reserve ratio). The remaining $900 becomes excess reserves, which can fuel a further increase in the money supply.

Round Two

Suppose Home Bank is your regular bank, and you apply for a $900 student loan to help pay student fees. Home Bank approves your loan and increases your checking account by $900. *Home Bank has converted your promise to repay, your IOU, into a $900 checkable deposit. Because checkable deposits are money, this action increases the money supply by $900.* The money supply has increased by a total of $1,900 to this point—the $1,000 increase in the securities dealer's checkable deposits and now the $900 increase in your checkable deposits. In the process, what had been $900 in Home Bank's excess reserves now back up its loan to you (remember, a bank can lend no more than its excess reserves). As shown in Exhibit 5, Home Bank's loans increase by $900 on the assets side because your IOU becomes the bank's asset. On the bank's liabilities side, checkable deposits increase by $900 because the bank has increased your account by that amount. In short, Home Bank has created $900 in checkable deposits based on your promise to repay the loan.

Exhibit 5

Changes in Home Bank's Balance Sheet After Lending $900 to You

Assets		Liabilities and Net Worth	
Loans	+ $900	Checkable deposits	+ $900

When you write a $900 check for student fees, your college promptly deposits the check into its checking account at Merchants Trust, which increases the college's account by $900 and sends your check to the Fed. The Fed transfers $900 in reserves from Home Bank's account to Merchants Trust's account. The Fed then sends the check to Home Bank, which reduces your checkable deposits by $900. The Fed has thereby "cleared" your check by settling the claim that Merchants Trust had on Home Bank. Your $900 in checkable deposits at Home Bank has become your college's $900 in checkable deposits at Merchants Trust. The total increase in the money supply to this point is still $1,900.

Round Three

But Merchants Trust now has $900 more in reserves on deposit with the Fed. After setting aside $90 as required reserves, or 10 percent of your college's checkable deposit increase, the bank has $810 in excess reserves. Suppose Merchants Trust lends this $810 to an English major starting a new business called "Note This," an online note-taking service for students in large classes. Exhibit 6 shows that assets at Merchants Trust are up by $810 in loans, and liabilities are up by $810 in checkable deposits. At this point, checkable deposits in the banking system, and the money supply in the economy, are up by a total of $2,710 (= $1,000 + $900 + $810), all springing from the Fed's original $1,000 bond purchase.

Exhibit 6

**Changes in Merchants Trust's Balance Sheet
After Lending $810 to English Major**

Assets		Liabilities and Net Worth	
Loans	+ $810	Checkable deposits	+ $810

The $810 loan is spent at the college bookstore, which deposits the check in its account at Fidelity Bank. Fidelity credits the bookstore's checkable deposits with $810 and sends the check to the Fed for clearance. The Fed reduces Merchants Trust's reserves by $810 and increases Fidelity's by the same. The Fed then sends the check to Merchants, which reduces the English major's checkable deposits by $810. So checkable deposits are down by $810 at Merchants and up by the same amount at Fidelity. Checkable deposits are still up by $2,710, as the $810 in checkable deposits has simply shifted from Merchants Trust to Fidelity Bank.

Round Four and Beyond

We could continue the process with Fidelity Bank setting aside $81 in required reserves and lending $729 in excess reserves, but you get some idea of money creation by now. Notice the pattern of deposits and loans. Each time a bank gets a fresh deposit, 10 percent goes to required reserves. The rest becomes excess reserves, which fuel new loans or other asset acquisitions. The borrower writes a check, which the recipient deposits in a checking account, thereby generating excess reserves to support still more loans. Because this example began with the Fed, the Fed can rightfully claim, "The buck starts here"—a slogan that appears on a large plaque in the Federal Reserve chairman's office.

An individual bank can lend no more than its excess reserves. When the borrower spends those funds, reserves at one bank usually fall, but total reserves in the banking system do not. The recipient bank uses most of the new deposit to extend more loans, creating more checkable deposits. The potential expansion of checkable deposits in the banking system therefore equals some multiple of the initial increase in reserves. Note that our example assumes that banks do not allow excess reserves to sit idle, that borrowed funds do not idle in checking accounts, and that the public does not hold some of the newly created money as cash. If excess reserves remained just that or if borrowed funds idled in checking accounts, they could not fuel an expansion of the money supply. And if people chose to hold borrowed funds in cash rather than in checking accounts, that idle cash could not add to reserves in the banking system.

A Summary of the Rounds

Let's review the money creation process: *The initial and most important step is the Fed's injection of $1,000 in fresh reserves into the banking system.* By buying the bond from the securities dealer, the Fed immediately increased the money supply by $1,000. Home Bank set aside $100 as required reserves and lent you its $900 in excess reserves. You paid your college fees, and the $900 ended up in your college's checkable account. This fueled more money creation, as shown in the series of rounds of Exhibit 7. As you can see, during each round, the increase in checkable deposits (column 1) minus the increase in required reserves (column 2) equals the potential increase in loans (column 3). Checkable deposits in this example can potentially increase by as much as $10,000.

In our example, money creation results from the Fed's $1,000 bond purchase from the securities dealer, but excess reserves would also have increased if the Fed purchased a $1,000 bond from Home Bank, lent Home Bank $1,000, or freed up $1,000 in excess reserves by lowering the reserve requirement.

Exhibit 7

Summary of the Money Creation Resulting from the Fed's Purchase of $1,000 U.S. Government Bond

Bank	(1) Increase in Checkable Deposits	(2) Increase in Required Reserves	(3) Increase in Loans (3) = (1) − (2)
1. Home Bank	$ 1,000	$ 100	$ 900
2. Merchants Trust	900	90	810
3. Fidelity Bank	810	81	729
All remaining rounds	7,290	729	6,561
Totals	$10,000	$1,000	$9,000

What if the Fed paid the securities dealer in cash? By exchanging Federal Reserve notes, which become part of the money supply in the hands of the public, for a U.S. bond, which is not part of the money supply, the Fed would have increased the money supply by $1,000. Once the securities dealer put this cash into a checking account—or spent the cash, so the money ended up in someone else's checking account—the banking system's money creation process would have been off and running.

Reserve Requirements and Money Expansion

The banking system as a whole eliminates excess reserves by expanding the money supply. With a 10 percent reserve requirement, the Fed's initial injection of $1,000 in fresh reserves could support up to $10,000 in new checkable deposits in the banking system as a whole, *assuming no bank holds excess reserves, borrowed funds don't sit idle, and people don't want to hold more cash.*

The multiple by which the money supply increases as a result of an increase in the banking system's reserves is called the money multiplier. The simple money multiplier equals the reciprocal of the

money multiplier the multiple by which the money supply changes as a result of a change in fresh reserves in the banking system

simple money multiplier the reciprocal of the required reserve ratio, or $1/r$; the maximum multiple of fresh reserves by which the money supply can increase

required reserve ratio, or $1/r$, where r is the reserve ratio. In our example, the reserve ratio was 10 percent, or 0.1, so the reciprocal is $1/0.1$, which equals 10. The formula for the multiple expansion of money supply can be written as:

Change in the money supply = Change in fresh reserves × $1/r$

Again, the simple money multiplier assumes that banks hold no excess reserves, that borrowers do not let the funds sit idle, and that people do not want to hold more cash. The higher the reserve requirement, the greater the fraction of deposits that must be held as reserves, so the smaller the money multiplier. A reserve requirement of 20 percent instead of 10 percent would mean each bank must set aside twice as much in required reserves. The simple money multiplier in this case would be $1/0.2$, which equals 5. The maximum possible increase in checkable deposits resulting from an initial $1,000 increase in fresh reserves would therefore be $1,000 × 5, or $5,000. *Excess reserves fuel the deposit expansion process, and a higher reserve requirement drains this fuel from the banking system, thereby reducing the amount of new money that can be created.*

On the other hand, with a reserve requirement of only 5 percent, banks would set aside less for required reserves, leaving more excess reserves available for loans. The simple money multiplier in that case would be $1/0.05$, or 20. With $1,000 in fresh reserves and a 5 percent reserve requirement, the banking system could increase the money supply by a maximum of $1,000 × 20, which equals $20,000. Thus, the change in the required reserve ratio affects the banking system's ability to create money.

In summary: Money creation usually begins with the Fed injecting new reserves into the banking system. An individual bank lends an amount no greater than its excess reserves. The borrower's spending ends up in someone else's checking account, fueling additional loans. *The fractional reserve requirement is the key to the multiple expansion of checkable deposits.* If each $1 deposit had to be backed by $1 in required reserves, the money multiplier would be reduced to 1, which is no multiplier at all.

Limitations on Money Expansion

Various leakages from the multiple expansion process reduce the size of the money multiplier, which is why $1/r$ is called the *simple* money multiplier. You

$$\Delta \text{ money supply} = \Delta \text{ fresh reserves} \times 1/r$$

could think of "simple" as meaning maximum. To repeat, our example assumed (1) that banks do not let excess reserves sit idle, (2) that borrowers do something with the money, and (3) that people do not choose to increase their cash holdings. How realistic are these assumptions? With regard to the first, banks have a profit incentive to make loans or buy some higher interest-bearing asset with excess reserves. Granted, banks earn some interest on reserves deposited with the Fed but the rate is typically less than could be earned on loans or other interest-bearing assets. The second assumption is also easy to defend. Why would people borrow money if they didn't need it for something? The third assumption is trickier. Cash may sometimes be preferable to checking accounts because cash is more versatile, so people may choose to hold some of the newly created money as cash. To the extent that people prefer to hold more cash, this drains reserves from the banking system. With less excess reserves, banks are less able to make loans, reducing the money multiplier. Incidentally, for the money multiplier to operate, a particular bank need not use excess reserves in a specific way; it could use them to pay all its employees a Christmas bonus, for that matter. As long as the money ends up as checkable deposits in the banking system, away we go with the money expansion process.

Multiple Contraction of the Money Supply

We have already outlined the money creation process, so the story of how the Federal Reserve System can reduce bank reserves, thereby reducing the money supply, can be a brief one. Again, we begin by assuming that there are no excess reserves in the system and that the reserve requirement is 10 percent. Suppose the Fed *sells* a $1,000 U.S. bond to a securities dealer and gets paid with a check drawn on the security dealer's account at Home Bank. So the Fed gets paid by drawing down Home Bank's reserves at the Fed by $1,000. The Fed has thereby reduced the money supply by $1,000 in this first round.

Because the dealer's checking account was reduced by $1,000, Home Bank no longer needs to hold $100 in required reserves. But Home Bank is still short $900 in required reserves (remember, when we started, there were no excess reserves in the banking system). To replenish reserves, Home Bank must recall loans (ask for repayment before the due date), or sell some other asset. Suppose the bank calls in $900 loaned to a local

We begin by assuming that there are no excess reserves in the system. . . .

© RADIUS IMAGES/JUPITERIMAGES

business, and the loan is repaid with a check written against Merchants Trust. When the check clears, Home Bank's reserves are up by $900, just enough to satisfy its reserve requirement, but Merchants Trust's reserves and checkable deposits are down by $900. Checkable deposits are now down $1,900 as a result of the Fed's purchase of a $1,000 bond. Because there were no excess reserves at the outset, the loss of $900 in reserves leaves Merchants $810 short of its required level of reserves, forcing that bank to get more reserves.

And so it goes down the line. The Fed's sale of government bonds reduces bank reserves, forcing banks to recall loans or to somehow replenish reserves. This reduces checkable deposits each additional round. *The maximum possible effect is to reduce the money supply by the original reduction in bank reserves times the simple money multiplier, which again equals 1 divided by the reserve requirement, or 1/r.* In our example, the Fed's sale of $1,000 in U.S. bonds could reduce the money supply by as much as $10,000.

LO⁴ The Fed's Tools of Monetary Control

Now that you have some idea how fractional reserve banking works, we are in a position to summarize the Federal Reserve's role in the economy. As mentioned in the previous chapter, in its capacity as a bankers' bank, the Fed clears checks for, extends loans to, and holds deposits of banks. About half of the narrow definition of money (M1) consists of checkable deposits. The Fed's control over checkable deposits works indirectly through its control over reserves in the banking system. You are already familiar with the Fed's three tools for controlling reserves: (1) open-market operations, or the buying and selling of U.S. government bonds; (2) the discount rate, which is the interest rate the Fed charges for loans it makes to banks; and (3) the required reserve ratio, which is the minimum fraction of reserves that banks must hold against deposits. Let's examine each of these in more detail, then look at some other Fed matters.

Open-Market Operations and the Federal Funds Rate

The Fed carries out open-market operations whenever it buys or sells U.S. government bonds in the open market. Decisions about open-market operations are made by the Federal Open Market Committee, or FOMC, which meets every six weeks and during emergencies. To increase the money supply, the Fed directs the New York Fed to buy U.S. bonds. This is called an open-market purchase. To reduce the money supply, the New York Fed is directed to carry out an open-market sale. Open-market operations are relatively easy to carry out. They require no change in laws or regulations and can be executed in any amount—large or small—chosen by the Fed. Their simplicity and ease of use make them the tool of choice for the Fed.

> THROUGH OPEN-MARKET OPERATIONS, THE FED INFLUENCES BANK RESERVES AND THE FEDERAL FUNDS RATE.

Through open-market operations, the Fed influences bank reserves and the *federal funds rate,* which is the interest rate banks charge one another for borrowing excess reserves at the Fed, typically just for a day or two. Banks that need reserves can borrow excess reserves from other banks, paying the federal funds rate of interest. The federal funds rate serves as a good indicator of the "tightness" of monetary policy. For example, suppose the Fed buys bonds in the open market and thereby increases reserves in the banking system. As a result, more banks have excess reserves. Demand for excess reserves in the federal funds market falls and supply increases, so the federal funds rate—the interest rate for reserves in this market—declines. We can expect this lower federal funds rate to spread quickly to the economy at large: The excess reserves that have created the lower federal

open-market purchase
the purchase of U.S. government bonds by the Fed to increase the money supply

open-market sale
the sale of U.S. government bonds by the Fed to reduce the money supply

funds rate prompt banks to lower short-term interest rates in general and this increases the quantity of loans demanded by the public.

The Discount Rate

The second monetary policy tool available to the Fed is the discount rate, which is the interest rate the Fed charges for loans it makes to banks. Banks borrow from the Fed to satisfy their reserve requirements. A lower discount rate reduces the cost of borrowing, encouraging banks to borrow reserves from the Fed. The Fed usually does not encourage banks to borrow, but the Fed considers itself as the "lender of last resort" and a lender during a financial crisis, as occurred in 2007–2009 when some homeowners defaulted on their mortgages.

There are actually two discount rates. The *primary discount rate* is usually one percentage point above the federal funds rate. Thus, discount borrowing is less attractive than borrowing through the federal funds market. But during a financial crisis, the Fed could lower the primary discount rate to supply liquidity to the banking system as it did 10 times between August 2007 and December 2008, a response to the financial crisis. The Fed charges more interest on loans to banks considered less sound than to other banks. This *secondary discount rate* is usually about one-half a percentage point higher than the primary discount rate.

The Fed uses the discount rate more as a signal to financial markets about its monetary policy than as a tool for increasing or decreasing the money supply. The discount rate might also be thought of as an emergency tool for injecting liquidity into the banking system in the event of some financial crisis, such as the global credit crisis of 2008. Banks would prefer to borrow reserves from other banks in the federal funds market rather than borrow reserves directly from the Fed.

Reserve Requirements

The Fed also influences the money supply through reserve requirements, which are regulations regarding the minimum amount of reserves that banks must hold to back up deposits. Reserve requirements determine how much money the banking system can create with each dollar of fresh reserves. If the Fed increases the reserve requirement, then banks have less excess reserves to lend out. This reduces the banking system's ability to create money. On the other hand, a lower reserve requirement increases the banking system's ability to create money. Reserve requirements

discount rate
the interest rate the Fed charges banks that borrow reserves

{ Market Indicators:
The Federal Funds Rate }

Since World War II, the federal funds rate has often been a reliable market indicator during economic slumps. In past market slumps, when the Fed would target a lower rate, usually a second adjustment to its target proved sufficient encouragement to bring investors back into the market. During the latest recession, however, the Fed lowered its target federal funds rate 10 times between August 2007 and December 2008, practically reducing it to zero.

SOURCE: David Henry, "Waiting for the Bull to Return," *Business Week,* 16 March 2009, 24–29.

can be changed by a simple majority vote of the Board of Governors. But changes in the reserve requirement disrupt the banking system, so the Fed seldom makes such changes. As noted already, the current reserve requirement is 10 percent on checkable deposits and zero on other deposits. Some countries such as Australia, Canada, and the United Kingdom have no reserve requirement. Banks there still hold reserves to deal with everyday cash requirements and can borrow from their central banks (at high rates) if necessary.

Coping with Financial Crises

The Fed, through its regulation of financial markets, also tries to prevent major disruptions and financial panics. For example, during the uncertain days following the terrorist attacks of September 11, 2001, people used their ATM cards to load up on cash. Some were hoarding it. To ensure the banking system had sufficient liquidity, the Fed bought all the government securities offered for sale, purchasing a record $150 billion worth in two days.[1] The Fed also eased some regulations to facilitate bank clearances, especially for banks struck during the attacks. Likewise, when financial crises threatened in 1987, 1989, 1998, and 2008, the Fed worked to ensure the financial system had sufficient liquidity. For example, to calm fears during a rash of mortgage defaults in 2008, the Fed lowered the discount rate to nearly zero and encouraged banks to borrow from the Fed. And to help banks improve their balance sheets, the Fed also began paying interest on bank reserves held at the Fed. As a general approach, Ben Bernanke, the Fed Chairman, announced that the Fed would provide sufficient liquidity to reduce the harm of mortgage defaults on the overall economy. To prevent cash shortages during a crisis, the Fed stockpiles extra cash in bank vaults around the country and around the world.

❖❖❖

1. Anita Rachavan, Susan Pulliam, and Jeff Opdyke, "Banks and Regulators Drew Together to Calm Rattled Markets After Attack," *Wall Street Journal,* 18 October 2001.

The Fed Is a Money Machine

One way to get a better idea of the Fed is to review its balance sheet, shown as Exhibit 8, with assets on the left and liabilities and net worth on the right. In response the mortgage crisis and global financial meltdown of 2008, the Fed injected more that a trillion dollars of liquidity into the banking system. In that sense, the Fed's balance sheet in April 2009 was far from typical. Note that U.S. government bonds account for about 24 percent of Fed assets, although in more normal times these bonds might account for 90 percent of assets. These IOUs from the federal government result from open-market operations, and they earn the Fed interest. On the other side of the ledger, Federal Reserve notes outstanding account for about 43 percent of Fed liabilities. These notes—U.S. currency—are IOUs from the Fed and are therefore liabilities of the Fed, but the Fed pays no interest on these notes. Thus, one of the Fed's primary assets—U.S. government bonds—earns interest, whereas the Fed's primary liability—Federal Reserve notes—requires no interest payments by the Fed. *The Fed is therefore both literally and figuratively a money machine. It is literally a money machine because it supplies the economy with Federal Reserve notes; it is figuratively a money machine because a main asset earns interest, but its main liability requires no interest payments.* The Fed also earns revenue from various services it provides banks. After covering its operating costs, paying interest on bank reserves at the Fed, and paying a 6 percent dividend to the member banks, the Fed turns over any remaining income. In 2008, the Fed sent the Treasury $34.9 billion.

The asset side of Exhibit 8 also indicates the size of the Fed's discount loans relative to total assets. As of April 1, 2009, the Fed's discount lending stood at $133.1 billion. On the right side of the ledger, you can see that depository institutions' reserves at the Fed totaled $837.5 billion. This reflects a huge jump from the year before. One reason for the increase is that in late 2008, the Fed began paying interest on bank reserves held by the Fed. You can also see that the Fed held deposits of the U.S. Treasury, a reminder that the Fed is the federal government's banker.

Exhibit 8

Federal Reserve Bank Balance Sheet as of April 1, 2009 (Billions)

Assets		Liabilities and Net Worth	
Financial crisis liquidity efforts	$1,026.1	Federal Reserve notes outstanding	$864.5
U.S. Treasury securities	492.3	Depository institution reserves	837.5
Foreign currencies	308.8	U.S. Treasury balance	237.7
Discount loans to depository institutions	133.1	Other liabilities	95.2
Bank buildings	2.2		
Other assets	117.9	Net worth	45.5
Total	$2,080.4	Total	$2,080.4

SOURCE: Federal Reserve Bank at http://www.federalreserve.gov/releases/h41/Current/.

Final Word

Banks play a unique role in the economy because they can transform someone's IOU into a checkable deposit, and a checkable deposit is money. The banking system's ability to expand the money supply depends on the amount of excess reserves in that system. In our example, it was the purchase of a $1,000 U.S. bond that started the ball rolling. The Fed can also increase reserves by lowering the discount rate enough to stimulate bank borrowing from the Fed (although the Fed uses changes in the discount rate more to signal its policy than to alter the money supply). And, by reducing the required reserve ratio, the Fed not only instantly creates excess reserves in the banking system but also increases the money multiplier. In practice, the Fed rarely changes the reserve requirement because of the disruptive effect of such a change on the banking system. *To control the money supply, the Fed relies primarily on open-market operations.*

Open-market operations can have a direct effect on the money supply, as when the Fed buys bonds from the public. But the Fed also affects the money supply indirectly, as when the Fed's bond purchase increases bank reserves, which then serve as fuel for the money multiplier. In the next chapter, we consider how changes in the money supply affect the economy.

Through various policies and practices, the Fed can expand the money supply much like rolling a snowball into a snowman.

© CHINA PHOTOS/GETTY IMAGES

Monetary Theory *and* Policy

Learning Outcomes

LO **1** Describe the relationship between the demand and supply of money

LO **2** Explain how changes in the money supply affect aggregate demand in the short run

LO **3** Explain how changes in the money supply affect aggregate demand in the long run

LO **4** Evaluate targets for monetary policy

"Why do people hold money?"

Why do people maintain checking accounts and have cash in their pockets, purses, wallets, desk drawers, coffee cans—wherever? In other words, why do people hold money? How does the stock of money in the economy affect your ability to find a job, get a student loan, buy a car, or pay credit card bills? What have economic theory and the historical record taught us about the relationship between the amount of money in the economy and other macroeconomic variables? Answers to these and related questions are addressed in this chapter, which examines monetary theory and policy.

The amount of money in the economy affects you in a variety of ways, but to understand these effects, we must dig a little deeper. So far, we have focused on how banks create money. But a more fundamental question is how money affects the economy, a topic called *monetary theory*. Monetary theory explores the effect of the money supply on the economy's price level, employment, and growth. The Fed's control over the money supply is called *monetary policy*. In the short run, changes in the money supply affect the economy by working through changes in the interest rate. In the long run, changes in the money supply affect the price level. In this chapter, we consider the theory behind each time frame.

What do you think?

I use a credit card to make all my purchases.

Strongly Disagree						Strongly Agree
1	2	3	4	5	6	7

Topics discussed in Chapter 16 include:

- Demand and supply of money
- Money in the short run
- Money in the long run
- Velocity of money
- Monetary policy targets

LO^1 The Demand and Supply of Money

Let's begin by reviewing the important distinction between the *stock of money* and the *flow of income*. How much money do you have with you right now? That amount is a *stock*—an amount measured at a point in time. Income, in contrast, is a *flow*—an amount measured per period of time. Income is a measure of how much money you receive per period. Income has no meaning unless the period is specified. You would not know whether to be impressed that a friend earned $400 unless you knew whether this was per month, per week, per day, or per hour.

The **demand for money** is a relationship between the interest rate and how much money people want to hold. Keep in mind

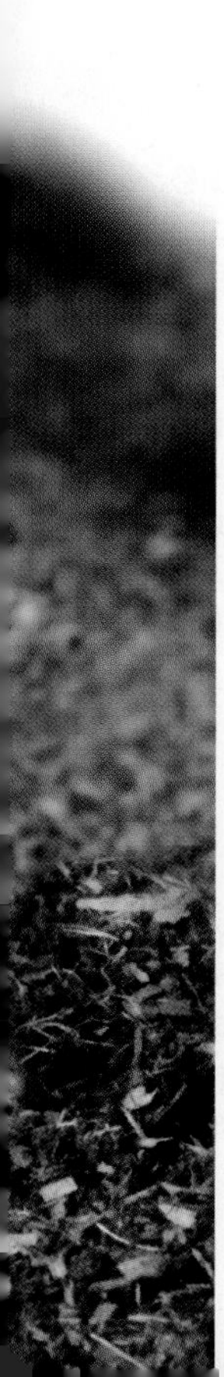

demand for money
the relationship between the interest rate and how much money people want to hold

that the quantity of money held is a stock measure. It may seem odd at first to be talking about the demand for money. You might think people would demand all the money they could get their hands on. But remember that money, the stock, is not the same as income, the flow. People express their demand for income by selling their labor and other resources. People express their demand for money by holding some of their wealth as money rather than holding other assets that earn more interest.

But we are getting ahead of ourselves. The question is: why do people demand money? Why do people have money with them, stash money around the house, and have money in checking accounts? The most obvious reason people demand money is that money is a convenient medium of exchange. *People demand money to pay for purchases.*

The Demand for Money

Because barter represents an insignificant portion of exchange in the modern industrialized economy, households, firms, governments, and foreigners need money to conduct their daily transactions. Consumers need money to buy products, and firms need money to buy resources. *Money allows people to carry out economic transactions more easily and more efficiently.* With credit cards, the short-term loan delays the payment of money, but all accounts must eventually be settled with money.

The greater the value of transactions to be financed in a given period, the greater the demand for money. *So the more active the economy is—that is, the more goods and services exchanged, reflected by real output—the more money demanded.* Obviously an econ-

omy with a real GDP of $14 trillion needs more money than an economy half that size. *Also, the higher the economy's price level, the greater the demand for money.* The more things cost on average, the more money is needed to buy them. Shoppers in economies suffering from hyperinflation need piles of cash.

You demand the money needed to fund your normal spending in the course of the day or week, and you may need money for unexpected expenditures. If you plan to buy lunch tomorrow, you will carry enough money to pay for it. But you may also want to be able to pay for other possible contingencies. For example, you could have car trouble or you could come across a sale on a favorite item. You can use checks, debit cards, or credit cards for some of these unexpected purchases, but you still feel safer with some extra cash. You may have a little extra money with you right now for who knows what. Even you don't know.

The demand for money is rooted in money's role as a medium of exchange. But as we have seen, money is more than a medium of exchange; it is also a store of value. People save for a new home, for college, for retirement. People can store their purchasing power as money or as some other financial assets, such as corporate and government bonds. When people buy bonds and other financial assets, they are lending their money and are paid interest for doing so.

The demand for any asset is based on the services it provides. The big advantage of money as a store of value is its liquidity: Money can be immediately exchanged for whatever is for sale. In contrast, other financial assets, such as corporate or government bonds, must first be *liquidated,* or exchanged for money, which can then be used to buy goods and services. Money, however, has one major disadvantage when compared to other financial assets. Money in the form of currency and traveler's checks earns no interest, and the rate earned on checkable deposits is well below that earned on other financial assets. So holding wealth as money means giving up some interest. For example, suppose a business could earn 3 percent more interest by holding financial assets other than money. The opportunity cost of holding $1 million as money rather than as some other financial asset would amount to $30,000 per year. *The interest forgone is the opportunity cost of holding money.*

Money Demand and Interest Rates

When the market interest rate is low, other things constant, the cost of holding money—the cost of maintaining liquidity—is low, so people hold more of their wealth in the form of money. When the interest rate is high, the cost of holding money is high, so people hold less of their wealth in money and more in other financial assets that pay higher interest. Thus, *other things constant, the quantity of money demanded varies inversely with the market interest rate.*

The money demand curve D_m in Exhibit 1 shows the quantity of money people demand at alternative interest rates, other things constant. Both the quantity of money and the interest rate are in nominal terms. *The money demand curve slopes downward because the lower the interest rate, the lower the opportunity cost of holding money.* Movements along the curve reflect the effects of changes in the interest rate on the quantity of money demanded, other things assumed constant. The quantity of money demanded is inversely related to the price of holding money, which is the interest rate. Assumed constant along the curve are the price level and real GDP. If either increases, the demand for money increases, as reflected by a rightward shift of the money demand curve.

The Supply of Money and the Equilibrium Interest Rate

The supply of money—the stock of money available in the economy at a particular time—is determined primarily by the Fed through its control over currency and over excess reserves in the banking system. The supply of money S_m is depicted as a vertical line in Exhibit 2. *A vertical supply curve implies that the quantity of money supplied is independent of the interest rate.*

The intersection of the demand for money D_m with the supply of money S_m determines the equilibrium interest rate, i—the interest rate that equates the quantity of money demanded with the quantity

supplied. At interest rates above the equilibrium level, the opportunity cost of holding money is higher, so the quantity of money people want to hold is less than the quantity supplied. At interest rates below the equilibrium level, the opportunity cost of holding money is lower, so the quantity of money people want to hold exceeds the quantity supplied.

If the Fed increases the money supply, the supply curve shifts to the right, as shown by the movement from S_m out to S'_m in Exhibit 2. At interest rate i, the quantity supplied now exceeds the quantity demanded. Because of the increased supply of money, people are *able* to hold more money. But at interest rate i they are *unwilling* to hold that much. Because people are now holding more of their wealth as money than they would like, they exchange some money for other financial assets, such as bonds. As the demand for bonds increases, bond sellers can pay less interest yet still attract enough buyers. The interest rate falls until the quantity of money demanded just equals the quantity supplied. With the decline in the interest rate to i' in Exhibit 2, the opportunity cost of holding money falls enough that the public is willing to hold the now-larger stock of money. Equilibrium moves from point a to point b. *For a given money demand curve, an increase in the money supply drives down the interest rate, and a decrease in the money supply drives up the interest rate.*

Now that you have some idea how money demand and money supply determine the market interest rate, you are ready to see how money fits into our model of the economy. Specifically, let's see how changes in the money supply affect aggregate demand and equilibrium output.

Exhibit 1

Demand for Money

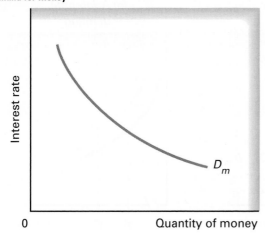

Exhibit 2

Effect of an Increase in the Money Supply

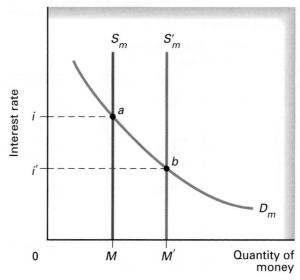

LO² Money and Aggregate Demand in the Short Run

In the short run, money affects the economy through changes in the interest rate. Monetary policy influences the market interest rate, which in turn affects investment, a component of aggregate demand. Let's work through the chain of causation.

Interest Rates and Investment

Suppose the Fed believes that the economy is producing less than its potential and decides to stimulate output and employment by increasing the money supply. Recall from the previous chapter that the Fed's primary tool for increasing the money supply is open-market purchases of U.S. government securities. The three panels of Exhibit 3 trace the links between changes in the money supply and changes in aggregate demand. We begin with equilibrium interest rate i, which is determined in panel (a) by the intersection of the money demand curve D_m with the money supply curve S_m. Suppose the Fed purchases U.S. government bonds and thereby increases the money supply, as shown by a rightward shift of the money supply curve from S_m to S'_m. After the increase in the supply of money, people are holding more money than they would prefer at interest rate i, so they try to exchange one form of wealth, money, for other financial assets. Exchanging dollars for financial assets has no direct effect on aggregate demand, but it does reduce the market interest rate.

A decline in the interest rate to i', other things constant, reduces the opportunity cost of financing new plants and equipment, thereby making new investment more profitable. Likewise, a lower interest rate reduces the cost of financing a new house. So a decline in the interest rate increases the amount of investment demanded. Panel (b) shows the demand for investment D_I first introduced several chapters back. When the interest rate falls from i to i', the quantity of investment demanded increases from I to I'.

The spending multiplier magnifies this increase in investment, leading to a greater increase in aggregate demand, reflected in panel (c) by a rightward shift of the aggregate demand curve from AD to AD'. At the given price level P, real GDP increases from Y to Y'.

The sequence of events can be summarized as follows:

$$M{\uparrow} \rightarrow i{\downarrow} \rightarrow I{\uparrow} \rightarrow AD{\uparrow} \rightarrow Y{\uparrow}$$

1. money supply, *M,* increases
2. reducing the interest rate, *i*
3. stimulating investment, *I*
4. increasing aggregate demand from *AD* to *AD'*
5. at a given price level, real GDP demanded increases from *Y* to *Y'*

The entire sequence is also traced out in each panel of Exhibit 3 by the movement from point *a* to point *b.*

Note that the graphs presented here ignore any feedback effects of changes in real GDP on the demand for money. Because the demand for money depends on the level of real GDP, an increase in real GDP would shift the money demand curve to the right in panel (a). If we had shifted the money

Exhibit 3

Effects of an Increase in the Money Supply on Interest Rates, Investment, and Aggregate Demand

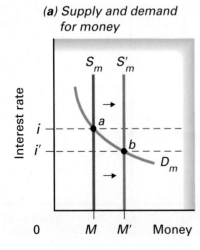
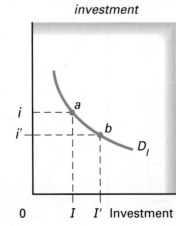
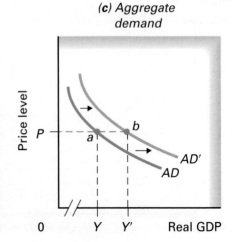

demand curve, the equilibrium interest rate would still have fallen, but not by as much, so investment and aggregate demand would not have increased by as much. Thus, Exhibit 3 is a simplified view, but it still captures the essentials of how changes in the money supply affect the economy.

Now let's consider the effect of a Fed-orchestrated *increase* in interest rates. In Exhibit 3 such a policy could be traced by moving from point b to point a in each panel, but we dispense with a blow-by-blow discussion of the graphs. Suppose the Federal Reserve decides to reduce the money supply to cool down an overheated economy. A decrease in the money supply would increase the interest rate. At the higher interest rate, businesses find it more costly to finance plants and equipment, and households find it more costly to finance new homes. Hence, a higher interest rate reduces the amount invested. The resulting decline in investment is magnified by the spending multiplier, leading to a greater decline in aggregate demand.

As long as the interest rate is sensitive to changes in the money supply, and as long as investment is sensitive to changes in the interest rate, changes in the money supply affect investment. The extent to which a given change in investment affects aggregate demand depends on the size of the spending multiplier.

Adding the Short-Run Aggregate Supply Curve

Even after tracing the effect of a change in the money supply on aggregate demand, we still have only half the story. To determine the effects of monetary policy on the equilibrium real GDP in the economy, we need the supply side. An aggregate supply curve helps show how a given shift of the aggregate demand curve affects real GDP and the price level. In the short run, the aggregate supply curve slopes upward, so the quantity supplied increases only if the price level increases. *For a given shift of the aggregate demand curve, the steeper the short-run aggregate supply curve, the smaller the increase in real GDP and the larger the increase in the price level.*

Suppose the economy is producing at point *a* in Exhibit 4, where the aggregate demand curve AD intersects the short-run aggregate supply curve SRAS$_{130}$, yielding a short-run equilibrium output of $13.8 trillion and a price level of 125. As you can see, the actual

Exhibit 4

Expansionary Monetary Policy to Close a Contractionary Gap

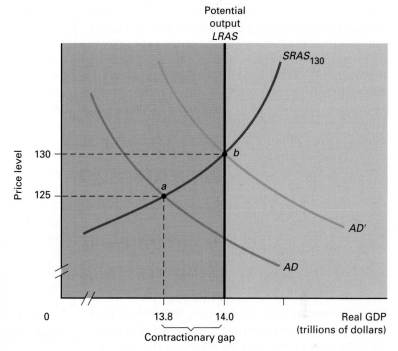

price level of 125 is below the expected price level of 130, and the short-run equilibrium output of $13.8 trillion is below the economy's potential of $14.0 trillion, yielding a contractionary gap of $0.2 trillion.

At point *a*, real wages are higher than had been negotiated and many people are looking for jobs. The Fed can wait to see whether the economy recovers on its own. Market forces could cause employers and workers to renegotiate lower nominal wages. This would lower production costs, pushing the short-run aggregate supply curve rightward, thus closing the contractionary gap. But if Fed officials are impatient with natural market forces, they could try to close the gap using an expansionary monetary policy. For example, during 2007 and 2008, the Fed aggressively cut the federal funds rate to stimulate aggregate demand. If the Fed lowers that rate by just the right amount, this stimulates investment, thus increasing the aggregate demand curve enough to achieve a new equilibrium at point *b*, where the economy produces its potential output. Given all the connections in the chain of causality between changes in the money supply and changes in equilibrium output, however, it would actually be quite remarkable for the Fed to execute monetary policy so precisely. If the Fed overshoots the mark and stimulates aggregate demand too much, this would open up an expansionary gap, thus creating inflationary pressure in the economy.

To review: As long as the money demand curve and the investment demand curve each slope downward, an increase in the money supply reduces the market interest rate, increasing investment and consequently increasing aggregate demand. And as long as the short-run aggregate supply curve slopes upward, the short-run effect of an increase in the money supply is an increase in both real output and the price level. But here is one final qualification: Lowering the interest rate may not always stimulate investment. Economic prospects may become so glum that lower interest rates may fail to achieve the desired increase in aggregate demand. In Japan, for example, the central bank lowered the interest rate nearly to zero, yet that economy remained lifeless for years during the 1990s.

LO³ Money and Aggregate Demand in the Long Run

When we looked at the impact of money on the economy in the short run, we found that **money influences aggregate demand and equilibrium output through its effect on the interest rate.** Here we look at the long-run effects of changes in the money supply on the economy. The long-run view of money is more direct: if the central bank supplies more money to the economy, sooner or later people spend more. But because the long-run aggregate supply curve is fixed at the economy's potential output, this greater spending simply increases the price level. In short, more money is chasing the same output. Here are the details.

The Equation of Exchange

Every transaction in the economy involves a two-way swap: The buyer exchanges money for goods and the seller exchanges goods for money. One way of expressing this relationship among key variables in the economy is the equation of exchange, first developed by classical economists. Although this equation can be arranged in different ways, depending on the emphasis, the basic version is

$$M \times V = P \times Y$$

where M is the quantity of money in the economy; V is the velocity of money, or the average number of times per year each dollar is used to purchase final goods and services; P is the average price level; and Y is real GDP. The equation of exchange says that the quantity of money in circulation, M, multiplied by V, the number of times that money changes hands, equals the average price level, P, times real output, Y. The price level, P, times real output, Y, equals the economy's nominal income and output, or nominal GDP.

By rearranging the equation of exchange, we find that velocity equals nominal GDP divided by the money stock, or:

$$V = \frac{P \times Y}{M}$$

For example, nominal GDP in 2008 was $14.3 trillion, and the money stock as measured by M1 averaged

equation of exchange
the quantity of money, *M*, multiplied by its velocity, *V*, equals nominal GDP, which is the product of the price level, *P*, and real GDP, *Y*; or *M* × *V* = *P* × *Y*

velocity of money
the average number of times per year each dollar is used to purchase final goods and services

$1.6 trillion. The velocity of money indicates how often each dollar is used on average to pay for final goods and services during the year. So in 2008, velocity was $14.3 trillion divided by $1.6 trillion, or 8.9. Given GDP and the money supply, each dollar in circulation must have been spent 8.9 times on average to pay for final goods and services. There is no other way these market transactions could have occurred. The value of velocity is implied by the values of the other variables. Incidentally, velocity measures spending only on final goods and services—not on intermediate products, secondhand goods, or financial assets, even though such spending also occurs. So velocity underestimates how hard the money supply works during the year.

The equation of exchange says that total spending ($M \times V$) is always equal to total receipts ($P \times Y$), as was the case in our circular-flow analysis. As described so far, however, the equation of exchange is simply an *identity*—a relationship expressed in such a way that it is true by definition. Another example of an identity would be a relationship equating miles per gallon to the distance driven divided by the gasoline required.

$$M \times V = P \times Y$$
$$V = \frac{P \times Y}{M}$$

The Quantity Theory of Money

If velocity is relatively stable over time, or at least predictable, the equation of exchange turns from an identity into a theory—the quantity theory of money. The quantity theory of money states that if the velocity of money is stable, or at least predictable, then the equation of exchange can be used to predict the effects of changes in the money supply on *nominal* GDP, $P \times Y$. For example, if M increases by 5 percent and V remains constant, then $P \times Y$, or nominal GDP, must also increase by 5 percent. For a while, some economists believed they could use the equation of exchange to predict nominal output in the short run. Now it's used primarily as a guide in the long run.

So an increase in the money supply results in more spending in the long run, meaning a higher nominal GDP. How is this increase in $P \times Y$ divided between changes in the price level and changes in real GDP? The answer does not lie in the quantity theory, for that theory is stated only in terms of nominal GDP. The answer lies in the shape of the aggregate supply curve.

The long-run aggregate supply curve is vertical at the economy's potential level of output. With real output, Y, fixed and the velocity of money, V, relatively stable, a change in the stock of money translates directly into a change in the price level. Exhibit 5 on the next page shows the effect of an increase in the money supply in the long run. An increase in the money supply causes a rightward shift of the aggregate demand curve, which increases the price level but leaves output unchanged at potential GDP. So the economy's potential output level is not affected by changes in the money supply. *In the long run, increases in the money supply, with velocity stable or at least not decreasing, result only in higher prices.* For example, an examination of 73 inflation periods across major economies since 1960 concludes that important triggers to inflation were expansionary monetary policies.

To review: If velocity is stable, or at least predictable, the quantity theory of money says that changes in the money supply will, in the long run, result in predictable effects on the economy's price level. Velocity's stability and predictability are key to the quantity theory of money.

What Determines the Velocity of Money?

Velocity depends on the customs and conventions of commerce. In colonial times, money might be tied up in transit for days as a courier on horseback carried a payment from a merchant

> **quantity theory of money**
> if the velocity of money is stable, or at least predictable, changes in the money supply have predictable effects on nominal GDP

Exhibit 5

In the Long Run, an Increase in the Money Supply Results in a Higher Price Level, or Inflation

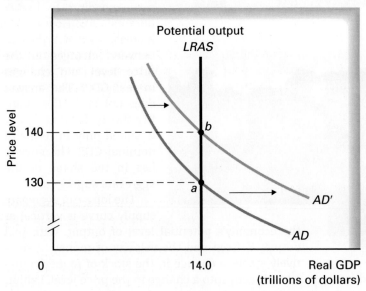

in Boston to one in Baltimore. Today, the electronic transmission of funds occurs in an instant, so the same stock of money can move around much more quickly to finance many more transactions. *The velocity of money has also increased because of a variety of commercial innovations that facilitate exchange.* For example, a wider use of charge accounts and credit cards has reduced the need for shoppers to carry cash. Likewise, automatic teller machines have made cash more accessible at more times and in more places. What's more, debit cards are used at a growing number of retail outlets, such as grocery stores and drug stores, so people need less "walking around" money.

Another institutional factor that determines velocity is the frequency with which workers get paid. Suppose a worker who earns $52,000 per year gets paid $2,000 every two weeks. Earnings are spent evenly during the two-week period and are gone by the end of the period. In that case, a worker's average money balance during the pay period is $1,000. If a worker earns the same $52,000 per year but, instead, gets paid $1,000 weekly, the average money balance during the week falls to $500. *Thus, the more often workers get paid, other things constant, the lower their average money balances, so the more active the money supply and the greater its velocity.* Payment prac-

> IN THE LONG RUN, INCREASES IN THE MONEY SUPPLY, WITH VELOCITY STABLE OR AT LEAST NOT DECREASING, RESULT ONLY IN HIGHER PRICES.

tices change slowly over time, and the effects of these changes on velocity are predictable.

Another factor affecting velocity depends on how stable money is as a store of value. *The better money serves as a store of value, the more money people hold, so the lower its velocity.* For example, the introduction of interest-bearing checking accounts made money a better store of value, so people were more willing to hold money in checking accounts and this financial innovation reduced velocity. On the other hand, when inflation increases unexpectedly, money turns out to be a poorer store of value. People become reluctant to hold money and try to exchange it for some asset that retains its value better. This reduction in people's willingness to hold money during periods of high inflation increases the velocity of money. During hyperinflations, workers usually get paid daily, boosting velocity even more. Thus, *velocity increases with a rise in the inflation rate, other things constant.* Money becomes a hot potato—nobody wants to hold it for long.

Again, the usefulness of the quantity theory in predicting changes in the price level in the long run hinges on how stable and predictable the velocity of money is over time.

How Stable Is Velocity?

Exhibit 6 graphs velocity since 1960, measured both as nominal GDP divided by M1 in panel (a) and as nominal GDP divided by M2 in panel (b). Between 1960 and 1980, M1 velocity increased steadily and in that sense could be considered at least predictable. M1 velocity bounced around during the 1980s. But in the early 1990s, more and more banks began offering money market funds that included limited check-writing privileges, or what is considered M2. Deposits shifted from M1 to M2, which increased the velocity of M1. Also in recent years, more people began using their ATM and debit cards to pay directly at grocery stores, drugstores, and a growing number of outlets, and this too increased the velocity of M1 because people had less need for walking-around money. M1 velocity increased from about 6.0 in 1993 to over 8.0 more recently. M2 velocity appears more stable, as you can see by comparing the two panels in Exhibit 6.

For a few years, the Fed focused on changes in the money supply as a target for monetary policy in the short run. Because M1 velocity became so unstable during the 1980s, the Fed in 1987 switched from targeting M1 to targeting M2. But when M2 velocity became volatile in the early 1990s, the Fed announced that money aggregates, including M2, would no longer be considered reliable guides for monetary policy in the short run. Since 1993, the equation of exchange has been considered more of a rough guide linking changes in the money supply to inflation in the long run.

What is the long-run relationship between increases in the money supply and inflation? Since the Federal Reserve System was established in 1913, the United States has suffered three episodes of high inflation, and each was preceded and accompanied by sharp increases in the money supply. These occurred from 1913 to 1920, 1939 to 1948, and 1967 to 1980.

Exhibit 6

The Velocity of Money

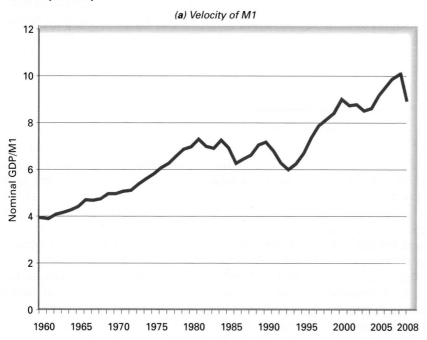

(a) Velocity of M1

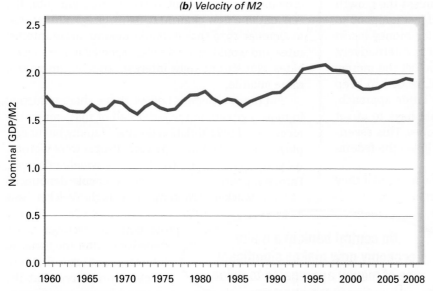

(b) Velocity of M2

SOURCE: *Economic Report of the President,* January 2009. To compute the latest velocity, go to http://www.gpoaccess.gov/eop/, find the statistical tables in the appendix then divide nominal GDP by M1 and by M2.

LO⁴ Targets for Monetary Policy

In the short run, monetary policy affects the economy largely by influencing the interest rate. In the long run, changes in the money supply affect the price level, though with an uncertain lag. Should monetary authorities focus on the interest rates in the short run or the supply of money in the long run? As we will see, the Fed lacks the tools to focus on both at the same time.

Contrasting Policies

To demonstrate the effects of different policies, we begin with the money market in equilibrium at point e in Exhibit 7. The interest rate is i and the money stock is M, values the monetary authorities find appropriate. Suppose there is an increase in the demand for money in the economy, perhaps because of an increase in nominal GDP. The money demand curve shifts to the right, from D_m to D'_m.

When confronted with an increase in the demand for money, monetary authorities can choose to do nothing, thereby allowing the interest rate to rise, or they can increase the money supply enough to hold the interest rate constant. If monetary authorities do nothing, the quantity of money in the economy remains at M, but the interest rate rises because the greater demand for money increases the

Exhibit 7

Targeting Interest Rates Versus Targeting the Money Supply

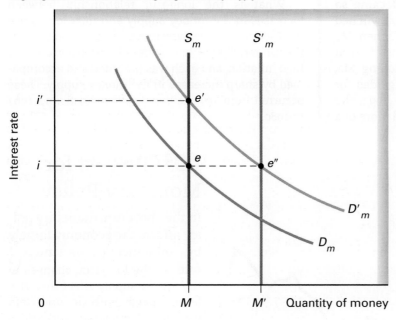

equilibrium combination from point *e* up to point *e'*. Alternatively, monetary authorities can try to keep the interest rate at its initial level by increasing the supply of money from S_m to S'_m. In terms of possible combinations of the money stock and the interest rate, monetary authorities must choose from points lying along the new money demand curve, D'_m.

A growing economy usually needs a growing money supply to pay for the increase in aggregate output. If monetary authorities maintain a constant growth in the money supply, and if velocity remains stable, the interest rate fluctuates unless the growth in the supply of money each period just happens to match the growth in the demand for money (as in the movement from *e* to *e''* in Exhibit 7). Alternatively, monetary authorities could try to adjust the money supply each period by the amount needed to keep the interest rate stable. With this latter approach, changes in the money supply would have to offset any changes in the demand for money. This essentially is what the Fed does when it holds the federal funds target constant.

Interest rate fluctuations could be harmful if they create undesirable fluctuations in investment. For interest rates to remain stable during economic expansions, the money supply would have to grow at the same rate as the demand for money. Likewise, for interest rates to remain stable during economic

> **No central bank in a major economy now makes significant use of money aggregates to guide policy in the short run.**

contractions, the money supply would have to shrink at the same rate as the demand for money. Hence, for monetary authorities to maintain the interest rate at some specified level, the money supply must increase during economic expansions and decrease during contractions. But an increase in the money supply during an expansion would increase aggregate demand even more, and a decrease in the money supply during a contraction would reduce aggregate demand even more. *Such changes in the money supply would thus tend to worsen fluctuations in economic activity, thereby adding more instability to the economy.* With this in mind, let's review monetary policy over the years.

Targets Before 1982

Between World War II and October 1979, the Fed attempted to stabilize interest rates. Stable interest rates were viewed as a prerequisite for an attractive investment environment and, thus, for a stable economy. Milton Friedman, a Nobel Prize winner, argued that this exclusive attention to interest rates made monetary policy a source of instability in the economy because changes in the money supply reinforced fluctuations in the economy. He said that the Fed should pay less attention to interest rates and instead should focus on a steady and predictable growth in the money supply. The debate raged during the 1970s, and Friedman won some important converts. Amid growing concern about a rising inflation rate, the Fed, under a new chairman, Paul Volcker, announced in October 1979 that it would deemphasize interest rates and would instead target specific money aggregates. Not surprisingly, interest rates became much more volatile.

But many observers believe that a sharp reduction in money growth in the latter half of 1981 caused the recession of 1982. Inflation declined rapidly, but unemployment climbed to 10 percent. People were worried. As you might expect, the Fed was widely criticized. Farmers, politicians, and businesspeople denounced Volcker. Emotions ran high. Volcker was reportedly even given Secret Service protection. In October 1982, three years after the focus on interest rates was dropped, Volcker announced that the Fed would again pay some attention to interest rates.

The Fed is always looking for signs about the direction of the economy.

Targets After 1982

The Fed is always feeling its way, looking for signs about the direction of the economy. The rapid pace of financial innovations and deregulation during the 1980s made the definition and measurement of the money supply more difficult. Alan Greenspan, who became the Fed chairman in 1987, said that, in the short run, changes in the money supply "are not linked closely enough with those of nominal income to justify a single-minded focus on the money supply."[1] In 1993, he testified in Congress that the Fed would no longer target money aggregates, such as M1 and M2, as a guide to monetary policy. As we've seen, the Fed in recent years has targeted the federal funds rate. *No central bank in a major economy now makes significant use of money aggregates to guide policy in the short run. Still, most policy makers also agree that in the long run, changes in the money supply influenced the price level and inflation.*

While monetary targets are important, also significant is what Fed officials have to say. For example, they might announce that they are following a prob-

❊❊❊

1. Quoted in "Greenspan Asks That Fed Be Allowed to Pay Interest," *Wall Street Journal,* 11 March 1992.

lem closely and are prepared to stabilize financial markets as needed. Such reassurance is sometimes all that's required to calm market jitters.

International Considerations

As national economies grow more interdependent, the Fed has become more sensitive to the global implications of its actions. What happens in the United States often affects markets overseas and vice versa. In both cases, the Fed tries to calm troubled waters. For example, the strength of the dollar relative to foreign currencies determines how competitive U.S. producers are in world markets. The stronger the dollar, the harder it is for U.S. producers to compete with foreign producers. In the mid-1980s, the dollar became quite strong. An expansionary monetary policy is one way to bring down the value of the dollar. As the money supply increases, interest rates fall in the short run, so

Fearing a collapsing housing market, the Fed lowered the target rate aggressively in 2008 to a range between zero and ¼ percent.

the U.S. economy is less attractive to foreign investors seeking high interest rates. The Fed pursued such a policy, and by 1987 the value of the dollar declined to a more competitive level.

The Fed has tried to soothe troubled world markets in a variety of ways. When Mexico faced financial difficulties in 1982 and again in 1994, Fed officials helped arrange loans to prevent financial crises. A worldwide financial panic in the fall of 1998 because of defaults on Russian bonds prompted the Fed to lower the federal funds rate to supply more liquidity here and abroad. And a worldwide shortage of credit in 2008–2009 caused by mortgage defaults in the United States prompted the Fed to supply additional liquidity to the banking system to ensure the orderly functioning of financial markets. Although not the main focus of monetary policy, international considerations are of growing importance to the Fed.

> The stronger the dollar, the harder it is for U.S. producers to compete with foreign producers.

focuses on the short run, an increase in the money supply means that people are holding more money than they would like at the prevailing interest rate, so they exchange one form of wealth, money, for other financial assets, such as corporate or government bonds. This greater demand for other financial assets has no direct effect on aggregate demand, but it does reduce the interest rate, and thereby stimulates investment. The higher investment gets magnified by the spending multiplier, increasing aggregate demand. The effect of this increase in demand on real output and the price level depends on the shape of the short-run aggregate supply curve.

In the model that focuses on the long run, changes in the money supply act more directly on the price level. If velocity is relatively stable or at least predictable, then a change in the money supply has a predictable effect on the price level in the long run. As long as velocity is not declining, an increase in the money supply means that people eventually spend more, increasing aggregate demand. But because long-run aggregate supply is fixed at the economy's potential output, increased aggregate demand leads simply to a higher price level, or to inflation.

Final Word

This chapter has described two ways of viewing the effects of money on the economy's performance, but we should not overstate the differences. In the model that

$14.3 trillion < U.S. nominal GDP in 2008

Average M1 money stock in 2008 > $1.6 trillion

8.9 < Velocity of M1 money in 2008

The years Alan Greenspan served as chairman of the Fed > 1987–2006

The Fed's target rate during the 2008–2009 housing crisis > 0–0.25%

CHAPTER 17

Macro Policy Debate:
Active *or* Passive?

Learning Outcomes

LO[1] Compare an active policy and a passive policy

LO[2] Consider the role of expectations

LO[3] Discuss policy rules versus discretion

LO[4] Explain the Phillips curve

"Does the economy work fairly well on its own, or does it require active government intervention?"

Does the economy work fairly well on its own, or does it require active government intervention? Does government intervention do more harm than good? If people expect government to intervene if the economy falters, does this expectation affect their behavior? Does this expectation affect government's behavior? What is the relationship between unemployment and inflation in the short run and in the long run? Answers to these and other questions are provided in this chapter, which discusses the appropriate role for government in economic stabilization.

What do you think?

The economy runs smoothly on its own without government involvement.

Strongly Disagree						Strongly Agree
1	2	3	4	5	6	7

You have studied both fiscal and monetary policy and are now in a position to consider the overall impact of public policy on the U.S. economy. This chapter distinguishes between two general approaches: the *active approach* and the *passive approach*. The active approach views the economy as relatively unstable and unable to recover from shocks when they occur. According to the active approach, economic fluctuations arise primarily from the private sector, particularly investment, and natural market forces may not help much or may be too slow once the economy gets off track. To move the economy to its potential output, the active approach calls for government intervention and discretionary policy. The passive approach, on the other hand, views the economy as relatively stable and able to recover from shocks when they do occur. When the economy derails, natural market forces and automatic stabilizers nudge it back on track in a timely manner. According to the passive approach, not only is active discretionary policy unnecessary, but such activism may do more harm than good.

In this chapter, we consider the pros and cons of *active* intervention in the economy versus *passive* reliance on natural market forces and automatic stabilizers. We also examine the role that expectations play in stabilization policy. You will learn why unanticipated stabilization policies have more impact on employment and output than do anticipated ones. Finally, the chapter explores the trade-off between unemployment and inflation.

Topics discussed in Chapter 17 include:

- Active versus passive approaches
- Self-correcting mechanisms
- Rational expectations
- Policy rules and policy credibility
- Short-run and long-run Phillips curves
- The time-inconsistency problem
- Natural rate hypothesis

LO¹ Active Policy Versus Passive Policy

According to the *active* approach, discretionary fiscal or monetary policy can reduce the costs of an unstable economy, such as higher unemployment. According to the *passive* approach, discretionary policy may contribute to the instability of the economy and is therefore part of the problem, not part of the solution. The two approaches differ in their assumptions about the effectiveness of natural market forces compared with government intervention.

Closing a Contractionary Gap

Perhaps the best way to describe each approach is by examining a particular macroeconomic problem. Suppose the economy is in short-run equilibrium at point *a* in panel (a) of Exhibit 1, with real GDP at $13.8 trillion, which is below the economy's potential of $14.0 trillion. The contractionary gap of $0.2 trillion drives unemployment above its natural rate (the rate when the economy produces potential GDP). This gap could result from lower-than-expected aggregate demand. What should public officials do?

Those who subscribe to the passive approach, as did their classical predecessors, have more faith in the *self-correcting forces* of the economy than do those who favor the active approach. In what sense is the economy self-correcting? According to the passive approach, wages and prices are flexible enough to adjust within a reasonable period to labor shortages or surpluses. High unemployment causes wages to fall, which reduces production costs, which shifts the short-run aggregate supply curve rightward in panel (a) of Exhibit 1. (Money wages need not actually fall; money wage increases need only lag behind price increases, so that real wages fall.) The short-run aggregate supply curve, within a reasonable period, shifts from $SRAS_{130}$ to $SRAS_{120}$, moving the economy to its potential output at point *b*. *According to the passive approach, the economy is stable enough, gravitating in a reasonable time toward potential GDP. Automatic stabilizers also help move the economy toward potential GDP. Consequently, advocates of passive policy see little reason for discretionary policy. The passive approach is to let natural market forces and automatic stabilizers close the contractionary gap. So the prescription of passive policy is to do nothing beyond the automatic stabilizers already built into taxes, transfers, and government purchases.*

Advocates of an active approach, on the other hand, believe that prices and wages are not that flexible, particularly in the downward direction. They think that when adverse supply shocks or sagging demand push unemployment above its natural rate, market forces may be too slow to respond. The longer market forces take to reduce unemployment to the natural rate, the greater the output lost and the greater the economic and psychological cost to those unemployed. *Because advocates of an active policy associate a high cost with the passive approach, they favor an active stabilization policy to stimulate aggregate demand.*

Exhibit 1

Closing a Contractionary Gap

(a) The passive approach

(b) The active approach

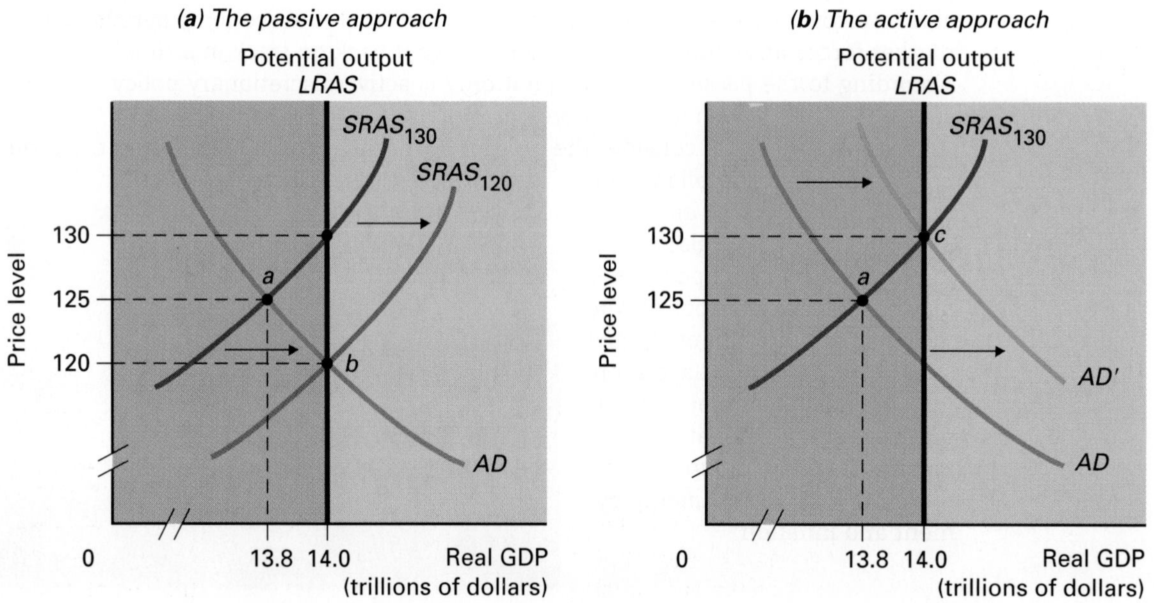

A decision by public officials to intervene in the economy to achieve potential output—that is, a decision to use discretionary policy—reflects an active approach. In panel (b) of Exhibit 1, we begin at the same point *a* as in panel (a). At point *a*, short-run equilibrium output is below potential output, so the economy is experiencing a contractionary gap. Through discretionary monetary policy, discretionary fiscal policy, or some of both, as occurred in 2009, active policy attempts to increase aggregate demand from AD to AD', moving equilibrium from point *a* to point *c*, thus closing the contractionary gap.

In 2009, policy makers tried to revive a slowing economy using both fiscal and monetary policy. Barack Obama's $787 billion stimulus plan, the largest on record, was approved by Congress in February and was aimed at counteracting the deep recession caused by the financial and subprime mortgage crisis. Meanwhile, throughout 2008, as noted in the previous chapter, the Fed cut its target interest rate a record amount to nearly zero. This combination of fiscal and monetary policy was the most concentrated attempt to boost aggregate demand ever. One possible cost of using discretionary policy to stimulate aggregate demand is an increase in the price level, or inflation. Another cost of fiscal stimulus is the increase in the budget deficit, which was projected to exceed one trillion dollars in 2009.

Closing an Expansionary Gap

Let's consider the situation in which the short-run equilibrium output exceeds the economy's poten-

tial. Suppose the actual price level of 135 exceeds the expected price level of 130, opening up an expansionary gap of $0.2 trillion, as shown in Exhibit 2. The passive approach argues that natural market forces prompt workers and firms to negotiate higher wages. These higher nominal wages increase production costs, shifting the short-run supply curve leftward, from $SRAS_{130}$ to $SRAS_{140}$, as shown in panel (a). Consequently, the price level increases and output decreases to the economy's potential. So the natural adjustment process results in a higher price level, or inflation.

An active approach sees discretionary policy as a way to reach potential output without increasing the price level. Advocates of an active policy believe that if aggregate demand can be reduced from AD" to AD', as shown in panel (b) of Exhibit 2, then the equilibrium point moves down along the initial aggregate supply curve from *d* to *c*. *Whereas the passive approach relies on natural market forces and automatic stabilizers to close an expansionary gap through a decrease in the short-run aggregate supply curve, the active approach relies on just the right discretionary policy to close the gap through a decrease of the aggregate demand curve.* In the long run, the passive approach results in a higher price level and the active approach results in a lower price level. Thus, the correct discretionary policy can relieve the inflationary pressure associated with an expansionary gap. Whenever the Fed attempts to cool down an overheated economy by increasing its target interest rate, as it did in 17 steps between mid-2004 and mid-2006, it employs an active monetary policy to close an expansionary gap. The Fed tried

Exhibit 2

Closing an Expansionary Gap

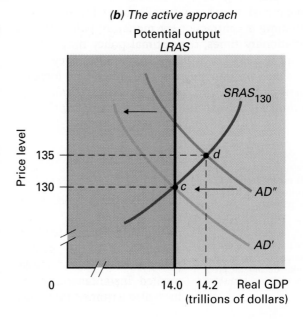

(a) The passive approach

(b) The active approach

to orchestrate a so-called *soft landing* to gently slow the rate of growth before that growth triggered unacceptably high inflation.

Problems with Active Policy

The timely adoption and implementation of an active policy is not easy. One problem is identifying the economy's potential output and the natural rate of unemployment. Suppose the natural rate of unemployment is 5 percent, but policy makers mistakenly believe it's 4 percent. As they pursue their elusive goal of 4 percent, they push aggregate output beyond its potential, fueling higher prices in the long run but with no permanent reduction in unemployment. Recall that when output exceeds the economy's potential, this opens up an expansionary gap, causing a leftward shift of the short-run aggregate supply curve until the economy returns to its potential output at a higher price level.

Even if policy makers can accurately estimate the economy's potential output and the natural rate of unemployment, formulating an effective policy requires detailed knowledge of current and future economic conditions. Policy makers must be able to predict what would happen with a passive approach.

Congress and the president pursue fiscal policy while the Fed pursues monetary policy; these groups often fail to coordinate their efforts. If an active policy requires coordination, the policy may not work as desired. In early 1995, for example, Congress was considering an expansionary tax cut while the Fed was pursuing a contractionary monetary policy. During inflationary times, the optimal policy may call for a tax increase or a tighter monetary policy—policies that are unpopular because they may increase unemployment. Finally, as we see next, timing lags complicate the execution of an active policy.

> Even if policy makers can accurately estimate the economy's potential output and the natural rate of unemployment, formulating an effective policy requires detailed knowledge of current and future economic conditions.

The Problem of Lags

So far, we have ignored the time required to implement policy. That is, we have assumed that the desired policy is selected and implemented instantaneously. We have also assumed that, once

recognition lag
the time needed to identify a macroeconomic problem and assess its seriousness

decision-making lag
the time needed to decide what to do once a macroeconomic problem has been identified

implemented, the policy works as advertised—again, in no time. Actually, there may be long, sometimes unpredictable, lags at several stages in the process. These lags reduce the effectiveness and increase the uncertainty of active policies.

First is a recognition lag—the time it takes to identify a problem and determine how serious it is. For example, time is required to accumulate evidence that the economy is indeed performing below its potential. Even if initial data look troubling, data are usually revised later. For example, the government releases three estimates of quarterly GDP growth coming weeks apart—an *advanced* estimate, a *preliminary* estimate, and a *final* estimate. What's more, these estimates are often revised years later or even a decade later. Therefore, policy makers sometimes wait for more proof before responding to what may turn out to be a false alarm. Because a recession is not identified as such until more than 6 months after it begins and because the average recession since 1945 has lasted only about 11 months, a typical recession is nearly over before officially recognized as such.

Even after enough evidence accumulates, policy makers often need time to decide what to do, so there is a decision-making lag. In the case of discretionary fiscal policy, Congress and the president must agree on an appropriate course of action. Fiscal policy usually takes months to develop and approve; it could take more than a year. On the other hand, the Fed can implement monetary policy more quickly and does not even have to wait for regular meetings. For example, as the economy weakened in 2008, the Fed announced interest rate cuts seven times. So the decision-making lag is shorter for monetary policy than for fiscal policy.

Once a decision has been made, the new policy must be introduced, which usually involves an implementation lag. Again, monetary policy has the advantage: After a policy has been adopted, the Fed can immediately begin buying or selling bonds to influence bank reserves and thereby change the federal funds rate. The implementation lag is longer for fiscal policy. If tax rates change, new tax forms must be printed and distributed advising employers of changes in tax withholding. If government spending changes, the appropriate government agencies must get involved. The implementation of fiscal policy can take more than a year. For example, in February 1983, the nation's unemployment rate reached 10.3 percent, with 11.5 million people unemployed. The following month, Congress passed the Emergency Jobs Appropriation Act providing $9 billion to create what supporters claimed would be hundreds of thousands of new jobs. Fifteen months later, only $3.1 billion had been spent and only 35,000 new jobs had been created, according to a U.S. General Accounting Office study. By that time, the economy was already recovering on its own, lowering the unemployment rate from 10.3 percent to 7.1 percent and adding 6.2 million new jobs. So this public spending program was implemented only after the recession had bottomed out and recovered. Likewise, in spring 1993, President Clinton proposed a $16 billion stimulus package to boost what appeared to be a sluggish recovery. The measure was defeated because it would have increased an already large federal deficit, yet the economy still added 5.6 million jobs over the next two years anyway. As a final example of an implementation lag, in February 2009, Congress approved a $787 billion stimulus plan, which President Obama said would save or create up to four million jobs. The idea was to spend the money quickly by funding "shovel ready" projects. But six months after passage, only 20 percent of expenditures had occurred; meanwhile the number unemployed swelled by three million.

Once a policy has been implemented, there is an effectiveness lag before the full impact of the policy registers on the economy. With monetary policy, the

lag between a change in the federal funds rate and the change in aggregate demand and output can take from months to a year or more. Fiscal policy, once enacted, usually requires 3 to 6 months to take effect and between 9 and 18 months to register its full effect. Because of the effectiveness lag, the economy may turn around on its own before the policy registers its full impact. A stimulus package may end up merely adding more inflationary pressure to a recovering economy.

These lags make active policy difficult to execute. The more variable the lags, the harder it is to predict when a particular policy will take hold and what the state of the economy will be at that time. To advocates of passive policy, these lags are reason enough to avoid active discretionary policy. *Advocates of a passive approach argue that an active stabilization policy imposes troubling fluctuations in the price level and real GDP because it often takes hold only after market forces have already returned the economy to its potential output level.*

Talk in the media about "jump-starting" the economy reflects the active approach, which views the economy as a sputtering machine that can be fixed by an expert mechanic. The passive approach views the economy as more like a supertanker on automatic pilot. The policy question then becomes whether to trust that automatic pilot (the self-correcting tendencies of the economy) or to try to override the mechanism with active discretionary policies.

implementation lag
the time needed to introduce a change in monetary or fiscal policy

effectiveness lag
the time needed for changes in monetary or fiscal policy to affect the economy

A Review of Policy Perspectives

The active and passive approaches reflect different views about the stability and resiliency of the economy and the ability of Congress or the Fed to implement appropriate discretionary policies. As we have seen, advocates of an active approach think that the natural adjustments of wages and prices can be excruciatingly slow, particularly when unemployment is high. Prolonged high unemployment means that much output must be sacrificed, and the unemployed must suffer personal hardship during the slow adjustment period. If high unemployment lasts a long time, labor skills may grow rusty, and some people may drop out of the labor force. Therefore, prolonged unemployment may cause the economy's potential GDP to fall.

Thus, active policy advocates see a high cost of ignoring discretionary policy. Despite the lags involved, they prefer action—through discretionary fiscal policy, discretionary monetary policy, or some combination of the two—to inaction. Passive policy advocates, on the other hand, believe that uncertain lags and ignorance about how the economy works undermine active policy. Rather than pursue a misguided activist policy, passivists prefer to sit back and rely on the economy's natural ability to correct itself just using automatic stabilizers.

LO² The Role of Expectations

The effectiveness of a particular government policy depends in part on what people expect. As we saw in an earlier chapter, the short-run aggregate supply curve is drawn for a given expected price level reflected in long-term wage contracts. If workers and firms expect continuing inflation, their wage agreements reflect these inflationary expectations. One approach in macroeconomics, called rational expectations, argues that people form expectations on the basis of all available information, including information about the probable future actions of policy makers. Thus, aggregate supply depends on what sort of macroeconomic course policy makers are expected to pursue. For example, if people were to observe policy makers using discretionary policy to stimulate aggregate demand every time output falls below potential, people would come to anticipate the effects of this policy on the price level and output. Robert Lucas, of the University of Chicago, won the 1995 Nobel Prize for his studies of rational expec-

rational expectations
a school of thought that argues people form expectations based on all available information, including the likely future actions of government policy makers

tations. We will consider the role of expectations in the context of monetary policy. We could focus on fiscal policy, but monetary policy has been calling the shots for most of the last quarter century. Only with George W. Bush's tax cuts and then Barack Obama's stimulus plan did fiscal policy make a comeback.

Monetary Policy and Inflation Expectations

Monetary authorities must testify before Congress regularly to offer an assessment of the economy. The Fed also announces, after each meeting of the FOMC, any changes in its interest rate targets and the likely direction, or "bias," of future changes. And Fed officials often deliver speeches around the country. Those interested in the economy sift through all this material to discover the future path of monetary policy.

Let's examine the relationship between Fed policy pronouncements, Fed actions, and equilibrium output. Suppose the economy is producing potential output so unemployment is at its natural rate. At the beginning of the year, firms and employees must negotiate wage agreements. While negotiations are under way, the Fed announces that throughout the year, monetary policy will aim at sustaining potential output while keeping the price level stable. This seems the appropriate policy because unemployment is already at the natural rate. Workers and firms understand that the Fed's stable price policy appears optimal under the circumstances because an expansionary monetary policy would lead only to higher inflation in the long run. Until the year is under way and monetary policy is actually implemented, however, the public cannot know for sure what the Fed will do.

As long as wage increases do not exceed the growth in labor productivity, the Fed's plan of a stable price level should work. Alternatively, workers could try for higher wage growth, but that would ultimately lead to inflation. Suppose workers and firms believe the Fed's pronouncements and agree on wage settlements based on a constant price level. If the Fed follows through as promised, the price level should turn out as expected. Output remains at the economy's potential, and unemployment remains at the natural rate. The situation is depicted in Exhibit 3. The short-run aggregate supply curve, $SRAS_{130}$, is based on wage contracts reflecting an expected price level of 130. If the Fed follows the announced course, the aggregate demand curve will be AD and equilibrium will be at point a, where the price level is as expected and the economy is producing \$14.0 trillion, the potential output.

Exhibit 3

Short-Run Effects of an Unexpected Expansionary Monetary Policy

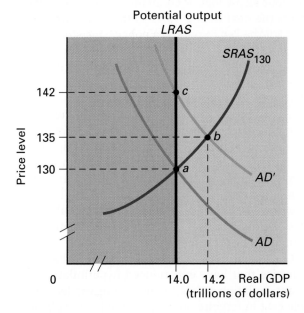

Suppose, however, that after workers and firms have agreed on nominal wages—that is, after the short-run aggregate supply curve has been determined—public officials become dissatisfied with the unemployment rate. Perhaps election-year concerns with unemployment, a false alarm about a recession, or overestimating potential output convinces the Fed to act. An expansionary monetary policy increases the aggregate demand curve from AD, the level anticipated by firms and employees, to AD'. This unexpected policy stimulates output and employment in the short run to equilibrium point b. Output increases to $14.2 trillion, and the price level increases to 135. This temporary boost in output and reduction in unemployment may last long enough to help public officials get reelected.

So the price level is now higher than workers expected, and their agreed-on wage buys less in real terms than workers bargained for. At their earliest opportunity, workers will negotiate higher wages. These higher wage agreements will eventually cause the short-run aggregate supply curve in Exhibit 3 to shift leftward, intersecting AD' at point c, the economy's potential output (to reduce clutter, the shifted short-run aggregate supply curve is not shown). So output once again returns to the economy's potential GDP, but in the process the price level rises to 142.

Thus, the unexpected expansionary policy causes a short-run pop in output and employment. But in the long run, the increase in the aggregate demand curve yields only inflation. The time-inconsistency problem arises when policy makers have an incentive to announce one policy to shape expectations

but then to pursue a different policy once those expectations have been formed and acted on.

Anticipating Monetary Policy

Suppose Fed policy makers become alarmed by the high inflation. The next time around, the Fed once again announces a monetary policy aimed at producing potential output while keeping the price level stable at 142. Based on their previous experience, however, workers and firms have learned that the Fed is willing to accept higher inflation in exchange for a temporary boost in output. Workers may be fooled once by the Fed's actions, but they won't be fooled again. Workers and their employers take the Fed's announcement with a grain of salt. Workers, in particular, do not want to get caught again with their real wages down should the Fed implement a stimulative monetary policy. Workers and firms expect the Fed's actions will increase the price level. The bottom line is that workers and firms negotiate a high wage increase.

In effect, workers and firms are betting the Fed will pursue an expansionary policy regardless of pronouncements to the contrary. The short-run aggregate supply curve reflecting these higher wage agreements is depicted by $SRAS_{152}$ in Exhibit 4, where 152 is the expected price level. Note that AD' would result if the Fed followed its announced policy; that demand curve intersects the potential output line at point c, where the price level is 142. But AD″ is the aggregate demand that workers and firms expect based on an expansionary monetary policy. They have agreed to wage settlements that will produce the economy's potential output if the Fed behaves as *expected*, not as *announced*. Thus, a price level of 152 is based on rational expectations. In effect, workers and firms expect the expansionary monetary policy to shift aggregate demand from AD' to AD″.

Monetary authorities must now decide whether to stick with their announced plan of a stable price level or follow a more expansionary monetary policy. If they pursue the constant-price-level policy, aggregate demand turns out to be AD' and short-run equilibrium occurs at point d. Short-run output falls below the economy's potential, resulting in unemployment exceeding the natural rate. If monetary authorities want to keep output at its potential, they have only one alternative—to match public expectations. Monetary authorities will likely pursue an expansionary monetary policy, an

> **time-inconsistency problem**
> when policy makers have an incentive to announce one policy to influence expectations but then pursue a different policy once those expectations have been formed and acted on

Exhibit 4

Short-Run Effects of the Fed Pursuing a More Expansionary Policy Than Announced

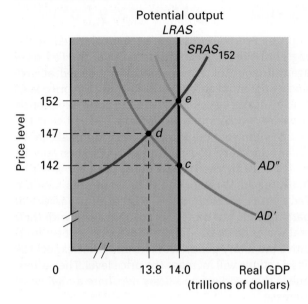

action that increases inflation and reinforces public skepticism of policy announcements. This expansionary policy results in an aggregate demand of AD″, leading to equilibrium at point e, where the price level is 152 and output equals the economy's potential.

Thus, workers and firms enter negotiations realizing that the Fed has an incentive to pursue an expansionary monetary policy. So workers and firms agree to higher wage increases, and the Fed follows with an expansionary policy, one that results in more inflation. Once workers and firms come to expect an expansionary monetary policy and the resulting inflation, such a policy does not spur even a temporary increase in output beyond the economy's potential. *Economists of the rational expectations school believe that if the economy is already producing its potential, an expansionary policy, if fully anticipated, has no effect on output or employment, not even in the short run. Only unanticipated changes in policy can temporarily push output beyond its potential.*

Policy Credibility

cold turkey
the announcement and execution of tough measures to reduce high inflation

If the economy was already producing its potential, an unexpected expansionary monetary policy would

increase output and employment temporarily. The costs, however, include not only inflation in the long term but also a loss of credibility in Fed pronouncements the next time around. Is there any way out of this? For the Fed to pursue a policy consistent with a constant price level, its announcements must somehow be *credible*, or believable. Worker and firms must believe that when the time comes to make a hard decision, the Fed will follow through as promised. Perhaps the Fed could offer some sort of guarantee to convince people it will stay the course—for example, the Fed chairman could promise to resign if the Fed does not follow the announced policy. Ironically, policy makers are often more credible and therefore more effective if they have some of their discretion taken away. In this case, a hard-and-fast rule could be substituted for a policy maker's discretion. We examine policy rules in the next section.

Consider the problems facing central banks in countries that have experienced hyperinflation. For an anti-inflation policy to succeed at the least possible cost in forgone output, the public must believe central bankers. How can central bankers in an economy ripped by hyperinflation establish credibility? Some economists believe that the most efficient anti-inflation policy is cold turkey, which is to announce and execute tough measures to stop inflation, such as halting the growth in the money supply. For example, in 1985, the annual rate of inflation in Bolivia was running at 20,000 percent when the new government announced a stern policy. The restrictive measures worked, and inflation was stopped within a month, with little loss in output. Around the world, credible anti-inflation policies have been successful.[1] Drastic measures sometimes involve costs. For example, some economists argue that the Fed's dramatic efforts to curb high U.S. inflation in the early 1980s triggered what was then the worst recession since the Great Depression. Some say that the Fed's pronouncements were simply not credible and therefore resulted in a recession.

Much depends on the Fed's time horizon. If policy makers take the long view, they will not risk their long-term policy effectiveness for a temporary

> ❝ How can central bankers in an economy ripped by hyperinflation establish credibility? ❞

---

1. For a discussion about how four hyperinflations in the 1920s ended, see Thomas Sargent, "The Ends of Four Big Inflations," in *Inflation: Causes and Consequences,* edited by Robert Hall (Chicago: University of Chicago Press, 1982): 41–98.

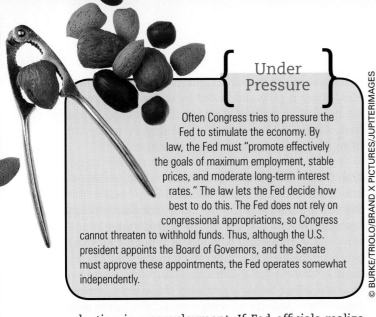

Under Pressure

Often Congress tries to pressure the Fed to stimulate the economy. By law, the Fed must "promote effectively the goals of maximum employment, stable prices, and moderate long-term interest rates." The law lets the Fed decide how best to do this. The Fed does not rely on congressional appropriations, so Congress cannot threaten to withhold funds. Thus, although the U.S. president appoints the Board of Governors, and the Senate must approve these appointments, the Fed operates somewhat independently.

reduction in unemployment. If Fed officials realize that their credibility is hard to develop but easy to undermine, they will be reluctant to pursue policies that ultimately just increase inflation.

LO³ Policy Rules Versus Discretion

Again, the active approach views the economy as unstable and in need of discretionary policy to cut cyclical unemployment when it arises. The passive approach views the economy as stable enough that discretionary policy is not only unnecessary but may actually worsen economic fluctuations. In place of discretionary policy, the passive approach often calls for predetermined rules to guide the actions of policy makers. In the context of fiscal policy, these rules take the form of automatic stabilizers, such as unemployment insurance, a progressive income tax, and transfer payments, all of which aim to dampen economic fluctuations. In the context of monetary policy, passive rules might be the decision to allow the money supply to grow at a predetermined rate, to maintain interest rates at some predetermined level, or to keep inflation below a certain rate. For example, the European Central Bank announced a rule that it would not lower its target interest rate as long as inflation exceeded 2.0 percent a year. Most central banks have committed to achieving low **inflation targets**, usually specifying a particular rate for the next year or two. Advocates of inflation targets say such targets encourage workers, firms, and investors to plan on a low and stable inflation rate. Opponents of inflation targets worry that the Fed would pay less attention to jobs and economic growth. In this section, we examine the arguments for policy rules versus discretion mostly in the context of monetary policy, the policy focus in recent decades.

Limitations on Discretion

The rationale for the passive approach rather than the use of active discretion arises from different views of how the economy works. One view holds that *the economy is so complex and economic aggregates interact in such obscure ways and with such varied lags that policy makers cannot comprehend what is going on well enough to pursue an active monetary or fiscal policy.* For example, if the Fed adopts a discretionary policy that is based on a misreading of the current economy or a poor understanding of the lag structure, the Fed may be lowering the target interest rate when a more appropriate course would be to leave the rate unchanged or even to raise it. As a case in point, during a meeting of the FOMC, one member lamented the difficulty of figuring out what was going on with the economy, noting, "As a lesson for the future, I'd like to remind us all that as recently as two meetings ago we couldn't see the strength that was unfolding in the second half [of the year]. . . . It wasn't in our forecast; it wasn't in the other forecasts; and it wasn't in the anecdotal reports. We were standing right on top of it and we couldn't see it. That's just an important lesson to remember going forward."[2]

A comparison of economic forecasters and weather forecasters may shed light on the position of those who advocate the passive approach. Suppose you are in charge of the heating and cooling system at a major shopping mall. You realize that weather forecasts are unreliable, particularly in the early spring, when days can be warm or cold. Each day you must guess what the temperature will be and, based on that guess, decide whether to fire up the heater, turn on the air conditioner, or leave them both off. Because the mall is huge, you must start the system long before you know for sure what the weather will be. Once the system is turned on, it can't be turned off until much later in the day.

Suppose you guess the day will be cold, so you turn on the heat. If the day turns out to be cold, your policy is correct and the mall temperature will be just right. But if the day turns out to be warm, the heating system will make the mall unbearable. You would have been better off with nothing. In contrast, if you turn on the air conditioning system expecting a warm day but the day turns out to be cold, the mall will be freezing. The lesson

❖❖❖
2. FOMC board member Thomas Melzer, in a transcript of the 22 December 1992 meeting of the Federal Open Market Committee, p. 14. Meeting transcripts are published after a five-year lag and are available at http://www.federalreserve.gov/ fomc/transcripts/.

inflation target
central bankers commit to keep the inflation below a certain rate for the next year or two

is that if you are unable to predict the weather, you should use neither system. Similarly, if policy makers cannot predict the course of the economy, they should not try to fine-tune monetary or fiscal policy. Complicating the prediction problem is the fact that policy officials are not sure about the lags involved with discretionary policy. The situation is comparable to your not knowing how long the system actually takes to come on once you flip the switch.

This analogy applies only if the cost of doing nothing—using neither heat nor air conditioning—is relatively low. In the early spring, you can assume that there is little risk of weather so cold that water pipes freeze or so hot that walls sweat. A similar assumption in the passive view is that the economy is fairly stable and periods of prolonged unemployment are unlikely. In such an economy, the costs of *not* intervening are relatively low. In contrast, advocates of active policy believe that wide and prolonged swings in the economy (analogous to wide and prolonged swings in temperature) make doing nothing risky.

> If policy makers cannot predict the course of the economy, they should not try to fine-tune it with monetary or fiscal policy.

Rules and Rational Expectations

Another group of economists also advocates the passive approach, but not because they believe the economy is too complex. Proponents of the rational expectations approach, discussed earlier, claim that people have a pretty good idea how the economy works and what to expect from government policy makers. For example, people know enough about monetary policies pursued in the past to forecast, with reasonable accuracy, future policies and their effects on the economy. Some individual forecasts are too high and some too low, but on average, fore-

casts turn out to be about right. *To the extent that monetary policy is fully anticipated by workers and firms, it has no effect on the level of output; it affects only the price level.* Thus, only unexpected changes in policy can bring about short-run changes in output.

In the long run, changes in the money supply affect only inflation, not potential output, so followers of the rational expectations theory believe that the Fed should avoid discretionary monetary policy. Instead, the Fed should follow a predictable monetary rule. A monetary rule would reduce policy surprises and keep output near the natural rate. *Whereas some economists favor rules over discretion because of ignorance about the lag structure of the economy, rational expectations theorists advocate a predictable rule to avoid surprises, because surprises result in unnecessary departures from potential output.*

Despite support by some economists for explicit rules rather than discretion, central bankers are reluctant to follow hard-and-fast rules about the course of future policy. Discretion has been used more than explicit rules since the early 1980s, though policy has become more predictable because the Fed now announces the probable trend of future target rate changes. As former Fed Chairman Paul Volcker argued:

The appeal of a simple rule is obvious. It would simplify our job at the Federal Reserve, make monetary policy easy to understand, and facilitate monitoring of our performance. And if the rule worked, it would reduce uncertainty. . . . But unfortunately, I know of no rule that can be relied on with sufficient consistency in our complex and constantly evolving economy.[3]

Volcker's successor, Alan Greenspan, expressed similar sentiment:

The Federal Reserve should, some conclude, attempt to be more formal in its operations by tying its actions solely to the prescriptions of a formal policy rule. That any approach along these lines would lead to an improvement in economic performance, however, is highly doubtful.[4]

❖❖❖

3. Former Federal Reserve Chairman Paul Volcker, before the Committee on Banking, Finance, and Urban Affairs, U.S. House of Representatives, August 1983.
4. Chairman Alan Greenspan, "Monetary Policy Under Uncertainty," remarks at a symposium sponsored by the Federal Reserve Bank of Kansas City, Jackson Hole, Wyoming, 29 August 2003, which can be found at http://www.federalreserve.gov/ boarddocs/speeches/ 2003/20030829/ default.htm.

And, Ben Bernanke, the current Fed chairman, views the matter now mostly as a nonissue:

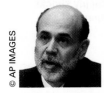
© AP IMAGES

[T]he argument that monetary policy should adhere mechanically to a strict rule, made by some economists in the past, has fallen out of favor in recent years. Today most monetary economists use the term "rule" more loosely to describe a general policy strategy, one that may include substantial scope for policymaker discretion and judgment.[5]

So far, we have looked at active stabilization policy, which focuses on shifts of the aggregate demand curve, and passive stabilization policy, which relies more on natural shifts of the short-run aggregate supply curve. In the final section, we focus on an additional model, the Phillips curve, to shed more light on the relationship between aggregate demand and aggregate supply in the short and long runs.

LO⁴ The Phillips Curve

At one time, policy makers thought they faced a long-run trade-off between inflation and unemployment. This view was suggested by the research of New Zealand economist A. W. Phillips, who in 1958 published an article that examined the historical relation between inflation and unemployment in the United Kingdom.[6] Based on about 100 years of evidence, his data traced an inverse relationship between the unemployment rate and the rate of change in nominal wages (serving as a measure of inflation). This relationship implied that the opportunity cost of reducing unemployment was higher inflation, and the opportunity cost of reducing inflation was higher unemployment.

The Phillips Framework

The possible options with respect to unemployment and inflation are illustrated by the hypothetical Phillips curve in Exhibit 5. The unemployment rate is measured along the horizontal axis and the inflation rate along the vertical axis. Let's begin at point a, which depicts one possible combination of unemployment and inflation. Fiscal or monetary

***

5. Ben Bernanke, "The Logic of Monetary Policy," remarks before the National Economists Club, Washington D.C., 2 December 2004, which can be found at http://www.federalreserve.gov/ boarddocs/Speeches/ 2004/20041202/default.htm.
6. A. W. Phillips, "Relation Between Unemployment and the Rate of Change in Money Wage Rates in the United Kingdom, 1861–1957," *Economica* 25 (November 1958): 283–299.

Exhibit 5

Hypothetical Phillips Curve

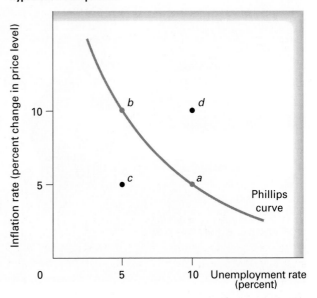

policy could be used to stimulate output and thereby reduce unemployment, moving the economy from point a to point b. Notice, however, that the reduction in unemployment comes at the cost of higher inflation. A reduction in unemployment with no change in inflation would be represented by point c. But as you can see, this alternative is not available.

Most policy makers of the 1960s came to believe that they faced a stable, long-run trade-off between unemployment and inflation. The Phillips curve was based on an era when inflation was low and the primary disturbances in the economy were shocks to aggregate demand. The effect of changes in aggregate demand can be traced as movements along a given short-run aggregate supply curve. If aggregate demand increases, the price level rises but unemployment falls. If aggregate demand decreases, the price level falls but unemployment rises. With appropriate demand-management policies, policy makers believed they could choose any point along the Phillips curve. The 1970s proved this view wrong in two ways. First, some of the biggest disturbances were adverse *supply* shocks, such as those created by oil embargoes and worldwide crop failures. These shocks shifted the aggregate supply curve leftward. A reduction of the aggregate supply curve led to both higher inflation *and* higher unemployment. Stagflation was at odds with the Phillips curve. Second, economists learned that when short-run output exceeds potential, an expansionary gap opens. As this gap closes by a leftward shift of the short-run aggregate supply curve, greater

Phillips curve
a curve showing possible combinations of the inflation rate and the unemployment rate

<< Long lines at gas stations like this one were not uncommon in 1974. The oil embargo created adverse supply shocks leading to both higher inflation and unemployment.

© AP IMAGES

inflation and higher unemployment result—again, an outcome inconsistent with a Phillips curve.

The increases in both inflation and unemployment caused by a decrease in aggregate supply can be represented by an outcome such as point *d* in Exhibit 5. By the end of the 1970s, increases in both inflation and unemployment suggested either that the Phillips curve had shifted outward or that it no longer described economic reality. The dilemma called for a reexamination of the Phillips curve, and this led to a distinction between the short-run Phillips curve and the long-run Phillips curve.

The Short-Run Phillips Curve

To discuss the underpinnings of the Phillips curve, we must return to the short-run aggregate supply curve. Suppose the price level this year is reflected by a price index of, say, 100, and that people expect prices to be about 3 percent higher next year. So the price level expected for next year is 103. Workers and firms therefore negotiate wage contracts based on an expected price level of 103. As the short-run aggregate supply curve in panel (a) of Exhibit 6 indicates, if *AD* is the aggregate demand curve and the price level is 103, as expected, output equals the economy's potential, shown here to be $14.0 trillion. Recall that when the economy produces its potential, unemployment is at the natural rate.

The short-run relationship between inflation and unemployment is presented in panel (b) of Exhibit 6 under the assumption that people expect inflation to be 3 percent. Unemployment is measured along the horizontal axis and inflation along the vertical axis. Panel (a) shows that when inflation is 3 percent, the economy produces its potential. Unemployment is at the natural rate, assumed in panel (b) to be 5 percent. The combination of 3 percent inflation and 5 percent unemployment is reflected by point *a* in panel (b), which corresponds to point *a* in panel (a).

What if aggregate demand turns out to be greater than expected, as indicated by *AD′*? In the short run, the greater demand results in point *b*, with a price level of 105 and output of $14.1 trillion. Because the price level exceeds that reflected in wage contracts, inflation also exceeds expectations. Specifically, inflation turns out to be 5 percent, not 3 percent. Because output exceeds potential, unemployment falls below the natural rate to 4 percent. The new combination of unemployment and inflation is depicted by point *b* in panel (b), which corresponds to point *b* in panel (a).

What if aggregate demand turns out to be lower than expected, as indicated by *AD″*? In the short run, the lower demand results in point *c*, where the price level of 101 is less than expected and output of $13.9 trillion is below potential. Inflation of 1 percent is less than the expected 3 percent, and unemployment of 6 percent exceeds the natural rate. This combination is reflected by point *c* in panel (b), which corresponds to point *c* in panel (a).

Note that the short-run aggregate supply curve in panel (a) can be used to develop the inverse relationship between inflation and unemployment shown in panel (b), called a **short-run Phillips curve**. This curve is created by the intersection of alternative aggregate demand curves along a given short-run aggregate supply curve. *The short-run Phillips curve is based on labor contracts that reflect a given expected price level, which implies a given expected rate of inflation.* The short-run Phillips curve in panel (b) is based on an expected inflation of 3 percent. If inflation turns out as expected, unemployment equals the natural rate. If inflation exceeds expectations, unemployment in

Exhibit 6

Aggregate Supply Curve and Phillips Curves in the Short Run and Long Run

(a) *Short-run aggregate supply curve*

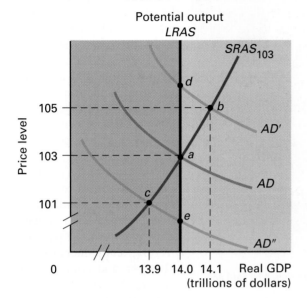

(b) *Short-run and long-run Phillips curves*

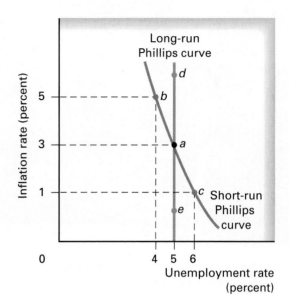

the short run falls below the natural rate. If inflation is less than expected, unemployment in the short run exceeds the natural rate.

The Long-Run Phillips Curve

If inflation exceeds expectations, output exceeds the economy's potential in the short run but not in the long run. Labor shortages and shrinking real wages prompt higher wage agreements. The short-run aggregate supply curve shifts leftward until it passes through point *d* in panel (a) of Exhibit 6, returning the economy to its potential output. The unexpectedly higher aggregate demand curve has no lasting effect on output or unemployment. Point *d* corresponds to a higher price level, and thus higher inflation. Closing the expansionary gap generates both higher unemployment and higher inflation, a combination depicted by point *d* in panel (b). Note that whereas points *a, b,* and *c* are on the same short-run Phillips curve, point *d* is not.

To trace the long-run effects of a lower-than-expected price level, let's return to point *c* in panel (a), where the actual price level is below the expected level, so output is below its potential. If workers and firms negotiate lower money wages (or if the growth in nominal wages trails inflation), the short-run aggregate supply curve could shift rightward until it passes through point *e*, where the economy returns once again to its potential output. Both infla-

tion and unemployment fall, as reflected by point *e* in panel (b).

Note that points *a, d,* and *e* in panel (a) depict long-run equilibrium points; the expected price level equals the actual price level. At those same points in panel (b), expected inflation equals actual inflation, so unemployment equals the natural rate. We can connect points *a, d,* and *e* in the right panel to form the long-run Phillips curve. *When workers and employers adjust fully to any unexpected change in aggregate demand, the long-run Phillips curve is a vertical line drawn at the economy's natural rate of unemployment.* As long as prices and wages are flexible enough, the rate of unemployment, in the long run, is independent of the rate of inflation. *Thus, according to proponents of this type of analysis, policy makers cannot, in the long run, choose between unemployment and inflation. They can choose only among alternative rates of inflation.*

The Natural Rate Hypothesis

The natural rate of unemployment occurs at the economy's potential output, discussed extensively already. An important idea that emerged from this reexamination of the Phillips curve is the

> **long-run Phillips curve**
> a vertical line drawn at the economy's natural rate of unemployment that traces equilibrium points that can occur when workers and employers have the time to adjust fully to any unexpected change in aggregate demand

1960 and 1969; the blue points for those years fit neatly along the blue curve. In the early part of the decade, inflation was low but unemployment relatively high; as the 1960s progressed, unemployment declined but inflation increased. Inflation during the decade averaged only 2.5 percent, and unemployment averaged 4.8 percent.

The short-run Phillips curve shifted to the right for the period from 1970 to 1973 (in red), when inflation and unemployment each climbed to an average of 5.2 percent. In 1974, sharp increases in oil prices and crop failures around the world reduced aggregate supply, which sparked another rightward shift of the Phillips curve. During the 1974–1983 period (in orange), inflation averaged 8.2 percent and unemployment 7.5 percent. After the Fed reduced inflationary expectations in the early 1980s, the short-run Phillips curve shifted leftward, or inward. Average inflation for 1984–1996 (in **black**) fell to 3.7 percent and average unemployment fell to 6.1 percent. Finally, data for 1997 to 2007 (in green) suggest a new, lower short-run Phillips curve, with average inflation of only 2.5 percent and average unemployment of 4.9 percent. Thus,

> > The short-run Phillips curve is based on labor contracts, like the one signed by Ford and the UAW in 2007, that reflect a given expected price level.

natural rate hypothesis, which states that in the long run, the economy tends toward the natural rate of unemployment. This natural rate is largely independent of any *aggregate demand* stimulus provided by monetary or fiscal policy. Policy makers may be able to push output beyond its potential temporarily, but only if the policy surprises the public. The natural rate hypothesis implies that *the policy that results in low inflation is generally the optimal policy in the long run.*

Evidence of the Phillips Curve

What has been the actual relationship between unemployment and inflation in the United States? In Exhibit 7, each year since 1960 is represented by a point, with the unemployment rate measured along the horizontal axis and the inflation rate measured along the vertical axis. Superimposed on these points is a series of short-run Phillips curves showing patterns of unemployment and inflation during what turns out to be five distinct periods since 1960. Remember, each short-run Phillips curve is drawn for a given *expected inflation rate.* A change in inflationary expectations shifts the short-run Phillips curve.

The clearest trade-off between unemployment and inflation occurred between

natural rate hypothesis
the natural rate of unemployment is largely independent of the stimulus provided by monetary or fiscal policy

Exhibit 7

Short-Run Phillips Curves Since 1960

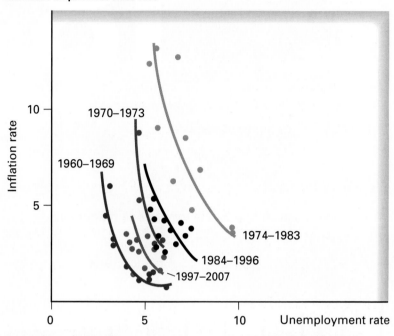

SOURCES: Based on inflation and unemployment figures from the *Economic Report of the President,* January 2009, at http://www.gpoaccess.gov/eop/index.html and the U.S. Bureau of Labor Statistics at http://www.bls.gov/.

the Phillips curve shifted rightward between the 1960s and the early 1980s. Since then, the Fed has learned more about how to control inflation, thereby reducing inflation expectations and shifting the Phillips curve back nearly to where it started in the 1960s.

The results for 2008 do not fit the 1997–2007 curve. In 2008, inflation increased to 3.8 percent, especially driven by high prices for oil and food early in the year. Unemployment averaged 5.8 percent for the year, but spiked to 7.2 percent in December 2008 as the recession deepened. It remains to be seen if the 2008–2009 recession coincides with another shift of the Phillips curve or whether these years are exceptions to the recent trend.

Final Word

This chapter examined the implications of active and passive policy. The important question is whether the economy is essentially stable and self-correcting when it gets off track or essentially unstable and in need of active government intervention. Advocates of active policy believe that the Fed or Congress should reduce economic fluctuations by stimulating aggregate demand when output falls below its potential level and by dampening aggregate demand when output exceeds its potential level. Advocates of active policy argue that government attempts to reduce the ups and downs of the business cycle may not be perfect but are still better than nothing. Some activists also believe that high unemployment may be self-reinforcing, because some unemployed workers lose valuable job skills and grow to accept unemployment as a way of life, as may have happened in Europe.

Advocates of passive policy, on the other hand, believe that discretionary policy may worsen cyclical swings in the economy, leading to higher inflation in the long run with no permanent boost in potential output and no permanent reduction in the employment rate. This group favors passive rules for monetary policy and automatic stabilizers for fiscal policy.

The active-passive debate in this chapter has focused primarily on monetary policy because discretionary fiscal policy was hampered by large federal deficits that ballooned the national debt. But the recession of 2008–2009 was so severe that most Washington policy makers decided to worry later about deficits and debt.

11 months   < average length of U.S. recessions since 1945

minimum lag time from when a recession begins and when it is identified > 6 months

3 to 6 months   < typical time required for fiscal policy to take effect

typical time required for fiscal policy to reach its full effect > 9 to 18 months

Learning Outcomes

LO   Describe the gains that trade brings

LO   Discuss the reasons for international specialization

LO   Explain trade restrictions and welfare loss

LO   Describe ways countries have reduced or eliminated trade barriers

LO   List and describe the arguments in favor of trade restrictions

International
Trade

> ❝If the United States is such a rich and productive country, why do we import so many goods and services?❞

This morning you pulled on your Levi's jeans from Mexico, pulled your Benetton sweater from Italy over your head, and laced up your Timberland boots from Thailand. After a breakfast that included bananas from Honduras and coffee from Brazil, you climbed into your Volvo from Sweden fueled by Venezuelan oil and headed for a lecture by a visiting professor from Hungary. If the United States is such a rich and productive country, why do we import so many goods and services? Why don't we produce everything ourselves? And why do some producers try to restrict foreign trade? Answers to these and other questions are addressed in this chapter.

The world is a giant shopping mall, and Americans are big spenders. For example, the U.S. population is less than 5 percent of the world's population, but Americans buy more than half the Rolls Royces and diamonds sold around the world. Americans also buy Japanese cars, French wine, European vacations, Chinese products galore, and thousands of other goods and services from around the globe. Foreigners buy U.S. products too—grain, aircraft, movies, software, trips to New York City, and thousands of other goods and services. In this chapter, we examine the gains from international trade and the effects of trade restrictions on the allocation of resources. The analysis is based on the familiar tools of demand and supply.

LO¹ The Gains from Trade

Topics discussed in Chapter 18 include:

- Gains from trade
- Absolute and comparative advantage revisited
- Tariffs
- Quotas
- Welfare loss from trade restrictions
- Arguments for trade restrictions

A family from Virginia that sits down for a meal of Kansas prime rib, Idaho potatoes, and California string beans, with Georgia peach cobbler for dessert, is benefiting from interstate trade. You already understand why the residents of one state trade with those of another. Back in Chapter 2, you learned about the gains arising from specialization and exchange. You may recall how you and your roommate could maximize output when you each specialized. The law of comparative advantage says that the individual with the lowest opportunity cost of producing a particular good should specialize in that good. Just as individuals benefit from specialization and exchange, so do states and, indeed, nations.

© ARTPARTNER-IMAGES/PHOTOGRAPHER'S CHOICE/GETTY IMAGES

To reap the gains that arise from specialization, countries engage in international trade. *Each country specializes in making goods with the lowest opportunity cost.*

A Profile of Exports and Imports

Just as some states are more involved in interstate trade than others, some nations are more involved in international trade than others. For example, exports account for about one-quarter of the gross domestic product (GDP) in the United Kingdom; about one-third of GDP in Canada; and about half of GDP in Germany, Switzerland, and Sweden. Despite the perception that Japan has a huge export sector, exports make up only about one-seventh of its GDP.

U.S. Exports

U.S. exports of goods and services amounted to $1.6 trillion, or about 12 percent of GDP in 2007. The left panel of Exhibit 1 shows the composition by major category. The largest category is services, which accounted for 30.2 percent of U.S. exports. U.S. service exports include transportation, insurance, banking, education, consulting, and tourism. Capital goods ranked second at 27.2 percent of exports in 2007. Capital goods include high-tech products, such as computers and jet aircraft. Third most important are industrial supplies, at 19.2 percent of the total. Capital goods and industrial supplies help foreign producers make stuff and accounted for nearly half of U.S. exports. Consumer goods (except food, which appears separately) accounted for only 10.9 percent of exports. Consumer goods include entertainment products, such as movies and recorded music.

U.S. Imports

U.S. imports of goods and services in 2007 totaled $2.3 trillion, or about 17 percent relative to GDP. The right panel of Exhibit 1 shows the composition of U.S. imports. The most important category, at 27.1 percent, is industrial supplies, such as crude oil from Venezuela and raw metals, including lead, zinc, and copper, from around the world. Whereas consumer goods

accounted for only 10.9 percent of U.S. exports, they were 23.4 percent of imports. Imported consumer goods include electronics from Taiwan, shoes from Brazil, and all kinds of products from China. Ranked third in importance is capital goods, at 18.9 percent, such as printing presses from Germany. Note that services, which accounted for 30.2 percent of U.S. exports, were only 16.1 percent of imports.

Trading Partners

To give you some feel for America's trading partners, here are the top 10 destinations for merchandise exports in 2007: Canada, the European Union, Mexico, China, Japan, South Korea, Taiwan, Singapore, Brazil, and Hong Kong. The top 10 sources of merchandise imports are the European Union, China, Canada, Mexico, Japan, South Korea, Taiwan, Venezuala, Saudi Arabia, and Nigeria.

Production Possibilities Without Trade

The rationale behind most international trade is obvious. The United States grows little coffee because the climate is not suited to coffee. More revealing, however, are the gains from trade where the comparative advantage is not so obvious. Suppose that just two goods—food and clothing—are produced and consumed and that there are only two countries in the world—the United States, with a labor force of 100 million workers, and the mythical country of Izodia, with 200 million workers. The conclusions derived from this simple model have general relevance for international trade.

Exhibit 1

Composition of U.S. Exports and Imports in 2007

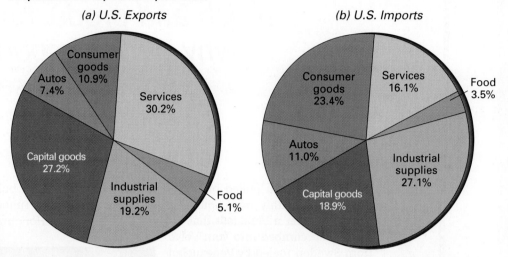

(a) U.S. Exports

(b) U.S. Imports

SOURCE: Based on government estimates in "International Data," *Survey of Current Business* 88 (December 2008), Table F, p. D-58.

Exhibit 2

Production Possibilities Schedules for the United States and Izodia

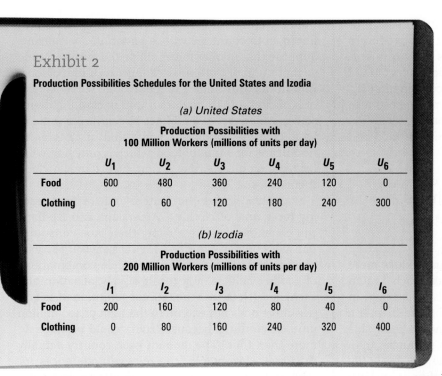

(a) United States

Production Possibilities with 100 Million Workers (millions of units per day)

	U_1	U_2	U_3	U_4	U_5	U_6
Food	600	480	360	240	120	0
Clothing	0	60	120	180	240	300

(b) Izodia

Production Possibilities with 200 Million Workers (millions of units per day)

	I_1	I_2	I_3	I_4	I_5	I_6
Food	200	160	120	80	40	0
Clothing	0	80	160	240	320	400

Exhibit 2 presents production possibilities tables for each country, based on the size of the labor force and the productivity of workers in each country. The exhibit assumes that each country has a given technology and that labor is efficiently employed. If no trade occurs between countries, Exhibit 2 also represents each country's *consumption possibilities* table. The production numbers imply that each worker in the United States can produce either 6 units of food or 3 units of clothing per day. If all 100 million U.S. workers produce food, they make 600 million units per day, as shown in column U_1 in panel (a). If all U.S. workers make clothing, they turn out 300 million

units per day, as shown in column U_6. The columns in between show some workers making food and some making clothing. Because a U.S. worker can produce either 6 units of food or 3 units of clothing, *the opportunity cost of 1 more unit of food is 0.5 units of clothing.*

Suppose Izodian workers are less educated, work with less capital, and farm less fertile soil than U.S. workers, so each Izodian worker can produce only 1 unit of food or 2 units of clothing per day. If all 200 million Izodian workers specialize in food, they can make 200 million units per day, as shown in column I_1 in panel (b) of Exhibit 2. If they all make clothing, total output is 400 million units per day, as shown in column I_6. Some intermediate production possibilities are also listed in the exhibit. Because an Izodian worker can produce either 1 unit of food or 2 units of clothing, *their opportunity cost of 1 more unit of food is 2 units of clothing.*

We can convert the data in Exhibit 2 to a production possibilities frontier for each country, as shown in Exhibit 3. In each diagram, the amount of food produced is measured on the vertical axis and the amount of clothing on the horizontal axis. U.S. combinations are shown in the left panel by U_1, U_2, and so on. Izodian combinations are shown in the right panel by I_1, I_2, and so on. Because we assume for simplicity that resources are perfectly adaptable to the production of each commodity, each production possibilities curve is a straight line. The slope of this line differs between countries because the opportunity cost of production differs between countries.

Exhibit 3 illustrates possible combinations of food and clothing that residents of each country can produce and consume if all resources are efficiently employed and there is no trade between the two countries. **Autarky** is the situation of national self-sufficiency, in which

> **autarky**
> national self-sufficiency; no economic interaction with foreigners

Exhibit 3

Production Possibilities Frontiers for the United States and Izodia Without Trade (millions of units per day)

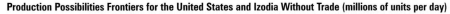

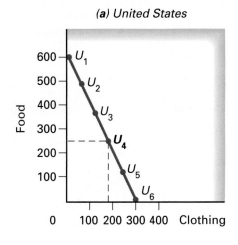

(a) United States

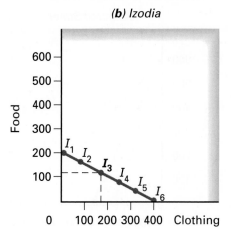

(b) Izodia

there is no economic interaction with foreign producers or consumers. Suppose that U.S. producers maximize profit and U.S. consumers maximize utility with the combination of 240 million units of food and 180 million units of clothing—combination U_4. This is called the *autarky equilibrium*. Suppose also that Izodians are in autarky equilibrium, identified as combination I_3, of 120 million units of food and 160 million units of clothing.

Consumption Possibilities Based on Comparative Advantage

In our example, each U.S. worker can produce more clothing and more food per day than can each Izodian worker, so Americans have an *absolute advantage* in the production of both goods. Recall from Chapter 2 that having an absolute advantage means being able to produce something using fewer resources than other producers require. Should the U.S. economy remain in autarky—that is, self-sufficient in both food and clothing productions—or could there be gains from specialization and trade?

As long as the opportunity cost of production differs between the two countries, there are gains from specialization and trade. *According to the law of comparative advantage, each country should specialize in producing the good with the lower opportunity cost.* The opportunity cost of producing 1 more unit of food is 0.5 units of clothing in the United States compared with 2 units of clothing in Izodia. Because the opportunity cost of producing food is lower in the United States than in Izodia, both countries gain if the United States specializes in food and exports some to Izodia, and Izodia specializes in clothing and exports some to the United States.

Before countries can trade, however, they must agree on how much of one good exchanges for another—that is, they must agree on the terms of trade. As long as Americans can get more than 0.5 units of clothing for each unit of food produced, and as long as Izodians can get more

terms of trade
how much of one good exchanges for a unit of another good

than 0.5 units of food for each unit of clothing produced, both countries will be better off specializing. Suppose that market forces shape the terms of trade so that 1 unit of clothing exchanges for 1 unit of food. Americans thus trade 1 unit of food to Izodians for 1 unit of clothing. To produce 1 unit of clothing themselves, Americans would have to sacrifice 2 units of food. Likewise, Izodians trade 1 unit of clothing to Americans for 1 unit of food, which is only half what Izodians would sacrifice to produce 1 unit of food themselves.

Exhibit 4 shows that with 1 unit of food trading for 1 unit of clothing, Americans and Izodians can consume anywhere along their blue consumption possibilities frontiers. *The consumption possibilities frontier shows a nation's possible combinations of goods available as a result of specialization and exchange.* (Note that the U.S. consumption possibilities curve does not extend to the right of 400 million units of clothing, because Izodia could produce no more than that.) The amount each country actually consumes depends on the relative preferences for food and clothing. Suppose Americans select combination U in panel (a) and Izodians select point I in panel (b).

Without trade, the United States produces and consumes 240 million units of food and 180 million units of clothing. With trade, the Americans specialize to produce 600 million units of food; they eat 400 million units and exchange the rest for 200 million units of Izodian clothing. This consumption combination is reflected by point U. Through exchange, Americans increase their consumption of both food and clothing.

Without trade, Izodians produce and consume 120 million units of food and 160 million units of clothing. With trade, Izodians specialize to produce

Exhibit 4

Production (and Consumption) Possibility Frontiers with Trade (millions of units per day)

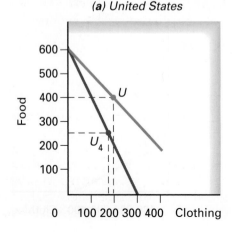

(a) United States

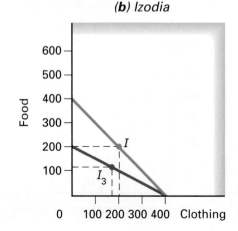

(b) Izodia

400 million units of clothing; they wear 200 million and exchange the rest for 200 million units of U.S. food. This consumption combination is shown by point I. Through trade, Izodians, like Americans, are able to increase their consumption of both goods. How is this possible?

Because Americans are more efficient in the production of food and Izodians are more efficient in the production of clothing, total output increases when each specializes. Without specialization, total world production was 360 million units of food and 340 million units of clothing. With specialization, food increases to 600 million units and clothing to 400 million units. Thus, both countries increase consumption with trade. *Although the United States has an absolute advantage in both goods, differences in the opportunity cost of production between the two nations ensure that specialization and exchange result in mutual gains.* Remember that comparative advantage, not absolute advantage, creates gains from specialization and trade. The only constraint on trade is that, for each good, *total world production must equal total world consumption.*

We simplified trade relations in our example to highlight the gains from specialization and exchange. We assumed that each country would completely specialize in producing a particular good, that resources were equally adaptable to the production of either good, that the costs of transporting goods from one country to another were inconsequential, and that there were no problems in arriving at the terms of trade. The world is not that simple. For example, we don't expect a country to produce just one good. Regardless, specialization based on the law of comparative advantage still leads to gains from trade.

LO² Reasons for International Specialization

Countries trade with one another—or, more precisely, people and firms in one country trade with those in another—because each side expects to gain from exchange. How do we know what each country should produce and what each should trade?

Differences in Resource Endowments

Differences in resource endowments often create differences in the opportunity cost of production across countries. Some countries are blessed with an abundance of fertile land and favorable growing seasons. The United States, for example, has been called the "breadbasket of the world" because of its rich farmland ideal for growing corn. Coffee grows best in the climate and elevation of Colombia, Brazil, and Jamaica. Honduras has the ideal climate for bananas. Thus, the United States exports corn and imports coffee and bananas. Seasonal differences across countries also encourage trade. For example, in the winter, Americans import fruit from Chile, and Canadians travel to Florida for sun and fun. In the summer, Americans export fruit to Chile, and Americans travel to Canada for camping and hiking.

Resources are often concentrated in particular countries: crude oil in Saudi Arabia, fertile soil in the United States, copper ore in Chile, rough diamonds in South Africa. The United States grows abundant supplies of oil seeds such as soybeans and sunflowers, but does not have enough crude oil to satisfy domestic demand. Thus, the United States exports oil seeds and imports crude oil. More generally, *countries export products they can produce more cheaply in return for products that are unavailable domestically or are cheaper elsewhere.* Remember, trade is based on comparative advantage, which is the ability to produce something at a lower opportunity cost than other producers face.

Exhibit 5 on the next page shows, for 12 key commodities, U.S. production as a percentage of U.S. consumption. If production falls short of consumption, this means the United States imports the difference. For example, because America grows coffee only in Hawaii, U.S. production is only 1 percent of U.S. consumption, so nearly all coffee is imported. The exhibit also shows that U.S. production falls short of consumption for oil and for metals such as lead, zinc, copper, and aluminum. If production exceeds consumption, the United States exports the difference. For example, U.S.-grown cotton amounts to 281 percent of U.S. cotton consumption, so most U.S. grown cotton is exported. U.S. production also exceeds consumption for other crops, including wheat, oil seeds, and coarse grains (corn, barley, oats). In short, when it comes to basic commodities, the United States is a net importer of oil and metals and a net exporter of farm crops.

Economies of Scale

If production is subject to *economies of scale*—that is, if the long-run average cost of production falls as a firm expands its scale of operation—countries can gain from trade if each nation specializes. Such specialization allows firms in each nation to produce more, which reduces average costs. The primary reason for establishing the single integrated market

Exhibit 5

U.S. Production as a Percentage of U.S. Consumption for Various Commodities

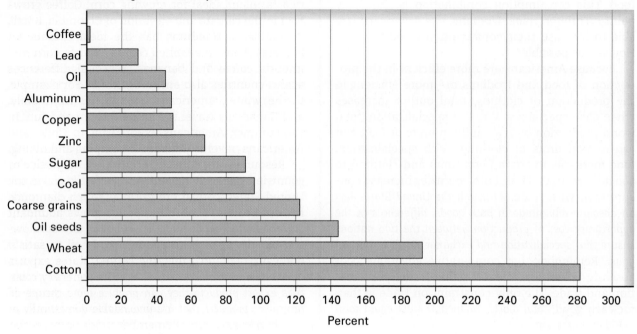

SOURCE: Based on annual figures from *The Economist World in Figures: 2007 Edition* (London: Profile Books, 2007).

of the European Union was to offer producers there a large, open market of now more than 500 million consumers. Producers could thereby achieve economies of scale. Firms and countries producing at the lowest opportunity costs are most competitive in international markets. For example, 60 percent of the world's buttons come from a single Chinese city.

Differences in Tastes

Even if all countries had identical resource endowments and combined those resources with equal efficiency, each country would still gain from trade as long as tastes differed among countries. Consumption patterns differ across countries and some of this results from differences in tastes. For example, the Czechs and Irish drink three times as much beer per capita as do the Swiss and Swedes. The French drink three times as much wine as do Australians. The Danes eat twice as much pork as do Americans. Americans eat twice as much chicken as do Hungarians. Soft drinks are four times more popular in the United States than in Europe. The English like tea; Americans, coffee. Algeria has an ideal climate for growing grapes (vineyards there date back to Roman times). But Algeria's population

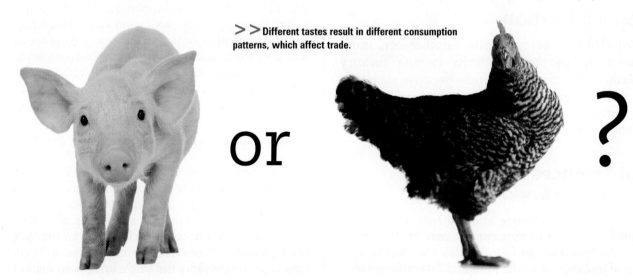

> > Different tastes result in different consumption patterns, which affect trade.

or

?

is 99 percent Muslim, a religion that forbids alcohol consumption. Thus, Algeria exports wine.

LO³ Trade Restrictions and Welfare Loss

Despite the benefits of exchange, nearly all countries at one time or another erect trade barriers, which benefit some domestic producers but harm other domestic producers and all domestic consumers. In this section, we consider the effects of trade barriers and the reasons they are imposed.

Consumer Surplus and Producer Surplus from Market Exchange

Before we explore the net effects of world trade on social welfare, let's develop a framework showing the benefits that consumers and producers get from market exchange. Consider a hypothetical market for chicken, shown in Exhibit 6. As discussed way back in Chapter 4, the height of the demand curve shows what consumers are willing and able to pay for each additional pound of chicken. In effect, the height of the demand curve shows the *marginal benefit* consumers expect from that pound of chicken. For example, the demand curve indicates that some consumers in this market are willing to pay $1.50 or more per pound for the first few pounds of chicken. But

every consumer gets to buy chicken at the market-clearing price, which here is $0.50 per pound. Most consumers thus get a bonus, or a surplus, from market exchange.

The blue-shaded triangle below the demand curve and above the market price reflects the *consumer surplus* in this market, which is the difference between the most that consumers would pay for 60 pounds of chicken per day and the actual amount they do pay. We all enjoy a consumer surplus from most products we buy.

Producers usually derive a similar surplus. The height of the supply curve shows what producers are willing and able to accept for each additional pound of chicken. That is, the height of the supply curve shows the expected *marginal cost* from producing each additional pound of chicken. For example, the supply curve indicates that some producers face a marginal cost of $0.25 or less per pound for supplying the first few pounds of chicken. But every producer gets to sell chicken for the market-clearing price of $0.50 per pound. The gold-shaded triangle above the supply curve and below the market price reflects the *producer surplus,* which is the difference between the actual amount that producers receive for 60 pounds of chicken and what they would accept to supply that amount.

The point is that market exchange usually generates a surplus, or a bonus, for both consumers and producers. In the balance of this chapter, we will continue to look at the gains from international trade and how trade restrictions affect consumer and producer surplus.

Tariffs

A *tariff,* a term first introduced in Chapter 3, is a tax on imports. (Tariffs can apply to exports, too, but we will focus on import tariffs.) A tariff can be either *specific,* such as a tariff of $5 per barrel of oil, or *ad valorem,* such as 10 percent on the import price of jeans. Consider the effects of a specific tariff on a particular good. In Exhibit 7 on the next page, D is the U.S. demand for sugar and S is the supply of sugar from U.S. growers (there were about 10,000 U.S. sugarcane growers in 2007). Suppose that the world price of sugar is $0.10 per pound, as it was in June 2007. The world price is determined by the world supply and demand for a product. It is the price at which any supplier can sell output on the world market and at which any demander can purchase output on the world market.

world price
the price at which a good is traded on the world market; determined by the world demand and world supply for the good

Exhibit 6

Consumer Surplus and Producer Surplus

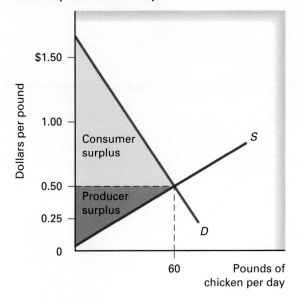

With free trade, any U.S. consumers could buy any amount desired at the world price of $0.10 per pound, so the quantity demanded is 70 million pounds per month, of which U.S. producers supply 20 million pounds and importers supply 50 million pounds. Because U.S. buyers can purchase sugar at the world price, U.S. producers can't charge more than that. Now suppose that a specific tariff of $0.05 is imposed on each pound of imported sugar, raising its price from $0.10 to $0.15 per pound. U.S. producers can therefore raise their own price to $0.15 per pound as well without losing business to imports. At the higher price, the quantity supplied by U.S. producers increases to 30 million pounds, but the quantity demanded by U.S. consumers declines to 60 million pounds. Because quantity demanded has declined and quantity supplied by U.S. producers has increased, U.S. imports fall from 50 million to 30 million pounds per month.

Because the U.S. price is higher after the tariff, U.S. consumers are worse off. Their loss in consumer surplus is identified in Exhibit 7 by the combination of the blue- and pink-shaded areas. Because both the U.S. price and the quantity supplied by U.S. producers have increased, their total revenue increases by the areas *a* plus *b* plus *f*. But only area *a* represents an increase in producer surplus. Revenue represented by the areas *b* plus *f* merely offsets the higher marginal cost U.S. producers face in expanding sugar output from 20 million to 30 million pounds

Exhibit 7

Effect of a Tariff

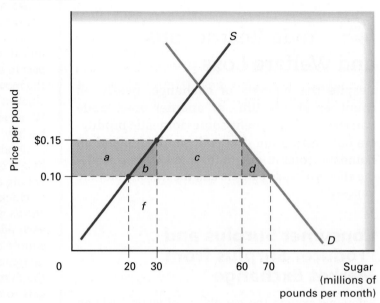

per month. Area *b* represents part of the net welfare loss to the domestic economy because those 10 million pounds could have been imported for $0.10 per pound rather than produced domestically at a higher marginal cost.

Government revenue from the tariff is identified by area *c*, which equals the tariff of $0.05 per pound multiplied by the 30 million pounds imported, for tariff revenue of $1.5 million per month. Tariff revenue is a loss to consumers, but because the tariff goes to the government, it can be used to lower taxes

or to increase public services, so it's not a loss to the U.S. economy. Area *d* shows a loss in consumer surplus because less sugar is consumed at the higher price. This loss is not redistributed to anyone else, so area *d* reflects part of the net welfare loss of the tariff. Therefore, areas *b* and *d* show the domestic economy's net welfare loss of the tariff; *the two triangles measure a loss in consumer surplus that is not offset by a gain to anyone in the domestic economy.*

In summary: Of the total loss in U.S. consumer surplus (areas *a, b, c,* and *d*) resulting from the tariff, area *a* goes to U.S producers, area *c* becomes government revenue, but areas *b* and *d* are net losses in domestic social welfare.

Import Quotas

An *import quota* is a legal limit on the amount of a commodity that can be imported. Quotas usually target imports from certain countries. For example, a quota may limit furniture from China or shoes from Brazil. To have an impact on the domestic market, a quota must be set below what would be imported with free trade. Consider a quota on the U.S. market for sugar. In panel (a) of Exhibit 8, *D* is the U.S. demand curve and *S* is the supply curve of U.S. sugar producers. Suppose again that the world price of sugar is $0.10 per pound. With free trade, that price would prevail in the U.S. market as well, and a total of 70 million pounds would be demanded per month. U.S. producers would supply 20 million pounds and importers, 50 million pounds. With a quota of 50 million pounds or more per month, the U.S. price would remain the

same as the world price of $0.10 per pound, and quantity would be 70 million pounds per month. In short, a quota of at least 50 million pounds would not raise the U.S. price above the world price because 50 million pounds were imported without a quota. A more stringent quota, however, would cut imports, which, as we'll see, would raise the U.S. price.

Suppose U.S. trade officials impose an import quota of 30 million pounds per month. As long as the U.S. price is at or above the world price of $0.10 per pound, foreign producers will supply 30 million pounds. So at prices at or above $0.10 per pound, the total supply of sugar to the U.S. market is found by adding 30 million pounds of imported sugar to the amount supplied by U.S. producers. U.S. and foreign producers would never sell in the U.S. market for less than $0.10 per pound because they can always get that price on the world market. Thus, the supply curve that sums domestic production and imports is horizontal at the world price of $0.10 per pound and remains so until the quantity supplied reaches 50 million pounds.

Again, for prices above $0.10 per pound, the new supply curve, S′, adds horizontally the 30-million-pound quota to S, the supply curve of U.S. producers. The U.S. price is found where this new supply curve, S′, intersects the domestic demand curve, which in the left panel of Exhibit 8 occurs at point *e*. By limiting imports, *the quota raises the domestic price of sugar above the world price and reduces quantity below the free trade level.* (Note that to compare more easily the effects of tariffs and quotas, this quota is designed to yield the same equilibrium price and quantity as the tariff examined earlier.)

Exhibit 8

Effect of a Quota

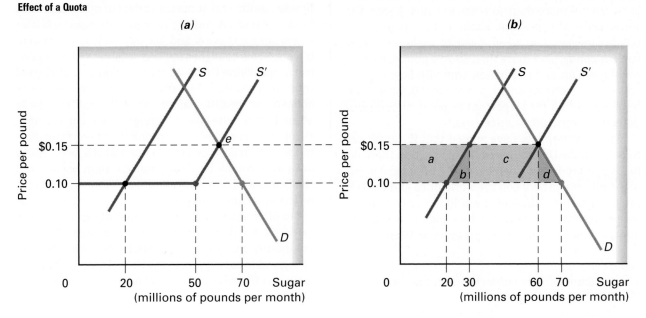

Panel (b) of Exhibit 8 shows the distribution and efficiency effects of the quota. As a result of the quota, U.S. consumer surplus declines by the combined blue and pink areas. Area *a* becomes producer surplus and thus involves no loss of U.S. welfare. Area *c* shows the increased economic profit to those permitted by the quota to sell Americans 30 million pounds for $0.15 per pound, or $0.05 above the world price. If foreign exporters rather than U.S. importers reap this profit, area *c* reflects a net loss in U.S. welfare.

Area *b* shows a welfare loss to the U.S. economy, because sugar could have been purchased abroad for $0.10 per pound, and the U.S. resources employed to increase sugar production could have been used more efficiently producing other goods. Area *d* is also a welfare loss because it reflects a reduction in consumer surplus with no offsetting gain to anyone. Thus, areas *b* and *d* in panel (b) of Exhibit 8 measure the minimum U.S. welfare loss from the quota. If the profit from quota rights (area *c*) accrues to foreign producers, this increases the U.S. welfare loss.

Quotas in Practice

The United States has granted quotas to specific countries. These countries, in turn, distribute these quota rights to their exporters through a variety of means. *By rewarding domestic and foreign producers with higher prices, the quota system creates two groups intent on securing and perpetuating these quotas.* Lobbyists for foreign producers work the halls of Congress, seeking the right to export to the United States. This strong support from producers, coupled with a lack of opposition from consumers (who remain rationally ignorant for the most part), has resulted in quotas that have lasted decades. For example, sugar quotas have been around more than 50 years. In January 2009, the world price of sugar was about $0.12 a pound, but U.S. businesses that need sugar to make products, such as candy, paid more than $0.20 a pound, costing consumers an extra $2 billion annually. Sugar growers, who account for only 1 percent of U.S. farm sales, have accounted for 17 percent of political contributions from agriculture since 1990.[1]

Some economists have argued that if quotas are to be used, the United States should auction them off to foreign producers, thereby capturing at least some of the difference between the world price and the U.S. price. Auctioning off quotas would not only increase federal revenue but would reduce the profitability of quotas, which would reduce pressure on Washington

❦❦❦

1. Michael Schroeder, "Sugar Growers Hold Up Push for Free Trade," *Wall Street Journal,* 3 February 2004.

to perpetuate them. American consumers are not the only victims of sugar quotas. Thousands of poor farmers around the world miss out on an opportunity to earn a living growing sugarcane for export to America.

Tariffs and Quotas Compared

Consider the similarities and differences between a tariff and a quota. Because both have identical effects on the price in our example, they both lead to the same change in quantity demanded. In both cases, U.S. consumers suffer the same loss of consumer surplus, and U.S. producers reap the same gain of producer surplus. The primary difference is that the revenue from the tariff goes to the U.S. government, whereas the revenue from the quota goes to whomever secures the right to sell foreign goods in the U.S. market. *If quota rights accrue to foreigners, then the domestic economy is worse off with a quota than with a tariff.* But even if quota rights go to domestic importers, quotas, like tariffs, still increase the domestic price, restrict quantity, and thereby reduce consumer surplus and economic welfare. Quotas and tariffs can also raise production costs. For example, U.S. candy manufacturers face higher production costs because of sugar quotas, making them less competitive on world markets. Finally, and most importantly, *quotas and tariffs encourage foreign governments to retaliate with quotas and tariffs of their own, thus shrinking U.S. export markets, so the loss is greater than shown in Exhibits 7 and 8.*

Other Trade Restrictions

Besides tariffs and quotas, a variety of other measures limit free trade. A country may provide *export subsidies* to encourage exports and *low-interest loans* to foreign buyers. Some countries impose *domestic content requirements* specifying that a certain portion of a final good must be produced domestically. Other requirements concerning health, safety, or technical standards often discriminate against foreign goods. For example, European countries once prohibited beef from hormone-fed cattle, a measure aimed at U.S. beef. Purity laws in Germany bar many non-German beers. Until the European Community adopted uniform standards, differing technical requirements forced manufacturers to offer as many as seven different versions of the same TV for that market. Sometimes exporters will voluntarily limit exports, as when Japanese automakers agreed to cut exports to the United States. The point is that *tariffs and quotas are only two of many devices used to restrict foreign trade.*

Recent research on the cost of protectionism indicates that international trade barriers slow the introduction of new goods and better technologies. So, rather than simply raising domestic prices, trade restrictions slow economic progress.

LO⁴ Reduction of Trade Barriers

In recent decades, countries have worked to reduce trade barriers and increase the flow of international trade. Let's examine multilateral agreements, the World Trade Organization, and common markets more closely.

Freer Trade by Multilateral Agreement

Mindful of how high tariffs cut world trade during the Great Depression, the United States, after World War II, invited its trading partners to negotiate lower tariffs and other trade barriers. The result was the General Agreement on Tariffs and Trade (GATT), an international trade treaty adopted in 1947 by 23 countries, including the United States. Each GATT member agreed to (1) reduce tariffs through multinational negotiations, (2) reduce import quotas, and (3) treat all members equally with respect to trade.

Trade barriers have been reduced through trade negotiations among many countries, or "trade rounds," under the auspices of GATT. Trade rounds offer a package approach rather than an issue-by-issue approach to trade negotiations. Concessions that are necessary but otherwise difficult to defend in domestic political terms can be made more acceptable in the context of a package that also contains politically and economically attractive benefits. Most early GATT trade rounds were aimed at reducing tariffs. The Kennedy Round in the mid-1960s included new provisions against *dumping*, which is selling a commodity abroad for less than is charged in the home market or less than the cost of production. The Tokyo Round of the 1970s was a more sweeping attempt to extend and improve the system.

The most recently completed round was launched in Uruguay in September 1986 and ratified by 123 participating countries in 1994. The number of signing countries now exceeds 140. This so-called *Uruguay Round*, the most comprehensive of the eight postwar multilateral trade negotiations, included 550 pages of tariff reductions on 85 percent of world trade. The Uruguay Round also created the World Trade Organization (WTO) to succeed GATT.

The World Trade Organization

The *World Trade Organization (WTO)* now provides the legal and institutional foundation for world trade.

{ No Dumping! }

The Bush Administration was often accused of being soft on China regarding trade, but on December 19, 2008, the United States filed a broad petition with the WTO alleging that China was using subsidies and cheap loans to provide Chinese exporters an unfair advantage. China has frequently been accused of dumping by American manufacturers, particularly steel makers. Between April 2008 and the end of the year, China's monthly steel exports to the United States nearly tripled, while U.S. steel mills had reduced production to 43% of capacity. China currently produces about 40% of global steel, though only six years before, it barely produced any. And while controversial, in many cases it is yet to be seen whether China's policies have actually been illegal.

SOURCE: Pete Engardio, "China: An Early Test for Obama," *Business Week,* 12 January 2008. pp.19–20.

General Agreement on Tariffs and Trade (GATT)
an international tariff-reduction treaty adopted in 1947 that resulted in a series of negotiated "rounds" aimed at freer trade; the Uruguay Round created GATT's successor, the World Trade Organization (WTO)

dumping
selling a product abroad for less than charged in the home market or for less than the cost of production

Uruguay Round
the final multilateral trade negotiation under GATT; this 1994 agreement cut tariffs, formed the World Trade Organization (WTO), and will eventually eliminate quotas

World Trade Organization (WTO)
the legal and institutional foundation of the multilateral trading system that succeeded GATT in 1995

© LEE JAE-WON/REUTERS/LANDOV

Whereas GATT was a multilateral agreement with no institutional foundation, the WTO is a permanent institution in Geneva, Switzerland. A staff of about 500 economists and lawyers helps shape policy and resolves trade disputes between member countries. Whereas GATT involved only merchandise trade, the WTO also covers services and trade-related aspects of intellectual property, such as books, movies, and computer programs. The WTO will eventually phase out quotas, but tariffs will remain legal. As a result of the Uruguay Round, average tariffs fell from 6 percent to 4 percent of the value of imports (when GATT began in 1947, tariffs averaged 40 percent).

Whereas GATT relied on voluntary cooperation, the WTO settles disputes in a way that is faster, more automatic, and less susceptible to blockage than the GATT system was. The WTO resolved more trade disputes in its first decade than GATT did in nearly 50 years. Since 2000, developing countries have filed 60 percent of the disputes. But the WTO has also become a lightning rod for globalization issues.

Common Markets

Some countries looked to the success of the U.S. economy, which is essentially a free trade zone across 50 states, and have tried to develop free trade zones of their own. The largest and best known is the European Union, which began in 1958 with a half dozen countries and expanded by 2007 to 27 countries and about 500 million people. The idea was to create a barrier-free European market like that of the United States in which goods, services, people, and capital are free to flow to their highest-valued use. Sixteen members of the European Union have also adopted a common currency, the *euro,* which replaced national currencies in 2002.

The United States, Canada, and Mexico have developed a free trade pact called the North American Free Trade Agreement (NAFTA). Through NAFTA, Mexico hopes to attract more U.S. investment by guaranteeing companies that locate there duty-free access

to U.S. markets, which is where over two-thirds of Mexico's exports go. Mexico's 110 million people represent an attractive export market for U.S. producers, and Mexico's oil reserves could ease U.S. energy problems. The United States would also like to support Mexico's efforts to become more market oriented, as is reflected, for example, by Mexico's privatization of its phone system and banks. Creating job opportunities in Mexico also reduces pressure for Mexicans to cross the U.S. border illegally. After more than a decade of NAFTA, agricultural exports to Mexico have doubled, as has overall trade among the three nations, but Americans still buy much more from Mexicans and Canadians than the other way around.

Free trade areas are springing up around the world. The United States and other countries signed a free trade agreement with the Dominican Republic and five Central American countries, called DR-CAFTA. Ten Latin American countries form Mercosur. In southeast Asia, ten nations have come together to form ASEAN, the Association of Southeast Asian Nations. And South Africa and its four neighboring countries form the Southern African Customs Union. Regional trade agreements require an exception to WTO rules because bloc members can make special deals among themselves and thus discriminate against outsiders. Under WTO's requirements, any trade concession granted one country must usually be granted to *all other* WTO members.

LO⁵ Arguments for Trade Restrictions

Trade restrictions are often little more than handouts for the domestic industries they protect. Given the loss in social welfare that results from these restrictions, it would be more efficient simply to transfer money from domestic consumers to domestic producers. But such a bald transfer would be politically unpopular. Arguments for trade restrictions avoid mention of transfers to domestic producers and instead cite loftier goals. As we shall now see, none of these goals makes a strong case for restrictions, but some make more sense than others.

National Defense Argument

Some industries claim they need protection from import competition because their output is vital for national defense. Products such as strategic metals and military hardware are often insulated from foreign competition by trade restrictions. Thus, national defense considerations outweigh concerns about efficiency and equity. How valid is this argument? Trade restrictions may shelter the defense industry, but other means, such as government subsidies, might be more efficient. Or the government could stockpile basic military hardware so that maintaining an ongoing productive capacity would become less essential. Still, technological change could make certain weapons obsolete. Because most industries can play some role in national defense, instituting trade restrictions on this basis can get out of hand. For example, many decades ago U.S. wool producers secured trade protection at a time when some military uniforms were made of wool.

Infant Industry Argument

The infant industry argument was formulated as a rationale for protecting emerging domestic industries from foreign competition. In industries where a firm's average cost of production falls as output expands, new firms may need protection from imports until these firms grow enough to become competitive. Trade restrictions let new firms achieve the economies of scale necessary to compete with mature foreign producers.

But how do we identify industries that merit protection, and when do they become old enough to look after themselves? Protection often fosters inefficiencies. The immediate cost of such restrictions is the net welfare loss from higher domestic prices. These costs may become permanent if the industry never realizes the expected economies of scale and thus never becomes competitive. As with the national defense argument, policy makers should be careful in adopting trade restrictions based on the infant industry argument. Here again, temporary production subsidies may be more efficient than import restrictions.

Antidumping Argument

As we have noted already, *dumping* is selling a product abroad for less than in the home market or less than the cost of production. Exporters may be able to sell the good for less overseas because of export subsidies, or firms may simply find it profitable to sell for less in foreign markets where consumers are more sensitive to prices. But why shouldn't U.S. consumers pay as little as possible? If dumping is persistent, the increase in consumer surplus would more than offset losses to domestic producers. *There*

is no good reason why consumers should not be allowed to buy imports for a persistently lower price.

> There is no good reason why consumers should not be allowed to buy imports for a persistently lower price.

An alternative form of dumping, termed *predatory dumping,* is the *temporary* sale abroad at prices below cost to eliminate competitors in that foreign market. Once the competition is gone, so the story goes, the exporting firm can raise the price in the foreign market. The trouble with this argument is that if dumpers try to take advantage of their monopoly position by sharply increasing the price, then other firms, either domestic or foreign, could enter the market and sell for less. There are few documented cases of predatory dumping.

Sometimes dumping may be *sporadic,* as firms occasionally try to unload excess inventories. Retailers hold periodic "sales" for the same reason. Sporadic dumping can be unsettling for domestic producers, but the economic impact is not a matter of great public concern. Regardless, all dumping is prohibited in the United States by the Trade Agreements Act of 1979, which calls for the imposition of tariffs when a good is sold for less in the United States than in its home market or less than the cost of production. In addition, WTO rules allow for offsetting tariffs when products are sold for "less than fair value" and when there is "material injury" to domestic producers. For example, U.S. producers of lumber and beer often accuse their Canadian counterparts of dumping.

Jobs and Income Argument

One rationale for trade restrictions that is commonly heard in the United States, and is voiced by WTO protestors, is that they protect U.S. jobs and wage levels. Using trade restrictions to protect domestic jobs is a strategy that dates back centuries. One problem with such a policy is that other countries usually retaliate by restricting *their* imports to save *their* jobs, so international trade is reduced, jobs are lost in export industries, and potential gains from trade fail to materialize. That happened big time during the Great Depression, as high tariffs choked trade and jobs.

Wages in other countries, especially developing countries, are often a small fraction of wages in the United States. Looking simply at differences in wages, however, narrows the focus too much. Wages represent just one component of the total production cost and may not necessarily be the most important. Employers are interested in the labor cost per unit of output, which depends on both the wage and labor productivity. Wages are high in the United States partly because U.S. labor productivity remains the highest in the world. High productivity can be traced to better education and training and to the abundant computers, machines, and other physical capital that make workers more productive. U.S. workers also benefit greatly from a stable business climate.

But what about the lower wages in many developing countries? Low wages are often linked to workers' lack of education and training, to the meager physical capital available to each worker, and to a business climate that is less stable and hence less attractive for producers. But once multinational firms build plants and provide technological know-how in developing countries, U.S. workers lose some of their competitive edge, and their relatively high wages could price some U.S. products out of the world market. This has already happened in the consumer electronics and toy industries. China makes 80 percent of the toys sold in the United States. Some U.S. toy sellers, such as the makers of Etch A Sketch, would no longer survive if they had not outsourced manufacturing to China.

Domestic producers do not like to compete with foreign producers whose costs are lower, so they often push for trade restrictions. But if restrictions negate any cost advantage a foreign producer might have, the law of comparative advantage becomes inoperative and domestic consumers are denied access to the lower-priced goods.

Over time, as labor productivity in developing countries increases, wage differentials among countries will narrow, much as wage differentials narrowed between the northern and southern United States. As technology and capital spread, U.S. workers, particularly unskilled workers, cannot expect to maintain wage levels that are far above those in other countries. So far, research and development has kept U.S. producers on the cutting edge of technological developments, but staying ahead in the technological race is a constant battle.

Declining Industries Argument

Where an established domestic industry is in jeopardy of closing because of lower-priced imports, could there be a rationale for *temporary* import restrictions?

After all, domestic producers employ many industry-specific resources—both specialized labor and specialized machines. This human and physical capital is worth less in its best alternative use. If the extinction of the domestic industry is forestalled through trade restrictions, specialized workers can retire voluntarily or can gradually pursue more promising careers. Specialized machines can be allowed to wear out naturally.

Thus, in the case of declining domestic industries, trade protection can help lessen shocks to the economy and can allow for an orderly transition to a new industrial mix. But the protection offered should not be so generous as to encourage continued investment in the industry. Protection should be of specific duration and should be phased out over that period.

The clothing industry is an example of a declining U.S. industry. The 22,000 U.S. jobs saved as a result of one trade restriction paid an average of less than $30,000 per year. But a Congressional Budget Office study estimated that the higher domestic clothing prices resulting from trade restrictions meant that U.S. consumers paid two to three times more than apparel workers earned. Trade restrictions in the U.S. clothing and textile industry started phasing out in 2005 under the Uruguay Round of trade agreements.

Free trade may displace some U.S. jobs through imports, but it also creates U.S. jobs through exports. When people celebrate a ribbon-cutting ceremony for a new software company, nobody credits free trade for those jobs, but when a steel plant closes, everyone talks about how those jobs went overseas. What's more, many foreign companies have built plants in the United States and employ U.S. workers. For example, a dozen foreign television manufacturers and all major Japanese automakers now operate plants in the United States.

The number of jobs in the United States has more than doubled in the last four decades. To recognize this job growth is not to deny the problems facing workers displaced by imports. Some displaced workers, particularly those in blue-collar jobs in steel and other unionized industries, are not likely to find jobs

Protecting one stage of production usually requires protecting downstream stages of production as well.

that will pay nearly as well as the ones they lost. As with infant industries, however, the problems posed by declining industries need not require trade restrictions. To support the affected industry, the government could offer wage subsidies or special tax breaks that decline over time. The government has also funded programs to retrain affected workers for jobs that are in greater demand.

Problems with Trade Protection

Trade restrictions raise a number of problems in addition to those already mentioned. First, protecting one stage of production usually requires protecting downstream stages of production as well. Protecting the U.S. textile industry from foreign competition, for example, raised the cost of cloth to U.S. apparel makers, reducing their competitiveness. Thus, when the government protected domestic textile manufacturers, the domestic garment industry also needed protection. Second, the cost of protection includes not only the welfare loss from the higher domestic price but also the cost of the resources used by domestic producer groups to secure the favored protection. The cost of *rent seeking*—lobbying fees, propaganda, and legal actions—can sometimes equal or exceed the direct welfare loss from restrictions. A third problem with trade restrictions is the transaction costs of enforcing the myriad quotas, tariffs, and other trade restrictions. These often lead to smuggling and black markets. A fourth problem is that economies insulated from foreign competition become less innovative and less efficient. The final and biggest problem with imposing trade restrictions is that other countries usually retaliate, thus shrinking the gains from trade. Retaliation can set off still greater trade restrictions, leading to an outright trade war.

Final Word

International trade arises from voluntary exchange among buyers and sellers pursuing their self-interest. Since 1950, world output has risen eightfold, while world trade has increased nearly twentyfold. World trade offers many advantages to the trading countries: access to markets around the world, lower costs through economies of scale, the opportunity to utilize abundant resources, better access to information about markets and technology, improved quality honed by competitive pressure, and, most importantly, lower prices for consumers. Comparative advantage, specialization, and trade allow people to use their scarce resources most efficiently to satisfy their unlimited wants.

Despite the clear gains from free trade, restrictions on international trade date back centuries, and pressure on public officials to impose trade restrictions continues today. Domestic producers (and their resource suppliers) benefit from trade restrictions in their markets because they can charge domestic consumers more. Trade restrictions insulate domestic producers from the rigors of global competition, in the process stifling innovation and leaving the industry vulnerable to technological change from abroad. With trade quotas, the winners also include those who have secured the right to import goods at the world prices and sell them at the domestic prices. Consumers, who must pay higher prices for protected goods, suffer from trade restrictions, as do the domestic producers who import resources. Other losers include U.S. exporters, who face higher trade barriers as foreigners retaliate with their own trade restrictions.

Producers have a laser-like focus on trade legislation, but consumers remain largely oblivious. Consumers purchase thousands of different goods and thus have no special interest in the effects of trade policy on any particular good. Congress tends to support the group that makes the most noise, so trade restrictions often persist, despite the clear and widespread gains from freer trade.

>> This kiosk is the gateway to New York City's garment district, an area that continues to be severely affected by low-price competition from overseas markets.

Learning Outcomes

LO^1 Explain how the balance of payments works

LO^2 Discuss foreign exchange rates and markets

LO^3 Define fixed and flexible exchange rates

LO^4 Describe the development of the international monetary system

International
Finance

"Why do nations try to influence the value of their currency?"

How can the United States export more than any other country yet still have the world's highest trade deficit? Are high trade deficits a worry? What's the official "fudge factor" used in computing the balance of payments? What's a "strong dollar"? Why do nations try to influence the value of their currency? And what's up with China? Answers to these and other questions are explored in this chapter, which focuses on international finance.

If Starbucks wants to buy 1,000 espresso machines from the German manufacturer, Krups, it will be quoted a price in euros. Suppose the machines cost a total of 1 million euros. How much is that in dollars? The dollar cost will depend on the exchange rate. When trade takes place across international borders, two currencies are usually involved. Supporting the flows of goods and services are flows of currencies that fund international transactions. The *exchange rate* between currencies—the price of one in terms of the other—is how the price of a product in one country translates into the price quoted a buyer in another country. Cross-border trade therefore depends on the exchange rate. In this chapter we examine the market forces that affect the relative value of one currency in terms of another.

What do you think?

The current euro exchange rate makes this a good time for a European vacation.

Strongly Disagree						Strongly Agree
1	2	3	4	5	6	7

Topics discussed in Chapter 19 include:

- Balance of payments
- Trade deficits and surpluses
- Foreign exchange markets
- Purchasing power parity
- Flexible exchange rates
- Fixed exchange rates
- International monetary system
- Bretton Woods agreement
- Managed float

LO¹ Balance of Payments

A country's gross domestic product, or GDP, measures the economy's income and output during a given period. To account for dealings abroad, countries must also keep track of international transactions. A country's *balance of payments,* as introduced in Chapter 3, summarizes all economic transactions during a given period between residents of that country and residents of other countries. *Residents* include people, firms, organizations, and governments.

International Economic Transactions

The balance of payments measures economic transactions between a country and the rest of the world, whether these transactions involve goods and services, real and financial assets, or transfer payments. The balance of payments measures a *flow* of transactions during a particular period, usually a year. Some transactions do not involve actual payments. For example, if *Time* magazine ships a new printing press to its Australian subsidiary, no payment is made, yet an economic transaction involving another country has occurred. Similarly, if CARE sends food to Africa or the Pentagon provides military assistance to the Middle East, these transactions must be captured in the balance of payments. So remember, although we speak of the *balance of payments,* a more descriptive phrase would be the *balance of economic transactions.*

Balance-of-payments accounts are maintained according to the principles of *double-entry bookkeeping.* Some entries are called *credits,* and others are called *debits.* As you will see, the balance of payments consists of several individual accounts. An individual account may not balance, but a deficit in one or more accounts must be offset by a surplus in the other accounts. Because total credits must equal total debits, there is a *balance* of payments—hence, the name. During a given period, such as a year, the inflow of receipts from the rest of the world, which are entered as credits, must equal the outflow of payments to the rest of the world, which are entered as debits.

The first of two major categories in the balance of payments is the current account. The current account records *current* flows of funds into and out of the country, including imports and exports of goods and services, net income earned by U.S. residents from foreign assets, and net transfer payments from abroad. These are discussed in turn.

The Merchandise Trade Balance

The *merchandise trade balance,* a term introduced in Chapter 3, equals the value of merchandise exports minus the value of merchandise imports. The merchandise account reflects trade in goods, or tangible products (stuff you can put in a box), like French wine or U.S. computers, and is often referred to simply as the *trade balance.* The value of U.S. mer-

chandise exports is a credit in the U.S. balance-of-payments account because U.S. residents get *paid* for the exported goods. The value of U.S. merchandise imports is a debit in the balance-of-payments account because U.S. residents *pay* foreigners for imported goods.

If merchandise exports exceed merchandise imports, the trade balance is in *surplus.* If merchandise imports exceed merchandise exports, the trade balance is in *deficit.* The merchandise trade balance, which is reported monthly, influences foreign exchange markets, the stock market, and other financial markets. The trade balance depends on a variety of factors, including the relative strength and competitiveness of the domestic economy compared with other economies and the relative value of the domestic currency compared with other currencies. Strong economies with growing incomes tend to buy more of everything, including imports.

U.S. merchandise trade since 1960 is depicted in Exhibit 1, where exports, the blue line, and imports, the red line, are expressed as a percentage of GDP. During the 1960s, exports exceeded imports, and the resulting trade surpluses are shaded blue. Since 1976, imports have exceeded exports, and the resulting trade deficits are shaded pink. Trade deficits as a percentage of GDP increased from 1.3 percent in 1991 to 5.9 percent in 2007, when the deficit reached $819.4 billion. Notice in Exhibit 1 that exports as a percentage of GDP dipped during the 1980s, when the value of the dollar rose sharply relative to other currencies (more on this later). Despite that dip, merchandise exports since 1980 have remained in the range of about 5 percent to 9 percent of GDP. But merchandise imports have trended up from about 9 percent in 1980 to more than 14 percent in 2007.

Exhibit 1

U.S. Imports Have Exceeded Exports Since 1976, and the Trade Deficit Has Widened

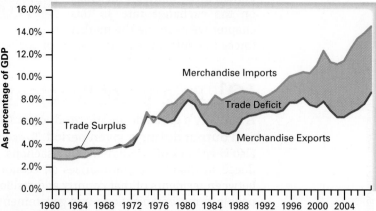

SOURCE: Developed from merchandise trade data from "GDP and the Economy," March 2008, Bureau of Economic Analysis. For the latest data, go to http://www.bea.gov.

Because per capita income in the United States is the highest in the world, the United States imports more goods from each of the world's major economies than it exports to them. Exhibit 2 shows the U.S. merchandise trade deficit with major economies or regions of the world in 2008. The $246 billion trade deficit with China was by far the largest, triple that with Japan, Canada, or the European Union. The large trade deficit with the OPEC nations represents the high price of oil in mid-2008. The Chinese bought $66 billion in U.S. goods in 2008, but Americans bought $313 billion in Chinese goods, or about $2,700 per U.S. household. So China sells America five times more than it buys from America. Chances are, most of the utensils in your kitchen were made in China; most toys are also Chinese made. The United States does not have a trade surplus with any major economy in the world and is the world's biggest importer.

Balance on Goods and Services

The merchandise trade balance focuses on the flow of goods, but services are also traded internationally. *Services* are intangibles, such as transportation, insurance, banking, education, consulting, and tourism. Services are often called "invisibles" because they are not tangible. The value of U.S. service exports, as when an Irish tourist visits New York City, is listed as a credit in the U.S. balance-of-payments account because U.S. residents get paid for these services. The value of U.S. service imports, like computer programming outsourced to India, is listed as a debit in the balance-of-payments account because U.S. residents must pay for the imported services.

Because the United States exports more services than it imports, services have been in surplus for the last three decades. The balance on goods and services is the export value of goods and services minus the import value of goods and services, or *net exports*, a component of GDP.

Net Investment Income

U.S. residents earn investment income, such as interest and dividends, from assets owned abroad. This investment income flows to the United States and is a credit in the balance-of-payments account. On the other side, foreigners earn investment income on assets owned in the United States, and this payment flows out of the country. This outflow is a debit in the balance-of-payments account. Net investment income from abroad is U.S. investment earnings from foreign assets minus foreigners' earnings from their U.S. assets. From year to year, this figure bounces around between a positive and a negative number. In 2007, net investment income from foreign holdings was $81.7 billion.

Unilateral Transfers

Unilateral transfers consist of government transfers to foreign residents, foreign aid, money workers send to families abroad, personal gifts to friends and relatives abroad, charitable donations, and the like. Money sent out of the country is a debit in the balance-of-payments account. For example, immigrants to the United

balance on goods and services the portion of a country's balance-of-payments account that measures the value of a country's exports of goods and services minus the value of its imports of goods and services

net investment income from abroad investment earnings by U.S. residents from their foreign assets minus investment earnings by foreigners from their assets in the United States

Exhibit 2

U.S. Merchandise Trade Deficits in 2008 by Country or Grouping

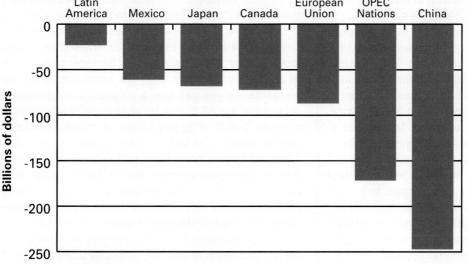

SOURCE: Developed from data in "Exports, Imports, and Balance of Goods by Selected Countries and Areas—2008," Exhibit 14, U.S. Bureau of Economic Analysis, 13 January 2009, at http://www.bea.gov/newsreleases/international/trade/2009/pdf/trad1108.pdf.

States often send money to families back home. Net unilateral transfers abroad equal the unilateral transfers received from abroad by U.S. residents minus unilateral transfers sent to foreign residents by U.S. residents. U.S. net unilateral transfers have been negative since World War II, except for 1991, when the U.S. government received sizable transfers from foreign governments to help pay their share of the Persian Gulf War. In 2007, net unilateral transfers were a negative $112.7 billion, with private transfers accounting for nearly two-thirds of that. Net unilateral transfers abroad averaged about $360 per U.S. resident in 2007.

The United States places few restrictions on money sent out of the country. Other countries, particularly developing countries, strictly limit the amount that may be sent abroad. More generally, many developing countries, such as China, restrict the convertibility of their currency into other currencies.

When we add net unilateral transfers to net exports of goods and services and net income from assets owned abroad, we get the balance on current account, which is reported quarterly. Thus, *the current account includes all international transactions in currently produced goods and services, net income from foreign assets, and net unilateral transfers*. It can be negative, reflecting a current account deficit; positive, reflecting a current account surplus; or zero.

The Financial Account

The current account records international transactions in goods, services, asset income, and unilateral transfers. The financial account records international purchases of assets, including financial assets such as stocks, bonds, and bank balances, and real assets such as land, housing, factories, and other physical assets. For example, U.S. residents purchase foreign securities to earn a higher return and to diversify their portfolios. Money flows out when Americans buy foreign assets or build factories overseas. Money flows in when foreigners buy U.S. assets or build factories here. The international purchase or sale of assets is recorded in the financial account.

Between 1917 and 1982, the United States ran a finan-cial account deficit, meaning that U.S. residents purchased more foreign assets than foreigners purchased assets from the United States. The net income from these foreign assets improved our current account balance. But in 1983, for the first time in 65 years, foreigners bought more assets in the United States than U.S. residents purchased abroad. Since 1983, foreigners have continued to buy more U.S. assets most years than the other way around, meaning there has usually been a surplus in the financial account.

By 2007, foreigners owned $20.1 trillion in U.S. assets and U.S. residents owned $17.6 trillion in foreign assets. Thus, foreigners owned $2.5 trillion more assets in the United States than U.S. residents owned abroad. This is not as bad as it sounds, because foreign purchases of assets in the United States add to America's productive capacity and promote employment and labor productivity here. But the income from these assets flows to their foreign owners, not to Americans. Remember, the investment income from these assets shows up in the current account.

Deficits and Surpluses

Nations, like households, operate under a budget constraint. Spending cannot exceed income plus cash on hand and borrowed funds. We have distinguished between *current* transactions, which include exports, imports, asset income, and unilateral transfers, and *financial* transactions, which reflect purchases of foreign real and financial assets. Any surplus or deficit in one account must be offset by deficits or surpluses in other balance-of-payments accounts.

Exhibit 3 presents the U.S. balance-of-payments statement for 2007. All transactions requiring payments from foreigners to U.S. residents are entered as credits, indicated by a plus sign (+), because they result in an inflow of funds from foreign residents to U.S. residents. All transactions requiring payments to foreigners from U.S. residents are entered as debits, indicated by a minus sign (−), because they result in an outflow of funds from U.S. residents to foreign residents. As you can see, a surplus in the financial account of $767.8 billion more than offsets a current account deficit of $731.3 billion. A *statistical discrepancy* is required to balance the payments, and that amounts to a negative $36.5 billion. Think of the statistical discrepancy as the official "fudge factor" that (1) measures the error in the balance of payments and (2) satisfies the double-entry bookkeeping requirement that total debits must equal total credits.

Foreign exchange is the currency of another country needed to carry out international transactions. A country runs a deficit in its current account when the amount of foreign exchange received from exports,

net unilateral transfers abroad the unilateral transfers (gifts and grants) received from abroad by U.S. residents minus the unilateral transfers U.S. residents send abroad

balance on current account the portion of the balance-of-payments account that measures that country's balance on goods and services, net investment income from abroad, plus net unilateral transfers abroad

financial account the record of a country's international transactions involving purchases or sales of financial and real assets

from holding foreign assets, and from unilateral transfers falls short of the amount needed to pay for imports, pay foreigners for their U.S. assets, and make unilateral transfers. If the current account is in deficit, the necessary foreign exchange must come from a net inflow in the financial account. Such an inflow in the financial account could stem from borrowing from foreigners, selling domestic stocks and bonds to foreigners, selling a steel plant in Pittsburgh or a ski lodge in Aspen to foreigners, and so forth.

If a country runs a current account surplus, the foreign exchange received from exports, from holding assets abroad, and from unilateral transfers exceeds the amount needed to pay for imports, to pay foreign holders for U.S. assets, and to make unilateral transfers. If the current account is in surplus, this excess foreign exchange results in a net outflow in the financial account through lending abroad, buying foreign stocks and bonds, buying a shoe plant in Italy or a villa on the French Riviera, and so forth.

When all transactions are considered, accounts must always balance, though specific accounts usually don't. A deficit in a particular account should not necessarily be viewed as a source of concern, nor should a surplus be a source of satisfaction. The deficit in the U.S. current account in recent years has been offset by a financial account surplus. As a result, foreigners are acquiring more claims on U.S. assets.

Exhibit 3

U.S. Balance of Payments for 2007 (billions of dollars)

Current Accounts	
1. Merchandise exports	+1,148.5
2. Merchandise imports	−1,967.9
3. Merchandise trade balance (1 + 2)	−819.4
4. Service exports	+497.2
5. Service imports	−378.1
6. Goods and services balance (3 + 4 + 5)	−700.3
7. Net investment income from abroad	+81.7
8. Net unilateral transfers	−112.7
9. Current account balance (6 + 7 + 8)	−731.3
Financial Accounts	
10. Change in U.S.-owned assets abroad	−1,289.9
11. Change in foreign-owned assets in U.S.	+2,057.7
12. Financial account balance (10 + 11)	+767.8
13. Statistical discrepancy	−36.5
TOTAL (9 + 12 + 13)	**0.0**

SOURCE: "U.S. International Transactions Accounts Data," Bureau of Economic Analysis, U.S. Department of Commerce, Table 1, 15 December 2008, at http://www.bea.gov/international/xls/table1.xls.

LO² Foreign Exchange Rates and Markets

Now that you have some idea about international flows, we can take a closer look at the forces that determine the underlying value of the currencies involved. Let's begin by looking at exchange rates and the market for foreign exchange.

Foreign Exchange

Foreign exchange, recall, is foreign money needed to carry out international transactions. The exchange rate is the price measured in one country's currency of buying one unit of another country's currency. Exchange rates are determined by the interaction of the households, firms, private financial institutions, governments, and central banks that buy and sell foreign exchange. The exchange rate fluctuates to equate the quantity of foreign exchange demanded with the quantity supplied. Typically, foreign exchange is made up of bank deposits denominated in the foreign currency. When foreign travel is involved, foreign exchange often consists of foreign paper money.

The foreign exchange market incorporates all the arrangements used to buy and sell foreign exchange. This market is not so much a physical place as a network of telephones and computers connecting financial centers all over the world. Perhaps you have seen pictures of foreign exchange traders in New York, Frankfurt, London, or Tokyo in front of computer screens amid a tangle of phone lines. The foreign exchange market is like an all-night diner—it never closes. A trading center is always open somewhere in the world.

We will consider the market for the euro in terms of the dollar. But first, a little more about the euro. For decades the nations of Western Europe have tried to increase their economic cooperation and trade. These countries believed they would be more productive and more competitive with the United States if they acted less like many separate economies and more like the 50 United States, with a single set of trade regulations and one currency. Imagine the hassle involved if each of the 50 states had its own currency.

In 2002, euro notes and coins entered circulation in the 12 European countries adopting the common currency. The big advantage of a

exchange rate
the price measured in one country's currency of purchasing 1 unit of another country's currency

The Demand for Foreign Exchange

Whenever U.S. residents need euros, they must buy them in the foreign exchange market, which could include their local banks, paying for them with dollars. Exhibit 4 depicts a market for foreign exchange—in this case, euros. The horizontal axis shows the quantity of foreign exchange, measured here in millions of euros. The vertical axis shows the price per unit of foreign exchange, measured here in dollars per euro. The demand curve D for foreign exchange shows the inverse relationship between the dollar price of the euro and the quantity of euros demanded, other things assumed constant. Assumed constant along the demand curve are the incomes and preferences of U.S. consumers, expected inflation in the United States and in the euro area, the euro price of goods in the euro area, and interest rates in the United States and in the euro area. People have many reasons for demanding foreign exchange, but in the aggregate, the lower the dollar price of foreign exchange, other things constant, the greater the quantity of foreign exchange demanded.

A drop in the dollar price of foreign exchange, in this case the euro, means that fewer dollars are needed to purchase each euro, so the dollar prices of euro area products (like German cars, Italian shoes, tickets to Euro Disney, and euro area securities), which list prices in euros, become cheaper. The cheaper it is to buy euros, the lower the dollar price of euro area products to U.S. residents, so the greater the quantity of euros demanded by U.S. residents, other things constant. For example, a cheap enough euro might persuade you to tour Rome, climb the Austrian Alps, wander the museums of Paris, or crawl the pubs of Dublin.

common currency is that Europeans no longer have to change money every time they cross a border or trade with another country in the group. Again, the inspiration for this is the United States, arguably the most successful economy in world history.

So the euro is the common currency of the *euro area*, or *euro zone*, as the now 16-country region is usually called. The price, or exchange rate, of the euro in terms of the dollar is the number of dollars required to purchase one euro. An increase in the number of dollars needed to purchase a euro indicates weakening, or depreciation, of the dollar. A decrease in the number of dollars needed to purchase a euro indicates strengthening, or appreciation, of the dollar. Put another way, a decrease in the number of euros needed to purchase a dollar is a depreciation of the dollar, and an increase in the number of euros needed to purchase a dollar is an appreciation of the dollar.

Because the exchange rate is usually a market price, it is determined by demand and supply: The equilibrium price is the one that equates quantity demanded with quantity supplied. To simplify the analysis, suppose that the United States and the euro area make up the entire world, so the demand and supply for euros in international finance is the demand and supply for foreign exchange from the U.S. perspective.

currency depreciation with respect to the dollar, an increase in the number of dollars needed to purchase 1 unit of foreign exchange in a flexible rate system

currency appreciation with respect to the dollar, a decrease in the number of dollars needed to purchase 1 unit of foreign exchange in a flexible rate system

Exhibit 4

The Foreign Exchange Market

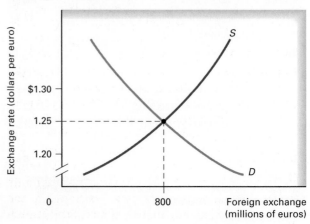

The Supply of Foreign Exchange

The supply of foreign exchange is generated by the desire of foreign residents to acquire dollars—that is, to exchange euros for dollars. Euro area residents want dollars to buy U.S. goods and services, acquire U.S. assets, make loans in dollars, or send dollars to their U.S. friends and relatives. Euros are supplied in the foreign exchange market to acquire the dollars people want. An increase in the dollar-per-euro exchange rate, other things constant, makes U.S. products cheaper for foreigners because foreign residents need fewer euros to get the same number of dollars. For example, suppose a Dell computer sells for $600. If the exchange rate is $1.20 per euro, that computer costs 500 euros; if the exchange rate is $1.25 per euro, it costs only 480 euros. The number of Dell computers demanded in the euro area increases as the dollar-per-euro exchange rate increases, other things constant, so more euros will be supplied on the foreign exchange market to buy dollars.

The positive relationship between the dollar-per-euro exchange rate and the quantity of euros supplied on the foreign exchange market is expressed in Exhibit 4 by the upward-sloping supply curve for foreign exchange (again, euros in our example). The supply curve assumes that other things remain constant, including euro area incomes and tastes, expectations about inflation in the euro area and in the United States, and interest rates in the euro area and in the United States.

Determining the Exchange Rate

Exhibit 4 brings together the demand and supply for foreign exchange to determine the exchange rate. At a rate of $1.25 per euro, the quantity of euros demanded equals the quantity supplied—in our example, 800 million euros. Once achieved, this equilibrium rate will remain constant until a change occurs in one of the factors that affect supply or demand. If the exchange rate is allowed to adjust freely, or to *float,* in response to market forces, the market will clear continually, as the quantities of foreign exchange demanded and supplied are equated.

What if the initial equilibrium is upset by a change in one of the underlying forces that affect demand or supply? For example, suppose higher U.S. incomes increase American demand for all normal goods, including those from the euro area. This shifts the U.S. demand curve for foreign exchange to the right, as Americans buy more Italian marble, Dutch

If the exchange rate is allowed to adjust freely, or to float, in response to market forces, the market will clear continually, as the quantities of foreign exchange demanded and supplied are equated.

chocolate, German machines, Parisian vacations, and euro area securities.

This increased demand for euros is shown in Exhibit 5 on the next page by a rightward shift of the demand curve for foreign exchange. The demand increase from D to D' leads to an increase in the exchange rate per euro from $1.25 to $1.27. Thus, the euro increases in value, or appreciates, while the dollar falls in value, or depreciates. An increase in U.S. income should not affect the euro supply curve, though it does increase the *quantity of euros supplied.* The higher exchange value of the euro prompts those in the euro area to buy more American products and assets, which are now cheaper in terms of the euro.

To review: Any increase in the demand for foreign exchange or any decrease in its supply, other things constant, increases the number of dollars required to purchase one unit of foreign exchange, which is a depreciation of the dollar. On the other hand, any decrease in the demand for foreign exchange or any increase in its supply, other things constant, reduces the number of dollars required to purchase one unit of foreign exchange, which is an appreciation of the dollar.

Arbitrageurs and Speculators

Exchange rates between two currencies are nearly identical at any given time in markets around the world. For example, the dollar price of a euro is the same in New York, Frankfurt, Tokyo, London, Zurich, Hong Kong, Istanbul, and other financial centers.

Exhibit 5

Effect on the Foreign Exchange Market of an Increased Demand for Euros

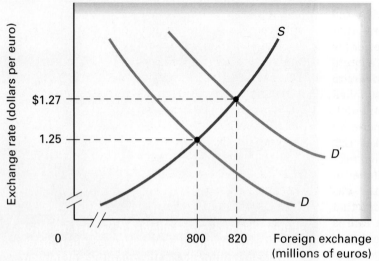

Arbitrageurs—dealers who take advantage of any difference in exchange rates between markets by buying low and selling high—ensure this equality. Their actions help to equalize exchange rates across markets. For example, if one euro costs $1.24 in New York but $1.25 in Frankfurt, an arbitrageur could buy, say, $1,000,000 worth of euros in New York and at the same time sell them in Frankfurt for $1,008,060, thereby earning $8,060 minus the transaction costs of the trades.

Because an arbitrageur buys and sells simultaneously, little risk is involved. In our example, the arbitrageur increased the demand for euros in New York and increased the supply of euros in Frankfurt. These actions increased the dollar price of euros in New York and decreased it in Frankfurt, thereby squeezing down the difference in exchange rates. Exchange rates may still change because of market forces, but they tend to change in all markets simultaneously.

The demand and supply of foreign exchange arises from many sources—from importers and exporters, investors in foreign assets, central banks, tourists, arbitrageurs, and speculators. Speculators buy or sell foreign exchange in hopes of profiting by trading the currency at a more favorable exchange rate later.

arbitrageur
someone who takes advantage of temporary geographic differences in the exchange rate by simultaneously purchasing a currency in one market and selling it in another market

speculator
someone who buys or sells foreign exchange in hopes of profiting from fluctuations in the exchange rate over time

purchasing power parity (PPP) theory
the idea that the exchange rate between two countries will adjust in the long run to equalize the cost between the countries of a basket of internationally traded goods

By taking risks, speculators aim to profit from market fluctuations—they try to buy low and sell high. In contrast, arbitrageurs take less risk, because they *simultaneously* buy currency in one market and sell it in another.

Finally, people in countries suffering from economic and political turmoil, such as occurred in Russia, Indonesia, and the Philippines, may buy *hard* currency as a hedge against the depreciation and instability of their own currencies. The dollar has long been accepted as an international medium of exchange. It is also the currency of choice in the world markets for oil and illegal drugs. But the euro eventually may challenge that dominance, in part because the largest euro denomination, the 500 euro note, is worth about six times the largest U.S. denomination, the $100 note. So it would be six times easier to smuggle euro notes than U.S. notes of equal value.

Purchasing Power Parity

As long as trade across borders is unrestricted and as long as exchange rates are allowed to adjust freely, the purchasing power parity (PPP) theory predicts that the exchange rate between two currencies will adjust in the long run to reflect price differences between the two currency regions. *A given basket of internationally traded goods should therefore sell for about the same around the world (except for differences reflecting transportation costs and the like).* Suppose a basket of internationally traded goods that sells for $10,000 in the United States sells for 8,000 euros in the euro area. According to the purchasing power parity theory, the equilibrium exchange rate should be $1.25 per euro. If this were not the case—if the exchange rate were, say, $1.20 per euro—then you could exchange $9,600 for 8,000 euros, with which you buy the basket of commodities in the euro area. You could then sell that basket of goods in the States for $10,000, yielding you a profit of $400 minus any transaction costs. Selling dollars and buying euros will also drive up the dollar price of euros.

The purchasing power parity theory is more of a long-run predictor than a day-to-day indicator of the relationship between changes in the price level and the exchange rate. For example, a country's currency generally appreciates when inflation is low compared with other countries and depreciates when inflation is high. Likewise, a country's currency generally appreciates when its real interest rates are higher than those in the rest of the world, because foreigners are more willing to buy and hold investments denominated in that high-interest currency. As a case in point, the dollar appreciated during the first half of the 1980s, when real U.S. interest rates were relatively high, and depreciated during 2002 to 2004, when real U.S. interest rates were relatively low. The dollar was expected to depreciate during 2009 because of historically low real interest rates, recession, and high government borrowing.

Because of trade barriers, central bank intervention in exchange markets, and the fact that many products are not traded or are not comparable across countries, the purchasing power parity theory usually does not explain exchange rates at a particular point in time that well. For example, if you went shopping in London tomorrow, you would soon notice a dollar does not buy as much there as it does in the United States.

LO³ Fixed and Flexible Exchange Rates

Flexible Exchange Rates

For the most part, we have been discussing a system of flexible exchange rates, with rates determined by demand and supply. Flexible, or *floating,* exchange rates adjust continually to the myriad forces that buffet foreign exchange markets. Consider how the exchange rate is linked to the balance-of-payments accounts. Debit entries in the current or financial accounts increase the demand for foreign exchange, resulting in a depreciation of the dollar. Credit entries in these accounts increase the supply of foreign exchange, resulting in an appreciation of the dollar.

Fixed Exchange Rates

When exchange rates are flexible, governments usually have little direct role in foreign exchange markets. But if governments try to set exchange rates, active and ongoing central bank intervention is often necessary to establish and maintain these fixed exchange rates. Suppose the European Central Bank selects what it thinks is an appropriate rate of exchange between the dollar and the euro. It attempts to *fix,* or to *peg,* the exchange rate within a narrow band around the particular value selected. If the euro threatens to climb above the maximum acceptable exchange rate, monetary authorities must sell euros and buy dollars, thereby keeping the dollar price of the euro down. Conversely, if the euro threatens to drop below the minimum acceptable exchange rate, monetary authorities must sell dollars and

buy euros. This increased demand for the euro will keep its value up relative to the dollar. Through such intervention in the foreign exchange market, monetary authorities try to stabilize the exchange rate, keeping it within the specified band.

If monetary officials must keep selling foreign exchange to keep the value of their domestic currency from falling, they risk running out of foreign exchange reserves. Faced with this threat, the government has several options for eliminating the exchange rate disequilibrium. First, the pegged exchange rate can be increased, which is a devaluation of the domestic currency. (A decrease in the pegged exchange rate is called a revaluation.) Second, the government can reduce the domestic demand for foreign exchange directly by imposing restrictions on imports or on financial outflows. Many developing countries do this. Third, the government can adopt policies to slow the domestic economy, increase interest rates, or reduce inflation relative to that of the country's trading partners, thereby indirectly decreasing the demand for foreign exchange and increasing the supply of foreign exchange. Several Asian economies, such as South Korea and Indonesia, pursued such policies to stabilize their currencies. Finally, the government can allow the disequilibrium to persist and ration the available foreign reserves through some form of foreign exchange control.

This concludes our introduction to the theories of international finance. Let's examine international finance in practice.

LO⁴ Development of the International Monetary System

From 1879 to 1914, the international financial system operated under a gold standard, whereby the major currencies were convertible

flexible exchange rate rate determined in foreign exchange markets by the forces of demand and supply without government intervention

fixed exchange rate rate of exchange between currencies pegged within a narrow range and maintained by the central bank's ongoing purchases and sales of currencies

currency devaluation an increase in the official pegged price of foreign exchange in terms of the domestic currency

currency revaluation a reduction in the official pegged price of foreign exchange in terms of the domestic currency

gold standard an arrangement whereby the currencies of most countries are convertible into gold at a fixed rate into gold at a fixed rate. For example, the U.S. dollar could be redeemed at the U.S. Treasury for one-twentieth of an ounce of gold. The British pound could be redeemed at the British Exchequer, or treasury, for one-fourth of an ounce of gold. Because each British pound could buy five times as much gold as each dollar, one British pound exchanged for $5.

The gold standard provided a predictable exchange rate, one that did not vary as long as currencies could be redeemed for gold at the announced rate. But the money supply in each country was determined in part by the flow of gold between countries, so each country's monetary policy was influenced by the supply of gold. A balance-of-payments deficit resulted in a loss of gold, which theoretically caused a country's money supply to shrink. A balance-of-payments surplus resulted in an influx of gold, which theoretically caused a country's money supply to expand. The supply of money throughout the world also depended on the vagaries of gold discoveries. When gold production did not keep pace with the growth in economic activity, the price level dropped. When gold production exceeded the growth in economic activity, the price level rose. For example, gold discoveries in Alaska and South Africa in the late 1890s expanded the U.S. money supply, leading to inflation.

The Bretton Woods Agreement

During World War I, many countries could no longer convert their currencies into gold, and the gold standard eventually collapsed, disrupting international trade during the 1920s and 1930s. Once an Allied victory in World War II appeared certain, the Allies met in Bretton Woods, New Hampshire, in July 1944 to formulate a new international monetary system. Because the United States had a strong economy and was not ravaged by the war, the dollar was selected as the key reserve currency in the new international monetary system. All exchange rates were fixed in terms of the dollar, and the United States, which held most of the world's gold reserves, stood ready to convert foreign holdings of dollars into gold at a rate of $35 per ounce. Even though the rate that dollars could be exchanged for gold was fixed by the Bretton Woods agreement, *other* countries could adjust their exchange rates relative to the U.S. dollar if they found a chronic disequilibrium in their balance of payments— that is, if a country faced a large and persistent deficit or surplus.

International Monetary Fund (IMF)
an international organization that establishes rules for maintaining the international monetary system and makes loans to countries with temporary balance-of-payments problems

The Bretton Woods agreement also created the **International Monetary Fund (IMF)** to set rules for maintaining the international monetary system, to standardize financial reporting for international trade, and to make loans to countries with temporary balance-of-payments problems. The IMF lends a revolving fund of about $200 billion to economies in need of reserves. Headquartered in Washington, D.C., the IMF has more than 180 member countries and a staff of 2,600 drawn from around the world.

The Demise of the Bretton Woods System

During the latter part of the 1960s, inflation began heating up in the United States. Because of U.S. inflation, the dollar had become *overvalued* at the official exchange rate, meaning that the gold value of the dollar exceeded the exchange value of the dollar. In 1971, U.S. merchandise imports exceeded merchandise exports for the first time since World War II. Foreigners exchanged dollars for gold. To stem this gold outflow, the United States stopped exchanging gold for dollars, but this just made the dollar less attractive. In December 1971, the world's 10 richest countries met in Washington and devalued the dollar by 8 percent. They hoped this devaluation would put the dollar on firmer footing and would save the "dollar standard." With prices rising at different rates around the world, however, an international monetary system based on fixed exchange rates was doomed.

When the U.S. trade deficit tripled in 1972, it became clear that the dollar was still overvalued. In early 1973, the dollar was devalued another 10 percent, but this did not quiet foreign exchange markets. The dollar, for three decades the anchor of the international monetary system, suddenly looked vulnerable, and speculators began betting that the dollar would fall even more. Dollars were exchanged for German marks because the mark appeared to be the most stable currency. Bundesbank, Germany's central bank, tried to defend the dollar's official exchange rate by selling marks and buying dollars. Why didn't Germany want the mark to appreciate? Appreciation would make German goods more expensive abroad and foreign goods cheaper in Germany, thereby reducing German exports and increasing German imports. So the mark's appreciation would reduce German output and employment. But after selling $10 billion worth of marks, the Bundesbank gave up defending the dollar. As soon as the value of the dollar was allowed to float against the mark, the Bretton Woods system, already on shaky ground, collapsed.

The Resilience of Gold

Despite the breakdown of the gold standard, most countries still hold a substantial gold reserve, and gold has often been considered a safe haven for investment in volatile markets. However, during the economic crisis of 2008, even gold was affected by market turmoil. In March, gold had reached a record high of $1,003.20 per troy ounce, leaving the metal in line with many other assets such as oil, stocks, and grain commodities. A rising dollar pushed gold down further, where it hit a low of $712 in November. It managed a slight recovery, closing 2008 around $870, leaving it up only 4% for the year, though it still outperformed most other asset classes, such as the S&P 500-stock index—down 41%—and crude oil—down 61%. Gold remained volatile at the start of 2009, passing $1000 again in late February but slipping to $930 by early July.

SOURCE: David Gaffen, "Gold, Not So Golden in 2008, Loses Chance to Be Market Star," *Wall Street Journal,* 29 December 2008. Available at http://online.wsj.com/article/SB123052519180239011.html (accessed 29 December 2008). Matt Whittaker, "Gold Tumbles 2.7% as Optimism Grows," *Wall Street Journal,* 6 April 2009. Available at http://online.wsj.com/article/SB123906170679495133.html (accessed 7 April 2009).

The Current System: Managed Float

The Bretton Woods system has been replaced by a managed float system, which combines features of a freely floating exchange rate with sporadic intervention by central banks as a way of moderating exchange rate fluctuations among the world's major currencies. Most small countries, particularly developing countries, still peg their currencies to one of the major currencies (such as the U.S. dollar) or to a "basket" of major currencies. What's more, in developing countries, private international borrowing and lending are severely restricted; some governments allow residents to purchase foreign exchange only for certain purposes. In some countries, different exchange rates apply to different categories of transactions.

Critics of flexible exchange rates argue that they are inflationary, because they free monetary authorities to pursue expansionary policies, and they have often been volatile. This volatility creates uncertainty and risk for importers and exporters, increasing the transaction costs of international trade. Furthermore, exchange rate volatility can lead to wrenching changes in the competitiveness of a country's export sector. These changes cause swings in employment, resulting in louder calls for import restrictions. For example, the exchange rate between the Japanese yen and the U.S. dollar has been relatively unstable, particularly because of international speculation.

Policy makers are always on the lookout for a system that will perform better than the current managed float system, with its fluctuating currency values. *Their ideal is a system that will foster international trade, lower inflation, and promote a more stable world economy.* International finance ministers have acknowledged that the world must find an international standard and establish greater exchange rate stability.

Final Word

The United States is very much a part of the world economy, not only as the largest exporter nation but also as the largest importer nation. Although the dollar remains the unit of transaction in many international settlements—OPEC, for example, still states oil prices in dollars—gyrations of exchange rates have made those involved in international finance wary of putting all their eggs in one basket. The international monetary system is now going through a difficult period as it gropes for a new source of stability nearly four decades after the collapse of the Bretton Woods agreement.

managed float system
an exchange rate system that combines features of freely floating rates with sporadic intervention by central banks

Learning Outcomes

LO¹ Describe the worldwide variation in economic vitality

LO² Explain why productivity is the key to development

LO³ Discuss international trade and development

LO⁴ Describe the role of foreign aid in economic development

LO⁵ Define transitional economies

LO⁶ Discuss markets and institutions

Developing *and* Transitional Economies

> **"Although there is no widely accepted theory of how best to achieve economic development, one approach is the introduction of market forces."**

People around the world face the day under quite different circumstances. Even during a recession, most Americans rise from a comfortable bed in a nice home, select the day's clothing from a wardrobe, choose from a variety of breakfast foods, and drive to school or to work in one of the family's personal automobiles. But many of the world's 6.8 billion people have little housing, clothing, or food. They have no automobile and no formal job. Their health is poor, as is their education. Many cannot read or write. A billion people need eyeglasses but can't afford them. Why are some countries so poor while others are so rich? What determines the wealth of nations?

In this chapter, we sort out rich nations from poor ones and try to explain the difference. Although there is no widely accepted theory of how best to achieve economic development, one approach that seems to be gaining favor is the introduction of market forces, especially in formerly socialist countries. Around the world, the demise of central planning has been stunning and pervasive. We close the chapter with a discussion of these rich experiments—these works in progress.

Topics discussed in Chapter 20 include:

- Developing countries
- Obstacles to development
- Import substitution
- Export promotion
- Foreign aid
- Transitional economies
- Big bang versus gradualism
- Privatization

LO¹ Worlds Apart

Differences in economic vitality among countries are huge. Countries are classified in a variety of ways based on their economic development. The yardstick most often used to compare living standards across nations is the amount an economy produces per capita, or *output per capita*. The World Bank, an economic development institution affiliated with the United Nations (UN), estimates output per capita figures and then uses these figures to classify economies. The measure used by the World Bank to classify countries begins with *gross national income (GNI)*. GNI measures the market value of all goods and services produced by resources supplied by the countries' residents and firms, regardless of the location of the resource. For example, U.S. GNI includes profit earned by a Ford factory in Great Britain but excludes profits earned by a Toyota factory in Kentucky.

© YELLOW DOG PRODUCTIONS/STONE/GETTY IMAGES

GNI measures both the value of output produced and the income that output generates. The World Bank computes the GNI per capita, which also measures income per capita, then adjusts figures across countries based on the purchasing power of that income in each country. Using this measure, the World Bank sorts countries around the world into three major groups: *high-income economies, middle-income economies, and low-income economies.*

Data on world population and world output are summarized in Exhibit 1. High-income economies in 2007 made up only 16 percent of the 6.8 billion people on Earth, but accounted for 74 percent of world output. So high-income economies, *with only about one-sixth of the world's population, produced three-fourths of the world's output.* Middle-income economies made up 64 percent of the world's population, but accounted for 25 percent of the world output. And low-income countries made up 20 percent of the world's population, but accounted for only 1 percent of the world output.

Developing and Industrial Economies

The low- and middle-income economies are usually referred to as **developing countries**. Most high-income economies are also referred to as **industrial market countries**. So low- and middle-income economies, what are called developing countries, had 84 percent of the world's population in 2007 but produced only 26 percent of the output. Compared to industrial market countries, developing countries usually have higher rates of illiteracy, higher unemployment, faster population growth, and exports consisting mostly of agricultural products and raw materials.

On average, more than 50 percent of the labor force in developing countries works in agriculture, versus only about 3 percent in industrial market countries. Because farming methods are relatively primitive in developing countries, farm productivity is low and many barely subsist. Industrial market countries, or *developed countries,* are primarily the economically advanced capitalist countries of Western Europe, North America, Australia, New Zealand, and Japan. They were the first to experience long-term economic growth during the 19th century.

developing countries
nations typified by high rates of illiteracy, high unemployment, high fertility rates, and exports of primary products; also known as low-income and middle-income economies

industrial market countries
economically advanced capitalist countries of Western Europe, North America, Australia, New Zealand, and Japan; also known as developed countries and high-income economies

Exhibit 1

Share of World Population and Output from High-, Middle-, and Low-Income Economies

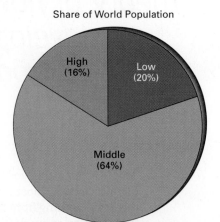

Share of World Population

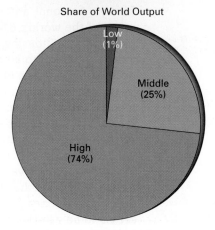

Share of World Output

SOURCE: Based on population and output estimated from the *World Bank's World Development Report: 2009,* Table 1. Find the World Bank at http://web.worldbank.org.

Exhibit 2 presents income per capita in 2007 for a sample of high-, middle-, and low-income economies. Because most countries in the sample have a large population, together they account for 54 percent of world population. Countries are listed from top to bottom in descending order based on income per capita. Again, figures have been adjusted to reflect the actual purchasing power of the native currency in its respective economy. The bars in the chart are color-coded, with high-income economies in blue, middle-income economies in orange, and low-income economies in red. Per capita income in the United States, the exhibit's top-ranked country, was more than eight times that of China, a middle-income economy. But per capita in China, in turn, was about four times that of Haiti and 18 times that of Burundi. Residents of China likely feel poor relative to America, but they appear well off compared to the poorest developing nations. U.S per capita income was 35 times that of Haiti, and 153 times that

Exhibit 2

Per Capita Income for Selected Countries in 2007

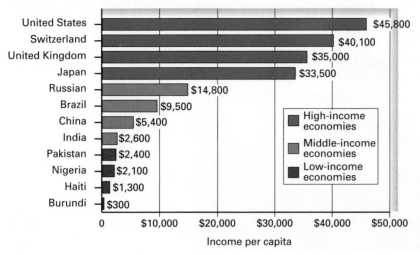

SOURCE: Developed from estimates from the Central Intelligence Agency *World Factbook: 2008* at www.cia.gov/library/publications/the-world-factbook/index.html. Figures are based on the purchasing power of each country's currency.

of Burundi. Thus, there is a tremendous range in productive performance around the world.

Health and Nutrition

Differences in stages of development among countries are reflected in a number of ways besides per capita income. For example, many people in developing countries suffer from poor health as a result of malnutrition and disease. AIDS is devastating some developing countries, particularly those in sub-Saharan Africa. In 2007, one in four adults in Swaziland and Botswana had HIV, compared to only one in 200 among those living in high-income economies. In sub-Saharan Africa, life expectancy at birth averaged 51 years, versus 79 years in high-income economies, 69 years in middle-income economies, and 57 years in all low-income economies.

Malnutrition

Those in the poorest countries consume only half the calories of those in high-income countries. Even if an infant survives the first year, malnutrition can turn normal childhood diseases, such as measles, into life-threatening events. Malnutrition is a primary or contributing factor in more than half of the deaths of children under the age of 5 in low-income countries. Diseases that are well controlled in the industrial countries—malaria, whooping cough, polio, dysentery, typhoid, and cholera—can become epidemics in poor countries. Many of these diseases are water-borne, as safe drinking water is often hard to find. In low-income countries, about 29 percent of children under the age of 5 suffered from malnutrition in 2007. Among middle-income countries the figure was about 23 percent. Among high-income countries, it was 3 percent.

Infant Mortality

Health differences among countries are reflected in child mortality. Child mortality rates are much greater in low-income countries than in high-income countries. As of 2006, the mortality rate for children up to 5 years of age was 7 per 1,000 live births in high-income economies, 49 in middle-income economies, and 135 in low-income economies. Rates for our representative sample of high-, middle-, and low-income economies appear in Exhibit 3. Again, high-income economies appear as blue bars, middle-income as orange

Exhibit 3

Child Mortality Rates Per 1,000 Live Births for the Sample of High-, Middle-, and Low-Income Economies

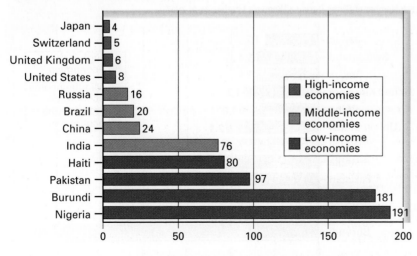

SOURCE: Based on figures from the World Bank's *World Development Report: 2009,* Table 2. Find the World Bank at http://web.worldbank.org.

countries because children are viewed as a source of farm labor and as economic and social security as the parents age. Most developing countries have no pension or social security system for the aged. The higher child mortality rates in poorer countries also engender higher birth rates, as parents strive to ensure a sufficiently large family.

Sub-Saharan African nations are among the poorest in the world and have the fastest-growing populations. Because of high fertility rates in the poorest countries, children under 15 make up 40 percent of the population there. In industrial countries, children make up less than a fifth of the population. Italy, an industrial economy, became the first country in history with more people over the age of 65 than under the age of 15. Germany, Greece, Spain, Portugal, and Japan have since followed.

In some developing countries, the population growth rate has exceeded the growth rate in total production, so the standard of living as measured by per capita output has declined. Still, even in the poorest of countries, attitudes about family size are changing. According to the United Nations, the birth rate during a typical woman's lifetime in a developing country has fallen from six children in 1965 to

bars, and low-income as red bars. Among the dozen countries shown, child mortality was highest in the sub-Saharan African nations of Nigeria and Burundi. Child mortality among all 47 sub-Saharan African countries averaged 22 times that in high-income countries.

High Birth Rates

Developing countries are identified not only by their low incomes and high mortality rates but also by their high birth rates. This year, more than 80 million of the 90 million people added to the world's population will be born in developing countries. In fact, the birth rate is one of the clearest ways of distinguishing between industrial and developing countries. Very few low-income economies have a fertility rate below 3.1 births per woman, but only three of 66 high-income countries have fertility rates above that level (Saudi Arabia, Equatorial Guinea, and Oman).

Exhibit 4 presents total fertility rates per woman for selected countries as of 2008. Burundi had one the world's highest fertility rates at 6.4. This means each woman in Burundi on average gives birth to 6.4 children during her lifetime. Note that the four low-income economies, shown as red bars, have the highest fertility rates. Historically, families tend to be larger in poor

Exhibit 4

Average Number of Births During a Woman's Lifetime as of 2008

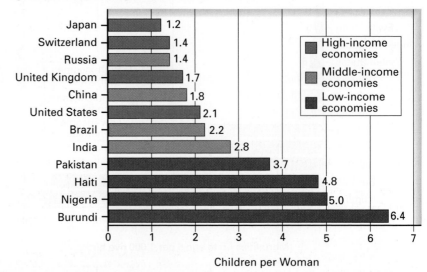

Children per Woman

Japan	1.2
Switzerland	1.4
Russia	1.4
United Kingdom	1.7
China	1.8
United States	2.1
Brazil	2.2
India	2.8
Pakistan	3.7
Haiti	4.8
Nigeria	5.0
Burundi	6.4

Legend: High-income economies / Middle-income economies / Low-income economies

SOURCE: Developed from estimates from the Central Intelligence Agency *World Factbook: 2008* at www.cia.gov/library/publications/the-world-factbook/index.html.

under three children today. Evidence from developing countries more generally indicates that when women have employment opportunities outside the home, fertility rates decline. And as women become better educated, they earn more and tend to have fewer children.

Women in Developing Countries

Throughout the world, poverty is greater among women than men, particularly women who head households. The percentage of households headed by women varies from country to country, but nears 50 percent in some areas of Africa and the Caribbean. Because women often must work in the home as well as in the labor market, poverty can impose a special hardship on them. In many cultures, women's responsibilities include gathering firewood and carrying water, tasks that are especially burdensome if firewood is scarce and water is far from home.

Women in developing countries tend to be less educated than men. In the countries of sub-Saharan Africa and South Asia, for example, only half as many women as men complete high school. And in Indonesia, girls are six times more likely than boys to drop out of school before the fourth grade. Women have fewer employment opportunities and earn lower wages than men do. For example, Sudan's Muslim fundamentalist government bans women from working in public places after 5:00 P.M. In Algeria, Egypt, Jordan, Libya, and Saudi Arabia, women account for only about one-quarter of the workforce. Women are often on the fringes of the labor market, working long hours in agriculture. They also have less access to other resources, such as land, capital, and technology.

LO² Productivity: Key to Development

We have examined some symptoms of poverty in developing countries, but not why poor countries are poor. At the risk of appearing simplistic, we might say that poor countries are poor because they do not produce many goods and services. In this section, we examine why some developing countries experience such low productivity.

Low Labor Productivity

Labor productivity, measured in terms of output per worker, is by definition low in low-income countries. Why? Labor productivity depends on the quality of the labor and on the amount of capital, natural resources, and other inputs that combine with labor. For example, as mentioned earlier, one certified public accountant with a computer and specialized software can sort out a company's finances more quickly and more accurately than can a thousand high-school–educated file clerks with pencils and paper.

One way a country raises its productivity is by investing more in human and physical capital. This investment must be financed by either domestic savings or foreign funds. Income per capita in the poorest countries is often too low to support much investment. In poor countries with unstable governments, the wealthy minority frequently invests in more stable foreign economies. This leaves less to invest domestically in either human or physical capital; without sufficient capital, workers remain less productive.

Technology and Education

What exactly is the contribution of education to the process of economic development? Education helps people make better use of the resources available. If knowledge is lacking, other resources may not be used efficiently. For example, a country may

{ **Cellphones Provide a Gateway to the Internet for Developing Nations** }

Developing nations are becoming important drivers of mobile-technology growth. Many countries like Indonesia, a nation comprised of more than 17,000 islands, have poor wire-line telecommunications services. Decreasing costs, higher bandwidths, and new technologies that speed up data transfers, however, have made it much easier to access the Internet via mobile devices. Many people, especially in poorer nations, cannot afford a PC, but they can afford cellphones, which allow them Internet and e-mail access almost anywhere. Technology for mobile web-browsers is allowing increasingly faster data transfer. Cellphones operating high-performance web browsers, like Internet Explorer, Firefox, and Safari, are expected to number 700 million by 2013, up from 76 million in 2007.

SOURCE: Tom Wright, "Poorer Nations Go Online on Cellphones," *Wall Street Journal,* 5 December 2008, B4.

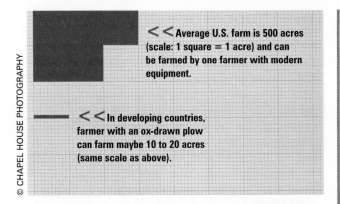

<<Average U.S. farm is 500 acres (scale: 1 square = 1 acre) and can be farmed by one farmer with modern equipment.

<<In developing countries, farmer with an ox-drawn plow can farm maybe 10 to 20 acres (same scale as above).

be endowed with fertile land, but farmers may lack knowledge of irrigation and fertilization techniques. Or farmers may not know how to rotate crops to avoid soil depletion. In low-income countries in 2005, 39 percent of those 15 and older were illiterate, compared to 10 percent in middle-income countries and 1 percent in high-income countries. In the low-income economies of Burundi and Pakistan only about one-quarter complete ninth grade. In the middle-income economies of Brazil and Mexico about half do. Children drop out of school because the family can't afford it or would rather put the child to work. Child labor in developing countries obviously limits educational opportunities.

Education also makes people more receptive to new ideas and methods. Countries with the most advanced educational systems were also the first to develop. In the 20th century, the leader in schooling and economic development was the United States. In Latin America, Argentina was the most educationally advanced nation 100 years ago, and it is one of the most developed Latin American nations today. The growth of education in Japan during the 19th century contributed to a ready acceptance of technology and thus to Japan's remarkable economic growth in the 20th century.

Inefficient Use of Labor

Another feature of developing countries is that they use labor less efficiently than do industrial nations. Unemployment and underemployment reflect inefficient uses of labor. *Underemployment* occurs when skilled workers are employed in low-skill jobs or when people are working less than they would like—a worker seeking full-time employment may find only a part-time job. *Unemployment* occurs when those willing and able to work can't find jobs.

Unemployment is measured primarily in urban areas, because in rural areas farm work is usually an outlet for labor even if many workers are underemployed there. The unemployment rate in develop-

ing nations on average is about 10 to 15 percent of the urban labor force. Unemployment among young workers—those aged 15 to 24—is typically twice that of older workers. In developing nations, about 30 percent of the combined urban and rural workforces is either unemployed or underemployed. In Zimbabwe the unemployment rate was 80 percent in 2007.

In some developing countries, the average farm is as small as two acres. Productivity is also low because few other inputs, such as capital and fertilizer, are used. *Although more than half the labor force in developing countries works in agriculture, only about one-third of output in these countries stems from agriculture.* In the United States, where farmers account for only 2 percent of the labor force, a farmer with modern equipment can farm hundreds or even thousands of acres (the average farm is about 500 acres). In developing countries, a farmer with a hand plow or an ox-drawn plow can farm maybe 10 to 20 acres. U.S. farmers, though only one-fiftieth of the labor force, grow enough to feed a nation and to lead the world in farm exports. The average value added per U.S. farm worker is about 72 times that of farm workers in low- and middle-income countries.

Low productivity obviously results in low income, but low income can, in turn, affect worker productivity. Low income means less saving and less saving means less investment in human and physical capital. Low income can also mean poor nutrition during the formative years, which can retard mental and physical development. These difficult beginnings may be aggravated by poor diet and insufficient health care in later life, making workers poorly suited for regular employment. Poverty can result in less saving, less education, less capital formation, a poor diet, and little health care—all of which can reduce a worker's productivity. Thus, *low income and low productivity may reinforce each other in a cycle of poverty.*

Natural Resources

Some countries are rich in natural resources. The difference is most striking when we compare countries with oil reserves and those without. The Middle East countries of Bahrain, Kuwait, Qatar, Saudi Arabia, and the United Arab Emirates are developing countries classified as high-income economies because they were lucky enough to be sitting atop huge oil reserves. But oil-rich countries are the exception. Many developing countries, such as Chad and Ethiopia, have little in the way of natural resources. Most developing countries without oil reserves were in trouble when oil prices rose in 2006 and peaked in 2008. Since oil must be imported, high oil prices drained oil-poor countries of precious foreign exchange.

Oil-rich countries also show us that an abundant supply of a natural resource is not in itself enough to create a modern industrial economy. On the other hand, Japan has one of the most developed economies in the world, yet has few natural resources. Connecticut is consistently the most productive of the United States measured in per capita income, but the state has little in the way of natural resources (its main natural resource is gravel). In fact, many researchers believe that reliance on resource wealth can be something of a curse for a nation.

Financial Institutions

Another requirement for development is an adequate and trusted system of financial institutions. An important source of funds for investment is the savings of households and firms. People in some developing countries have little confidence in their currency because some governments finance a large fraction of public outlays by printing money. This practice results in high inflation and sometimes very high inflation, or hyperinflation, as has occurred recently in Zimbabwe, where annual inflation topped 11 million percent in 2008. High and unpredictable inflation discourages saving and hurts development.

Developing countries have special problems because banks are often viewed with suspicion. At the first sign of economic problems, many depositors withdraw their funds. Because banks cannot rely on a continuous supply of deposits, they cannot make loans for extended periods. If financial institutions fail to serve as intermediaries between savers and borrowers, the lack of funds for investment becomes an obstacle to growth. During the global financial crisis of 2008–2009, banks in industrial market countries also suffered from decreased confidence. One measure of banking presence is the credit provided by banks as a percent of a nation's total output. This percentage is more than five times greater in high-income countries than in low-income countries.

Capital Infrastructure

Production and exchange depend on a reliable infrastructure of transportation, communication, sanitation, and electricity. Roads, bridges, airports, harbors, and other transportation facilities are vital to commercial activity. Reliable mail service, telephone communication, clean water, and electricity are also essential for advanced production techniques. Imagine how difficult it would be to run even a personal computer if the supply of electricity and access to the Internet were unavailable or continually interrupted, as is often the case in many developing countries.

Some developing countries have serious deficiencies in their physical infrastructures. As just one measure, Exhibit 5 shows the number of fixed and mobile telephone lines per 1,000 people in 2006–2007 for the 12 countries examined earlier. The top four countries, three of which are high-income economies, have about 7 times more phones per 1,000 people than the bottom four countries, three of which are low-income economies. The United Kingdom, the top-rated in this category, had 1,734 phone lines per 1,000 people. Bottom-ranked Burundi had just 33 phone lines per 1,000 people.

Phone lines help knit together an economy's communications network. Countries without reliable phone service have difficulty not only communicating but reaping the benefits of other technology advances, such as the Internet. Exhibit 6 on the next page shows Internet users as a percent of the population in 2007–2008 for our sample countries. There is an unmistakable digital divide between high-income and low-income economies. In the four high-income economies, an average 67.3 percent of the population used the Internet. The United States, which developed the Internet, topped the group at 73.4 percent. In low-income economies, just 7.2 percent used the Internet on average. At the bottom is Burundi, where only 0.7 percent, or seven out of every 1,000 people, used the Internet. Even in India, which has

Exhibit 5

Phone Lines Per 1,000 People for the Sample of High-, Middle-, and Low-Income Economies

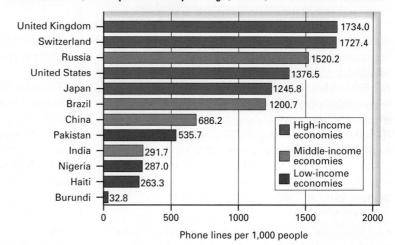

SOURCE: Computed based on fixed and mobile line estimates from the Central Intelligence Agency's *World Factbook: 2008* at www.cia.gov/library/publications/the-world-factbook/index.html.

Exhibit 6

Internet Users as Percent of Population for the Sample of High-, Middle-, and Low-Income Economies

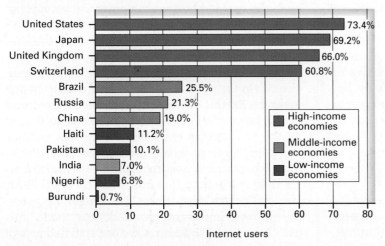

United States	73.4%
Japan	69.2%
United Kingdom	66.0%
Switzerland	60.8%
Brazil	25.5%
Russia	21.3%
China	19.0%
Haiti	11.2%
Pakistan	10.1%
India	7.0%
Nigeria	6.8%
Burundi	0.7%

Legend:
- High-income economies
- Middle-income economies
- Low-income economies

Internet users

SOURCE: Computed from used estimates in the Central Intelligence Agency's *World Factbook: 2008* at www.cla.gov/library/publications/the-world-factbook/index.html.

a reputation as computer savvy, what with all the online support centers and software companies we read about, only 7.0 percent of the population were Internet users. Indian colleges average only one computer for every 229 students.[1]

Entrepreneurial Ability

An economy can have abundant supplies of labor, capital, and natural resources, but without entrepreneurial ability, the other resources will not be combined efficiently to produce goods and services. Unless a country has entrepreneurs who are able to bring together resources and take the risk of profit or loss, development may never get off the ground. Many developing countries were once under colonial rule, a system of government that offered the local population fewer opportunities to develop entrepreneurial skills.

Government officials sometimes decide that entrepreneurs are unable to generate the kind of economic growth the country needs. State enterprises are therefore created to do what government believes the free market cannot do. But state-owned enterprises may have objectives other than producing goods efficiently—objectives that could include providing jobs for friends and relatives of government officials.

social capital
the shared values and trust that promote cooperation in the economy

***
1. Shailaja Neelakantan, "India's Prime Minister Assails Universities as Below Average and 'Dysfunctional,'" *Chronicle of Higher Education,* 25 June 2007.

Rules of the Game

Finally, in addition to human capital, natural resources, financial institutions, capital infrastructure, and entrepreneurial ability, a successful economy needs reliable *rules of the game.* Perhaps the most elusive ingredients for development are the formal and informal institutions that promote production and exchange: the laws, customs, conventions, and other institutional elements that sustain an economy. A stable political environment with well-defined property rights is important. Little private-sector investment will occur if potential investors believe their capital might be appropriated by government, destroyed by civil unrest, or stolen by thieves.

High-income economies have developed a reliable and respected system of property rights and customs and conventions that nurture productive activity. These successful economies have cultivated the social capital that helps the economy run more smoothly. Social capital consists of the shared values and trust that promote cooperation in the economy. Low-income economies typically have poorly defined property rights, less social capital, and, in the extreme, customs and conventions where bribery is commonplace and government corruption is an everyday practice. Worse still, civil wars have ravaged some of the poorest countries on Earth. Such violence and uncertainty make people less willing to invest in their own future or in the future of their country.

Although it is common to sort countries into advanced industrial economies and developing economies, there are broad differences among developing economies.

Income Distribution Within Countries

Thus far the focus has been on income differences across countries, and these differences can be vast. But what about income differences within a country. Are poor countries uniformly poor or are there sizable income differences within a given nation's population. One way to measure inequality across households is to look at the share of national income going to the poorest fifth of the population. As a point of reference, in the unlikely event that income in an economy were evenly distributed across all households, then the poorest fifth would also receive exactly one-fifth, or 20 percent, of national income. More realistically, the poorest fifth receives less than 20 percent of the income, but how much less? Is the percentage of income going to the poorest fifth higher for low-income countries than for high-income countries? In other words, is income more evenly distributed among people in poor countries than among people in rich countries? Not necessarily. Among our 12 nations, the poorest fifth of the population got an average of 7.4 percent of the income in the high-income countries, 5.4 percent in middle-income countries, and 5.4 percent in low-income countries. So, at least in this sample, income was less evenly distributed in middle- or low-income countries than in high-income countries.

LO³ International Trade and Development

Developing countries need to trade with developed countries to acquire the capital and technology that will increase labor productivity on the farm, in the factory, in the office, and in the home. To import capital and technology, developing countries must first acquire the funds, or foreign exchange, needed to pay for imports. Exports usually generate more than half of the annual flow of foreign exchange in developing countries. Foreign aid and private investment make up the rest.

Trade Problems for Developing Countries

Primary products, such as agricultural goods and other raw materials, make up the bulk of exports from developing countries, just as manufactured goods make up the bulk of exports from industrial countries. About half the merchandise exports from low-income

> **EXPORTS USUALLY GENERATE MORE THAN HALF OF THE ANNUAL FLOW OF FOREIGN EXCHANGE IN DEVELOPING COUNTRIES.**

countries consist of raw materials, compared to only 20 percent from high-income countries. A problem for developing countries is that the prices of primary products, such as coffee, cocoa, sugar, and rubber, fluctuate more widely than do the prices of finished goods, because crop supply fluctuates with the weather.

When developing countries experience trade deficits, they often try to restrict imports. Because imported food is sometimes critical to survival, developing countries are more likely to cut imports of capital goods—the very items needed to promote long-term growth and productivity. Thus many developing countries cannot afford the modern machinery that will help them become more productive. Developing countries must also confront industrial countries' trade restrictions, such as tariffs and quotas, which often discriminate against primary products. For example, the United States strictly limits sugar imports.

Migration and the Brain Drain

Migration plays an important role in the economies of developing countries. A major source of foreign exchange in some countries is the money sent home by migrants who find jobs in industrial countries. According to the World Bank, migrants sent home about $283 billion in 2008. Thus migration provides a valuable safety valve for poor countries. But there is a downside. Often the best and the brightest professionals, such as doctors, nurses, and engineers, migrate to developed countries. For example, every year thousands of nurses migrate from countries such as Kenya and the Philippines to the United States, where half the world's nurses are employed. The financial attraction is powerful: a nurse in the Philippines would start there at less than $2,000 a year, compared with at least $36,000 in the United States.[2]

The Philippines economy benefits from the billions sent home by overseas workers. So the upside of the brain drain for the poor country is the remittances sent home by overseas workers. Still, a nation is hurt when its best and brightest leave for opportunities elsewhere. Some African countries are demanding compensation for educating the doctors and nurses who move to high-income economies.

© FOODPIX/JUPITERIMAGES

2. Celia Dugger, "U.S. Plan to Lure Nurses May Hurt Poor Countries," *New York Times,* 24 May 2006.

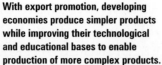

With export promotion, developing economies produce simpler products while improving their technological and educational bases to enable production of more complex products.

Import Substitution Versus Export Promotion

An economy's progress usually involves moving up the production chain from agriculture and raw material to manufacturing and then to services. If a country is fortunate, this transformation occurs gradually through natural market forces. For example, in 1850 most U.S. jobs were in agriculture. Now most jobs are in the service sector. Sometimes governments try to speed up the evolution. Many developing countries, including Argentina and India, pursued a strategy called import substitution, whereby domestic manufacturers would make products that until then had been imported. To insulate domestic manufacturers from foreign competition, the government imposed stiff tariffs and quotas. This development strategy became popular for several reasons. First, demand already existed for these products, so the "what to produce" question was easily answered. Second, import substitution provided infant industries a protected market. Finally, import substitution was popular with those who supplied resources to the favored domestic industries.

Like all trade protection, however, import substitution erased the gains from specialization and comparative advantage among countries. Often the developing country replaced low-cost foreign goods with high-cost domestic goods. And domestic producers, shielded from foreign competition, usually failed to become efficient. Worse still, other countries often retaliated with their own trade restrictions.

Critics of import substitution claim that export promotion is a surer path to economic development. Export promotion concentrates on producing for the export market. This development strategy begins with relatively simple products, such as textiles. As a developing country builds its technological and educational base—that is, as the developing economy learns by doing—producers can then make more complex products for export.

import substitution a development strategy that emphasizes domestic manufacturing of products that had been imported

export promotion a development strategy that concentrates on producing for the export market

Economists favor export promotion over import substitution because the emphasis is on comparative advantage and trade expansion rather than on trade restriction. Export promotion also forces producers to become more efficient in order to compete on world markets. Research shows that facing global competition boosts domestic efficiency.[3] What's more, export promotion requires less government intervention in the market than does import substitution.

Of the two approaches, export promotion has been more successful around the world. For example, the newly industrialized countries of East Asia have successfully pursued export promotion, while Argentina, India, and Peru have failed with their import substitution approach. In 1965, the newly industrialized economies of Hong Kong, Korea, Singapore, and Taiwan had an average income only 20 percent that of high-income countries. Now these four are themselves high-income countries. Most Latin American nations, which for decades had favored import substitution, are now pursuing free trade agreements with each other and with the United States. Even India is dismantling trade barriers, with an emphasis on importing high-technology capital goods. One slogan of Indian trade officials is "Microchips, yes! Potato chips, no!"

Trade Liberalization and Special Interests

Although most people would benefit from freer international trade, some would be worse off. Consequently, governments in some developing countries have difficulty pursuing policies conducive to development. Often the gains from economic development are widespread, but the beneficiaries, such as consumers, do not recognize their potential gains. On the other hand, the losers tend to be concentrated, such as producers in an industry that had been sheltered from foreign competition, and they know quite well the source of their losses. So the government often lacks

***

3. See Martin Baily and Hans Gersbach, "Efficiency in Manufacturing and the Need for Global Competition," in *Brookings Papers on Economic Activity: Microeconomics,* M. Baily, P. Reiss, and C. Winston, eds. (Brookings Institution, 1995): 307–347.

© INSIDEOUT PIX/JUPITER IMAGES / © STOCKBYTE/GETTY IMAGES

the political will and support to remove impediments to development, because the potential losers fight reforms that might harm their livelihood while the potential winners remain largely unaware of what's at stake. What's more, consumers have difficulty organizing even if they become aware of what's going on. A recent study by the World Bank suggests a strong link in Africa between governments that cater to special-interest groups and low rates of economic growth.

Nonetheless, many developing countries have been opening their borders to freer trade. People around the world have been exposed to information about the opportunities and goods available on world markets. So consumers want the goods and firms want the technology and capital that are available abroad. Both groups want government to ease trade restrictions. Studies by the World Bank and others have underscored the successes of countries that have adopted trade liberalization policies.

> Because poor countries do not generate enough savings to fund an adequate level of investment, these countries often rely on foreign financing.

LO⁴ Foreign Aid and Economic Development

We have already seen that because poor countries do not generate enough savings to fund an adequate level of investment, these countries often rely on foreign financing. Private international borrowing and lending are heavily restricted by the governments of developing countries. Governments may allow residents to purchase foreign exchange only for certain purposes. In some developing countries, different exchange rates apply to different categories of transactions. Thus the local currency is not easily convertible into other currencies. Some developing countries also require foreign investors to find a local partner who must be granted controlling interest. All these restrictions discourage foreign investment. In this section, we will look primarily at foreign aid and its link to economic development.

Foreign Aid

Foreign aid is any international transfer made on *concessional* (i.e., especially favorable) terms for the purposes of promoting economic development. Foreign aid includes grants, which need not be repaid, and loans extended on more favorable repayment terms than the recipient could normally secure. Concessional loans have lower interest rates, longer repayment periods, or grace periods during which repayments

are reduced or even waived (similar to some student loans). Foreign aid can take the form of money, capital goods, technical assistance, food, and so forth.

Some foreign aid is granted by a specific country, such as the United States, to another specific country, such as the Philippines. Country-to-country aid is called *bilateral* assistance. Other foreign aid goes through international bodies such as the World Bank. Assistance provided by organizations that use funds from a number of countries is called *multilateral*. For example, the World Bank provides loans and grants to support activities that are viewed as prerequisites for development, such as health and education programs or basic development projects like dams, roads, and communications networks. And the International Monetary Fund extends loans to countries that have trouble with their balance of payments.

During the last four decades, the United States has provided the developing world with over $400 billion in aid. Since 1961, most U.S. aid has been coordinated by the U.S. Agency for International Development (USAID), which is part of the U.S. Department of State. This agency concentrates primarily on health, education, and agriculture, providing both technical assistance and loans. USAID emphasizes long-range plans to meet the basic needs of the poor and to promote self-sufficiency. Foreign aid is a controversial, though relatively small, part of the federal budget. Since 1993, official U.S. aid has been less than 0.2 percent of U.S. GDP, compared to an average of 0.3 percent from 21 other industrialized nations.

Does Foreign Aid Promote Economic Development?

In general, foreign aid provides additional purchasing power and thus the possibility of increased investment, capital imports, and consumption. But it remains unclear whether foreign aid *supplements* domestic saving, thus increasing investment, or simply *substitutes* for domestic saving, thereby increasing consumption rather than investment. What is clear is that foreign aid often becomes a source of discretionary funds that benefit not the poor but their leaders. Historically, more than 90 percent of the funds distributed by USAID have gone to governments, whose leaders assume responsibility for distributing these funds.

Much bilateral funding is tied to purchases of

foreign aid
an international transfer made on especially favorable terms for the purpose of promoting economic development

goods and services from the donor nation, and such programs can sometimes be counterproductive. For example, in the 1950s, the United States began the Food for Peace program, which helped sell U.S. farm products abroad, but some recipient governments sold that food to finance poorly conceived projects. Worse yet, the availability of low-priced food from abroad drove down farm prices in the developing countries, hurting poor farmers there.

Foreign aid may have raised the standard of living in some developing countries, but it has not necessarily increased their ability to become self-supporting at that higher standard of living. Many countries that receive aid are doing less of what they had done well. Their agricultural sectors have suffered. For example, though we should be careful when drawing conclusions about causality, per capita food production in Africa has fallen since 1960. Outside aid has often insulated government officials from their own incompetence and fundamental troubles of their own economies. No country receiving U.S. aid in the past 25 years has moved up in status from developing to industrial. And most countries today that have achieved industrial status did so without foreign aid.

Because of disappointment with the results of government aid, the trend is toward channeling funds through private nonprofit agencies such as CARE. More than half of foreign aid now flows through private channels. The privatization of foreign aid follows a larger trend toward privatization around the world. We discuss that important development in the balance of this chapter.

LO⁵ Transitional Economies

As we have seen, there is no widely accepted theory of economic development, but around the world, markets have replaced central plans in once-socialist countries. Economic developments in these emerging market economies have tremendous significance for those who study economics. Like geologists, economists must rely primarily on natural experiments to figure out how things work. *The attempt to replace central planning with markets has been one of the greatest economic experiments in history.* In the study of geology, this would be comparable to a huge earthquake. In this section, we take a look at these so-called transitional economies.

Types of Economic Systems

First, let's briefly review economic systems. Chapter 2 considered the three questions that every economic system must answer: what to produce, how to produce it, and for whom to produce it. Laws regarding resource ownership and the role of government in resource allocation determine the "rules of the game"—the incentives and constraints that guide the behavior of individual decision makers. Economic systems can be classified based on the ownership of resources, the way resources are allocated to produce goods and services, and the incentives used to motivate people.

As we discussed in Chapter 2, resources in *capitalist* systems are owned mostly by individuals and are allocated through market coordination. In socialist economies, resources other than labor are owned by the state. For example, a country such as Cuba or North Korea carefully limits the private ownership of resources such as land and capital. Each country employs a slightly different system of resource ownership, resource allocation, and individual incentives to answer the three economic questions.

So under capitalism, the rules of the game include private ownership of most resources and the coordination of economic activity by price signals generated by market forces; market coordination answers the three questions. Under socialism, the rules of the game include government ownership of most resources and the allocation of resources through central plans.

Enterprises and Soft Budget Constraints

In the socialist system, enterprises that earn a "profit" see that profit appropriated by the state. Firms that end up with a loss find that loss covered by a state subsidy. Thus socialist enterprises face what has been called a soft budget constraint. This can lead to inefficiency, a lack of response to changes in supply or demand, and poor investment decisions. Quality has also been a problem under central planning, because plant managers would rather meet production quotas than satisfy consumer demand. For example, plant managers do not score extra bureaucratic points by producing garments that are in style and in popular sizes. Tales of shoddy products in socialist systems abound.

Most prices in centrally planned economies are established not by market forces but by central planners. As a result, consumers have less say in what to produce. Once set, prices tend to be inflexible. For example, in the former Soviet Union, the price of a cabbage slicer was stamped on the metal at the factory. In the spirit of equity, Soviet planners priced most consumer goods below the market-clearing level, so shortages (or "interruptions in supply," as they were called) were common. For example, as of 1990, the price of bread in the former Soviet Union

soft budget constraint the budget condition faced by socialist enterprises that are subsidized if they lose money

had not changed since 1954, and that price in 1990 amounted to just 7 percent of bread's production cost. Meat prices had not changed since 1962. Some rents had not changed in 60 years.

Capitalist economies equate quantity demanded with quantity supplied through the *invisible hand* of market coordination; centrally planned economies try to equate the two using the *visible hand* of bureaucratic coordination assisted by taxes and subsidies. If quantity supplied and quantity demanded are not in balance, something has to give. In a capitalist system, what gives is the price. In a centrally planned economy, what usually gives is the central plan itself. A common problem in the Soviet system was that the amount produced often fell short of planned production. When the quantity supplied fell below the planned amount, central planners reduced the amount supplied to each sector, cutting critical sectors such as heavy industry and the military the least and cutting lower-priority sectors such as consumer products the most. Evidence of shortages of consumer goods included long waiting lines at retail stores; empty store shelves; the "tips," or bribes, shop operators expected for supplying scarce consumer goods; and higher prices for the same goods on the black market. Shoppers would sometimes wait in line all night and into the next day. Consumers often relied on "connections" through acquaintances to obtain most goods and services. Scarce goods were frequently diverted to the black market.

LO⁶ Markets and Institutions

A study of economic systems underscores the importance of institutions in the course of development. *Institutions,* or "rules of the game," are the incentives and constraints that structure political, economic, and social interaction. They consist of (1) formal rules of behavior, such as a constitution, laws, and property rights, and (2) informal constraints on behavior, such as sanctions, manners, customs, traditions, and codes of conduct. Throughout history, institutions have been devised by people to create order and reduce uncertainty in exchange. Thus underlying the surface of economic behavior is a grid of informal, often unconscious, habits, customs, manners, and norms that make markets possible. *A reliable system of property rights and enforceable contracts is a prerequisite for creating incentives that support a healthy market economy.*

Together with the standard constraints of economics, such as income, resource availability, and prices, institutions shape the incentive structure of an economy. As the incentive structure evolves, it can direct economic change toward growth, stagnation, or decline. Economic history is largely a story of economies that have failed to produce a set of economic rules of the game that lead to sustained economic growth. After all, most of the world's economies are still developing—still trying to get their act together.

Customs and conventions can sometimes be obstacles to development. In developed market economies, resource owners tend to supply their resources where they are most valued; but in developing countries, links to the family or clan may be the most important consideration. For example, in some cultures, children, particularly male children, are expected to remain in their father's occupation even though some are better suited for other lines of work. Family businesses may resist growth because such growth would involve hiring people from outside the family.

Institutions and Economic Development

> " A reliable system of property rights and enforceable contracts is a prerequisite for creating incentives that support a healthy market economy. "

Institutions shape the incentive structure of an economy, but, as already noted, most countries in the world have failed to come up with the rules of the game that lead to sustained economic growth. Although political and judicial decisions may change formal rules overnight, informal constraints embodied in manners, customs, traditions, and codes of conduct are more immune to deliberate policies. For example, respect for the law cannot be legislated.

Prior to the market reforms in the former Soviet Union, widespread corruption and a lack of faith in formal institutions were woven into the social fabric. Workers bribed officials to get good jobs, and consumers bribed clerks to get desired products. Bribery became a way of life, a way of dealing with the distortions that arise when prices are not allowed to allocate resources efficiently.

In centrally planned economies, the exchange relationship was typically personal, based as it was on bureaucratic ties on the production side and inside connections on the consumption side. But in the United States and other market economies, successful institutional evolution permits the impersonal exchange necessary to capture the potential economic benefits of specialization and modern technology. Impersonal exchange allows for a far greater division of labor, but it requires a richer and more stable institutional setting.

The Big Bang Versus Gradualism

The Hungarian economist Janos Kornai believes that a market order should be grown from the bottom up. First, small-scale capitalism in farming, trade, light manufacturing, and services thrives. These grassroots markets can serve as a foundation for the privatization of larger industrial sectors. Large industrial enterprises should quickly find the market-clearing price so that input and output decisions are consistent with market preferences. In the meantime, state-owned enterprises should be run more like businesses in which state directors attempt to maximize profit. Money-losing enterprises should be phased out. This "bottom-up" approach proposed by Kornai could be termed gradualism, which can be contrasted with a big-bang theory, whereby the transition from central planning to a market economy would occur in a matter of months.

One example of gradualism is taking place in China. In 1978, the government began dismantling agricultural communes in favor of a "household-responsibility" system of small-farm agriculture. Land was assigned to individual families, who could keep any excess production after meeting specific state-imposed goals. Initially the system was to be applied only to the poorest 20 percent of rural areas. Once the positive effects became apparent, however, the system spread on its own. Eventually farmers established their own wholesale and retail marketing systems and were allowed to sell directly to urban areas at market-clearing prices. This gave rise to a market for truckers to buy, transport, and resell farm products. Over the next seven years, agricultural output increased by an impressive 8 to 10 percent per year.

gradualism
a "bottom-up" approach to moving gradually from a centrally planned to a market economy by establishing markets at the most decentralized level first, such as on small farms or in light industry

big-bang theory
the argument that the transition from a centrally planned to a market economy should be broad and swift, taking place in a matter of months

privatization
the process of turning public enterprises into private enterprises

transparent finances
a firm's financial records that clearly indicate the economic health of the company

Privatization

Privatization is the process of turning public enterprises into private enterprises. It is the opposite of *nationalization* (what Hugo Chávez has been doing in Venezuela). For example, Russian privatization began in April 1992 with the sale of municipally owned shops. Although most property in countries of the former Soviet Union was nominally owned by the state, it often remained unclear who had the authority to sell the property and who should receive the proceeds. This ambiguity resulted in cases in which the same property was purchased from different officials by different buyers. Yet *there was no clear legal process for resolving title disputes*. Worse still, some enterprises have been stripped of their assets by self-serving managers, a process that derisively came to be called "spontaneous" privatization. The necessarily complex process of privatization was undermined because the general population perceived it as unfair.

Privatization also requires modern accounting and other information systems, the training of competent managers, and the installation of adequate facilities for telecommunication, computing, travel, and transportation. This transformation cannot be accomplished overnight. Consider just the accounting problem. A market economy depends on financial accounting rules as well as on an independent system for auditing financial reports. The needed information must show up in a company's balance sheet and income statement. Prospective buyers of enterprises need such information, as do banks and other lenders. Thus, a firm's finances should be transparent, meaning someone should be able to look at the books and the balance sheet and tell exactly what's going on.

By all reports, the accounting systems of most formerly socialist firms are almost worthless. For decades, data had been aimed more at central planners, who wanted to know about *physical* flows, than at someone who wanted to know about the efficiency and financial promise of the firm. So there is much information, but little that is relevant. Incidentally, the major advantage of the market economy is that it minimizes the need for the kind of resource-flow data that had been reported under central planning. *Prices convey most of the information necessary to coordinate economic activity among firms.*

Institutional Requirements of Efficient Markets

Some may look at the initial instability that resulted from the dismantling of socialist states and argue that the move toward markets has been a failure. But in the former Soviet Union the state dismantled central controls before institutions such as property rights, customs, codes of conduct, and a legal system were in place.

Tax laws are applied unevenly and the rates change frequently. For example, the personal income tax in Russia jumped from a graduated rate topping at 13 percent to a flat rate of 60 percent, to a graduated rate topping at 40 percent, then 30 percent, then to a flat rate of 13 percent. The low flat rate seems to be popular and has increased revenue more than 10 percent a year since its adoption in 2001. Russian expert Marshall Goldman has argued that "tax evasion by both enterprises and individuals is a source of pride dating back to czarist times."[4] Millions of Russians carry out their business in the underground economy.

The shift from central planning to a market economy has been rough going in Russia. Simply loosening constraints to create private property may not be enough for successful reform. The development of supporting institutions is essential, but *there is no unified economic theory of how to construct the institutions that are central to the success of capitalism.* Most so-called economists employed in Soviet-type systems did not understand even the basics of how markets work. They had been trained to regard the alleged "anarchy" of the market as a primary defect of capitalism.

A more fundamental problem is that, although Western economic theory focuses on the operation of efficient markets, *even market economists usually do not understand the institutional requirements of efficient markets.* Market economists often take the necessary institutions for granted. Those involved in the transition must develop a deeper appreciation for the institutions that nurture and support impersonal market activity.

So the jury is still out on the transition to markets. Exhibit 7 presents, for 10 key transitional economies, the gross domestic product (GDP) per capita in 2008 based on the purchasing power of the domestic currency. Notice the dramatic differences across these economies, with GDP per capita in the Czech Republic more than nine times greater than that of Vietnam. Russia ranked about halfway between those two. Seven of the 10 countries are middle-income economies. Vietnam is a low-income economy but on the

---

4. Marshall Goldman, "Russian Tax Evasion Is Source of Pride," letter to the editor, *New York Times,* 9 August 1998.

Exhibit 7

GDP Per Capita for Transitional Economies in 2008

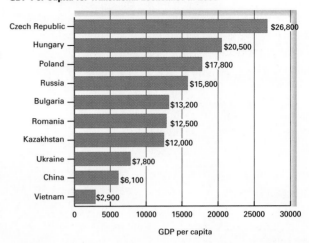

GDP per capita

SOURCE: Computed from estimates in the Central Intelligence Agency's *World Factbook: 2008* at www.cia.gov/library/publications/the-world-factbook/index.html. Figures are based on the purchasing power of the local currency.

way up. So far, only the Czech Republic and Hungary have become high-income nations.

Lessons about the nature of economic processes will likely emerge from the analysis of these transitional economies. The course of economic reform will provide insights into both the potential and the limits of economics itself.

Final Word

Because no single theory of economic development has become widely accepted, this chapter has been more descriptive than theoretical. We can readily identify the features that distinguish developing from industrial economies. Education is key to development, both because of its direct effect on productivity and because those who are more educated tend to be more receptive to new ideas. A physical infrastructure of transportation and communication systems and utilities is needed to link economic participants. And trusted financial institutions help link savers and borrowers. A country needs entrepreneurs with the vision to move the economy forward. Finally, the most elusive ingredients are the laws, manners, customs, and ways of doing business that nurture economic development. Economic history is largely a story of economies that have failed to produce a set of economic rules of the game that lead to sustained economic growth. Some newly emerging industrial countries in Asia show that economic development is still achievable.

Problems Appendix

CHAPTER 1

LO¹ Explain the economic problem of scarce resources and unlimited wants

1.1. *(Definition of Economics)* What determines whether or not a resource is scarce? Why is the concept of scarcity important to the definition of economics?

LO² Describe the forces that shape economic choices

2.1. *(Rational Self-Interest)* Discuss the impact of rational self-interest on each of the following decisions:
   a. Whether to attend college full time or enter the workforce full time
   b. Whether to buy a new textbook or a used one
   c. Whether to attend a local college or an out-of-town college
2.2. *(Rational Self-Interest)* If behavior is governed by rational self-interest, why do people make charitable contributions of time and money?
2.3. *(Marginal Analysis)* The owner of a small pizzeria is deciding whether to increase the radius of delivery area by one mile. What considerations must be taken into account if such a decision is to increase profitability?
2.4. *(Time and Information)* It is often costly to obtain the information necessary to make good decisions. Yet your own interests can be best served by rationally weighing all options available to you. This requires informed decision making. Does this mean that making uninformed decisions is irrational? How do you determine how much information is the right amount?

LO³ Explain the relationship between economic theory and economic reality

3.1. *(Role of Theory)* What good is economic theory if it can't predict the behavior of a specific individual?

LO⁴ Identify some pitfalls of economic analysis

4.1. *(Pitfalls of Economic Analysis)* Review the discussion of pitfalls in economic thinking in this chapter. Then identify the fallacy, or mistake in thinking, in each of the following statements:
   a. Raising taxes always increases government revenues.
   b. Whenever there is a recession, imports decrease. Therefore, to stop a recession, we should increase imports.
   c. Raising the tariff on imported steel helps the U.S. steel industry. Therefore, the entire economy is helped.

   d. Gold sells for about $900 per ounce. Therefore, the U.S. government could sell all the gold in Fort Knox at $900 per ounce and reduce the national debt.
4.2. *(Association Versus Causation)* Suppose I observe that communities with lots of doctors tend to have relatively high rates of illness. I conclude that doctors cause illness. What's wrong with this reasoning?

LO⁵ Describe several reasons to study economics

5.1. *(Studying Economics)* According to the text, economics majors on average make more money than most other majors and have more job opportunities. Are these the primary motivations one might have for studying economics? What are your motivations for studying economics?

CHAPTER 2

LO¹ Describe the impact of choice on opportunity

1.1. *(Sunk Cost and Choice)* Suppose you go to a restaurant and buy an expensive meal. Halfway through, despite feeling quite full, you decide to clean your plate. After all, you think, you paid for the meal, so you are going to eat all of it. What's wrong with this thinking?
1.2. *(Opportunity Cost)* You can either spend spring break working at home for $80 per day for five days or go to Florida for the week. If you stay home, your expenses will total about $100. If you go to Florida, the airfare, hotel, food, and miscellaneous expenses will total about $700. What's your opportunity cost of going to Florida?

LO² Explain how comparative advantage, specialization, and exchange affect economic outcomes (output)

2.1. *(Absolute and Comparative Advantage)* You have the following information concerning the production of wheat and cloth in the United States and the United Kingdom:

| | **Labor Hours Required to Produce One Unit** | |
	United Kingdom	**United States**
Wheat	2	1
Cloth	6	5

   a. What is the opportunity cost of producing a unit of wheat in the United Kingdom? In the United States?
   b. Which country has an absolute advantage in producing wheat? In producing cloth?
   c. Which country has a comparative advantage in producing

wheat? In producing cloth?

    d. Which country should specialize in producing wheat? In producing cloth?

2.2. *(Specialization)* Provide some examples of specialized markets or retail outlets. What makes the Web so conducive to specialization?

LO³ Outline how economies function as production systems

3.1. *(Shape of the PPF)* Suppose a production possibilities frontier includes the following combinations:

Cars	Washing Machines
0	1,000
100	600
200	0

    a. Graph the PPF, assuming that it has no curved segments.

    b. What is the cost of producing an additional car when 50 cars are being produced?

    c. What is the cost of producing an additional car when 150 cars are being produced?

    d. What is the cost of producing an additional washing machine when 50 cars are being produced? When 150 cars are being produced?

    e. What do your answers tell you about opportunity costs?

3.2. *(Production Possibilities)* Suppose an economy uses two resources (labor and capital) to produce two goods (wheat and cloth). Capital is relatively more useful in producing cloth, and labor is relatively more useful in producing wheat. If the supply of capital falls by 10 percent and the supply of labor increases by 10 percent, how will the PPF for wheat and cloth change?

3.3. *(Production Possibilities)* There's no reason why a production possibilities frontier could not be used to represent the situation facing an individual. Imagine your own PPF. Right now—today—you have certain resources—your time, your skills, perhaps some capital. And you can produce various outputs. Suppose you can produce combinations of two outputs, call them studying and partying.

    a. Draw your PPF for studying and partying. Be sure to label the axes of the diagram appropriately. Label the points where the PPF intersects the axes, as well as several other points along the frontier.

    b. Explain what it would mean for you to move upward and to the left along your personal PPF. What kinds of adjustments would you have to make in your life to make such a movement along the frontier?

    c. Under what circumstances would your personal PPF shift outward? Do you think the shift would be a "parallel" one? Why, or why not?

3.4. *(Shifting Production Possibilities)* Determine whether each of the following would cause the economy's PPF to shift inward, outward, or not at all:

    a. An increase in average length of annual vacations

    b. An increase in immigration

    c. A decrease in the average retirement age

    d. The migration of skilled workers to other countries

LO⁴ Describe different economic systems and the decision-making rules that define them

4.1. *(Economic Systems)* The United States is best described as having a mixed economy. What are some elements of command in the U.S. economy? What are some elements of tradition?

CHAPTER 3

LO¹ Explain the role of the household in an economic system

1.1. *(Evolution of the Household)* Determine whether each of the following would increase or decrease the opportunity costs for mothers who choose not to work outside the home. Explain your answers.

    a. Higher levels of education for women

    b. Higher unemployment rates for women

    c. Higher average pay levels for women

    d. Lower demand for labor in industries that traditionally employ large numbers of women

1.2. *(Household Production)* Many households supplement their food budget by cultivating small vegetable gardens. Explain how each of the following might influence this kind of household production:

    a. Both husband and wife are professionals who earn high salaries.

    b. The household is located in a city rather than in a rural area.

    c. The household is located in a region where there is a high sales tax on food.

    d. The household is located in a region that has a high property tax rate.

1.3. *(Household Production)* What factors does a householder consider when deciding whether to produce a good or service at home or buy it in the marketplace?

1.4. *(Objectives of the Economic Decision Makers)* In economic analysis, what are the assumed objectives of households, firms, and the government?

LO² Identify the different types of firms and describe their roles in the economy

2.1. *(Corporations)* How did the institution of the firm get a boost from the advent of the Industrial Revolution? What type of business organization existed before this?

2.2. *(Sole Proprietorships)* What are the disadvantages of the sole proprietorship form of business?

2.3. *(Cooperatives)* How do cooperatives differ from typical businesses?

2.4. *(Evolution of the Firm)* Explain how production after the Industrial Revolution differed from production under the cottage industry system.

LO³ Outline the ways governments affect their economies

3.1. *(Government)* Complete each of the following sentences:

    a. When the private operation of a market leads to overproduction or underproduction of some good, this is known as a(n) _____.

b. Goods that are nonrival and nonexcludable are known as
_____.

c. _____ are cash or in-kind benefits given to individuals as outright grants from the government.

d. A(n) _____ confers an external benefit on third parties that are not directly involved in a market transaction.

e. _____ refers to the government's pursuit of full employment and price stability through variations in taxes and government spending.

3.2. *(Tax Rates)* Suppose taxes are related to income level as follows:

Income	Taxes
$1,000	$200
$2,000	$350
$3,000	$450

a. What percentage of income is paid in taxes at each level?

b. Is the tax rate progressive, proportional, or regressive?

c. What is the marginal tax rate on the first $1,000 of income? The second $1,000? The third $1,000?

3.3. *(Government Revenue)* What are the sources of government revenue in the United States? Which types of taxes are most important at each level of government? Which two taxes provide the most revenue to the federal government?

3.4. *(Externalities)* Suppose there is an external cost, or negative externality, associated with production of a certain good. What's wrong with letting the market determine how much of this good will be produced?

LO⁴ Outline the international influences on an economy

4.1. *(International Trade)* Why does international trade occur? What does it mean to run a deficit in the merchandise trade balance?

4.2. *(International Trade)* Distinguish between a tariff and a quota. Who benefits from and who is harmed by such restrictions on imports?

CHAPTER 4

LO¹ Explain how the law of demand affects market activity

1.1. *(Shifting Demand)* Using demand and supply curves, show the effect of each of the following on the market for cigarettes:

a. A cure for lung cancer is found.

b. The price of cigars increases.

c. Wages increase substantially in states that grow tobacco.

d. A fertilizer that increases the yield per acre of tobacco is discovered.

e. There is a sharp increase in the price of matches, lighters, and lighter fluid.

f. More states pass laws restricting smoking in restaurants and public places.

1.2. *(Substitutes and Complements)* For each of the following pair of goods, determine whether the goods are substitutes, complements, or unrelated:

a. Peanut butter and jelly

b. Private and public transportation

c. Coke and Pepsi

d. Alarm clocks and automobiles

e. Golf clubs and golf balls

LO² Explain how the law of supply affects market activity

2.1. *(Supply)* What is the law of supply? Give an example of how you have observed the law of supply at work. What is the relationship between the law of supply and the supply curve?

LO³ Describe how the interaction between supply and demand creates markets

3.1. *(Demand and Supply)* How do you think each of the following affected the world price of oil? (Use demand and supply analysis.)

a. Tax credits were offered for expenditures on home insulation.

b. The Alaskan oil pipeline was completed.

c. The ceiling on the price of oil was removed.

d. Oil was discovered in the North Sea.

e. Sport utility vehicles and minivans became popular.

f. The use of nuclear power declined.

3.2. *(Demand and Supply)* What happens to the equilibrium price and quantity of ice cream in response to each of the following? Explain your answers.

a. The price of dairy cow fodder increases.

b. The price of beef decreases.

c. Concerns arise about the fat content of ice cream. Simultaneously, the price of sugar (used to produce ice cream) increases.

LO⁴ Describe how markets reach equilibrium

4.1. *(Equilibrium)* "If a price is not an equilibrium price, there is a tendency for it to move to its equilibrium level. Regardless of whether the price is too high or too low to begin with, the adjustment process will increase the quantity of the good purchased." Explain, using a demand and supply diagram.

4.2. *(Equilibrium)* Assume the market for corn is depicted as in the table that appears below.

a. Complete the table below.

b. What market pressure occurs when quantity demanded exceeds quantity supplied? Explain.

c. What market pressure occurs when quantity supplied exceeds quantity demanded? Explain.

d. What is the equilibrium price?

e. What could change the equilibrium price?

f. At each price in the first column of the table below, how much is sold?

Price per Bushel	Quantity Demanded (millions of bushels)	Quantity Supplied (millions of bushels)	Surplus/ Shortage	Will Price Rise or Fall?
$1.80	320	200	_____	_____
2.00	300	230	_____	_____
2.20	270	270	_____	_____
2.40	230	300	_____	_____
2.60	200	330	_____	_____
2.80	180	350	_____	_____

4.3. *(Market Equilibrium)* Determine whether each of the following statements is true, false, or uncertain. Then briefly explain each answer.
   a. In equilibrium, all sellers can find buyers.
   b. In equilibrium, there is no pressure on the market to produce or consume more than is being sold.
   c. At prices above equilibrium, the quantity exchanged exceeds the quantity demanded.
   d. At prices below equilibrium, the quantity exchanged is equal to the quantity supplied

4.4. *(Changes in Equilibrium)* What are the effects on the equilibrium price and quantity of steel if the wages of steelworkers rise and, simultaneously, the price of aluminum rises?

4.5. *(Price Floor)* There is considerable interest in whether the minimum wage rate contributes to teenage unemployment. Draw a demand and supply diagram for the unskilled labor market, and discuss the effects of a minimum wage. Who is helped and who is hurt by the minimum wage?

LO⁵ Explain how markets react during periods of disequilibrium.

5.1. *(Price Floor)* There is considerable interest in whether the minimum wage rate contributes to teenage unemployment. Draw a demand and supply diagram for the unskilled labor market, and discuss the effects of a minimum wage. Who is helped and who is hurt by the minimum wage?

CHAPTER 5

LO¹ Discuss macroeconomics and the national economy

1.1. *(The National Economy)* Why do economists pay more attention to national economies (for example, the U.S. or Canadian economies) than to state or provincial economies (such as California or Ontario)?

LO² Discuss economic fluctuations and growth

2.1. *(Economic Fluctuations)* Describe the various components of fluctuations in economic activity over time. Because economic activity fluctuates, how is long-term growth possible?

LO³ Explain aggregate demand and aggregate supply

Aggregate Demand Curve

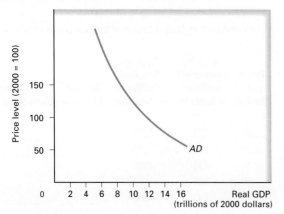

Aggregate Demand and Aggregate Supply in 2008

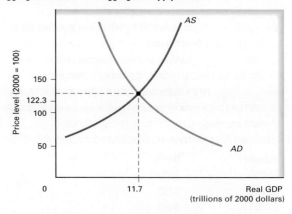

3.1. *(Aggregate Demand and Supply)* Review the information on demand and supply curves in Chapter 4. How do the aggregate demand and aggregate supply curves presented in this chapter differ from the market curves of Chapter 4?

3.2. *(Aggregate Demand and Supply)* Determine whether each of the following would cause a shift of the aggregate demand curve, a shift of the aggregate supply curve, neither, or both. Which curve shifts, and in which direction? What happens to aggregate output and the price level in each case?
   a. The price level changes.
   b. Consumer confidence declines.
   c. The supply of resources increases.
   d. The wage rate increases.

LO⁴ Describe the history of the U.S. economy

4.1. *(Supply-Side Economics)* One supply-side measure introduced by the Reagan administration was a cut in income tax rates. Use an aggregate demand/aggregate supply diagram to show what effect was intended. What might happen if such a tax cut also shifted the aggregate demand curve?

CHAPTER 6

LO¹ Explain the theory of productivity and growth

1.1. *(Growth and the PPF)* Use the production possibilities frontier (PPF) to demonstrate economic growth.
   a. With consumption goods on one axis and capital goods on the other, show how the combination of goods selected this period affects the PPF in the next period.
   b. Extend this comparison by choosing a different point on this period's PPF and determining whether that combination leads to more or less growth over the next period.

1.2. *(Shifts in the PPF)* Terrorist attacks foster instability and may affect productivity over the short and long term. Do you think the September 11, 2001, terrorist attacks on the World Trade Center and the Pentagon affected short- and/or long-term productivity in the United States? Explain your response and show any movements in the PPF.

LO^2 Describe productivity and growth in practice

2.1. *(Long-Term Productivity Growth)* Suppose that two nations start out in 2010 with identical levels of output per work hour—say, $100 per hour. In the first nation, labor productivity grows by 1 percent per year. In the second, it grows by 2 percent per year. Use a calculator or a spreadsheet to determine how much output per hour each nation will be producing 20 years later, assuming that labor productivity growth rates do not change. Then, determine how much each will be producing per hour 100 years later. What do your results tell you about the effects of small differences in productivity growth rates?

LO^3 Discuss other issues of technology and growth

3.1. *(Technological Change and Unemployment)* What are some examples, other than those given in the chapter, of technological change that has caused unemployment? And what are some examples of new technologies that have created jobs? How do you think you might measure the net impact of technological change on overall employment and GDP in the United States?

CHAPTER 7

LO^1 Explain the gross domestic product

1.1. *(Income Approach to GDP)* How does the income approach to measuring GDP differ from the expenditure approach? Explain the meaning of *value added* and its importance in the income approach. Consider the following data for the selling price at each stage in the production of a 5-pound bag of flour sold by your local grocer. Calculate the final market value of the flour.

Stage of Production	Sale Price
Farmer	$0.30
Miller	0.50
Wholesaler	1.00
Grocer	1.50

1.2. *(Expenditure Approach to GDP)* Given the following annual information about a hypothetical country, answer questions a through d.

	Billions of Dollars
Personal consumption expenditures	$200
Personal taxes	50
Exports	30
Depreciation	10
Government purchases	50
Gross private domestic investment	40
Imports	40
Government transfer payments	20

a. What is the value of GDP?
b. What is the value of net domestic product?
c. What is the value of net investment?
d. What is the value of net exports?

1.3. *(Investment)* Given the following data, answer questions a through c.

	Billions of Dollars
New residential construction	$500
Purchases of existing homes	250
Sales value of newly issued stocks and bonds	600
New physical capital	800
Depreciation	200
Household purchases of new furniture	50
Net change in firms' inventories	100
Production of new intermediate goods	700

a. What is the value of gross private domestic investment?
b. What is the value of net investment?
c. Are any intermediate goods counted in gross investment?

LO^2 Discuss the circular flow of income and expenditure

2.1. *(Leakages and Injections)* What are the leakages from and injections into the circular flow? How are leakages and injections related in the circular flow?

LO^3 Assess the limitations of national income accounting

3.1. *(Limitations of National Income Accounting)* Explain why each of the following should be taken into account when GDP data are used to compare the "level of well-being" in different countries:
a. Population levels
b. The distribution of income
c. The amount of production that takes place outside of markets
d. The length of the average workweek
e. The level of environmental pollution

LO^4 Explain how to account for price changes

4.1. *(Consumer Price Index)* Calculate a new consumer price index for the data in the following exhibit. Assume that current-year prices of Twinkies, fuel oil, and cable TV are $0.95/package, $1.25/gallon, and $15.00/month, respectively. Calculate the current year's cost of the market basket and the value of the current year's price index. What is this year's percentage change in the price level compared to the base year?

Product	(1) Quantity in Market Basket	(2) Prices in Base Year	(3) Cost of Basket in Base Year (3) = (1) × (2)	(4) Prices in Current Year	(5) Cost of Basket in Current Year (5) = (1) × (4)
Twinkies	365 packages	$0.89/package	$324.85	$0.79	$288.35
Fuel oil	500 gallons	1.00/gallon	500.00	1.50	750.00
Cable TV	12 months	30.00/month	360.00	30.00	360.00
			$1,184.85		$1,398.35

4.2. *(Consumer Price Index)* Given the following data, what was the value of the consumer price index in the base year? Calculate the annual rate of consumer price inflation in 2011 in each of the following situations:
   a. The CPI equals 200 in 2010 and 240 in 2011.
   b. The CPI equals 150 in 2010 and 175 in 2011.
   c. The CPI equals 325 in 2010 and 340 in 2011.
   d. The CPI equals 325 in 2010 and 315 in 2011.

CHAPTER 8

LO¹ Discuss the effects of unemployment on the economy

1.1. *(Measuring Unemployment)* Determine the impact on each of the following if 2 million formerly unemployed workers decide to return to school full time and stop looking for work:
   a. The labor force participation rate
   b. The size of the labor force
   c. The unemployment rate

1.2. *(Measuring Unemployment)* Suppose that the U.S. noninstitutional adult population is 230 million and the labor force participation rate is 67 percent.
   a. What would be the size of the U.S. labor force?
   b. If 85 million adults are not working, what is the unemployment rate?

1.3. *(Types of Unemployment)* Determine whether each of the following would be considered frictional, structural, seasonal, or cyclical unemployment:
   a. A UPS employee who was hired for the Christmas season is laid off after Christmas.
   b. A worker is laid off due to reduced aggregate demand in the economy.
   c. A worker in a DVD rental store becomes unemployed as video-on-demand cable service becomes more popular.
   d. A new college graduate is looking for employment.

LO² Discuss the effects of inflation on the economy

2.1. (Inflation) Here are some recent data on the U.S. consumer price index:

Year	CPI	Year	CPI	Year	CPI
1988	118.3	1994	148.2	2000	172.2
1989	124.0	1995	152.4	2001	177.1
1990	130.7	1996	156.9	2002	179.9
1991	136.2	1997	160.5	2003	184.0
1992	140.3	1998	163.0	2004	188.9
1993	144.5	1999	166.6	2005	195.3
				2006	201.8

Compute the inflation rate for each year 1989–2006 and determine which were years of inflation. In which years did deflation occur? In which years did disinflation occur? Was there hyperinflation in any year?

2.2. *(Sources of Inflation)* Using the concepts of aggregate supply and aggregate demand, explain why inflation usually increases during wartime.

2.3. *(Inflation and Interest Rates)* Using a demand-supply diagram for loanable funds (like the exhibit below), show what happens to the nominal interest rate and the equilibrium quantity of loans when both borrowers and lenders increase their estimates of the expected inflation rate from 5 percent to 10 percent.

The Market for Loanable Funds

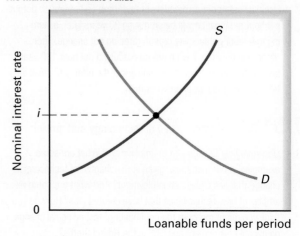

CHAPTER 9

LO¹ Explain the role of consumption

1.1. *(Consumption)* Use the following data to answer the questions below:

Consumption Real Disposable Income (billions)	Expenditures (billions)	Saving (billions)
$100	$150	$ _____
$200	$200	_____
$300	$250	_____
$400	$300	_____

   a. Graph the consumption function, with consumption spending on the vertical axis and disposable income on the horizontal axis.
   b. If the consumption function is a straight line, what is its slope?
   c. Fill in the saving column at each level of income. If the saving function is a straight line, what is its slope?

1.2. *(MPC and MPS)* If consumption increases by $12 billion when disposable income increases by $15 billion, what is the value of the MPC? What is the relationship between the MPC and the MPS? If the MPC increases, what must happen to the MPS? How is the MPC related to the consumption function? How is the MPS related to the saving function?

1.3. *(Consumption and Saving)* Suppose that consumption equals $500 billion when disposable income is $0 and that each increase of $100 billion in disposable income causes consumption to increase by $70 billion. Draw a graph of the saving function using this information.

LO² Discuss gross private domestic investment

2.1. *(Investment Spending)* Review the exhibit below. If the operators of the golf course revised their revenue estimates so that each cart is expected to earn $100 less, how many carts would they buy at an interest rate of 8 percent? How many would they buy if the interest rate is 3 percent?

Rates of Return on Golf Carts and the Opportunity Cost of Funds

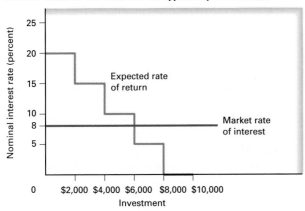

LO³ Analyze the effects of government purchases of goods and services

3.1. *(Government Spending)* How do changes in disposable income affect government purchases and the government purchase function? How do changes in net taxes affect the consumption function?

LO⁴ Explain how net exports affect aggregate expenditure

4.1. *(Net Exports)* What factors are assumed constant along the net export function? What would be the impact on net exports of a change in real disposable income?

LO⁵ Examine aggregate spending as a whole

5.1. *(Impact of Government Spending)* Based on the following exhibit, describe the net result of the overall changes in government spending over the last five decades.

U.S. Spending Components as Percentages of GDP Since 1959

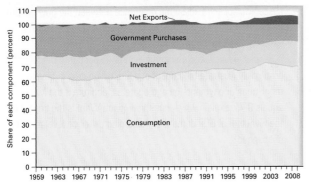

CHAPTER 10

LO¹ Explain how total spending in the economy changes with income

1.1. *(Aggregate Expenditure)* What are the components of aggregate expenditure? In the model developed in this chapter, which components vary with changes in the level of real GDP? What determines the slope of the aggregate expenditure line?

LO² Discuss how the simple spending multiplier accounts for changes in spending plans

2.1. *(Simple Spending Multiplier)* For each of the following values for the MPC, determine the size of the simple spending multiplier and the total change in real GDP demanded following a $10 billion decrease in spending:
   a. $MPC = 0.9$
   b. $MPC = 0.75$
   c. $MPC = 0.6$

2.2. *(Simple Spending Multiplier)* Suppose that the MPC is 0.8 and that $14 trillion of real GDP is currently being demanded. The government wants to increase real GDP demanded to $15 trillion at the given price level. By how much would it have to increase government purchases to achieve this goal?

2.3. *(Simple Spending Multiplier)* Suppose that the MPC is 0.8, while investment, government purchases, and net exports sum to $500 billion. Suppose also that the government budget is in balance.
   a. What is the sum of saving and net taxes when desired spending equals real GDP? Explain.
   b. What is the value of the multiplier?
   c. Explain why the multiplier is related to the slope of the consumption function.

2.4. *(Investment and the Multiplier)* This chapter assumes that investment is autonomous. What would happen to the size of the multiplier if investment increases as real GDP increases? Explain.

LO³ Describe the aggregate demand curve

3.1. *(Shifts of Aggregate Demand)* Assume the simple spending multiplier equals 10. Determine the size and direction of any changes of the aggregate expenditure line, real GDP demanded, and the aggregate demand curve for each of the following changes in spending:
   a. Spending rises by $8 billion at each income level.
   b. Spending falls by $5 billion at each income level.
   c. Spending rises by $20 billion at each income level.

CHAPTER 11

LO¹ Explain how aggregate supply operates in the short run

1.1. *(Natural Rate of Unemployment)* What is the relationship between potential output and the natural rate of unemployment?

a. If the economy currently has a frictional unemployment rate of 2 percent, structural unemployment of 2 percent, seasonal unemployment of 0.5 percent, and cyclical unemployment of 2 percent, what is the natural rate of unemployment? Where is the economy operating relative to its potential GDP?

b. What happens to the natural rate of unemployment and potential GDP if cyclical unemployment rises to 3 percent with other types of unemployment unchanged from part (a)?

c. What happens to the natural rate of unemployment and potential GDP if structural unemployment falls to 1.5 percent with other types of unemployment unchanged from part (a)?

1.2. *(Real Wages)* In the exhibit below, how does the real wage rate at point *c* compare with the real wage rate at point *a*? How do nominal wage rates compare at those two points? Explain your answers.

Long-Run Adjustment When the Price Level Exceeds Expectations

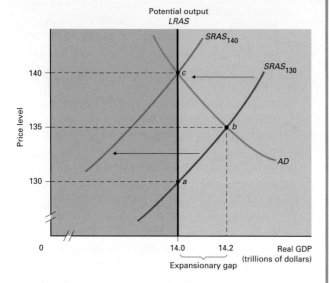

LO² Discuss short-run aggregate supply in relation to the long run

2.1. *(Expansionary and Contractionary Gaps)* Answer questions a through f on the basis of the following graph:

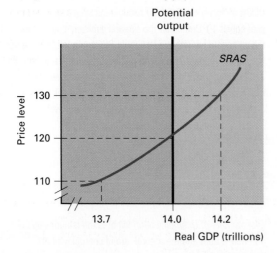

a. If the actual price level exceeds the expected price level reflected in long-term contracts, real GDP equals _____ and the actual price level equals _____ in the short run.

b. The situation described in part (a) results in a(n) _____ gap equal to _____.

c. If the actual price level is lower than the expected price level reflected in long-term contracts, real GDP equals _____ and the actual price level equals _____ in the short run.

d. The situation described in part (c) results in a(n) _____ gap equal to _____.

e. If the actual price level equals the expected price level reflected in long-term contracts, real GDP equals _____ and the actual price level equals _____ in the short run.

f. The situation described in part (e) results in a(n) _____ gap equal to _____.

2.2. *(Long-Run Adjustment)* The ability of the economy to eliminate any imbalances between actual and potential output is sometimes called self-correction. Using an aggregate supply and aggregate demand diagram, show why this self-correction process involves only temporary periods of inflation or deflation.

LO³ Analyze shifts of the aggregate supply curve

3.1. *(Changes in Aggregate Supply)* List three factors that can change the economy's potential output. What is the impact of shifts of the aggregate demand curve on potential output? Illustrate your answers with a diagram.

3.2. *(Supply Shocks)* Give an example of an adverse supply shock and illustrate graphically. Now do the same for a beneficial supply shock.

CHAPTER 12

LO¹ Explain the theory of fiscal policy

1.1. *(Changes in Government Purchases)* Assume that government purchases decrease by $10 billion, with other factors held constant, including the price level. Calculate the change in the level of real GDP demanded for each of the following values of the MPC. Then, calculate the change if the government, instead of reducing its purchases, increased autonomous net taxes by $10 billion.
a. 0.9
b. 0.8
c. 0.75
d. 0.6

1.2. *(Fiscal Multipliers)* Explain the difference between the government purchases multiplier and the net tax multiplier. If the MPC falls, what happens to the tax multiplier?

1.3. *(Changes in Net Taxes)* Using the income-expenditure model, graphically illustrate the impact of a $15 billion drop in government transfer payments on aggregate expenditure if the MPC equals 0.75. Explain why it has this impact. What is the impact on the level of real GDP demanded, assuming the price level remains unchanged?

1.4. *(Multipliers)* Suppose investment, in addition to having an autonomous component, also has a component that varies directly with the level of real GDP. How would this affect the size of the government purchase and net tax multipliers?

LO² Describe how aggregate supply affects fiscal policy

2.1. *(Fiscal Policy)* Chapter 12 shows that increased government purchases, with taxes held constant, can eliminate a contractionary gap. How could a tax cut achieve the same result? Would the tax cut have to be larger than the increase in government purchases? Why or why not?

2.2. *(Fiscal Policy with an Expansionary Gap)* Using the aggregate demand–aggregate supply model, illustrate an economy with an expansionary gap. If the government is to close the gap by changing government purchases, should it increase or decrease those purchases? In the long run, what happens to the level of real GDP as a result of government intervention? What happens to the price level? Illustrate this on an *AD–AS* diagram, assuming that the government changes its purchases by exactly the amount necessary to close the gap.

LO³ Discuss the evolution of fiscal policy

3.1. *(Evolution of Fiscal Policy)* What did classical economists assume about the flexibility of prices, wages, and interest rates? What did this assumption imply about the self-correcting tendencies in an economy in recession? What disagreements did Keynes have with classical economists?

CHAPTER 13

LO¹ Examine the federal budget process

1.1. *(The Federal Budget Process)* The federal budget passed by Congress and signed by the president shows the relationship between *budgeted* expenditures and *projected* revenues. Why does the budget require a forecast of the economy? Under what circumstances would actual government spending and tax revenue fail to match the budget as approved?

LO² Discuss the fiscal impact of the federal budget

2.1. *(Budget Philosophies)* Explain the differences among an annually balanced budget, a cyclically balanced budget, and functional finance. How does each affect economic fluctuations?

2.2. *(Crowding Out)* Is it possible for U.S. federal budget deficits to crowd out investment spending in other countries? How could German or British investment be hurt by large U.S. budget deficits?

LO³ Explain the national debt

3.1. *(The National Debt)* Try the following exercises to better understand how the national debt is related to the government's budget deficit.

a. Assume that the gross national debt initially is equal to $3 trillion and the federal government then runs a deficit of $300 billion.
  i. What is the new level of gross national debt?
  ii. If 100 percent of the deficit is financed by the sale of securities to federal agencies, what happens to the amount of debt held by the public? What happens to the level of gross debt?
  iii. If GDP increased by 5 percent in the same year that the deficit is run, what happens to gross debt as a percentage of GDP? What happens to the level of debt held by the public as a percentage of GDP?

b. Now suppose that the gross national debt initially is equal to $2.5 trillion and the federal government then runs a deficit of $100 billion.
  i. What is the new level of gross national debt?
  ii. If 100 percent of this deficit is financed by the sale of securities to the public, what happens to the level of debt held by the public? What happens to the level of gross debt?
  iii. If GDP increases by 6 percent in the same year as the deficit is run, what happens to gross debt as a percentage of GDP? What happens to the level of debt held by the public as a percentage of GDP?

CHAPTER 14

LO¹ Discuss the evolution of money

1.1. *(Origins of Banking)* Discuss the various ways in which London goldsmiths functioned as early banks.

1.2. *(Types of Money)* Complete each of the following sentences:
  a. If the face value of a coin exceeds the cost of coinage, the resulting revenue to the issuer of the coin is known as _____.
  b. A product that serves both as money and as a commodity is

  _____.
  c. Most coins and paper money circulating in the United States have face values that exceed the value of the materials from which they are made. Therefore, they are forms of _____.
  d. If the government declares that creditors must accept a form of money as payment for debts, the money becomes _____.
  e. A common unit for measuring the value of every good or service in the economy is known as a(n) _____.

1.3. *(Fiat Money)* Most economists believe that the better fiat money serves as a store of value, the more acceptable it is. What does this statement mean? How could people lose faith in money?

1.4. *(The Value of Money)* When the value of money was based on its gold content, new discoveries of gold were frequently followed by periods of inflation. Explain.

LO² Identify types of financial institutions in the United States

2.1. *(Depository Institutions)* What is a depository institution, and what types of depository institutions are found in the United States? How do they act as intermediaries between savers and borrowers? Why do they play this role?

LO³ Discuss the origin and powers of the Federal Reserve

3.1. *(Federal Reserve System)* What are the main powers and responsibilities of the Federal Reserve System?

LO⁴ Describe the history of the U.S banking system from the Great Depression to today

4.1. *(The Structure of U.S. Banking)* Discuss the impact of bank mergers on the structure of American banking. Why do banks merge?

4.2. *(Bank Deregulation)* Some economists argue that deregulating the interest rates that could be paid on deposits combined with deposit insurance led to the insolvency of many depository institutions. On what basis do they make such an argument?

CHAPTER 15

LO¹ Examine definitions of money aggregates

1.1. *(Monetary Aggregates)* Calculate M1 and M2 using the following information:

Large-denomination time deposits	$304 billion
Currency and coin held by the non-banking public	$438 billion
Checkable deposits	$509 billion
Small-denomination time deposits	$198 billion
Traveler's checks	$18 billion
Savings deposits	$326 billion
Money market mutual fund accounts	$637 billion

LO² Explain how banks work

2.1. *(Reserve Accounts)* Suppose that a bank's customer deposits $4,000 in her checking account. The required reserve ratio is 0.25. What are the required reserves on this new deposit? What is the largest loan that the bank can make on the basis of the new deposit? If the bank chooses to hold reserves of $3,000 on the new deposit, what are the excess reserves on the deposit?

LO³ Describe how banks create money

3.1. *(Money Creation)* Suppose Bank A, which faces a reserve requirement of 10 percent, receives a $1,000 deposit from a customer.
   a. Assuming that it wishes to hold no excess reserves, determine how much the bank should lend. Show your answer on Bank A's balance sheet.
   b. Assuming that the loan shown in Bank A's balance sheet is redeposited in Bank B, show the changes in Bank B's balance sheet if it lends out the maximum possible.
   c. Repeat this process for three additional banks: C, D, and E.
   d. Using the simple money multiplier, calculate the total change in the money supply resulting from the $1,000 initial deposit.
   e. Assume Banks A, B, C, D, and E each wish to hold 5 percent excess reserves. How would holding this level of excess reserves affect the total change in the money supply?

3.2. *(Money Multiplier)* Suppose that the Federal Reserve lowers the required reserve ratio from 0.10 to 0.05. How does this affect the simple money multiplier, assuming that excess reserves are held to zero and there are no currency leakages? What are the money multipliers for required reserve ratios of 0.15 and 0.20?

3.3. *(Money Creation)* Show how each of the following would initially affect a bank's assets and liabilities.
   a. Someone makes a $10,000 deposit into a checking account.
   b. A bank makes a loan of $1,000 by establishing a checking account for $1,000.
   c. The loan described in part (b) is spent.
   d. A bank must write off a loan because the borrower defaults.

3.4. *(Money Creation)* Show how each of the following *initially* affects bank assets, liabilities, and reserves. Do *not* include the results of bank behavior resulting from the Fed's action. Assume a required reserve ratio of 0.05.
   a. The Fed purchases $10 million worth of U.S. government bonds from a bank.
   b. The Fed loans $5 million to a bank.
   c. The Fed raises the required reserve ratio to 0.10.

LO⁴ Discuss the Fed's tools for monetary control

4.1. *(Monetary Control)* Suppose the money supply is currently $500 billion and the Fed wishes to increase it by $100 billion.
   a. Given a required reserve ratio of 0.25, what should it do?
   b. If it decided to change the money supply by changing the required reserve ratio, what change should it make?

CHAPTER 16

LO¹ Describe the relationship between the demand and supply of money

1.1. *(Money Demand)* Suppose that you never carry cash. Your paycheck of $1,000 per month is deposited directly into your checking account, and you spend your money at a constant rate so that at the end of each month your checking account balance is zero.
   a. What is your average money balance during the pay period?
   b. How would each of the following changes affect your average monthly balance?
      i. You are paid $500 twice monthly rather than $1,000 each month.
      ii. You are uncertain about your total spending each month.
      iii. You spend a lot at the beginning of the month (e.g., for rent) and little at the end of the month.
      iv. Your monthly income increases.

LO² Explain how changes in the money supply affect aggregate demand in the short run

2.1. *(Money and Aggregate Demand)* Would each of the following increase, decrease, or have no impact on the ability of open-market operations to affect aggregate demand? Explain your answer.

a. Investment demand becomes less sensitive to changes in the interest rate.

b. The marginal propensity to consume rises.

c. The money multiplier rises.

d. Banks decide to hold additional excess reserves.

e. The demand for money becomes more sensitive to changes in the interest rate.

2.2. *(Monetary Policy and Aggregate Supply)* Assume that the economy is initially in long-run equilibrium. Using an *AD–AS* diagram, illustrate and explain the short-run and long-run impacts of an increase in the money supply.

2.3. *(Monetary Policy and an Expansionary Gap)* Suppose the Fed wishes to use monetary policy to close an expansionary gap.

a. Should the Fed increase or decrease the money supply?

b. If the Fed uses open-market operations, should it buy or sell government securities?

c. Determine whether each of the following increases, decreases, or remains unchanged in the short run: the market interest rate, the quantity of money demanded, investment spending, aggregate demand, potential output, the price level, and equilibrium real GDP.

LO³ Explain how changes in the money supply affect aggregate demand in the long run

3.1. *(Equation of Exchange)* Calculate the velocity of money if real GDP is 3,000 units, the average price level is $4 per unit, and the quantity of money in the economy is $1,500. What happens to velocity if the average price level drops to $3 per unit? What happens to velocity if the average price level remains at $4 per unit but the money supply rises to $2,000? What happens to velocity if the average price level falls to $2 per unit, the money supply is $2,000, and real GDP is 4,000 units?

3.2. *(Quantity Theory of Money)* What basic assumption about the velocity of money transforms the equation of exchange into the quantity theory of money? Also:

a. According to the quantity theory, what will happen to nominal GDP if the money supply increases by 5 percent and velocity does not change?

b. What will happen to nominal GDP if, instead, the money supply decreases by 8 percent and velocity does not change?

c. What will happen to nominal GDP if, instead, the money supply increases by 5 percent and velocity decreases by 5 percent?

d. What happens to the price level in the short run in each of these three situations?

LO⁴ Evaluate targets for monetary policy

4.1. *(Money Supply Versus Interest Rate Targets)* Assume that the economy's real GDP is growing.

a. What will happen to money demand over time?

b. If the Fed leaves the money supply unchanged, what will happen to the interest rate over time?

c. If the Fed changes the money supply to match the change in money demand, what will happen to the interest rate over time?

d. What would be the effect of the policy described in part (c) on the economy's stability over the business cycle?

CHAPTER 17

LO¹ Compare an active policy and a passive policy

1.1. *(Active Versus Passive Policy)* Discuss the role each of the following plays in the debate between the active and passive approaches:

a. The speed of adjustment of the nominal wage

b. The speed of adjustment of expectations about inflation

c. The existence of lags in policy creation and implementation

d. Variability in the natural rate of unemployment over time

1.2. *(Problems with Active Policy)* Use an *AD–AS* diagram to illustrate and explain the short-run and long-run effects on the economy of the following situation: Both the natural rate of unemployment and the actual rate of unemployment are 5 percent. However, the government believes that the natural rate of unemployment is 6 percent and that the economy is overheating. Therefore, it introduces a policy to reduce aggregate demand.

LO² Consider the role of expectations

2.1. *(Rational Expectations)* Using an *AD–AS* diagram, illustrate the short-run effects on prices, output, and employment of an increase in the money supply that is correctly anticipated by the public. Assume that the economy is initially at potential output.

LO³ Discuss policy rules versus discretion

3.1. *(Policy Lags)* What lag in discretionary policy is described in each of the following statements? Why do long lags make discretionary policy less effective?

a. The time from when the government determines that the economy is in recession until a tax cut is approved to reduce unemployment

b. The time from when the money supply is increased until the resulting effect on the economy is felt

c. The time from the start of a recession until the government identifies the existence and severity of the recession

d. The time from when the Fed decides to reduce the money supply until the money supply actually declines

LO⁴ Explain the Phillips curve

4.1. *(Long-Run Phillips Curve)* Suppose the economy is at point *d* on the long-run Phillips curve shown in the accompanying exhibit. If that inflation rate is unacceptably high, how can policy makers get the inflation rate down? Would rational expectations help or hinder their efforts?

Phillips Curves in the Short Run and Long Run

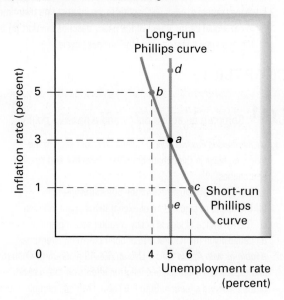

CHAPTER 18

LO¹ Describe the gains that trade brings

1.1. *(Comparative Advantage)* Suppose that each U.S. worker can produce 8 units of food or 2 units of clothing daily. In Izodia, which has the same number of workers, each worker can produce 7 units of food or 1 unit of clothing daily. Why does the United States have an absolute advantage in both goods? Which country enjoys a comparative advantage in food? Why?

1.2. *(Comparative Advantage)* The consumption possibilities frontiers shown in the following exhibit assume terms of trade of 1 unit of clothing for 1 unit of food. What would the consumption possibilities frontiers look like if the terms of trade were 1 unit of clothing for 2 units of food?

Production (and Consumption) Possibility Frontiers with Trade (millions of units per day)

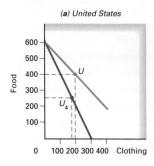
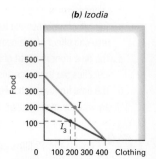

LO² Discuss the reasons for international specialization

2.1. *(Reasons for International Specialization)* What determines which goods a country should produce and export?

LO³ Explain trade restrictions and welfare loss

3.1. *(Import Quotas)* How low must a quota be in effect to have an impact? Using a demand-and-supply diagram, illustrate and explain the net welfare loss from imposing such a quota. Under what circumstances would the net welfare loss from an import quota exceed the net welfare loss from an equivalent tariff (one that results in the same price and import level as the quota)?

3.2. *(Trade Restrictions)* Suppose that the world price for steel is below the U.S. domestic price, but the government requires that all steel used in the United States be domestically produced.

  a. Use a diagram like the one below to show the gains and losses from such a policy.

  b. How could you estimate the net welfare loss (deadweight loss) from such a diagram?

  c. What response to such a policy would you expect from industries (like automobile producers) that use U.S. steel?

  d. What government revenues are generated by this policy?

Effect of a Tariff

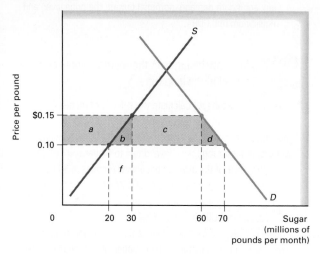

Effect of a Quota

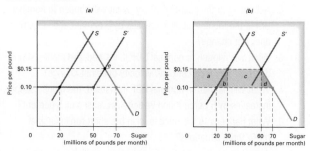

3.3. *(Trade Restrictions)* The previous three graphs show net losses to the economy of a country that imposes tariffs or quotas on imported sugar. What kinds of gains and losses would occur in the economies of countries that export sugar?

LO⁴ Describe ways countries have reduced or eliminated trade barriers

4.1. *(The World Trade Organization)* What is the World Trade Organization (WTO) and how does it help foster multilateral trade? (Check the WTO Web site at http://www.wto.org/.)

LO⁵ List and describe the arguments in favor of trade restrictions

5.1. *(Arguments for Trade Restrictions)* Explain the national defense, declining industries, and infant industry arguments for protecting a domestic industry from international competition.

5.2. *(Arguments for Trade Restrictions)* Firms hurt by cheap imports typically argue that restricting trade will save U.S. jobs. What's wrong with this argument? Are there ever any reasons to support such trade restrictions?

CHAPTER 19

LO¹ Explain how the balance of payments works

1.1. *(Balance of Payments)* The following are hypothetical data for the U.S. balance of payments. Use the data to calculate each of the following:
a. Merchandise trade balance
b. Balance on goods and services
c. Balance on current account
d. Capital account balance
e. Statistical discrepancy

	Billions of Dollars
Merchandise exports	350.0
Merchandise imports	2,425.0
Service exports	170.0
Service imports	2,145.0
Net income and net transfers	221.5
Outflow of U.S. capital	245.0
Inflow of foreign capital	70.0

1.2. *(Balance of Payments)* Explain where in the U.S. balance of payments an entry would be recorded for each of the following:
a. A Hong Kong financier buys some U.S. corporate stock.
b. A U.S. tourist in Paris buys some perfume to take home.
c. A Japanese company sells machinery to a pineapple company in Hawaii.
d. U.S. farmers make a gift of food to starving children in Ethiopia.
e. The U.S. Treasury sells a bond to a Saudi Arabian prince.
f. A U.S. tourist flies to France on Air France.
g. A U.S. company sells insurance to a foreign firm.

LO² Discuss foreign exchange rates and markets

2.1. *(Determining the Exchange Rate)* Use these data to answer the following questions about the market for British pounds:

Pound Price (in $)	Quantity Demanded (of pounds)	Quantity Supplied (of pounds)
$4.00	50	100
3.00	75	75
2.00	100	50

a. Draw the demand and supply curves for pounds, and determine the equilibrium exchange rate (dollars per pound).
b. Suppose that the supply of pounds doubles. Draw the new supply curve.
c. What is the new equilibrium exchange rate?
d. Has the dollar appreciated or depreciated?
e. What happens to U.S. imports of British goods?

LO³ Define fixed and flexible exchange rates

3.1 *(Exchange Rates)* Discuss the differences between a flexible exchange rate and a fixed exchange rate. What measures can the government take to maintain fixed exchange rates?

LO⁴ Describe the development of the international monetary system

4.1. *(The Current System: Managed Float)* What is a managed float? What are the disadvantages of freely floating exchange rates that led countries to the managed float system?

CHAPTER 20

LO¹ Describe the worldwide variation in economic vitality

1.1. *(Worlds Apart)* Assume that GDP per capita income is about 63 times greater in the richest country on Earth than in the poorest country. Suppose GDP per capita grows an average of 3 percent per year in the richest country and 6 percent per year in the poorest country. Assuming such growth rates continue indefinitely into the future, how many years would it take before per capita in the poorest country exceed that of the richest country? (To simplify the math, suppose at the outset per capita income is $63,000 in the richest country and $1,000 in the poorest country.)

LO² Explain why productivity is the key to development

2.1. *(Import Substitution Versus Export Promotion)* Explain why domestic producers who supply a good that competes with imports would prefer an import-substitution approach to trade policy rather than an export-promotion approach. Which policy would domestic consumers prefer and why?

LO³ Discuss international trade and development

3.1. *(International Trade and Development)* From the perspective of citizens in a developing country, what are some of the benefits and drawbacks of international trade?

3.2. *(Import Substitution Versus Export Promotion)* Explain why domestic producers who supply a good that competes with imports would prefer an import-substitution approach to trade policy rather than an export-promotion approach. Which policy would domestic consumers prefer and why?

LO⁴ Describe the role of foreign aid in economic development

4.1. *(Foreign Aid and Economic Development)* Foreign aid, if it is to be successful in enhancing economic development, must lead to a more productive economy. Describe some of the problems in achieving such an objective through foreign aid.

LO⁵ Define transitional economies

5.1. *(Transitional Economies)* What special problems are faced by Eastern European economies as they make the transition from central planning to competitive markets?

LO⁶ Discuss markets and institutions

6.1. *(Markets and Institutions)* Why is a system of well-defined and enforceable property rights crucial when a country is converting to a market-based system of resource allocation?

 or  ?

Learning Your Way

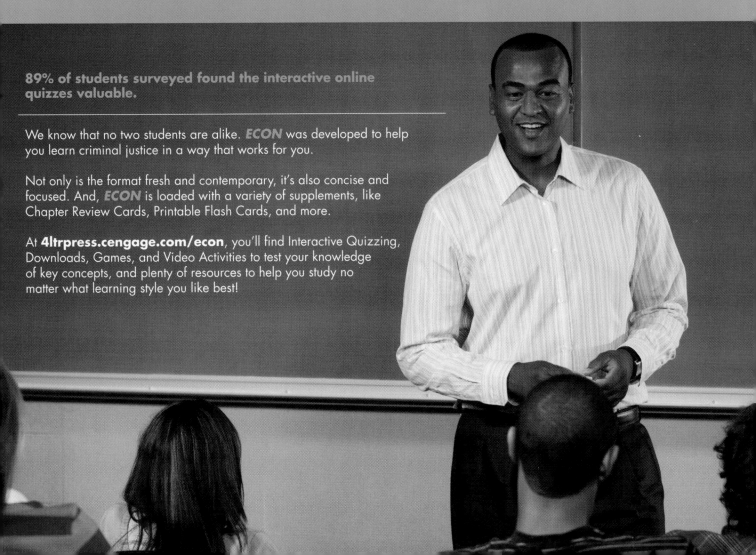

89% of students surveyed found the interactive online quizzes valuable.

We know that no two students are alike. *ECON* was developed to help you learn criminal justice in a way that works for you.

Not only is the format fresh and contemporary, it's also concise and focused. And, *ECON* is loaded with a variety of supplements, like Chapter Review Cards, Printable Flash Cards, and more.

At **4ltrpress.cengage.com/econ**, you'll find Interactive Quizzing, Downloads, Games, and Video Activities to test your knowledge of key concepts, and plenty of resources to help you study no matter what learning style you like best!

Test coming up? Now what?

With *ECON* you have a multitude of study aids at your fingertips. After reading the chapters, check out these ideas for further help.

Chapter in Review cards include all learning outcomes, definitions, and summaries for each chapter.

Online printable flash cards give you three additional ways to check your comprehension of key concepts.

Other great ways to help you study include **interactive quizzes** and **videos**.

You can find it all at **4ltrpress.cengage.com/econ**.

Chapter in Review

KEY TERMS

economics
the study of how people use their scarce resources to satisfy their unlimited wants

resources
the inputs, or factors of production, used to produce the goods and services that people want; resources consist of labor, capital, natural resources, and entrepreneurial ability

labor
the physical and mental effort used to produce goods and services

capital
the buildings, equipment, and human skills used to produce goods and services

natural resources
so-called "gifts of nature" used to produce goods and services; exhaustible res...

entrepreneu...
managerial and...
start a firm, combined with the willingness to take the risk of profit or loss

entrepreneur
a profit-seeking decision maker who starts with an idea, organizes an enterprise to bring that idea to life, and assumes the risk of the operation

wages
payment to resource owners for their labor

interest
payment to resource owners for the use of their capital

rent
payment to resource owners for the use of their natural resources

profit
reward for entrepreneurial ability; sales revenue minus resource cost

good
a tangible product used to satisfy human wants

service
an activity, o...
human want...

scarcity
occurs whe...
the amount...

market
a set of arra...
sellers carry...
terms

product m...
a market in v...
and sold

resource r...
a market in v...

circular-fl...
a diagram th...
products, inc...
decision ma...

> Here, you'll find the key terms and definitions in ithe order they appear in the chapter.

How to use the Card:

1. Look over the card to preview the new concepts you'll be introduced to in the chapter.

2. Read your chapter to fully understand the material.

3. Go to class (and pay attention).

4. Review the card one more time to make sure you've registered the key concepts.

5. Don't forget, this card is only one of many ECON learning tools available to help you succeed in your economics course.

LO¹ Explain the economic problem of scarce resources and unlimited
wants. The problem is that, although your wants, or desires, are virtually unlimited, the resources available to satisfy these wants are scarce. Because... must choose from among your many wants, and whenever yo... satisfying some other wants. Without scarcity, there would b... need for prices.

> In this column, you'll find summary points supported by the exhibits from the chapters. Exhibits have short explanations to help further cement the concepts in your mind.

The Simple Circular-Flow Model for Households and Firms

Households earn income by supplying resources to the resource market, as shown in the lower portion of the model. Firms demand these resources to produce goods and services, which they supply to the product market, as shown in the upper portion of the model. Households spend their income to demand these goods and services. This spending flows through the product market as revenue to firms.

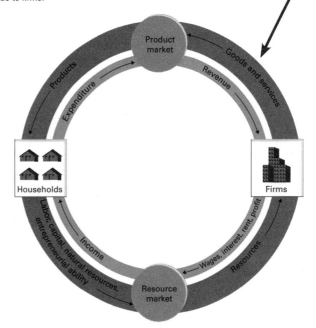

LO² Describe the forces that shape economic choices. An economy results
from the choices that millions of individuals make in attempting to satisfy their unlimited wants. A key economic assumption is that individuals, in making choices, rationally select alternatives they perceive to be in their best interests. Economic choice is based on a comparison of the expected marginal benefit and the expected marginal cost of the action under consideration.

LO³ Explain the relationship between economic theory and economic
reality. An economic theory is a simplification of economic reality that is used to make predictions about the real world. A theory, or model, captures the important elements of the problem under study but need not spell out every detail and interrelation. You might think of economic theory as a streamlined version of economic reality.

> When it's time to prepare for exams, use the Card and the technique to the left to ensure successful study sesions.

rational self-interest
individuals try to maximize the expected benefit achieved with a given cost or to minimize the expected cost of achieving a given benefit

marginal
incremental, additional, or extra; used to describe a change in an economic variable

microeconomics
the study of the economic behavior in particular markets, such as that for computers or unskilled labor

macroeconomics
the study of the economic behavior of entire economies

economic theory (economic model)
a simplification of reality used to make predictions about cause and effect in the real world

variable
a measure, such as price or quantity, that can take on different values at different times

other-things-constant assumption
the assumption, when focusing on the relation among key economic variables, that other variables remain unchanged; in Latin, *ceteris paribus*

behavioral assumption
an assumption that describes the expected behavior of economic decision makers, what motivates them

hypothesis
a theory about how key variables relate

positive economic statement
a statement that can be proved or disproved by reference to facts

normative economic statement
a statement that reflects an opinion, which cannot be proved or disproved by reference to the facts

association-is-causation fallacy
the incorrect idea that if two variables are associated in time, one must necessarily cause the other

fallacy of composition
the incorrect belief that what is true for the individual, or part, must necessarily be true for the group, or the whole

secondary effects
unintended consequences of economic actions that may develop slowly over time as people react to events

The Scientific Method: Step by Step

The steps of the scientific method are designed to develop and test hypotheses about how the world works. The objective is a theory that predicts outcomes more accurately than the best alternative theory. A hypothesis is rejected if it does not predict as accurately as the best alternative. A rejected hypothesis can be modified in light of the test results.

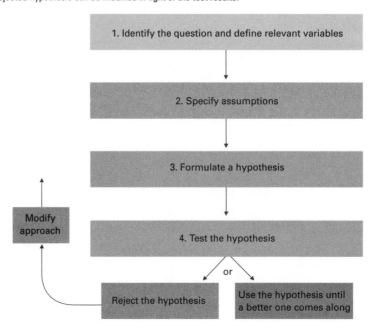

LO⁴ Identify some pitfalls of economic analysis. Economic analysis, like other forms of scientific inquiry, is subject to common mistakes in reasoning that can lead to faulty conclusions. Three sources of confusion are the fallacy that association is causation, the fallacy of composition, and the mistake of ignoring secondary effects.

LO⁵ Describe several reasons to study economics. The economics profession thrives because its models usually do a better job of making economic sense out of a confusing world than do alternative approaches. Studies show that economics majors earn more than most and they experience no pay difference based on gender.

APPENDIX TERMS

origin
on a graph depicting two-dimensional space, the zero point

horizontal axis
line on a graph that begins at the origin and goes to the right and left; sometimes called the *x* axis

vertical axis
line on a graph that begins at the origin and goes up and down; sometimes called the *y* axis

graph
a picture showing how variables relate in two-dimensional space; one variable is measured along the horizontal axis and the other along the vertical axis

dependent variable
a variable whose value depends on that of the independent variable

independent variable
a variable whose value determines that of the dependent variable

positive relation (direct relation)
occurs when two variables increase or decrease together; the two variables move in the same direction

negative relation (inverse relation)
occurs when two variables move in opposite directions; when one increases, the other decreases

slope of a line
a measure of how much the vertical variable changes for a given increase in the horizontal variable; the vertical change between two points divided by the horizontal increase

tangent
a straight line that touches a curve at a point but does not cut or cross the curve; used to measure the slope of a curve at a point

Chapter in Review

KEY TERMS

economics
the study of how people use their scarce resources to satisfy their unlimited wants

resources
the inputs, or factors of production, used to produce the goods and services that people want; resources consist of labor, capital, natural resources, and entrepreneurial ability

labor
the physical and mental effort used to produce goods and services

capital
the buildings, equipment, and human skills used to produce goods and services

natural resources
so-called "gifts of nature" used to produce goods and services; includes renewable and exhaustible resources

entrepreneurial ability
managerial and organizational skills needed to start a firm, combined with the willingness to take the risk of profit or loss

entrepreneur
a profit-seeking decision maker who starts with an idea, organizes an enterprise to bring that idea to life, and assumes the risk of the operation

wages
payment to resource owners for their labor

interest
payment to resource owners for the use of their capital

rent
payment to resource owners for the use of their natural resources

profit
reward for entrepreneurial ability; sales revenue minus resource cost

good
a tangible product used to satisfy human wants

service
an activity, or intangible product, used to satisfy human wants

scarcity
occurs when the amount people desire exceeds the amount available at a zero price

market
a set of arrangements by which buyers and sellers carry out exchange at mutually agreeable terms

product market
a market in which a good or service is bought and sold

resource market
a market in which a resource is bought and sold

circular-flow model
a diagram that traces the flow of resources, products, income, and revenue among economic decision makers

LO¹ Explain the economic problem of scarce resources and unlimited wants. The problem is that, although your wants, or desires, are virtually unlimited, the resources available to satisfy these wants are scarce. Because resources are scarce, you must choose from among your many wants, and whenever you choose, you must forgo satisfying some other wants. Without scarcity, there would be no economic problem and no need for prices.

The Simple Circular-Flow Model for Households and Firms

Households earn income by supplying resources to the resource market, as shown in the lower portion of the model. Firms demand these resources to produce goods and services, which they supply to the product market, as shown in the upper portion of the model. Households spend their income to demand these goods and services. This spending flows through the product market as revenue to firms.

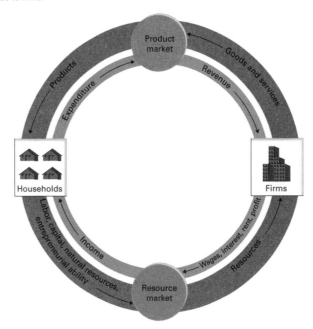

LO² Describe the forces that shape economic choices. An economy results from the choices that millions of individuals make in attempting to satisfy their unlimited wants. A key economic assumption is that individuals, in making choices, rationally select alternatives they perceive to be in their best interests. Economic choice is based on a comparison of the expected marginal benefit and the expected marginal cost of the action under consideration.

LO³ Explain the relationship between economic theory and economic reality. An economic theory is a simplification of economic reality that is used to make predictions about the real world. A theory, or model, captures the important elements of the problem under study but need not spell out every detail and interrelation. You might think of economic theory as a streamlined version of economic reality.

rational self-interest
individuals try to maximize the expected benefit achieved with a given cost or to minimize the expected cost of achieving a given benefit

marginal
incremental, additional, or extra; used to describe a change in an economic variable

microeconomics
the study of the economic behavior in particular markets, such as that for computers or unskilled labor

macroeconomics
the study of the economic behavior of entire economies

economic theory (economic model)
a simplification of reality used to make predictions about cause and effect in the real world

variable
a measure, such as price or quantity, that can take on different values at different times

other-things-constant assumption
the assumption, when focusing on the relation among key economic variables, that other variables remain unchanged; in Latin, *ceteris paribus*

behavioral assumption
an assumption that describes the expected behavior of economic decision makers, what motivates them

hypothesis
a theory about how key variables relate

positive economic statement
a statement that can be proved or disproved by reference to facts

normative economic statement
a statement that reflects an opinion, which cannot be proved or disproved by reference to the facts

association-is-causation fallacy
the incorrect idea that if two variables are associated in time, one must necessarily cause the other

fallacy of composition
the incorrect belief that what is true for the individual, or part, must necessarily be true for the group, or the whole

secondary effects
unintended consequences of economic actions that may develop slowly over time as people react to events

The Scientific Method: Step by Step

The steps of the scientific method are designed to develop and test hypotheses about how the world works. The objective is a theory that predicts outcomes more accurately than the best alternative theory. A hypothesis is rejected if it does not predict as accurately as the best alternative. A rejected hypothesis can be modified in light of the test results.

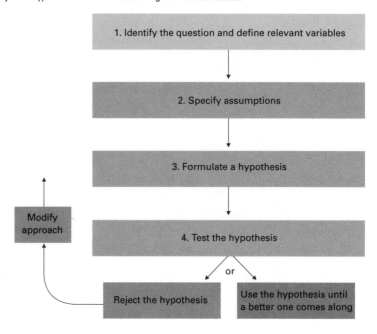

LO⁴ Identify some pitfalls of economic analysis. Economic analysis, like other forms of scientific inquiry, is subject to common mistakes in reasoning that can lead to faulty conclusions. Three sources of confusion are the fallacy that association is causation, the fallacy of composition, and the mistake of ignoring secondary effects.

LO⁵ Describe several reasons to study economics. The economics profession thrives because its models usually do a better job of making economic sense out of a confusing world than do alternative approaches. Studies show that economics majors earn more than most and they experience no pay difference based on gender.

APPENDIX TERMS

origin
on a graph depicting two-dimensional space, the zero point

horizontal axis
line on a graph that begins at the origin and goes to the right and left; sometimes called the *x* axis

vertical axis
line on a graph that begins at the origin and goes up and down; sometimes called the *y* axis

graph
a picture showing how variables relate in two-dimensional space; one variable is measured along the horizontal axis and the other along the vertical axis

dependent variable
a variable whose value depends on that of the independent variable

independent variable
a variable whose value determines that of the dependent variable

positive relation (direct relation)
occurs when two variables increase or decrease together; the two variables move in the same direction

negative relation (inverse relation)
occurs when two variables move in opposite directions; when one increases, the other decreases

slope of a line
a measure of how much the vertical variable changes for a given increase in the horizontal variable; the vertical change between two points divided by the horizontal increase

tangent
a straight line that touches a curve at a point but does not cut or cross the curve; used to measure the slope of a curve at a point

Chapter in Review

2

KEY TERMS

opportunity cost
the value of the best alternative forgone when an item or activity is chosen

sunk cost
a cost that has already been incurred, cannot be recovered, and thus is irrelevant for present and future economic decisions

law of comparative advantage
the individual, firm, region, or country with the lowest opportunity cost of producing a particular good should specialize in that good

absolute advantage
the ability to make something using fewer resources than other producers use

comparative advantage
the ability to make something at a lower opportunity cost than other producers face

barter
the direct exchange of one good for another without using money

division of labor
breaking down the production of a good into separate tasks

specialization of labor
focusing work effort on a particular product or a single task

production possibilities frontier (PPF)
a curve showing alternative combinations of goods that can be produced when available resources are used efficiently; a boundary line between inefficient and unattainable combinations

efficiency
the condition that exists when there is no way resources can be reallocated to increase the production of one good without decreasing the production of another; getting the most from available resources

law of increasing opportunity cost
to produce more of one good, a successively larger amount of the other good must be sacrificed

economic growth
an increase in the economy's ability to produce goods and services; reflected by an outward shift of the economy's production possibilities frontier

rules of the game
the formal and informal institutions that support the economy—laws, customs, manners, conventions, and other institutional underpinnings that encourage people to pursue productive activity

economic system
the set of mechanisms and institutions that resolve the what, how, and for whom questions

LO¹ Describe the impact of choice on opportunity. Resources are scarce, but human wants are unlimited. Because you cannot satisfy all your wants, you must choose, and whenever you choose, you must forgo some option. Choice involves an opportunity cost. The opportunity cost of the selected option is the value of the best alternative forgone.

LO² Explain how comparative advantage, specialization, and exchange affect economic outcomes (output). The law of comparative advantage says that the individual, firm, region, or country with the lowest opportunity cost of producing a particular good should specialize in that good. Specialization according to the law of comparative advantage promotes the most efficient use of resources. The specialization of labor increases efficiency by (a) taking advantage of individual preferences and natural abilities, (b) allowing each worker to develop expertise and experience at a particular task, (c) reducing the need to shift between different tasks, and (d) allowing for the introduction of more specialized machines and large-scale production techniques.

LO³ Outline how economies function as production systems. The production possibilities frontier, or PPF, shows the productive capabilities of an economy when all resources are used efficiently. The frontier's bowed-out shape reflects the law of increasing opportunity cost, which arises because some resources are not perfectly adaptable to the production of different goods. Over time, the frontier can shift in or out as a result of changes in the availability of resources, in technology, or in the rules of the game. The frontier demonstrates several economic concepts, including efficiency, scarcity, opportunity cost, the law of increasing opportunity cost, economic growth, and the need for choice.

The Economy's Production Possibilities Frontier

If the economy uses its available resources and technology efficiently in producing consumer goods and capital goods, that economy is on its production possibilities frontier, *AF*. The *PPF* is bowed out to reflect the law of increasing opportunity cost: additional units of capital goods require the economy to sacrifice more and more units of consumer goods. Note that more consumer goods must be given up in moving from *E* to *F* than in moving from *A* to *B*, although in each case the gain in capital goods is 10 million units. Points inside the *PPF*, such as *I*, represent inefficient use of resources. Points outside the *PPF*, such as *U*, represent unattainable combinations.

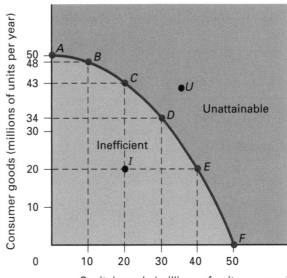

Shifts of the Economy's Production Possibilities Frontier

When the resources available to an economy change, the *PPF* shifts. If more resources become available or if technology improves, the *PPF* shifts outward, as in panel (a), indicating that more output can be produced. A decrease in available resources causes the *PPF* to shift inward, as in panel (b). Panel (c) shows a change affecting consumer goods production. More consumer goods can now be produced at any given level of capital goods. Panel (d) shows a change affecting capital goods production.

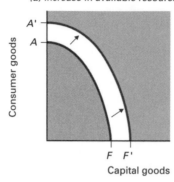

(a) Increase in available resources

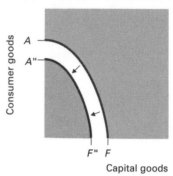

(b) Decrease in available resources

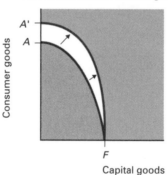

(c) Change in resources, technology, or rules that benefits consumer goods

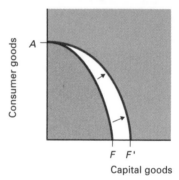

(d) Change in resources, technology, or rules that benefits capital goods

LO⁴ Describe different economic systems and the decision-making rules that define them. All economic systems, regardless of their decision-making processes, must answer three basic questions: What is to be produced? How is it to be produced? And for whom is it to be produced? Economies answer the questions differently, depending on who owns the resources and how economic activity is coordinated. Economies can be directed by market forces, by the central plans of government, or, in most cases, by a mix of the two.

Chapter in Review

3

KEY TERMS

utility
the satisfaction received from consumption; sense of well-being

transfer payments
cash or in-kind benefits given to individuals as outright grants from the government

Industrial Revolution
development of large-scale factory production that began in Great Britain around 1750 and spread to the rest of Europe, North America, and Australia

firms
economic units formed by profit-seeking entrepreneurs who employ resources to produce goods and services for sale

sole proprietorship
a firm with a single owner who has the right to all profits but who also bears unlimited liability for the firm's losses and debts

partnership
a firm with multiple owners who share the profits and bear unlimited liability for the firm's losses and debts

corporation
a legal entity owned by stockholders whose liability is limited to the value of their stock ownership

cooperative
an organization consisting of people who pool their resources to buy and sell more efficiently than they could individually

not-for-profit organizations
groups that do not pursue profit as a goal; they engage in charitable, educational, humanitarian, cultural, professional, or other activities, often with a social purpose

market failure
a condition that arises when the unregulated operation of markets yields socially undesirable results

monopoly
a sole supplier of a product with no close substitutes

natural monopoly
one firm that can supply the entire market at a lower per-unit cost than could two or more firms

private good
a good that is both rival in consumption and exclusive, such as pizza

LO¹ Explain the role of the household in an economic system. Households play the starring role in a market economy. Their demand for goods and services determines what gets produced, and their supplies of labor, capital, natural resources, and entrepreneurial ability produce that output. As demanders of goods and services and suppliers of resources, households make all kinds of choices in an attempt to maximize utility.

Where U.S. Personal Income Comes From and Where It Goes

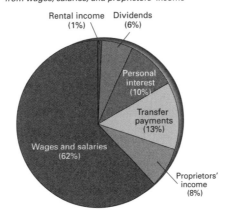

(a) Over two-thirds of personal income in 2007 was from wages, salaries, and proprietors' income

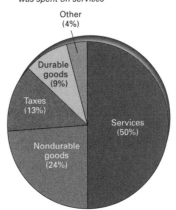

(b) Half of U.S. personal income in 2007 was spent on services

LO² Identify the different types of firms and describe their roles in the economy. Firms are economic units formed by entrepreneurs who combine labor, capital, and natural resources to produce goods and services in an attempt to maximize profit. For-profit firms organize in one of three ways: as a sole proprietorship, as a partnership, or as a corporation. Not-for-profit organizations engage in activities that often have a social purpose, while cooperatives are groups that organize with the goal of minimizing costs.

Number and Sales of Each Type of Firm

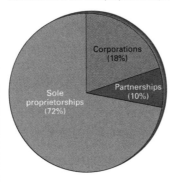

(a) Most firms are sole proprietorships

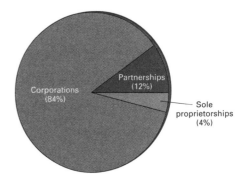

(b) Corporations account for most sales

LO³ Outline the ways governments affect their economies. Governments attempt to improve society's overall welfare by intervening in cases of market failure. Beneficial government interventions in markets include establishing and enforcing the rules of the game, promoting competition, regulating natural monopolies, providing public goods, dealing with externalities, more equally distributing income, and pursuing full employment, price stability, and economic growth.

public good
a good that, once produced, is available for all to consume, regardless of who pays and who doesn't; such a good is nonrival and nonexclusive, such as a safer community

externality
a cost or a benefit that affects neither the buyer or seller, but instead affects people not involved in the market transaction

fiscal policy
the use of government purchases, transfer payments, taxes, and borrowing to influence economy-wide variables such as inflation, employment, and economic growth

monetary policy
regulation of the money supply to influence economy-wide variables such as inflation, employment, and economic growth

ability-to-pay tax principle
those with a greater ability to pay, such as those earning higher incomes or those owning more property, should pay more taxes

benefits-received tax principle
those who get more benefits from the government program should pay more taxes

tax incidence
the distribution of tax burden among taxpayers; who ultimately pays the tax

proportional taxation
the tax as a percentage of income remains constant as income increases; also called a flat tax

progressive taxation
the tax as a percentage of income increases as income increases

marginal tax rate
the percentage of each additional dollar of income that goes to the tax

regressive taxation
the tax as a percentage of income decreases as income increases

merchandise trade balance
the value during a given period of a country's exported goods minus the value of its imported goods

balance of payments
a record of all economic transactions during a given period between residents of one country and residents of the rest of the world

foreign exchange
foreign money needed to carry out international transactions

tariff
a tax on imports

quota
a legal limit on the quantity of a particular product that can be imported

Redistribution Has Grown and Defense Has Declined as Share of Federal Outlays Since 1960

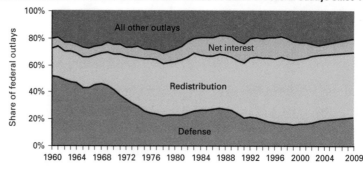

Payroll Taxes Have Grown as a Share of Federal Revenue Since 1960

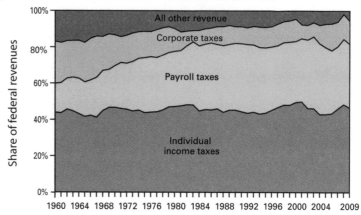

Top Marginal Rate on Federal Personal Income Tax Since 1913

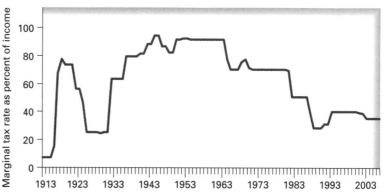

LO⁴ Outline the international influences on an economy. The rest of the world affects what U.S. households consume and what U.S. firms produce. U.S. households and firms are consumers and suppliers of manufactured goods and raw materials from and to foreign economies, and these transactions impact U.S. prices, wages, and profits. International trade, exchange rates, and trade restrictions all affect the U.S. economy.

Chapter in Review

4

KEY TERMS

demand
a relation between the price of a good and the quantity that consumers are willing and able to buy per period, other things constant

law of demand
the quantity of a good that consumers are willing and able to buy per period relates inversely, or negatively, to the price, other things constant

substitution effect of a price change
when the price of a good falls, that good become cheaper compared to other goods so consumers tend to substitute that good for other goods

money income
the number of dollars a person receives per period, such as $400 per week

real income
income measured in terms of the goods and services it can buy; real income changes when the price changes

income effect of a price change
a fall in the price of a good increases consumers' real income, making consumers more able to purchase goods; for a normal good, the quantity demanded increases

demand curve
a curve showing the relation between the price of a good and the quantity consumers are willing and able to buy per period, other things constant

quantity demanded
the amount of a good consumers are willing and able to buy per period at a particular price, as reflected by a point on a demand curve

individual demand
a relation between the price of a good and the quantity purchased by an individual consumer per period, other things constant

market demand
the relation between the price of a good and the quantity purchased by all consumers in the market during a given period, other things constant; sum of the individual demands in the market

normal good
a good, such as new clothes, for which demand increases, or shifts rightward, as consumer income rises

inferior good
a good, such as used clothes, for which demand decreases, or shifts leftward, as consumer income rises

substitutes
goods, such as Coke and Pepsi, that relate in such a way that an increase in the price of one shifts the demand for the other rightward

complements
goods, such as milk and cookies, that relate in such a way that an increase in the price of one shifts the demand for the other leftward

tastes
consumer preferences; likes and dislikes in consumption; assumed to remain constant along a given demand curve

LO¹ Explain how the law of demand affects market activity. Demand is a relationship between the price of a product and the quantity consumers are willing and able to buy per period, other things constant. According to the law of demand, quantity demanded varies negatively, or inversely, with the price. A demand curve slopes downward because a price decrease makes consumers (a) more willing to substitute this good for other goods and (b) more able to buy the good because the lower price increases real income.

The Demand Curve for Pizza

The market demand curve *D* shows the quantity of pizza demanded, at various prices, by all consumers. Price and quantity demanded are inversely related.

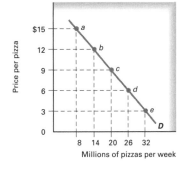

LO² Explain how the law of supply affects market activity. Supply is a relationship between the price of a good and the quantity producers are willing and able to sell per period, other things constant. According to the law of supply, price and quantity supplied are usually postitively, or directly, related, so the supply curve typically slopes upward. The supply curve slopes upward because higher prices make producers (a) more willing to supply this good rather than supply other goods that use the same resources and (b) more able to cover the higher marginal cost associated with greater output rates.

The Supply Curve for Pizza

Market supply curve *S* shows the quantity of pizza supplied, at various prices, by all pizza makers. Price and quantity supplied are directly related.

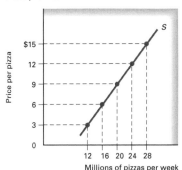

LO³ Describe how the interaction between supply and demand creates markets. Demand and supply come together in the market for the good. A market provides information about the price, quantity, and quality of the good. In doing so, a market reduces the transaction costs of exchange—the costs of time and information required for buyers and sellers to make a deal. The interaction of demand and supply guides resources and products to their highest-valued use.

movement along a demand curve
change in quantity demanded resulting from a change in the price of the good, other things constant

shift of a demand curve
movement of a demand curve right or left resulting from a change in one of the determinants of demand other than the price of the good

supply
a relation between the price of a good and the quantity that producers are willing and able to sell per period, other things constant

law of supply
the amount of a good that producers are willing and able to sell per period is usually directly related to its price, other things constant

supply curve
a curve showing the relation between price of a good and the quantity producers are willing and able to sell per period other things constant

quantity supplied
the amount offered for sale per period at a particular price, as reflected by a point on a given supply curve

individual supply
the relation between the price of a good and the quantity an individual producer is willing and able to sell per period, other things constant

market supply
the relation between the price of a good and the quantity all producers are willing and able to sell per period, other things constant

relevant resources
resources used to produce the good in question

alternative goods
other goods that use some or all of the same resources as the good in question

movement along a supply curve
change in quantity supplied resulting from a change in the price of the good, other things constant

shift of a supply curve
movement of a supply curve left or right resulting from a change in one of the determinants of supply other than the price of the good

transaction costs
the costs of time and information required to carry out market exchange

surplus
at a given price, the amount by which quantity supplied exceeds quantity demanded; a surplus usually forces the price down

shortage
at a given price, the amount by which quantity demanded exceeds quantity supplied; a shortage usually forces the price up

equilibrium
the condition that exists in a market when the plans of buyers match those of sellers, so quantity demanded equals quantity supplied and the market clears

disequilibrium
the condition that exists in a market when the plans of buyers do not match those of sellers; a temporary mismatch between quantity supplied and quantity demanded as the market seeks equilibrium

Equilibrium in the Pizza Market

Market equilibrium occurs at the price where quantity demanded equals quantity supplied. This is shown at point c. Price pressure occurs at all other points on the curves.

(a) Market schedules

	Millions of Pizzas per Week			
Price per Pizza	Quantity Demanded	Quantity Supplied	Surplus or Shortage	Effect on Price
$15	8	28	Surplus of 20	Falls
12	14	24	Surplus of 10	Falls
9	20	20	Equilibrium	Remains the same
6	26	16	Shortage of 10	Rises
3	32	12	Shortage of 20	Rises

(b) Market curves

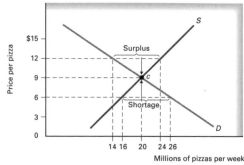

LO⁴

Describe how markets reach equilibrium. Impersonal market forces reconcile the personal and independent plans of buyers and sellers. Market equilibrium, once established, will continue unless there is a change in a determinant that shapes demand or supply.

Effects of an Increase in Demand

An increase in demand is shown by a shift of the demand curve rightward from D to D'. Both price and quantity are higher following the rightward shift of the demand curve.

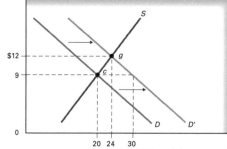

Effects of an Increase in Supply

An increase in supply is shown by a shift of the supply curve rightward, from S to S'. At the new equilibrium, quantity is greater and the price is lower than before the increase in supply.

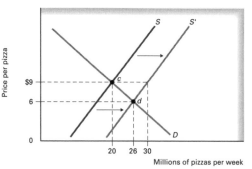

LO⁵

Explain how markets react during periods of disequilibrium. Markets can't always achieve equilibrium quickly. Until they do, a period of disequilibrium occurs. Governments often impose price floors or price ceilings to manage the uncomfortable market effects of disequilibrium, like falling income or product surplus.

price floor
a minimum legal price below which a product cannot be sold; to have an impact, a price floor must be set above the equilibrium price

price ceiling
a maximum legal price above which a product cannot be sold; to have an impact, a price ceiling must be set below the equilibrium price

Chapter in Review

5

KEY TERMS

economy
the structure of economic activity in a community, a region, a country, a group of countries, or the world

gross domestic product (GDP)
the market value of all final goods and services produced in the nation during a particular period, usually a year

gross world product
the market value of all final goods and services produced in the world during a given period, usually a year

flow variable
a variable that measures something over an interval of time, such as your income per week

stock variable
a variable that measures something at a particular point in time, such as the amount of money you have with you right now

mercantilism
the incorrect theory that a nation's economic objective should be to accumulate precious metals in the public treasury; this theory prompted trade barriers to cut imports, but other countries retaliated, reducing trade and the gains from specialization

economic fluctuations
the rise and fall of economic activity relative to the long-term growth trend of the economy; also called business cycles

expansion
a period during which the economy's output increases

contraction
a period during which the economy's output declines

depression
a sharp reduction in an economy's total output accompanied by high unemployment lasting more than a year

recession
a sustained decline in the economy's total output lasting at least two consecutive quarters, or six months; an economic contraction

inflation
an increase in the economy's average price level

leading economic indicators
variables that predict, or lead to, a recession or recovery; examples include consumer confidence, stock market prices, business investment, and big-ticket purchases, such as automobiles and homes

LO¹ Discuss macroeconomics and the national economy. Macroeconomics concerns the overall performance of the national economy. A standard measure of performance is the growth of real gross domestic product, or real GDP, the value of final goods and services produced in the nation during the year.

LO² Discuss economic fluctuations and growth. The economy fluctuates between two phases: periods of expansion and periods of contraction. No two business cycles are the same. Before 1945, expansions averaged 29 months and contractions 21 months. Since 1945, expansions have averaged 57 months and contractions 11 months. Despite the Great Depression and later recessions, the economy's output has grown thirteenfold since 1929 and jobs have grown faster than the population.

Hypothetical Business Cycles

Business cycles reflect movements of economic activity around a trend line that shows long-term growth. An expansion (shaded in blue) begins when the economy starts to grow and continues until the economy reaches a peak. After an expansion has peaked, a contraction (shaded in pink) begins and continues until the economy reaches a trough.

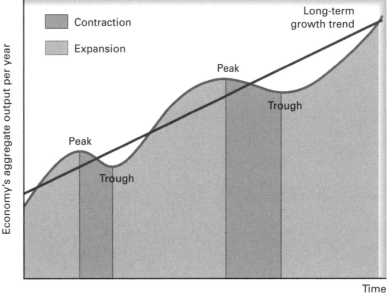

Annual Percentage Change in U.S. Real GDP Since 1929

Years of declining real GDP are shown as red bars and years of growth as blue bars. Note that the year-to-year swings in output became less pronounced after World War II.

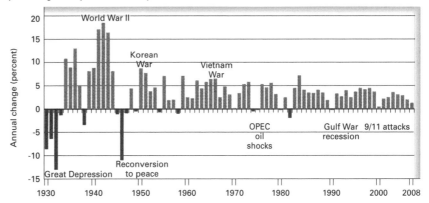

LO³ Explain aggregate demand and aggregate supply. The aggregate demand curve slopes downward, reflecting a negative, or inverse, relationship between the price level and real GDP demanded. The aggregate supply curve slopes upward, reflecting a positive, or direct, relationship between the price level and real GDP supplied. The intersection of the two curves determines the economy's real GDP and price level.

Aggregate Demand Curve

The quantity of aggregate output demanded is inversely related to the price level, other things constant. This inverse relationship is reflected by the aggregate demand curve *AD*.

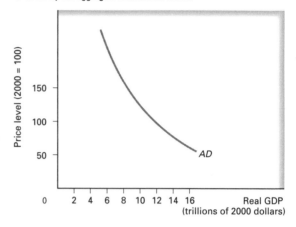

Aggregate Demand and Aggregate Supply in 2008

The total output of the economy and its price level are determined at the intersection of the aggregate demand and aggregate supply curves. This point reflects real GDP and the price level for 2008 using 2000 as the base year.

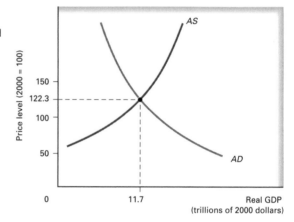

LO⁴ Describe the history of the U.S. economy. The Great Depression and earlier depressions prompted John Maynard Keynes to argue that the economy is unstable, largely because business investment is erratic. Keynes did not believe that contractions were self-correcting. His demand-side policies of increased government spending and decreased taxes dominated macroeconomic thinking between World War II and the late 1960s.

During the 1970s, higher oil prices and global crop failures reduced aggregate supply. The result was stagflation, the troublesome combination of declining real GDP and rising inflation. Supply-side tax cuts in the early 1980s were aimed at increasing aggregate supply, thereby increasing output while dampening inflation. Unfortunately, federal spending increased faster than federal tax revenue, resulting in budget deficits that grew into the early 1990s. Tax increases, a slower growth in government spending, and an expanding economy all helped erase budget deficits by 1998, creating a federal budget surplus. The economy then experienced an eight-month recession that ended in late 2001, but unemployment continued to rise into 2003. Tax cuts and a sluggish recovery boosted the federal deficit. Jobs began growing once again in late 2003, and by the end of 2007, the economy added more than 8 million jobs. This growth cut the federal deficit in half by 2007 to $200 billion. The recession that began officially in December 2007 reversed those recent gains. After spikes in the price of oil and other commodities and the collapse of the housing market, the U.S. economy lost 2.5 million jobs in 2008. The federal budget deficit increased to $450 billion in 2008. With lower tax revenues and increased stimulus spending, the deficit will be even higher in 2009.

Chapter in Review

6

KEY TERMS

productivity
the ratio of a specific measure of output, such as real GDP, to a specific measure of input, such as labor; in this case productivity measures real GDP per hour of labor

labor productivity
output per unit of labor; measured as real GDP divided by the hours of labor employed to produce that output

per-worker production function
the relationship between the amount of capital per worker in the economy and average output per worker

capital deepening
an increase in the amount of capital per worker; one source of rising labor productivity

rules of the game
the formal and informal institutions that promote economic activity; the laws, customs, manners, conventions, and other institutional elements that determine transaction costs and thereby affect people's incentive to undertake production and exchange

industrial market countries
economically advanced capitalist countries of Western Europe, North America, Australia, New Zealand, and Japan, plus the newly industrialized Asian economies of Taiwan, South Korea, Hong Kong, and Singapore

developing countries
countries with a low living standard because of less human and physical capital per worker

basic research
the search for knowledge without regard to how that knowledge will be used

applied research
research that seeks answers to particular questions or to apply scientific discoveries to develop specific products

industrial policy
the view that government—using taxes, subsidies, and regulations—should nurture the industries and technologies of the future, thereby giving these domestic industries an advantage over foreign competition

convergence
a theory predicting that the standards of living in economies around the world will grow more similar over time, with poorer countries eventually catching up with richer ones

LO¹ Explain the theory of productivity and growth. If the population is continually increasing, an economy must produce more goods and services simply to maintain its standard of living, as measured by output per capita. If output grows faster than the population, the standard of living rises.

The per-worker production function shows the relationship between the amount of capital per worker in the economy and the output per worker. As capital per worker increases, so does output per worker but at a decreasing rate. Technological change and improvements in the rules of the game shift the per-worker production function upward.

Economic Growth Shown by Shifts Outward in the Production Possibilities Frontier

An economy that produces more capital goods will grow more, as reflected by a shift outward of the production possibilities frontier. More capital goods and fewer consumer goods are produced in panel (b) than in panel (a), so the PPF shifts out more in panel (b).

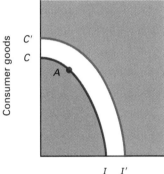

(a) Lower growth   *(b) Higher growth*

Per-Worker Production Function

The per-worker production function, *PF*, shows a direct relationship between the amount of capital per worker, *k*, and the output per worker, *y*. The bowed shape of *PF* reflects the law of diminishing marginal returns from capital, which holds that as more capital is added to a given number of workers, output per worker increases but at a diminishing rate and eventually could turn negative.

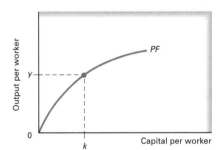

Impact of a Technological Breakthrough on the Per-Worker Production Function

A technological breakthrough increases output per worker at each level of capital per worker. Better technology makes workers more productive. This is shown by a rotation upward in the per-worker production function from *PF* to *PF'*. An improvement in the rules of the game would have a similar effect.

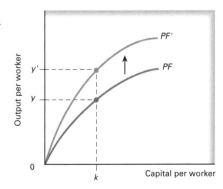

LO² Describe productivity and growth in practice.

Since 1870, U.S. labor productivity growth has averaged 2.1 percent per year. The *quality* of labor and capital is much more important than the *quantity* of these resources. Labor productivity growth slowed between 1974 and 1982, in part because of spikes in energy prices and implementation of costly but necessary environmental and workplace regulations. Since 1983, productivity growth has picked up, especially since 1996, due primarily to information technology. Among the seven major industrial market economies, the United States has experienced the second highest growth rate in real GDP per capita over the last quarter of a century and most recently experienced the highest real GDP per capita.

Long-Term Trend in U.S. Labor Productivity Growth: Annual Average by Decade

Annual productivity growth, measured as the growth in real output per work hour, is averaged by decades. For the entire period since 1870, labor productivity grew an average of 2.1 percent per year. Note the big dip during the Great Depression of the 1930s and the big bounce back during World War II. Productivity growth slowed during the 1970s and 1980s but recovered.

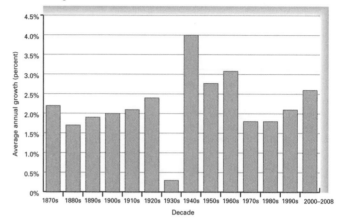

LO³ Discuss other issues of technology and growth.

Technological change sometimes costs jobs in the short run when workers fail to adjust. Over time, however, most displaced workers find other jobs, sometimes in new industries created by technological change. There is no evidence that, in the long run, technological change increases unemployment in the economy.

Some governments use industrial policy in an effort to nurture the industries and technologies of the future, giving domestic industries an advantage over foreign competitors. But critics are wary of the government's ability to pick the winning technologies of the future.

Convergence is a theory predicting that the standards of living around the world will grow more alike, as poorer countries catch up with richer ones. Some Asian countries that had been poor are catching up with the leaders, but many poor countries around the world have failed to close the gap.

U.S. Labor Productivity Growth Slowed During 1974 to 1982 and Then Rebounded

The growth in labor productivity declined from an average of 2.9 percent per year between 1948 and 1973 to only 1.0 percent between 1974 and 1982. A jump in the price of oil helped contribute to three recessions during that stretch, and new environmental and workplace regulations, though necessary and beneficial, slowed down productivity growth temporarily. The information revolution powered by the computer chip has boosted productivity in recent years.

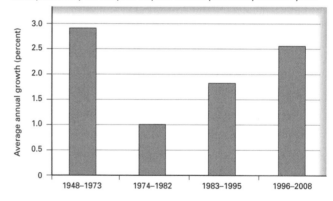

U.S. Real GDP per Capita Has Nearly Tripled Since 1959

Despite eight recessions since 1959, real GDP per capita has nearly tripled. Periods of recession are indicated by the pink-shaded bars.

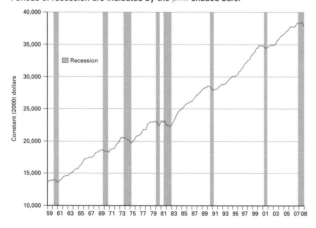

Chapter in Review

7

KEY TERMS

expenditure approach to GDP
calculating GDP by adding up spending on all final goods and services produced in the nation during the year

income approach to GDP
calculating GDP by adding up all earnings from resources used to produce output in the nation during the year

final goods and services
goods and services sold to final, or end, users

intermediate goods and services
goods and services purchased by firms for additional processing and resale

double counting
the mistake of including both the value of intermediate products and the value of final products in calculating gross domestic product; counting the same production more than once

consumption
household purchases of final goods and services, except for new residences, which count as investment

investment
the purchase of new plants, new equipment, new buildings, and new residences, plus net additions to inventories

physical capital
manufactured items used to produce goods and services; includes new plants and new equipment

residential construction
building new homes or dwelling places

inventories
producers' stocks of finished and in-process goods

government purchases
spending for goods and services by all levels of government; government outlays minus transfer payments

net exports
the value of a country's exports minus the value of its imports

aggregate expenditure
total spending on final goods and services in an economy during a given period, usually a year

aggregate income
all earnings of resource suppliers in an economy during a given period, usually a year

value added
at each stage of production, the selling price of a product minus the cost of intermediate goods purchased from other firms

LO¹ Explain the gross domestic product. Gross domestic product, or GDP, measures the market value of all final goods and services produced during the year by resources located in the United States, regardless of who owns those resources. The expenditure approach to GDP adds up the market value of all final goods and services produced in the economy during the year. The income approach to GDP adds up all the income generated as a result of that production.

LO² Discuss the circular flow of income and expenditure. The circular-flow model summarizes the flow of income and spending through the economy. Saving, net taxes, and imports leak from the circular flow. These leakages equal the injections into the circular flow from investment, government purchases, and exports.

Circular Flow of Income and Expenditure

The circular-flow model captures important relationships in the economy. The bottom half depicts the income arising from production. At juncture (1), GDP equals aggregate income. Taxes leak from the flow at (2), but transfer payments enter the flow at (3). Taxes minus transfers equals net taxes, NT. Aggregate income minus net taxes equals disposable income, DI, which flows to households at juncture (4). The top half of the model shows the flow of expenditure. At (5), households either spend disposable income or save it. Consumption enters the spending flow directly. Saving leaks from the spending flow into financial markets, where it is channeled to borrowers. At (6), investment enters the spending flow. At (7), government purchases enter the spending flow. At (8), imports leak from the spending flow, and at (9), exports enter the spending flow. Consumption plus investment plus government purchases plus net exports add up to the aggregate expenditure on GDP received by firms at (10).

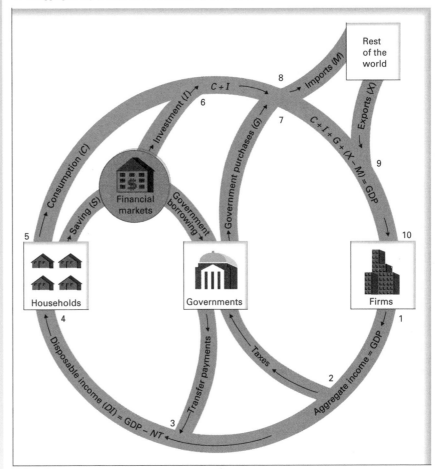

disposable income (DI)
the income households have available to spend or to save after paying taxes and receiving transfer payments

net taxes (NT)
taxes minus transfer payments

financial markets
banks and other financial institutions that facilitate the flow of funds from savers to borrowers

injection
any spending other than by households or any income other than from resource earnings; includes investment, government purchases, exports, and transfer payments

leakage
any diversion of income from the domestic spending stream; includes saving, taxes, and imports

underground economy
market transactions that go unreported either because they are illegal or because people involved want to evade taxes

depreciation
the value of capital stock used up to produce GDP or that becomes obsolete during the year

net domestic product
gross domestic product minus depreciation

nominal GDP
GDP based on prices prevailing at the time of production

base year
the year with which other years are compared when constructing an index; the index equals 100 in the base year

price index
a number that shows the average price of products; changes in a price index over time show changes in the economy's average price level

consumer price index (CPI)
a measure of inflation based on the cost of a fixed market basket of goods and services

GDP price index
a comprehensive inflation measure of all goods and services included in the gross domestic product

chain-weighted system
an inflation measure that adjusts the weights from year to year in calculating a price index, thereby reducing the bias caused by a fixed-price weighting system

LO³ Assess the limitations of national income accounting. GDP reflects market production in a given period, usually a year. Most household production and the underground economy are not captured by GDP. Improvements in the quality and variety of products also are often missed in GDP. In other ways GDP may overstate production. GDP fails to subtract for the depreciation of the capital stock or for the depletion of natural resources and fails to account for any negative externalities arising from production.

LO⁴ Explain how to account for price changes. Nominal GDP in a particular year values output based on market prices when the output was produced. To determine real GDP, nominal GDP must be adjusted for price changes. The consumer price index, or CPI, tracks prices for a market basket of goods and services over time. The GDP price index tracks price changes for all output. No adjustment for price changes is perfect, but current approaches offer a reasonably good estimate of real GDP both at a point in time and over time.

U.S. Gross Domestic Product in Nominal Dollars and Chained (2000) Dollars

Real GDP, the red line, shows the value of output measured in chained (2000) dollars. The blue line measures GDP in current dollars, or nominal dollars, of each year shown. The two lines intersect in 2000, when real GDP equaled nominal GDP. Year-to-year changes in current-dollar GDP reflect changes in real GDP and in the price level. Year-to-year changes in chained-dollar GDP reflect changes in real GDP only. Current-dollar GDP grows faster than chained-dollar GDP. Prior to 2000, current-dollar prices are less than chained-dollar prices, so current-dollar GDP is less than chained-dollar GDP.

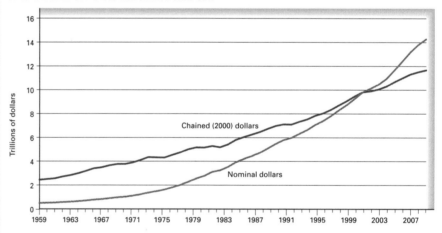

CHAPTER EQUATIONS

Aggregate Expenditure

$$C + I + G + (X - M) = \text{Aggregate expenditure} = GDP$$
$$C = \text{Consumption}$$
$$I = \text{Investment}$$
$$G = \text{Government purchases}$$
$$(X - M) = \text{Net exports} = \text{Exports} - \text{Imports}$$

Aggregate Income

$$GDP = \text{Aggregate income} = DI + NT$$

Disposable Income

$$DI = C + S$$
$$C + I + G + (X - M) = DI + NT$$
$$C + I + G + (X - M) = C + S + NT$$
$$I + G + X = S + NT + M$$

GDP Price Index

$$\text{GDP price index} = \frac{\text{Nominal GDP}}{\text{Real GDP}} \times 100$$

Chapter in Review

8

KEY TERMS

labor force
those 16 years of age and older who are either working or looking for work

unemployment rate
the number unemployed as a percentage of the labor force

discouraged workers
those who drop out of the labor force in frustration because they can't find work

labor force participation rate
the labor force as a percentage of the adult population

frictional unemployment
unemployment that occurs because job seekers and employers need time to find each other

seasonal unemployment
unemployment caused by seasonal changes in the demand for certain kinds of labor

structural unemployment
unemployment because (1) the skills demanded by employers do not match those of the unemployed, or (2) the unemployed do not live where the jobs are

cyclical unemployment
unemployment that fluctuates with the business cycle, increasing during contractions and decreasing during expansions

full employment
employment level when there is no cyclical unemployment

unemployment benefits
cash transfers to those who lose their jobs and actively seek employment

underemployment
workers are overqualified for their jobs or work fewer hours than they would prefer

hyperinflation
a very high rate of inflation

deflation
a sustained decrease in the price level

disinflation
a reduction in the rate of inflation

demand-pull inflation
a sustained rise in the price level caused by a rightward shift of the aggregate demand curve

cost-push inflation
a sustained rise in the price level caused by a leftward shift of the aggregate supply curve

LO¹ Discuss the effects of unemployment on the economy. The unemployment rate is the number of people looking for work divided by the number in the labor force. The unemployment rate masks differences among particular groups and across regions. The rate is lowest among white adults and highest among black teenagers.

There are four sources of unemployment. Frictional unemployment arises because employers and qualified job seekers need time to find one another. Seasonal unemployment stems from the effects of weather and the seasons on certain industries, such as construction and agriculture. Structural unemployment arises because changes in tastes, technology, taxes, and competition reduce the demand for certain skills and increase the demand for other skills. And cyclical unemployment results from fluctuations in economic activity caused by the business cycle. Policy makers and economists are less concerned with frictional and seasonal unemployment. Full employment occurs when cyclical unemployment is zero.

The Adult Population Sums the Employed, the Unemployed and Those Not in the Labor Force: February 2009 (in millions)

The labor force, depicted by the left circle, consists of those employed plus those unemployed. Those not working, depicted by the right circle, consists of those not in the labor force and those unemployed.

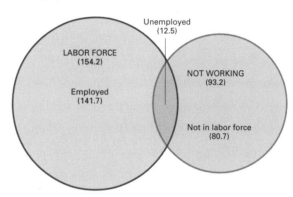

LO² Discuss the effects of inflation on the economy. Inflation is a sustained rise in the average price level. An increase in aggregate demand can cause demand-pull inflation. A decrease in aggregate supply can cause cost-push inflation. Prior to World War II, both inflation and deflation were common, but since then the price level has increased virtually every year.

Anticipated inflation causes fewer distortions in the economy than unanticipated inflation. Unanticipated inflation arbitrarily creates winners and losers, and forces people to spend more time and energy coping with the effects of inflation. Because not all prices change by the same amount during inflationary periods, people have trouble keeping track of the changes in relative prices. Unexpected inflation makes long-term planning more difficult and more risky.

The intersection of the demand and supply curves for loanable funds yields the market interest rate. The real interest rate is the nominal interest rate minus the inflation rate. Borrowers and lenders base decisions on the expected real interest rate.

Inflation Caused by Shifts of Aggregate Demand and Aggregate Supply Curves

Panel (a) illustrates demand-pull inflation. An outward shift of the aggregate demand to AD' "pulls" the price level up from P to P'. Panel (b) shows cost-push inflation. A decrease of aggregate supply to AS' "pushes" the price level up from P to P'.

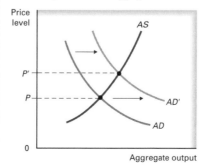

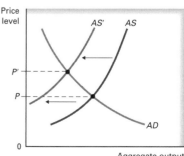

interest
the dollar amount paid by borrowers to lenders

interest rate
interest per year as a percentage of the amount loaned

nominal interest rate
the interest rate expressed in dollars of current value (that is, not adjusted for inflation) as a percentage of the amount loaned; the interest rate specified on the loan agreement

real interest rate
the interest rate expressed in dollars of constant purchasing power as a percentage of the amount loaned; the nominal interest rate minus the inflation rate

COLA
cost-of-living adjustment; an increase in a transfer payment or wage that is tied to the increase in the price level

CHAPTER EQUATIONS

Unemployment Rate

\# Unemployed ÷ Labor force

Labor Force Participation Rate

Labor force ÷ Adult population

Real Interest Rate

Nominal interest rate − Inflation rate

Consumer Price Index Since 1913

Panel (a) shows that, despite fluctuations, the price level, as measured by the consumer price index, was lower in 1940 than in 1920. Since 1940, the price level has risen nearly every year. Panel (b) shows the annual rate of change in the price level. Since 1948, the inflation rate has averaged 3.8 percent annually.

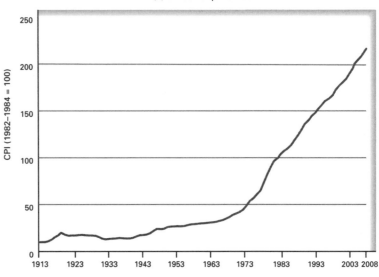

(a) Consumer price index

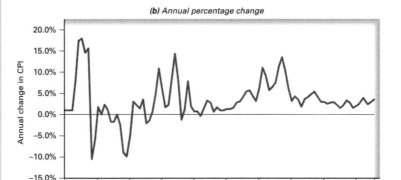

(b) Annual percentage change

The Market for Loanable Funds

The upward-sloping supply curve, S, shows that more loanable funds are supplied at higher interest rates. The downward-sloping demand curve, D, shows that the quantity of loanable funds demanded is greater at lower interest rates. The two curves intersect to determine the market interest rate, i.

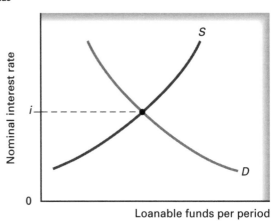

Chapter in Review

KEY TERMS

consumption function
the relationship in the economy between consumption and income, other things constant

marginal propensity to consume (MPC)
the fraction of a change in income that is spent on consumption; the change in consumption divided by the change in income that caused it

marginal propensity to save (MPS)
the fraction of a change in income that is saved; the change in saving divided by the change in income that caused it

saving function
the relationship between saving and income, other things constant

net wealth
the value of all assets minus liabilities

life-cycle model of consumption and saving
young people borrow, middle-agers pay off debts and save, and older people draw down their savings; on average, net savings over a lifetime is usually little or nothing

investment function
the relationship between the amount businesses plan to invest and the economy's income, other things constant

autonomous
a term that means "independent"; for example, autonomous investment is independent of income

government purchase function
the relationship between government purchases and the economy's income, other things constant

net export function
the relationship between net exports and the economy's income, other things constant

CHAPTER EQUATION

$$MPC + MPS = 1$$

LO^1 Explain the role of consumption. The most predictable and most useful relationship in macroeconomics is between consumption and income. The more people have available to spend, the more they spend on consumption, other things constant. The consumption function shows the link between consumption and income in the economy. The slope of the consumption function reflects the marginal propensity to consume, which is the change in consumption divided by the change in income. The slope of the saving function reflects the marginal propensity to save, which is the change in saving divided by the change in income. Increases in net wealth, higher price levels, increases in interest rates, and expectations about future incomes are all factors that can cause consumers to change the amount they want to spend at each income level.

The Consumption Function

The consumption function, C, shows the relationship between consumption and disposable income, other things constant.

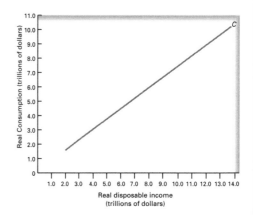

Marginal Propensities to Consume and to Save

The slope of the consumption function equals the marginal propensity to consume. For the straight-line consumption function in panel (a), the slope is the same at all levels of income and is given by the change in consumption divided by the change in disposable income that causes it. Thus, the marginal propensity to consume equals $\Delta C/\Delta DI$, or 0.4/0.5 = 4/5. The slope of the saving function in panel (b) equals the marginal propensity to save, $\Delta S/\Delta DI$, or 0.1/0.5 = 1/5. Both consumption and disposable income are in real terms.

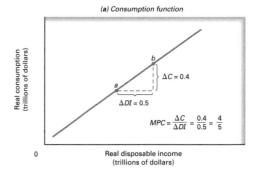

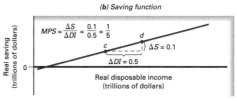

Shifts of the Consumption Function

A downward shift of the consumption function, such as from C to C', can be caused by a decrease in wealth, an increase in the price level, an unfavorable change in consumer expectations, or an increase in the interest rate. An upward shift, such as from C to C'', can be caused by an increase in wealth, a decrease in the price level, a favorable change in expectations, or a decrease in the interest rate.

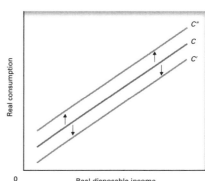

LO² Discuss gross private domestic investment.
Investment depends on the market interest rate and on business expectations. Investment fluctuates from year to year but averaged about one-sixth of GDP during the last decade. We'll assume for now that investment in the economy is unrelated to income.

Investment Demand Curve for the Economy

The investment demand curve for the economy sums the investment demanded by each firm at each interest rate. At lower interest rates, more investment projects become profitable for individual firms, so total investment in the economy increases.

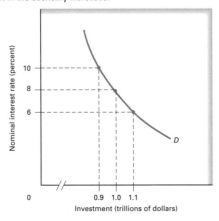

Investment Function

Investment is assumed to be independent of income, as shown by the horizontal lines. Thus, investment is assumed to be autonomous. An increase in the interest rate or less favorable business expectations would decrease investment at every level of income, as shown by the downward shift from *I* to *I'*. A decrease in the interest rate or more upbeat business expectations would increase investment at every level of income, as shown by the upward shift from *I* to *I''*.

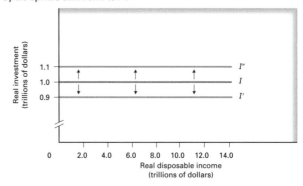

LO³ Analyze the effects of government purchases of goods and services.
Government purchases, which exclude transfer payments, averaged a little less than one-fifth of GDP during the last decade. Government purchases are based on the public choices of elected officials and are assumed to be autonomous, or independent of the economy's income level. Net taxes, or taxes minus transfer payments, are also assumed for now to be unrelated to income.

LO⁴ Explain how net exports affect aggregate expenditure.
Net exports equal the value of exports minus the value of imports. U.S. exports depend on foreign income, not on U.S. income. Imports increase with U.S. income. So net exports decline as income increases. For simplicity, however, we initially assume that net exports are autonomous, or unrelated to domestic income.

Net Export Function

Net exports here are assumed to be independent of disposable income, as shown by the horizontal lines. $X - M$ is the net export function when autonomous net exports equal −$400 billion. An increase in the value of the dollar relative to other currencies would decrease net exports at each level of income, as shown by the shift down to $X' - M'$. A decrease in the value of the dollar would increase net exports at each level of income, as shown by the shift up to $X'' - M''$.

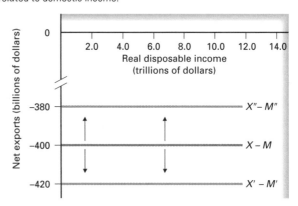

LO⁵ Examine aggregate spending as a whole.
Consumption's share of total spending increased from about 62 percent during the 1960s to 69 percent during the most recent decade. The share reflected by government purchases fell from about 22 percent to 18 percent. Investment's share bounced around but averaged about 17 percent of GDP during the period. Net exports' share turned negative, meaning that imports exceeded exports.

U.S. Spending Components as Percentages of GDP Since 1959

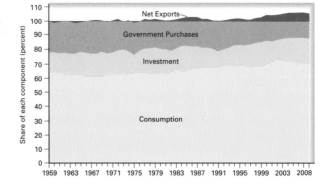

Chapter in Review

KEY TERMS

aggregate expenditure line
a relationship tracing, for a given price level, spending at each level of income, or real GDP; the total of $C + I + G + (X - M)$ at each level of income, or real GDP

income-expenditure model
a relationship that shows how much people plan to spend at each income level; this model identifies, for a given price level, where the amount people plan to spend equals the amount produced in the economy

simple spending multiplier
the ratio of a change in real GDP demanded to the initial change in spending that brought it about; the numerical value of the simple spending multiplier is $1/(1 - MPC)$; called "simple" because only consumption varies with income

CHAPTER EQUATIONS

Simple Spending Multiplier =

$$\frac{1}{1 - MPC} = \frac{1}{MPS}$$

LO^1 Explain how total spending in the economy changes with income. The aggregate expenditure line indicates, for a given price level, spending plans at each income level. At a given price level, real GDP demanded is found where the amount that people plan to spend equals the amount produced.

Deriving the Real GDP Demanded for a Given Price Level

Real GDP demanded for a given price level is found where aggregate expenditure equals aggregate output—that is, where spending equals the amount produced, or real GDP. This occurs at point *e*, where the aggregate expenditure line intersects the 45-degree line.

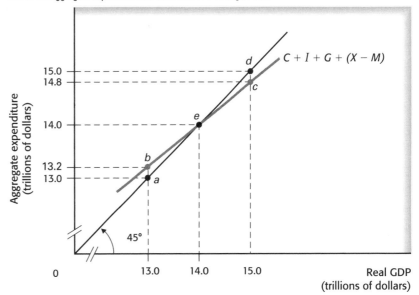

LO^2 Discuss how the simple spending multiplier accounts for changes in spending plans. The spending multiplier indicates the multiple by which a change in the amount people plan to spend changes real GDP demanded. The simple spending multiplier developed in this chapter is $1/(1 - MPC)$. The larger the MPC, the more is spent and the less is saved, so the larger the simple spending multiplier. This multiplier is called "simple" because only consumption changes with changes in income.

Tracking the Rounds of Spending Following a $100 Billion Increase in Investment (billions of dollars)

Round	New Spending This Round	Cumulative New Spending	New Saving This Round	Cumulative New Saving
1	100	100	—	—
2	80	180	20	20
3	64	244	16	36
⋮	⋮	⋮	⋮	⋮
10	13.4	446.3	3.35	86.6
⋮	⋮	⋮	⋮	⋮
∞	0	500	0	100

LO³ Describe the aggregate demand curve.

A higher price level causes a downward shift of the aggregate expenditure line, leading to a lower real GDP demanded. A lower price level causes an upward shift of the aggregate expenditure line, increasing real GDP demanded. By tracing the impact of price changes on real GDP demanded, we can derive an aggregate demand curve.

The aggregate expenditure line and the aggregate demand curve portray real output from different perspectives. The aggregate expenditure line shows, for a given price level, how much people plan to spend at each income level. Real GDP demanded is found where spending equals income, or real GDP. The aggregate demand curve shows, for various price levels, the quantities of real GDP demanded. At a given price level, a change in spending plans shifts the aggregate demand curve.

The Income-Expenditure Approach and the Aggregate Demand Curve

At the initial price level of 130, the aggregate expenditure line is *AE*, which identifies real GDP demanded of $14.0 trillion. This combination of a price level of 130 and a real GDP demanded of $14.0 trillion determines one combination (point *e*) on the aggregate demand curve in panel (b). At the higher price level of 140, the aggregate expenditure line shifts down to *AE'*, and real GDP demanded falls to $13.5 trillion. This price-quantity combination is plotted as point *e"* in panel (b). At the lower price level of 120, the aggregate expenditure line shifts up to *AE"*, which increases real GDP demanded. This combination is plotted as point *e* in panel (b). Connecting points *e, e',* and *e"* in panel (b) yields the downward-sloping aggregate demand curve, which shows the inverse relation between price and real GDP demanded.

A Shift of the Aggregate Expenditure Line That Shifts the Aggregate Demand Curve

A shift of the aggregate expenditure line at a given price level shifts the aggregate demand curve. In panel (a), an increase in investment of $0.1 trillion, with the price level constant at 130, causes the aggregate expenditure line to increase from $C + I + G + (X - M)$ to $C + I' + G + (X - M)$. As a result, real GDP demanded increases from $14.0 trillion to $14.5 trillion. In panel (b), the aggregate demand curve has shifted from *AD* out to *AD'*. At the prevailing price level of 130, real GDP demanded has increased by $0.5 trillion.

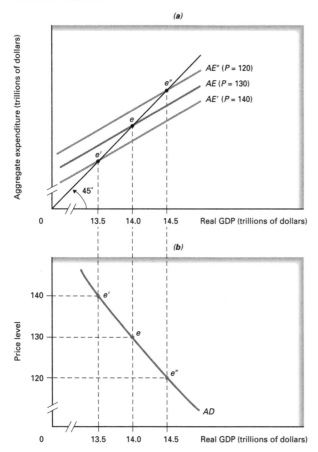

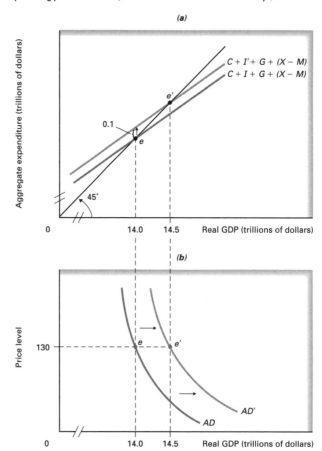

Chapter in Review

11

KEY TERMS

nominal wage
the wage measured in dollars of the year in question; the dollar amount on a paycheck

real wage
the wage measured in dollars of constant purchasing power; the wage measured in terms of the quantity of goods and services it buys

potential output
the economy's maximum sustainable output, given the supply of resources, technology, and rules of the game; the output level when there are no surprises about the price level

natural rate of unemployment
the unemployment rate when the economy produces its potential output

short run
in macroeconomics, a period during which some resource prices, especially those for labor, are fixed by explicit or implicit agreements

short-run aggregate supply (SRAS) curve
a curve that shows a direct relationship between the actual price level and real GDP supplied in the short run, other things constant, including the expected price level

short-run equilibrium
the price level and real GDP that result when the aggregate demand curve intersects the short-run aggregate supply curve

expansionary gap
the amount by which actual output in the short run exceeds the economy's potential output

long run
in macroeconomics, a period during which wage contracts and resource price agreements can be renegotiated; there are no surprises about the economy's actual price level

long-run equilibrium
the price level and real GDP that occurs when (1) the actual price level equals the expected price level, (2) real GDP supplied equals potential output, and (3) real GDP supplied equals real GDP demanded

contractionary gap
the amount by which actual output in the short run falls short of the economy's potential output

LO^1 Explain how aggregate supply operates in the short run. Short-run aggregate supply is based on resource demand and supply decisions that reflect the expected price level. If the price level turns out as expected, the economy produces its potential output. If the price level exceeds expectations, short-run output exceeds the economy's potential, creating an expansionary gap. If the price level is below expectations, short-run output falls short of the economy's potential, creating a contractionary gap.

Short-Run Aggregate Supply Curve

The short-run aggregate supply curve is drawn based on a given expected price level, in this case, 130. Point a shows that if the actual price level equals the expected price level of 130, producers supply potential output. If the actual price level exceeds 130, firms supply more than potential. If the actual price level is below 130, firms supply less than potential. Output levels that fall short of the economy's potential are shaded red; output levels that exceed the economy's potential are shaded blue.

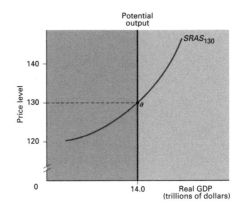

LO^2 Discuss short-run aggregate supply in relation to the long run. Output can exceed the economy's potential in the short run, but in the long run, higher nominal wages will be negotiated at the earliest opportunity. This increases the cost of production, shifting the short-run aggregate supply curve leftward along the aggregate demand curve until the economy produces its potential output.

Long-Run Adjustment When the Price Level Exceeds Expectations

If the expected price level is 130, the short-run aggregate supply curve is SRAS$_{130}$. If the actual price level turns out as expected, the quantity supplied is the potential output of $14.0 trillion. Given the aggregate demand curve shown here, the price level ends up higher than expected, and output exceeds potential, as shown by the short-run equilibrium at point b. The amount by which actual output exceeds the economy's potential output is called the expansionary gap. In the long run, price level expectations and nominal wages will be revised upward. Costs will rise and the short-run aggregate supply curve will shift leftward to SRAS$_{140}$. Eventually, the economy will move to long-run equilibrium at point c, thus closing the expansionary gap.

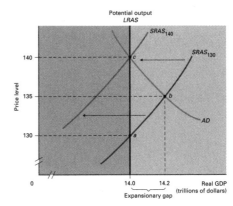

Long-Run Adjustment When the Price Level Is Below Expectations

When the actual price level is below expectations, as indicated by the intersection of the aggregate demand curve AD" with the shortrun aggregate supply curve SRAS$_{130}$, short-run equilibrium occurs at point d. Production below the economy's potential opens a contractionary gap. If prices and wages are flexible enough in the long run, nominal wages will be renegotiated lower. As resource costs fall, the short-run aggregate supply curve eventually shifts rightward to SRAS$_{120}$ and the economy moves to long-run equilibrium at point e, with output increasing to the potential level of $14.0 trillion.

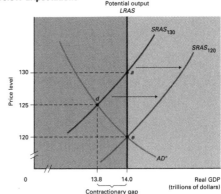

long-run aggregate supply (LRAS) curve

a vertical line at the economy's potential output; aggregate supply when there are no surprises about the price level and all resource contracts can be renegotiated

coordination failure

a situation in which workers and employers fail to achieve an outcome that all would prefer

supply shocks

unexpected events that affect aggregate supply, sometimes only temporarily

beneficial supply shocks

unexpected events that increase aggregate supply, sometimes only temporarily

adverse supply shocks

unexpected events that reduce aggregate supply, sometimes only temporarily

hysteresis

the theory that the natural rate of unemployment depends in part on the recent history of unemployment; high unemployment rates increase the natural rate of unemployment

Long-Run Aggregate Supply Curve

In the long run, when the actual price level equals the expected price level, the economy produces its potential. In the long run, $14.0 trillion in real GDP will be supplied regardless of the actual price level. As long as wages and prices are flexible, the economy's potential GDP is consistent with any price level. Thus, shifts of the aggregate demand curve will, in the long run, not affect potential output. The long-run aggregate supply curve, LRAS, is a vertical line at potential GDP.

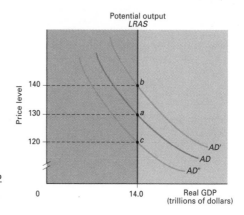

LO³ Analyze shifts of the aggregate supply curve. If output in the short run is less than the economy's potential and if wages and prices are flexible enough, lower nominal wages will reduce production costs in the long run. These lower costs shift the short-run aggregate supply curve rightward along the aggregate demand curve until the economy produces its potential output.

Evidence suggests that when output exceeds the economy's potential, nominal wages and the price level increase. But there is less evidence that nominal wages and the price level fall when output is below the economy's potential. Wages appear to be "sticky" in the downward direction. What usually closes a contractionary gap is an increase in aggregate demand.

The long-run aggregate supply curve, or the economy's potential output, depends on the amount and quality of resources available, the state of technology, and formal and informal institutions, such as patent laws and business practices, that shape production incentives. Increases in resource availability, improvements in technology, or institutional changes that provide more attractive production incentives increase aggregate supply and potential output.

Supply shocks are unexpected, often temporary changes in aggregate supply. Beneficial supply shocks increase output, sometimes only temporarily. Adverse supply shocks reduce output and increase the price level, a combination called stagflation. Adverse supply shocks may be temporary.

Effect of a Gradual Increase in Resources on Aggregate Supply

A gradual increase in the supply of resources increases the potential GDP—in this case, from $14.0 trillion to $14.5 trillion. The long-run aggregate supply curve shifts to the right.

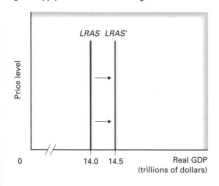

Effects of a Beneficial Supply Shock on Aggregate Supply

Given the aggregate demand curve, a beneficial supply shock that has a lasting effect, such as a breakthrough in technology, will permanently shift both the short-run aggregate supply curve and the long-run aggregate supply curve, or potential output. A beneficial supply shock lowers the price level and increases output, as reflected by the change in equilibrium from point a to point b. A temporary beneficial supply shock, such as would result from an unusually favorable growing season, will shift the aggregate supply curves only temporarily. If the next growing season returns to normal, the aggregate supply curves will return to their original equilibrium position at point a.

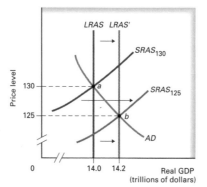

Effects of an Adverse Supply Shock on Aggregate Supply

Given the aggregate demand curve, an adverse supply shock, such as an increased threat of terrorism, shifts the short-run and long-run aggregate supply curves to the left, increasing the price level and reducing real GDP, a movement called stagflation. This change is shown by the move in equilibrium from point a to point c. If the shock is just temporary, the curves will be temporary.

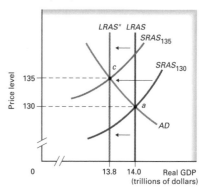

FISCAL POLICY
Chapter in Review

KEY TERMS

automatic stabilizers
structural features of government spending and taxation that reduce fluctuations in disposable income, and thus consumption, over the business cycle

discretionary fiscal policy
the deliberate manipulation of government purchases, taxation, and transfer payments to promote macroeconomic goals, such as full employment, price stability, and economic growth

simple tax multiplier
the ratio of a change in real GDP demanded to the initial change in autonomous net taxes that brought it about; the numerical value of the simple tax multiplier is $-MPC/(1 - MPC)$

expansionary fiscal policy
an increase in government purchases, decrease in net taxes, or some combination of the two aimed at increasing aggregate demand enough to reduce unemployment and return the economy to its potential output; fiscal policy used to close a contractionary gap

contractionary fiscal policy
a decrease in government purchases, increase in net taxes, or some combination of the two aimed at reducing aggregate demand enough to return the economy to potential output without worsening inflation; fiscal policy used to close an expansionary gap

classical economists
a group of 18th- and 19th-century economists who believed that economic downturns corrected themselves through natural market forces; thus, they believed the economy was self-correcting and needed no government intervention

Employment Act of 1946
law that assigned to the federal government the responsibility for promoting full employment and price stability

political business cycles
economic fluctuations that occur when discretionary policy is manipulated for political gain

permanent income
income that individuals expect to receive on average over the long term

LO¹ Explain the theory of fiscal policy. The tools of fiscal policy are automatic stabilizers and discretionary fiscal measures. Automatic stabilizers, such as the federal income tax, once implemented, operate year after year without congressional action. Discretionary fiscal policy results from specific legislation about government spending, taxation, and transfers. If that legislation becomes permanent, then discretionary fiscal policies often become automatic stabilizers.

Effect of a $0.1 Trillion Increase in Government Purchases on Aggregate Expenditure and Real GDP Demanded

As a result of a $0.1 trillion increase in government purchases, the aggregate expenditure line shifts up by $0.1 trillion, increasing the level of real GDP demanded by $0.5 trillion. This model assumes the price level remains unchanged.

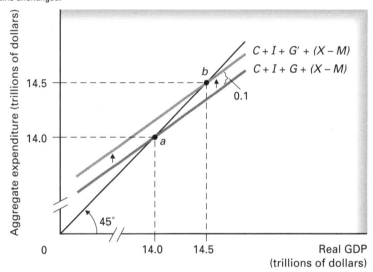

Effect of a $0.1 Trillion Decrease in Net Taxes on Aggregate Expenditure and Real GDP Demanded

As a result of a decrease in net taxes of $0.1 trillion, or $100 billion, consumers, who are assumed to have a marginal propensity to consume of 0.8, spend $80 billion more and save $20 more billion at every level of GDP. The consumption function shifts up by $80 billion, or $0.08 trillion, as does the aggregate expenditure line. An $80 billion increase of the aggregate expenditure line eventually increases real GDP demanded by $0.4 trillion. Keep in mind that the price level is assumed to remain constant during all this.

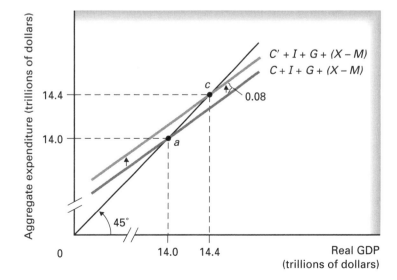

LO² Describe how aggregate supply affects fiscal policy.

An expansionary fiscal policy can close a contractionary gap by increasing government purchases, reducing net taxes, or both. Because the short-run aggregate supply curve slopes upward, an increase in aggregate demand raises both output and the price level in the short run. A contractionary fiscal policy can close an expansionary gap by reducing government purchases, increasing net taxes, or both. Fiscal policy that reduces aggregate demand to close an expansionary gap reduces both output and the price level.

Discretionary Fiscal Policy to Close a Contractionary Gap

The aggregate demand curve AD and the short-run aggregate supply curve, $SRAS_{130}$, intersect at point e. Output falls short of the economy's potential. The resulting contractionary gap is $0.5 trillion. This gap could be closed by discretionary fiscal policy that increases aggregate demand by just the right amount. An increase in government purchases, a decrease in net taxes, or some combination could shift aggregate demand out to AD^*, moving the economy out to its potential output at e^*.

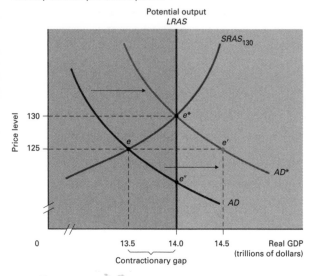

Discretionary Fiscal Policy to Close an Expansionary Gap

The aggregate demand curve AD' and the short-run aggregate supply curve, $SRAS_{130}$, intersect at point e', resulting in an expansionary gap of $0.5 trillion. Discretionary fiscal policy aimed at reducing aggregate demand by just the right amount could close this gap without inflation. An increase in net taxes, a decrease in government purchases, or some combination could shift the aggregate demand curve back to AD^* and move the economy back to potential output at point e^*.

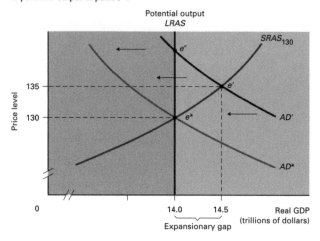

LO³ Discuss the evolution of fiscal policy.

Fiscal policy focuses primarily on the demand side, not the supply side. The problems of the 1970s, however, resulted more from a decline of aggregate supply than from a decline of aggregate demand, so demand-side remedies seemed less effective.

The tax cuts of the early 1980s aimed to increase aggregate supply. But government spending grew faster than tax revenue, creating budget deficits that stimulated aggregate demand. These huge deficits discouraged additional discretionary fiscal policy, but success in erasing deficits in the late 1990s spawned renewed interest in discretionary fiscal policy, as reflected by President Bush's tax cuts in the face of the 2001 recession.

Tax cuts and new spending increased deficits into 2004, but the economy added over 8 million jobs by 2007. The added output and income cut the federal deficit from about $400 billion in 2004 to under $200 billion in 2007. The recession that began officially in December 2007 reversed those recent gains. The federal budget deficit increased to $450 billion in 2008. With lower tax revenues, bailouts, and increased stimulus spending, some forecast deficits as high as $1 trillion.

When Discretionary Fiscal Policy Overshoots Potential Output

If public officials underestimate the natural rate of unemployment, they may attempt to stimulate aggregate demand even if the economy is already producing its potential output, as at point a. This expansionary policy yields a short-run equilibrium at point b, where the price level and output are higher and unemployment is lower, so the policy appears to succeed. But the resulting expansionary gap will, in the long run, reduce the short-run aggregate supply curve from $SRAS_{130}$ to $SRAS_{140}$, eventually reducing output to its potential level of $14.0 trillion while increasing the price level to 140. Thus, attempts to increase production beyond potential GDP lead only to inflation in the long run.

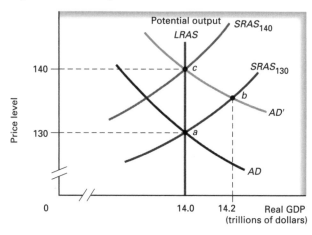

CHAPTER EQUATIONS

Δ Real GDP Demanded

$$\Delta G \times \frac{1}{1 - MPC}$$

Δ Real GDP Demanded

$$(- MPC \times \Delta NT) \times \frac{1}{1 - MPC}$$

Δ Real GDP Demanded

$$\Delta NT \times \frac{-MPC}{1 - MPC}$$

Chapter in Review

13

KEY TERMS

federal budget
a plan for federal government outlays and revenues for a specified period, usually a year

budget resolution
a congressional agreement about total outlays, spending by major category, and expected revenues; it guides spending and revenue decisions by the many congressional committees and subcommittees

continuing resolutions
budget agreements that allow agencies, in the absence of an approved budget, to spend at the rate of the previous year's budget

entitlement programs
guaranteed benefits for those who qualify for government transfer programs such as Social Security and Medicare

annually balanced budget
budget philosophy prior to the Great Depression; aimed at matching annual revenues with outlays, except during times of war

cyclically balanced budget
a budget philosophy calling for budget deficits during recessions to be financed by budget surpluses during expansions

functional finance
a budget philosophy using fiscal policy to achieve the economy's potential GDP, rather than balancing budgets either annually or over the business cycle

crowding out
the displacement of interest-sensitive private investment that occurs when higher government deficits drive up market interest rates

crowding in
the potential for government spending to stimulate private investment in an otherwise dead economy

national debt
the net accumulation of federal budget deficits

LO¹ Examine the federal budget process. The federal budget is a plan of outlays and revenues for a specified period, usually a year. The federal budget process suffers from a variety of problems, including overlapping committee jurisdictions, lengthy budget deliberations, budgeting by continuing resolutions, budgeting in too much detail, failure to distinguish between operating costs and capital costs, and a lack of control over most of the budget. Suggested improvements include instituting a biennial budget, budgeting in less detail, and distinguishing between an operating budget and a capital budget.

Defense's Share of Federal Outlays Declined Since 1960 and Redistribution Increased

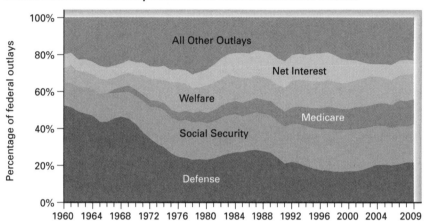

LO² Discuss the fiscal impact of the federal budget. Historically, deficits increase during wars and severe recessions. Deficits remained high, however, during the economic expansions of the 1980s. Those deficits arose from a combination of tax cuts during the early 1980s and growth in federal spending. After peaking at $290 billion in 1992, the federal deficit turned into a surplus by 1998 because of higher tax rates and reduced outlays, especially for defense. The recession of 2001 and terrorist attacks prompted tax cuts to "get the economy moving again." The weak recovery plus tax cuts and federal spending increases brought about a deficit of $400 billion in 2004. But by 2007 the economy added more than 8 million jobs, which helped cut the federal deficit by more than 50 percent. However, stimulus spending, bailouts, and lower tax revenues during the recession of 2008–2009 caused great increases in deficits.

To the extent that deficits crowd out private capital formation, this decline in private investment reduces the economy's ability to grow. This is one cost of deficit spending. Foreign holdings of debt also impose a burden on future generations because debt payments go to foreigners. Thus, the deficits of one generation of Americans can reduce the standard of living of the next.

During the 1990s, Federal Outlays Declined Relative to GDP and Revenues Increased, Turning Deficits into Surpluses, But Not for Long

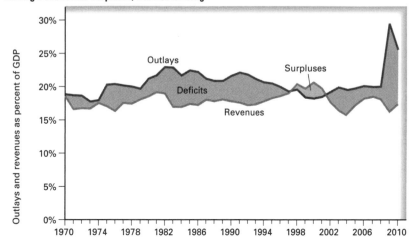

Government Outlays as a Percentage of GDP Declined Between 1994 and 2008 in Most Major Economies

Government outlays relative to GDP shrank in 7 of the 10 industrial economies during the time period. The average dropped from 46 percent to 42 percent. The demise of the Soviet Union in the early 1990s reduced defense spending, and the failure of the socialist experiment shifted sentiment more toward private markets, thus diminishing the role of government.

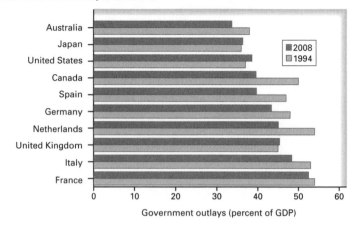

Government outlays (percent of GDP)

LO³ Explain the national debt. The federal or national debt is a stock variable measuring the net accumulation of past deficits, the amount owed by the federal government. Most recently the U.S. federal debt measured relative to GDP was somewhat above the average for major industrial countries and was relatively low compared to U.S. historical levels stretching back to 1940. But the federal debt is projected to grow and federal deficits are projected to worsen.

Federal Debt Held by the Public as a Percentage of GDP Since 1940

The huge cost of World War II rocketed federal debt from 44 percent of GDP in 1940 to over 100 percent by 1946. During the next few decades, GDP grew faster than federal debt so by 1980, federal debt had dropped to only 26 percent of GDP. But high deficits of the 1980s and early 1990s nearly doubled debt to 49 percent of GDP by 1993. Debt then trended lower to 37 percent of GDP by 2007, slightly lower than in 1940. Deficits caused by the 2008–2009 recession caused the percent relative to GDP to increase.

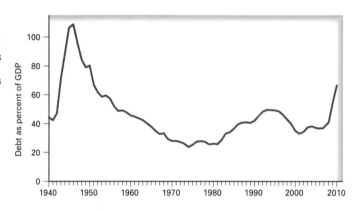

Relative to GDP, U.S. Net Public Debt in 2008 Was About Average for Major Economies

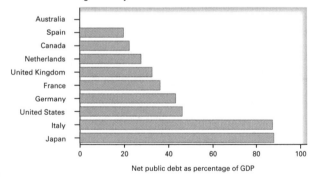

Net public debt as percentage of GDP

Interest Payments on Federal Debt Held by the Public as a Percentage of Federal Outlays Peaked in 1996

After remaining relatively constant during the 1960s and 1970s, interest payments as a share of federal outlays climbed during the 1980s and early 1990s because of growing deficits and higher interest rates. After peaking in 1996 at 15.4 percent of outlays, interest payments declined first because of budget surpluses and later because of declining interest rates. Interest's share of federal outlays will likely climb as interest rates rise from historic lows of recent years.

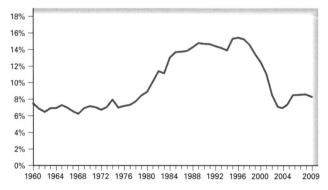

Chapter in Review

14

KEY TERMS

double coincidence of wants
two traders are willing to exchange their products directly

money
anything that is generally accepted in exchange for goods and services

medium of exchange
anything that facilitates trade by being generally accepted by all parties in payment for goods or services

commodity money
anything that serves both as money and as a commodity; money that has intrinsic value

unit of account
a common unit for measuring the value of each good or service

store of value
anything that retains its purchasing power over time

Gresham's Law
people tend to trade away inferior money and hoard the best

seigniorage
the difference between the face value of money and the cost of supplying it; the "profit" from issuing money

token money
money whose face value exceeds its cost of production

check
a written order instructing the bank to pay someone from an amount deposited

fractional reserve banking system
bank reserves amount to only a fraction of funds on deposit with the bank

bank notes
originally, pieces of paper promising a specific amount of gold or silver to anyone who presented them to issuing banks for redemption; today, Federal Reserve notes are mere paper money

representative money
bank notes that exchange for a specific commodity, such as gold

fiat money
money not redeemable for any commodity; its status as money is conferred initially by government decree but eventually by common experience

legal tender
currency that constitutes a valid and legal offer of payment of debt

LO¹ Discuss the evolution of money. Barter was the first form of exchange. As specialization grew, it became more difficult to discover the double coincidence of wants that barter required, bringing about the adoption of money. Anything that acquires a high degree of acceptability throughout an economy becomes money. The first monies were commodities, such as gold, then pieces of paper that could be redeemed for such commodities. As paper money became widely accepted, governments introduced fiat money—money by law or by government fiat. People accept fiat money because, through experience, they believe that other people will do so as well.

The value of money depends on what it buys. If money fails to serve as a medium of exchange, traders find other means of exchange. If a monetary system breaks down, more time must be devoted to exchange, leaving less time for production, so efficiency suffers. No machine increases an economy's productivity as much as a properly functioning money.

Purchasing Power of $1 Measured in 1982–1984 Constant Dollars

An increase in the price level over time reduces what $1.00 buys. The price level has risen every year since 1960, so the purchasing power of $1.00 (measured in 1982–1984 constant dollars) has fallen from $3.38 in 1960 to $0.46 in 2008.

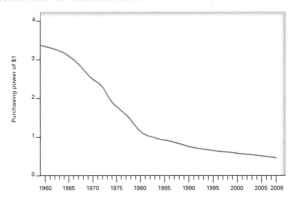

LO² Identify types of financial institutions in the United States. Financial institutions, or intermediaries, earn a profit by paying a lower interest rate to savers than they charge borrowers. Of these, depository institutions, which obtain funds primarily through customer deposits, can be classified broadly into commercial banks, which primarily extend loans for commercial ventures, and thrift institutions. Thrifts can be classified into savings banks, which specialize in home mortgage loans, and credit unions, which primarily finance loans for members' consumer purchases.

LO³ Discuss the origin and powers of the Federal Reserve. The Federal Reserve System, or the Fed, was established in 1913 to regulate the banking system and issue the nation's currency. After a third of the nation's banks failed during the Great Depression, the Fed's powers were increased and centralized. The primary powers of the Fed became (a) to conduct open-market operations (buying and selling U.S. government securities), (b) to set the discount rate (the interest rate the Fed charges borrowing banks), and (c) to establish reserve requirements (the share of deposits banks must hold in reserve).

The Twelve Federal Reserve Districts

The map shows by color the area covered by each of the 12 Federal Reserve districts. Black dots note the locations of the Federal Reserve Bank in each district. Identified with a star is the Board of Governors headquarters in Washington, D.C.

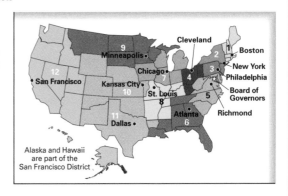

financial intermediaries
institutions such as banks, mortgage companies, and finance companies that serve as go-betweens, borrowing from people who have saved to make loans to others

depository institutions
commercial banks and thrift institutions; financial institutions that accept deposits from the public

commercial banks
depository institutions that historically made short-term loans primarily to businesses

thrift institutions (thrifts)
savings banks and credit unions; depository institutions that historically lent money to households

Federal Reserve System (the Fed)
the central bank and monetary authority of the United States

reserves
funds that banks use to satisfy the cash demands of their customers and the reserve requirements of the Fed; reserves consist of cash held by banks plus deposits at the Fed

Federal Open Market Committee (FOMC)
the 12-member group that makes decisions about open-market operations—purchases and sales of U.S. government securities by the Fed that affect the money supply and interest rates; consists of the seven Board governors plus five of the 12 presidents of the Reserve Banks

open-market operations
purchases and sales of government securities by the Fed in an effort to influence the money supply

money market mutual fund
a collection of short-term interest-earning assets purchased with funds collected from many shareholders

bank branches
a bank's additional offices that carry out banking operations

bank holding company
a corporation that owns banks

LO4 Describe the history of the U.S banking system from the Great Depression to today. In response to the Great Depression, the banking industry became much more closely regulated. Reforms in the 1980s gave banks more flexibility to compete for deposits with other kinds of financial intermediaries. Some banks used this flexibility to make risky loans, but these gambles often failed, causing bank failures. In 1989, Congress approved a measure to close failing banks, pay off insured depositors, and impose tighter regulations. By the mid-1990s, U.S. banks were thriving once again. However, the subprime mortgage and global financial crises caused an increase in the number of commercial bank failures in 2008 and early 2009. Mergers and holding companies are creating larger banks that span the nation, but U.S. banks are still not that large by world standards.

Organization Chart of the Federal Reserve System

Members of the Board of Governors are appointed by the president and confirmed by the Senate. The seven board members also belong to the 12-member Federal Open Market Committee, which advises the board. The Board of Governors controls the reserve banks in each of the 12 districts, which in turn control the U.S. banking system.

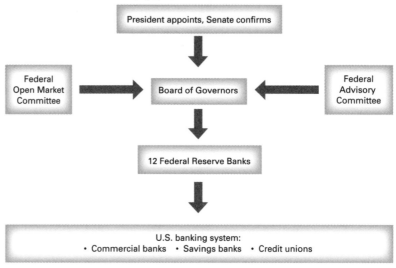

The Number of Commercial Banks Declined over the Last Two Decades, but the Number of Branches Continues to Grow

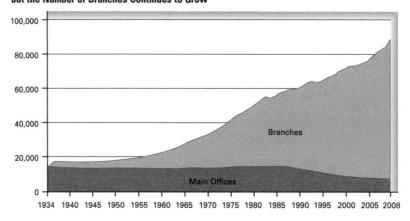

Chapter in Review

15

KEY TERMS

checkable deposits
bank deposits that allow the account owner to write checks to third parties; ATM or debit cards can also access these deposits and transmit them electronically

money aggregates
measures of the economy's money supply

M1
the narrow measure of the money supply, consisting of currency and coins held by the nonbanking public, checkable deposits, and traveler's checks

savings deposits
deposits that earn interest but have no specific maturity date

time deposits
deposits that earn a fixed interest rate if held for the specified period, which can range from several months to several years; also called certificates of deposit

M2
a money aggregate consisting of M1 plus savings deposits, small-denomination time deposits, and money market mutual funds

debit card
card that taps directly into the depositor's bank account to fund purchases; also called a check card, and often doubles as an ATM card

asymmetric information
a situation in which one side of the market has more reliable information than the other side

net worth
assets minus liabilities; also called owners' equity

balance sheet
a financial statement at a given point in time that shows assets on one side and liabilities and net worth on the other side; because assets must equal liabilities plus net worth, the two sides of the statement must be in balance

asset
anything of value that is owned

liability
anything that is owed to other people or institutions

required reserves
the dollar amount of reserves a bank is obligated by regulation to hold as cash in the bank's vault or on account at the Fed

LO¹ Examine definitions of money aggregates. The money supply is narrowly defined as M1, which consists of currency held by the nonbanking public plus checkable deposits and traveler's checks. A broader money aggregate, M2, includes M1 plus savings deposits, small-denomination time deposits, money market mutual funds, and other near-monies.

Measures of the Money Supply (February 2009)

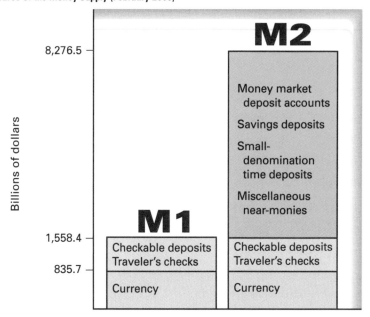

LO² Explain how banks work. Banks are unlike other financial intermediaries because they can turn a borrower's IOU into money—they can create money. Banks also evaluate loan applications and diversify portfolios of assets to reduce the risk to any one saver. In acquiring portfolios of assets, banks try to maximize profit while maintaining enough liquidity to satisfy depositors' requests for money. Assets that earn the bank more interest are usually less liquid.

LO³ Describe how banks create money. Any single bank can expand the money supply by the amount of its excess reserves. For the banking system as a whole, however, the maximum expansion of the money supply equals a multiple of fresh bank reserves. The simple money multiplier is the reciprocal of the reserve ratio, or 1/r. This multiplier is reduced to the extent that (a) banks allow excess reserves to remain idle, (b) borrowers sit on their proceeds, and (c) the public withdraws cash from the banking system and holds it.

LO⁴ Discuss the Fed's tools for monetary control. The key to changes in the money supply is the Fed's impact on excess reserves in the banking system. To increase excess reserves and thus increase the money supply, the Fed can buy U.S. government bonds, reduce the discount rate, or lower the reserve requirement. To reduce excess reserves and thus reduce the money supply, the Fed can sell U.S. government bonds, increase the discount rate, or increase the reserve requirement. The Fed's most important tool by far is the buying or selling of U.S. bonds.

required reserve ratio
the ratio of reserves to deposits that banks are obligated by regulation to hold

excess reserves
bank reserves exceeding required reserves

liquidity
a measure of the ease with which an asset can be converted into money without a significant loss of value

federal funds market
a market for overnight lending and borrowing of reserves among banks; the interbank market for reserves on account at the Fed

federal funds rate
the interest rate charged in the federal funds market; the interest rate banks charge one another for overnight borrowing; the Fed's target interest rate

money multiplier
the multiple by which the money supply changes as a result of a change in fresh reserves in the banking system

simple money multiplier
the reciprocal of the required reserve ratio, or $1/r$; the maximum multiple of fresh reserves by which the money supply can increase

open-market purchase
the purchase of U.S. government bonds by the Fed to increase the money supply

open-market sale
the sale of U.S. government bonds by the Fed to reduce the money supply

discount rate
the interest rate the Fed charges banks that borrow reserves

CHAPTER EQUATIONS

Assets

$$\text{Assets} = \text{Liabilities} + \text{Net worth}$$

Simple Money Multiplier

$$\Delta \text{ money supply} = \Delta \text{ fresh reserves} \times 1/r$$

NOTES

Chapter in Review

16

KEY TERMS

demand for money
the relationship between the interest rate and how much money people want to hold

equation of exchange
the quantity of money, *M,* multiplied by its velocity, *V,* equals nominal GDP, which is the product of the price level, *P,* and real GDP, *Y,* or $M \times V = P \times Y$

velocity of money
the average number of times per year each dollar is used to purchase final goods and services

quantity theory of money
if the velocity of money is stable, or at least predictable, changes in the money supply have predictable effects on nominal GDP

CHAPTER EQUATIONS

Effects of an Increase in the Money Supply

$$M\uparrow \rightarrow i\downarrow \rightarrow I\uparrow \rightarrow AD\uparrow \rightarrow Y\uparrow$$

Equation of Exchange

$$M \times V = P \times Y$$

Velocity

$$V = \frac{P \times Y}{M}$$

Total Spending

$$M \times V$$

Total Receipts

$$P \times Y$$

LO¹ Describe the relationship between the demand and supply of money. The opportunity cost of holding money is the higher interest forgone by not holding other financial assets instead. Along a given money demand curve, the quantity of money demanded relates inversely to the interest rate. The demand for money curve shifts rightward as a result of an increase in the price level, an increase in real GDP, or an increase in both.

Demand for Money

The money demand curve, *D_m*, slopes downward. As the interest rate falls, other things constant, so does the opportunity cost of holding money; the quantity of money demanded increases.

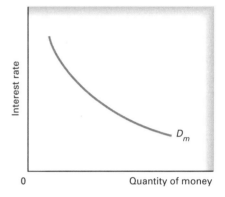

Effect of an Increase in the Money Supply

Because the supply of money is determined by the Federal Reserve, it can be represented by a vertical line. At point *a,* the intersection of supply of money, *S_m*, and the demand for money, *D_m*, determines the market interest rate, *i.* Following an increase in the money supply to *S'_m,* the quantity of money supplied exceeds the quantity demanded at the original interest rate, *i.* People attempt to exchange money for bonds or other financial assets. In doing so, they push down the interest rate to *i'*, where quantity demanded equals the new quantity supplied. This new equilibrium occurs at point *b.*

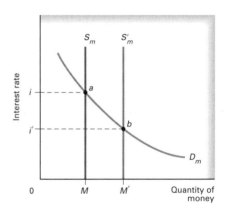

LO² Explain how changes in the money supply affect aggregate demand in the short run. The Fed determines the supply of money, which is assumed to be independent of the interest rate. The intersection of the supply and demand curves for money determines the market interest rate. In the short run, an increase in the supply of money reduces the interest rate, which increases investment. This boosts aggregate demand, which increases real output and the price level.

Effects of an Increase in the Money Supply on Interest Rates, Investment, and Aggregate Demand

In panel (a), an increase in the money supply drives the interest rate down to *i'*. With the cost of borrowing lower, the amount invested increases from *I* to *I'*, as shown in panel (b). This sets off the spending multiplier process, so the aggregate output demanded at price level *P* increases from *Y* to *Y'*. The increase is shown by the shift of the aggregate demand curve to the right in panel (c).

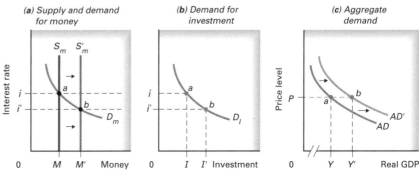

Expansionary Monetary Policy to Close a Contractionary Gap

At point *a*, the economy is producing less than its potential in the short run, resulting in a contractionary gap of $0.2 trillion. If the Federal Reserve increases the money supply by just the right amount, the aggregate demand curve shifts rightward from *AD* to *AD'*. A short-run and long-run equilibrium is established at point *b*, with the price level at 130 and output at the potential level of $14.0 trillion.

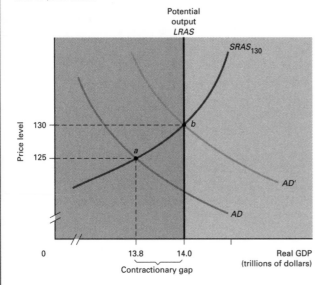

The Velocity of Money

M1 velocity fluctuated so much during the 1980s that M1 growth was abandoned as a short-run policy target. M2 velocity appears more stable than M1 velocity, but both are now considered by the Fed as too unpredictable for short-run policy use.

LO³ Explain how changes in the money supply affect aggregate demand in the long run.

The long-run approach focuses on the role of money through the equation of exchange, which states that the quantity of money, *M,* multiplied by velocity, *V,* the average number of times each dollar gets spent on final goods and services, equals the price level, *P,* multiplied by real output, *Y.* So $M \times V = P \times Y.$ Because the aggregate supply curve in the long run is a vertical line at the economy's potential output, a change in the money supply affects the price level but not real output.

In the Long Run, an Increase in the Money Supply Results in a Higher Price Level, or Inflation

The quantity theory of money predicts that if velocity is stable, then an increase in the supply of money in the long run results in a higher price level, or inflation. Because the long-run aggregate supply curve is fixed, increases in the money supply affect only the price level, not real output.

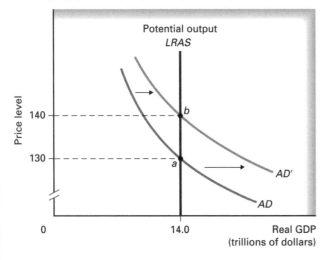

LO⁴ Evaluate targets for monetary policy.

Between World War II and October 1979, the Fed tried to maintain stable interest rates as a way of promoting a stable investment environment. During the 1980s and early 1990s, the Fed paid more attention to growth in money aggregates, first M1 and then M2. To pursue its main goals of price stability and sustainable economic growth, the Fed adjusts the federal funds rate, raising the rate to prevent higher inflation and lowering the rate to stimulate economic growth.

Targeting Interest Rates Versus Targeting the Money Supply

An increase in the price level or in real GDP, with velocity stable, shifts rightward the money demand curve from D_m to D'_m. If the Federal Reserve holds the money supply at S_m, the interest rate will rise from *i* (at point *e*) to *i'* (at point *e'*). Alternatively, the Fed could hold the interest rate constant by increasing the supply of money to S'_m. The Fed may choose any point along the money demand curve D'_m.

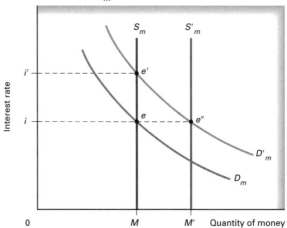

Chapter in Review

17

KEY TERMS

recognition lag
the time needed to identify a macroeconomic problem and assess its seriousness

decision-making lag
the time needed to decide what to do once a macroeconomic problem has been identified

implementation lag
the time needed to introduce a change in monetary or fiscal policy

effectiveness lag
the time needed for changes in monetary or fiscal policy to affect the economy

rational expectations
a school of thought that argues people form expectations based on all available information, including the likely future actions of government policy makers

time-inconsistency problem
when policy makers have an incentive to announce one policy to influence expectations but then pursue a different policy once those expectations have been formed and acted on

cold turkey
the announcement and execution of tough measures to reduce high inflation

inflation target
central bankers commit to keep the inflation below a certain rate for the next year or two

Phillips curve
curve showing possible combinations of the inflation rate and the unemployment rate

short-run Phillips curve
based on an expected inflation rate, a curve that reflects an inverse relationship between the inflation rate and the unemployment rate

long-run Phillips curve
a vertical line drawn at the economy's natural rate of unemployment that traces equilibrium points that can occur when workers and employers have the time to adjust fully to any unexpected change in aggregate demand

natural rate hypothesis
the natural rate of unemployment is largely independent of the stimulus provided by monetary or fiscal policy

LO¹ Compare an active policy and a passive policy. Advocates of active policy view the private sector—particularly fluctuations in investment—as the primary source of economic instability in the economy. Activists argue that achieving potential output through natural market forces can be slow and painful, so the Fed or Congress should stimulate aggregate demand when actual output falls below potential.

Advocates of passive policy argue that the economy has enough natural resiliency to return to potential output within a reasonable period if upset by some shock. They point to the variable and uncertain lags associated with discretionary policy as reason enough to steer clear of active intervention.

Closing a Contractionary Gap

At point a in both panels, the economy is in short-run equilibrium, with unemployment exceeding its natural rate. According to the passive approach, shown in panel (a), high unemployment eventually causes wages to fall, reducing the cost of doing business. The decline in costs shifts the short-run aggregate supply curve rightward from $SRAS_{130}$ to $SRAS_{120}$, moving the economy to its potential output at point b. In panel (b), the government employs an active approach to shift the aggregate demand curve from AD to AD'. If the active policy works perfectly, the economy moves to its potential output at point c.

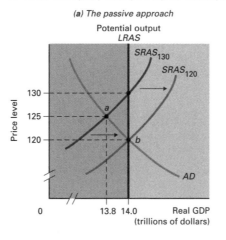

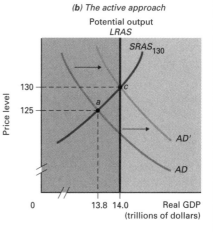

Closing an Expansionary Gap

At point d in both panels, the economy is in short-run equilibrium, producing \$14.2 trillion, which exceeds the economy's potential output. Unemployment is below its natural rate. In the passive approach reflected in panel (a), the government makes no change in policy, so natural market forces eventually bring about a higher negotiated wage, increasing firm costs and shifting the short-run supply curve leftward to $SRAS_{140}$. The new equilibrium at point e results in a higher price level and lower output and employment. An active policy reduces aggregate demand, shifting the equilibrium in panel (b) from point d to point c, thus closing the expansionary gap without increasing the price level.

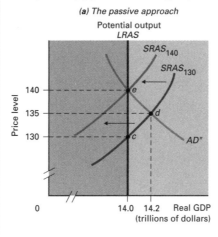

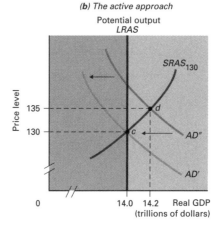

LO² Consider the role of expectations. The theory of rational expectations holds that people form expectations based on all available information, including past behavior by public officials. According to the rational expectations school, government policies are mostly anticipated by the public, and therefore have less effect than unexpected policies.

LO³ Discuss policy rules versus discretion. The active approach views the economy as unstable and in need of discretionary policy to eliminate excess unemployment. The passive approach, however, suggests that discretionary policy is not necessary and may even be harmful. The passive approach suggests that the government should follow clear and predictable policies and avoid discretionary intervention to stimulate or dampen aggregate demand. Passive policies are reflected in automatic fiscal stabilizers and in explicit monetary rules, such as keeping inflation below a certain rate.

LO⁴ Explain the Phillips curve. At one time, public officials thought they faced a stable trade-off between higher unemployment and higher inflation. More recent research suggests that if there is a trade-off, it exists only in the short run, not in the long run. The hypothetical Phillips curve illustrates the relationship between inflation and unemployment. Expansionary fiscal or monetary policies may stimulate output and employment in the short run. But if the economy is already at or near its potential output, these expansionary policies, in the long run, result only in more inflation.

Hypothetical Phillips Curve

The Phillips curve shows an inverse relation between unemployment and inflation. Points *a* and *b* lie on the Phillips curve and represent alternative combinations of inflation and unemployment that are attainable as long as the curve itself does not shift. Points *c* and *d* are off the curve. ⟶

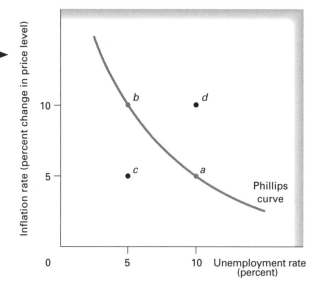

Aggregate Supply Curve and Phillips Curves in the Short Run and Long Run

If people expect a price level of 103, which is 3 percent higher than the current level, and if *AD* turns out to be the aggregate demand curve, then the price level is 103 and output is at its potential. Point *a* in both panels represents this situation. Unemployment is the natural rate, assumed to be 5 percent in panel (b). If aggregate demand turns out to be greater than expected (*AD′* instead of *AD*), the economy in the short run will be at point *b* in panel (a), where the price level of 105 will exceed expectations and output will exceed its potential. The resulting higher inflation and lower unemployment are shown as point *b* in panel (b). If aggregate demand turns out to be less than expected (*AD″* instead of AD), short-run equilibrium will be at point *c* in panel (a), where the price level of 101 will be lower than expected and output will be short of potential. Lower inflation and higher unemployment are shown as point *c* in panel (b). In panel (b), points *a, b,* and *c* trace a short-run Phillips curve. In the long run, the actual price level equals the expected price level. Output is at the potential level, $14.0 trillion, in panel (a). Unemployment is at the natural rate, 5 percent, in panel (b). Points *a, d,* and *e* depict long-run points in each panel. In panel (a) these points trace potential output, or long-run aggregate supply. In panel (b), these points trace a long-run Phillips curve.

(a) *Short-run aggregate supply curve*

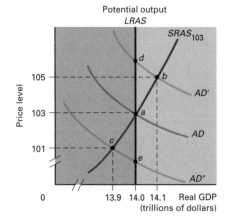

(b) *Short-run and long-run Phillips curves*

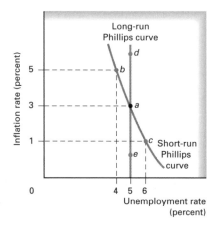

INTERNATIONAL TRADE
Chapter in Review

18

KEY TERMS

autarky
national self-sufficiency; no economic interaction with foreigners

terms of trade
how much of one good exchanges for a unit of another good

world price
the price at which a good is traded on the world market; determined by the world demand and world supply for the good

General Agreement on Tariffs and Trade (GATT)
an international tariff-reduction treaty adopted in 1947 that resulted in a series of negotiated "rounds" aimed at freer trade; the Uruguay Round created GATT's successor, the World Trade Organization (WTO)

dumping
selling a product abroad for less than charged in the home market or for less than the cost of production

Uruguay Round
the final multilateral trade negotiation under GATT; this 1994 agreement cut tariffs, formed the World Trade Organization (WTO), and will eventually eliminate quotas

World Trade Organization (WTO)
the legal and institutional foundation of the multilateral trading system that succeeded GATT in 1995

LO¹ Describe the gains that trade brings. The law of comparative advantage says that the individual with the lowest opportunity cost of producing a particular good should specialize in that good. Just as individuals benefit from specialization and exchange, so do states and, indeed, nations. To reap the gains that arise from specialization, countries engage in international trade. Each country specializes in making goods with the lowest opportunity cost. Before countries can trade, however, they must agree on how much of one good exchanges for another (i.e., the terms of trade).

Production Possibilities Frontiers for the United States and Izodia Without Trade (millions of units per day)

Panel (a) shows the U.S. production possibilities frontier; its slope indicates that the opportunity cost of an additional unit of food is 1/2 unit of clothing. Panel (b) shows production possibilities in Izodia; an additional unit of food costs 2 units of clothing. Food is produced at a lower opportunity cost in the United States.

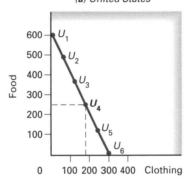

Production (and Consumption) Possibility Frontiers with Trade (millions of units per day)

If Izodia and the United States can trade at the rate of 1 unit of clothing for 1 unit of food, both can benefit. Consumption possibilities at these terms of trade are shown by the blue lines. The United States was previously producing and consuming U_4. By trading with Izodia, it can produce only food and still consume combination U, which has more food and more clothing than U_4. Likewise, Izodia can attain preferred combination I by trading its clothing for U.S. food. Both countries are better off as a result of international trade.

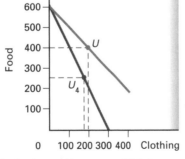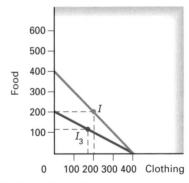

U.S. Production as a Percentage of U.S. Consumption for Various Commodities

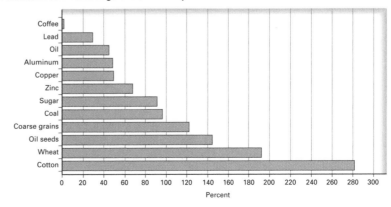

LO² Discuss the reasons for international specialization. Countries export products they can produce more cheaply in return for products that are unavailable domestically or are cheaper elsewhere. If production is subject to economies of scale (i.e., if the long-run average cost of production falls as a firm expands its scale of operation), countries can gain from trade if each nation specializes. Consumption patterns differ across countries, and some of this results from differences in tastes, a situation that allows countries to gain from trade.

LO³
Explain trade restrictions and welfare loss. Market exchange usually generates a surplus, or a bonus, for both consumers and producers. Governments try to regulate surpluses by imposing tariffs (either specific or *ad valorem*) and import quotas, granting export subsidies, or extending low-interest loans to foreign buyers. Loss in U.S. consumer surplus resulting from tariffs is divided three ways: a portion goes to domestic producers; a portion becomes government revenue; and the last portion represents net losses in domestic social welfare. Welfare loss occurs when consumers must pay a higher price for products that could have been imported and sold at a lower price.

Effect of a Tariff

At a world price of $0.10 per pound, U.S. consumers demand 70 million pounds of sugar per month, and U.S. producers supply 20 million pounds per month; the difference is imported. After the imposition of a $0.05 per pound tariff, the U.S. price rises to $0.15 per pound. U.S. producers increase production to 30 million pounds, and U.S. consumers cut back to 60 million pounds. Imports fall to 30 million pounds. At the higher U.S. price, consumers are worse off; their loss of consumer surplus is the sum of areas *a, b, c,* and *d.* Area *a* represents an increase in producer surplus; this area is transferred from consumers to producers. Area *b* reflects the higher marginal cost of domestically producing sugar that could have been produced more cheaply abroad; thus *b* is a net U.S. welfare loss. Area *c* shows government revenue from the tariff. Area *d* reflects the loss of consumer surplus resulting from the drop in consumption. The net welfare loss to the U.S. economy consists of areas *b* and *d.*

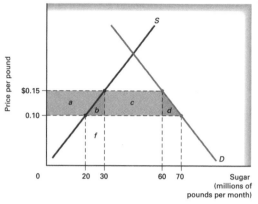

Effect of a Quota

In panel (a), *D* is the U.S. demand curve and *S* is the supply curve of U.S. producers. When the government establishes a sugar quota of 30 million pounds per year, the supply curve from both U.S. production and imports becomes horizontal at the world price of $0.10 per pound and remains horizontal until the quantity supplied reaches 50 million pounds. For higher prices, the supply curve equals the horizontal sum of the U.S. supply curve, *S,* and the quota. The new U.S. price, $0.15 per pound, is determined by the intersection of the new supply curve, *S′,* with the U.S. demand curve, *D.* Panel (b) shows the welfare effect of the quota. As a result of the higher U.S. price, consumer surplus

(a) *(b)*

is cut by the shaded area. Area *a* represents a transfer from U.S. consumers to U.S. producers. Triangular area *b* reflects a net loss; it represents the amount by which the cost of producing an extra 10 million pounds of sugar in the United States exceeds the cost of buying it from abroad. Rectangular area *c* shows the gain to those who can sell foreign-grown sugar at the higher U.S. price instead of the world price. Area *d* also reflects a net loss—a reduction in consumer surplus as consumption falls because of the price increase. Thus, the blue-shaded areas illustrate the loss in consumer surplus that is captured by domestic producers and those who are permitted to fulfill the quota, and the pink-shaded triangles illustrate the net welfare cost of the quota on the U.S. economy.

LO⁴
Describe ways countries have reduced or eliminated trade barriers. Trade restrictions impose a variety of strains on the economy besides the higher costs to consumers, so countries have worked to create free trade agreements and common markets to reduce or eliminate trade barriers. The General Agreement on Tariffs and Trade (GATT) was an international treaty ratified in 1947 to reduce trade barriers. Subsequent negotiations lowered tariffs and reduced trade restrictions. The Uruguay Round, ratified in 1994, lowered tariffs, phased out quotas, and created the World Trade Organization (WTO) as the successor to GATT.

LO⁵
List and describe the arguments in favor of trade restrictions. Arguments used by producer groups to support trade restrictions include promoting national defense, nurturing infant industries, preventing foreign producers from dumping goods in domestic markets, protecting domestic jobs, and allowing declining industries time to wind down and exit the market.

INTERNATIONAL FINANCE

Chapter in Review

KEY TERMS

balance on goods and services
the portion of a country's balance-of-payments account that measures the value of a country's exports of goods and services minus the value of its imports of goods and services

net investment income from abroad
investment earnings by U.S. residents from their foreign assets minus investment earnings by foreigners from their assets in the United States

net unilateral transfers abroad
the unilateral transfers (gifts and grants) received from abroad by U.S. residents minus the unilateral transfers U.S. residents send abroad

balance on current account
the portion of the balance-of-payments account that measures that country's balance on goods and services, net investment income from abroad, plus net unilateral transfers abroad

LO¹ Explain how the balance of payments works. The balance of payments reflects all economic transactions between one country and the rest of the world. The current account measures flows from (a) goods; (b) services, including consulting and tourism; (c) income from holdings of foreign assets; and (d) unilateral transfers, or public and private transfer payments to and from foreign residents. The financial account measures international transactions in real and financial assets.

U.S. Balance of Payments for 2007 (billions of dollars)

Current Accounts	
1. Merchandise exports	+1,148.5
2. Merchandise imports	−1,967.9
3. Merchandise trade balance (1 + 2)	−819.4
4. Service exports	+497.2
5. Service imports	−378.1
6. Goods and services balance (3 + 4 + 5)	−700.3
7. Net investment income from abroad	+81.7
8. Net unilateral transfers	−112.7
9. Current account balance (6 + 7 + 8)	−731.3
Financial Accounts	
10. Change in U.S.-owned assets abroad	−1,289.9
11. Change in foreign-owned assets in U.S.	+2,057.7
12. Financial account balance (10 + 11)	+767.8
13. Statistical discrepancy	−36.5
TOTAL (9 + 12 + 13)	**0.0**

U.S. Imports Have Topped Exports Since 1976, and the Trade Deficit Has Widened

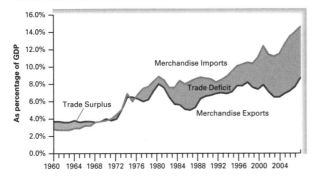

U.S. Merchandise Trade Deficits in 2008 by Country or Grouping

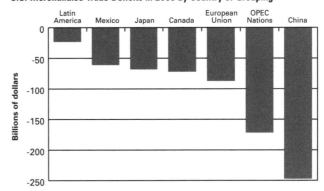

financial account
the record of a country's international transactions involving purchases or sales of financial and real assets

exchange rate
the price measured in one country's currency of purchasing 1 unit of another country's currency

currency depreciation
with respect to the dollar, an increase in the number of dollars needed to purchase 1 unit of foreign exchange in a flexible rate system

currency appreciation
with respect to the dollar, a decrease in the number of dollars needed to purchase 1 unit of foreign exchange in a flexible rate system

arbitrageur
someone who takes advantage of temporary geographic differences in the exchange rate by simultaneously purchasing a currency in one market and selling it in another market

speculator
someone who buys or sells foreign exchange in hopes of profiting from fluctuations in the exchange rate over time

purchasing power parity (PPP) theory
the idea that the exchange rate between two countries will adjust in the long run to equalize the cost between the countries of a basket of internationally traded goods

flexible exchange rate
rate determined in foreign exchange markets by the forces of demand and supply without government intervention

fixed exchange rate
rate of exchange between currencies pegged within a narrow range and maintained by the central bank's ongoing purchases and sales of currencies

currency devaluation
an increase in the official pegged price of foreign exchange in terms of the domestic currency

currency revaluation
a reduction in the official pegged price of foreign exchange in terms of the domestic currency

gold standard
an arrangement whereby the currencies of most countries are convertible into gold at a fixed rate

International Monetary Fund (IMF)
an international organization that establishes rules for maintaining the international monetary system and makes loans to countries with temporary balance-of-payments problems

managed float system
an exchange rate system that combines features of freely floating rates with sporadic intervention by central banks

LO² Discuss foreign exchange rates and markets. Under a system of fixed exchange rates, monetary authorities try to stabilize the exchange rate, keeping it between a specified ceiling and floor value. A country may try to hold down the value of its currency, so that exports will be cheaper to foreigners and imports will cost more to domestic consumers. One objective here is to increase domestic production and employment.

The Foreign Exchange Market

The fewer dollars needed to purchase 1 unit of foreign exchange, the lower the price of foreign goods and the greater the quantity of foreign goods demanded. The greater the quantity of foreign goods demanded, the greater the quantity of foreign exchange demanded. Thus, the demand curve for foreign exchange slopes downward. An increase in the exchange rate makes U.S. products cheaper for foreigners. The increased demand for U.S. goods implies an increase in the quantity of foreign exchange supplied. The supply curve of foreign exchange slopes upward.

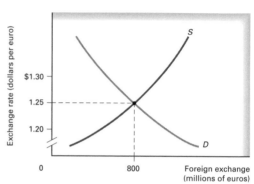

Effect on the Foreign Exchange Market of an Increased Demand for Euros

The intersection of the demand curve for foreign exchange, *D,* and the supply curve for foreign exchange, *S,* determines the exchange rate. At an exchange rate of $1.25 per euro, the quantity of euros demanded equals the quantity supplied. An increase in the demand for euros from *D* to *D'* increases the exchange rate from $1.25 to $1.27 per euro.

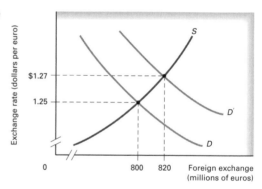

LO³ Define fixed and flexible exchange rates. Under a system of flexible, or floating, exchange rates, the value of the dollar varies inversely with respect to changes in the demand for foreign exchange and directly with respect to changes in the supply of foreign exchange. If governments, however, try to impose fixed exchange rates, active and ongoing central bank intervention is often necessary to establish and maintain them.

LO⁴ Describe the development of the international monetary system. For much of this century, the international monetary system was based on fixed exchange rates. A managed float system has been in effect for the major currencies since the demise of the Bretton Woods system in the early 1970s. Although central banks often try to stabilize exchange rates, fluctuations in rates persist. These fluctuations usually reflect market forces, but they still raise the transaction costs of international trade and finance.

Chapter in Review

20

KEY TERMS

developing countries
nations typified by high rates of illiteracy, high unemployment, high fertility rates, and exports of primary products; also known as low-income and middle-income economies

industrial market countries
economically advanced capitalist countries of Western Europe, North America, Australia, New Zealand, and Japan; also known as developed countries and high-income economies

social capital
the shared values and trust that promote cooperation in the economy

import substitution
a development strategy that emphasizes domestic manufacturing of products that had been imported

export promotion
a development strategy that concentrates on producing for the export market

foreign aid
an international transfer made on especially favorable terms for the purpose of promoting economic development

soft budget constraint
the budget condition faced by socialist enterprises that are subsidized if they lose money

gradualism
a "bottom-up" approach to moving gradually from a centrally planned to a market economy by establishing markets at the most decentralized level first, such as on small farms or in light industry

big-bang theory
the argument that the transition from a centrally planned to a market economy should be broad and swift, taking place in a matter of months

privatization
the process of turning public enterprises into private enterprises

transparent finances
a firm's financial records that clearly indicate the economic health of the company

LO¹ Describe the worldwide variation in economic vitality. The most common measure of comparison of standards of living between different countries is output per capita. Developing countries are distinguished by low output per capita, poor health and nutrition, high fertility rates, and poor education.

Share of World Population and Output from High-, Middle-, and Low-Income Economies

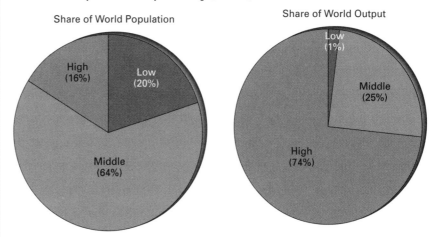

Per Capita Income for Selected Countries in 2007

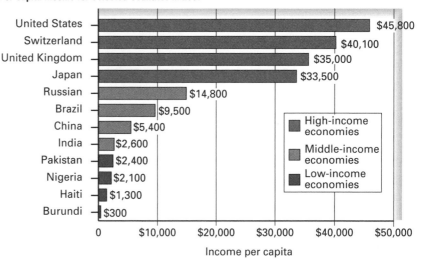

LO² Explain why productivity is the key to development. Labor productivity, measured in terms of output per worker, is by definition low in low-income countries, as it depends on the quality of the labor and other inputs that combine with labor, such as capital and natural resources. The key to a rising standard of living is increased productivity. To foster productivity, developing nations must stimulate investment, support education and training programs, provide sufficient infrastructure, and foster supportive rules of the game.

LO³ Discuss international trade and development. Developing countries need to trade with developed countries to acquire the capital and technology that will increase labor productivity. Exports usually generate more than half of the annual flow of foreign exchange in developing countries. Foreign aid and private investment make up the rest. Developing countries often use either import substitution or export promotion strategies to improve production. With import substitution, domestic manufacturers make products that had previously been imported and the government supports them with tariffs and quotas. Export promotion concentrates on producing for the export market. Export promotion has proven generally more successful.

LO⁴ Describe the role of foreign aid in economic development. Foreign aid has been a mixed blessing for most developing countries. In some cases, that aid has helped countries build the roads, bridges, schools, and other capital infrastructure necessary for development. In other cases, foreign aid has simply increased consumption and insulated government from painful but necessary reforms. Worse still, subsidized food from abroad has undermined domestic agriculture, hurting poor farmers.

LO⁵ Define transitional economies. Transitional economies are primarily defined by the attempt to replace central planning with markets. Major reforms have been introduced in recent years in formerly socialist economies to decentralize decision making, to provide greater production incentives to workers, and to introduce competitive markets.

LO⁶ Discuss markets and institutions. Institutions, or "rules of the game," are the formal and informal incentives and constraints that structure political, economic, and social interaction. Throughout history, institutions have been devised by people to create order and reduce uncertainty in exchange. As many countries tried to create efficient markets, central controls were dismantled before the institutional framework had developed to support a market economy. The gradual transition from a centrally planned economy to a market economy seems to be working better than a faster transition. That's because a gradual transition takes into account the fact that underlying the surface of economic behavior is a grid of informal, often unconscious, habits, customs, manners, and norms that make markets possible.

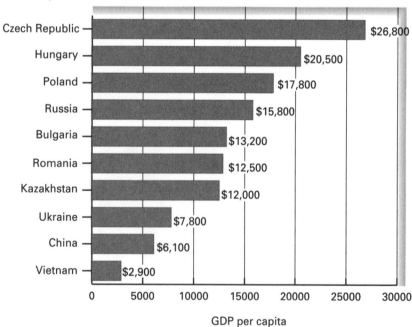

GDP Per Capita for Transitional Economies in 2008

Country	GDP per capita
Czech Republic	$26,800
Hungary	$20,500
Poland	$17,800
Russia	$15,800
Bulgaria	$13,200
Romania	$12,500
Kazakhstan	$12,000
Ukraine	$7,800
China	$6,100
Vietnam	$2,900

Case Study

The Opportunity Cost of College (Chapter 2)

What is your opportunity cost of attending college full time this year? What was the best alternative you gave up? If you held a full-time job, you have some idea of the income you gave up to attend college. Suppose you expected to earn $20,000 a year, after taxes, from a full-time job. As a full-time college student, you plan to work part time during the academic year and full time during the summer, earning a total of $10,000 after taxes. Thus, by attending college this year, you gave up after-tax earnings of $10,000 (= $20,000 − $10,000).

There is also the direct cost of college itself. Suppose you are paying $6,000 this year for in-state tuition, fees, and books at a public college (paying out-of-state rates would add another $6,000 to that, and attending a private college would add about $15,000). The opportunity cost of paying for tuition, fees, and books is what you and your family could otherwise have purchased with that money.

How about room and board? Expenses for room and board are not necessarily an opportunity cost because, even if you were not attending college, you would still need to live somewhere and eat something, though these could cost more in college. Likewise, whether or not you attended college, you would still buy goods such as CDs, clothes, and toiletries, and services such as laundry, haircuts, and DVD rentals. Your spending for such products is not an opportunity cost of attending college but the personal cost that arises regardless of what you do. So for simplicity, assume that room, board, and personal expenses are the same whether or not you attend college. The forgone earnings of $10,000 plus the $6,000 for tuition, fees, and books yield an opportunity cost of $16,000 this year for a student paying in-state rates at a public college. Opportunity cost jumps to about $22,000 for students paying out-of-state rates and to about $31,000 for those at private colleges. Scholarships, but not loans, would reduce your opportunity cost (why not loans?).

This analysis assumes that other things remain constant. But if, in your view, attending college is more of a pain than you expected your next best alternative to be, then the opportunity cost of attending college is even higher. In other words, if you are one of those people who find college difficult, often boring, and in most ways more unpleasant than a full-time job, then the cost in money terms understates your opportunity cost. Not only are you incurring the expense of college, but you are also forgoing a more pleasant quality of life. If, on the other hand, you believe the wild and crazy life of a college student is more enjoyable than a full-time job would be, then the dollar figures overstate your opportunity cost, because your next best alternative involves a less satisfying quality of life.

Apparently, you view college as a wise investment in your future, even though it's costly and perhaps even painful. College graduates on average earn about twice as much per year as high school graduates, a difference that exceeds $1 million over a lifetime. These pay gains from college encourage a growing fraction of college students to pile up debts to finance their education.

Still, college is not for everyone. Some find the opportunity cost too high. For example, Bill Gates and Paul Allen dropped out of college to cofound Microsoft (Gates was the second richest person on earth in 2007; Allen ranked 19th). Tiger Woods, once an economics major at Stanford, dropped out after two years to earn his fortune in professional golf. And Paula Creamer, who skipped college to play golf, won her first $1 million sooner than any LPGA player in tour history. High school basketball players who believe they are ready for the pros also skip college, as do most tennis pros. Many actors even drop out of high school to pursue their craft, including Jim Carrey, Tom Cruise, Johnny Depp, Robert DeNiro, Cameron Diaz, Colin Farrell, Nicole Kidman, Jude Law, Demi Moore, Keanu Reeves, Kiefer Sutherland, Hilary Swank, Charlize Theron, and Kate Winslet.

SOURCES: "Tuition and Fees, 2006–7," *Chronicle of Higher Education Facts and Figures,* http://chronicle.com/stats/tuition/; Hillary Chura, "Cracking the Books for Financial Aid to College," *New York Times,* 27 January 2007; "The World's Billionaires," *Forbes,* 3 July 2007; and "College Board Connect to College Success" at http://www.collegeboard.com/.

THINK ABOUT IT

During the Vietnam War, colleges and universities were overflowing with students. Was this bumper crop of students caused by a greater expected return on a college education or by a change in the opportunity cost of attending college? Explain.

---

*Remember

There are more case studies to illustrate economic concepts at 4ltrpress.cengage.com/econ.

Case Study

User-Generated Products (Chapter 3)

In a market economy, new products and processes are usually developed by profit-seeking entrepreneurs, but sometimes sheer curiosity and the challenge of solving problems lead to new and better ways of doing things. For example, loose communities of computer programmers have been collaborating for decades. By the early 1990s, they formed a grass roots movement known as "open source," which was fueled by the Internet. In 1991, Linus Torvalds, a student at the University of Helsinki in Finland, wrote the core for what would become known as the Linux operating system. He posted his program online and invited anyone to tinker with the coding. Word spread, and computer aficionados around the world began spending their free time making Linux better.

Other software has developed in the open-source arena. For example, from the University of Illinois came web server software named Apache, and Swedish researchers developed database software called MySQL. The *Free Software Directory* lists more than 6,000 free software packages. The term *free* refers not only to the dollar cost of the software, which is zero, but to what you can do with the software—you can examine it, modify it, and redistribute it to anyone. Free user-generated software now includes the second most popular desktop operating system (Linux), web browser (Firefox), and office suite (OpenOffice), and the most widely used web server (Apache).

But most software sold is copyrighted to prevent redistribution, and buyers usually cannot even see the code, let alone tinker with it. Some for-profit start-up companies are piggybacking on user-generated products to create new software. For example, the developers of Zimbra email software drew from more than 40 open-source programs, including Apache and MySQL, to build the basics of their email system. Those 40 programs had been tested and improved by users over many years. Once Zimbra took shape, the company posted it online as open-source software for fine-tuning. Software junkies helped debug and improve it. The company now sells Zimbra online for much less than Microsoft charges for its email system.

Other user-generated products include some familiar names—Wikipedia, MySpace, Facebook, and YouTube. Wikipedia is a free online encyclopedia written and edited by volunteers. The idea is that collaboration over time will improve content much the way that open-source software has evolved. Wikipedia claims to be one of the most visited online sites. Founder Jimmy Wales says he spent a half million dollars getting Wikipedia going, but now the project relies on volunteers and donations.

MySpace and Facebook are social networking sites that allow users to post personal profiles, blogs, photos, music, videos, and more. So the main attraction of the sites is material provided by users. The companies simply provide the software and hardware framework to support the network. MySpace, founded in July 2003, was sold in July 2005 for about $330 million. Facebook was started by a college sophomore in 2004; in 2006 that founder turned down a $1 billion offer from Yahoo.

YouTube is an online video site that allows users to post their own videos and to view those posted by others. Searching for particular subjects is easy. For example, "comparative advantage" turned up "KaratEconomics Lesson 1." When YouTube was sold to Google in October 2006, YouTube had only 67 employees and no profit. Still, because visitors were viewing more than 100 million videos a day, all those eyeballs gave YouTube tremendous advertising potential. Google paid $1.65 billion for a company with no profit. Google still has its own video site; so does Yahoo.

User-generated products are not new. Radio call-in shows have been making money off callers for decades. But the Internet has increased opportunities for users to create new products and to improve existing products. Most of the users are just having fun. The more users involved, the more valuable that product is to each user. That's why networking and video sites are trying to dominate their markets.

SOURCES: Robert Guth, "Trolling the Web for Free Labor, Software Upstarts Are a New Force," *Wall Street Journal,* 13 November 2006; Pui-Wing Tam, "Google's YouTube Pact Spawns Big Payday," *Wall Street Journal,* 8 February 2007; and Robert Guth, "Linux Starts to Find Home on Desktops," 13 March 2007. The Free Software Directory is found at http://directory.fsf.org/.

THINK ABOUT IT

Why are users willing to help create certain products even though few, if any, users are paid for their efforts?

---

*Remember

There are more case studies to illustrate economic concepts at 4ltrpress.cengage.com/econ.

Case Study

Income and Happiness (Chapter 6)

The Declaration of Independence in 1776 identified "certain unalienable Rights, that among these are Life, Liberty, and the Pursuit of Happiness." This did not guarantee happiness but did establish the pursuit of happiness as an "unalienable" right, meaning that right cannot be taken away, given away, or sold. Eighteenth-century philosopher and social reformer Jeremy Bentham argued that government policy should promote the greatest happiness for the greatest number of people.

Many people today apparently agree. In recent polls, 77 percent of Australians and 81 percent of Brits believed that a government's prime objective should be promoting the greatest happiness rather than the greatest wealth. The United Nations in 2007 sponsored an international conference on "Happiness and Public Policy." Thailand now compiles a monthly Gross Domestic Happiness Index. Even China has joined in the fun, reporting a happiness index based on polling results about living conditions, income, the environment, social welfare, and employment. Australia, Canada, and the United Kingdom are also developing happiness indexes.

Economists have long shied away from asking people how they feel, preferring instead to observe their behavior. But more now see some value in asking questions. In the most extensive of polls, the Gallup organization asked people in 130 countries: "How satisfied are you with your life, on a scale of zero to ten?" The results, reported in 2007, are not surprising. Most people in the high income areas, such as the United States, Europe, and Japan, said they are happy. Most people in the poor areas, especially in Africa, said they are not. Also, within a given country, income and happiness are positively related. After evaluating all the results of the Gallup world poll, Angus Deaton of Princeton concluded: "The very strong international relationship between per capita GDP and life satisfaction suggests that, on average, people have a good idea of how income, or the lack of it, affects their lives."[1]

So these results are no surprise. What does puzzle economists is that other surveys suggest that in affluent countries people do not seem any happier over time even though each generation became richer than the last. For example, in the United States, the proportion of people who say they are happy has stayed about the same despite 60 years of economic growth. In Japan, happiness responses actually declined despite a substantial increase in real income over the last 50 years.

Here are two possible explanations. First, people begin taking for granted those luxuries they most desired. For example, two generations ago color TVs, automobiles, and major appliances were luxuries, but now they are must-have items for most households. Computers and flat screen HDTVs will soon move from luxuries to necessities. As each generation attains a higher standard of living, people become less sensitive to the benefits, they take them for granted, and thus they say they are no happier.

Second, research suggests that what matters is not just the absolute level of income but income relative to other people in the reference group. Imagine you have a choice between (1) earning $50,000 a year while others in your reference group make $25,000 or (2) earning $100,000 a year while others make $250,000 (suppose, too, that prices remain the same, so $100,000 is double the real income of $50,000). Which would you prefer? Studies show that when people face this hypothetical choice, most pick the $50,000 option. That is, they prefer to make more than others even if that means a lower real income. Thus, if all incomes rise on average over time, this does not affect that aspect of happiness linked to one's relative standing. As the social critic H. L. Mencken long ago observed, "A wealthy man is one who earns $100 a year more than his wife's sister's husband."

1. Angus Deaton, "Income, Aging, Health, and Wellbeing Around the World: Evidence from the Gallup World Poll," Princeton Working Paper (August 2007): 31.

SOURCES: Daniel Gilbert, *Stumbling On Happiness* (New York: Knopf, 2006); Marina Kamenev, "Rating Countries for the Happiness Factor," *Business Week*, 11 October 2006; Angus Deaton, "Income, Aging, Health, and Wellbeing Around the World: Evidence from the Gallup World Poll," Princeton Working Paper, (August 2007); and "Where Money Seems to Talk," *Economist*, 12 July 2007.

THINK ABOUT IT

How would you explain the finding that people in high-income economies seem happier than people in low-income economies, but, over time, people in high income economies do not seem to be happier even though their country grows richer?

> ***Remember**
>
> There are more case studies to illustrate economic concepts at 4ltrpress.cengage.com/econ.

Case Study

The Hassle of Small Change (Chapter 14)

About 8 billion U.S. pennies were minted in 2006, and about 140 billion pennies circulated. That's nearly 500 pennies per U.S. resident. About 60 percent of pennies are resting in change jars, drawers, or other gathering places for the lowly coin. Pennies are abandoned in the tiny bins and donation cans at store counters. Many people won't bother to pick one up on the sidewalk. The penny, like all U.S. currency, has over time been robbed of its exchange value by inflation. Today's penny buys only one-seventh as much as it did in the 1950s. Pennies can't be used in parking meters, vending machines, or pay telephones, and penny candy has been long gone. To avoid the hassle of small change, some restaurants, such as the Vanilla Bean Café in Pomfret, Connecticut, charge prices exactly divisible by 25 cents. That way, pennies, nickels, and dimes need not be part of any transaction.

The exchange value of the penny has declined as the cost of minting it has risen. For more than a century, the penny was 95 percent copper. In 1982, copper prices reached record levels, so the U.S. Mint began making pennies from zinc, with just a thin copper finish. Then, the price of zinc quadrupled, boosting the metal cost of a penny to 0.8 cents. Add to that the 0.7-cent minting cost per penny, and you get 1.5 cents per coin. So the government loses a half a cent on each. The government lost $41 million minting pennies in 2006—this, for a coin headed for the change jar. Nickels are also money losers; they cost 5.5 cents to make.

Has the penny outlived its usefulness? In the face of rising metal prices, the government has some options. First option: mint them from a lower-cost alloy. This would buy some time, but inflation would eventually drive the metallic cost above the exchange value of the coin. Second option: abolish the penny. Take it out of circulation. Many countries have eliminated their smallest coin, including Australia, Britain, Finland, Hong Kong, and the Netherlands. The United States abolished the half-cent piece in 1857, at a time when it was worth 8 cents in today's purchasing power.

Third option: decree that the penny is worth five cents, the same as a nickel. At the same time, the government could withdraw nickels from circulation. With pennies worth so much more, there would be no incentive to hoard them for their metallic value (a current problem), and it would likely be decades before the metallic value caught up with the exchange value. Rebasing the penny to 5 cents would increase the money supply by about $6 billion, a drop in the bucket compared to a total money supply exceeding $1 trillion, so the move would have virtually no effect on inflation.

If the penny gets so little respect, why did production increase from 6.8 billion pennies in 2003 to 8.2 billion in 2006? As noted, some people are hoarding pennies, waiting for the day when the metallic value exceeds the exchange value. For example, one hoarder accumulated 700,000 pennies (about two tons of them). Another source of demand is the sales tax, which adds pennies to transactions in 44 states. The sales tax helps explain why efforts to abolish the penny go nowhere. Charities also collect millions from change cans located at check-out counters. And zinc producers lobby heavily to keep the penny around, since it's a major user of the metal. Thus, the penny still has its boosters. That's why retailers continue to order pennies from their banks, these banks order pennies from the Fed, the Fed orders them from the Mint, and the Mint presses yet more pennies into idle service.

SOURCES: Austan Goolsbee, "Now that the Penny Isn't Worth Much, It's Time to Make It Worth 5 Cents," *New York Times,* 1 February 2007; Floyd Norris, "A Penny for Your Thoughts, and 1.4 Cents for the Penny," *New York Times,* 22 April 2006; "A Penny Unsaved," *Wall Street Journal,* 20 July 2006; and Thomas Sargent and Francois Velde, *The Big Problem of Small Change* (Princeton, NJ: Princeton University Press, 2002). View the rounded prices on Vanilla Bean Café's menu at http://www.thevanillabeancafe.com/.

THINK ABOUT IT

In what sense are coins a hassle for you? Are you more inclined to use credit and debit cards in order to avoid carrying cash, particularly coins?

*Remember

There are more case studies to illustrate economic concepts at 4ltrpress.cengage.com/econ.

Case Study

Faking It (Chapter 15)

As noted earlier, as much as 60 percent of U.S. currency is held abroad, mostly as a safe, liquid, and portable store of value. One possible threat to the integrity of U.S. currency is the so-called supernote—a counterfeit $100 note of extremely high quality that began circulating around 1990. It's a remarkable forgery, including sequential serial numbers and a polymer security thread that took Crane & Company, the supplier of paper for U.S. currency since 1879, years to develop. By perfectly emulating the ferrous oxide inked in Benjamin Franklin's portrait, the supernote sometimes fools currency-scanning machines at the nation's 12 Federal Reserve Banks.

Expert engravers produced the supernote, but technological improvements in copy machines, computers, and printers now allow even amateurs to make counterfeits. About half the fake notes found in a recent year were produced with computers, copiers, and printers, up from just 1 percent in 1995. On U.S. soil, the Secret Service seizes most counterfeit money before it circulates. But foreign counterfeiting poses a problem for the U.S. Secret Service, which is primarily a domestic police force (few of the 2,000 agents work abroad). Most counterfeit money seized here is printed abroad, and seizures abroad have been growing.

To combat technological improvements in counterfeiting, the U.S. Treasury now redesigns U.S. currency every 7 to 10 years. The $100 note was redesigned in 1996 for the first time since 1928. Other denominations have added extra colors other than green and black for the first time in modern American history. The $100 note was scheduled to get the same colorful treatment in late 2008. The $1 note is not popular with counterfeiters and will not get a facelift. Vending machine owners also oppose any change in the $1 note.

The $20 note is most popular among domestic counterfeiters, and the $100 note most popular among foreign counterfeiters. Colombia is the world's largest source of bogus American currency. Colombia borders on Ecuador, which converted to the U.S. dollar in 2000 and thus offers a ready outlet for counterfeits. As noted earlier, in some countries the U.S. dollar circulates alongside the native currency, which offers more outlets for counterfeiters.

The U.S. Treasury concludes that counterfeiting is not a threat to the nation's currency. Even abroad, merchants are able to spot most fakes and they have an abiding interest in doing so. According to the Treasury, the chance of encountering a fake abroad is no greater than in the United States, and in either case it's quite low—only about one counterfeit in every 10,000 notes.

The United States has a policy of never recalling currency for fear that the world's hoarders of dollars might switch to other currencies, such as euros (remember, we want foreigners to keep hoarding their U.S. dollars). Over time, preference for the new currency and the replacement of old notes as they pass through the Fed will eventually eliminate old notes. But different designs of the same denomination will circulate side by side for some time, especially $100 notes. To give you some idea how long this could take, U.S. notes of $500 and up were last printed in 1946, and the Fed began taking them out of circulation in 1969. Yet hundreds of thousands of these big denominations are still hoarded by the public and remain legal tender. Some still show up at Federal Reserve Banks, where they are destroyed. Every U.S. note issued since 1861 remains legal tender today. That's one reason U.S. dollars are prized around the world. They all come with a lifetime money-back guarantee, so to speak.

SOURCES: Benny Avni, "U.N. Officials Knew Earlier of North Korean Fake Currency," *New York Sun,* 3 April 2007; Bill Fairies, "Made in South America: New Breed of Fake U.S. Dollars," *Christian Science Monitor,* 14 April 2005; and "The Use and Counterfeiting of U.S. Currency Abroad, Part 3," *A Final Report to the Congress by the Secretary of the Treasury,* September 2006. The U.S. Treasury also has a Web site providing information about new notes at http://www.moneyfactory.gov/section.cfm/4.

THINK ABOUT IT

Why did the U.S. government consider it important to redesign the $100 note in order to combat the effects of the "supernote"?

---

*Remember

There are more case studies to illustrate economic concepts at 4ltrpress.cengage.com/econ.

Case Study

What About China? (Chapter 19)

The U.S. trade deficit with China of $233 billion in 2006 exceeded America's combined deficits with the European Union and Latin America. The deficit with China grew well over 20 percent annually between 2000 and 2006. Americans spend five times more on Chinese products than the Chinese spend on American products.

Many economists, politicians, and union officials argue that China manipulates its currency, the yuan, to keep Chinese products cheaper abroad and foreign products more expensive at home. This stimulates Chinese exports and discourages imports, thereby boosting Chinese production and jobs. At the same time, the average Chinese consumer is poorer because the yuan buys fewer foreign products.

As we have seen, any country that establishes a fixed exchange rate that undervalues or overvalues the currency must intervene continuously to maintain that rate. Thus, if the official exchange rate chronically undervalues the Chinese yuan relative to the dollar, as appears to be the case, then Chinese authorities must continuously exchange yuan for dollars in foreign exchange markets. The increased supply of yuan keeps the yuan down, and the increased demand for dollars keeps the dollar up.

But the charge that China manipulates its currency goes beyond simply depressing the yuan and boosting the dollar. China's trading partners increasingly feel they are being squeezed out by Chinese producers without gaining access to Chinese markets. For example, China offers some producers tax rebates and subsidies to promote exports, while imposing quotas and tariffs to discourage imports, such as a 25 percent tariff on auto-parts imports.

China has tried to sooth concerns about the trade deficit. Most importantly, Chinese authorities in 2005 began allowing the yuan to rise modestly against the dollar. As a result, the yuan rose a total of 8.3 percent against the dollar between July 2005 and July 2007. China also announced plans to cut tax rebates paid to its exporters and to lower some import duties. But these measures seemed to have had little effect on America's monster deficit with China.

Facing political pressure to do something, a bipartisan group of U.S. senators introduced a bill in June 2007 intended to punish countries that "unfairly undervalue their currencies," a measure aimed primarily at China. The bill was crafted to stay within WTO guidelines about trade disputes, but the upshot would be that China could lose some prestige and trading privileges that it values.

Also in June 2007, the International Monetary Fund (IMF) announced new rules to give "clear guidance to our members on how they should run their exchange-rate policies, on what is acceptable to the international community and what is not." IMF officials said that any nation publicly identified as an exchange rate manipulator would be shamed into changing its practices. As an emerging economic power and host of the 2008 Olympics, China faces mounting pressure to allow its currency to seek a sustainable level.

SOURCES: Lee Branstetter and Nicholas Lardy, "China's Embrace of Globalization," NBER Working Paper 12373 (July 2006); John McCary, "Bill Targets China's Policy on Currency," *Wall Street Journal,* 14 June 2007; John McCary and Andrew Batson, "Punishing China: Will It Fly?" *Wall Street Journal,* 23 June 2007; and Jeremy Peters, "Rising Exports Putting a Dent in Trade Gap," *New York Times,* 14 May 2007.

THINK ABOUT IT

Why would China want its own currency to be undervalued relative to the U.S. dollar? How does China maintain an undervalued currency?

---

*Remember

There are more case studies to illustrate economic concepts at <u>4ltrpress.cengage.com/econ</u>.